Critical Issues
in Modern Religion

ROGER A. JOHNSON
Wellesley College

and

ERNEST WALLWORK
Harvard University (Visiting Scholar)

with

CLIFFORD GREEN
Goucher College

H. PAUL SANTMIRE
Wellesley College

HAROLD Y. VANDERPOOL
Wellesley College

PRENTICE-HALL, INC., Englewood Cliffs, New Jersey

Library of Congress Cataloging in Publication Data

JOHNSON, ROGER A
    Critical issues in modern religion.

    Includes bibliographies.
        1. Religion and science—1946–
2. Religion—Addresses, essays, lectures.
I. Wallwork, Ernest, joint author. II. Title.
BL240.2.J55   200'.1   72-10829
ISBN 0-13-193987-4
ISBN 0-13-193979-3 (pbk)

Printed in the United States of America

10 9 8 7 6 5

Prentice-Hall International, Inc., *London*
Prentice-Hall of Australia, Pty. Ltd., *Sydney*
Prentice-Hall of Canada, Ltd., *Toronto*
Prentice-Hall of India Private Limited, *New Delhi*
Prentice-Hall of Japan, Inc., *Tokyo*

Acknowledgments

For permission to reprint copyrighted material from the following books, thanks
are gratefully expressed to the several publishers.

A. & C. Black Ltd. and Stanford University Press, for David Hume, *The Natu-
    ral History of Religion*, ed., H. E. Root. London, A. & C. Black Ltd., 1956;
    Stanford, California: Stanford University Press, 1956.

The Clarendon Press, for David Hume, *Dialogues Concerning Natural Re-
    ligion*, ed., Norman Kemp Smith, Oxford, England, 1935. By permission
    of The Clarendon Press, Oxford.

Dover Publications, Inc., for *The Autobiography of Charles Darwin and Se-
    lected Letters*, New York.

The New American Library, Inc., for Charles Darwin, *The Origin of the
    Species*, New York.

Schocken Books Inc., for Karl Marx and Friedrich Engels, *On Religion*. Introduction by Reinhold Niebuhr. Reprinted by permission of Schocken Books Inc., copyright © 1964 by Schocken Books Inc.

Charles Scribner's Sons, for Reinhold Niebuhr, *Moral Man and Immoral Society*, New York, 1960.

Dimension Books, Inc. and Sheed and Ward Limited, for Dom Helder Camara, *The Church and Colonialism*, trans. by William McSweeney. Denville, New Jersey: Dimension Books, 1969.

Orbis Books, for José de Broucker, *Dom Helder Camara: The Violence of a Peacemaker*, trans. by Herma Briffault. Maryknoll, New York: Orbis Books, 1970.

Seabury Press, for James H. Cone, *Black Theology and Black Power*, New York, 1969.

SCM Press Ltd. and The Macmillan Company, for Dietrich Bonhoeffer, *Letters and Papers from Prison*, New Enlarged Edition, SCM Press, London and Macmillan Co., New York. © SCM Press 1953, 1971.

W. W. Norton & Company and Faber and Faber, Ltd., for Erik H. Erikson, *Young Man Luther: A Study in Psychoanalysis and History*, New York and London, 1958; and *Identity: Youth and Crisis*, New York and London. 1968. Reprinted by permission of W. W. Norton & Company and Faber and Faber, Ltd.

University of Chicago Press, for Paul Tillich, *Systematic Theology*, vol. II, © 1957 by The University of Chicago. All rights reserved. Published 1957. Ninth Impression 1969. Vol. III, © 1963 by the University of Chicago. All rights reserved. Published 1963.

Yale University Press, for Paul Tillich, *The Courage to Be*, New Haven, 1966, from pp. 34f., 50, 111, 156, 172, 185.

Columbia University Press, for Paul Tillich, *Christianity and the Encounter of the World Religions*, New York, 1963. Paperback edition, 1964.

Doubleday & Company and Faber and Faber, Ltd., for Theodore Roethke, first stanza of "The Far Field." Copyright © 1962 by Beatrice Roethke, Administratrix of the Estate of Theodore Roethke, from *Collected Poems of Theodore Roethke*. Reprinted by permission of Doubleday & Company, Inc. and Faber and Faber, Ltd.

Houghton Mifflin Company, for Archibald MacLeish, "The End of the World," from *Collected Poems 1917–1952*. Copyright 1926, 1952 by Archibald MacLeish. Reprinted by permission of the publisher, Houghton Mifflin Company.

CONTENTS

PREFACE   vii

INTRODUCTION   1
Johnson

I: NATURAL SCIENCE AND RELIGION

1   *DAVID HUME:* A Skeptic Examines Religious Beliefs   13
Johnson

2   *RUDOLF BULTMANN:* Beyond the Conflict of Science and Religion—
An Existential Faith   39
Johnson

II: BIOLOGY AND RELIGION

3   *CHARLES DARWIN AND DARWINISM:* A Naturalized World
and a Brutalized Man?   77
Vanderpool

4   *PIERRE TEILHARD DE CHARDIN:* The Christianization of Evolution   114
Santmire

v

III: SOCIAL THEORY AND RELIGION

5   **KARL MARX:** Religion—Social Narcotic and Reactionary Ideology   143
     Green

6   **REINHOLD NIEBUHR:** Religion Fosters Social Criticism
     and Promotes Social Justice   175
     Vanderpool

7   **RELIGIOUS RADICALS—CAMARA AND CONE:** Christians
     in the Revolution of the Oppressed   209
     Wallwork

IV: PSYCHOANALYSIS AND RELIGION

8   **SIGMUND FREUD:** The Psychoanalytic Diagnosis—Infantile Illusion   251
     Wallwork

9   **DIETRICH BONHOEFFER:** Religionless Christianity—Maturity,
     Transcendence, and Freedom   284
     Johnson

10   **ERIK H. ERIKSON:** Psychosocial Resources for Faith   322
     Wallwork

V: HISTORY AND RELIGION

11   **ERNST TROELTSCH:** Modern Historical Thought and the
     Challenge to Individual Religions   365
     Santmire

12   **PAUL TILLICH:** The Relative and the Ultimate in the Encounter of Religions   400
     Green

     EPILOGUE: The Birthing of Post-Modern Religion   435
     Santmire

     INDEX OF NAMES   461

     SUBJECT INDEX   463

PREFACE

Like many others teaching in the field of religion, we have long felt the need for an interdisciplinary approach to the subject of modern religious thought. During the past two centuries, the natural sciences and the social sciences have engendered a body of new knowledge, insights, and theories that have undermined traditional religious beliefs and decisively influenced the reformulation of religion in the modern era. Through the impact of these secular disciplines, patterns of religious belief and thought, which had been normative in the pre-modern era, have been either abandoned or radically altered by twentieth-century religious thinkers. Because the transformation of theological traditions in the modern era is so closely linked with new intellectual movements, we are convinced that an interdisciplinary approach provides the most effective vehicle for understanding the changing shape of modern religious thought.

We have not attempted to present a comprehensive survey of the interaction of modern thought and theological reflection. Because of the quantity of material characteristic of a survey, the treatment of particular figures tends to be superficial and the reader depends for his conclusions on the author's generalizations. By presenting a thorough discussion of a limited number of positions, we intend to give the reader an adequate basis to make his own judgment concerning the issues debated. Neither have we sought to articulate a single, consistent theological position throughout the book. We assume that the religious convictions of our readers are at least as diverse as the positions presented. As a result, we only presuppose an openness to religious concerns and a willingness to come to terms with those critical issues that have loomed so large in the development of modern religious thought. Our goal is to inform, clarify, and stimulate our reader's reflection, but not to provide a set of answers for the issues discussed. Finally, we do not approach the subject matter of religion with a single methodology or synthetic meta-methodology. Rather, in studying religious issues arising from various disciplines and differing theological perspectives, the reader will encounter a diversity of methods used to interpret religion. Thus, for example, a concept as basic as 'religion' does not have a consistent meaning throughout the text; instead, the definitions of religion in the several chapters are those of the positions under discussion.

The following information may prove helpful for the reader's use of the book. One may begin with any of the five sections of the book or, for that matter, with any of the twelve chapters. Both sections and chapters are relatively self-contained and independent of each other. While each chapter concentrates on a set of central issues, these issues are treated within the broader framework of the author's thought as a whole, though without purporting to offer an exhaustive account of every facet of his work. In an academic context, the book may prove useful not only for religious studies but also in the several disciplines represented. Furthermore, because of its interdisciplinary approach and historical scope, it may also be appropriate within the study of modern intellectual history. To assist further study, bibliographies are found at the end of each chapter. References in parentheses throughout the chapter refer to the books as numbered in the chapter's bibliography.

Our book grew out of a corporate teaching venture in the Department of Religion and Biblical Studies at Wellesley College. We remember with affection our many students whose suggestions and criticisms have contributed to this book. We are especially indebted to Ellison Banks for her preparation of the index and to Ann Suzedell and Kathryn Woodward for their assistance in proofreading. As colleagues in teaching and writing, we have enjoyed and profited from the process of working together. While each of us accepts responsibility for his own chapters, we happily acknowledge that we have learned much from each other in this joint endeavor.

Writing this book has been an intellectually stimulating and personally rewarding venture for its authors. We wish the same for our readers.

Roger A. Johnson
Ernest Wallwork
Clifford Green
H. Paul Santmire
Harold Vanderpool

INTRODUCTION

The middle of the twentieth century seems to mark a watershed in the religious history of the West. For two hundred years since the Enlightenment, many seminal figures had turned a critical eye upon Christianity, the predominant religion of Western culture. By mid-century, popular education gave the critical ideas of men like Darwin, Marx, and Freud a broad social impact, catalyzing the contemporary religious crisis. This crisis was heightened by a curious ignorance in the popular religious mind. While people were aware of the collision of science and psychology with religious belief, there was considerably less familiarity with the creative developments in new religious thinking. The names of Bultmann, Teilhard, and Bonhoeffer are hardly household words like those of Darwin, Marx, and Freud. This book is an encounter between critics and modern religious thinkers.

The emergence of modern science informed the empiricism and philosophical skepticism which shaped David Hume's attack upon Christianity. Even those who know little of Hume are acutely aware that belief in miracles is incompatible with a scientific view of the world. Darwin's theory of evolution provoked such religious controversy that schools banned the teaching of his views on the origin of the human species: such views undermined the belief that the world was created in seven days by a benevolent Creator who gave special dignity to man; they further eroded the credibility of the Bible which for centuries had fostered man's special status and his trust in the goodness of the Creator. Marx taught that religion is "the opium of the people," a reactionary social ideology encouraging the industrial masses to look for heavenly bliss, and sanctioning oppression by the capitalist class. Marx's teachings have fed into the current criticism of "institutional religion" and have engendered suspicion about the social function of belief in a life after death. Freud, espousing atheism chiefly for psychological reasons, diagnosed belief in a heavenly Father as an "illusion," a regression to infantile dependency in a self-defeating effort to cope with anxiety. And, while the name of Ernst Troeltsch is less famous outside academic circles, the question he posed is well-known: in light of new knowledge about the diverse religions of the world, how can anyone still believe the Christian claim to preach the one true revelation of God for all humanity? Natural science, evolution, social theory, psychology and historical relativism have beaten like eroding waves upon the traditional belief structure of Christianity.

Forceful and inescapable though such critiques are, modern religious thinkers have honestly grappled with them. Rudolf Bultmann insisted that the miracle stories of the Bible are pre-scientific, and that they are set within a whole mythological world view. His method of "demythologizing" was specifically intended to free the authentic meaning of the Bible from mythological misunderstanding. Teilhard de Chardin, a Jesuit priest and paleontologist, appropriated and extended Darwin's evolutionary vision, not as an enemy of the faith but as a natural ally. Reinhold Niebuhr and Bishop Camara in their different social contexts, Niebuhr in America during the 1930's to 1950's and Camara in the Third-World country of Brazil in the 1960's and 1970's, recognized the validity of Marx's analysis of the reactionary role of religious institutions; nevertheless, both men persuasively argued that biblical religion required a commitment to social justice which included the possibility of revolution. James Cone, a contemporary black theologian, has seen true Christianity as a radical religious ally for the revolutionary Black Power movement in America. Dietrich Bonhoeffer, a Christian theologian martyred by the Nazis, and Erik Erikson, an American psychoanalyst and humanist, affirmed that faith can support the ego autonomy and psychological maturity found among modern men while rejecting the religion of infantile dependency. Paul Tillich acknowledged the presence of the divine in all religions as a way of overcoming religious parochialism and intolerance, without sacrificing the integrity of his own—or any other—particular faith. Such religious thinkers creatively engaged the new knowledge, insights, and theories generated by modern thought. Like the critics of religion, they were themselves modern men who nevertheless believed that faith continued to be humanizing and transforming.

Such engagement is no mere accommodation. For these religious spokesmen not only reinterpreted faith in relation to modern thought, but also articulated the transforming possibilities of that faith in relation to the urgent crises of their times. Their religious convictions enabled them to diagnose the ills of modern life and to offer healing insights. Some called men away from the false offers of security in a technological society in order to discover their authentic freedom in their personal life histories. Some offered religious resources for hope and courage over against the despair engendered by a depersonalized society and disintegrating culture. Some, by their example and writing, struggled against political tyranny and social injustice, holding all men accountable to transcendent norms of justice, freedom and love in public life. In varying ways, then, they all testified to an authentic transcendence as a power of transformation engaging their world.

This brief introduction to the figures discussed in the book highlights two themes crucial for the development of modern religious thought: crises of *belief*, and the quest for a new understanding of *transcendence.*

Belief was not always a problem for religion. Prior to the Enlightenment, religious believers of various persuasions, and even heretics, shared a common view of man and his world. All could agree concerning the reality of God, his miracles and revelation, man's sin and need for redemption, the authority of Scripture and the saving work of Christ, and the necessity of a Christian basis for public morality. The existence of Jewish and Islamic communities within the geographical territory of Christendom was not sufficient to disturb the cultural consensus concerning these self-evident truths. While Protestants and Catholics of the seventeenth century could engage in intense theological and military conflict over their beliefs, this struggle occurred within a theologically formed view of reality which they all shared. For the basic beliefs of pre-modern Christendom transcended even the hostile confrontations of a divided Church.

With the Enlightenment, however, the shared religious beliefs of the West began to disintegrate. The criticism of belief developed along two levels: a rejection of particular beliefs, and a critique of belief itself as dishonest, debilitating, and dehumanizing. The new knowledge and perspective on reality developed by modern thought called into question the truth claims of a variety of beliefs: miracles, the divine creation of man and the world, the literal truth of the Bible as the inspired Word of God, the hope for a life after death with rewards and punishments, Heaven and Hell, conscience as the inner voice of God, earthly suffering as punishment for sin, the state as the temporal agent of God's rule, the sacrificial death of Christ to atone for the sin of men, the mission of converting the whole world to Christ, and the necessity of orthodox faith for good public morality; and above all, God as the Supreme Being, omnipotent and omniscient, whose revelation is the source of all these beliefs. In brief, beliefs which had been self-evident in the pre-modern era became increasingly incredible under the impact of the modern critical intellect.

But the criticism of belief itself was more fundamental than the rejection of particular beliefs. The very posture of believing was attacked as superstitious, oppressive, and regressive; in short, being religious was fundamentally alien to man's humanity. David Hume identified belief as a mask for man's ignorance and anxious search for happiness; strip away the facade of belief and one discovers only superstition and fear. For Karl Marx, belief was an ally of those in power, pacifying the oppressed. When men believed that their sin was the cause of their suffering and that their docility in this world would be rewarded with a good life in the world to come, they would hardly rise up in revolt against their oppressors. Freud described belief as an illusion, snaring man in self-deceptive and self-destructive fantasies. Unwilling to give up their infantile wish for happiness and face the insecurity of the real world, men project in religion their need for a protective Father concerned for their safety. Belief is regressive, exacting the high price of perpetual immaturity and psychic suffering. For all these critics, religious beliefs were not simply erroneous when examined by the light of reason; rather, the very posture of believing was thoroughly dysfunctional and destructive, preventing the realization of rationality, social justice, and psychological maturity. The critics were humanists, and they attacked the religious attitude as dehumanizing.

The repudiation of particular beliefs was not confined to the critics of religion. Not only agnostics and atheists who attacked religion, but also Christians who spoke from *within* their religious communities rejected many of the traditional beliefs which were in conflict with their changing perception of reality. For example, Rudolf Bultmann, while a Lutheran Christian devoted to his church and the preaching of the Word of God, did not believe in the literal truth of the Bible and its miracle stories any more than David Hume. Nor did Teilhard find his Catholic faith requiring him to believe that plants, animals, and men were created by separate acts of God within a seven-day span of time. And, while there are individual variations in belief, the other religious spokesmen do not differ substantially from this pattern. Indeed, a retrospective view of the development of modern religious thought discloses a steady erosion within religious communities of many beliefs considered normative in the pre-modern era. In light of this development, it is not surprising that many people, for whom traditional beliefs formed a vital part of their faith, should find themselves confused and distressed by the loss of beliefs once regarded as sacred.

In addition to jettisoning many particular beliefs, the religious spokesman shared with the critics a basic suspicion about belief itself. While men of faith, most of them were not also men of belief. Here also Bultmann's position is typical. He finds that religious belief generally functions as an inauthentic resolution to the genuine human problem of insecurity. In an effort to overcome the anxiety intrinsic to their freedom, men cling to a system of beliefs supposed to give them security. In contrast, faith for Bultmann is not belief, but a new understanding of oneself, an existential decision crucial for the life history of the individual. Bonhoeffer concurs with the general thrust of Bultmann's proposal, and so criticizes dogmatic claims for belief in Christian revelation. However, Bonhoeffer also insists that Bultmann has not been radical enough. While Bultmann rejected a mythological form of belief, he failed to see the deeper problem of religious dependency on an all-powerful God. Like Freud, Bonhoeffer regards this belief in God as an emotional crutch to support weak egos in times of crisis. Faith, for Bonhoeffer, is not belief, but participation in the being of Jesus which transforms man's life with others. Tillich also was a critic of belief. He found that beliefs too often were simply the product of authoritarian claims of religious institutions; they did not express the depths of man's own concern and experience but the supposed truths he was taught to believe as the condition for his eventual salvation. Such beliefs cannot unite man with the Ultimate, but only estrange him from his true being. Therefore, Tillich speaks of faith not as belief, but as ultimate concern, or participation in the Ground of Being. Thus, each of these theologians clearly distinguishes faith from belief, affirming the former and denying the latter. A recent book of essays by the sociologist Robert Bellah exemplifies this trend of modern religious thought in its title, *Beyond Belief: Essays on Religion in a Post-Traditional World.**

In an unexpected way, both the religious spokesmen and the critics shared in common a concern for authentic transcendence, though the latter used words like "reflection" and "projection" rather than transcendence. However, by attacking spurious claims for transcendence, the critics cleared the way for new understandings of genuine transcendence. Spurious transcendence is dramatically portrayed in the critical theories of religion developed by Freud and Marx.

* New York: Harper & Row, 1970.

Freud's criticism of spurious transcendence focuses on the psychic function of the religious belief in the Father-God. According to Freud, in situations of anxiety the religious person regresses in search of the security and parental protection known in childhood. This regression evokes the figure of the powerful Father, who is then projected as a transcendent Supreme Being, the cosmic Father of all men. Although the believer may find some comfort in this dependence on the heavenly Father, he is not freed from his anxieties or his infantile attempt to handle them. The transcendent Father does not provide new and realistic ways of coping with the causes of anxiety, and does not cultivate mature independence, autonomy, freedom and self-responsibility. On the contrary, the power, authority, and moral demands of the transcendent Father will probably add religious guilt and anxiety to natural anxiety; so the process of regression and projection is repeated over and over again and the believer is trapped in the posture of infantile dependence. The Father-God, in Freud's analysis, is a spurious transcendence because it simply grows out of, and reinforces, an established psychic pattern. Pseudo-transcendence does not bring any new, transforming and liberating possibilities to the self. It is a circular and self-replicating process.

Marx's analysis of spurious transcendence focuses upon the social function of belief in the kingdom of Heaven. In Marx's view, the oppressed proletariat turn away from the pain of their earthly suffering, looking to Heaven where they will receive after death abundance, freedom and happiness as compensation for their miserable lot on earth. But this is a fantasy-compensation with very reactionary social consequences. Longing for a transcendent Heaven directs men's desire for a radically different society into an other-worldly life after death. Further, in order to gain the heavenly reward, the proletariat must be submissive to the oppressive, established order and must accept its religious rationalization of their suffering. Belief in a transcendent kingdom of Heaven, then, only serves to reinforce man's acquiescence in his own exploitation. This is again a spurious transcendence. It arises from and reflects the prevailing conditions in society, and it helps to replicate them indefinitely. It does not bring revolutionary new insights to men which would enable them to transform the unjust conditions of society. As in the psychic realm explored by Freud, this is again a circular and self-perpetuating process. Spurious transcendence only reflects; it never transforms. In contrast, authentic transcendence brings new life-possibilities which enable men to transcend psychic bondage and dehumanized society.

In the pre-modern era the theistic idea of God provided the basic model for understanding transcendence. God was popularly understood as a separate and objective Being beyond the transience of worldly history. His eternal nature and will were known through a particular revelation guaranteed by miracles and the authority of the Bible and church doctrine. Omnipotence and omniscience were his primary attributes, expressed in mercy and benevolent care for all his earthly children. He ruled over the world through his appointed powers in the state and in his church which ministered to the souls of men, preparing them for their heavenly destiny. The intellectual, social and psychological problems inherent in this theistic conception of God have already been suggested. It is not surprising that virtually none of the Protestant or Catholic spokesmen included in this book adopt or defend this theistic idea of God. Nor is it surprising that there was such a widespread popular response to the "death of God" slogan advertised in the 1960's. For this idea of God no longer communicated authentic transcendence to the experience of modern man.

Like the critics, modern religious thinkers turned away from the theistic idea of God as a spurious mode of transcendence; unlike the critics, they confidently proposed new interpretations of transcendence which, while faithful to their religious heritage, both transcended the problems of theism and were relevant to the achievements and crises of modern man. Thus Bultmann and Tillich were typical of others in denying the religious viability of any conception of God as a separate and objective Being. For both of them, authentic transcendence was an experience of the whole self and not a theoretical and abstract belief in a Supreme Being. Similarly, Bonhoeffer located transcendence not in an omnipotent Deity beyond the world, but in the transforming presence of Jesus in the world. For Bonhoeffer, encounter with Jesus, "the man for others," is the catalytic experience liberating men from their narcissistic bondage to self. Authentic transcendence is therefore documented in the new freedom which men find for their personal and political lives. Other religious spokesmen relate authentic transcendence to processes of cosmic evolution, struggles for social justice, the formation of ego strengths and psychological maturity, and the viability of a personal faith for people living in a global village.

Such explorations of authentic transcendence involve a major debate between the critics and exponents of modern religion: the latter, by affirming transcendence, call into question the *reductionism* of many of the former. Briefly, reductionism means an oversimplified explanation of a complex phenomenon like religion, usually by means of one set of causal factors. Accordingly, several of the critics contend that religion has no independent reality in itself, but is merely a by-product of some other, more basic human process. Thus, some claim that religion is nothing but a distorted expression of psychic dynamics. Others contend that religion is simply a reflection of underlying social factors. Still others argue that religion is only a primitive antecedent of scientific thinking. Without denying that many important insights into the nature of religion have been discovered by disciplines such as psychology and sociology, the reductionist approach is now widely discredited in many disciplines, not only religious studies.

The organization of this book highlights the demise of belief and the quest for a new understanding of transcendence. Five intellectual disciplines have been selected as particularly decisive for the reinterpretation of religion; the natural sciences, biological science, social theory, psychoanalysis, and the theory of history. These five fields have been selected because the religious issues they raised have had a broad social impact. Religion is a social phenomenon, and issues which once were confined to intellectual elites have, through education and the popular media, now forced their way into the foreground of the public religious consciousness. Within these five intellectual movements, presented in the order of their historical appearance, one representative has been selected because he addressed himself specifically to the religious implications of his field and because his thought marked a crucial turning point in modern intellectual history. Juxtaposed to the critics of religion are twentieth-century religious thinkers whose writings confronted a specific critical issue. Thus, Bultmann focuses on the conflict between natural science and mythological forms of faith. Teilhard grapples with the impact of Darwinism; Niebuhr, Camara, and Cone appropriate and criticize the legacy of Marx; Bonhoeffer and Erikson take up the psychological questions raised by Freud; and Tillich in his later years seeks to overcome the problem of historical relativism.

While the broad category of religion is used throughout the book, the focus falls consistently on Western Christian traditions. Both the religious spokesmen and the critics discuss the issues in terms of Christianity. Hume and Freud, for example, may refer in passing to primitive religions, but it is always clear that the focus of their analysis and criticism is that form of the Christian religion predominant in their social milieu. The criticism of religion and its reformulation does not occur in a vacuum or in the abstract realm of pure theory, but is always an event rooted in a particular social-cultural context. The issues debated, however, are not confined or peculiar to Christianity, but have proven to be problems for any religion confronting modernity. Thus, Bultmann's proposal of demythologizing has been used by Western Jewish thinkers and Japanese Buddhists; the crisis in belief created by the emergence of the scientific world view extends beyond the limits of any particular religious tradition. Modernity, however, first developed in the midst of Western culture where Christianity was the predominant religion, and for this reason Christianity was caught up in the great experiment of modernity.

The rationale of the book, then, is apparent. It does not deal with religion in an encyclopedic manner. Religion is an extremely complex phenomenon. It encompasses beliefs and doctrines, myths and rituals, devotional life, piety, and religious experience, personal and social ethics, sacred scriptures and cultic objects, and the manifestation of Transcendence in these many aspects. From this rich and variegated subject matter, this book, for the reasons we have indicated, focuses on the themes of belief and transcendence. To be sure, this thematic focus does not exclude numerous discussions relevant to other facets of religion. However, the reader should be alerted that not all aspects of religion have been equally problematic and prominent in the modern period. Furthermore, it is hardly possible to pursue the other areas of religious study without first coming to terms with these inescapable problems.

Consistent with this focus on subject matter and the inter-disciplinary approach, the book inevitably introduces the reader to several different methods widely used in the study of religion. However, methodology is not treated in the abstract. And some methods, like phenomenology of religion, are not included at all. Yet, in the course of examining the substantive issues, the reader will meet philosophical, sociological, psychological, and historical methods; furthermore, each of these methods is represented by a pioneering figure in his field. This enables the reader to acquire considerable competence in several important methods of religious studies. For pedagogical purposes, it seems most fruitful to introduce methodological considerations through an examination of substantive religious issues.

NATURAL SCIENCE
AND RELIGION

1

A Skeptic Examines Religious Beliefs

At the time of David Hume's burial, a large crowd gathered near his home. A bystander remarked, as the coffin passed by, "Ah, he was an atheist." "No matter," his companion replied, "he was an honest man."

This story, reported by Hume's biographer E. C. Mossner, suggests the new direction in religious studies developed by David Hume (1711–1776). Hume was in no sense a believer—though technically he was an agnostic and not an atheist—but he was committed to intellectual honesty with a passion. For the sake of this honesty, Hume cultivated doubt just as men in earlier times had cultivated belief. Credulity he found to be the enemy of intellectual honesty and skepticism a staunch ally. Religion, therefore, became for Hume not a subject for belief, but an object of inquiry, analysis, and criticism. The age of analysis superseded the age of belief in his writings, and the modern critical study of religion was born.

Hume was a more thoroughgoing skeptic than most of his Enlightenment contemporaries. His critical scrutiny was directed at the claims of science as well as the claims of religion. Thus, the laws of nature are not inherent in the universe itself, but belong to the interpretation of the scientist. In a similar manner, the sacred texts of religion do not contain the revelation of God but only the beliefs of ancient men. In both cases, Hume divested so-called objective truths of their solid objectivity and reinserted them into the looser texture of human experience and reflection. The pervasiveness of his skepticism prevented him from developing a constructive position in either science or religion. His own religious attitude appears only as an indirect implication of his criticism of others. The task of reconstruction was left for later generations.

In Hume's quest for honesty rather than belief, he established a style of critical, analytical thinking which has characterized the modern study of religion. Indeed, Hume's critical insights expressed in the eighteenth century anticipated a wide range of issues prominent in the scholarly discussion of religion throughout the nineteenth and twentieth centuries. Darwin's vision of an organic cosmos shaped by developmental laws intrinsic to it and not by an external Creator God, Marx's view of the oppressive role of religion in society, Freud's description of the psychological sources of religious belief in anxiety and projection, and Troeltsch's examination of Christian revelation claims in the context of other world religions reflect themes originally set forth by Hume. In addition, Hume's insistence on the separation of religious faith from all forms of scientific knowledge became decisive for the development of nineteenth- and twentieth-century theology, including the work of existentialists like Søren Kierkegaard and Rudolf Bultmann. To read Hume on the subject of religion today, almost two centuries after his death, is to encounter an intellectual revolutionary whose innovative methods of inquiry and radical proposals set the direction for the development of modern religious thought.

Hume's legacy may be identified in terms of three of his intellectual roles: as historian, social critic, and philosopher. As an historian, Hume's approach to religion marks the beginning of what is now called "the scientific study of religion." In *The Natural History of Religion* Hume poses the question of the origin of religion. Traditionally, the answer had been given either in terms of divine revelation or the apprehension of metaphysical properties. Hume, in contrast, offers his explanation for the origins of religious belief solely within the limits of this world, with no reference to a world beyond. His history of religion is a "natural history," not a "supernatural history." In writing this history, Hume adopts the detached attitude and empirical method of the scientist. He gathers empirical data from many primitive religions and compares them with each other. Hume's attitude, method, and goal all show the application of the methodology of the natural sciences to the subject matter of religion.

As a social critic, Hume paints a stark picture of the psychological and social consequences of Christianity in eighteenth-century Scotland. Hume's childhood left him with memories of the frightening harshness of Scottish Calvinism. As an adult, Hume also experienced Calvinism as a form of cultural repression inhibiting intellectual freedom; he was twice threatened with excommunication and on two occasions the powers of the church thwarted his efforts to obtain a university position. As a result, Hume's critique of religion is informed by personal passion and social concern as well as empirical methods. Religion represented for Hume a condition of bondage because it inhibited intellectual freedom, created unnecessary internal conflicts, and fostered cultural repression. In these respects, Hume's critique of religion anticipated later social critics like Karl Marx.

In his philosophical study of religion, Hume was the first to establish the respective independence of scientific knowledge and religious belief. Opposing the traditional doctrine that science and religion, reason and revelation, are inherently complementary, Hume maintained that scientific knowledge and religious belief are mutually exclusive. The scientist does not need to consult the claims of religion in the pursuit of empirical information; his findings may even contradict religious claims. The religious believer, in turn, does not depend upon scientific knowledge or rational arguments for his beliefs. In fact, religion is not even a form of knowing; it is, rather, a complex type of feeling. As a corollary of this bifurcation between science and religion, Hume argued that believers cannot legitimately employ either natural events (in the form of miracles) or rational arguments (such as the inference that the complexity of the world implies a creator God) in support of theistic claims. For Hume, the religious man can only be a fideist: one who believes without recourse to science or reason.

As an historian, social critic, and philosopher, David Hume introduced a new set of problems and issues for religion which came to constitute the agenda for the study of religion during the modern period. Because of the innovative thrust and comprehensive scope of his thought, David Hume's writings provide an appropriate point of departure for our examination of critical issues in modern religious thought.

1. THE ORIGINS OF RELIGION

Hume distinguishes between two basically different kinds of questions which may be asked about religion. In the first place, one may examine the historical and psychological origins of religion. This kind of inquiry requires the method of the scientist, who gathers empirical evidence from diverse religions and constructs hypotheses to account for the data. This question of origins is pursued by Hume in his now-classical essay, *The Natural History of Religion*. Secondly, one may inquire concerning the truth of religious claims or, to use Hume's phrase, their "foundation in reason" (4:21). Such an inquiry requires a philosophical clarification of terms and a logical analysis of the arguments used to validate religious assertions. This second question provides the theme of Hume's *Dialogues Concerning Natural Religion.*

Hume's analysis of the first of these issues in *The Natural History of Religion* begins with the claim that religion first arose among the crude tribal forebears of modern man. Hume's arguments in support of this claim reflect his indebtedness to earlier Enlightenment students of religion. Adopting a developmental view of history similar to that formulated by Bernard Fontenelle (1657–1757), Pierre Bayle (1647–1706), and other Enlightenment scholars, Hume likens the history of mankind to the growth of an individual, which, beginning with the pre-rational stage of infancy, moves in the direction of fully developed, adult rationality.[1] Like other Enlightenment figures, Hume looks back on his primitive childlike ancestors from the adult end of an upward curve representing the "natural progress of human thought" (4:24). He does not condemn his ancient forebears, but views them, rather, with pity. With Bernard Fontenelle, he adopts the superior attitude reflected in the French scholar's dictum: "What can one expect of *les pauvres sauvages* who knew nothing of weights, levers, or measurement?" Like Fontenelle and Bayle, Hume assumes an "improvement of human society, from rude beginnings to a state of greater perfection" (4:23). Unlike his French predecessors, however, Hume views historical development as a more limited process; he does not extend progress indefinitely into the future. The developmental thesis for Hume does not imply a doctrine of progress promising a new age of reason for all mankind. Rather, it simply indicates the primitive historical framework within which religion first appeared and in which its origins must be examined.

With this developmental thesis in mind, Hume argues that primitive polytheism was "the first and most ancient religion of mankind" (4:23). This claim represented a major break with the prevalent view of religious origins in the eighteenth century.[2] For the defenders of a rational religion of nature, polytheism appeared to be an isolated deviation from mankind's original belief in a single Creator. In refuting this theory, Hume gathers together a large quantity of evidence demonstrating the chronological priority and widespread prevalence of polytheism. Like other eighteenth-century students of religion, Hume had new data concerning primitive religions from the accounts of recent voyages of exploration. He cites examples from classical Egypt, Greece, and Rome as well as from "the savage tribes of America, Africa, and Asia" (4:23). Indeed, he finds that the historical evidence all points to the same conclusion: "The north, the south, the east, the west, give their unanimous testimony to the same fact. . . . Polytheism, the primitive religion of uninstructed mankind" (4:23,26).

Hume concludes from the historical priority of polytheism that religion originated and remains in the non-rational dimensions of human nature. If religion had begun as a creation of reason, then all men at all times would have recognized a single creator of this "vast machine," the cosmos.[3]

> Were men led into the apprehension of invisible, intelligent power by a contemplation of the works of nature, they could never possibly entertain any conception but of one single being, who bestowed existence and order on this vast machine and adjusted all its parts, according to one regular plan or connected system (4:26).

The pre-rational status of primitive man and the abundance of polytheistic religions all point away from human rationality as a possible point of origin for religion. Hume thus locates the origin of religion in the not-yet-rational nature of primitive man.

If religion is non-rational in its origins, is it nevertheless "an original instinct or primary impression of nature" (4:21)? Hume answers this question in the negative. In contrast to the universality of primary instincts, such as sexuality, hunger, and affection, Hume finds that religion is not "absolutely universal in all nations and ages" (4:21). There are individuals and even cultures which apparently lack any significant religious practices. Furthermore, the primary instincts invariably pursue a definite object, e.g. sexual gratification, food, or human fellowship. The objects of religious devotion, however, vary from culture to culture. Hume therefore concludes that religion is neither rooted in reason nor in a primary instinct.

Because religion does not spring from either reason or instinct, the question concerning its origins is complex. Hume warns his reader that it may be difficult to disentangle the multiple factors which lie at the root of religion. We may clarify Hume's interpretation of these roots by reference to three factors: the condition, the motive, and the operative principle of religion. In Hume's theory, religion originates in the condition of ignorance, it is motivated by fear, and it is elaborated by the imagination.

The first condition necessary for the birth of religion is *ignorance,* especially ignorance of scientific causality. Because primitive men were ignorant of the natural laws responsible for thunderstorms, earthquakes, and the like, they invented miracle stories and supernatural beings to explain both natural and historical events. Later, as they became more enlightened, their world view became more realistic and valid. Only then were they able to give a true account of natural laws and historical developments. The stories of primitive people, so busy with gods and demons acting in miracles, only reflects their condition of ignorance and their corresponding pre-scientific world view.

Because ignorance is a condition essential to the origins of religion, Hume often speaks of religion quite simply as "superstition," meaning, as Webster defines it, "a belief, conception, act or practice resulting from ignorance, unreasonable fear of the unknown or mysterious . . . a false conception of causation" (Webster's Third, p. 2296). In terms of Hume's developmental schema, superstition is primitive man's surrogate for science.

While ignorance is a necessary condition for religion, it is not a sufficient cause. Psychological motivation is equally essential. In attempting to explain the motivational origins of religious belief, Hume directs our attention away from the regularity of the natural environment and towards the uncertainties of human life.

> We are placed in this world, as in a great theatre, where the true springs and causes of every event are entirely concealed from us; nor have we either sufficient wisdom to foresee, or power to prevent those ills, with which we are continually threatened. We hang in perpetual suspense between life and death, health and sickness, plenty and want; which are distributed amongst the human species by secret and unknown causes, whose operation is oft unexpected, and always unaccountable (4:28,29).

It is only by understanding the anxiety of man's situation in such a world that we can understand the origins of religion.[4]

Hume identifies man's affective response to the insecurity of his life-situation as the principle *motive* for religion. He delineates a pattern of response that is diametrically opposite to that of the scientist. Whereas science requires detachment from one's feelings as a necessary prerequisite for the objective study of nature, religion considers "these admirable works in a more confined and selfish view" (4:47). Religion stems not from detachment, but from self-concern, especially from "anxious concern for happiness," "dread of future misery," and "terror of death" (4:28). Indeed, the greater the insecurity, the more "religious" man becomes; as in the case of war, "where the event is so uncertain" (4:30). Religion flourished in primitive times because men were comparatively more insecure: "All human life, especially before the institution of order and good government, being subject to fortuitous accidents; it is natural, that superstition should prevail . . ." (4:30).

Whereas science penetrates "into the secret structure of vegetable or animal bodies" in order to discern the cause-effect structure, religion simply postulates a variety of unknown causes as "the perpetual objects of hopes and fears, wishes and apprehensions" (4:47). However, religious man is not content simply to acknowledge such unknown causes. Instead, his *imagination* supplies what his reason lacks.

> As the *causes*, which bestow happiness or misery, are, in general, very
> little known and very uncertain, our anxious concern endeavors to attain
> a determinate idea of them; and finds no better expedient than to rep-
> resent them as intelligent voluntary agents, like ourselves; only somewhat
> superior in power and wisdom (4:40).

This is the operative principle of religion, the imaginative conversion of
unknown causes of anxiety into knowable beings like ourselves. Hume
attributes this process to "the active imagination"; today it is more frequently called projection.[5]

> By degrees, the active imagination of men, uneasy in this abstract concep-
> tion of objects, about which it is incessantly employed, begins to render
> them more particular, and to clothe them in shapes more suitable to its
> natural comprehension. It represents them to be sensible, intelligent be-
> ings, like mankind; actuated by love and hatred, and flexible by gifts and
> entreaties, by prayers and sacrifices. Hence the origin of religion (4:47).

Because of this cooperation of anxious need and imaginative projection, Hume often labels religion "idolatry." By this term, he refers primarily to the concrete visible images of gods portrayed in polytheistic
religions. However, "idolatry" also refers to any religion engendered by
human need and imaginative projection.[6] In Hume's view, any deity born
of this matrix, including the monotheistic God of Judaism and Christianity, is not genuinely ultimate.

Hume locates the origins of religion in the following conspiracy of
confusion: the conditions of ignorance, the motive of anxiety, and the
operative principle of the imaginative projection of human qualities onto
unknown causes. Hume neither presented an attractive picture of religion
nor made it appealing to men of his own age. Indeed, as we shall see,
Hume's analysis of ancient religious origins was, for the most part, a pro-
logue to his critique of that form of Christianity which he found so destructive and oppressive in his own life-situation.

2. THE SOCIAL CRITICISM OF RELIGION

The critical passion which informs Hume's study of religion becomes
apparent for the first time in his discussion of Calvinist Christianity.
Hume intends to expose, and thereby weaken, the religious beliefs and
practices characteristic of his own childhood and society. He is engaged
in an existential project, not simply a theoretical and objective reconstruction of primitive religion.

In two respects, primitive polytheism serves as a foil for Hume's
critique of contemporary religion. First, polytheism provides Hume with
a neutral territory within which it was relatively non-controversial to

establish the non-rational origins of religion. Having demonstrated the irrational roots of religion, Hume then proceeds to demonstrate the essential continuity between ancient polytheism and modern Christian theism. For Hume, Christianity begins in the same womb of ignorance, anxiety, and fantasy which gave birth to the primitive gods. Second, consideration of the benign consequences of polytheism provides Hume with an opportunity to discuss the undesirable, even demonic, psychological and social consequences of Calvinism. Calvin's religion may share the same origins as ancient polytheism, but its consequences are far more harmful for both individual and political life. As an institution destructive of both psychological harmony and individual freedom, Calvinism is viewed by Hume as an extremely dysfunctional social force. It is primarily for this reason that Hume utilized all the information at his command as well as his immense intellectual talents to diminish Calvinism's widespread authority.

Curiously, however, Hume seldom uses the term "Calvinism" or even "Christianity." Instead, he speaks of "modern religion." "Modern religion" refers neither to Hume's own religious attitude—which he calls "true religion"—nor to that form of rational theism which was prevalent among eighteenth-century intellectuals. Occasionally, he extends his use of the phrase "modern religion" to include Roman Catholicism and Anglicanism, but the term usually refers to the Orthodox Calvinism which was the prevailing form of religion in his own country.

Like other children in eighteenth-century Scotland, young David attended church for at least three hours on Sunday. His own family were members at Chirnside Parish Church where David's uncle, George Home, was the pastor. The sabbath service included a sermon and a lecture in which the preacher was expected to review the main points in the drama of salvation. The bleak economic conditions of the period tended to reinforce the harsher aspects of Calvin's teachings. The fall, man's condition of sin and degradation, his present hopelessness and future judgment were strongly emphasized. Because of his continuing offense against God, man had accumulated an enormous burden of guilt which provoked in God an appropriate response of wrath and condemnation. As one historian of the Scottish church observes,

> During the seventeenth century, Scottish religion had fallen greatly under the influence of English puritanism. . . . [It] depicted God as an implacable despot, swift to wrath . . . it held by the doctrines of election and reprobation in all their severity (5:4).

By the age of seventeen or eighteen, David had turned away from the religion of his childhood. Nevertheless, his experience with Calvinism in these early years continued to play a decisive role in his later thought. As Norman Kemp Smith points out, Calvinism

> continued to typify for him what he meant by religion; and owing to the very strength of aversion which he had come to feel towards it, it was an important factor in determining the contrary character of the beliefs to which . . . he definitively committed himself (5:8).

Later in his career Hume became acquainted with representatives of a more moderate form of Calvinism, but his view of "modern religion" was already formed by that time.

According to Hume, the popular Christian theism of modern Europe is no less rooted in ignorance than primitive polytheism. "Even at this day . . . the vulgar, in nations which have embraced the doctrine of theism, still build it upon irrational and superstitious principles" (4:41, 42). As evidence of contemporary Christian ignorance, Hume cites the continuing belief in miracles. In his eyes, the fact that a large number of people believe in miracles violating the laws of nature and human rationality provides no proof of their validity. Even if all English historians should agree that Queen Elizabeth had died, was declared dead by physicians and mourned by members of the court, was buried for a month, and then returned to rule for three years, Hume writes, "I should not have the least inclination to believe so miraculous an event" (6:135). Yet, Christianity continues to rely upon ancient books which recount absurd miracle stories. The stories in the Old Testament, for example, are "presented to us by a barbarous and ignorant people, written in an age when they were still more barbarous . . . and resembling those fabulous accounts, which every nation gives of its origins" (6:137). If barbarous ancient Hebrews believed miracle stories innocently, modern man believes such stories only by violating his rational integrity. To maintain modern man's rational integrity by eliminating miracles in Christianity would, however, virtually destroy its popular basis and appeal (6:134). Hume therefore concludes his analysis of the superstitious bases of popular Christianity by envisioning a perpetual conflict between the miraculous aspects of Christianity and the emerging rational, scientific world view.

If popular Christianity is rooted in ignorance, fear and anxiety provide its chief motivational roots. The monotheistic God of Christianity simply expresses an extension of the same anxiety which gave birth to the less powerful deities of polytheism:

> the same anxious concern for happiness, which begets the idea of these invisible, intelligent powers, allows not mankind to remain long in the first conception of them; as powerful, but limited beings. . . . Men's ex-

aggerated praises and compliments still swell their ideas upon them; and elevating their deities to the utmost bounds of perfection, at last beget the attributes of unity and infinity, simplicity, and spirituality (4:47).

Rooted in fear, monotheism represents a partial transformation of the object of worship in order to meet man's developing rational need for a more abstract and spiritual deity.

Hume's most eloquent critique of modern religion is found in his exposé of the role of fear in generating Calvinist faith. From his own experience, Hume knew how Scottish preachers played with the natural fears of men in attempting to drive them towards faith in Christ. "No topic," he writes, "is more usual with all popular divines than to display the advantages of affliction, in bringing men to a due sense of religion; by subduing their confidence and sensuality, which, in times of prosperity, make them forgetful of a divine providence" (4:31). This emphasis upon fear, which Hume finds in Calvinist preaching, not only reflects man's true condition in this world; it also includes an increment introduced by the Calvinist imagination itself. Hume accordingly distinguishes between the roots of fear which "springs from the essential and universal properties of human nature" and the inventions of men which "aggravate our natural infirmities and follies of this kind, but never originally beget them" (4:73). The trouble with Calvinism, in Hume's opinion, is its intensification of the natural fears of man which polytheism simply expresses. Whereas the element of fear is a minor motif in pagan religions, the "active imagination" of the Calvinist heightens human anxiety by characterizing the deity in terms of "wrath, fury, vengeance, and all the blackest vices" (4:69).

In short, Hume finds that ignorance, anxiety, and imaginative projection are elements constitutive of Calvinism as well as of paganism. The fact that both these religions are grounded in similar causal factors does not mean that they are equally benign. Christianity, in Hume's opinion, is far more destructive than polytheism. Indeed, it is precisely because modern Christianity has so intensified fear that it has a greater destructive capacity. If religion cannot be abolished, Hume argues, it is, nevertheless, possible to mitigate its malign influences. In arguing for such mitigation, Hume contrasts the innocence of pagan polytheism with the demonic power of Calvinism.[7]

The first of these contrasts compares the pagan freedom to doubt religious claims with the hypocritical assurance of modern Calvinists. In primitive religions, doctrinal beliefs are vague and shrouded in darkness, for their teachings consist primarily of loose collections of stories which have yet to be shaped into "determinate articles of faith," "fixed dogmas and principles" (4:61). This "complex, contradictory, and, on many occasions, doubtful" religious tradition encourages pagans to "faulter and hesitate more in maintaining their principles," and is apt to produce a qualified assent to the claims of religious stories (4:61). In contrast, modern religions, especially Calvinism, demand unconditional acceptance of strict doctrinal tenets. Faced with this demand for unquestioned faith and its re-enforcement by the emotional "enthusiasm" and commitment generated by worship services, modern believers tend to deny, even in their own hearts, the doubts they actually entertain regarding religious issues. "They make a merit of implicit faith; and disguise to themselves their real infidelity, by the strongest asseverations and most positive bigotry" (4:60). The result is hypocrisy, inasmuch as doubt continues to exist underneath great professions of faith. Indeed, under these conditions, the man who makes "a great profession of religion and devotion" becomes so untrustworthy as to induce prudent men to put up "their guard lest they be cheated and deceived by him" (5:275). Primitive hesitation is thus replaced by hypocritical credulity.

(2) Second, Hume contrasts the manly virtues generated by paganism with the self-depreciation, abasement, and humility engendered by Calvinism. Because the gods of polytheism are only slightly superior to man, the primitive is "at ease in addressing them, and may even, without profaneness, aspire sometimes to a rivalship and emulation of them" (4:52). The psychological effects of such worship are "activity, spirit, courage, magnanimity, love of liberty, and all the virtues which aggrandize a people" (4:52). By way of contrast, all forms of Christianity, Roman Catholic as well as Protestant, foster "the monkish virtues of mortification, penance, humility, and passive suffering" (4:52). Hume's explanation of this self-depreciation is identical with Friedrich Nietzsche's claim that there is an intimate connection between the exaltation of a deity and the diminution of the self: "Where the deity is represented as infinitely superior to mankind, this belief, though altogether just, is apt, when joined with superstitious terrors, to sink the human mind into the lowest submission and abasement" (4:52).[8]

(3) The tendency of Calvinism to destroy the psychic equilibrium maintained by polytheism is a third contrast introduced by Hume. Primitive religions do not plunge their adherents into psychic conflicts by inducing an exaggerated sense of terror. Pagan fables are "light, easy, and familiar; without devils, or seas of brimstone, or any object that could much terrify the imagination" (4:61). In marked contrast, Calvinism portrays a God bereft of ordinary benevolence and preoccupied with vengeance. Given the opportunity, Hume contends, Christians would disavow such a deity as "a species of demonism." They cannot do so, however, without fear of reprisal. Hence, Christians are plunged into deep intra-psychic conflict:

The heart secretly detests such measures of cruel and implacable vengeance; but the judgment dares not but pronounce them perfect and
adorable. And the additional misery of this inward struggle aggravates
all the other terrors, by which these unhappy victims to superstition
are forever haunted (4:67).

Finally, Hume censures Calvinism for inducing a heavier burden of
guilt than primitive religion. Whereas guilt is scarcely mentioned in
primitive religions, self-accusation is heightened by Calvinist sermons on
sin and judgment. The resulting sense of unworthiness and self-con-
demnation does not succeed in fostering morality; it, rather, drives *homo
religiosus* to useless and compulsive acts of self-mortification ("fasting or
whipping") designed "to allay those terrors with which he is haunted"
(4:72). Religion, therefore, does not necessarily engender moral virtue.
Quite the contrary, it may generate cruelty towards oneself and others.

Hume condemns Calvinism for inducing hypocrisy, self-effacement,
intra-psychic conflict, and guilt. Yet, religion need not always be so ma-
lignant. Over against these destructive consequences of Calvinism, Hume
sets forth the *"traditional, mythological* religion" of primitive man "which,
however groundless . . . sits also so easy and light on men's minds
that . . . it happily makes no such deep impression on the affections
and understanding" (4:65). The theoretical conclusion to be drawn from
this comparison is clear: the less serious a religion, the more humane it
is likely to be.

Hume's negative evaluation of modern religion in its Calvinist form
remains undiminished as he turns from the individual to society. In his
own age, it was axiomatic to regard religion as a positive social good,
which restrained the evil in man by fostering moral virtue. Indeed, most
people then believed that religion provided the only viable foundation
for morality in society. Hume rejected this view. Having learned from
science to trust the orderliness of the external world of nature, Hume saw
no reason not to trust natural human inclinations, sentiments, and instincts. Virtue, in his opinion, is simply a natural sentiment brought to
its fruition. It is human nature, not religion, that is the real foundation
of morality. Religion, in fact, may be an enemy of natural virtues if it
misdirects man's innate benevolence. Instead of supporting the moral
foundations of society, religion may undermine both political stability
and individual freedom.

In attempting to demonstrate the undesirable political consequences
of religion, Hume cites several historical examples dealing with religious
fanaticism. "Factions, civil wars, persecutions, subversions of government, oppression, slavery: these are the dismal consequences which
always attend its [religion's] prevalency over the minds of men" (5:271-
72). The dogmatism engendered by religion undermines the tolerant

attitude required for political stability and good government. As one of the characters in Hume's *Dialogues* observes, happy and prosperous periods of history are those during which religion is least regarded (5:272). For religious intolerance threatens both civil harmony and good government.

Hume also objects to the way modern religions tend to inhibit individual freedom, especially intellectual freedom. In the loose doctrinal texture of the ancient world this was not the case. Philosophical freedom, for example, flourished alongside religion. Ancient Greece never produced anything resembling the inquisitions in Rome and Madrid (4:51). In the dogmatic atmosphere of eighteenth-century Scotland, Hume knew from personal experience that religious intolerance flourished and philosophy suffered. "Even at the present, when she [philosophy] may be supposed more hardy and robust, she bears with much difficulty the inclemency of the seasons, and those harsh winds of calumny and persecution which blow upon her" (6:140). Hume sees philosophy itself partially responsible for the transition from the open spirit of pagan antiquity to the dogmatic fanaticism of Calvinism. Philosophy's role in this transition resulted from extending her mantle of reason to religion:

> This pertinacious bigotry, of which you complain, as so fatal to philosophy, is really her offspring, who, after allying with superstition, separates himself entirely from the interest of his parent, and becomes her most inveterate enemy and persecutor (6:140).

Philosophers must mend their ways if the demonic power of religion is to be checked. Hume accordingly admonishes his philosophical colleagues, most of whom were content with the harmony of scientific reason and religious faith in natural theology, to abandon their efforts to bless religion with the grace of reason. Only by separating reason from religion will philosophy become genuinely free of the dominant and harmful effects of religion.

3. A PHILOSOPHICAL CRITIQUE OF NATURAL THEOLOGY

Hume's criticism of popular Calvinism, while offensive to churchmen of his native Scotland, did not greatly disturb his intellectual contemporaries. As men of science, they did not share the prevailing popular faith. They adhered, rather, to a form of natural theology that combined Newtonian science with the biblical idea of God as Creator and Moral Judge. Hume nowhere directly attacks this species of natural theology in any of the works published during his lifetime. In these publications, he continues to pay lip service to the rational theism of natural theology.

In the introduction to *The Natural History of Religion,* for instance, Hume expresses the central creed of natural theology:

> The whole frame of nature bespeaks an intelligent author; and no rational enquirer can, after serious reflection, suspend his belief a moment with regard to the primary principles of genuine Theism and Religion (4:21).

At the same time that he was professing this central creed of natural theology, however, Hume was also writing the *Dialogues Concerning Natural Religion* in which he developed a decisive refutation of that creed. Written in 1751, the book was so controversial that Hume delayed its publication until after his death in 1776. His closest intellectual friends and colleagues were sufficiently disturbed by the book to advise him against publishing it in any form at any time. Yet, the book was obviously an extremely important one for Hume. He labored on the manuscript through many revisions, and stipulated in his will that it be published after his death. In these *Dialogues,* Hume turned his attention from popular forms of faith to the rational theology prevalent among his sophisticated contemporaries.

Although rational theism or natural theology eventually became popular among educated classes throughout Northern Europe, it flourished first in England at the end of the seventeenth century, where it developed in close conjunction with the orthodox Christianity of the Anglican Church. Its outstanding spokesmen included John Tillotson (the Archbishop of Canterbury), John Locke (the well-known philosopher), Samuel Clarke (the most eminent theologian of the era), and Sir Isaac Newton.[9] By the time the young Hume first encountered natural theology in the writings of Samuel Clarke, the new movement was being widely praised by the foremost intellectuals of the day. Hume's reaction was quite different. In describing his adolescent reaction to Clarke, for example, Hume states that Clarke's failure to rationally justify religion convinced him of the folly of the entire enterprise. Indeed, his negative reaction to Clarke became decisive in his repudiation of religion itself (5:97).

Three distinctive features characterize the Christian natural theology of Tillotson, Locke, Clarke, and Newton. First, religion is seen not as an emotional feeling or instinctual act but as a set of intellectual propositions verifiable by evidence and rational argument. Hence, there is no qualitative distinction between the science of physics and the science of natural theology:

> The arguments employed in all [sciences] are of a similar nature and contain the same force and evidence. Or if there be any difference among them, the advantage lies entirely on the side of theology and natural religion (5:170).

Second, spokesmen for natural theology view historic Christianity as thoroughly consistent with a religion grounded in reason. The title of John Locke's *The Reasonableness of Christianity as Delivered in the Scriptures* (1695) and a book by his student, John Toland, entitled *Christianity Not Mysterious* (1696) illustrate this contention.[10] Even Archbishop Tillotson regards Christianity as essentially a rationally grounded set of propositions. The revelation of God given in Scriptures may be a practical aid, given because of human sin and intellectual weakness, our spokesmen argue, but revelation does not contradict rationally justified propositions. Thus Locke, utilizing criteria designed to test the rationality of religions, finds that Christianity contains truth in agreement with reason (such as the existence of a Creator) and truth above reason (such as the resurrection of the body), but no truth in contradiction with reason, like the superstitious beliefs of pagans. For this reason, the representative of natural theology in Hume's *Dialogues* credits Locke with being

> the first Christian, who ventured openly to assert, that *faith* was nothing but a species of *reason*, that religion was only a branch of philosophy, and that a chain of arguments, similar to that which established any truth in morals, politics, or physics, was always employed in discovering all the principles of theology, natural and revealed (5:171).

Third, exponents of natural theology argue for the existence of God from the design of nature. This argument has three distinct elements. The first is simply the complex order of nature. Having recently learned a great deal about the natural world from the new science of physics, natural theologians marvel at the intricate and complex interconnections between the parts and the whole.[11] The anatomy of the eye is a favorite example employed both by theologians and scientists. The second element is the image of nature as a vast machine. This mechanistic image of nature had its origins in the Renaissance, but it did not become the predominant image until Newton articulated the laws by which the cosmic machine was governed. A third element is the principle of analogy. The whole of nature disclosing a design, order, and purpose similar to human constructs, it seems reasonable to assume that such a design or order is not the result of chance or accident. From similar effects, natural theologians infer similar causes. Just as the mind of man makes a machine, and just as no machine is ever constructed by chance, similarly, a Cosmic Intelligence, a First Cause, or the Mind of God must have made the whole of nature. In other words, "the Author of nature is somewhat similar to the mind of man; though possessed of much larger faculties . . ." (6:176).

Against these several aspects of natural theology, Hume hurls the battery of brilliant arguments contained in the *Dialogues*. Three different characters develop the thrust of Hume's argument in a dialogical form: Cleanthes, the spokesman for natural theology; Philo, the philosophical skeptic who most directly expresses Hume's own position; and Demea, the pious Calvinist.[12] Through these spokesmen, Hume sets forth three basic objections to the rational theism of natural theology:

1. Reason is limited to the realm of human experience; therefore, it cannot decide ultimate questions, like the origin of the cosmos or the existence of God.

2. The argument for the existence of God from the design of nature depends upon an illegitimate, and therefore invalid, application of the principle of analogy.

3. Science may account for the order of nature without recourse to a transcendent Creator. If the whole of nature is understood as an organism, instead of as a machine, then the principle of order may be understood as immanent in nature, not transcendent of it. Science would then be free to abandon the God-hypothesis.[13]

Early in the *Dialogues*, Philo expresses Hume's views regarding the first of these objections to natural theology. Referring to his "skeptical considerations on the uncertainties and narrow limits of reason," Philo reminds his disputants of the errors to which reason is liable even in judgments concerning objects in the natural world (5:165). All the sciences constantly depend upon experiments to verify the conclusions of reason. With what assurance, therefore, could reason offer any judgment concerning the origin of the cosmos or the nature of a First Cause (5:162)? In addition, Philo argues that reason not only depends upon experience for its verification, but reason itself is constituted within the limits of experience. For Philo, as for Hume, all ideas are mental impressions derived from experience.[14] He therefore concludes that reason violates its very nature when it attempts to transcend the "narrow limits" of ordinary experience by pontificating on ultimate questions.

> Our ideas reach no farther than our experience: we have no experience of divine attributes and operations: I need not conclude my syllogism: you can draw the inference yourself (5:176).

In addition to this first critique, Hume also refutes the attempt to argue for the existence of God from the design of nature. According to Hume, the principle of analogy only applies to instances of species when we know the cause and effect of the species. For example, if we find a house on an uninhabited desert island, we infer that the house was built by a man. For every instance of the species "house" known to us has been built by a man. Therefore, when we find a house in an uninhabited place, we conclude that the house (effect) has also been built by a man (cause). However, in the creation of the universe, we are not considering one instance of a species but a single unique event. Inasmuch as we have not witnessed the process of creation or seen a world-maker at work, we are not in a position to make any inference concerning the cause of the unique effect. Unlike our knowledge of builders and houses, we only know the effects of creation; we have no knowledge of the cause.

In refuting the argument from design, Hume does not—and cannot—ignore the fact of order in nature. How, then, can we account for order, if it is not the work of a Creator? Hume responds with what he regards as a far simpler explanation: matter contains within itself its own principle of order. Philo asks why it is necessary to postulate a cause of order beyond the cosmos itself. Why is it not sufficient to simply recognize order as a characteristic of nature itself? In proposing this hypothesis, Hume suggests abandoning the mechanistic image of nature in favor of an organic image. If the cosmos is seen as a vast machine, it is necessary to account for order by reference to a transcendent cause; but if nature is viewed as an organism, the principle of order may be understood as immanent in nature.[15]

Hume's three-pronged critique of natural theology had little impact in the English-speaking world in either the eighteenth or early nineteenth centuries. In part, this was due to the literary device which he employed to conceal the main thrust of the argument. At the end of the *Dialogues,* Pamphilus, who is cast as the neutral observer and reporter, concludes that "Philo's principles are more probable than Demea's . . . but those of Cleanthes approach still nearer to the truth" (5:282). In part, the concluding words of Pamphilus were accepted because they were more consistent with the scientific, philosophical, and religious climate of the eighteenth century than Hume's own position. Only after Charles Darwin provided evidence for viewing the natural world as an organism and Immanuel Kant found a way of separating scientific knowledge from religious faith without depreciating religion could Hume's penetrating critique of natural theology be fully appreciated.

4. AN AGNOSTIC VERSION OF "TRUE RELIGION"

Hume's repudiation of both popular and rational religion did not entail a rejection of religion *per se.* In the closing chapter of the *Dialogues,* Philo reminds Cleanthes that

> you are sensible that . . . no one has a deeper sense of religion impressed upon his mind, or pays more profound adoration to the divine Being, as he discovers himself to reason (5:264).

In another context, Hume describes his own religious position by the phrase "true religion" and relates his respect for true religion to his criticism of popular religion: "In proportion to my veneration for true religion is my abhorrence of vulgar superstition" (5:271). Although Hume was more concerned with criticizing religious views prevalent in the eighteenth century than with explicating his own position, it is, none-theless, possible to identify two characteristic themes associated with "true religion."

First, Hume acknowledges a dimension of mystery given in and with man's rational knowledge of the cosmos. Rejecting atheism as well as theism, Hume maintains that reason can neither prove nor disprove the existence of God. Second, the dimension of mystery Hume acknowledges is irreducibly vague and opaque. As a result, he could not convert this apprehension of mystery, by means of images or concepts, into a definite Being or Beings. "Suspense of judgment" thus becomes the salient char-acteristic of "true religion." As Hume puts it:

> The whole is a riddle, an aenigma, an inexplicable mystery. Doubt, un-
> certainty, suspence of judgment appear the only result of our most ac-
> curate scrutiny, concerning this subject (4:76).

Hume suspends judgment regarding most religious issues, including the nature or attributes of God. Near the end of the *Dialogues*, Philo ac-cepts Cleanthes' argument that "the cause or causes of order in the uni-verse probably bears some remote analogy to human intelligence" (5:281). Hume quickly adds, however, that even this remote analogy between human intelligence and the ultimate cause of order in the universe is limited. The possibility that this ultimate cause may be analogous to human intelligence does not provide a basis for attributing any other human qualities to the deity. For example, Hume refuses to characterize the deity in terms of human will or particular moral attributes, such as justice and mercy. An ultimate being characterized by something analo-gous to human intelligence is about as close as Hume comes to a positive religious assertion.

Hume also asks what evidence is available to support belief in the goodness of the deity. Human misery and evil abound; the virtues and strengths of created beings are minimal resources sufficient for survival but little else. Does such evidence support the goodness of the Creator? Hume responds, on the basis of the evidence, human and non-human, that man must conclude that if God is all-powerful, He is not good; or, if He is good, He is not all-powerful. In contrast with both popular and rational religion, Hume steadfastly refuses to make any judgment con-cerning the nature of the unknown.

"Suspense of judgment" also dominates Hume's view of religious activities. Both popular and rational religions agree in acknowledging cult and ritual as an appropriate expression of man's religious response. The deities of polytheism had their own priests, forms of worship, and religious communities. The sacred literature and worship of the Christian church were accepted by most natural theologians as appropriate religious expressions for rational man. For Hume, the practice of true religion is limited to "philosophical assent to the proposition . . . that the cause or causes of order in the universe probably bears some remote analogy to human intelligence" (5:281). True religion neither entails the adoption of sacred literature nor includes participation in sacred ritual. Indeed, any form of worship going beyond rational assent is idolatrous.

> "To know god is to worship him." All other worship is indeed absurd, superstitious, and even impious (5:280).

Finally, Hume refuses to grant religious knowledge of future rewards and punishments. In both popular religion and natural theology, future expectations of divinely administered rewards and punishments were deemed essential for morality. Because the just frequently suffer while the unjust prosper here on earth, it was felt that only a judgment beyond history could rectify the imbalance in history and so guarantee moral behavior. For Hume, true religion excludes any knowledge of the future:

> No new fact can ever be inferred from the old religious hypothesis; no event foreseen or foretold; no reward or punishment expected or dreaded, beyond what is actually known by practice and observation (6:155).

Consequently, "true religion" cannot exert any direct influence on morality. It is neither a source of morality in society nor a motive for individual moral behavior. For Hume, a natural sentiment, not religion, provides the only genuine basis for morality;

> A sentiment of order and moral obligation joins its force to . . . natural ties, and the whole man, if truly virtuous, is drawn to his duty, without any effort or endeavour (4:71).

Hume realized that his version of "true religion" would neither replace popular Calvinism nor supplant natural theology. "The philosophical skeptics" who were willing "to suspend, or endeavour to suspend all judgments with regard to such sublime and such extraordinary subjects" were few in number. They constituted an extremely rare sect (5:281). Like his Calvinist ancestors, Hume envisioned a select theological elite;

indeed, those destined for "true religion" were rarer than those predestined for salvation in Calvin's theology.[16]

5. THE LEGACY AND LIMITS OF HUME'S CRITIQUE

David Hume's writings offer the most comprehensive critique of traditional religion developed by any author in the eighteenth century. Yet, Hume's writings on religion were largely ignored, especially in the English-speaking world. His most radical work, *Dialogues Concerning Natural Religion,* was misunderstood until the early decades of this century. Natural theology continued to flourish in England without any significant detraction from Hume for over a century after his death. In assessing Hume's significance for the modern study of religion, we must follow a more indirect route than his direct impact on Anglo-Saxon philosophy and theology: first, we shall identify the significant ways in which Hume anticipated later theories of religion; second, we shall note his decisive impact on the development of continental philosophy and theology.

Hume's account of the origin of religion anticipated the development of anthropology and comparative religion in the nineteenth and twentieth centuries. Among the scholars responsible for the development of these fields, F. Max Mueller, E. B. Tylor, and James G. Fraser set forth diverse theories of religion.[17] Like Hume, they gathered data from the many different religions of the world. They also refused to grant biblical religion a privileged status, since it was only one among many world religions. Like Hume, they sought a single point of origin of all religious phenomena. In recent decades, this quest for a single point of origin has been abandoned for more fruitful lines of inquiry. However, Hume's cross-cultural method of gathering data from diverse religions and his inclusion of biblical materials alongside other sacred literature for comparative purposes continue to serve as working principles in the scientific study of religion.

At several points, Hume also anticipated the theory of religion formulated by Sigmund Freud. Like the founder of psychoanalysis, Hume sees psychic conflict—though he did not have the phrase available to him—as a significant factor in the genesis of religious belief. Specifically, both Hume and Freud agree that religion originates in man's insecurity and anxiety in the face of the unknown and threatening. In comparison with Freud's extensive use of clinical data or in comparison with the modern anthropologist's use of abundant field data, Hume's resources seem limited and his methods crude. Nevertheless, Hume's insights are striking in their anticipation of the more sophisticated studies of religion developed in the nineteenth and twentieth centuries.

Although Hume exercised little direct influence on the development of Anglo-Saxon religious thought, his writings did function as a significant catalyst in the formation of German philosophy and theology. At least two major continental schools of thought—which will be more fully explained in the following chapter—owe a considerable debt to Hume's writings on religion. The first is the philosophy of Immanuel Kant. Kant was first "awakened from his dogmatic slumber" by Hume's skepticism.[18] It goaded him to develop a critical philosophy in which moral and religious knowledge was sharply differentiated from scientific forms of knowing. Subsequently, Kant's philosophy provided the systematic basis for acceptance in modern Protestant theology of Hume's separation of religious faith from scientific knowledge. While religion and morality remained bound together in Kant's own philosophical work, the Neo-Kantians at the end of the nineteenth century separated religion from morality as well as from scientific forms of knowledge. In this Neo-Kantian revision, Hume's view of religion as separated from both morality and scientific knowledge finally found systematic philosophical expression.

The second continental school of thought influenced by Hume is existentialism. When one of the earliest anticipators of existentialism, Johann Georg Hamann (1730–1788), received a copy of Hume's *Dialogues,* he was so impressed by the book that he translated it into German. As a critic of eighteenth-century rationalism, Hamann found an ally in Hume. He especially appreciated the fact that Hume "took faith seriously in his philosophical system and knew that it could not be derived from reason." Hamann, however, developed a very distinctive theological position over against Hume's "true religion" in which the Christian act of faith supplants the English skeptic's vague apprehension of mystery. While little known for his own writings, Hamann's theology of faith played a significant role in the life and writings of the founder of existentialism, Søren Kierkegaard.[19] In the following chapter, we shall examine the writings of Rudolf Bultmann, a twentieth-century German theologian who combined Neo-Kantian philosophy with Kierkegaard's existential theology.

Having briefly indicated the scope and legacy of Hume's writings on religion, we now turn to several critical objections to his critique of religion.

First, we need to qualify our earlier assertion that Hume was a pioneer in the scientific study of religion. It is true that Hume gathered data from a variety of world religions, interpreted this data in the context of natural history, and, in this way, extended scientific inquiry to religion. However, a genuinely scientific interpretation would not attempt at the outset to offer a single explanation for a phenomenon as complex as religion. The manifold richness of religious phenomena and the variety of causal factors that have influenced the world's religions are simply too complex. For this reason twentieth-century scholars of religion have characteristically limited themselves to the task of describing the complex interrelationships affecting a particular religion in a specific socio-cultural context. Hume's mono-causal theory has not been particularly helpful for modern scholars interested in understanding the diversified and often conflicting forces that have inspired religious belief.

Second, Hume's explanation of the dynamics of religion—anxiety, ignorance, and imagination—is not supported by contemporary knowledge of religious traditions. Anxiety may have been a factor in the genesis of some religions and may continue to motivate some individuals, but Pure Land Buddhism and Pauline Christianity, to select two examples, are best characterized as religions primarily expressive of our ability to love and trust one another.[20] Amita Buddha and the Lord Jesus are experienced as figures who evoke trust and confidence in their believers. Similarly, ignorance of natural causality is not a necessary condition for religious piety. In the seventeenth century, when the Royal Society of science was founded in England, a majority of its members were Puritans, and many historians have pointed out the close connection between religious faith and the development of the sciences throughout modern history. Finally, while man's imaginative faculties do find expression in religion through images, symbols, legends and myths, this imaginative enterprise is not necessarily in conflict with rational reflection or with truth. Rationality and faith may be different dimensions of the human spirit, but this does not necessarily imply a conflict. Plato claimed the *mythos* of imagination as an ally for the *logos* of reason and many contemporary scientists would agree with his claim. The religious utilization of imagination may itself be a mode of access to truth and not simply the substitution of fantasy for fact.

Finally, we must question Hume's moral theory. In developing his critique of Calvinism, Hume argues in favor of natural moral sentiments and individual freedom. He was therefore critical of Calvinism for restraining free expression of innate benevolence and intellectual freedom. At this point, Hume's moral theory is similar to the economic theory of his close friend Adam Smith. Smith also sought to eliminate all restraints on the free activity of the entrepreneur. In Smith's theory of *laissez-faire* capitalism, the marketplace provided an automatic and sufficient regulator of man's acquisitive instincts. Similarly, Hume trusts that man's natural moral sentiments are sufficient for a life of moral duty and beneficence toward others. If freed from oppressive restraints like religion, man's intrinsic virtues will find expression in his life with others. In light of Freud's diagnosis of man's aggressive instincts and in light of the dramatization of man's capacity for destruction at Auschwitz and Hiroshima, we might well doubt Hume's confidence in the adequacy of the individual's natural sentiments as a basis for morality.

Whatever the limitations of Hume's position, they do not seriously detract from his contribution to our understanding of religion. In his commitment to intellectual honesty, Hume thoroughly explored the nature and legitimacy of religious claims. As a scientific historian, Hume called attention to the irrational origins and functions of religious belief. His theory of religion as rooted in ignorance, anxiety, and imagination did not prove fruitful for understanding the complexity and variety of religious phenomena, but did illumine important aspects of religious belief often hidden from the believer. As a philosopher, Hume undermined that fusion of faith and reason which had been a cornerstone of earlier Christian civilization. While his version of "true religion" did not provide an adequate substitute for an historical faith, his distinction between religious faith and scientific knowledge did play a formative role in the development of modern religious thought.

After Hume, credulity was no longer an ultimate virtue, for all beliefs were placed under the moral jurisdiction of honesty.

NOTES

1 Prior to Hume, early French Enlightenment figures Bernard Fontenelle and Pierre Bayle had already articulated the developmental hypothesis and the notion of primitive ignorance of the natural world as the context for understanding the origins of religion. Through his travels and residence in France, Hume became familiar with Bayle's writings. For a discussion of these French Enlightenment figures, see Frank Manuel, *The Eighteenth Century Confronts the Gods* (7:24-56).

2 Representatives of natural theology in England, like Sir Isaac Newton, John Toland, and Matthew Tindal, had argued that monotheism was the original religion of humanity. In their view, primitive man had an instinctive attraction to monotheism, temporarily deflected towards polytheism by fear and other passions, and now restored by Christian Revelation and/or enlightened Reason. Hume's collection of religious data from diverse nations is deliberately intended to refute this hypothesis of "primitive monotheism" (7:57-69 and 118ff.).

3 While Hume can use the mechanical model of the universe which is prevalent in his Newtonian culture, he is himself committed to the older Greek view of the cosmos as an organism; (see above, p. 29). A clear contrast between organic and mechanical models of nature is depicted in R. G. Collingwood, *The Idea of Nature* (Oxford: Clarendon Press, 1945).

4 Many contemporary sociologists identify the basic functions of religion in relation to natural conditions of human life like scarcity, contingency, and powerlessness. For a discussion of functional theories of religion in sociology, see Thomas F. O'Dea, *The Sociology of Religion* (Englewood Cliffs: Prentice-Hall, 1966), ch. I.

5 Ludwig Feuerbach used the notion of projection to characterize the dynamics of man's religious life in his 1841 theological study, *The Essence of Christianity* (New York: Harper & Row, 1957), p. 29ff. Projection became a technical term in religious studies after Freud's psychoanalytic interpretation of religion appeared in *The Future of an Illusion;* see ch. 8 below.

6 Christian theologians like Karl Barth and Dietrich Bonhoeffer have also identified religion as "idolatry" or "unbelief" if it is rooted in human need rather than a genuine revelation of God. For Barth's critique of religion as "Unbelief," see *Church Dogmatics,* I:2 (Edinburgh: T. & T. Clark, 1956), pp. 297-324. Bonhoeffer's repudiation of religion is discussed in ch. 9 below.

7 Hume's appreciation of the pagan religiosity of Greek and Roman antiquity, as an alternative to Western Christianity, was a characteristic motif of a variety of Enlightenment figures. The Enlightenment recovery of pagan religious attitudes, as well as the rationality of the classical world is a theme highlighted in: Peter Gay, *The Enlightenment: An Interpretation—The Rise of Modern Paganism* (New York: Alfred A. Knopf, 1966).

8 In Nietzsche's view, the "slave morality" and guilty conscience of Western man was a correlate of the Christian belief in God. Friedrich Nietzsche, *Genealogy of Morals* (Garden City, N. Y.: Doubleday, 1956), pp. 217-224. Nietzsche's proclamation of the death of God for the sake of human liberation was a prominent theme of the Death-of-God theologies of the late 1960's. William Hamilton and Thomas J. J. Altizer, *Radical Theology and the Death of God* (New York: Bobbs-Merrill, 1966).

9 For a brief summary and comparison of the positions of Tillotson, Locke, Clark and other spokesmen for natural theology, see A. C. McGiffert, *Protestant Thought before Kant* (New York: Scribner's, 1942), pp. 189-242. John Dillenberger summarizes "The Science and Theology of Isaac Newton" in *Protestant Thought and Natural Science* (Nashville: Abingdon Press, 1960).

10 While the natural theologies of John Locke and Isaac Newton had a strong Christian orientation, the later positions of John Toland and Matthew Tindal were more critical of Christianity as a "religion of revelation" and more akin to anti-Christian forms of Deism; see G. R. Cragg, *From Puritanism to the Age of Reason* (Cambridge: University Press, 1950). Brief selections of the religious writings of Locke, Clarke, Toland and Tindal are printed in *Religious Thought in the Eighteenth Century,* eds. J. M. Creed and J. S. Bayssmith (Cambridge: University Press, 1939).

11 In his theological writings, Newton compiled an impressive list of recent scientific discoveries which pointed towards "an incorporeal, living, intelligent, omnipresent being"; cited in Edwin A. Burtt, *The Metaphysical Foundations of Modern Science* (1:284). Not only did the findings of science point towards the existence of God, but the existence of God was an essential hypothesis of Newton's scientific cosmology. Burtt provides a clear analysis of the relationship between Newton's scientific theories and his natural theology; *op. cit.,* pp. 202-300.

12 Norman Kemp Smith has stated the most convincing case for regarding Philo as most expressive of Hume's own position. See Smith's introduction to Hume's *Dialogues Concerning Natural Religion* (5:73-96). For a critical revision of Smith's interpretation of Hume's identification with Philo, see "Hume's Agnosticism" by James Noxon (2:361-383).

13 The notion of the "God-hypothesis" and its dispensability for science is associated with the famous exchange of Pierre Simon Laplace and Napoleon Bonaparte. Upon receiving a copy of Laplace's *Mécanique Céleste,* Napoleon remarked, "You have written this huge book on the system of the world with-

out once mentioning the author of the universe." To this, Laplace replied, "Sire, I have no need of that hypothesis." While Newton required the God-hypothesis to account for the correction of irregularities in the universe, Laplace apprehended the cosmos as intrinsically stable, its irregularities periodical and subject to an immanent and eternal law. Dietrich Bonhoeffer frequently cites the abandonment of the God-hypothesis in science as one of the turning points in the emergence of post-religious Western culture. See chapter 9 below.

14 Hume develops his theory of knowledge in *The Treatise on Human Nature* and *An Enquiry Concerning Human Understanding* available in the Modern Library Edition, *Hume Selections* (New York: Scribner's, 1927).

15 In an essay entitled "Hume's Immanent God," George Nathan argues that Hume's principle of order is incomprehensible, rational, eternal, and internal to nature—in other words, an immanent Deity (2:396-423).

16 Hume realized the limited impact of his writings on the religious beliefs of his countrymen. In a conversation with Adam Smith shortly before his death, Hume discussed several possible excuses which he might offer to Charon (the mythological boatman for the dead) in explaining why his death should be delayed: " 'Have a little patience, good Charon: I have been endeavouring to open the eyes of the public. If I live a few years longer, I may have the satisfaction of seeing the downfall of the prevailing systems of superstition.' But Charon would then lose all temper and decency. 'You loitering rogue, that will not happen these many hundred years. Do you fancy I will grant you a lease for so long a term? Get into the boat this instant, you lazy, loitering rogue' " (6:xxi).

17 Frederick Streng offers a brief discussion of the contributions of Mueller, Tylor, Fraser and other nineteenth- and early twentieth-century historians of religion together with a criticism of their quest for a single point of origin for religion in *Understanding Religious Man* (Belmont, Cal.: Dickenson, 1969), pp. 16-23.

18 Norman Kemp Smith clarifies the philosophical significance of Hume for Kant in *A Commentary to Kant's "Critique of Pure Reason"* (London: Macmillan, 1918), pp. xxv-xxxiii.

19 Walter Lowrie offers a brief account of Hamann's role in mediating Hume to Kierkegaard in *Kierkegaard* (London: Oxford Press, 1938), p. 164ff. For a more substantive discussion of the relationship of Hume to Hamann and Hamann to Kierkegaard, see Walter Lowrie, *Johann Georg Hamann, an Existentialist* (Princeton: Princeton Theological Seminary, 1950).

20 For an introduction to Japanese Pure Land Buddhism, see Alfred Bloom, *Shinran's Gospel of Pure Grace* (Tucson: University of Arizona Press, 1965).

BIBLIOGRAPHY

1. BURTT, EDWIN A., *The Metaphysical Foundations of Modern Science.* New York: Harcourt, Brace, 1925.
2. CHAPPELL, V. C., ed., *Hume.* Garden City, N. Y.: Doubleday, 1966.
3. FLEW, ANTHONY, *Hume's Philosophy of Belief.* London: Routledge & Kegan Paul, 1961.
4. HUME, DAVID, *The Natural History of Religion,* ed. H. E. Root. Stanford: Stanford University Press, 1956.

5. ———, *Dialogues Concerning Natural Religion*, ed. Norman Kemp Smith. Oxford: Clarendon Press, 1935.

6. ———, *An Enquiry Concerning Human Understanding* and selections from *A Treatise of Human Nature*. Chicago: Open Court Publishing Company, 1927. This edition includes Hume's autobiography and a letter from Adam Smith.

7. MANUEL, FRANK, *The Eighteenth Century Confronts the Gods*. Cambridge: Harvard University Press, 1959.

8. MOSSNER, ERNEST C., *The Life of David Hume*. Austin: University of Texas Press, 1954.

9. PASSMORE, J. A., *Hume's Intentions*. Cambridge: University Press, 1952.

10. PEARS, D. F., ed., *David Hume: A Symposium*. London: Macmillan, 1963.

11. SMITH, NORMAN KEMP, *The Philosophy of David Hume*. London: Macmillan, 1941.

SUGGESTED READINGS

1. *Primary Readings*

A convenient one-volume collection of Hume's writings on religion, edited by Richard Wollheim, is *Hume on Religion* (New York: World Publishing, n.d.). This includes selections from *The Natural History of Religion, Dialogues Concerning Natural Religion*, the essays "Of Miracles" and "Of a Particular Providence and of a Future State," and Hume's autobiography. Though presently out of print, this volume may still be available in libraries. *The Natural History of Religion* (4) offers a good introduction in Hume's lively prose to his historical and psychological analysis of religion. The two essays mentioned above provide a concise summary of Hume's philosophical criticism of religion; they appear also in *An Enquiry Concerning Human Understanding* (6). The *Dialogues Concerning Natural Religion* (5) is a longer and more difficult statement of Hume's mature philosophical position on religion.

2. *Secondary Readings*

Norman Kemp Smith's study of Hume (11) is one of the most reliable introductions to Hume's philosophy, while Mossner's excellent biography (8) is especially helpful for understanding Hume's personal religious background and perspective.

3. *Additional Bibliography*

A complete bibliography of Hume's writings and books about Hume published before 1938 is available in T. E. Jessop, ed., *A Bibliography of David Hume and of Scottish Philosophy* (London: A. Brown, 1938), pp. 5-67. A bibliography of more recent articles and books about Hume is included in Chappell's collection of essays (2:424-429).

2

Beyond the Conflict of
Science and Religion:
An Existential Faith

The scientific criticism of religion that was first developed during the Enlightenment had little impact on most eighteenth-century men and women. Only a small group of intellectuals were familiar with the presuppositions and results of scientific study. The majority of people continued to live in a world informed by traditional religious beliefs, rather than in the new world governed by the scientific laws discovered by Newton. The natural world was regarded as surrounded—and infiltrated—by a supernatural realm. God and his angels, not to mention the Devil and his legions of demons, were held responsible for miracles and visions, sicknesses and floods, poverty and death. Little wonder that critics of religion, like David Hume, had so little hope of changing the views of their fellow citizens. For science had yet to radically alter the ordinary man's perception of reality.

By the mid-twentieth century, this situation had dramatically changed. The scientific perspective formerly confined to a narrow circle of intellectual elites had been communicated—via educational institutions, radio, and television—throughout all classes of society. As a result, modern man came to view reality and even himself in a new way. For he now envisioned the world in terms of scientific laws that affected everything from the movement of stars to the behavior of his friends. Disease was no longer a result of sins which repentance might remedy, but an illness to be diagnosed by a doctor and cured with a complicated prescription. Floods were not a sign of divine displeasure which a priest might remedy through prayers to the deity, but a problem for irrigation engineers to resolve. Man himself was no longer a plaything of spiritual forces beyond his control, but a source of powerful resources which, when pooled and concentrated on a given problem, could land a man on the moon—an event as dramatic for modern man perhaps as the landing of a god on earth would have been for men of old. In these and countless other ways, scientific achievements gradually eroded older religious views of the world. As a result, the scientific world view, which had been a mark of privilege in the eighteenth century, gradually became, by our time, the common property of most men.

The emergence of science created a profound crisis for religion, insofar as it was in fundamental conflict with the traditional world view. Caught between the competing claims of science and religion, many individuals felt compelled either to opt for science or to effect an inherently uneasy compromise between the new and the old. Those who opted for an exclusively scientific orientation tended to dismiss religion as an obsolete and irrelevant heritage from an unenlightened past. Religious books like the Bible, they reasoned, told clearly inaccurate stories about the creation of the world in six days and Joshua's successful order to the sun to stop moving. If the Bible was so unreliable in its stories about the natural world, how could anyone trust its religious and ethical claims? Far better, they argued, to limit oneself to scientifically verifiable truths and other plausible modern assumptions. Others, of course, accepted most aspects of the all-pervasive scientific culture, but refused to allow science to influence their traditional religious beliefs. For the more conservative in this group, the earth was still surrounded by a heaven above and a hell below, despite the failure of astronauts to encounter angels or gods on their journeys through space. Similarly, biblical stories were literally true—including the Genesis account of the creation and Joshua's order to the sun—despite the geological, astronomical, and biological evidence to the contrary. Even the most conservative of modern believers, nevertheless, were confronted by precisely the same problem that struck their scientific detractors, namely, the modern crisis in belief. Unlike their ancestors, whose religious and secular concerns were joined together in a single world view, they found their religious beliefs to be in conflict with their ordinary, scientifically informed view of the world.

Among modern scholars who have explored the encounter of science and religion, few have been more original and influential than Rudolf Bultmann (b. 1884). For Bultmann did not side with either scientific debunkers of religion or religious conservatives, but provided a fundamental new understanding of the nature of the science–faith conflict. Contrary to earlier opinion, he argued that the real conflict between science and religion was not to be located at the point of their differing world views. In Bultmann's judgment, the primitive world view presented in the Bible was an accident of history and not an essential part of biblical faith. The biblical world view simply reflected the prevalent beliefs of its surrounding culture, and not the distinctive faith of either the Jewish or Christian communities. As a result, the modern Christian or Jew was not obliged to believe in the world view presupposed by the Bible, nor need he defend as true the miracle stories which were simply an expression of ancient cosmology. While Bultmann did not take seriously the biblical world view as a point of conflict with science, he did insist that there was a genuine conflict between science and faith at the level of personal self-understanding. He found that modern culture, dominated by science, tended to depersonalize human life and to entice men to self-destructive relationships with themselves, others, and their environment. Bultmann thus criticized modern scientific culture from the perspective of his personal faith while accepting the scientific criticism of the Bible.

As an heir of both Christianity and the scientific history and philosophy of the Enlightenment, Bultmann was particularly well suited to reformulate the science–religion problem. The son of a German Lutheran pastor, he appropriated the Christian faith early in his life and became a leading interpreter of that faith, both in his New Testament studies and in his theological writings.[1] As a student at the University of Marburg, and later as a university professor, he was also committed to the scientific study of religion and made significant contributions to our understanding of the history and literature of religion during the Hellenistic period. In Bultmann the claims of intellectual honesty and scientific discipline were joined with a profound personal faith.

As a descendant of the Enlightenment tradition of scientific thought, Bultmann found the traditional claims of Christianity to be increasingly dubious and irrelevant. He described the picture of the world presupposed by the New Testament as a primitive three-story universe, with earth in the middle, heaven above, and hell below. Joining together these three were escalators on which demons and angels, Satan and God—and sometimes even men—would move up or down, from one level to another. Bultmann could not take seriously such a primitive view of the world, nor did he think that any other Christian was obliged to believe such absurdities. For him, no story or teaching of the Bible, regardless of its importance for the Christian religion, was exempt from the critical scrutiny of scientific inquiry. Even the story of the resurrection of Jesus was subjected to radical criticism. Like other men of modern culture, Bultmann was committed to the norm of intellectual honesty in all matters, including religious belief. He would not condone superstition, ignorance, or error, even if these were cloaked in the sacred claims of prevalent religious beliefs.

As a Christian believer, Bultmann articulated the meaning of faith in explicit conflict with the predominant social ethos of our technological society. From the existentialist philosophy of Søren Kierkegaard and Martin Heidegger, Bultmann learned that each man must realize his own particular selfhood through the process of his historical decisions.[2] We are as we choose. Precisely because of this, we are also somewhat anxious, for each of us is finally responsible for actualizing—or failing to reach— our own authentic humanity. Modern society, however, would conceal this truth from us and confine us in bondage to itself. Its bureaucracy invites us to exchange our freedom for the reward of a secure place in the system; its culture teaches that our own essential nature is rationality, not the particularity of our lived history; its economy seduces us to understand ourselves solely in terms of the bourgeois work ethos, as if our personal value depended strictly on our achievements; and its government holds out the promise of constantly increasing the security and well-being of humanity through the indefinite extension of the powers of science and technology. For Bultmann, such enticements—however pervasive and persuasive they may seem—are bogus promises which have not been—and cannot be—fulfilled. The deceptive lures of modernity may undermine our freedom, they may diminish the quality of our lived experience, but they cannot deliver the panacea which has so long been promised. In his own life history, Bultmann experienced the New Testament message of faith as the decisive encounter which changed his own understanding of himself and liberated him from the dominant self-understanding of his society. He therefore proposes an existentialist interpretation of the Christian faith, not simply to update the New Testament for the modern world, but as an effective instrument of change in the lives of those who hear and respond.

1. THE ENLIGHTENMENT CRITIQUE: DEMYTHOLOGIZING

Rudolf Bultmann is an intellectual heir of David Hume in two respects. First, Bultmann's biblical scholarship compelled him to agree with Hume's contention that the stories of the Old Testament and New Testament do not present factually accurate historical accounts. Biblical stories of demon possession, for example, like the religious stories of other ancient peoples, presuppose a basic ignorance of the scientific laws of nature and a capacity for imaginative fantasy. To be sure, stories of demon possession may refer to genuine incidents of strange behavior, but they do not present an adequate interpretation of that behavior. Such fanciful explanations of events express that peculiar way of thinking which Bultmann calls "mythological" and which Hume described as a mixture of ignorance and fantasy. Second, as a Christian theologian, Bultmann also agrees with Hume's argument that God is not an appropriate object for rational discourse. For Bultmann, as for Hume, all talk of God falls outside the limits of reason. While any believer may acknowledge God in the experiential language of faith, no man may prove—or disprove—the existence or attributes of God in the objective language of reason.

Despite these points of agreement with Hume, Bultmann did not formulate his criticism of traditional religious literature and theology in direct relation to the writings of the Scottish philosopher. For his biblical criticism, Bultmann is indebted to a group of eighteenth- and nineteenth-century German historians and biblical scholars. For his theological criticism, he drew extensively upon the very specific tradition of German Neo-Kantian philosophy and theology. Therefore, we must first examine these two major schools of criticism before turning to Bultmann's own thought.

Shortly after Hume published *The Natural History of Religion* in 1757, a significant number of European intellectuals from a variety of disciplines became engaged in the task of examining and explaining the strange religious ideas of their ancestors.[3] One of these scholars, working on classical Greek and Roman texts, was C. G. Heyne. Heyne clarified a point of semantic confusion by introducing a very specific, technical meaning to the category of "mythology." Previously, critical studies of the beliefs of ancient peoples had spoken vaguely of "fable," "legend," "myth," or "religion." In clarifying the specific intention of these Enlightenment critics, Heyne defined mythology as a pre-rational mode of thought characteristic of all peoples in early stages of their development and manifest in a pre-scientific view of the world. This definition of mythology, while scarcely typical of ordinary usage as interpreted by Webster's *Dictionary*, became the basic meaning of "mythology" for a large number of Enlightenment critics, including—at a much later date—Rudolf Bultmann.

Mythology, according to this concept, has three component elements: 1) it is identified with a distinct mode of thought, 2) limited to an early epoch in human history, and 3) manifest in a pre-scientific view of the world. These three aspects of mythology may be clarified by reference to the work of two early biblical scholars: J. G. Eichorn, *Introduction to the Old Testament* (1780–1783) and D. F. Strauss, *Life of Jesus* (1835).[4]

1. Like Hume, Eichorn and Strauss describe the mode of thought of ancient peoples in terms of ignorance and imagination. The ancient Hebrew authors of the Old Testament did not possess knowledge of "the

nature of things and the causes of their changes" or "the immutable laws by which all the workings of Nature are regulated" (12:35). In addition, their imagination was uninhibited by the discipline of critical reasoning. They freely projected their own feelings on to nature, creating in the process a world populated with "ghosts, demons, divinities [and other such] invisible beings" (12:35). According to Strauss, most ancient religions created "a new world of mere imagination . . . a sphere of divine existences whose relations to one another, actions and influences, can be represented only after human analogy" (20:62). An ignorance of the actual operations of nature, combined with the free projection of human feelings: this is the mythological mode of thought.

2. Again in terms reminiscent of Hume, Eichorn and Strauss describe the characteristic thought pattern of the Bible as a product of early stages in human history. The Bible was written in "the lowest step of civilization," in "an infant and unscientific age," by an intellect limited to "puerile representations" (12:3; 12:36; 20:21). A developmental view of human history is one essential presupposition for this Enlightenment concept of mythology. Enlightenment men saw their age as the apex of human development in sharp contrast with the primitive and undeveloped age of mythology.

3. In addition to contrasting the mythological and Enlightenment periods of history, these authors employed a scientific view of the world as their criterion for identifying a mythological mode of thought. Eichorn saw the modern world as fundamentally different from the ancient world because of the scientific idea that "all changes are connected with one another like the links of a long chain"; and Strauss contends that "the progress of mental cultivation mainly consists in the gradual recognition of a chain of causes and effects connecting natural phenomena with each other" (12:35; 20:11). Modern men see the world scientifically: as a closed, unified system of causal relations governed by fixed laws. Primitive and ancient men experienced their world in just the opposite way. The world was an arena in which conflicting causal agencies—divine and demonic—struggled for supremacy; it was not a world of regularity governed by law, but a world in which literally anything could—and did—happen. Both Eichorn and Strauss regard this pre-scientific world view as an essential presupposition for the biblical stories of revelation and miracles; both men also agree on the necessity for eliminating all expressions of such a mythological mode of thought in a scientific age.

Bultmann appropriated this Enlightenment idea of mythology as one means of clarifying the meaning of the New Testament.[5] Like Eichorn and Strauss, he found the New Testament to presuppose a basic mythological perspective. He also understood mythology to mean a pre-scientific mode of thought and a world view characteristic of a pre-Enlightenment epoch of history. He thus defined mythology as "a particular mode of thought" which is "the opposite of scientific thinking" (7:180). Mythological thinking is more subjective than scientific thinking; it "arises out of astonishment, fright, and questioning," and so takes the form of projection of divine activity on to the sphere of nature (6:197; 8:100). Mythological thinking is also more arbitrary than science, less governed by laws of logic and causality. While scientific thinking understands all worldly events in terms of a single, self-contained system of cause–effect relations, mythological thinking may explain any event by reference to a variety of independent causal agencies. Some things happen because of natural or human causes; others are caused by "other-worldly" powers. Even these "other-worldly" powers do not all belong to the same sphere: some "other-worldly" powers are divine, "from above," and some are demonic, "from below." As a result, a variety of earthly events are understood to be the direct result of the actions of "other-worldly" powers: demon possession—the invasion of a person by a power "from below"; exorcism—the driving out of a demonic power by a power "from above"; miracles—the actions of power "from above" in healing illness, changing the course of nature, or raising the dead; and revelations—the descent of divine powers "from above" to teach the secrets of the heavenly sphere to men on earth.

Bultmann, like earlier biblical critics, insists that the mythological perspective is a product of particular historical circumstances rather than genuine religious insight. Mythology is a characteristic of a given historical epoch, and not an essential or distinctive characteristic of Christianity or any other world religion. Bultmann therefore identifies mythology with "a very definite historical phenomenon" and sets "the mythical epoch" in sharp contrast with "the epoch of the Enlightenment" (7:180; 1:47).[6] While many of his readers may cite examples of mythology in modern times—for example, knocking on wood or throwing salt over one's shoulder —Bultmann rejects such a use of "mythology" as illegitimate. For such practices, however prevalent they may be, are not consistent with the modern world view. They linger on as relics of an earlier age of history. Even if some "credulous people" of the present period of history continue to to believe "in spirits and miracles," and even if certain groups deliberately foster magic, witchcraft, and anti-scientific attitudes, such beliefs do not fall within the limits of "mythology" as Bultmann defines it (6:5). For mythology designates a way of thinking about the world characteristic of a total culture and society; the remnants of mythology in a scientific age of history Bultmann prefers to call "superstition" (6:5).

By identifying mythology with an earlier mode of thought, Bultmann is able to clearly differentiate between the claims of mythology and the claims of Christian faith. For Bultmann, as for Hume, the claims of mythology are dead. He believes that all men live today in a practical world shaped by science. When we are ill, we seek the diagnosis of a doctor; we do not seek an exorcist. We cannot be honest about our beliefs if we live our daily life in a scientific world and then return to a quite different world as the context for our religious life. For the sake of his own integrity and intellectual honesty, the Christian believer, as well as the philosophical skeptic, needs to repudiate the mythological claims which traditional religious loyalties have imposed upon him. Further-more, as an historian, Bultmann knows that mythology is in no way distinctive to the Christian faith. First-century Gnostics, mystery religions, and quasi-religious forms of cosmological speculation shared the same world view presupposed by the New Testament. In light of this, Bultmann proposed to "demythologize" the New Testament, that is, to strip away the belief claims of this ancient world view and mode of thought. Only in this way will the genuine religious message of the New Testament become freed from the mythological veil under which it has been concealed; only in this way will modern man be able to hear and respond to that message of faith.

Bultmann uses mythology, then, to designate a false way of thinking about the world based on a pre-scientific mode of reasoning. Mythological thinking, according to this definition, is false because it subjectifies the world, that is, worldly events are understood in terms of human feelings and attitudes projected on to nature. Bultmann also employs the concept of mythology to designate a false way of thinking about God. According to this second meaning of the term, mythological thinking is false because it objectifies God, that is, God is understood as if he were a discrete object like other objects of the world. Just as all worldly objects have a definite location in space, so God is pictured in mythology as residing in a heavenly realm above the earth. While the first use of mythology was derived from the tradition of Enlightenment historians, the second use of the concept grew out of the Kantian school of philosophy.

Immanuel Kant's theory of knowledge is important for Bultmann insofar as it criticizes all attempts to know God by using the intellectual categories appropriate to our everyday world. Kant reached this criticism of traditional ways of thinking about God by analyzing the nature of human knowledge.[7] Unlike Hume, Kant did not believe that knowledge is merely the result of data received through the senses. For Kant, there are no unstructured sense experiences. There are, in fact, two different ways in which the mind organizes sense data. First, sensations are received by the mind in spatio-temporal forms of intuition. For example, a pool ball rolling on a green table is not perceived as a chaotic mass of color; rather, it is seen as moving from a definite location—at one end of the table—to another location at a later moment of time. Second, the intellect is also an active agent in the process of knowing. It synthesizes sensations by means of the categories of reason, such as causality. If we see a pool ball move immediately after it has been struck by a cue ball, we automatically conclude that the cue ball has "caused" the other ball to move. Causality is thus an expression of the synthesizing activity of reason which gives order to all our experiences of the world. Between the knowing mind and the known objects of the world, there is an appropriate reciprocity which makes possible valid knowledge of the world.

Precisely because the human mind structures worldly experience in this way, knowledge of God is impossible. God's transcendence of the world cannot be grasped by a mind limited to spatio-temporal forms of intuition and rational categories. Therefore, Kant agrees with Hume that knowledge of God falls outside the limits of cognition. In addition to Hume's argument that there is no empirical evidence for God's existence, Kant argues that a mind well adapted to apprehending worldly phenomena cannot also apprehend a transcendent God.

The significance of Kant's theory of knowledge for the apprehension of God may be illustrated by an analogy. Imagine a man wearing a pair of intense magnifying lenses as glasses. Such glasses would enable him to apprehend clearly the small type on a printed page, but they would necessarily prevent him from seeing the horizon in the distance. In a similar manner, Kant described our rational consciousness, structured by the forms of space and time together with the categories of reason, like causality, as the glasses through which we experience the world. While this rational consciousness is an effective means for our perception and conception of the experienced world, it necessarily excludes from our vision the horizon of the world as a whole, or the transcendent reality of God. The Buddhist religion presents a similar teaching in its doctrine of Nirvana. According to Buddhism, all our sensations, perceptions, conceptions and forms of consciousness are barriers to the experience of the Ultimate or Nirvana, precisely because these forms of experience and thought are bound to this world. Similarly, the Kantian tradition denies the possibility of apprehending God in a worldly form of consciousness.

For Bultmann, mythology presents a false understanding of God precisely because it employs worldly forms of consciousness in thinking about God. Thus, the New Testament uses the notion of space in speaking of the transcendence of God and of the power of evil: God is described as residing in heaven, "up above"; evil is depicted as located in hell, "down below" (5:20). Similarly, the New Testament employs the notion of time in portraying God's eschatological deed; the *eschaton*, that is, the end of world history and the second coming of Christ, is envisaged as an imminent event in future time, expected "within this generation"

(5:22). Finally, the New Testament presupposes the category of causality in setting forth the actions of God: God intervenes in a series of natural or historical events, "causing" miracles to happen (5:61). Space, time, causality—these conceptual forms of thought so appropriate for understanding worldly phenomena, are naively and improperly used to express the transcendence of God. In Bultmann's terms, such talk of God is mythological because it "expresses the other-worldly in terms of this-world . . . the other-side in terms of this-side" (6:10). In another characteristic German phrase, he describes mythology as objectifying transcendence in terms of this world (5:19).

Like space, time, and causality, the category of "objectifying" is another characteristic of worldly knowledge which Bultmann appropriates from the tradition of Kantian philosophy. Especially for the Marburg Neo-Kantians who influenced Bultmann, the terms "objective" and "objectivity" acquired a specific technical meaning.[8] In ordinary speech, the term "objective" generally refers to something "real," something standing over against us in its otherness, something which is the opposite of "subjective" or "unreal." For the Neo-Kantians, however, the "object" of the "subject-object relation of knowledge" designates, not a real entity external to the knower, but a construct of reason posited in accordance with consistent logical principles. They did not consider either empirical evidence or the correspondence of an idea with an existing independent reality to be necessary to establish objective validity. For example, Einstein's theory of relativity was established as valid on purely mathematical grounds long before there was any empirical evidence to confirm it. Indeed, it was precisely this kind of knowledge characteristic of mathematical physics which provided the Neo-Kantians with their model for all human knowledge. As a result, they considered the "object given for thought" in earlier theories of knowledge to be the "objectified construct of thought."[9]

To speak of God objectively within this Neo-Kantian perspective is not to speak of God in his genuine otherness. Quite the contrary, it is to speak only of an idea of God constructed by human reason. Bultmann therefore regards such objectifying speech of God as idolatrous. Man remains the master of all his objectified constructs, and an objectified conception of God turns out to be simply an exalted product of human handicraft. As a result, Bultmann repudiates all conceptual patterns which objectify God. Mythology is a prime example of this false mode of conceptualizing God, but it is not the only offender. Biblical historians may objectify God by identifying him with certain sacred events of the past; dogmatic theologians may objectify God by making him the subject of a series of propositions for belief; moralists may objectify God by inferring certain moral laws from the "fact" of God's existence; metaphysical thinkers may objectify God by including him in a general theory of reality. In order to avoid any objectifying view of God, Bultmann refuses to take seriously any general idea about God or the role of God in any kind of world view—mythological, scientific, or other (5:83).

In summary, Bultmann's concept of mythology is a complex and eclectic construct which gathers together a series of significant developments in recent intellectual history. On the one hand, Bultmann's idea of mythology appropriates the earlier use of mythology developed by Enlightenment historians and biblical scholars. By identifying the world view of the biblical period as mythological, in contrast with the scientific world view of the modern period, these historians were able to relativize the supernaturalistic claims of the Bible. Stories about miraculous happenings in nature or unambiguous divine revelations in history did not necessarily reflect the uniqueness of either Judaism or Christianity but simply expressed the culturally conditioned world view prevalent at that time. On the other hand, Bultmann's concept of mythology also presupposed the Kantian theory of knowledge, especially as this was refined by later Neo-Kantians. Human reason, with its categories of space, time, and causality and its objectification of worldly phenomena, is effective in gaining scientific knowledge of the world but inappropriate for approaching transcendence. In light of the dual origins of his concept of mythology, demythologizing also has a double significance for Bultmann. It means the elimination of any understanding of nature or history which presupposes a pre-scientific world view and the exclusion of any objectifying or worldly form of thought about God.

2. ANXIETY AND SELF-UNDERSTANDING: EXISTENTIAL INTERPRETATION

Hume did not confine his critique of religion to the primitive nature of religious thought. He also called attention to the role of anxiety and fear in motivating religious belief. Bultmann similarly extends his analysis of mythology beyond the particular mode of thought characterized as pre-scientific. Like Hume, he realized that religion is not simply a product of reason or its pre-rational antecedents, but an expression of a deeper human concern. For Bultmann, the most decisive factor in religion, as well as in human life as a whole, is anxiety. But his understanding of anxiety and its role in human existence differs considerably from Hume's view of this subject.

The anxiety of which Bultmann speaks is quite different from the fear which primitive man experienced in the face of natural dangers like floods, earthquakes, and storms. This kind of fear has been significantly alleviated by the development of technological means for controlling the forces of nature that threaten human existence. But real anxiety, unlike fear of a specific danger, does not have a definite object. Hence, it is not dissipated by increasing scientific mastery of the environment. Anxiety is a free-floating fear, an object-less fear; it is being afraid of something, like the dark or like death, without knowing what that "something" is. For this reason, modern man, while less fearful of natural threats, is likely to be as anxious as his primitive ancestors. Bultmann's understanding of anxiety is also different from the neurotic anxiety described by modern psychology.[10] Neurotic anxiety is engendered by severe psychic conflicts which may cause a person to behave in abnormal ways. Insofar as neurotic anxiety is caused by specific psychological processes, it is like the particular fears of primitive men. The anxiety of which Bultmann speaks is more universal than neurotic anxiety and more pervasive than the fears of primitive men. He calls this anxiety "existential anxiety" precisely because it belongs to the structure and dynamics of human existence itself. All men experience existential anxiety without regard to the level of their technological development or mental health. Three structural characteristics of human life may be identified as sources of existential anxiety.

First, man is an historical self who faces a fundamental dilemma. On the one hand, he has a clear sense of responsibility for his own existence. Men create their own particular selfhood through the many decisions they make during their lives. The human self is not given automatically by nature, society, or culture, nor is man able to create willfully a particular self-identity. We are what we have become through the specific choices made in our past (2:159). Each of us is therefore responsible for the person we have become. On the other hand, man does not have complete control over his existence or the power to dispose of his future. Historical events—wars, social or economic developments, cultural changes—may dramatically alter the course of his life, either frustrating hopes or bringing new possibilities for a future which he had not previously envisioned. While we are responsible for our own lives, our lives do not fall entirely within the scope of our own powers; we are not the masters of our own destiny (2:163).[11]

This structural characteristic of human existence can be illustrated by an analogy. Railroads once developed a track-laying machine which set both ties and track in front of the vehicle while running on the track just laid behind.[12] Imagine a personified track-laying machine moving through an uncharted wilderness, without any guidelines for direction before it, without knowledge of environmental obstacles ahead of it, not even knowing the ultimate destination of the track, yet always committed to moving forward on the basis of track already laid. Such is the historicity of man, as Bultmann sees him. Looking to the future, he constantly confronts a variety of choices without clear guidelines for making them. Some decisions may prove more decisive for the trajectory of his personal life than others, but all will contribute to the particularity of his experience and sense of self. He must not only make each decision without definite knowledge of the future, he is unable to say at any given moment who he will be in the future or what his destiny will finally be. Looking to the past, he sees only the track of previous decisions stretching backwards through time as a pattern of life determining his present. He is not able to return to an earlier moment of time to alter a decision made then. Every zig and zag become a part of his historical identity. To be human is to be responsible for the self we have chosen to become, although we are not able to determine in advance what we shall be in the future.

(2) A second structural characteristic of human existence is its setting in the midst of transitory and, sometimes, decaying social institutions. This aspect of Bultmann's thought reflects the cultural and social shock precipitated by World War I. The war had a profound effect on German intellectuals, including Bultmann, much like the impact of the Vietnam War on American intellectuals. Basic institutions of society, like government, education, economic organizations, and the family, were suddenly revealed to be far less trustworthy and reliable than previously supposed. Cultural meanings, religious traditions, and moral values, which once appeared eminently reasonable and even divinely sanctioned, were disclosed as historically relative constructs of human ingenuity, the bearers of irrational opinion, and sometimes the agencies of human destruction. In a 1917 sermon, Bultmann describes his experience of confronting for the first time "the abyss of life and its opposing forces" (3:25). The veil of human deception had been removed from his eyes and he saw his world, not as a sphere of rational order and value, but as "an abysmal darkness," "a sphere of uncanny, mysterious, enigmatic powers" (3:24-30). The existentialist interpretation of anxiety was born in this confrontation with the Emptyness concealed within the apparent Substance of civilization. In terms of our analogy, it is as if the personified track-laying machine were proceeding along the shifting sands of a desert, or on top of a seacoast bluff, steadily being eroded by the waves below.

(3) A third structural characteristic of human existence is the self's anticipation of its own Nothingness in death. When Bultmann speaks of death, he does not refer to the abstract idea that all men must die or to the loss of a loved one. The death of which he speaks is always "my own death," the death of one's own particular self.[13] He does not speak of one's own death as a morbid fascination with an event in the future, but as an existential actuality in the present. For that anxiety which so

troubles human existence is due to the shadow which our future death casts upon our present. Because men unconsciously seek to avoid this kind of anxiety, they construct a variety of death-denying beliefs and practices. For example, we ordinarily assume that our present everyday activity will extend indefinitely into the future, although we secretly know that it will come to an end. In terms of our analogy, it is as if the track-laying machine contained a self-destruct device, automatically detonated at the point of its unknown destination.

Self-responsibility before an unknown future, the transitory and unstable nature of established forms of civilization, and the finality of death are the most basic conditions of human existence. The anxiety engendered by these conditions is universally characteristic of man, that is to say, it is existential anxiety. For Bultmann, this anxiety is not simply one universal phenomenon among others, it is the most decisive and pervasive characteristic of human life. What sexuality is for Sigmund Freud, anxiety is for Rudolf Bultmann. For anxiety is not limited to one segment or expression of man's life but pervades the whole of his existence: his work, his relations with friends and family, his participation in political and cultural activities, and even—and especially—his relation with transcendence or God. According to the way in which a man comes to terms with anxiety, he finds self-fulfill-ment or self-destruction. Bultmann describes the different ways in which men come to terms with existential anxiety by means of the category of self-understanding.

Self-understanding does not refer to a theoretical or abstract under-standing of the nature of the self, nor to the kind of self-picture we acquire through introspection, by sitting back and looking at ourselves. Self-understanding is more a matter of who we are than of what we think. Our self-understanding appears in our attitudes, our actions, our inter-actions with other persons, and our response to events that happen to us. Every person, whether adult or child, has his own particular self-understanding. This self-understanding may be conscious, and open to critical scrutiny, or it may be unconscious and wholly hidden from us. In either case, our self-understanding plays a decisive role in shaping the course of our life history (5:74).

The meaning of self-understanding for Bultmann appears most clearly in his discussion of two particular kinds of self-understanding. The first kind is developed through work. Work extends our power through organized endeavor to gain mastery over some segment of our objective environment. The second kind of self-understanding is formed through encounters with other persons, historical events, and/or the transcendent. Encounters disclose the diverse factors that limit our per-sonal lives and also provide new occasions for self-actualization. For heuristic purposes, we will refer to the first as an impersonal self-understanding of work and the second as a personal self-understanding of encounter.[14]

From the perspective of an impersonal self-understanding, one begins with a sense of power as the way of resolving anxiety: the abilities and talents which enable one to attain status and power in the community of men; the powers of scientific reason which allow one to understand the workings of nature and, through cooperation with others, to control and change nature technologically for the sake of a more secure human life. In an impersonal self-understanding, the self is primarily an agent of control. One seeks to control biological instincts and drives, as well as imaginative fantasies, while developing corresponding patterns of conscientious introspection and self-discipline. Other individuals and groups appear as rivals in conflict with our own sphere of control or as objects to be manipulated. One envisages his ultimate destiny as a participant in an indefinite and unlimited process of expanding powers of control to encompass the total environment.

From the standpoint of a personal self-understanding, I begin with an acknowledgment of my own limits: my need for other human beings and my lack of self-sufficiency; my inability to predict or control the forces of world history, however much they disrupt my personal life; and my status as a finite creature who lives out of a source of life greater than myself. In interpersonal relations, I experience myself as a person bound to other persons in relations of trust and love. I recognize dimensions of mystery and depth in my embodied existence which may become, not enemies to be subdued, but allies to be trusted. I experience others in situations of honest encounter as persons in their own right, not as objects for me to manipulate, but persons who may make new demands on me or who may bring new possibilities of life to me. I envisage a future which, while not known or under my control, I anticipate as offering occasions for actualizing that existence which is most distinctively my own.

While Bultmann sets these two kinds of self-understanding in sharp opposition to each other, he does not ascribe either kind of self-understanding to particular individuals or groups of people. Both kinds of self-understanding are possibilities for all men. No one's self-understanding is exclusively impersonal, just as no man lives out of an exclusively personal self-understanding. Bultmann sees these two self-understandings as the basic ways in which men come to terms with existential anxiety. His own concern is with the dynamic interaction and relative balance of these two self-understandings in the life of any given individual.

Bultmann's discussion of science and biblical religion is informed by the distinction between an impersonal and personal self-understanding. According to Bultmann, science embodies that impersonal self-understanding which attempts to resolve anxiety by increasing human knowledge and control.[15] Biblical religion is essentially a personal self-understanding which transcends anxiety—without eliminating it—by setting human life in its ultimate context.

At the level of existential self-understanding, Bultmann sees science as a form of work. Here we need to note the very particular understanding of work which Bultmann presupposes. He consistently cites two dynamics as constitutive of work life. First, the sense of anxiety or the longing for security is the basic drive motivating work. Because men are anxious for their future, they submit themselves to toil in the present. We study books, construct buildings, and organize communities in order to make human life more secure, both individually and corporately. Second, the sufficiency of human power to attain the desired goal of security is the basic belief which informs work. Men would not strive to secure their life through endeavor if they did not believe, consciously or unconsciously, that their powers were adequate to reach their goal. Like other forms of work, science expresses both man's desire for security and confidence in the sufficiency of his powers (2:18). For Bultmann, science is simply the self-understanding of work writ large across the face of modern culture.

While Bultmann has no objection to science as a mode of thought, he is highly critical of science as self-understanding. In the first place, he objects to the cultural role of science because of its constricting impact on man's personal life. In pre-modern societies, religious pageants and festivals provided opportunities for personal self-expression which enriched man's work life. In the modern period, however, the scientific domination of culture has tended to exclude these richer forms of social life. In this restricted context, man tends to lose touch with the deepest roots of his inner life, including his freedom of choice and the anxieties and possibilities intrinsic to it. Failing to recognize his freedom for the future, he becomes trapped in conformist patterns of behavior as he is increasingly driven by unacknowledged anxiety regarding the future. The loss of his future also entails the loss of his past. He cuts himself off from the genuine historical roots of his own particular selfhood and comes instead to identify himself exclusively with the ideal of rational man. His life in the present is shaped by the dominant bourgeois work ethos, which devalues personal relations of trust and love and reduces all human relationships to the narrow limits of achievement-oriented tasks. The worth of other people, and even a person's sense of his own worth, comes to depend solely on their work status. From Bultmann's point of view, this consistent depersonalizing of human life is one consequence of the predominant role of science, and its implicit self-understanding, in modern culture.

In the second place, Bultmann attacks the self-understanding associated with science because of its religious pretensions. The dynamics of work express man's longing for self-security and self-sufficiency which, in the classical biblical tradition, have always been regarded as *hubris* or sin.[16] For sin is man's effort to deny his status as a finite creature while claiming for himself the self-sufficiency or aseity of God. Bultmann therefore sets the existential orientation of science in explicit opposition to the existential attitude of faith as depicted in biblical religion.

Biblical religion, in Bultmann's view, begins with an acknowledgment of the reality of human insecurity and the limitation of human powers (5:40). Bultmann finds this sense of the precarious condition of human life to be rooted in two biblical attributes of God: God as Creator and Judge. To accept God as Creator is to accept oneself as a finite creature inseparably bound to the contingencies of history; it is not to indulge in speculation concerning the origins of the cosmos. To accept God as Judge is to accept the ambiguity always present in man's moral life with others; it is not to subscribe to a particular theory concerning the origins of moral norms. Insecurity, from a biblical point of view, is therefore a basic condition of human life, not a temporary problem to be resolved by new knowledge, technology, or agencies of social control. To seek escape from this insecurity through schemes of self-reliance is both a hopeless wish, in conflict with man's real historical–ethical life situation, and an idolatrous belief, negating the transcendent ground of human life.

Bultmann finds that the Bible sets faith in explicit conflict with man's innate desire for self-security. For example, Bultmann cites a continuing tradition which links together his own polemic against the self-understanding of work with Paul's critique of justification by works. Just as Paul criticizes man's attempt to establish his ultimate security by obeying the ceremonial and moral works prescribed in the Jewish Torah (Law), so Bultmann questions modern man's search for security through the extension of scientific means of control. In both cases, man has taken something originally good—the Jewish Torah or scientific laws—and distorted them to meet his security needs. Both the Torah and science were originally intended to serve man's life of love with others; both became instead pseudo-religions used to avoid concrete encounters with other men. Bultmann finds that the Gospel of John raises this same polemical issue. John presents the opponents of Jesus as men who use their religion, not to become aware of their own creaturehood, but to answer for their security needs (10:27ff). Pseudo-religions are determined by the dynamics of man's work life, as they claim to supplement human powers with superhuman powers to satisfy man's innate desire for security. In contrast, biblical religion both acknowledges insecurity as intrinsic to human life and engages in a polemic against any use of religion as a defense against the insecure—but liberating—possibility of new historical encounters.

While biblical religion accepts man's insecurity, it does not leave man as a helpless victim of that insecurity. On the contrary, biblical religion fosters personal qualities like confidence, love, hope, and joy which enable men to realize their true humanity precisely in the midst of insecurity (9:314–330). But these personal strengths are clearly differentiated from the illusion that human power is sufficient to eliminate anxiety. For Bultmann, these personal strengths are not possessions which men may claim to have at their disposal, but are realized only in concrete moments of interpersonal encounter. Biblical religion not only shatters that self-understanding which desires security, it simultaneously calls forth a new self-understanding of trust and hope which opens men toward the future and the needs of others.

Bultmann's concern to free biblical religion from pseudo-security is expressed in his demythologizing project. For mythology mixes together man's genuine acknowledgement of insecurity with his effort to protect himself against it. On the one hand, mythology attempts to express the precarious quality of human life and the limits of human powers, describing the everyday world as threatened by mysterious, uncanny powers which could destroy its order and set loose the forces of primeval chaos (6:10–11). Mythology also speaks of man as one whose destiny and fulfillment depend on powers greater than his own (6:10–11). In these ways, mythology attempts to acknowledge the mysterious and enigmatic forces which constitute the ultimate context of human life.

On the other hand, mythology, while recognizing the limits of human existence, conceals man's insecurity under a veil of stories about supernatural powers, beings, and deities. Mythology depicts such deities as if they were objectively real in the same way that objects of the everyday world are real (5:19). Thus, the deities in mythology may resemble fire, thunder, a great military hero, or a founder of a human community. In these cases, mythological deities have the same kind of reality as worldly objects and they differ only in that they enjoy greater power than natural phenomena (5:19). For Bultmann, this mythological view of transcendence is not only the result of a defect in primitive modes of thought; it is also an expression of a flaw in the human spirit. For the objective deities of mythology invite men to seek security and power in the sphere of the ultimate. Thus, it is natural that these same mythological deities are presented as allies in man's quest for security or as the ground and guarantor of his moral and cultural world order. Furthermore, through cultic activities, man may extend his own powers by sacrificial offerings which propitiate the gods and alter the disposition of their will for the sake of the security and well-being of the cultic community. For Bultmann, it is precisely the quality of worldly objectivity that mythology claims for transcendence which corrupts its original intention. Instead of disclosing the insecurity of human existence and the limits of human powers, mythology deceives men by leading them to believe that the security which they cannot find in this world may be obtained in a world-beyond.

Because biblical religion was born in the midst of a mythological age, it often borrowed mythological imagery to express its own meaning. For example, when the New Testament portrays Jesus as the Christ, it does so by mythological stories: he was born of a virgin mother, rose from death to life, and ascended into heaven. For many believers, these stories provided objective evidence for the existence of God and his presence in Jesus. Especially in the midst of the uncertainties of modern life, some people find comfort in these miraculous stories testifying to the divinity of Christ. Demythologizing attempts to undermine this form of belief. For Bultmann, belief in the miraculous events of biblical times leads men out of the real world of present history into a make-believe world that offers pseudo-security. Demythologizing the mythological stories of biblical religion entails the elimination of any religious belief which may be used as a crutch for human insecurity.

At the level of existential self-understanding, Bultmann is critical of mythology and science for the same reason: both claim, implicitly or explicitly, to resolve man's personal anxiety by extending his knowledge and control to the sphere of the ultimate. Mythology does this by positing an objective deity apprehended by belief and influenced by religious rites; science does this by constructing an objective view of reality open to rational knowledge and technological manipulation. Bultmann seeks to clarify the mythological dramatization of human insecurity and limitations through a demythologized interpretation. He also wishes to restore science to its proper role as a tool of man's work world.

Bultmann thus intends to eliminate any mythological understanding of biblical religion. He regards the mythological motifs employed in the New Testament as a remnant of Hellenistic culture which, if taken literally, can only confuse the biblical meaning of faith. In his judgment, such mythological motifs are not only obsolete because of the scientific world view, but they also conceal and distort the primary intention of biblical religion. Because of its ambiguity, mythology preserves the dynamics of man's work life, his longing for security and exaggerated confidence in the sufficiency of his powers, and extends them to the religious sphere of ultimacy. In contrast with mythology, biblical faith accepts the insecurity of historical existence and enables men to discover personal strengths of trust and hope which renew their freedom and enable them to transcend the insecurities of existence. For Bultmann, existential interpretation makes explicit the distinctive dynamics of biblical faith while exposing the ambiguities of mythology. For these reasons, Bultmann proposes a systematic existential interpretation of biblical religion to clarify the mixture of existential and mythological themes characteristic of traditional forms of the Christian religion.

3. FAITH, KERYGMA, AND AUTHENTIC EXISTENCE

Demythologizing and existential interpretation have become the trademarks of Bultmann's reformulation of religious thought. We would do Bultmann an injustice, however, if we understood his thought only in relation to the philosophical and historical issues involved in his analysis of mythology and existential self-understanding. For Bultmann is primarily a Christian theologian and an interpreter of the New Testament message.[17] His analysis of mythology and human existence are not ends in themselves, but means for the explication of the faith which he found decisive in his own life. We therefore need to turn our attention to the task of describing that faith which Bultmann presents as a Christian believer.[18]

First, Bultmann understands Christian faith as an existential act. Faith occurs only in the mode of encounter and always involves a decision concerning self-understanding. As previously noted, encounter and work are antithetical modes of human experience. In working, we are masters of the situation; our calculating and manipulating egos are actively engaged. In encounters, something happens to us; our sense of self is affected. Faith is realized only in encounter because faith is a response to someone outside the self. Similarly, the decision of faith is essentially a decision concerning our personal lives. Faith is not primarily a decision concerning the credibility of biblical stories, the reliability of beliefs from the past, or the nature of reality in general, for it is our self-understanding that is called into question in a decision of faith. Indeed, faith is precisely that decision in which a new self-understanding replaces the old egocentric self (9:316).

Because faith results from an existential encounter and decision, Bultmann believes that traditional religious language must be redefined in terms of existential discourse. This discourse uses the primary language of self-expression with which we are all familiar. We speak of loving and trusting another person, of suffering and joy, of gaining new insights into ourselves. In speaking this way, we use words to describe something very personal that has happened to us. This existential discourse, while not consistent with the language of scientific thought or philosophical reflection, is the medium through which we realize our own sense of identity, both as individuals and as members of communities.

Bultmann uses this primary language of existential discourse to reinterpret the meaning of the phrase "act of God." An act of God is not a supernatural interference with the natural order, but a decisive event known only through human interpretation. Some events are so significant for us that they evoke from us the response: this must be an act of God. This is not simply an ordinary experience of everyday life; in this experience, we feel touched by a transcendent power. Because of its existential significance, we call this kind of event an act of God even if, to outside observers, it appears to be simply a natural event (5:62).[19]

Bultmann recognizes that even such existential forms of God-talk may not prove agreeable to all men. Depending on one's previous history and present experience, an individual may find any way of speaking of God to be unacceptable. In place of Bultmann's dramatic and theological forms of existential speech, some may prefer to say, more simply, that such and such an event was particularly meaningful to me—without regard to its significance as a moment of transcendence. Bultmann acknowledges the plausibility of such an objection to his theological position. He only insists that this objection be based on a genuine existential issue, such as a sense of self-sufficiency. He does not think it is legitimate for men to reject God simply because they have a false idea of God as a cosmic object or supernatural being who interferes with the natural order. For Bultmann, faith involves self-understanding, not a world view.

Faith is not only an existential decision of self-understanding, it is also a response to a concrete instance of revelation. Faith does not mean the same thing as "belief in God" nor is faith equivalent to holding in high regard the idea of transcendence (2:161; 9:318). Above all, faith is not a quality or attitude that is self-generated. Faith is a possibility that is only realized in a concrete situation of encounter. In this way, faith is like love. We are not able to love alone. We experience love only as we encounter another who enables us to love; similarly, we experience faith only as we encounter the divine Other who profoundly alters our self-understanding.

Bultmann uses the phrase "word of God" to designate the encounter situation which has proven decisive for his own self-understanding. In the first instance, word of God refers to an event which happens when the Gospel is preached in the Christian community. To be sure, there is nothing supernatural or magical about the words used by a minister in his sermon. However, they are intended to call the hearer to a decision concerning himself. Any sermon becomes a word of God only as the hearers find their egocentric self-understanding called into question. The criterion for a sermon becoming a word of God is its existential efficacy, not its religious views, moral teachings, or sincerity. In addition, a word of God may also be heard in secular experiences. While preaching is, for Bultmann, the clear and decisive point of God's meeting with men, those who have heard the word in proclamation may also hear a word of God in an encounter with a friend or in a political movement. Whether the word of God is heard in the preaching of the Christian community or in the more ordinary and familiar contexts of human experience, it is always a contemporary word which intersects the existential history of the hearer. The word of God is not, for Bultmann, a body of religious doctrine or a story of events that happened long ago. It only occurs in the present.

While men hear God's word only in a present moment of their lives, Bultmann understands this contemporary word in terms of its historical origins in the kerygma or proclamation of the early Christian church. Kerygma means proclamation: the announcement of the deed of God in the life and death of Jesus of Nazareth. Like most other New Testament scholars, Bultmann understands this kerygma to be the eschatological message at the core of New Testament faith.[20] The Greek word *eschaton* refers to the ultimate or end: specifically, the end of the world. Both Jesus' preaching of the kingdom of God and the Church's proclamation of the act of God in Jesus announce the imminent end of an old age and the inauguration of a new age. In its mythological New Testament form, this eschatological message included the expectation that the world would literally come to an end within the lifetime of the first generation of disciples.[21] God was expected to judge the unrighteous and to invite the faithful to share in the blessings of the reign of Christ. While this eschatological theme has receded into the background of contemporary Christianity, Christians continue to pray in the Lord's Prayer, "Thy kingdom come, thy will be done," as an expression of the hope that the kingdom of Christ will come.

Twenty centuries later, it is no longer possible to believe the eschatological message of the kerygma in its literal form. The end of the world did not come. The expectation of the early Christians and authors of the New Testament was not fulfilled. In this situation, the contemporary Christian could choose to ignore this aspect of New Testament faith but, as Bultmann points out, this would entail a loss of the initial message of the church. He therefore challenges his readers to take the kerygma seriously, if not literally, existentially but not mythologically.

In Bultmann's view, the real meaning of the kerygma does not lie in its chronology of history, with a set date for the end of the world, but in the existential history of the individual believer and the Christian community. The end which the kerygma announces is not the end of the world, but the end of a worldly self-understanding; the new age which the kerygma promises is not a new heaven and a new earth, but a new self-understanding which includes a new perspective on the whole of reality. The contemporary believer, like the first-century Christian, is invited to die with Christ, to let his hankering for security be judged by the word of God, to give up his pretensions to power and self-sufficiency. The believer is also promised a new life with Christ, meaning a new self-understanding involving freedom from the domination of the past and anxiety about the future. The dynamics of death and rebirth, accompanied by a new freedom for others in the present, are, in Bultmann's judgment, the decisive marks of the life of faith, both in the days of the New Testament and in the present.

Bultmann claims that it is only by hearing the Christian proclamation that this decisive alteration in self-understanding may occur. It is only after one has heard the message in the Christian community that one can interpret secular experiences in similar terms. For example, one may see God's hand at work in liberating interpersonal relationships only after one has been freed by faith in Christ. Bultmann realizes that the exclusiveness of this Christian claim, that self-understanding is radically changed only in response to the church's proclamation, is offensive to modern men. Enlightened men of the twentieth century, aware of the diverse religions of the world and the divergent philosophical and poetic interpretations of human existence, may be scandalized by the notion that men only gain authentic self-understanding through hearing a particular proclamation from the past.[22] Yet, Bultmann is not willing to give up, or to minimize, the offense caused by the particularity of Christian faith. Indeed, he regards this offense as an essential element in the process of changing one's self-understanding.

In the first place, the kerygma—because of the literary particularity of the New Testament and the historical specificity of the life of Jesus—meets us as a distinct message over against us. None of us has made this kerygma to be what it is, nor is the figure of Jesus a creation of our reason, esthetic imagination, moral ideals, or spiritual powers. The believer therefore hears this word of God in the mode of encounter and not as part of the world reality he has constructed. Just because of its concrete otherness, this word is able to change our self-understanding by inviting us to abandon constraining self-images previously imposed upon us and by freeing us for a new discovery of self in the actualities of our lived history. Bultmann sees man as imprisoned by his ego rationality and past identity-forming experiences. Only through explicit confrontation with a word that stands beyond the limits of reason and previous achievements of civilization are men freed from that bondage.

A second reason for insisting on the decisive role of the New Testament kerygma is its challenge to man's religious quest for security. Vague and general religious beliefs tend to posit an omnipotent deity who compensates for our sense of inadequacy. In sharp contrast with man's natural religious inclinations, the New Testament presents God, not as a supernatural, superhuman figure, but as a man whose weakness and humanity is like our own. He is not immune from the natural limits of the body and the cruelties of society, but he suffers betrayal and death on a cross. This story does not appeal to man's natural religiosity and security needs. It does not encourage men to escape from the limits and insecurities of historical existence, but invites men to take up the cross of Christ in the midst of their own life with others. The cross which is the center of the Christian kerygma is an offense not because it is mythology, for it was an historical event, but because it undermines man's longing for that security which the world—including all its religious beliefs—can never provide.

Bultmann thus emphasizes the offense of the kerygma as the polemical edge of the Gospel. He sees man as basically self-centered, hostile and manipulative towards others, and frightened of the future.[23] He does not invest much hope in changing these basic attitudes and behavior by philosophical truths or vague religious beliefs. Man is so locked in his egocentric posture that he is likely to adapt any general religious or philosophical perspective to fit his own self-interest. Only a specific word from beyond, a word which always stands over against man exposing his natural perversity, is able to liberate man for a new life. For Bultmann, that word from beyond comes through the Christian kerygma.

Bultmann describes the transformation of self which occurs in response to the kerygma as "authentic existence." Authentic existence does not designate a certain type of personality, but a dynamic process that persists throughout the whole of life. On the one hand, authentic existence is a natural possibility that is open to all men; it is not some new magical or supernatural power superimposed on humanity, but is simply human existence brought to its fruition. On the other hand, authentic existence is something of a "miracle." It is not a possibility which men may choose to realize for themselves, but depends upon an encounter with transcendence, a hearing of the word of God. Authentic existence may be characterized as a dynamic process involving liberation from the past, a new confidence and trust in the future, and a freedom for others in the present.

Liberation from the past is the experience of losing the self one has become. In the process of becoming a self, all of us experience a variety of life-enhancing and life-destroying relationships. Family, racial environment, social institutions, and cultural symbols all contribute their distinctive strengths and liabilities to our current existence. None of us knows a past freed from these ambiguities. Yet, none of us has the power to alter the past that makes us who we are in the present (2:159). This past, in its totality, is so determinative for our present identity that we find ourselves bound by it, for good or ill. Not only does the past determine our present, it also leaves us with a burden of guilt. It is not simply the guilt we might have incurred for violating our own moral norms, but also the guilt we know for having failed to realize our own potentialities in this past.

Liberation from our existential past—its ambiguities, its determinative role in our present, and its guilt—is one of the characteristics of authentic existence. To hear a word from beyond in our present is also to die to our natural but inauthentic past (2:158). To illustrate this process, we may return briefly to our personified track-laying machine. Only for inauthentic existence does the past appear as a single set of tracks stretching from our point of origin to the present. For authentic existence, the past looks more like the Chicago railroad yards, in which there are many sets of tracks, joined together by a variety of junctures and switches. Freedom from a dominant past at the center of present existence is also freedom for a recovery of the genuine complexity and diversity of our past.

The self-understanding of faith also alters our perception of the future. As long as we seek to establish our own existence by means at our control, the future is always experienced as threatening. For the future promises changes which we do not choose, new possibilities which threaten to undermine established positions of power and security. The existential anxiety of which Bultmann speaks is a correlate of this threatening future. But if we give up the pretense of controlling our life by the powers at our disposal in response to a word from beyond, we also become freed for the future and open to all the changes which it might bring (5:77). Instead of appearing as a threat, the unknown future then appears as an invitation, offering us the opportunity to actualize unknown possibilities of our existence. Instead of dreading this future in a state of anxiety, we are enabled to step into this future with confidence. In terms of our analogy, the unknown environment ahead of the track-laying machine suddenly discloses vague outlines or contours which offer support and direction for the track. For Bultmann, such a new vision of the future is not a possibility we can conjure up on our own; it is a gift which accompanies the hearing of the kerygma. For the God of the future encountered in the kerygma, while bringing death to our natural self-understanding, is also a gracious God whose promise of new life enables us to experience the unknown future with hope. Hope, like confidence, is a distinctive characteristic of the authentic life of faith, in New Testament times as well as in the present.

Finally, the self-understanding of faith brings a new freedom for loving others in the present. Most of us have some experience of the ways in which anxiety distorts our loving relationships. Parents sometimes love their children insofar as the children conform to parental expectations and so confirm the parents' own sense of well-being and security. A man and a woman may love each other out of a common need for a sense of security, and so their love tends to be possessive and manipulative. As long as we love others to alleviate our anxiety or insecurity, we are never free to love other persons as they really are, in their own particularity. We must always reduce the other person to the status of a love object that fits our security needs.

The love of which Bultmann speaks is a different kind of love and derives its specific meaning from the New Testament understanding of faith. It is a love rooted in the freedom of the lover; it is not a love that grows out of the lover's needs. It is a love motivated by the intention of bringing benefit to the other, involving respect for the particularity of the other and responding to his needs (2:155). In Bultmann's view, such a free and gracious love arises spontaneously and naturally from the self-understanding of faith. Men freed from bondage to anxious self-concern will also become free for others: free to let others be, to love them without claims of possession, domination, or pity; free to wait, listen, or act, whichever is appropriate.

Within the context of this new relationship with others, work, including the use of science and technology, acquires a new ethical status. The resources of scientific research and technology, which Bultmann rejects as symbols of unlimited control, become restored to their rightful status as tools, tools placed in the service of beneficent love (2:161–162). Bultmann, therefore, does not admonish his readers to flee from the complexities and temptations of modern civilization to a more simple form of life. Instead, he proposes that men of faith remain in the midst of the modern world, but in a spirit of detachment (2:162). By stripping away the symbolic significance of science and technology as sources of human security and unlimited power, Bultmann is able to claim these same instruments as resources for the upbuilding of the human community. It is no accident that the biblical passage which Bultmann cites most frequently is I Corinthians 7:29–31:

Let those who have wives live as though they had none, and those who mourn as though they were not mourning, and those who rejoice as though they were not rejoicing, and those who buy as though they had no goods, and those who deal with the world as though they had no dealings with it.

For Bultmann, this passage vividly expresses the meaning of detachment, "dealing with the world in a spirit of 'as if not'" (6:20). A sense of detachment from the world, and all its spurious claims and promises, is the decisive quality of the new life of faith, even as it is the precondition for a love born of freedom.

4. THE SCIENCE-FAITH DILEMMA RESOLVED: NEW PROBLEMS

The explosion of scientific knowledge in the twentieth century altered decisively the consciousness of men in the modern world. One result of this explosion was the creation of a chasm separating modern man from his religious origins. When contemporary men read the religious stories of their Jewish and Christian ancestors, they do not find their religious convictions and sense of historical continuity confirmed. More often than not, they are simply confounded by a strange world of belief quite alien to their own. Stories of the miraculous exodus of the Hebrews from Egypt or the healings and resurrection of Jesus are more likely to evoke a sense of cognitive dissonance than religious awe. Such narratives simply do not fit with the reader's ordinary knowledge of reality; rather, they leave him baffled, puzzled and frustrated, but hardly inspired.

Rudolf Bultmann was not the first theologian to confront the gulf between modern consciousness and its religious origins. The early work of eighteenth-century critics like David Hume was later incorporated by nineteenth-century theologians like Friedrich Schleiermacher, Adolf Harnack, and Wilhelm Herrmann. Yet none of these figures played the decisive role in reshaping modern religious thought that Rudolf Bultmann did. For Bultmann was both more radical and more conservative than his predecessors. He was more radical in that he would not allow any contrived compromise between science and the Bible. He would not give his reader the privilege of holding on to some miracles while dismissing others. He would not allow the absurdity of a biblical narrative—such as Jesus' exorcism of demons into a herd of swine—to be concealed behind a sympathetic interpretation. If he erred in any direction, he tended to overstate the mythological tendencies of the biblical narrative in order to compel his readers to confront within themselves the hiatus between their world and the Bible. At the same time, Bultmann was also more conservative than his liberal theological precursors in his insistence on the centrality of the kerygma as the heart of New Testament Christianity. He would not ignore the mythological themes of the kerygma in order to extract from the New Testament certain ethical teachings agreeable to modern men. Nor would he minimize the scandal of the proclamation of the cross for the sake of cultivating general religious sentiments. In his proposal of demythologizing and existential interpretation, radical criticism and orthodox fidelity to the kerygma of the primitive Christian community are inseparably joined together.

While Bultmann was himself a Lutheran Christian, in his theological style and church life, his thought has been appropriated by religious thinkers from a wide variety of other traditions. Innumerable Protestant theologians have incorporated demythologizing themes and existential categories in their own thought. Catholic theologians like Leslie Dewart and Jewish thinkers like Richard Rubenstein have also employed Bultmann's categories in reinterpreting their own traditions.[24] In Japan, where science and technology have also come to play a dominant role, Buddhist scholars from both the Zen and Pure Land traditions have also borrowed from Bultmann. The ecumenical and international scope of Bultmann's influence reflects the basic turn of direction which he effected in modern religious thought. For Bultmann brought to a conclusion that chapter of modern religious thought which Hume initiated with his critique of the pre-scientific origins of religious belief.

While Bultmann's resolution of the science-faith dilemma had obvious strengths, it also engendered new problems. Basic to his reinterpretation of religion is the absolute dichotomy of scientific reason and existential faith. According to Bultmann, faith is not able to make any cognitive claims about reality; this falls under the jurisdiction of reason. Rational processes, in turn, are not able to illumine or inform the mysteries of existential freedom and anxiety; this falls under the jurisdiction of faith. Man is thus divided into two parts: his *reason* which comprehends every aspect of his objective environment—natural, historical, political, social, and moral; and his *existential freedom* as a subject who realizes himself through his historical decisions. There is no bridge which joins together the depths of existential freedom and the scope of objective reason. This dualism is presupposed in every aspect of Bultmann's thought.

One consequence of this dichotomy is Bultmann's individualism. Just as the objective environment is excluded from the domain of existential faith, so is man's life with others in community or sociopolitical bodies. Bultmann tends to be suspicious of man's concern with social forms of life as a possible escape from the anxiety of an individual's existential freedom. Social life often appears as a temptation, luring men to give up their individuality and authenticity in order to become part of the crowd. Like other existentialists, Bultmann addresses himself to "the solitary individual" who takes upon himself the anxiety of his freedom and opens himself to the unknown future. Every aspect of his theology is interpreted strictly within the limits of this individualistic perspective. The experience of worship, which occurs in the context of Christian community, is understood by Bultmann as an occasion for encounter between the individual believer and the word of God. Worship does not lead an individual out of his isolation into shared experiences with others; it rather intensifies his sense of inwardness and individuality which separates him from others. Eschatology is also thoroughly individualized by Bultmann. The "eschatological moment" of which he speaks is an event in the life history of the individual in which his old self-understanding is judged and a new freedom for his future is awakened.

Many contemporary theologians have sharply criticized Bultmann for the individualistic focus of his theology. Harvey Cox, for example, has described Bultmann's individualism as a remnant of the dying bourgeois social order of nineteenth-century Europe: "the last child of a cultural epoch, born in its mother's senility" (11:252). Future-oriented theologians, like Jürgen Moltmann and Rubem Alves, have criticized Bultmann's individualized eschatology on biblical grounds.[25] Moltmann insists that biblical eschatology looks forward to political transformations. The word of God is both a judgment on those social structures which institutionalize exploitation and oppression and a call for commitment to a more just and humane society in the future. In Moltmann's view, the kerygma cannot be interpreted solely as addressed to the individual. Still other theologians have emphasized the communal dimensions of worship over against Bultmann's individualized experience of encounter. For Sam Keen, worship does not isolate man in the depths of his inner life, but calls him to share with others the ecstatic joys and the sufferings of life.

A final problem intrinsic to Bultmann's resolution of the science–faith conflict is his Christian exclusivism. Because he has excluded any rational use of objective standards in evaluating faith, Bultmann is required to ground faith in a single decisive instance of revelation, namely the Christian kerygma. Without such a clear locus for faith outside the individual, Bultmann fears that faith would be reduced to an arbitrary, subjective decision. Hence, Bultmann insists that while authentic existence is a "theoretical possibility" for all men, it is an "actual possibility" only for those who hear and respond to the Christian kerygma (6:29). His position does not allow him to consider the possibility that the authentic existence known through Christianity might also be realized through other modes of self-transformation. As a result, authentic existence, which first appeared as a universal possibility, becomes finally confined to Christian believers.

Bultmann's exclusive focus on the Christian kerygma was ideally suited to the religious-political context of his era. The German Nationalists had formulated a religious ideology that appealed to the so-called "God of Nature" to justify genocidal and militaristic ventures. In confronting the demonic religious claims of the Nazis, Bultmann and other Christians found it necessary to repudiate all other forms of religious belief by a forceful declaration of the kerygma as the one true source of faith. Later theologians, writing in a quite different religious-political context, have found it equally necessary to reject Bultmann's exclusivism. Seiicho Yagi, a Bultmannian theologian in Japan, refuses to ground faith in any single instance of historical revelation. Instead, he identifies faith solely with that particular understanding of human existence which he finds in both the Zen tradition and in Bultmann's version of Christian existentialism. Schubert Ogden, an American Bultmannian theologian, has also criticized Bultmann's exclusivism.[26] For Ogden, Christian revelation provides a decisive disclosure of authentic existence, but not the sole means through which it may be realized. In their critique of Bultmann, both of these theologians reflect a secular, pluralistic religious context which does not allow any one religious tradition to make imperialist claims.

The problems of dualism, individualism, and exclusivism should not overshadow the basic contribution of Bultmann's theology. Each significant development in human thought generates its own problems. While Bultmann's entire theology may not be fully adequate today, he does provide new ways of dealing with important contemporary religious issues. By pointing to the pre-scientific mythology expressed in the Bible and distinguishing the essentials of faith from this primitive world view, he enables us to appropriate the faith of our Western religious origins without sacrificing our intellectual integrity. After Bultmann, the old battles between scientists and believers become obsolete.

NOTES

[1] Bultmann's brief "Autobiographical Reflections" are printed in *Existence and Faith* (3:283-288) and *The Theology of Rudolf Bultmann* (14:xix-xxv).

[2] While Bultmann borrowed a variety of anthropological categories from Martin Heidegger's existentialist philosophy, he never appropriated Heidegger's basic

philosophical schema as the conceptual foundation for his own thought. Unnecessary confusion has been created because so many interpreters of Bultmann have continued to presuppose Heidegger's existentialism as the fundamental philosophical source for Bultmann's theology. Bultmann remained a Kantian, not an existentialist, in his basic philosophical position. His so-called existentialist theology is a consistent development and modification of the Lutheran-Neo-Kantian theology of Wilhelm Herrmann, Bultmann's beloved theological mentor (19:33-36). Therefore, I give relatively little attention to Heidegger's philosophy in this chapter. For a typical Heideggerean interpretation of Bultmann, see John Macquarrie, *An Existentialist Theology: A Comparison of Heidegger and Bultmann* (New York: Macmillan, 1955). For a more detailed analysis of the relationship between Bultmann's theology, Heidegger's existentialism, and Neo-Kantian philosophy and theology, see my longer study of Bultmann, *The Origins of Demythologizing* (13).

3 For a comprehensive survey of these eighteenth-century critics of religion, see Frank Manuel, *The Eighteenth Century Confronts the Gods* (Cambridge: Harvard University Press, 1959).

4 Eichorn was a student of Heyne and the first biblical scholar to use the concept of mythology as a critical tool in Old Testament studies. For a definitive study of the use of "mythology" by Eichorn, Strauss, and other early nineteenth-century biblical scholars, see C. Hartlich and W. Sachs, *Der Ursprung des Mythosbegriffes in der modernen Bibelwissenschaft* (Tuebingen: J. C. B. Mohr, 1952). Strauss' essay, "Myth in the New Testament," has been reprinted in B. M. G. Reardon, *Religious Thought in the Nineteenth Century* (Cambridge: University Press, 1966). Albert Schweitzer offers a helpful introduction to the work of Strauss as a biblical critic in *The Quest of the Historical Jesus* (New York: Macmillan, 1957), chs. VII and VIII. Karl Barth has written a provocative theological interpretation of Strauss in *From Rousseau to Ritschl* (London: SCM Press, 1959), ch. X.

5 Bultmann first used the Enlightenment idea of mythology in a 1930 essay, "Mythus und Mythologie im Neuen Testament," *Die Religion in Gechichte und Gegenwart,* 2nd ed. (Tuebingen: Mohr, 1927-1931), vol. IV, cols. 204-208. Prior to this time, he understood myth simply as a soteriological narrative enacted in a cultic context and in the form of a cosmic drama. For examples of Bultmann's early use of myth, see his 1920 essay, "Ethical and Mystical Religion in Primitive Christianity," *The Beginnings of Dialectical Theology,* ed. James Robinson (Richmond: John Knox Press, 1968), pp. 221-235, or his 1921 form critical study, *The History of the Synoptic Tradition* (New York: Harper & Row, 1963).

6 Many of Bultmann's critics did not understand the Enlightenment periodization of history which Bultmann presupposed in his use of myth. Hence, they mistakenly identified mythology with contemporary phenomena like political ideologies, philosophical or scientific theories of reality, or popular superstitious practices and habits of thought. Several of the essays in *Kerygma and Myth,* I (6) illustrate this confusion.

7 Norman Kemp Smith provides a brief but reliable introduction to Kant's theory of knowledge in *A Commentary to Kant's "Critique of Pure Reason"* (New York: Humanities Press, 1962), pp. xxxiii-xvlii.

8 By Marburg Neo-Kantians, I refer to the philosophers Hermann Cohen and Paul Natorp and the theologian, Wilhelm Herrmann. Natorp and Cohen revised Kant's theory of knowledge in light of the mathematical physics predominant at the turn of the century. Their logical idealism rejected sense data as a given for knowledge and they repudiated Kant's notion of the "tran-

scendental object." For a discussion of Kant's theory of sensibility and transcendental object, see Norman Kemp Smith's *Commentary . . .*, pp. 79-85, 204-208. Essays by Fritz Kaufmann and William Workmeister include a discussion of philosophical themes characteristic of Marburg Neo-Kantianism and are published in *The Philosophy of Ernst Cassirer*, ed. Paul Schillp (Evanston: Library of Living Philosophers, 1949), pp. 757-797 and 798-854. For a clear example of Bultmann's appropriation of Neo-Kantian philosophical categories, see his 1920 essay, "Religion and Culture," *The Beginnings of Dialectical Theology*, pp. 205-220.

9 By virtue of their emphasis on the active role of reason in establishing valid knowledge, the Neo-Kantians prefer the verbal forms of "objectifying" or "objectified" to the noun "object." Bultmann also employs this Neo-Kantian terminology in his theological writings.

10 Paul Tillich has clarified the distinction between existential anxiety and neurotic anxiety in *The Courage to Be* (New Haven: Yale University Press, 1952), pp. 32-42 and 64-78.

11 Bultmann first articulates his understanding of human existence in terms of self-responsibility and insecurity in an essay of 1925, "What Does it Mean to Speak of God?" (4:62-63). After 1925, Bultmann presupposes and extends this basic understanding of human existence throughout the whole range of his theological writings. For example, see his interpretation of Pauline anthropology in *Theology of the New Testament*, I (9:227), or his original proposal for demythologizing, *Kerygma and Myth*, I (6:18).

12 I am indebted to Professor Louis Mink of Wesleyan University for first suggesting the "track-laying machine" analogy as part of his presentation of R. G. Collingwood's philosophy of history for The New Haven Theological Discussion Group.

13 For an existentialist interpretation of death, see Martin Heidegger, *Being and Time* (London: SCM Press, 1962), pp. 279-311.

14 Work, for Bultmann, encompasses both a particular kind of thought—the objectifying and unifying thought of science—and a particular self-understanding—the existential attitude of self-reliance, seeking security by one's own strength and the disposable resources of the world. In Bultmann's theological critique of the work ethic predominant in Protestant culture, sin becomes identified with the self-understanding of work: "But this is basically the sin of the world in general: to estimate itself and God by achievement and work. . . . Wonder [in the sense of a genuine act of God] confronts man with the critical question of how far he understands the world rightly when he understands it as the working world amenable to his control; how far he rightly understands himself when he estimates himself by his work and aims at making himself secure through his work. Thus the concept of wonder radically negates the character of the world as the controllable, working world, because it destroys man's understanding of himself as made secure through his work" (4:254-255).

15 In Bultmann's judgment, Wilhelm Herrmann first recognized the connection between the natural laws of modern science and the primitive idea of work (4:248).

16 See Bultmann's discussion of "Flesh, Sin and World" (9:227-269).

17 While Bultmann's theological writings are the focus of this chapter, his contributions to New Testament scholarship are of equal importance. With Martin Dibelius, Bultmann was a pioneer in developing "form criticism": a literary analysis of Synoptic Gospel story units and their changing shape in oral tradition: *The History of the Synoptic Tradition* (New York: Harper & Row,

1963). His 1926 study of Jesus—*Jesus and the Word* (New York: Scribner's, 1934), his 1941 commentary on the Gospel of John, and his two-volume *Theology of the New Testament* (8 and 9) remain as classics in the field of New Testament scholarship. The philosophical and theological themes described in this chapter are equally prominent in his New Testament studies, except for those publications written before the creative turn in Bultmann's thought which occurred in the period 1925-1933.

18 Bultmann has consistently understood demythologizing as a method of interpreting the Christian Gospel for the sake of preaching in the contemporary Church. Walter Schmithals highlights this point in his study of Bultmann, *An Introduction to the Theology of Rudolf Bultmann* (18), esp. p. 249ff. For a collection of Bultmann's own sermons, see *This World and the Beyond: Marburg Sermons* (New York: Scribner's, 1960).

19 An "act of God" for Bultmann is always an event open to two interpretations: from the objectifying perspective of reason, it appears to be an ordinary event which can be explained in terms of natural causes; from an existential perspective of faith, it is an extraordinary event—a "wonder"—which breaks in upon a closed self-understanding, calls for a radical new self-understanding, and invites a response of faith in God.

20 Biblical scholars began to recognize the prominence of an eschatological perspective in the New Testament at the turn of the century. One effect of this discovery was to radically undermine the liberal theological picture of Jesus as a wise and loving moral and religious teacher; see Albert Schweitzer, *The Quest of the Historical Jesus*, chs. 15, 16, 19, 20. The eschatology of the New Testament also required a radical reinterpretation of modern theology, of which Karl Barth's 1918 commentary on Romans is a classic example. For Bultmann's discussion of eschatology, in addition to works already cited, see *Primitive Christianity in Its Contemporary Setting* (New York: Meridian Books, 1956) and *History and Eschatology* (New York: Harper Torchbooks, 1957).

21 The preaching of Jesus, the epistles of Paul, and the Gospels of Mark and Matthew all share the expectation of an imminent eschatological event in the future. In the Gospels of Luke and John, the eschatological theme is reinterpreted and the expectation of an imminent future event recedes into the background.

22 Bultmann's insistence on the unique role of Christian proclamation as the way to authentic existence is one of the central issues in the debate between himself and existentialist philosopher Karl Jaspers: *Myth and Christianity* (New York: Noonday Press, 1958).

23 Bultmann's radical doctrine of sin also divides him from his existentialist philosophical colleagues; in addition to his debate with Jaspers, see his discussion with Wilhelm Kamlah, *Kerygma and Myth*, I (6:25-33).

24 Catholic theologian Leslie Dewart proposes to extend the demythologizing of the Bible to a dehellenizing of dogma: *The Future of Belief* (New York: Herder & Herder, 1966). Richard Rubenstein extends demythologizing in a psychoanalytic interpretation of Judaism: *After Auschwitz* (New York: Bobbs-Merrill, 1966).

25 Rubem Alves calls attention to the Kantian dualism of the rational/objective and existential/individual which leads Bultmann to his individualistic interpretation of New Testament eschatology: *A Theology of Human Hope* (New York: Corpus Books, 1969), pp. 34-43.

26 The writings of Seiicho Yagi, while popular in Japan, have not been translated into English; Schubert Ogden's criticism of Bultmann appears in *Christ With-*

out Myth: a Study Based on the Theology of Rudolf Bultmann (New York: Harper, 1961).

BIBLIOGRAPHY

1. BULTMANN, RUDOLF, *Die Christliche Hoffnung und das Problem der Entmythologisierung.* Stuttgart: Evangelisches Verlagswerk, 1954.
2. ———, *Essays: Philosophical and Theological.* London: SCM Press, 1955.
3. ———, *Existence and Faith.* New York: Meridian Books, 1960.
4. ———, *Faith and Understanding.* New York: Harper & Row, 1969.
5. ———, *Jesus Christ and Mythology.* New York: Scribner's, 1958.
6. ———, *Kerygma and Myth,* I, ed. H. W. Bartsch. London: SPCK, 1957.
7. ———, *Kerygma und Mythos,* II, ed. H. W. Bartsch. Hamburg: Reich & Heindrich, 1951.
8. ———, "On the Problem of Demythologizing," *Journal of Religion,* 42 (1962), 96-102.
9. ———, *Theology of the New Testament,* I. New York: Scribner's, 1951.
10. ———, *Theology of the New Testament,* II. New York: Scribner's, 1955.
11. COX, HARVEY, *The Secular City.* New York: Macmillan, 1966.
12. EICHORN, JOHANN GOTTFRIED, *Introduction to the Old Testament: Selections.* London: E. Sotheran, 1888.
13. JOHNSON, ROGER A., *The Origins of Demythologizing.* Leiden: Brill, 1973.
14. KEGLEY, CHARLES W., ed., *The Theology of Rudolf Bultmann.* New York: Harper & Row, 1966.
15. MACQUARRIE, JOHN, *The Scope of Demythologizing.* London: SCM Press, 1960.
16. OGDEN, SCHUBERT, *Christ Without Myth.* New York: Harper, 1961.
17. PERRIN, NORMAN, *The Promise of Bultmann.* Philadelphia: Lippincott, 1969.
18. SCHMITHALS, WALTER, *An Introduction to the Theology of Rudolf Bultmann.* Minneapolis: Augsburg, 1968.
19. SMART, JAMES, *The Divided Mind of Modern Theology.* Philadelphia: Westminster Press, 1967.
20. STRAUSS, DAVID FRIEDRICH, *The Life of Jesus Critically Examined,* 4th ed. New York: Calvin Blanchard, 1860.

SUGGESTED READINGS

1. *Primary Readings*

Bultmann first proposed the demythologizing of the New Testament in his 1941 essay, "New Testament and Mythology," *Kerygma and Myth,* I (6).

However, the most thorough and clear statement of demythologizing appears in *Jesus Christ and Mythology* (5). This book was originally prepared as a series of lectures for American audiences and incorporates Bultmann's response to many of the issues raised in the demythologizing debate.

2. Secondary Readings

Essays in *Kerygma and Myth*, I (6) and II (London: SPCK, 1962) offer a variety of critical responses to demythologizing. For a selection of mostly Lutheran responses to Bultmann's theology, see Carl Braaten and Roy Harrisville, eds., *Kerygma and History* (Nashville: Abingdon Press, 1962). For a cross-section of Catholic views of Bultmann's theology, see Thomas F. O'Meara and Donald M. Weisser, *Rudolf Bultmann in Catholic Thought* (New York: Herder & Herder, 1968); and also Heinrich Fries, *Bultmann-Barth and Catholic Theology* (Pittsburgh: Duquesne University Press, 1967). For a sympathetic and non-technical introduction to Bultmann's theology, see Norman Perrin, *The Promise of Bultmann* (17).

3. Additional Bibliography

For a complete list of Bultmann's publications from 1908 through 1965, see Charles Kegley, *The Theology of Rudolf Bultmann* (14:289-310). For books and articles written about Bultmann's theology, see the bibliographies in any of the following: *Existence and Faith* (3), *The Origins of Demythologizing* (13), *The Promise of Bultmann* (17), and *Kerygma and Myth*, II (London: SPCK, 1962).

BIOLOGY AND RELIGION

CHARLES DARWIN AND DARWINISM 3

A Naturalized World and a Brutalized Man?

In 1925 John T. Scopes was charged with the crime of teaching the theory of evolution in public schools in the state of Tennessee. Three years earlier William Jennings Bryan, who was to be the prosecutor at the trial, stated in an article published in the *New York Times* that Darwinism

> entirely changes one's view of life and undermines faith in the Bible. Evolution has no place for the miracle or the supernatural. . . . Evolution proposes to bring all the processes of nature within the comprehension of man (1:26).
>
> The evolution that is harmful—distinctly so—is the evolution that destroys man's family tree as taught by the Bible and makes him a descendent of the lower forms of life. This, as I shall try to show, is a very vital matter (1:23).

Even if we are not inclined to accept the derisive geographical description of Bryan as the "orator of the Platte" because that river, which has its origin in Bryan's home state of Nebraska, is six miles wide but only six inches deep at the mouth, we cannot avoid the fact that Charles Darwin's theory of evolution had challenged and offended Bryan to the bottom of his conservative soul. At the Scopes trial Bryan claimed that Darwin traced man's moral nature "back to the animals" and cried out: "It is all

77

animal, animal, animal, with never a thought of God or of religion"
(13:326).

To be sure, by the time Darwin's views were placed on trial in
Tennessee, the issues of science versus religion, evolution versus the Bible,
created man versus animal man had been painted in the overly contrasted colors of fundamentalism.[1] But still the basic issues raised by
Darwin's research were apparent. Specific questions were raised about
the nature of man, the accuracy and worth of the Bible and the validity
of traditional proofs for the existence of God, but the over-arching issue
involved the way Darwin divorced knowledge about the nature of man
and the biological world from cardinal Western religious convictions.
Man and nature were understood apart from the existence of God and
his creation and providence. This is the essence of naturalization—the
removal of things from a religious or spiritual realm to the realm of the
natural and the ordinary. To Bryan, this Darwinian impulse seemed
positively debasing. Separated from the doctrines of creation and providence, nature could no longer point to the existence of God; and man,
now stripped of his divine properties, appeared lonely and brutalized.

Two of Darwin's critics further illustrate the nature and gravity of
the issues raised by *The Origin of Species* (1859). The Reverend Adam
Sedgwick (1785–1873), Professor of Geology at the University of Cambridge and one of Darwin's most important scientific mentors, wrote to
Darwin just as the *Origin* was being published stating that he had been
"greatly shocked" by Darwin's book. "There is," he cried

> a moral or metaphysical part of nature as well as a physical [part]. A
> man who denies this is deep in the mire of folly. 'Tis the crown and glory
> of organic science that it does . . . link material and moral. . . . You
> have ignored this link; and, if I do not mistake your meaning, you have
> done your best in one or two pregnant cases to break it. Were it possible
> (which, thank God, it is not) to break it, humanity, in my mind, would
> suffer damage that might brutalize it, and sink the human race into a
> lower grade of degradation than any into which it has fallen since its
> written records tell us of its history (2:229).

In jest Sedgwick alluded to himself as "a son of a monkey and an old
friend of yours," but he quickly added that he humbly accepted "God's
revelation of Himself both in His works and in His word" (2:230). Darwin's conclusions concerning the origins of animal life, developed independently from religious and moral concerns, had threatened the aging
professor's world view. To Sedgwick, the removal of religion from the
discussion of man and nature brutalized humankind and ruptured the
affectionate relation between science and the Bible that had been a
reigning assumption in the universities of England.

The reaction of the eloquent, reforming Bishop of Oxford, Samuel Wilberforce (1805–1873), was no less intense. Wilberforce was the bishop who attacked Darwin's ideas in grim earnest at Oxford, only to be met with the equally forceful reply of T. H. Huxley, self-styled as "Darwin's bulldog." Fed by information supplied to him by the eminent anatomist and paleontologist, Richard Owen, Wilberforce said that it was "solely on scientific grounds" that he found *The Origin of Species* an *"utterly rotten fabric of guess and speculation"* (12:253,256). His real differences with Darwin, however, lay not in scientific evidence but in Wilberforce's conviction that Darwin's ideas were

> absolutely incompatible not only with single expressions in the word of God . . . but . . . of far more importance, with the whole representation of that moral and spiritual condition of man which is its proper subject matter. Man's derived supremacy over the earth; man's power of articulate speech; man's gift of reason . . . man's fall and man's redemption; the incarnation of the Eternal Son . . . all are equally and utterly irreconcilable with the degrading notion of the brute origin of him who was created in the image of God, and redeemed by the Eternal Son assuming to himself his nature (12:258).

The assumed religious verities of creation, redemption and providence as taught in the Bible had preserved mankind's dignity and articulated his uniqueness. To refute or ignore these revealed truths was to cut the umbilical cord between God and man, leaving nature secularized and man brutalized.

The traditional view of man and nature shared by Bryan the politician, Sedgwick the scientist and Wilberforce the bishop was based upon the Bible and natural theology. The Bible depicted God as creating the natural world and man and sustaining them by his providential care and concern. Mankind's dignity and honor lay in its unique possession of the "image of God" and its divine commission to exercise sovereignty over the natural world. Natural theology at the time was a form of philosophical speculation that, independently from scripture, sought to prove that the natural world reflects the existence and providential character of God. Since Darwin's work could not be harmonized with the common, literal interpretation of the Bible, and since it ran counter to the "proofs" offered by natural theology, Darwinism seemed to cut away the ground from beneath the interrelated beliefs about the existence of God and the dignity of man. For Darwin, man and nature were to be understood in the context of the secular domain of science. Their origins, development and character were to be explained in terms of ordinary, natural, cause-and-effect relationships. To understand man in this naturalized context, in which the existence of God and his relationship to man were either questioned or dismissed, seemed to deny man's importance and transcendence.

Darwin's revolutionary approach to man and nature accounts for his image as the Copernicus of the natural world. Even as Copernicus showed that the earth was not the center of the cosmos, but rather was one of several planets revolving around the sun, so Darwin radically questioned whether man was the focal point of the created order. Was man not, rather, only one of thousands of creatures, all emerging from the same set of environmental conditions? In the Bible man is pictured as the central concern of God and the uniquely endowed, high point of creation to whom the world of nature was affectionately entrusted. In evolution, man appears as a belated variety of mammals, emerging so late on the scene that during most of its vast history the earth was entrusted to other animals. Men and women who had believed that they were a "little lower than the angels" discovered that they were but a "little higher than the brutes" (6:337).

The reactions of Bryan, Sedgwick, and Wilberforce to Charles Darwin's ideas highlight three interrelated religious issues basic to the naturalization of the biological order. Darwinism gave birth to intense discussions and debates over the nature of man, the status of the traditional, literal interpretation of the Bible and the validity of natural theology's argument for God from the principle of design. All three themes, however, are related to the broader question of attempting to understand man and the natural world apart from those religious convictions mediated to the West through the biblical literature.

1. DARWIN'S SCIENTIFIC AND RELIGIOUS HERITAGE

Intellectuals in early nineteenth-century England were consciously committed to the cultivation of an harmonious relationship between science and religion. Charles Darwin (1809–1882) received his own education in this intellectual milieu and shared this point of view in the early stages of his development. Christianity, it was affirmed, had "everything to hope and nothing to fear" from the advancement of science, since the God of nature and the God of revelation were the same (12:257). On that issue scientists and clergymen had slight disagreement —so little, in fact, that the roles of clergymen and scientists were often intermeshed. Surely one of the reasons why Darwin was attracted for a season to the cloth was his belief that as a salaried country parson he could continue collecting and observing organisms in an almost uninterrupted fashion. Indeed, to be a natural historian could be a way to participate in a form of piety. This is seen in the life style of the man who by Darwin's own admission was the greatest single influence on his whole career. On "most days," said Darwin, he and the Reverend John Stevens Henslow, professor of botany at Cambridge, would take long walks together (2:22). From Henslow Darwin learned "to draw conclusions from long-continued minute observations." And through Henslow's life Darwin saw the example of a model clergyman-scientist—a man who was "deeply religious and so orthodox," observed Darwin, "that he told me one day he should be grieved if a single word of the Thirty-nine Articles were altered" (2:22).

The marriage between religion and natural science was consummated so that biological investigation did not conflict with the Bible. Scientific data were gathered and organized in such a way that they would not disagree with the acceptance of the historical and scientific accuracy of the Bible. For example, excluding a few rare exceptions, biologists in England were "creationists." They believed that all species had been created by God and possessed unique and permanent features. The great Swedish naturalist Carolus Linnaeus (1707–1778) spent his life classifying "as many species as issued in pairs from the hands of the Creator" (6:131-137,182-187). The brilliant Frenchman, Georges Cuvier (1769–1832), sought to relate the findings of Linnaeus to the vast quantity of newly gathered biological information. He supported the theory that there were successive periods of creation, and thus approved a compromise between new scientific discoveries, like the recognition that many species had become extinct, and the traditional, biblical view of creation. In English-speaking countries only more eccentric thinkers like James Burnet (Lord Monboddo) (1714–1799) and Charles Darwin's grandfather, Erasmus (1713–1802), speculated respectively that man could greatly develop his intellectual capacities or that general evolution occurred. The views of neither man became normative or, for that matter, widely influential within the context of the universities. Undisposed to accept what Coleridge called "orang-outang theology," the great majority of English scientists believed that most factual evidence supported the theory that the species were created immutable.

In the middle decades of the nineteenth century most Englishmen still assumed that the Bible was literally true. By and large the history and ideas of the Bible served as *a priori* assumptions concerning the nature of man, human history, and the structure of the cosmos. Those who had begun to question the literal accuracy of the Bible—and their numbers were increasing at mid-century—still believed that science and scripture could be harmonized.[2] To compel science to speak according to the Bible was rejected by clergymen and scientists alike. Bishop Wilberforce himself called such compulsion a "feebleminded dishonesty of lying for God" (12:256). Nevertheless, most mid-century Victorians had great faith that patient investigation would vindicate the accuracy of the biblical world view. The Bible still hovered over England like a huge bird, mothering the ideas which were to bear ultimately her image.

In order for the Bible to maintain its intellectual respectability, it had to be reinterpreted constantly in the light of new scientific evidence and to be defended elaborately by learned, orthodox spokesmen. Reinterpretation and defense were also necessarily applied to the arguments for God from natural theology. Given David Hume's cogent critique of the rational theism of the eighteenth century, we can well ask how natural theology maintained its esteem in the post-Humean period. The answer lies in part in the emergence of sophisticated, orthodox apologists who shifted the focus of natural theology away from Hume by concentrating on anatomy, on the marvelous balance between structure and function in biological organisms, rather than the whole cosmos.[3] Orthodox thinkers thus re-established proofs for design and harmony in the natural world by shifting to the intricate world of biology. We can illuminate the character of the new defenses of the Bible and natural theology by referring to the ideas of one of the truly representative and influential orthodox voices at the turn of the century—William Paley (1743–1805).

Paley's theology had two major divisions, the first dealing with those truths which may be affirmed about God without revelation, the second with those doctrines which are based on scripture. For the first he wrote *Natural Theology* (1802) in which he sought to prove "that there must be something in the world more than what we see" and "that, amongst the invisible things of nature, there must be an intelligent mind" (10:486). He began his argument with the famous analogy based upon one's stumbling across a watch.

> This mechanism being observed . . . the inference, we think, is inevitable, that the watch must have had a maker; that there must have existed, at some time, and at some place or other, an artificer or artificers, who formed it for the purpose which we find it actually to answer; who comprehended its construction, and designed its use (10:388).

Paley then, avoiding Hume's argument that the entire universe hardly functions so smoothly that one can argue that it was formed by one designing mind, focused on individual biological mechanisms.

> I mean, that the contrivances of nature surpass the contrivances of art, in the complexity, subtlety, and curiosity, of the mechanism . . . yet, in a multitude of cases, are not less evidently accommodated to their end, or suited to their office, then are the most perfect productions of human ingenuity.
>
> I know no better method of introducing so large a subject, than that of comparing a single thing with a single thing; an eye, for example, with a telescope (10:391).

Is not the eye more complex, more marvelous than the telescope or part of a watch? Is not its structure admirably suited for its function? And can it not be argued that so regulated, so compact, so functionally perfect an instrument points to the necessity of an intelligent Creator? And if the eye, also the ear, the foot, the hand, the organs; intermeshed, they work together like the parts of an intricate, cosmic watch (10:435). "It is an immense conclusion, that there is a God; a perceiving, intelligent, designing Being; at the head of creation, and from whose will it proceeded" (10:468). The argument for God from design in its new, anatomical form is completed. The mind is awe-stricken. The orthodox sing:

> Deep in unfathomable mines
> Of never-failing skill,
> He treasures up His bright designs,
> And works His gracious will.[4]

Paley's line of argumentation, however, was only partially given in his *Natural Theology*. A Deist could agree with him up to that point. The next step involved asking whether such a Creator might not reveal himself more particularly. "The true theist will be the first to listen to *any* credible communication of Divine knowledge" (10:486). Paley, of course, believed that God had communicated with man in a way which went far beyond the limitations of the series of proofs from natural reflection. He revealed himself in the Bible; and in defense of it Paley wrote his famous *Evidences of Christianity* (1794). In that book he gave a long series of arguments in favor of the historical veracity of the Bible, utilizing the great store of information from Greco-Roman and Christian antiquity which had been gathered by early orthodox biblical critics. Given the accuracy of the New Testament documents in such matters as their depiction of Jewish and Roman customs, given the sincerity, honesty, and moral sacrifices made by the apostles who wrote the books in the canon, and given such proofs as the admission by both the skeptical opponents and loyal adherents of Christianity that Christ and the apostles could work miracles, was not the Christian religion and the revelation which presents it true? Christianity

> contradicted the most fixed persuasions and prejudices of the persons to whom it was addressed; it required from those who accepted it, not a simple, indolent assent, but a change, from thenceforward, of principles and conduct, a submission to consequences the most serious and the most deterring, to loss and danger, to insult, outrage, and persecution. How such a story should be false, or, if false, how under such circumstances it should make its way, I think impossible to be explained; yet such the Christian story was . . . and in opposition to such difficulties did it prevail (10:384).

It is immediately apparent that Paley's apologetic is essentially rational.[5] Like any Enlightenment scientist or historian he is amassing factual "evidence" to prove his case, or perhaps more accurately put, to show how irrational it is to *reject* his case. Even if such arguments could not prove the infallibility of the Bible, they were thought to produce respect for its historicity and to rout thoroughly Deist assertions that it was little less than a pious hoax.

It is in the light of this still intact, biblically informed, God-imbued world view that the pre-Darwinian understanding of man must be seen. Enlightened orthodox Christianity enshrined and encased Western interpretations of man. It should not be assumed, however, that before Darwin man was in no way linked rather closely to the animal kingdom. As early as 1735 man was identified biologically with animal species. In that year Linnaeus ranked man with the quadrupeds, a group in which he also included apes and sloths. In the twelfth and last edition of his *System of Nature* (1758) Linnaeus still held that there were no adequate physical characteristics which would lead him to place man in a distinct category (6:173–175,184–187).[6] On the other hand, Linnaeus was careful to point to man's mental and spiritual superiority over all other creatures. One of the problems with Linnaeus' handling of men and apes was the fact that he knew next to nothing about the latter. Travelers from Africa had brought home stories about tailed men, and Linnaeus believed them. When more accurate information about monkeys and apes became available, such biologists as Cuvier separated humans from apes, heightening man's biological uniqueness and supporting traditional notions regarding his God-given capacities. Except for Lord Monboddo, who believed that orang-outangs were uncultured men, scholars before Darwin had little reason to question the strikingly unique qualities of man.

In the light of the constant and cordial relationships between science and religion, of the fact that man and the biological world were inextricably related to the biblical notions of creation, design and providence, and of the defenses of the literal truth of the Bible, our earlier quotations from Adam Sedgwick and Bishop Wilberforce can be seen as reflecting the common assumptions of the time. Religion and science informed one another, and there is no better example of this than the intellectual world of pre-Darwinian scientists and clergymen. The complexities and mysteries of nature and the varied physical, mental and moral capacities of mankind were directly linked to the existence and creative power of God as manifested in the Bible.

The young Charles Darwin fully participated in the world view which has been sketched above. Given the mode of scientific teaching in his time, Darwin could hardly have avoided accepting this traditional

Weltanschauung. His intention to become a parson intensified that acceptance. Concerning his father's request that he should become a clergyman, Darwin said:

> He was very properly vehement against my turning into an idle sporting man, which then seemed my probable destination. I asked for some time to consider, as from what little I had heard or thought on the subject I had scruples about declaring my belief in all the dogmas of the Church of England; though otherwise I liked the thought of being a country clergyman. Accordingly I read with great care . . . books on divinity; and as I did not then in the least doubt the strict and literal truth of every word in the Bible, I soon persuaded myself that our Creed must be fully accepted (2:17-18).

And whom did Darwin study en route? None other than William Paley. He said in his *Autobiography:*

> In order to pass the B. A. examination, it was also necessary to get up Paley's *Evidences of Christianity,* and his *Moral Philosophy.* This was done in a thorough manner, and I am convinced that I could have written out the whole of the *Evidences* with perfect correctness, but not of course in the clear language of Paley. The logic of this book and, as I may add, of his *Natural Theology,* gave me as much delight as did Euclid (2:19).

Darwin added that he was "charmed and convinced" by Paley's long line of argumentation (2:19). It is surely not overstated that an image of the older world view was sketched on the mind of the young Darwin. The harmony of science and religion, feelings of wonder and mystery towards a natural world informed by the belief that that world was created by God and reflects structurally his designing hand, respect for Scripture and its teachings, and an image of man which reflects the marriage between biology and the Bible—these all composed the world view of Darwin and the great majority of his intelligent contemporaries.

This world view would be cracked if someone were to refute William Paley's form of natural theology in which the existence of complex organic structures was explained by the notion that they were designed by God. Still more shattering would be a truly cogent point of view that could serve as an unequivocal, forceful platform for the rejection of the traditional understanding of the factual accuracy of the Bible. Darwin's researches were to do both. In one book he antiquated Paley and rewrote the first two chapters of Genesis. Symbolically and literally *The Origin of Species* confirmed and extended previous doubts about traditional opinion. At once the inherited concepts of creation and design were undermined, and with that man was to experience a fall second only to Lucifer's exclusion from heaven. Only instead of into hell, man was to fall into the lap of a naturalized world.

2. EVOLUTION AND NATURAL SELECTION
OPPOSE CREATION AND DESIGN

Charles Darwin left England as a naturalist aboard the *Beagle* in 1831 with a Bachelor of Arts degree in theology and the classics. His heart had been long attached to the out-of-doors. He enjoyed hunting birds and beetle collecting. By the time the *Beagle* dropped anchor at Falmouth, England, some five years later, his mind had found its true object of devotion—science. "The voyage of the *Beagle*," he said, "has been by far the most important event in my life, and has determined my whole career . . . I was led to attend closely to several branches of natural history, and thus my powers of observation were improved . . ." (2:28). When he returned he was his own man. His passion for science gradually eclipsed his love for all other activities. Hints about the reactions from leading scientists concerning his work fired him with zeal that he might "take a fair place among scientific men" (2:31). Also, during his more than five years' absence from home he became emancipated from the authority of his father.[7]

He began the voyage fully convinced of the creative power of God in nature. But he was open to new insights. As he collected plankton during the first weeks of the voyage, he spoke of his "feeling of wonder that so much beauty should be apparently created for such little purpose" (7:23). Darwin was so deeply moved by the grandeur of the Brazilian forests that he recorded in his journal that, "it is not possible to give an adequate idea of the higher feelings of wonder, admiration, and devotion which fill and elevate the mind" (2:65). The nature-piety of William Paley was being experienced first hand. Upon reaching the Galapagos Islands, however, Darwin was questioning the validity of the concept of the immutability of the species. Already he had found evidence of numerous extinct fossils and had observed how similar animals replaced others as they pushed southward down the continent (2:41-42). Then at the Galapagos he observed the similarities and yet differences between the island species and those on the South American continent. An individual species, such as the finch, appeared to have become differentiated when exploiting various biological niches on the islands. Such facts, he believed "would undermine the stability of species" (7:44). He was haunted by "the supposition that species gradually became modified," but until he could explain how plant and animal organisms became so "beautifully adapted to their habits of life," it seemed useless for him to speculate about their evolution (2:42).

Paley still loomed large. His argument was that complex structures were adapted so perfectly for particular functions that one must conclude that an intelligent mind made or created them precisely that way. To presuppose that species originated or are changed by some other method would require the devising of another explanation for this structure-function relation. Darwin's observations were leading him to link together areas and eras into an organic whole. By the end of the *Beagle*'s voyage he was thinking in terms of the mutability, rather than the permanence or fixity, of species. But he lacked an explanation for the mechanism behind such change.

Two presuppositions were especially important for Darwin's changing world view: the age of the earth and the nature of geological change. Both ideas are included in the one term, "uniformitarianism," which was strongly advocated in the work of the geologist Charles Lyell.[8] In opposition to "catastrophists," who believed that the great changes in the earth's surface were due to successive cataclysms, Lyell argued that the earth changed over a far more lengthy period of time, always subject to the same type of forces which are presently operative. Catastrophists greatly shortened the age of the earth by arguing that natural catastrophies brought the earth to its present condition more rapidly than any gradualist theory. That position was well suited for biologists such as Cuvier, who believed in the creation of plant and animal life, but who were forced by the newer evidence to recognize more than one creative epoch. Catastrophism, therefore, was a mediating position between uniformitarianism and the traditional understanding of the age of the earth (approximately six thousand years) as well as the traditional, biblical understanding of creation (in one short period of time). It was a perfect refuge for progressive traditionalists.

Just as Darwin was leaving on the voyage of the *Beagle* he was given a copy of the first volume of Lyell's *Principles of Geology* by his conservative botanist friend, Professor Henslow. Henslow warned Darwin at the time that "on no account" was he to accept the views set forward by Lyell (2:35). Predictably, Henslow held to both creationism and catastrophism. During the voyage Darwin received Lyell's second volume; and as he travelled, he became convinced "of the infinite superiority of Lyell's views over those advocated in any other work known to me" (2:36). He was thus thinking in terms of a natural world which was extremely old and which always changed as it now changes. One cannot forget that when Darwin began to formulate his ideas on evolution, he presupposed that species changed over the course of exceedingly vast periods of time. In that way very slight changes could eventually become significant ones.

Within nine months of his return to England Darwin began to gather information in notebooks which he entitled *The Transmutation of Species.* His intent was to collect all facts "which bore in any way on the variation of animals and plants under domestication and nature" in order to determine some of the factors that lay behind such modification or transmutation. By scouring through numerous books and even whole series of journals and by extended inquiries with breeders and gardeners,

> I soon perceived that selection was the keystone of man's success in making useful races of animals and plants. But how selection could be applied to organisms living in a state of nature remained for some time a mystery to me (2:42).

Another part of the puzzle was in place, one which clearly proved something about the way species were altered. But he still could account neither for the marvelous adaptive structures and actions within nature nor for the mechanism behind the variation of animals and plants which were not under domestication. Paley's explanation was still worthy of respect. Even as man's mind could steer the process of change of a limited series of creatures, so also the Divine mind could supervise change throughout the natural world.

Then in October of 1838, fifteen months after Darwin's systematic inquiry was initiated, he read "for amusement" Malthus's morose "Essay on the Principle of Population." Suddenly his long-standing awareness of the competitive side of nature was given specific focus. There were too many plants and animals by the very nature of their reproductive processes; hence there ensued a grave and constant struggle for survival. Darwin now had the answer:

> It at once struck me that under these circumstances favourable variations would tend to be preserved and unfavourable ones to be destroyed. The result of this would be the formation of new species. Here, then, I had at last got a theory by which to work . . . (2:42-43).

"Natural selection" in the context of a competitive world was indeed Darwin's own unique theory—one which explained how evolution or transmutation occurred by the pressures innate to the natural world itself. He could explain now why a limited number of species on the Galapagos exploited every possible crevice on those islands. He wrote in his notebook at the time that, "one may say there is a force like a hundred thousand wedges trying to force every kind of structure into the gaps in the economy of nature" (7:55). He could explain also why nature produced more complex structures—those structures simply gave the organism an advantage in the struggle for survival. In "natural selection" he had a truly unified theory which was to become the basis for his life's work.

"Natural selection" was to become the *coup de grace* of a static view of nature. It was in its own right a new "law" of nature and was treated by Darwin as such (5:449). Only this was not a law of Newtonian cosmic order, but a *statistical* law, a "law" of chance. Species in nature survive and evolve in the context of random variations among organisms competing for life and space in an overcrowded world. One German scholar called it the law of "higglety-pigglety." Ironically, Darwin's theory gave an orderly defense of the priorities of chance and change in nature. His law was to provide a basis for the development of whole new disciplines of study. It can well be argued, therefore, that Darwin was both the Copernicus and the Newton of the natural world.

Significant for an understanding of *The Origin of Species* (1859) is the fact that Darwin had been holding the theory set forth in that book for over twenty years; and even then he published his book under a form of scholarly duress. Why he took so long to publish his views is not altogether clear. At one point he had his "hands burned" by setting forth a geological explanation which was soon proven fallacious. He was always an exceedingly meticulous scholar and he also wanted to finish an enormous project on the study of barnacles. Surely involved, however, was his legitimate concern that his book would disturb the religious convictions of orthodox Christians, not the least of whom was his own wife.

The argument of the *Origin* is so intricate that Darwin once used it as evidence for his own power of reasoning (2:55). Impressive also is the range of his scientific study displayed in his essay. He argues from animal husbandry, morphology, botany, embryology, paleontology, and geology. Our concern, however, is not with the overall force of his argument or with the scientific accuracy of his study, even though both are impressive. We are primarily interested in the meaning and significance of two of the central concepts around which the evidence is gathered— the principles of "evolution" and of "natural selection" as the mechanism behind the evolutionary process.

To most present-day readers, the concept of "evolution," aside from bearing certain progressive connotations, signifies biologically that various types of organisms have their origin in other preexisting types, having received their distinguishing characteristics from successive modifications of previous organisms. From a biological point of view that is about what Darwin had in mind. But for Darwin evolution meant something more; it denoted a refutation of creationism. At one point in his correspondence, he affirmed that on the personal level he cared very much about the principle of natural selection, "but that seems to me utterly unimportant, compared to the question of Creation *or* Modification" (2:260). Behind much of the information that he gave in the *Origin* was his constant attempt to disprove one thesis as he established another. The *Origin's* introduction concludes with the assertion:

> Although much remains obscure, and will long remain obscure, I can entertain no doubt, after the most deliberate study and dispassionate judgment of which I am capable, that the view which most naturalists until recently entertained, and which I formerly entertained—namely, that each species has been independently created—is erroneous. I am fully convinced that species are not immutable. . . . Furthermore, I am convinced that Natural Selection has been the most important, but not the exclusive, means of modification (5:30).

The argument is thus: not creation, but evolution by natural selection. Darwin even refuted specific modifications of the creationist point of view, such as the idea that instead of all the species being created in one place, various species were created at several, centrally located regions (5:343-346). Against that opinion, which was designed to uphold the principle of creation and still explain why some species were confined to only certain continents or islands, Darwin argued that "a single birthplace" from which species dispersed slowly and naturally over the globe was "incomparably the safest" answer (5:345). Only in that way could he account for the similarities and differences between such species as those on the Galapagos Islands and those on the mainland of South America.

Darwin continued to oppose any creationalist point of view. It disturbed him that Charles Lyell, whom he had assumed was convinced that evolution occurred, kept writing about the principle circumspectly (2:268). He was even more disturbed that he once "truckled to public opinion, and used the Pentateuchal term of creation" by speaking of life's being "first breathed" into primordial matter instead of using a neutral term (2:272).

Similar to the way Darwin set his concept of evolution over against the doctrine of creation, he used his theory of natural selection to oppose the traditional notions of design and creation. "Natural selection" was Darwin's shorthand phrase for the mechanism behind evolution, although he did not deny other mechanisms like "sexual selection" which emerged prominently in his later investigation. But *natural* selection also meant for him that no providential activity of God was needed to account for the development of complex organisms. Rather, Darwin conceived of the biological world in terms of self-regulation, self-direction and chance, quite independent from the creative, purposeful action of God. Darwin even found it difficult to personify the term "nature," and asserted that that term meant "only the aggregate action and product of many natural laws" (5:88). To be sure, in the *Origin* he also spoke of the laws of nature as "secondary causes" that had been impressed in nature in the beginning by "the Creator" (5:449). He therefore entertained the belief that natural laws may have been initially established by divine action. God might be distant, not just absent. But either way the Darwinist hardly needed a God-hypothesis, which is one way of saying that Darwin had secularized the study of man and nature.

Darwin's lengthy argument in favor of natural selection presupposed that the entire process was due to "slowly acting and still existing" causes (uniformitarianism) (5:449, 89-95). His analysis assumed that the natural world was completely self-regulated, a view he believed was antithetical to that of special creation.

> Nature is prodigal in variety, but niggard in innovation. Why on the theory of Creation, would there be so much variety and so little real novelty? Why should all the parts and organs of many independent beings, each supposed to have been separately created for its proper place in nature, be so commonly linked together by graduated steps? . . . On the theory of natural selection, we can clearly understand why she should not; for natural selection acts only by taking advantage of slight successive variations; she can never take a great and sudden leap, but must advance by short and sure, though slow steps (5:181).

The principle of natural selection thus supported Darwin's overall image of nature: neither static nor disjunctured, and in no need of divine, providential supervision. For Darwin, however, no cogent explanation for evolution could be given unless it could explain how the complex organs of animal organisms were formed. He even said in the introduction of the *Origin* that any conclusion which held that species "had not been independently created" would be "unsatisfactory" unless "it could be shown how the innumerable species inhabiting this world have been modified, so as to acquire that perfection of structure and coadaptation which justly excites our admiration" (5:28). This is equivalent to Darwin's saying that his theory must give a *natural* explanation for the structures which William Paley declared were designed by God. He was ready to do just that.

Darwin developed his discussion with Paley by devoting three sections to facts relating to the latter's theological arguments, beginning with a section entitled "Organs of Extreme Perfection and Complications." And what example did he choose? The eye!

> To suppose that the eye with all its inimitable contrivances for adjusting the focus to different distances, for admitting different amounts of light, and for the correction of spherical and chromatic aberration, could have been formed by natural selection, seems I freely confess, absurd in the highest degree (5:168).

Suppose, he argued, there are many gradations of such an organ, which there are. Suppose that some of these organs are exceedingly simple, with the complex ones being but variations of others just a step down the biological scale, which is the case. When then?

> When we reflect on these facts, here given much too briefly, with respect to the wide, diversified, and graduated range of structure in the eyes of the lower animals; and when we bear in mind how small the number of all living forms must be in comparison with those which have become extinct, the difficulty ceases to be very great in believing that natural selection may have converted the simple apparatus of an optic nerve, coated with pigment and invested by transparent membrane, into an optical instrument as perfect as is possessed by any member of the Articulate Class (5:170).

Then fully entering Paley's world of examples, Darwin mused that it was "scarcely possible to avoid comparing the eye with a telescope." Since that instrument had been perfected "by the long-continued efforts of the highest human intellects," might it not be inferred "that the eye has been formed by a somewhat analogous process" (5:171)? Darwin answered with the observation that during the process of millions of years and millions of species within each year "a living optical instrument might thus be formed as superior to one of glass" (5:171). In short, natural selection produces such complex biological organisms and thus must be equated with the inventive process of "the Creator." He claimed that the only way that this theory would "break down" would be if it could be demonstrated "that any complex organ existed, which could not possibly have been formed by numerous, successive, slight modifications." Then immediately he added: "But I can find out no such case" (5:171).

Darwin seriously dulled the force of Paley's analogy. The latter had formulated his argument so as to convince the reader about the uniqueness and wonder of the creative handiwork of God. But Darwin so clearly identified the Creator with natural processes that the thrust of Paley's analogy between man's making a watch or a telescope and God's making an eye or ear was strained to the breaking point. Was there anything that could be described as "made" by man that took thousands of years and was filled with such enormous trial and error? If so, would it be a compliment to God to say that he worked in such an *ad hoc* fashion? And could one honestly describe such activity as singular, benevolent and purposeful? Had not Darwin in effect *reversed* the roles of God and man intended by Paley? Given Darwin's equation of the creative work of God with natural selection, was not man able to form mechanisms with greater facility and grace? Later, revealing his awareness of the nature of some of the problems involved Darwin confessed: "I see no necessity in the belief that the eye was expressly designed" (2:249). He at least knew that a God so closely tied to natural processes was at the outset not benevolent or kind. Thus God had bungled away thousands of years and millions of organisms in the process of designing an eye. At best he could later say that the natural world although filled with chance had not been produced by "brute force" alone (2:249).

Darwin's harsh treatment of the Paleyean argument for design did not fall on deaf ears. That he ignored the "moral or metaphysical part of nature," and worse, that he apparently desired "in one or two pregnant cases" to dispense with the religious aspects of natural history was precisely the factor that alarmed the aged scientist Adam Sedgwick to the point of believing that Darwin would "brutalize" humanity (2:229). Bishop Wilberforce believed that Darwin's statements about the ability of natural selection to produce an organ as complex as the eye were due to the latter's "wantonness of conjecture," and that in fact Darwin's assertions were "without the shadow of a fact" (12:249). Even Asa Gray, the celebrated Harvard botanist who defended Darwin so adeptly in America, wrote to Darwin claiming that "the weakest point in the book is the attempt to account for the formation of organs, the making of eyes, etc., by natural selection" (2:238).[9] Darwin's research and professional image were linked with evolution and *natural* selection in opposition to creationism and design. Piety and biology were at the point of having their marriage annulled.

3. DARWIN AND DARWINIANS DISCUSS
THE NATURE OF MAN

The day before the *Origin* was released from the press T. H. Huxley wrote an ecstatically enthusiastic letter about the proof copy he had received. Toward the end of his letter he remarked prophetically:

> I trust you will not allow yourself to be in any way disgusted or annoyed by the considerable abuse and misrepresentation which, unless I greatly mistake, is in store for you. . . . And as to the curs which will bark and yelp, you must recollect that some of your friends . . . are endowed with an amount of combativeness which . . . may stand you in good stead. I am sharpening up my claws and beak in readiness (2:226).

Huxley did not have to wait long for the skirmishes to begin, nor did it take long for him to find out that his claws and beak were to become some of the most fit instruments for Darwin's public survival.

The most momentous exchange that occurred in England came in Oxford about six months after the first edition of the *Origin* was released.[10] Undergraduates, clergymen, amateur and professional scientists alike congregated to hear Bishop Samuel Wilberforce marshal evidence against Darwin before one of the zoological section meetings of the British Association of Science. Wilberforce was armed to the teeth by one of Darwin's most caustic scientific critics, Richard Owen. With colorful invective the bishop concluded that Darwin's case was supported by almost no credible evidence. Then turning to Huxley, who had almost missed the meeting because he did not want to be "episcopally pounded," the bishop asked:

> I should like to ask Professor Huxley, who is sitting by me, and is about to tear me to pieces when I have sat down, as to his belief in being descended from an ape. Is it on his grandfather's or his grandmother's side that the ape ancestry comes in (2:251-252)?

Earlier, upon perceiving that the bishop was actually quite ill-informed, Huxley had whispered to an astounded old gentleman sitting next to him: "The Lord hath delivered him into mine hands" (2:254). Then rising and claiming that he had come only in the interest of science, Huxley defended Darwin. Not avoiding the question of his origins, Huxley declared that he was far less ashamed of an ape for a grandfather, than that of

> a *man*, a man of restless and versatile intellect, who, not content with . . . success in his own sphere of activity, plunges into scientific questions with which he has no real acquaintance, only to obscure them by an aimless rhetoric . . . eloquent digressions, and skilled appeals to religious prejudice (2:253).

Students thundered and one woman fainted in the commotion which ensued.

The recounting of the famous exchange above is significant for at least two reasons. First, it reveals something about the nature of Darwin's opponents. Bishop Wilberforce's reaction was similar to that of numerous religious traditionalists. In addition, behind the bishop was Richard Owen, whose professional status, like that of many other scientists, was threatened by Darwin's work. This led to ferocious theoretical infighting. Even national egos were on the line. The French, loyal to Cuvier and Lamarck, resisted the new approach. Without whitewashing the existing ecclesiastical ignorance, it is also worth noting that such leading churchmen as Charles Kingsley in England and James McCosh in America supported Darwin's opinions (2:241-242).[11] Even Bishop Wilberforce, not a man to bear grudges, remarked later that Darwin was "such a capital fellow" (2:256).

Second, much of the debate centered on what Darwin once referred to as "an uncommonly curious subject"—man (2:237). Even though Darwin said very little about man in the *Origin,* it is quite apparent why heated exchanges occurred. In opposing the doctrine of creation and in referring at points "to the first dawn of life, when all organic beings . . . presented the simplest structure," Darwin raised questions about *man's* origin (5:125). In also opposing the principle of special design, he brought forth even more serious questions. How did man get to be who he is? What is his nature? Darwin knew the direction in which his research was taking him. In a letter to the geologist Charles Lyell some four months after the publication of the *Origin* he remarked:

> I believe man is in the same predicament with other animals. It is in fact impossible to doubt it. I have thought (only vaguely) on man . . . I have one good speculative line, but a man must have entire credence in Natural Selection before he will even listen to it (2:236-237).

Darwin's "line" would be in print in a little over a decade.

With respect to the nature of man, the thought of the following four evolutionists will now be discussed: T. H. Huxley, Charles Lyell, Darwin himself, and Alfred Russel Wallace. The first of Darwin's converts to give special attention to the study of man was T. H. Huxley. More accurately, Huxley had been doing a great amount of research on the relationship of the skeletons of man and the higher apes; and Darwin's theory suddenly gave him his most adequate and exciting working model (9:vi-ix).[12]

In full awareness of the strong opposition to any views which would "break down the barrier between man and the rest of the animal world" even among the scientists of his day, Huxley published in 1863 *Man's Place in Nature* (9:viii). Immediately, said Huxley, the "Boreas of criticism blew his hardest blasts of misrepresentation and ridicule" against his conclusions (9:x).

In *Man's Place* Huxley argued on the basis of embryology, skeletal likenesses, and brain shapes and capacities that man possessed "structural unity" with the rest of the animal world, "more particularly and closely" with the apes (9:92). Man's embryo, for example, can hardly be distinguished in its earlier stages from that of a dog, or from that of an ape even in its later stages. On the basis of such biological evidence Huxley concluded that "the great law-giver of systematic zoology, Linnaeus," was correct in placing man in the same order (termed primates) with apes and lemurs. Instead of leading him to distinguish man and apes sharply, as was done by noted post-Linnaeus systematizers such as Cuvier, Huxley's research led him to confront the "arrogance of man" with his true proximity to other animals (9:146).

Given the fact that man is separated by no greater structural barriers from the apes than they are from one another, was there some theory which could account for man's origin? There was only one such theory, said Huxley—"that propounded by Mr. Darwin." Concerning it, he said:

> I, for one, am fully convinced, that if not precisely true, that hypothesis is as near an approximation to the truth as, for example, the Copernican hypothesis was to the true theory of the planetary motions (9:147,149).

Darwin's theory, argued Huxley, accounted for the origin of man, and in so doing gave a "complete and crushing" argument against "the intervention of any but what are termed secondary causes, in the production of all the phenomena of the universe" (9:151). This meant that man emerged from nature via chance and change in the context of a struggle for survival rather than via creation or special design. Huxley was convinced that there were no real breaks in "Nature's great progression, from the formless to the formed—from the inorganic to the organic—from blind force to conscious intellect and will" (9:151). He regarded any attempt to draw a sharp line of demarcation between man and the animal kingdom on the basis of psychic, emotional, or intellectual distinctions as futile—equally futile as past attempts to find anatomical lines of difference (9:152). The Darwinian die was cast. Man's body, emotions and intellect were affirmed to be products of natural selection, differing only in degree with those of other animals.

Huxley well knew that the belief in a single origin for man and brutes would bring charges concerning "the brutalization and degradation of the former" (9:153). He could not, however, accept that conclusion. Is man, he asked

> bound to howl and grovel on all fours because of the wholly unquestionable fact, that he was once an egg, which no ordinary power of discrimination could distinguish from that of a Dog? Or is the philanthropist, or the saint, to give up his endeavors to lead a noble life, because the simplest study of man's nature reveals, at its foundations, all the selfish passions, and fierce appetites of the merest quadruped? Is mother-love vile because a hen shows it, or fidelity base because dogs possess it? (9:154)

Instead, Huxley asserted that there was a vast gulf between civilized man and the brutes, for man alone "possesses the marvelous endowment of intelligible and rational speech" and remembers and learns from his past (9:155-156). Man could take heart that he had come so far from his lowly past. That fact was for Huxley the "best evidence of the splendour of his capacities" and was the reasonable ground for faith in an even "nobler future." Darwinian thought was developing its own form of eschatology. Future expectations could compensate for the skeletons in man's ancestral closet.

Throughout his life Huxley continued to insist on man's completely naturalistic origins as well as his immense differences with other animal species. If in no other way, man became the "superb animal" because of his success in the struggle for existence (8:51). But Huxley believed that in society, moral insights emerged which conflicted with natural selection. Sympathetic emotions, aesthetic and intellectual activities arose which were in constant contradiction with the hostile influences in the state of nature (8:33). Such societal ethics and activities should be encouraged. Against thinkers such as Herbert Spencer, who were seeking to expound evolutionary ethics based on the principle of the survival of the fittest, Huxley thought that man's savage instincts should be curbed (8:82-86). "Let us understand," he said in his famous Romanes' lecture, "that the ethical progress of society depends, not on imitating the cosmic process, still less in running away from it, but in combating it" (8:83).

Huxley's anthropology can best be described as a naturalistic humanism. He considered everything human to have evolved from lower animal forms, yet he valued human attainments so highly that human values could counteract former natural ones. For him the fact that man was a superb animal was at once humbling and ennobling. Through his intelligence and through the "exact knowledge" furnished by science, man should take command over all non-human nature and modify the conditions of existence which brought him into being (8:84-85).

Charles Lyell's *Antiquity of Man* was published in the same year (1863) as Huxley's *Man's Place in Nature*. Lyell's anthropology well illustrates Huxley's observation that in the 1860's scientists themselves "lay poles asunder" with respect to their estimates of man. Lyell was strongly opposed to "anything which tended to break down the barrier between man and the rest of the animal world" (9:vii-viii). He exasperated Darwin with his noncommittal statements about evolution in *Antiquity*, even though he claimed privately that his public reticence was designed to win Darwin a larger following (2:268-269,272).

Lyell, who had been so influential for the development of Darwin's own thinking, agreed with Darwin on the principle that man had evolved from lower forms of life. With Huxley, he also believed that man had a much older past than had been assumed and that the attempts to prove that there was a decisive difference between the human brain and those of the apes were in vain. However, Lyell believed that man's uniqueness could not be accounted for purely in terms of natural selection. Rather, he found a principle in life which defied and transcended scientific explanation—"a law of development so high as to stand nearly in the same relation as the deity himself to man's finite understanding" (6:314). He declared that any confusion of "natural selection" with such "creational laws" either deified secondary causes or "immeasurably" exaggerated their influences (6:314). He thus could not believe that the principle of natural selection adequately accounted for the uniqueness of man. He argued that when man emerged, there must have occurred some special exertion of creative power, some sudden leap forward (6:315). Only in that way could Lyell explain the significance of human intelligence.

Clearly, Lyell deviated from the evolutionary naturalism of Darwin and Huxley. He could not speak of "Nature's great progression" in terms suggesting that no break had occurred between "blind force" and "conscious intellect and will." When Darwin expressed his disappointment with Lyell's conclusions, the latter could only exclaim: "I have spoken out to the full extent of my present convictions, and even beyond my state of *feeling* as to man's unbroken descent from the brutes" (2:270).

Charles Darwin's own convictions about man were not finalized and articulated until some eight years after the monographs of Huxley and Lyell. The *Descent of Man* (1871) was, however, by Darwin's own description the product of 33 years of reflection and data-collecting. His views clearly lay in the direction of those already published by Huxley. In fact, when Darwin first heard of Huxley's views on man, he exclaimed: "By jove, you have attacked bigotry in its stronghold. I thought you would have been mobbed" (2:264). Nevertheless, Darwin himself decided to publish his more elaborate views about man when he became convinced that the theory of evolution had become widely accepted.

Two emphases in *Descent* are of special significance for Darwin's image of man: first, his insistence that man had indeed evolved from lower animal forms; second, that man's evolution was determined by natural means. Near the beginning of the chapter in which he argued for man's evolution, Darwin asserted that man's likenesses with animal species were notoriously extensive (4:6). He believed that evidence from anatomy and embryology as well as a study of certain vestigial organs made it so obvious that all animals shared in a "community of descent" that some day naturalists would marvel that anyone believed that each species was "a separate act of creation" (4:25). Man, "the wonder and glory of the Universe," proceeded through the Old World monkeys. He has a "pedigree of prodigious length" but not, Darwin emphasized, of any particularly noble quality (4:165).

> Unless we willfully close our eyes, we may, with our present knowledge, approximately recognize our parentage; nor need we feel ashamed of it. The most humble organism is something much higher than the inorganic dust under our feet; and no one with an unbiased mind can study any living creature, however humble, without being struck with enthusiasm at its marvelous structure and properties (4:165).

Paley's form of wonder towards nature remains. But its function is different. Instead of supporting the dignity and majesty of man and nature by pointing to the designing hand of God, it shores up man's pride by comparing his superior structure to inorganic matter and lower biological organisms.

Darwin's second aim was at the heart of his anthropology in *Descent of Man*. He maintained that he could account for man's bodily structure, his intellect, his ability to speak and write, his emotions, his aesthetic apprehensions and his morality on the exclusive basis of natural history (4:97-98). His argument begins, like that of the *Origin*, by contending that men vary in body and mind depending on various types of circumstances and hence possess changeable natures. When, therefore, man was exposed to the severe struggle for existence, he developed certain features which made him "the most dominant animal" on earth. He developed intellectual faculties, social habits which would "lead him to aid and defend his fellows," together with a unique bodily structure (4:48). Darwin was anxious that the reader did not underestimate the significance of man's corporeal structure, since such facts as erect posture and the free use of the hands encouraged the development of the brain (4:49-54). Against Alfred Russel Wallace, whose independent discovery of evolution had led to Darwin's publication of his own views, Darwin argued that natural selection alone enabled man to develop a brain far superior to that of an ape (4:49). Even the intellectual and moral faculties of man were "perfected or advanced" through natural selection (4:127-128). He also emphasized that for social animals such as man, natural selection involves the preservation of features which are beneficial to the community. In that way strength is gained through numbers, and tribal competition helps "raise man to his present high position in the organic scale" (4:62-64).

Darwin then entered into an extended discussion comparing men and animals. By showing that rudiments of the mental and emotional faculties of man are detectable among animals he intended to prove that there is no "fundamental difference" between the two. He argued that animals communicate with each other, enjoy excitement, imitate each other and other animals, possess certain powers of reason and even "suffer from ennui" (4:65-93). How can we be so sure that an old dog "never reflects on his past pleasures or pains in the chase" or is not distantly religious in his complete submission, love and fear of his master (4:83, 96)? Surely, many animals have a taste for beauty, especially during the periods when they mate (4:92).

Darwin's chapter on the natural development of what he called "the most noble of all the attributes of man"—his moral sense—is of special interest. His theory is quite easily described: 1) like many animals, man instinctively is a social animal with well-marked parental and filial affections; 2) but since man's mental abilities are great, he can remember and compare his actions and motives, approving or disapproving of them, he thus develops a conscious rule of conduct, a moral sense of "ought"; 3) the power of language enables the community to communicate its sense of common good to each member; 4) habit strengthens and perpetuates communal norms of right and wrong (4:97-99). For Darwin this moral sense emerged when developed social instincts and highly developed intelligence meet in the same creature (4:108-111). Only in that way did a comparison of past and present actions lead to a sense of responsibility, shame, or happiness. Any moral endorsement of socially cohesive instincts and condemnation of negative ones would, said Darwin, give one tribe an "immense advantage" over other tribes that lacked the same (4:132). Once such social instincts became consciously held and defined, they could be extended beyond tribal boundaries (4:ch. 5). Darwin thus believed that tribal norms became the basis for the moral beliefs of civilized nations, but he knew full well that refined moral values were not necessary for the perpetuation of the fittest. In one of his summary passages he stated that

> the social instincts, which no doubt were acquired by man as by the lower animals for the good of the community, will from the first have given to him some wish to aid his fellows, some feeling of sympathy, and have compelled him to regard their approbation and disapprobation. Such impulses will have served him at a very early period as a rude rule of right and wrong. But as man gradually advanced in intellectual power, and was enabled to trace the more remote consequences of his actions . . . and his sympathies became more tender and widely diffused, extending to men of all races, to the imbecile, maimed, and other useless members of society . . . so would the standard of his morality rise higher and higher (4:124-125).

Throughout his analysis Darwin was anxious to point out that although the difference between even the lowest man and the highest animal is "immense," certainly that difference is "one of degree and not of kind" (4:125-126). The bodies, minds, and emotions of animals evolved under natural evolutionary conditions into corporeal, intellectual, emotional and moral man. This view of man did not disturb him.

> Looking to future generations, there is no cause to fear that the social instincts will grow weaker, and we may expect that virtuous habits will grow stronger, becoming perhaps fixed by inheritance. In this case, the struggle between our higher and lower impulses will be less severe, and virtue will be triumphant (4:125).

Like T. H. Huxley, Darwin employed the new eschatology of evolutionary naturalism as an antidote for pessimism or moral cynicism. As Darwin said, it is both "truer and more cheerful . . . that progress has been much more general than retrogression" (4:145).

Darwin's convictions concerning man's status—both his lowly origins and his capacity for future development—were rooted in his unique, but still rudimentary, awareness of cultural evolution. Man's present civilized status presupposed not only a long history of biological evolution but also a definite process of cultural evolution. Darwin's opponents argued that it was incredible to assume that the progeny of an ape could write like Homer or speak like Huxley (2:252-253). This objection was not valid to the degree that it ignored the missing link between civilized man and the apes, namely the man of primitive culture. Darwin did have some first-hand knowledge of an exceedingly primitive tribe, and this enabled him to historicize man's development, culturally as well as biologically.

On board the *Beagle* were three South American Indians who had been taken as hostages from Tierra del Fuego three years earlier. After being schooled in Christian doctrine and proper English culture, they were sent back to the tip of South America with an English missionary, tea-trays, mahogany furniture, and fine white linen in order to redeem the area for Christ. With a kind of gingerly hope, the three Feugians—Jemmy Button, York Minister, Feugia Basket—and the Reverend Richard Matthews were deposited on their native soil for a week—only to have their goods plundered by the local inhabitants. They responded to the thieving with a typical sense of English justice. After Jemmy Button told Darwin that his own brother had been stealing from him, he asked "what fashion do you call that?" (3:136)

A year and two months later (March, 1834) the *Beagle* returned to Tierra del Fuego. At first Jemmy Button was unrecognizable. "I never saw so complete and grievous a change," observed Darwin (3:215). His hair was now down to his shoulders; except for a bit of blanket around his waist, he was unclothed. The crew was surprised "to find he had not the least wish to return to England" (3:216). The impression on Darwin was great. "I would not have believed how entire the difference between savage and civilized man is. It is greater than between a wild and domesticated animal . . ." (3:119).

> How little can the higher powers of the mind come into play: what is there for imagination to paint, for reason to compare, for judgment to decide upon? . . . Although essentially the same creature, how little must the mind of one of these beings resemble that of an educated man. . . . Whence have these people come? Have they remained in the same state since the creation of the world? (3:213)

Did the lack of the man-need of further cultural evolution cause primitive society?

The Feugians gave Darwin a vivid example of a living link between civilized man and his prehistoric ancestors. He drew extensively upon this encounter with the Feugians in his later work, *The Descent of Man* (4:65,133,143-145,178).

At no point does one find Darwin, like Lyell, willing to grant that with the coming of man, a new level or form of creative power entered the world. For Darwin, man's uniqueness lay in the higher functional capacities and social instincts which enabled him to triumph in the struggle for survival. Compared to other animals, man can remember more, reason more, appreciate more, but always like other species. His emphasis on man's relation to the animal kingdom led him to obliterate man–animal borderlines. In a sense he is as much humanizing the animal kingdom as he is animalizing the human one. He never appears, however, to have advocated vegetarianism, although he was well known for his great sympathy for the suffering of man and beast (2:303-304). He thus opposed vivisection out of "mere damnable and detestable curiosity" but believed that the kind of opposition to vivisection which would impede progress of physiology was a "crime against mankind" (2:304-306).

Man's functional superiority in comparison to the animals hardly places man at the center of the cosmos. A better image would be to place man on the top of the heap, on the top of the billions of organisms whose desperate struggles for survival gave birth to man. Clearly, Darwin had abandoned his former orthodox Christian view of man. Man has no "soul." He is neither created nor designed by God. The idea of Adam, who had been created by God, was dead.

Alfred Russel Wallace serves as our fourth and last thinker. Like Huxley, Lyell, and Darwin, he achieved the status of an highly respected scientist, wrote about the nature of man, and accepted the principle of evolution through the survival of the fittest. Indeed, he discovered that principle independently of Darwin. In 1889, eighteen years after the publication of *The Descent of Man*, Wallace wrote an essay entitled "Darwinism as Applied to Man." [13] He was fully a "Darwinian" in the sense that he believed that the biological evidence marshaled by himself, Darwin and others demonstrated "the essential identity of man's bodily structure with that of the higher mammalia, and his descent from some ancestral form common to man and the anthropoid apes" (11:254). The evidence for that view was "overwhelming and conclusive" (11:254).

However, Wallace could not agree with Darwin's thesis in *Descent of Man* that the intellectual and moral faculties of man had evolved naturally and progressively from the lower animals (11:256). He argued that variation and natural selection alone could not account for such abilities. Could it really be proved that music, art, mathematics, and metaphysics were developed as mere instruments of survival (11:257-265)?

> Each of these characteristics is totally inconsistent with any action of the law of natural selection in the production of the faculties referred to; and the facts, taken in their entirety, compel us to recognize some origin for them wholly distinct from that which has served to account for the animal characteristics—whether bodily or mental—of man.
>
> The special faculties we have been discussing clearly point to the existence in man of something which he has not derived from his animal progenitors—something which we may best refer to as being of a spiritual essence of nature, capable of progressive development under favorable conditions (11:266-267).

Only by recognizing man's unique endowment with a non-animal "essence," could Wallace account for the enormous influence of man's ideas, his delight in beauty, and his sense of justice.

He therefore outlined certain stages in the development of life in which new sources of vitality and creative power could be said to enter—for example, the movement from non-life to life and the unique intellectual and moral capacities of man which transcended the struggle for survival. Wallace emphasized that his point of view explained man's uniqueness without conflicting with evolution. Also, in contrast to the "hopeless and soul-deadening" naturalism of Darwin, he contended that his interpretation of the same evidence restored a sense of purpose:

> To us, the whole purpose, the only *raison d'être* of the world—with all its complexities of physical structure . . . the slow evolution of the vegetable and animal kingdoms . . . was the development of the human spirit in association with the human body (11:270).

There was, he believed, "another origin" that explained the phenomenon of man—"the unseen universe of Spirit" (11:271).

Darwinians who discussed man gave rise to at least two legacies. On the one hand, there were those like Huxley and Darwin who sought to discover the essence of man in terms of his natural and functional similarities and differences with other animals. Man was interpreted as not different in kind from the animals. On the other hand, there were scholars like Lyell and Wallace who believed that man's uniqueness could be accounted for only by appealing to categories which transcended animal existence. As apparent in the thought of Alfred Russel Wallace, this discussion of human superiority and dignity began to draw upon religious categories. For both groups the *permanent* legacy was the discovery of man's proximity to the natural world. Man was indeed related to the "brutes"; he was not "created" in the traditional meaning of that term.

Adam Sedgwick and Samuel Wilberforce had predicted that the acceptance of Darwin's theory of evolution would brutalize and degrade man, destroy his uniqueness and claims for supremacy, impugn his power of reason and lead him to shirk his responsibility. Such moral pessimism was ill-founded. Optimism was not the unique possession of any one school of thought. By demonstrating man's proximity to the animal kingdom, Darwin and Huxley did wound man's pride; but this wound was healed by their intense appreciation of man's functional superiority and their expectations of his further development in the future. Similarly, while Paley's theology was rejected, his methodology was retained. Under Darwin and Huxley, arguments concerning the functional complexity of biological organisms were used to prove the uniqueness of man rather than the existence of God. A naturalized world did not necessarily imply a brutalized man.[14] Finally and ironically, the disagreements of evolutionary biologists concerning the nature of man provided the context for nurturing new forms of religious thought. The spiritism of Alfred Russel Wallace and the cosmic evolutionary optimism of the Americans John Fisk and Lyman Abbot illustrate the fecundity of religious visions compatible with and encouraged by the hypothesis of evolution.

4. DARWIN AND HUXLEY ON RELIGION

Darwin's letters on religion are shot through with uncertainty, attitudes of "believe-what-you-will," and constant reservations about his competence to make any judgments on the subject. Given his scholarly care and his own affirmation that he had not thought about religion "deeply enough to justify any publicity," (2:60), we can even question the wisdom of setting forth Darwin's views. However, there are several reasons why it is significant to treat his religious beliefs. Not only did he become both hero and villain almost immediately (Karl Marx sought to dedicate Das Kapital to him), but, more important, the image of religion presupposed by Darwin is one that remains widely accepted. Also, Darwin's own position is a witness to the full-scale rout of the older orthodox apologetic and calls into question the romantic nature-pantheism of a number of early nineteenth-century thinkers.

Darwin's spiritual journey had three stages: orthodox Anglicanism, Deism, then agnosticism. In response to his father's wish that he become a minister, Darwin began a course of religious study which persuaded him that the 39 articles of the Church of England "must be fully accepted" (2:18). Later, on board the Beagle, he amused several of the officers of the ship with his Bible-quoting moralism (2:62). However, within three years after his return from the voyage of the *Beagle* (1836–1839), Darwin came to believe that the Old Testament was "no more to be trusted than the sacred books of the Hindoos," that miracles were "incredible," and that men at the time of the birth of Christianity "were ignorant and credulous to a degree almost incomprehensible to us" (2:62). At this time Darwin was in close contact with Charles Lyell, who, although "thoroughly liberal in his religious beliefs, or rather disbeliefs," remained a "strong theist" (2:35). While Darwin rejected "Christianity as a divine revelation" in this second stage of his religious development, he did not disbelieve in the existence of a deity. Darwin was still a Deist when he wrote *Origin of Species.* He was therefore able to talk about "the Creator" and the existence of a "First Cause having an intelligent mind in some degree analogous to that of man" (5:449-450, 2:66).

After 1859, however, he acknowledged that further disbelief crept over him until at last it became "complete" (2:62,64). He could no longer accept William Paley's defense of the existence of God because of the argument from design—no more than believing that the wind blew by design (2:63). Nor could he accept the idea that any God of nature was benevolent.[15] There was such a vast amount of suffering in the world, and that fact seemed to be a strong argument against the existence of an intelligent First Cause (2:63-64,67-68). After literally muddling through a letter to the American Asa Gray, he confessed that "the more I think the more bewildered I become; as indeed I have probably shown by this letter" (2:249). Genuinely confessing that the answers to religious questions lay beyond the range of human intelligence he said:

> I cannot pretend to throw the least light on such abstruse problems. The mystery of the beginning of all things is insoluble by us, and I for one must be content to remain an Agnostic (2:66).

During the course of his theological atrophy, he also gave up reading Milton, Coleridge, and Shakespeare, as well as the enjoyment of music. Almost clinically he observed that his mind "seems to have become a kind of machine for grinding general laws out of large collections of facts," and described the loss of his taste for music and literature as "a loss of happiness, which may possibly be injurious to the intellect, and more probably to the moral character, by enfeebling the emotional part of our nature" (2:53-54). Because of this loss of emotional and aesthetic sensibilities, Darwin found himself standing outside the tradition of romantic religious thought as represented by Friedrich Schleiermacher and Samuel Taylor Coleridge.[16] By his own confession, Darwin had become blind and deaf to the colors and sounds of any religious language (2:62,65), but he still wrote with superb felicity and in spite of his secluded life at Down manifested genuine interest in a number of public issues.

T. H. Huxley first created and popularized the term "agnosticism." For him the term was not to be equated with "atheism," since that position, like theism, presumed to know too much. Like David Hume, Huxley believed that the limitations of knowledge applied to nay-sayers as well as yea-sayers. Partially because of his refusal to adopt an atheistic instead of an agnostic position, Huxley never received a hero's welcome in the Soviet Union (7:80). Unlike Darwin, however, Huxley spoke out on numerous occasions on subjects relating to Christianity and Judaism. For example, in seeking to mar the image of the literal accuracy of the Bible in order to pave the way for a more popular acceptance of evolution and science, Huxley indulged in such mid-Victorian debates as whether in fact Christ had commanded a herd of swine to drown themselves. His opponent was none other than the statesman, William Gladstone. Still, Huxley appreciated the Bible as literature, as a moral tonic, and believed that there were no higher ethical values than those set forth by the Hebrew prophets.

Darwin conceived of religion as primarily pre-scientific speculation more false than true. This belief was predicated on his conviction that all "truth" was based on tangible, observable, cautiously-obtained "evidence." And for Darwin, scientific and historical evidence indicated that the Old and New Testaments were inaccurate and untrustworthy and that earlier, religious mankind had been extremely ignorant and credulous (2:62). He further believed that the arguments designed to prove the existence of God on the basis of human feeling and need lacked evidential value, particularly because he did not feel such need himself (2:65). The rational argument from the principle of design was the best ground for the defense of theism he thought, but he found that argument increasingly difficult to sustain (2:66-68,247).[17] He thus had no pressing rational grounds for remaining a theist, nor did he perceive of positive uses of religious language. As a recourse he could become either an atheist or an agnostic, and he preferred the "unaggressive attitude" of the latter.

5. CONTINUING CONCERNS

The claim is still made that Darwin almost single-handedly banished miracles, creation, and design from the world and "robbed God of his role of creator . . . and man of his divine origin" (7:126). Such declarations testify to Darwin's continual role as a formative influence in the making and breaking of world views, even if the singular achievement of Darwin is exaggerated. Actually, although the work initiated by Darwin did seriously undermine the older orthodoxy, the major issues that were debated in Darwin's time have been restated and reargued in new, often cogent forms. If religion is equated with the straw-man of traditional rational orthodoxy, Darwin can be seen as the heroic banisher of antiquated world views. But if religion is honestly identified with revised perceptions, the issues of the cosmological argument for God based on design, the significance of the Bible, and the nature of man are far from extinct.[18]

With respect to the argument from design, soon after the publication of the *Origin of Species,* a variety of thinkers—such as the Englishmen Charles Kingsley and Henry Drummond and the Americans John Fisk and Lyman Abbot—argued that Darwin's perspective, although invalidating the specific line of argumentation set forth by William Paley, established a new, more general and cosmic basis for some principle of purpose or design in nature.[19] These arguments have been given a new impetus through the work of Pierre Teilhard de Chardin, whose thought is the subject of the next chapter.

Positive affirmations of the religious significance of the Bible by no means ended with Darwin. When orthodox rationalists like William Paley assumed that the Genesis account of creation was intended to be accepted literally, the scientific theory of evolution constituted a proof that the Bible was false. This assumption lay behind Darwin's own rejection of the Bible and helped initiate a long series of debates between theological literalists and scientific empiricists. The famed *"conflict* between religion and science" in the Victorian era was sustained, in fact, by laymen and clergymen who still shared Paley's form of rationalism and biblical literalism.[20]

However, well before Darwin in Germany and contemporaneous with him in England and America, biblical scholars began to demonstrate the inadequacy of forcing upon the biblical literature a literal, empirical intentionality. Through the discovery of numerous ancient historical documents, Israel's history and thought have been linked to the history and ideas of the ancient Near East, and the early Christian literature has been related to the Hellenistic world. With the recovery of these world views, scholars have shown that the intention of the biblical writers lay more in the direction of conceiving of and establishing attitudes and relationships between mankind and God as well as nurturing human relationships rather than revealing factual information.[21] Rudolf Bultmann and Paul Tillich exemplify twentieth-century thinkers who find ultimate meaning disclosed in the Bible through mythical and symbolic categories instead of factual literalism.

Charles Darwin's continued expectations of an empirical validation of religion discloses his fixation at the point of Paley's rationalism. When the latter's conceptual world collapsed, Darwin was left with nothing but that discredited foundation for his religious faith. He seems to have never really seriously entertained newer points of view, but then again neither did the majority of churchmen in England and America in the same era. The continued attachment to empiricism, however, enabled scientific investigation to flourish as much as it caused orthodox rationalism to flounder. Scientists were further freed for their own spheres of investigation; and thinkers such as Huxley and Darwin found in science a renewed basis for personal commitment. Darwin found in his investigations a release from his discomforts and even a new biological form of teleology (2:40, 55,284,308).

The differing evaluations of man continued with even greater intensity and diversity than those which we have noted from the writings of Huxley, Lyell, Darwin, and Wallace. Some anthropologists, such as the American Alfred Louis Kroeber (1876–1960) believed that Darwinism commissioned them to account for man's history and culture on completely naturalistic grounds.[22] This "scientific anthropology" denied any "shred of ethnocentricity" or prevaluations in favor of human standards, and interpreted all human phenomena on terms equal with other animals. Man's ideas and morals are thereby viewed, like mutations in organic nature, as survival mechanisms in the evolutionary process. On the other hand, the celebrated zoologist Theodosius Dobzhansky regards attempts that account for man solely on the basis of his zoological past as myopic. Dobzhansky views man as unique and unprecedented. In man evolution transcends itself.[23]

Theologians like the Victorian Henry Drummond and the twentieth-century Jesuit Teilhard have insisted that man's past be read in light of his ascent rather than descent.[24] Others, like Søren Kierkegaard and Rudolf Bultmann have been concerned to explicate the particularly human aspects of man's emotional and existential depths. Theological issues relating to the nature of man are still very much alive.

Finally, ethical questions concerning man and his environment have expanded in significance. Contrary to what might be expected, Darwin's research did not immediately lead to new levels of concern for the preservation of the natural world of which man is so much a part. Scientists wanted to study, and technicians wanted to manipulate nature. In fact, until recently post-Darwinian scientists have probably been even less inclined to care for the natural world than the pre-Darwinian clergymen-scientists and romantics. Concerns over ecology, however, have radically changed the attitudes of many scientists. Barry Commoner argues that scientists must supplement their empirical investigations with social and moral concerns and maintains that ecological research must be given priority for the sake of human survival. The microbiologist, René Dubos even speaks of the necessity of a new ethic.[25] Man must learn to love the earth because he is umbilical to it. He must care for the ground and species out of which he emerged and with which he is one. A recovery of man's place in nature might also raise anew questions regarding that which is "natural" to man. New styles of life may be adopted as man integrates into his present the origins of his past.

Darwin's statement in the *Origin of Species* that his research might shed light on man was obviously one of the great understatements of all time. Western images of man, God, and nature have been profoundly altered. There is surely historical irony in the fact that the very research which appeared to so many to brutalize man and destroy his world view, may, through ecology, end in saving man from his own brutal self-destruction. In the process, a world view may also be established which enables the humane to flourish.

NOTES

[1] For the Scopes' trial, see Ray Ginger, *Six Days or Forever?* (Boston: Beacon Press, 1958), and Scopes' memoirs in John Thomas Scopes, *Center of the Storm* (New York: Holt, Reinhart and Winston, 1967).

[2] Both the new biblical criticism emanating for the most part from Germany and the problems arising over attempts to harmonize the Bible with impressive, new geological data led a number of English intellectuals to revise traditional opinions about the Bible before the publication of *The Origin of Species* in 1859. The most famous and alarming of English manifestos concerning the necessity of giving up biblical literalism were the essays by C. W. Goodwin and Benjamine Jowett in *Essays and Reviews* (1860), published almost contemporaneously with Darwin's *Origin*. On the basis of his knowledge of Hebraic thought and of geology, Goodwin argued that the creation narratives in Genesis were scientifically "untenable," although still meaningful. Like several notable early German critics, Jowett argued that the Bible should be interpreted "like any other book," meaning that it should be subject to ordinary canons of historical and linguistic analysis and thus regarded as a book manifesting pre-modern cosmology and literary standards. An intelligent, readable discussion on the history of early biblical criticism in England and the reception given to *Essays and Reviews* is found in Owen Chadwick, *The Victorian Church*, II (New York: Oxford University Press, 1970), pp. 40-97. For biblical criticism and geology in England, see also Willis B. Glover, *Evangelical Non-conformity and Higher Criticism in the Nineteenth Century* (London: Independent Press, 1954); *Essays and Reviews* (London, 1860); and Charles Coulston Gillispie, *Genesis and Geology* (New York: Harper and Row, 1951).

[3] The famous display of the newer natural theology in England is found in the numerous volumes of *The Bridgewater Treatises*, published, somewhat ironically, during and shortly following Darwin's voyage on the *Beagle* (1831-1836). The

treatises were subtitled, *On the Power, Wisdom and Goodness of God as Manifested in the Creation* and dealt with the human body (a whole volume discussed the design of the hand), animal habits, animal and plant physiology, chemistry, geology, and physics. Useful secondary discussions of biology and natural theology before and during the time of Darwin are the following: John C. Greene, *The Death of Adam* (6: chs. 1-8); Loren Eiseley, *Darwin's Century* (Garden City, N. Y.: Doubleday, 1958), pp. 13-16, 57-89, 325-352; and John Dillenberger, *Protestant Thought and Natural Science* (Nashville: Abingdon Press, 1960), pp. 104-162.

For Hume, see ch. one above and Hume's "Dialogues Concerning Natural Religion" in Hume *On Religion*, ed. Richard Wollheim (New York: World, 1963), pp. 99-204.

[4] These lines from the famous Protestant hymn "God Moves in a Mysterious Way" were written by William Cowper, probably England's most renowned poet in the last decades of the eighteenth century. Intellectually and temperamentally Cowper's poetry lies precisely between the natural theology of William Paley and the nature romanticism of William Wordsworth. See the collection of Cowper's verses and letters in Brian Spiller (ed.), *Cowper* (Cambridge: Harvard University Press, 1968), and the discussions of Cowper by Maurice J. Quinlan, *William Cowper* (Minneapolis: University of Minnesota Press, 1953), Norman Nicholson, *William Cowper* (London: John Lehmann, 1951), and Lodwick C. Hartley, *William Cowper* (Chapel Hill: University of North Carolina Press, 1938).

For discussions of other figures besides Paley and Cowper, see the sources cited in n. 3 above.

[5] This commonly employed, rational method of defending theism and the integrity of the Bible has been termed "supernatural rationalism" and is fully evident in the thought of John Locke (1632-1704) and numerous other post-Lockean, orthodox rationalists. Cf. the discussions in Dillenberger, *Protestant Thought and Natural Science*, pp. 133-162; and Conrad Wright, *The Liberal Christians* (Boston: Beacon Press, 1970), pp. 1-21.

[6] Cf. the fascinating background and elaboration of the thought of Linnaeus and others in John C. Greene, *The Death of Adam* (6:175-200).

[7] Interesting accounts of Darwin's maturation and his voyage on the *Beagle* are those by Sir Gavin de Beer, *Charles Darwin* (Garden City, N. Y.: Doubleday, 1964), pp. 21-134; Julian Huxley and H. B. D. Kettlewell, *Charles Darwin and His World* (7), Alan Moorehead, *Darwin and the Beagle* (N. Y.: Harper and Row, 1960); and, apart from her animus toward "natural selection," Gertrude Himmelfarb, *Darwin and the Darwinian Revolution* (Garden City, N. Y.: Doubleday, 1962), pp. 1-124. An excellent analysis of literature on Darwin and Darwinism as well as assessments and critiques of recent biographies is that by Bert James Loewenberg, "Darwin and Darwin Studies, 1959-1963," *History of Science*, IV (1965), 15-54.

[8] For a thorough discussion of Lyell and previous "catastrophist" geology, see Gillispie, *Genesis and Geology*, pp. 98-148.

[9] Gray was perhaps the leading American botanist at mid-century and did much to publicize Darwin's work in America as compatible with theism and the existing natural theology. Cf. Asa Gray, *Darwiniana*, ed. A. Hunter Dupree (Cambridge: Harvard University Press, 1963 [1876]), chs. II and III.

[10] For a collection of the exchanges between Darwin and Huxley and their critics, see Harold Y. Vanderpool (ed.), *Darwin's Impact: Revolutionary Insights Concerning Man, Nature, Religion and Society* (Lexington, Mass.: D. C. Heath,

1973). These accounts are narrated in the biographies cited in n. 7 above and in William Irvine, *Apes, Angels, and Victorians* (New York: McGraw-Hill, 1955.)

11 Kingsley was a famous Anglican novelist who wrote to Darwin manifesting positive enthusiasm toward *The Origin* and whose popular book for children entitled *Waterbabies* (London, 1863), contained several sympathetic references to evolution. McCosh was a Presbyterian who became president of Princeton University, and Henry Drummond was a widely read, amateur scientist and theologian in England. For the response of Kingsley to Darwin, see Charles Darwin, *The Autobiography of Charles Darwin* (2:241-242). See also Drummond's *The Assent of Man* (New York, 1894), and the discussion of Kingsley, McCosh, Drummond and other representative clergymen in Dillenberger, *Protestant Thought and Natural Science*, pp. 230-248.

12 A vivid, popular depiction of Darwin and Huxley's relationships and concerns is found in William Irvine's *Apes, Angels, and Victorians* (New York: McGraw-Hill, 1955), which is rivaled by the fascinating letters of the two men themselves in Charles Darwin, *The Autobiography of Charles Darwin* (2:esp. chs. XI-XIV).

13 For the primary sources on the Darwin-Wallace exchanges, see Bert James Loewenberg, ed., *Darwin, Wallace and the Theory of Natural Selection* (Cambridge: Arlington Books, 1959).

14 See the discussion of Darwin's optimistic appraisal of the future development of man and the variety of secular and religious visions that were encouraged by that optimism in Ernst Benz, *Evolution and Christian Hope* (Garden City, N. Y.: Doubleday, 1966), pp. 64-220.

15 Set in the perspective of history, the pervasive and popular attempts in Darwin's time to rely heavily on proving the existence of God from the principle of design was a reoccurring, but by no means persistent or essential element in the defense of theism in the West. For example, neither Martin Luther nor John Calvin believed that natural man could discern the purposeful activity of God in creation. In spite of classical religious thought and the critiques of rational theism by David Hume and Immanuel Kant, however, trust in "proofs" for the existence and benevolence of God was a marked feature of theology in the eighteenth and early nineteenth centuries. This reliance made theological systems particularly vulnerable at the time that Darwin released *The Origin of Species*. In a brilliant essay Donald Fleming rightly emphasized how Darwin's revulsion from pain and suffering encouraged him to reject the rational theism of his time. Cf. Donald Fleming, "Charles Darwin, the Anaesthetic Man," *Victorian Studies*, IV (1961), 219-236. On the use of rational proofs in the defense of theism, see the discussion by John Dillenberger, *Protestant Thought and Natural Science*, pp. 133-162, 193-212.

16 Well before the publication of *The Origin of Species* in 1859, Schleiermacher on the Continent and Coleridge in England argued that the older Enlightenment defenses of the faith were defunct and unnecessary. See Coleridge, *Aids to Reflection* (London, 1825): Schleiermacher, *On Religion: Speeches to Its Cultured Despisers* (New York: Harper and Row, 1958 [1799]); and the discussion by John Dillenberger and Claude Welch, *Protestant Christianity* (New York: Scribner's, 1954), pp. 179-206.

Donald Fleming has argued cogently that Darwin's pursuit of honesty and equation of art, music, and religion with feeling and illusion encouraged him to avoid all three areas. Fleming, "Charles Darwin, the Anaesthetic Man," *op. cit.*

17 See footnotes 3, 15, and 16 above.

[18] See, for example, the discussion of the beliefs of numerous, post-Darwinian religious thinkers on these subjects in Ian G. Barbour, *Issues in Science and Religion* (Englewood Cliffs, N. J.: Prentice-Hall, 1966), pp. 373-418; and the essay on evolution and purpose in Kenneth Cauthen, *Science, Secularization and God* (Nashville: Abingdon Press, 1969), pp. 90-130. For the revision of religious thought in Victorian England, see Owen Chadwick, *The Victorian Church*, II.

[19] For the ideas and significance of Fisk and Abbot in America, see Bert James Loewenberg, *Darwinism Comes to America, 1859-1900* (Philadelphia: Fortress Press, 1969), pp. 14-22; and Richard Hofstadter, *Social Darwinism in American Thought* (Boston: Beacon Press, 1955), ch. 1. See also n. 11 above.

[20] A scholarly, but one-sided elaboration of this conflict throughout Christian history is Andrew D. White, *History of the Warfare of Science with Theology in Christendom* (1893), 2 vols., still published in several paperback editions.

[21] The literature here is vast. Helpful, brief histories of the interpretation of the Bible after the Enlightenment are Robert M. Grant, *A Short History of the Interpretation of the Bible* (New York: Macmillan, 1963), chs. 11-15; and Samuel Terrien, "History of the Interpretation of the Bible: Modern Period," *The Interpreter's Bible*, II (Nashville: Abingdon Press, 1952), pp. 127-141. See also n. 2 above. For a helpful introduction to the analysis of the Hebrew Bible in the light of the culture of the ancient Near East, see James King West, *Introduction to the Old Testament* (New York: Macmillan, 1971).

[22] For an overview of Kroeber's theoretical position and numerous publications, see Julian H. Steward, "Alfred Lewis Kroeber, 1876-1960," *American Anthropologist*, 63 (October, 1961), 1038-1059.

[23] See especially Theodosius Dobzhansky, *Mankind Evolving* (New Haven: Yale University Press, 1962), and *The Biology of Ultimate Concern* (New York: New American Library, 1967).

[24] See footnotes 11 and 19 above and the following chapter.

[25] See René Dubos, *So Human an Animal* (New York: Scribner's, 1968).

BIBLIOGRAPHY

1. BRYAN, WILLIAM JENNINGS, "God and Creation," *Evolution and Religion*, ed. Gail Kennedy. Boston: D. C. Heath, 1957.

2. DARWIN, CHARLES, *The Autobiography of Charles Darwin and Selected Letters*. New York: Dover Publications, 1958.

3. ———, *The Beagle Diary, 1831-1836*. New York: Macmillan, 1933.

4. ———, *The Descent of Man and Selection in Relation to Sex*. New York: D. Appleton, 1896 [1871].

5. ———, *On the Origin of Species by Means of Natural Selection*. New York: New American Library, 1958 [1859].

6. GREENE, JOHN C., *The Death of Adam*. Ames, Iowa: Iowa State University Press, 1959.

7. HUXLEY, JULIAN and H. B. D. KETTLEWELL, *Charles Darwin and His World*. New York: Viking Press, 1965.

8. HUXLEY, T. H., *Evolution and Ethics and Other Essays*. London: Macmillan, 1895. New York: American Book, 1913.
9. ———, *Man's Place in Nature and Other Anthropological Essays*. London: Macmillan, 1895.
10. PALEY, WILLIAM, *The Works of William Paley*. Philadelphia: J. J. Woodward, 1831.
11. WALLACE, ALFRED RUSSEL, "Darwinism as Applied to Man," *Representative Essays in Modern Thought*. New York: American Book, 1913.
12. WILBERFORCE, SAMUEL, "On the Origin of Species, by Means of Natural Selection: or the Preservation of Favored Races in the Struggle for Life," *Quarterly Review*. 108 (July and October, 1860), 225-264.
13. *The World's Most Famous Court Trial*. Cincinnati: National Book, 1925.

SUGGESTED READINGS

1. *Primary Readings*

A collection of sources that highlights the momentous issues discussed by Darwin, Huxley, and their critics is found in Harold Y. Vanderpool (ed.), *Darwin's Impact: Revolutionary Insights Concerning Man, Nature, Religion and Society* in the *Problems in European Civilization* series (Lexington, Mass.: D. C. Heath, 1973). Section I contains selections from the Bible, William Paley, and English romantic poets and scientists which reflect traditional understandings of creation, man, and nature. Sections II and III contain selections from Darwin's *Origin, Descent of Man*, and *Autobiography*, as well as essays from such thinkers as T. H. Huxley, Bishop Wilberforce, and Alfred Russel Wallace that highlight problems related to the status of religion and the nature of man.

For Darwin's autobiographical account of his training as a divinity student at Cambridge (1828-1831) until he published *Descent of Man* in 1871, see *The Autobiography of Charles Darwin and Selected Letters* (2:17-51).

2. *Secondary Readings*

Helpful, brief descriptions of Darwin's research and its impact on religious thought are those by John Dillenberger, *Protestant Thought and Natural Science* (Garden City, N. Y.: Doubleday, 1960), pp. 217-251; and Ian G. Barbour, *Issues in Science and Religion* (Englewood Cliffs, N. J.: Prentice-Hall, 1966), pp. 80-114.

3. *Additional Bibliography*

For a brief, accessible bibliography of Darwin's writings as well as an annotated bibliography concerning his life, his cultural influence, and references to contemporary evolutionary theory, see Marston Bates and Philip S. Humphrey, *The Darwin Reader* (New York: Scribner's, 1956), pp. 445-455. For an excellent, lengthy, and critical review of primary and secondary sources on Darwin and Darwinism, see Bert James Loewenberg, "Darwin and Darwin Studies, 1959-1963," *History of Science*, IV (1965), 15-54.

4

The Christianization
of Evolution

Although Charles Darwin published his findings about evolution in 1859, the shock of that scientific theory is still reverberating in the sanctuaries of contemporary religion. Not that religious people are still fighting against evolution as William Jennings Bryan and Bishop Wilberforce did. The truth of the theory of evolution has been acknowledged by most theologians and by many lay people, as well as by all natural scientists. The problem for most religious people today is not whether to accept evolution as a fact, but what to do with this fact now that it has been accepted.

Is man merely a higher animal? Is he no more than a random outgrowth at one insignificant point in an infinite system of natural cause and effect? If man *is* a product of evolution through and through, what are we to say about his alleged "moral nature"? Can we expect anything more from him than a somewhat sophisticated form of animal behavior? In the same vein, in what sense, if any, does man have a Divine destiny? Has not his religious life been swallowed up by nature? Where if anywhere does God fit into the picture?

These are obviously pressing questions for anyone concerned to uphold the claims of traditional religion. Obviously? Well, not always. Indeed there is much evidence that these questions, and others like them, have been by-passed by many religious people rather than confronted directly. Among religious lay people this has occurred mainly in the form of a certain compartmentalization. By default, if not by conscious reflection, evolution has been consigned to the laboratory. Although many religiously concerned lay people have accepted the scientific theory of evolution as a fact, they have found one kind of excuse or another to forget about it as quickly as possible. They have held on to their traditional religious ways, more or less, without having allowed their convictions or their piety to be substantially altered by the theory of evolution. They have believed, for example, in a special Divine creation of man, although the scientific evidence seems to account quite adequately for the coming-into-being of man sheerly in terms of natural laws.

In a striking way, a number of sophisticated theologians have reacted to the scientific theory of evolution in much the same manner.[1] They have argued, in one fashion or another, that theology's proper concern is the life of man, not the laws of the cosmos.[2] They have been concerned chiefly with "the mighty acts of God in history," not with any relation God may or may not have with the processes of nature.[3] These theologians have been interested in human history not as a story embedded in the context of the whole universe—a universe with virtually infinite expanses of space and time, including a surprisingly long expanse of evolutionary development on the little planet Earth. They have not approached man as an *evolved* animal, but as a creature with a *spiritual* calling and a *moral* nature.[4] All these theologians have calmly accepted evolution as a scientific fact, but at the same time they have not really concerned themselves directly with the religious implications of evolution.

This is particularly true of those Protestant theologians—like Rudolf Bultmann—who have developed their thought as theologies of the Word of God, and who accordingly have given much of their attention to interpreting the Bible. Without any major exception, they have abandoned the traditional idea that the world was created in seven days, as that creation is portrayed in the book of Genesis. Nevertheless they have almost exclusively concerned themselves with man as a spiritual and historical creature. Correspondingly, they have emphasized God's dealings with man alone, and the role of Christ as the mediator of salvation for man alone. They have either deliberately or unconsciously neglected the religious questions implicit in the scientific theory of evolution.

Not all religiously concerned lay people and not all theologians have by-passed the theory of evolution in their piety and reflection. Evolution has been a central concern for a small but creative segment of religious thinkers. Among those who have chosen to wrestle spiritually and theologically with the theory of evolution, the most radical results and the most celebrated insights have appeared in the writings of the visionary French Jesuit and paleontologist, Pierre Teilhard de Chardin (1881–1955). The widespread attention his work has received exemplifies dramatically the deep need many modern religious men and women have felt for coming to terms with the theory of evolution, for integrating it into their world view, rather than passing it by, leaving its questions unanswered.

With a boldness and a rigor virtually unmatched in nineteenth- and twentieth-century religious thought, Teilhard sought to *Christianize evolution*.[5] Teilhard not only accepted evolution as a fact; he worked with the theory of evolution as *the key* for unlocking all the mysteries of the universe: not just the secrets of nature, but also the inmost movements of human history, the life of Christ and the Church, and the reality of God himself. Teilhard appropriated the theory of evolution —and in the process developed it far beyond anything Darwin ever dreamed of—as a way of establishing an integrated understanding of the whole of reality, as a way of unfolding a unified Christian vision of nature, man, and God.

Teilhard was a synthesizer in the venerable tradition of Thomas Aquinas. What Thomas Aquinas did with Aristotelian philosophy for the medieval world, Teilhard ventured to do with Darwinian science for the modern world. Teilhard accepted Darwin's view that man is but "a little higher than the brutes," yet the Jesuit thinker did so in a new and impressive way: he also forcefully affirmed the traditional theme that man is but "a little lower than the angels." For Teilhard, the story of the whole universe is the story of the *cosmic ascent of man*. In Teilhard's vision, the universal process of evolution is the unfolding of the Divine life and the building up of the glorified spiritual Body of Christ. With the touch of Teilhard's disciplined but artistic hands, then, the story of evolution becomes the narrative of Christian truth.

1. THE SHAPE OF TEILHARD'S VISION

Teilhard's thought is not automatically understandable. Some readers find it positively mystifying. This is especially due to Teilhard's peculiar-sounding terminology—cosmogenesis, noosphere, pleromatization, cephalization, and so on. The distinctiveness of Teilhard's vision comes out sharply when viewed in relationship to philosopher David Hume and scientist Charles Darwin, on the one hand, and theologian Rudolf Bultmann, on the other hand.

For Hume, religious faith or religious consciousness is definitely something *secondary* for human nature. More fundamental to human nature than religion, according to Hume, are the basic physical drives:

hunger, sex, and so on. At the same time, Hume sees the objective world of nature as a relatively self-enclosed, self-sufficient whole. The existence and the benevolent qualities of God, according to Hume, cannot be proved from observing nature. Darwin stands firmly in this Humean tradition, and in fact he accents it considerably. Darwin scarcely pays any attention to the religious consciousness, so secondary is it, as far as he is concerned. Darwin's rigorously objective doctrine of evolution, moreover, further solidifies the notion that nature is a self-enclosed, self-sufficient whole, and that any proof of a benevolent Creator from nature is untenable.

Hume and Darwin represent a widespread tendency in modern culture—to approach all aspects of life as objectively as possible, with as much detachment as possible. Most educated people today still reflect this tendency, insofar as they value an *objective* point of view, other things being equal, over anything *subjective*.

Bultmann takes a heroic stance over against the exclusively objectifying tendencies of modern culture, represented by Hume and Darwin. Following the father of modern existentialism, Søren Kierkegaard, Bultmann thinks of truth, at least in part, as subjectivity. For Bultmann the religious consciousness is not something secondary to human nature, to be scorned or neglected as one devotes one's major attention to a detached study of the natural world. For Bultmann the religious consciousness is *primary*. On this fundamental premise—the existential centrality of religious faith for human life—Bultmann builds his whole theological enterprise.

This is not to say that Bultmann turns his back on the findings of the natural sciences. On the contrary, he embraces the objective approach to nature championed by Hume and Darwin. But Bultmann embraces this objective approach to nature, paradoxically, without touching it. He simply accepts the objective findings of Newtonian and Darwinian science without giving them direct attention.[6] Then he finds another place not touched by them, the existential self, for religion. Bultmann's world has, as it were, two levels, two parallel lines: the objective level described by science and the subjective interpersonal level. The latter includes the dimension of the I-Thou relationship, the dimension of communion between God and man, depicted by theology and real for the believer who hears the proclaimed Word of God. When all has been said, for Bultmann these two levels remain parallel, like two boards glued together. Science and religion, detached study of the world and existential faith, do belong together, as far as Bultmann is concerned. But they do not interpenetrate each other so as to form an integrated whole.

Teilhard follows the course laid out by Bultmann, and the mainstream of modern theology, insofar as Teilhard assigns a primary place to the religious consciousness. For Teilhard, religion belongs to the inmost essence of human nature; it is not something secondary as it was for Hume and Darwin. But Teilhard's enterprise is more comprehensive and more ambitious than Bultmann's or virtually any other post-Darwinian theologian. Teilhard is not content with two levels, objective and subjective, which do not interpenetrate. He is not content to see faith in God rooted in man's religious consciousness and then to leave the world of nature to objective study by the natural sciences. Rather he sees human consciousness as a clue which allows the reflective individual to have a unified, integrated view of the world.[7] Teilhard affirms that human consciousness reveals a universal law, which applies not only to man, but also to the whole of nature and, indeed, to ultimate reality itself.

Teilhard affirms that the whole universe, not just man, has a subjective side. Teilhard thus stands over against Hume and Darwin not just by arguing that the inner side of man is decisive, as Bultmann does. He stands over against Hume and Darwin by maintaining that the *inner side of the whole universe,* man and nature, is decisive.[8] Yet at the same time, no less than Bultmann and most contemporary religious thinkers, Teilhard accepts the objective method of the natural sciences as an essential and indispensable avenue to truth about nature.

It will come as no surprise, then, to note that Teilhard enters into the natural scientific enterprise itself, a venture which his scientific training as a paleontologist permits him to make. Bultmann, in contrast, more or less accepted the scientific status quo, then proceeded to develop his theology. Teilhard actually works with the data of the natural world. He functions as an active scientist as well as a reflective theologian. In this way he seeks to show that the scientific and religious understandings of reality are united with each other. In his mind, and in his work, scientific and religious data continually interpenetrate each other.

That is one essential motif of Teilhard's vision, the quest for scientific and religious unity and coherence. To see only this, however, is not yet to identify the driving existential force which led Teilhard to undertake his scientific-religious synthesis. Teilhard wrote not just for intellectual reasons, to unify science and religion. Even more, he wrote for practical existential reasons. He desperately wanted to overcome the pessimism and the despair which he felt were dominating the heart of twentieth-century man. He wanted to offer a forceful, scientifically respectable optimism to our "Age of Anxiety."

Teilhard saw twentieth-century pessimism as arising mainly from two sources—the findings of modern science, particularly physics, and the events of modern history. The implication of the Second Law of

Thermodynamics, the concept of "entropy," seems to be that the whole universe is destined to end in a static state of dead frigidity. Our universe, according to modern physics, apparently is headed for an immense and inglorious "heat death." This cosmic pessimism, coupled with the historical pessimism growing out of the bitter experiences of two world wars and the dehumanizing effects of modern technology, has resulted in a profound sense of despair. Add to this the thermonuclear bomb, and we have identified the pathos of the twentieth century. It is precisely this cosmic and historical despair that has been articulated by such writers as Albert Camus and Jean-Paul Sartre.[9]

Teilhard believed that if man is filled with despair, as twentieth-century man seems to be, he will never be fully free to create a better future. He will be immobilized by the weight of his own anxiety. As Teilhard says at one point in his major study, *The Phenomenon of Man*, "Man will never take a step in a direction he knows to be blocked. There is precisely the ill that causes our disquiet" (13:229). The commitment to provide a real hope for despairing twentieth-century man was the driving practical concern behind Teilhard's intellectual synthesis. He *was* interested in unifying Darwinian science and the Christian religion. Even more, he was committed to undercutting the cosmic and the cultural pessimism of our century. He was committed to say to his contemporaries: look to nature and to history, and use the tools of science along with the insights of religion; see—the world is full of meaning, the world is full of hope.

As we look at the shape of Teilhard's vision, then, both in its intellectual and practical aspects, both with regard to his quest for a synthesis of religion and science and with regard to his quest for a new scientifically respectable optimism, we see motifs which are rather different from many of those with which we are most familiar. Ours is the "Age of Analysis" and the "Age of Anxiety." We are tutored by a natural scientific approach to reality which plays down the quest for synthesis, which accents careful, painstaking, detailed analysis. Likewise we are influenced in large measure by the dominant despair of our time. The world has an infinite number of profound problems, it seems; and in that mire the world seems to be bogged down. Hence, to encounter a thinker who emphasizes synthesis and optimism is, at least in some respects, to encounter someone strange, someone who speaks a foreign-sounding kind of language.

Indeed, Teilhard was a rather isolated intellectual figure in his own time. While many philosophers were restricting themselves to the relatively narrow areas of the theory of knowledge, the description of the structures of human existence as such ("existentialism"), or the analysis of language, Teilhard was outlining a comprehensive speculative philosophy. While natural scientists in increasing numbers were retreating to the modest task of research in areas of their own specialization, Teilhard was seeking to incorporate the whole sphere of the natural sciences into a coherent world view, which would draw on many disciplines and fields of knowledge. While many theologians were minimizing the role of "unaided human reason" in the creation of any theological synthesis, and emphasizing the decisive role of Divine revelation in the Bible, Teilhard was seeking to maximize the role of human reason and to harmonize the speculations of human reason with the elements of knowledge he believed he had received by the mediation of revelation. Likewise, Teilhard's analysis of the potential of his own culture set him apart from many others. Virtually at the same time as the German philosopher of history, Oswald Spengler, was writing his extensive work, *The Decline of the Western World*, Teilhard was describing his faith in Progress. Virtually at the same time as the Swiss theologian, Karl Barth, was inaugurating a "Theology of Crisis," which depicted a radical Divine judgment (*krisis*) resting on all things human, Teilhard was celebrating the potential of man to build a new world.[10] Of Teilhard it might be said, without discrediting his thought, that he was not really a child of our century, but that his deepest convictions made him more fittingly a child of another era, perhaps the time of the Enlightenment. Teilhard was optimistic, speculative, confident in man and human reason, and a firm believer in human progress. This cultural apartness was reinforced by the relative isolation, intellectual and social, in which he lived. Teilhard was very much aware of the cultural milieu of the twentieth century, as we have seen. But he saw it from a relative distance, as the biography indicates.[11]

Teilhard grew up intellectually in the protective atmosphere of a traditional Jesuit education. He spent most of his life abroad, in Egypt and China. He was a stretcher-bearer in the first World War, but that experience—so traumatic for many nineteenth-century believers in Progress—was not a formative influence on his thinking. Even his written works were somewhat isolated, because of the ban placed on some of them by the Roman Church. Teilhard never really was forced to enter into a worldwide dialogue with the thinkers of his time. He conversed mainly with friends and disciples. This is reflected in the complete freedom he felt to create his own terminology. His thought was more a monologue than a dialogue. He was chiefly concerned with formulating his own synthesis. He was not primarily interested in communicating his ideas in the language of his intellectual peers. He was surely a monument of intellectual integrity; there can be no question of that. But he was, when all has been said, a lonely thinker.

But Teilhard's relative intellectual and practical apartness from the main currents of our century by no means should be taken to imply that his thought is not germane, that it is "irrelevant." On the contrary, it might well be the case that Teilhard had the better perspective to interpret us and our world to ourselves, enmeshed as most of us are in our "Age of Analysis" and our "Age of Anxiety." It could be that Teilhard s relative cultural detachment gave him insights which others, much involved in the intellectual and existential currents of the twentieth century, cannot readily discover by themselves.

2. TEILHARD'S INTELLECTUAL INHERITANCE

Although Teilhard was a somewhat isolated intellectual figure in his own day, there is good reason to say that he stands firmly within the classical philosophical and theological traditions of the West. Teilhard himself was not a professional philosopher or theologian, to be sure, and his training in these areas seems to have been rather conventional. His Jesuit education included four years study in philosophy and four years in theology, but it was apparently a tradition-directed scholastic education in classical Thomism, which was neither exciting nor innovative.[12] Teilhard apparently did not study modern philosophy or the history of ideas in any great detail. But this is only to view Teilhard's intellectual inheritance externally, from "without" as it were. A glimpse at the "within" of Teilhard's intellectual inheritance gives a markedly different picture.

Although it is difficult to establish any direct influence of a thoroughgoing nature, it can be said that the life-blood of Teilhard's comprehensive intellectual synthesis was the philosophical and theological vitality of classical Western culture. With boundless imagination and insight, Teilhard revived and transformed the tradition of Plato, Aristotle, and Plotinus; Origen, Augustine, and Thomas Aquinas; Leibniz, Schelling, and Hegel. Perhaps the best way to indicate this succinctly is to draw on the study, *The Great Chain of Being*, by the eminent historian of ideas Arthur O. Lovejoy (5).

Throughout the history of the West, philosophers have sought to grasp and identify the ultimate structures and forces of reality. One of the dominating products of this intellectual quest, if not *the* dominating result, was the comprehensive idea of a Great Chain of Being. At the apex of the Chain is pure being, being itself, variously called the One, the Good, or God. The Chain then extends downward toward nothingness or non-being. There is a vast gradation of beings: nearest to God, the purely spiritual or angelic creatures; then man, the creature of embodied spirit; then the animals, plants, and material elements;

finally sheer non-being. This schema is thought of classically, moreover, under the rubric of "the One and the Many," the ultimate Being itself, on the one hand, and the virtually infinite number of creatures, on the other hand. Lovejoy identifies three major characteristics of the idea of the Great Chain of Being: 1) *plenitude* or universal fullness, 2) *continuity,* an idea which is deduced from the first (any gap between two species must be filled, since otherwise the creation would not be as full as it might otherwise be), and 3) *gradation,* the notion of a hierarchy of "perfection" extending from the apex to the nadir of the Chain of Being, from the One to the Many (the higher on the scale, the more Being a creature possesses and therefore the greater perfection).

The inner logic of the Great Chain of Being, classically envisioned, is the logic of "the Good." By its very nature the Good (the One) is pure perfection, and therefore it cannot contain itself; it overflows. This is how the third-century Neoplatonic philosopher Plotinus describes this ultimate process: "The One is perfect because it seeks for nothing, and possesses nothing, and has need of nothing; and being perfect, it overflows, and thus its superabundance produces an Other." Similarly:

> Whenever anything reaches its own perfection, we see that it cannot endure to remain in itself, but generates and produces some other thing. Not only beings having the power of choice, but also those which are by nature incapable of choice, and even inanimate things, send forth as much of themselves as they can; thus fire emits heat and snow cold and drugs act upon other things. . . . How then should the Most Perfect Being and the First Good remain shut up in itself, as though it were jealous or impotent—itself the potency of all things? . . . Something must therefore be begotten of it (5:62).

And for Plotinus this process of universal generation of the Many from the One will not end until every possibility of being is realized. For Plotinus there is thus a comprehensive, infinitely variegated, hierarchical process of *emanation* (an important philosophical term), from the One to the Many—a process which is eternal in Plotinus' schema, timeless, without beginning or end.

Sometimes this motif of emanation has been conceived of morphologically, that is, according to the idea that every creature in the Great Chain of Being is a distinct *form* of being; that it has its own particular gradation of Being. On occasion, the emanation from the One to the Many has also been thought of psychologically, that is, in terms of gradations of *consciousness.* The seventeenth-century German philosopher Leibniz is a good example of a thinker who depicted the Great Chain of Being in the second way, in psychological terms. Leibniz was a panpsychist; for him the whole of reality was essentially a gradation of varying levels of consciousness. God, at the apex of the Great Chain of Being, is for Leibniz pure consciousness or spirit; man is essentially a lesser form of consciousness; animals and even material entities have a certain small degree of consciousness. We will see presently that Teilhard adopts the fundamental motif of a Great Chain of Being, but that he does so in the tradition of Leibniz, with a philosophy of consciousness.

Perhaps the most decisive development in the history of the motif we are examining is what Lovejoy refers to as *temporalizing of the Chain of Being*, which occurred dramatically in the eighteenth century. Schematically, it is helpful here to think of that Chain of Being as now being tipped 45 degrees to the right, with the process of emanation moving now *not from the One to the Many, but from the Many to the One.* This is the shift of thought from the timeless vertical metaphysics of ancient philosophy, to the temporal, horizontal metaphysics of modernity. In the wake of this shift, the concept of emanation would eventually give way to the concept of *evolution.* This is how Lovejoy describes the temporalizing of the Chain of Being:

> The *plenum formarum* [fullness of metaphysical forms] came to be conceived by some, not as the inventory but as the program of nature, which is being carried out gradually and exceedingly slowly in the cosmic history. While all the possibles demand realization, they are not accorded it all at once. Some have attained it in the past and have apparently since lost it; many are embodied in the kind of creatures which now exist; doubtless infinitely many more are destined to receive the gift of actual existence in the ages that are to come. It is only of the universe in its entire temporal span that the principle of plenitude holds good. The Demiurgus [the Creator] is not in a hurry; and his goodness is sufficiently exhibited if, soon or late, every Idea finds its manifestation in the sensible order (5:244).

Interestingly, this temporalized Chain of Being appears forcefully in some of the writings of Leibniz, coupled with the familiar Enlightenment idea of indefinite Progress. The timeless Chain of Being thus becomes a program of endless Becoming, individual, biological, and cosmic (5:259). We will see that Teilhard follows Leibniz implicitly in this respect, too, as well as in the context of a metaphysics of consciousness. For Teilhard—who was profoundly influenced by Darwin's empirical conclusion that evolution is a fundamental law of nature—the metaphysical theme of a universal cosmic evolution is virtually indubitable.

There were many reasons for the shift in thinking from the idea of a timeless Chain of Being to a temporal Process of Becoming. Among the most important of these was a new influence exercised by *biblical eschatology.* Lovejoy does not deal with this theme in detail, but it is

worth attending to it in view of its evident significance for our understanding of Teilhard's thought.

Biblical thinking, in both the Old and the New Testaments, was
thoroughly "eschatological." [13] That is to say, time rather than space
was the predominating category.[14] Although some early Christian thinkers such as Origen set forth emanation-schemas like that of Plotinus,
the notion of temporal development or *history* was undoubtedly rightly
read as the fundamental premise of the Bible, wherever the biblical
writings were read on their own terms. Biblical thinking was predicated
on a movement of thought from Alpha to Omega, from the first things
to the last things (*ta eschata*). Generally speaking, this temporal, historical element tended to fall by the wayside, or be deemphasized, however, as early Christianity became more and more settled within the
Greek-speaking world. The timeless metaphysics (ontology) of thinkers
like Plotinus came to have a formative influence in Christian theology,
while the temporal, historical thought (eschatology) of the Bible tended
to become secondary. Yet this pattern did not go unquestioned. The
early Christian thinker Irenaeus, for example, self-consciously set forth
a theology of historical development.[15] A key figure in this tradition
(not even mentioned by Lovejoy) is the twelfth-century abbot, Joachim
of Fiore (1:35–48). Joachim was captivated by a new sense of the out-
pouring of the Spirit, not unlike the first-century experience of Pentecost.
On the basis of this existential involvement he developed a new periodization of history: the Age of the Father (the Old Testament era); the
Age of the Son (the time of the New Testament and the institutional
Church); and the Age of the Spirit (the period of his own time, with
the projected end of the institutional Church). Importantly, as Ernst
Benz points out in his study *Evolution and Christian Hope,* Joachim
did not define development and progress in history in human terms:
"They are, rather, considered as steps in the progressive self-realization
and self-revelation of the Divine Trinity in the history of mankind"
(1:37). That is to say, for Joachim, in a certain sense, *ultimate reality
is in process;* God himself has a history. Here, in the vision of Joachim,
the whole of reality has been temporalized.

The tradition of Joachim, it seems safe to say, flows into the thought
of Teilhard de Chardin, who self-consciously sought to take biblical
eschatology with a new kind of seriousness. When Teilhard longs for
a new stage in the history of evolution, the tradition of Joachim is not
far beneath the surface. Surely this tradition is mediated to Teilhard
through German romanticism, the German philosophers Hegel and
Schelling, and finally through the French philosopher Henri Bergson,
whose book *Creative Evolution* Teilhard read very carefully. Yet the

influence of the tradition of Joachim, and behind that the thought of the Bible, should not be underestimated as we seek to trace Teilhard's intellectual inheritance. Indeed, it might be said that the best way to think of Teilhard's achievement, in a positive light, is to think of it as a creative fusion of the philosophical tradition of the Great Chain of Being (as that motif more and more came to be temporalized in the form of a Great Process of Becoming) with the theological tradition of a historical Divine exfoliation: a creative fusion of the tradition of speculative ontology with the tradition of biblical eschatology.

This creative fusion is signaled in a particularly forceful way in Teilhard's confessional essay, "My Universe." On the one hand, we can see the now thoroughly temporalized Chain of Being:

> The picture, then, is perfectly clear: in light of the creative union the universe assumes the form of a huge cone, whose base expands indefinitely to the rear, into darkness, while its apex rises up and concentrates ever further into the light. Throughout the whole, the *same* creative influence makes itself felt, but always in a more conscious, more purified, more complex form. Initially, it is only vague affinities that set matter in motion; soon, however, the pull of the living can be felt; in lower forms it is an almost mechanical process, but in the human heart it becomes the infinitely rich and formidable power of love. Finally, at a still higher level, the passion is born for the realities that lie above the circles of man, realities in which in some vague way we feel we are immersed (14:48).

On the other hand, we can see the formative image of the Christ, who is the consummation of all things, an image drawn from New Testament eschatology:

> God did not will individually . . . the sun, the earth, plants, or Man. He willed his Christ;—and in order to have his Christ, he had to create the spiritual world, and man in particular, upon which Christ might germinate;—and to have man, he had to launch the vast process of organic life . . . ;—and the birth of that organic life called for the entire cosmic turbulence.

> At the beginning of the perceptible world what existed was the Multiple [the Many]; and that Multiple was already rising up, like one indissociable whole, towards spirit under the magnetic influence of the universal Christ who was being engendered in it (14:79).

3. THE ELEMENTS OF TEILHARD'S VISION

The elements of Teilhard's vision flow together like the parts of a beautifully simple but highly complex oriental brush drawing. From one standpoint the *unity* of the whole is the most striking aspect of the drawing. From another standpoint the attention to *individual detail* most captivates the onlooker.

The unity of Teilhard's vision is its *radical humanism*. This humanism informs every detail of his thought. For Teilhard, mankind is stationed at the very heart of reality. We live in an infinitely large universe, Teilhard grants, with regard both to time and space. Nevertheless mankind *is* at the center of the whole history of the universe. Teilhard emphasizes the cosmic and the universal; the whole of reality for him is an infinite process, a primordial flux. But it is a process with a direction, a flux with a goal. It moves from the Many to the One. It moves from an undifferentiated "Alpha," when all things are vague and undefinable, to a highly integrated "Omega," the final fulfillment of all things in the white heat of the Divine life. Precisely the coming into being and the final transformation of *mankind* at the final "Omega point" is the goal of the whole universal process.

To underline this point Teilhard revives a scientific concept which has been widely rejected, in its traditional form, by most biologists today: *orthogenesis*. Literally this word means coming into being in a straight line. By invoking this contested concept Teilhard seeks to reaffirm the centrality of man in the story of evolution. With Darwin and the neo-Darwinians, Teilhard does accept the anti-orthogenetic notion of natural selection. The process of evolution is not simply a straight line to man, by any means, according to Teilhard. The process of evolution, he holds, "proceeds step by step by dint of billionfold trial and error" (13:302). It is an infinite process of groping or "cosmic drift." That explains why the whole process has taken such an extended time.

At the same time, for Teilhard, evolution has always had *one* goal, it has followed a line toward the coming into being of man and the life of man or planet Earth. This line surely has been more like a highly erratic spiral upwards than a straight line, according to Teilhard. Nevertheless, he maintains, there has been, there is, and there always will be one inner drive—*one main axis of evolution*—of the whole universal evolutionary process, however random its morphology, until the final point Omega is reached.

In this connection Teilhard introduces the concept of a universal law, a law as fundamental to reality, he believes, as is the law of gravity, the Second Law of Thermodynamics, or the law of the conservation of energy. This is the *law of complexity and consciousness*. Teilhard refers to this law, again and again, and in this way he holds all the disparate individual elements of his vision together.

The law of complexity and consciousness means simply that the process of evolution represents an ever increasing development toward higher organization and more intense and unified forms of consciousness. There are, then, Teilhard points out, two axial lines in the universe, the impressive quantitative one which runs from the subatomic world to the galactic world, the axis of physical infinity. This material aspect of the world, Teilhard grants, is ultimately tending towards death, according to the Second Law of Thermodynamics. Then there is the evolutionary axis of complexity-consciousness. According to this law, in the midst of the dying physical cosmos, life and consciousness are gradually emerging and intensifying. *This* is the axis—complexity and consciousness—which Teilhard sees as the key to understanding the meaning of the whole universe and the history of evolution in particular. This is the orthogenetic line of evolution.

The law of complexity-consciousness, Teilhard maintains, applies everywhere, even where it cannot be observed. All entities in the universe have both a "without," a certain state of organization, and a "within," a certain state of consciousness. Where the one increases, the other will increase too. A larger and more organized brain, for example, will soon be the occasion for a more intense form of consciousness. The higher the level of organization of a natural entity, moreover, the more consciousness it will possess.

Now this seems to imply that even such apparently "dead" entities as rocks and trees, electrons and neutrons, have some consciousness. Is this to say, then, that Teilhard believes that all entities in nature have a soul? Does Teilhard believe in panpsychism? The answer is yes, and no. All things definitely have a "within," he maintains. But the "within" of electrons, for example, is extremely undifferentiated and disintegrated, approaching nothingness; much the same is true of a rock or a tree. There can be no question, then, of communion somehow with the "within" or the consciousness of the tree.

Yet Teilhard feels compelled to postulate such a primitive state of consciousness in all things on the basis of the scientific principle, much emphasized by Darwin, and intrinsic to the motif of the great Chain of Being, *natura non facit saltum*. Nature doesn't proceed by leaps. If consciousness is a reality now, of which we are subjectively certain, it must have been real in some sense at primitive levels of physical reality. Teilhard then compares this point to other well-known findings of science:

> The speed of a body must approach that of light for the variation in its mass to be apparent to us. Its temperature must reach 500 degrees C for its radiation to be visible to us. Is it not, then, reasonable to expect that through just the same mechanism, matter, until it begins to approach a complexity of a million or a half million, should appear "dead" . . . while beyond that figure it begins to show the red glow of life? (12:24)

The concept of orthogenesis and the law of complexity-conscious-ness show how deep the current of humanism is in Teilhard's thought, and why the term "radical" is appropriate at this point. The whole infinitely variegated evolutionary process of the universe has one axis, one goal: the life of man and his future. The ultimate law of the universe, complexity-consciousness, focuses finally on human reality; man is its final product, both in this world and in the world to come.

But Teilhard's humanism is more than just a passive scientific-theological observation of a universal process which has its final goal in the glorification of man—staggering to the imagination as that aspect of his vision may be. Teilhard's radically humanistic vision of reality also has an activist thrust, not unlike the thought of Karl Marx.[16] According-ing to Teilhard, man is now in a position to bring the whole universe to its originally intended fulfillment *by his own action*. In this sense, the future of the whole universe hinges on the proper exercise of human freedom. Mankind, Teilhard says, is "evolution conscious of itself." Evolution, therefore, will only move on to its next pinnacle through the proper use of human consciousness. In theological terms, the Kingdom of God will not come unless mankind consciously works to make it come.

This radical humanism, both in its reflective and its activist aspects, can be called Teilhard's own "Copernican revolution." In Teilhard's vision, mankind once again appears at the center of the whole of reality. Indeed, mankind occupies a position of importance that few thinkers have ever allotted to it before. No longer is man at the periphery of things, where Copernicus, Darwin, and Einstein placed him. Rather, for Teilhard, the history of the whole universe is the story of the cosmic ascent of man. In Teilhard's words:

> Man is not at the centre of the universe as once we thought in our sim-plicity, but something much more wonderful—the arrow pointing the way to the final unification of the world in terms of life (13:223).

That, then, is the unity of Teilhard's vision, its radical humanism. That is his thought when we consider it as a whole. When we examine the details of Teilhard's vision, in turn, we see that his argument has two major parts: first, his "science" or his "phenomenology," second, his specifically religious discourse, his theology. Employing science and theology is continuity with each other, Teilhard depicts a universal process of *genesis*, the coming into being of increasingly complex and conscious levels of reality. These levels he denotes by the terms cosmo-genesis, biogenesis, homogenesis, and Christogenesis.

The whole universal evolutionary process begins with _cosmogenesis_, the coming into being and the increasing organization of physical matter. Over a period of billions of years, from a state of virtually total disintegrated physical matter, the history of our universe began. By apparent accident, moreover, a habitable place finally came into being, the Earth. Again, through a billionfold process of trial and error, life emerged on planet Earth. This was _biogenesis_. Through a similarly lengthy process, life covered the Earth; henceforth this could be called the biosphere. In this sphere, complexification then proceeded on a vast scale. Retrospectively we can see that life's greatest density passed through those creatures possessing a central nervous system. Teilhard calls this facet of evolution _cephalization_ (from the Greek word for head). With cephalization, Teilhard points out, one can see the first signs of emergent consciousness.

Then comes a step in the history of evolution comparable only to the birth of life. This is the birth of mind or self-consciousness in the creature man, the most cephalized of the living creatures. This, Teilhard calls _noogenesis_ or _homogenesis_. Quantitatively speaking, the appearance of man was almost totally without significance. Here Teilhard agrees with Darwin and Darwin's twentieth-century followers. In almost all respects man _was_ dwarfed by other creatures; he appeared as but one weak product of a billionfold cosmic drift. As Teilhard says with his characteristic sense of drama, "Man came silently into the world" (13: 183). Nevertheless here was a phenomenon expressing the flow of the universe itself:

> However solitary his advent, man emerged from a general groping of the world. He was born a direct lineal descendent from a total effort of life, so that the species has an axial value and a preeminent dignity (13:188).

Man emerged, then, like everything else, as a result of natural selection, but it was a natural selection which was drawn forward by the very life force of the universe itself. With man, moreover, the interiority of matter, the "within," has finally become the dominant factor. Here, finally, spirit rules over matter; or it can. Man is a self-conscious being. He knows himself as a self and is free to lead a rational life.

But evolution doesn't stop here, Teilhard stresses. It continues to press forward and upward, in two partially overlapping phases. The first phase is expansion or _planetization_. Man multiplies and fills the earth. Concomitantly, his quality of life or culture develops or intensifies. This is the second phase, the phase of compression or _convergence_. As Teilhard writes,

Traditions became organized and a collective memory was developed. Slender and granular as the first membrane might be, the noosphere there and then began to close in upon itself and to encircle the earth (13:209).

From about the middle of the nineteenth century, roughly in our era, this dual process of human evolution by expansion and compression began to reach its limits, according to Teilhard. This process was helped along by the social compression of mankind on continents, and by the worldwide social interaction made possible by modern technology. Here we see Teilhard linking human culture and technology to the law of complexity-consciousness; in man's life, that is the way that law works, for the most part. This positive view of technology is obviously different from recent criticism of technology as a force of cosmic regression. For Teilhard, the radio and computer help to carry the process of evolution forward and upward.

In the human sphere, Teilhard believes, evolution is now approaching its limits; evolution is ready for another major step forward. Teilhard sees signs of this impending new development in the growing social organization of the world (11:39). He does see the evils of certain totalitarian states in the twentieth century, for example; but at the same time he sees them as pointing to new possibilities for a world society. More important than social organization, however, Teilhard sees the noosphere arriving at a critical point of development through the scientific discovery of evolution. *Now*, finally, in our period, evolution has become conscious of itself. This awareness Teilhard calls the *involution of evolution* (13:220). We men are now coming to realize that the whole universal process is passing through *us* and to that extent depends on us. As Teilhard writes, with reference to the similar Marxist point of view:

> Like sons who have grown up, like workers who have become "conscious," we are discovering that something is developing in the world by means of us, perhaps at our expense. And what is more serious still, is that we have become aware that, in the great game that is being played, we are the players as well as being the cards and the stakes. Nothing can go on if we leave the table. Neither can any power force us to remain (13:229).

This conception of a humanity which has reached the limits of its terrestrial expansion and is fast approaching the limits of its spiritual–cultural compression, leads Teilhard to pose the question of the Omega point: that is, the question whether it is not reasonable to assume that the whole evolutionary process has a final *cone*, which is the end-goal of the working of the law of complexity-consciousness. This takes Teilhard's thought to the boundary of metaphysics or theology, since he has discerned that the whole process is tending toward the production of purer and purer forms of personalized spirit.

As human life is progressively integrated and spiritualized, Teilhard asks, is it not conceivable that evolution will pass through one final cosmic involution into the reality of sheer personalized-spirit? This, for example, is what Teilhard has to say in an essay written in 1946:

> Ahead of, or rather in the heart of, a universe prolonged along its axis of complexity, there exists a divine center of convergence. That nothing may be prejudged, and in order to stress its synthesizing and personalizing function, let us call it the point Omega. Let us suppose that from this universal centre, this Omega point, there constantly emanate radiations hitherto only perceptible to those persons whom we call mystic . Let us further imagine that, as the sensibility or response to mysticism of the human race increases with planetization, the awareness of Omega becomes so widespread as to warm the earth psychically while physically it is growing cold.
>
> Is it not conceivable that mankind, at the end of its totalization, its folding in upon itself, may reach a critical level of maturity where, leaving earth and stars to lapse slowly back into the dwindling mass of primordial energy, it will detach itself from this planet and join the one true, irreversible essence of things, the Omega point? This will be an escape from the planet, not in space or outwardly, but spiritually and inwardly, such as the hyper-centration of cosmic matter upon itself allows (11:122).

When that time comes, evil—which for Teilhard is disintegration and disunion of reality—will have been abolished. Perfect union of spiritualized personal reality, an ultra-synthesized mankind, will have come into being.

One can see, then, how smoothly Teilhard's scientific account of evolution passes over into his theology of evolution. In this context Teilhard affirms that the exalted Jesus Christ is the central point of the whole universe, of all visible and invisible powers. Teilhard now states that the whole universal process of cosmogenesis, biogenesis, homogenesis, is ultimately a process of *Christogenesis*, the growth of the living, fulfilled Christ. The exalted, resurrected Christ and his body united to him, is the Omega point of the universe. Teilhard frequently alludes to Colossians and Ephesians in the New Testament as the biblical basis for his cosmic Christology. In particular, he often refers to Colossians 1:15f.:

> He is the image of the invisible God, the first-born of all creation; for in him all things were created, in heaven and on earth, visible and invisible, whether thrones or dominations or principalities or authorities—all things were created through him and for him. He is before all things, and in him all things hold together. He is the head of the body, the church; he is

the beginning, the firstborn from the dead, that in everything he might be pre-eminent. For in him all the fullness of God was pleased to dwell.

For Teilhard, then, Christ is the ultimate reality of the universe. Teilhard expressed this by drawing on the New Testament word *pleroma* ("fullness"), and refers to Christ's role in the universe as *pleromatization* or totalization, that is, drawing all things to himself. All things, Teilhard maintains, have their being and their becoming through the cosmic Christ.

In metaphysical terms, Teilhard sees the exalted cosmic Christ functioning as the First-Mover of the universe: not as its efficient cause, as the Enlightenment deity, as the "God way back there" who set all things in motion. No, God is not way back at the beginning, in isolation as the efficient cause, the watch-maker. Rather God is the *ever-present final cause*. Christ, in other words, is a kind of spiritual magnet which draws the universe to himself, and which organizes and orders the universe, a process which will allow it one day to attain fulfillment in Him. More specifically the ultimate spiritual energy which radiates from Christ and which draws all things to him and orders all things for him is—Divine Love. *Ultimate Reality is charity.* Charity is the spiritual force which draws all things toward final union with God in Christ. This is the spiritual force which was working at the beginning of time on the "within" of primordial matter, drawing it forward and upward along the axis of complexity-consciousness.

Teilhard further sees historical Christianity as being in some sense already at the Omega point. He holds that historical Christianity is the most universal religion open to man and the religion most able to inspire mankind to deeds of love and peace. More particularly, he implies that the Church of Rome occupies the portion closest to the main axis of evolution, according to the evolutionary principle of cephalization. The Roman Church, especially the Roman pontiff, Teilhard seems to suggest, is, as it were, the central nervous system of the Body of Christ. So, the way to final fulfillment, in that sense, seems to pass through the doors of St. Peter's. But it is not the organization of the Body of Christ as much as its reality which fascinates Teilhard, particularly the reality of the cosmic Christ experienced in the Eucharist. Celebration of the Eucharist, according to Teilhard, is participation in the fullness of the final cosmic Christ, the finally formed Body of Christ or the Divine Milieu. In the Eucharist, Ultimate Charity is real in our own period of evolutionary history.

Teilhard thus has a certain mystical bent, which he would never have wanted to deny. He deeply values the mysteries of the Church, as the reality of the End Time in our own time. Still, he is much more concerned with *moral action*. He holds that the logical–existential result of the evolutionary process is that Christians are called to join with all men of good will in building a world society of peace and justice. Indeed, insofar as *anybody* works on building that society, he is building up the Body of Christ. We should pause to hear again the radicalness of Teilhard's concept: he is saying that the *concluding cosmic works of Christ can only and will only be done by the hands and the minds of men.* The final Kingdom of God will come only if men work, as they are free and empowered to do, to make it come. Only then, when the just world society, highly synthesized but nevertheless allowing for individual rights—only when this ultra-synthesized state is attained, will mankind truly be ready to be transformed into its final spiritualized Christic life. As Teilhard suggested in a note in 1918, Christ needs the results of man's labor so that he can reach his plenitude, his own fullness.

When Christ does reach his own fullness, his highly intensified, infinitely spiritualized Body will be the only surviving reality. Sheer physical reality will die a death of heatlessness and will disintegrate toward nothingness. But human reality will be transfigured into the white spiritual heat of Ultimate Charity, in the fullness of Christ. The members of the mystical Body will then be united once and for all to the Head, the final cephalization of the universe, which Teilhard refers to as an act of spiritual ecstasy in God. Then the vast universal process of evolution—cosmogenesis, biogenesis, homogenesis, and Christogenesis—will come to an end. The cosmic ascent of man will have reached its final goal.

4. TEILHARD'S ACHIEVEMENT IN RETROSPECT

Of the comprehensiveness and the imaginativeness of Teilhard's vision there can be little doubt. Here was a scientist who was not willing to rest content with what psychologist Gordon Allport once called "the itsy-bitsy empiricisms." Here was a theologian who was not content to remain safely sheltered in what some wag once referred to as the "stained-glass foxhole" of theology. Here was an intellectual visionary whose name is worthy of inclusion in a list of the greatest religious thinkers the modern West has produced.

Teilhard was a brilliant synthesizer. The hallmark of his thought might be said to be, to use his own terminology, "creative union." As we had occasion to observe in our review of Teilhard's intellectual inheritance, Teilhard creatively fused the tradition of speculative metaphysics with the tradition of biblical eschatology. In like manner, it should now be apparent, he brought the tradition of Darwinian science and the tradition of the Church's theology into a harmonious inter-relationship. Science and religion become brother and sister, according to Teilhard's schema. Teilhard also brought theory and practice, piety and morality, together in a most creative way. For Teilhard there is no thought and no prayer, legitimately, without a commitment to moral action, and vice versa. In the same vein, Teilhard resolutely sought to hold the Church and the world in the most intimate of interrelationships. For Teilhard, there could legitimately be no Church which was not actively engaged in "building the earth," and no world which could attain its own fulfillment apart from the Church. Along with all this, Teilhard vigorously sought to protect both the rights of the individual and the creative function of the collective, through the doctrine of ultimate reality as a personalizing force. Finally, Teilhard compassionately and forcefully sought to forge a link between the (sometimes hidden) hopes of all men and women for justice and peace, and the promises which he saw to be implicit in the story of evolution itself. Teilhard was an artist of universal synthesis and compelling relevance.

A thinker of this stature naturally exposes himself to criticism on a variety of fronts. Let us review some of these criticisms by raising some questions in conclusion.

One of Teilhard's most vulnerable points seems to be his use of the term "science." Teilhard divides his exposition into two major parts, as we have noted, on the one hand what he calls "science" or "phenomenology," on the other hand his self-consciously religious discourse, his theology. The first part describes the process of evolution from cosmogenesis through homogenesis, and poses the question of an Omega point. The second part identifies Christ as the Omega point and therefore is called Christogenesis. Teilhard holds that the first part can be undertaken by any scientist, in principle. Any scientist with eyes to see, Teilhard feels, will be able to observe the workings of the law of complexity-consciousness as a law of nature alongside of other natural laws. The second portion of Teilhard's argument, he maintains, can only be undertaken by someone who has an acquaintance with Christian revelation.

Is the first part of Teilhard's argument truly "science"? Teilhard says that *The Phenomenon of Man,* for example, is "purely and simply . . . a scientific treatise" (13:29). Is that what this work actually is? After all, perhaps *the* most important feature of natural science, as it is commonly understood, is the principle of empirical verification. And *The Phenomenon of Man* includes not only empirically verifiable scientific findings, but also certain empirically unverifiable hypotheses and prognostications.

The well-known neo-Darwinian biologist, George Gaylord Simpson, has criticized Teilhard severely at this point. Simpson holds that the major thrust of Teilhard's argument is unscientific, that the Jesuit's religious preconceptions *vitiate* his science (8:232). Simpson allows that evolution *is* directional, as any historical process must be; but, he says, evolution is *multi*-directional. It proceeds in many directions at once: "it is erratic and opportunistic" (8:229). Simpson then criticizes Teilhard for arbitrarily rejecting a scientific consensus when Teilhard reaffirms the traditional notion that evolution is unidirectional, that is, orthogenetic (8:230). Empirical science shows, according to Simpson, that man is just one of the many paths evolution has followed; man is hardly the main axis of evolution, scientifically speaking. In what sense, then, is Teilhard's science (or "phenomenology") actually scientific?

A related question can be addressed to Teilhard from a philosophical standpoint. Can the notion of a cosmic purpose be inferred from the scientific data as Teilhard tries to do? First, how can one legitimately extrapolate from the past into the future? Things may have "progressed" in some sense from the rocks and plants through the various animals to man, but on what basis can we say scientifically that they will progress any further? As a matter of fact, man may well destroy himself with thermonuclear bombs or poison himself to extinction with his own pollution. What will become of the Omega point then? Second, if the purpose of the cosmos is to evolve mind, why has the whole process taken so long? Is not mind more accidental than essential in the vast evolutionary process? Is not the idea that the cosmos's purpose is to evolve mind further discredited when we think about the complete isolation (as far as we know) of mankind on that insignificant planet called Earth, in one solar system of one of the galaxies in a universe composed of millions of galaxies? When we consider our vast universe dispassionately, can we really maintain that its underlying purpose is to produce a rational animal? The philosopher Bertrand Russell raised questions like these in his 1935 essay, "Cosmic Purpose." Russell concluded, "The Copernican revolution will not have done its work until it has taught men more modesty than is to be found among those who think man sufficient evidence of cosmic purpose" (7:233). This is the question for Teilhard at this point, then: has he really reversed the Copernican revolution with his own "Copernical revolution"? Has he shown convincingly that man is at the center of the universe and that this is evidence of cosmic purpose?

Criticism has naturally come Teilhard's way from the ranks of the theologians, too. Much of it has centered on his admitted optimism. His thought has been called in question at this point, we should note, not because he has held up hope at the end of the cosmic process, but because he has allegedly underplayed the role of *evil* in the course of the cosmic process, particularly in human history. Teilhard views death and suffering rather biologically, as the price evolution has to pay for progress. Now that may be all right for lemmings, but is it all right for man? Can one easily say that Dachau and Buchenwald, Hiroshima and Nagasaki, Vietnam and Biafra, are part of a Divinely ordained process? Or is there finally no rational explanation for evil? Moreover, can one place so much trust in the evolution of world society towards peace and righteousness? Isn't Teilhard viewing world history through rose-colored glasses? Is it not conceivable that world history may move to a stage of monolithic *1984*-style dictatorships? And what will happen if we do not reverse the horrendous trends of the contemporary ecological crisis? Could not the next stage of world history easily be a period of Thirty-Year-War style of famine conflicts, which will drive us back to the stone age? If any one of these events is a possibility, then, should we not take a more realistic, less optimistic, approach to present-day politics? Some might even want to argue that radical pessimism is the only realistic attitude to take to world history today.

Then a theological question can be raised regarding Teilhard's New Testament interpretation. Teilhard clearly sets the cosmic Christ of Colossians and Ephesians in the center of his vision. What then becomes of the Jesus pictured in the Gospels? Is the Jesus of history swept aside, away from his roots in history, by the cosmic Christ? Related to this point is the question regarding the role of the *individual*. The Jesus depicted in the Gospels seeks out individuals. The Christ depicted in the Letter to the Colossians rules over nations and the universe. With this in mind one can ask: Is there a totalitarian thrust in Teilhard's thought, perhaps so much that the individual is finally lost in the mass collective? Teilhard argued repeatedly, to be sure, that the individual is never lost in the totality. He pointed out, for example, that when an individual enters into a marriage covenant he gives up some of his autonomy but that, when the marriage is right, the relationship will allow him to attain more depth and uniqueness as an individual than ever before. All the more so, correspondingly, for the right kind of society; the individual will find his deepest fulfillment as a citizen of a world government. Still, Teilhard's principle of cephalization makes one wonder. It makes one think of the totalitarian slogan that perfect freedom is perfect obedience—a slogan to which Teilhard himself adhered strictly in his Jesuit life, even when the fruits of his life-work were threatened by the Vatican. How does Teilhard safeguard the role of the individual, and the individual's freedom, in the evolutionary process?

A somewhat different question, ironical perhaps when directed to such an evolutionary thinker as Teilhard, also arises from a theological perspective. When all has been said, do we not detect in Teilhard's thought the ancient Greek dualism between matter and spirit? For all his attention to nature, does Teilhard really treat matter positively in a convincing way? If he does not, is his thought really compatible with the biblical emphasis on the goodness of matter and the goodness of the human body in particular? For Teilhard, unquestionably, the greatness of man is his *mind;* likewise for the whole universe. Spirit is the goal of all things, or more specifically, spiritualized matter, as far as Teilhard is concerned. In contrast, the biblical writings strongly emphasize—rather materialistically—the new creation of heaven and earth, and the resurrection of the body. For Teilhard, at the very end the stars and the planets and all matter will drift back into nothingness; hyper-intensified spirit will remain. For the Bible, not only man, but also the earth and the stars and the planets will be saved. Teilhard's vision seems to be rather cramped at this point, compared to biblical thinking. Is Teilhard too spiritualistic?

Finally, we come to the traditional philosophical and theological question concerning the relation of faith and reason. Is it not the case that Teilhard simply knows too much? Does he not claim to know more than he can possibly know as a mortal, and—from a Christian standpoint—a sinful mortal at that? Bertrand Russell was raising this kind of question in his own way about those who were arguing for "cosmic purpose" on the basis of reason. Centuries ago, moreover, the same kind of question was raised implicitly by St. Paul when he confessed, "for now we see through a glass darkly, but then face to face" (I Cor. 13:12). Is not Teilhard's vision un-Pauline precisely because it is a *vision?* Is Teilhard's kind of rational synthesis really possible on this side of the veil of heaven? Can human reasoning—sinful human reasoning—really accomplish all that Teilhard tries to do? Or does reason have a margin beyond which it becomes vanity?

These are some of the questions that can be directed to Teilhard. They are sweeping questions, surely, but they have an eminently worthy object. For, however we finally evaluate Teilhard's vision, the magnificence and the brilliance of his intellectual achievement cannot be doubted.

NOTES

1 The theologies of Karl Barth, Emil Brunner, and Rudolf Bultmann are particularly exemplary here. For an analysis of Bultmann's thought, see Chapter 2 above.

2 In this regard, much of contemporary theology parallels the characteristic concerns expressed by modern "existential philosophy." This "philosophy of existence" is fundamentally a philosophy of *human* existence. It is mainly, sometimes exclusively, concerned with the life of man. This emphasis is particularly evident in the writings of Søren Kierkegaard, the Christian philosopher and theologian generally acknowledged to be the father of existential philosophy. See further Karl Löwith, "Nature, History, and Existentialism," *Social Research*, IX:1 (March, 1952), 79-94.

3 This point has been identified as the dominant theological motif of the Bible, by a number of biblical scholars. See, for example, G. Ernest Wright, *God Who Acts* (Chicago: Alec. R. Allenson, 1952). For another view, see H. Paul Santmire, *Brother Earth: Nature, God, and Ecology in a Time of Crisis* (New York: Thomas Nelson, 1970), ch. IV.

4 In Protestant theology the influence of the philosopher Immanuel Kant has been decisive at this point. Kant identified morality as the definitive human characteristic, rather than embodiment in a cosmic whole. In his major philosophical works, Kant did not seek to set forth a philosophy of the cosmos as such; he more or less accepted the findings of the natural sciences of his day (above all, Newton's physics) as final. See S. Körner, *Kant* (Harmondsworth, England: Penguin Books, 1955).

5 This is not to suggest that other modern Christian thinkers did not embark on a similar intellectual quest or deal with similar themes. See Ernst Benz, *Evolution and Christian Hope* (1:chs. IX, X). Teilhard remains a preeminent figure, however.

6 In this respect, Bultmann is very much an heir of Kant. See note 4 above.

7 With this drive for universal comprehensiveness and rational coherence, Teilhard aligns himself, at least implicitly, with the classical tradition of speculative Western philosophy. See section two of this chapter, "Teilhard's Intellectual Inheritance." For Teilhard's own description of the scope of his thought, see "My Universe," *Science and Christ* (14, esp. p. 38f.).

8 For a succinct statement of this principle by Teilhard, see *ibid.*, p. 39ff.

9 See, for example, Albert Camus, *The Myth of Sisyphus*, trans. Justin O'Brien (New York: Vintage Books, 1955).

10 Karl Barth's most famous work in this connection is his *Epistle to the Romans*, trans. E. C. Hoskyns (London: Oxford University Press, 1933).

11 One vivid introduction to the story of Teilhard's life is *The Teilhard de Chardin Album* (16). See further, Claude Cuénot, *Teilhard de Chardin: A Biographical Study* (Baltimore: Helicon Press, 1965).

12 Emile Rideau, *The Thought of Teilhard de Chadin*, trans. René Hague (New York: Harper & Row, 1967), p. 26. Cf. Rideau's striking remark (also p. 26): "Both in quantity and quality Teilhard's reading was somewhat deficient."

13 For a brief but convincing justification of this point, see Carl Braaten, *Christ and Counter-Christ* (Philadelphia: Fortress Press, 1972).

14 See Paul Tillich's essay, "The Struggle between Time and Space," *Theology of Culture*, ed. Robert C. Kimball (New York: Oxford University Press, 1959).

15 See Gustaf Wingren, *Man and the Incarnation: A Study in the Biblical Theology of Irenaeus*, trans. Ross Mackenzie (Philadelphia: Muhlenberg Press, 1959).

16 Teilhard, of course, was generally familiar with the philosophy of Karl Marx, but it is not clear whether he ever studied Marx's works with any thoroughness. See Rideau, *op. cit.*, ch. I.

BIBLIOGRAPHY

1. BENZ, ERNST, *Evolution and Christian Hope: Man's Concept of the Future, From the Early Fathers to Teilhard de Chardin,* trans. Heinz G. Frank. Garden City, N. Y.: Doubleday, 1968.

2. FARICY, ROBERT L., *Teilhard de Chardin's Theology of the Christian in the World.* New York: Sheed and Ward, 1967.

3. HEFNER, PHILIP, *The Promise of Teilhard: The Meaning of the Twentieth Century in Christian Perspective.* Philadelphia: J. B. Lippincott, 1970.

4. HUXLEY, JULIAN, *Religion Without Revelation.* New York: New American Library, 1957.

5. LOVEJOY, ARTHUR O., *The Great Chain of Being.* New York: Harper & Brothers, 1936.

6. DE LUBAC, HENRI, *Teilhard de Chardin: The Man and His Meaning,* trans. René Hague. New York: New American Library, 1965.

7. RUSSELL, BERTRAND, "Cosmic Purpose," in *Religion and Science.* New York: Henry Holt, 1935.

8. SIMPSON, GEORGE GAYLORD, *This View of Life: The World of an Evolutionist.* New York: Harcourt, Brace & World, 1947, ch. III.

9. TEILHARD DE CHARDIN, PIERRE, *Building the Earth,* no trans. Wilkes-Barre, Pa.: Dimension Books, 1965.

10. ———, *The Divine Milieu: An Essay on the Interior Life,* no trans. New York: Harper & Row, 1965.

11. ———, *The Future of Man,* trans. N. Denny. New York: Harper & Row, 1964.

12. ———, *Man's Place in Nature,* no trans. New York: Harper & Row, 1966.

13. ———, *The Phenomenon of Man,* trans. Bernard Wall, introduction by Julian Huxley. New York: Harper & Row, 1959.

14. ———, *Science and Christ,* trans. René Hague. New York: Harper & Row, 1969.

15. ———, *The Vision of the Past,* trans. J. M. Cohen. New York: Harper & Row, 1966.

16. *The Teilhard de Chardin Album,* JEANNE MORTIER and MARIE-LOUISE AUBOUX, eds. New York: Harper & Row, 1966.

17. TRESMONTANT, CLAUDE, *Pierre Teilhard de Chardin: His Thought,* no trans. Baltimore: Helicon Press, 1959.

SUGGESTED READINGS

1. *Primary Readings*

The Divine Milieu (10:43-155). A meditative essay on "the inward vision," outlining Teilhard's approach to the spiritual life.

The Future of Man (11). A collection of shorter papers by Teilhard, written over a period of thirty years, dealing with philosophical and theological themes. Best read selectively as complementary material for Teilhard's major books and essays.

How I Believe, trans. René Hague (New York: Harper & Row, 1969). A readable outline of Teilhard's most fundamental beliefs.

"My Universe," in *Science and Christ* (14:37-85). Perhaps the best brief statement of Teilhard's thought available in English.

The Phenomenon of Man (13:esp. pp. 11-50, 53-66, 163-166, 174-176, 180-183f., 213-244f., 254-275f., 284-313). Teilhard's magnum opus, a book that must be read by the student at some point for a full appreciation of Teilhard's achievement.

2. *Secondary Readings*

Benz, Ernst, *Evolution and Christian Hope* (1). A historical survey which focuses on Teilhard's theological heritage.

Faricy, Robert, *Teilhard de Chardin's Theology of the Christian in the World* (2). A readable treatment of an important Teilhardian theme, in the context of his thought as a whole.

Hefner, Philip, *The Promise of Teilhard* (3) An excellent essay on the relevance of Teilhard for the contemporary cultural and theological milieu.

Lovejoy, Arthur O., *The Great Chain of Being* (5). A lengthy classic study which deals with a major Western intellectual theme. Although Teilhard is not treated, this work is important background reading.

Tresmontant, Claude, *Pierre Teilhard de Chardin: His Thought* (17). A clear exposition of the major themes of Teilhard's thought, with a glossary of Teilhard's terms.

3. *Additional Bibliography*

Almago, Romano, *A Basic Teilhard Bibliography* (New York: American Teilhard Association, 1968, 1970). Extensive citation.

Mooney, Christopher F., *Teilhard de Chardin and the Mystery of Christ* (New York: Doubleday, 1966), pp. 289-304. Cites basic primary and secondary materials.

III

SOCIAL THEORY
AND RELIGION

5

Religion: Social Narcotic and Reactionary Ideology

"Religion . . . is the *opium* of the people." Everyone who has heard the name of Karl Marx knows this celebrated dictum. Everyone knows that Marx was an atheist. He taught that the people had to abolish religion. The fantasy compensations of heaven must be destroyed. "Pie now, not pie in the sky when you die!" The energies of men must be liberated for the socialist revolution. True earthly happiness will be found in the communist society. In the new society religion will be rendered obsolete once and for all.

To comprehend the full force of Marx's critique of religion expressed by these slogans, we must clear the ground ahead. First, cold war rhetoric commonly anathematized the thought of Marx in the popular Western mind with the phrase "atheistic communism." [1] Yet it is an error to make a simplistic identification of Marx's social theory with the political system of Russian communism, particularly in its Stalinist form when the cold war was most intense. [2] Further, Marx himself did not advocate religious persecution and discrimination; he opposed it. His critique of religion would contradict itself if it justified attacks on religious people as such. One cannot, therefore, simply blame Marx's criticism of religion for antireligious actions by later communist governments.

The second preliminary observation concerns the nature of Marx's atheism. Marx is a "social atheist," and not an anti-theist; he is concerned with the *social function* of religion, not with philosophical disputes about the existence or non-existence of God. [3] Nowhere in his writings do we find any arguments designed to refute the traditional "proofs" for the existence of God, such as those advanced by theologians and philosophers like Anselm and Thomas Aquinas, Descartes and Spinoza. Marx refuses to attack religion on its own terms, and should not be classed with that type of atheism which is a reverse image of the theism it opposes. He is not an anti-theist, but a critic of the reactionary social role which religion plays in supporting an exploitative social system. He is engaged not in theoretical polemics but in criticism which is the fuse for political action. His aim is not to score debating points but to win a social revolution.

Having cleared the ground of these potential obstructions, we must now gather our resources. We need some knowledge of the personal careers of Marx and his lifelong friend and collaborator Friedrich Engels, seen in the context of the economic, industrial and political conditions of Europe and Britain at the time they worked and wrote. Then we need some information about the religious attitudes which were common in the national and international affairs of the period. We also need some familiarity with the philosophical currents in Germany in the early nineteenth century which flowed into the thought of Marx and Engels. The present-day English reader finds a number of important but unfamiliar terms and assumptions in their writings; so far as the criticism of religion is concerned, the background for understanding these concepts can be found chiefly in the writings of the philosophers Hegel and Feuerbach.

With these resources we will be able to understand the main theses of Marx's critique of religion: that the exploitation and class conflict of capitalist society produce human alienation; that religion is a projection reflecting this alienation; that this projection represents a protest of the exploited proletariat suffering under oppressive conditions; that it is a narcotic protest which provides relief and comfort at the price of addicting the proletariat to the status quo which exploits them; that the compensatory fantasy world of religion is an immobilizing drug which rationalizes and legitimates the oppressive capitalist system; that it inculcates the servile virtues of submission, suffering, weakness, humility, patience and forgiveness of enemies, thereby repressing revolutionary energies; that the capitalist class with its vested interest in the status quo is the true profiteer from religious sublimation and compensation; and that the revolutionary overthrow of the class structure of capitalist society will abolish the reactionary social role of religion and remove the conditions in which it thrives.

1. THE SOCIAL MATRIX OF MARX

Karl Marx (1818–1883) was born in the Rhineland of Germany into the family of a Jewish lawyer, and numbered rabbis among his ancestors on both sides of the family. Neither the family nor the young Marx were devout Jews, however; the father was a devotee of Voltaire and Rousseau rather than of Torah and Talmud. Indeed, like a number of other Jewish families in Germany at the time, Marx's parents wished to take advantage of the social emancipation which followed the Enlightenment ideal of tolerance and the principles of liberty and equality heralded in the French Revolution. So they made a *pro forma* conversion to Christianity in 1824 and young Karl was baptized at the age of six. But this was a rite of social transition, and not the occasion for a personal religious crisis. The church membership ticket represented not a passport to heaven but, as Marx's Jewish compatriot Heinrich Heine put it, "an entrance card into the community of European culture" (15:3). Thus, Marx's writings against religion do not bear the scars of a childhood religious trauma; while his writing is vivid, passionate and polemical, it is the passion of a social clinician, not the therapeutic involvement of a patient, which is evident.

Marx's criticism of religion is found in his earliest work. It appears in his doctoral dissertation of 1841, together with criticism of Hegel's philosophy. As a result of his alignment with the radical Hegelians he was prevented from gaining an academic post. His writings criticizing the Prussian government led to official pressure which forced him to leave Germany in 1843. The next year he met Friedrich Engels who soon became his most intimate friend, collaborator, and financial benefactor.

Engels (1820–1895) was born into a Calvinist family in Barmen, Germany; his father was a wealthy industrialist in one of the most typical enterprises of the period, namely, cotton manufacturing. In 1842 he went for a time to Manchester, England, where one of his father's cotton mills was located. When Engels returned to Germany he published a vivid and passionate indictment of industrial squalor in his book, *The Condition of the Working Class in England* (1845). By this time Marx was in Paris, already deeply immersed in the study of economics and philosophy, particularly French socialism and communism. Expelled from France because of continuing pressures from the Prussian Government, Marx went to Brussels where he and Engels collaborated on two books, joined the Communist League, and in 1848 jointly issued *The Communist Manifesto*. He was then expelled from Brussels and, after a brief time in Germany where he was acquitted of a charge of fomenting armed insurrection, he renounced his Prussian citizenship; in 1849 Marx went into exile in London where he spent the rest of his life.

Engels joined him in England the following year. From 1854 to 1870 he was a partner in his father's Manchester cotton mill, using his income to support Marx and his family who lived in great poverty. Marx and Engels both continued their research and individual writings in economics, politics, philosophy and history. They also lectured widely and organized the workers. In 1864 they founded the International Working-men's Association in London to replace the then defunct Communist League. From 1866 onwards they organized the several congresses of the International in various European cities.

The unifying purpose of all this activity was the critical analysis of capitalist society, and the preparation of the theoretical and political foundation for a communist society. This society, as described in the *Manifesto*, is to be a true democracy in which "the freedom of each is the condition for the free development of all." It will be a society without social classes. Private ownership of the means of production will be abolished; the economy will be governed not by profit but by rational planning. Goods and services will be equally distributed. The classless, communist society will not need the coercive apparatus of police, courts, and army which the dominant capitalist class now uses to oppress the proletariat.

Upon the death of Marx in 1883, Engels became his literary executor, editor, interpreter and defender. In his eulogy for Marx at the graveside in Highgate Cemetery, London, Engels summarized the contribution of his friend in the following words:

> As Darwin discovered the law of evolution in organic nature, so Marx discovered the law of evolution in human history: the simple fact, previously hidden under ideological growths, that human beings must first of all eat, drink, shelter and clothe themselves before they can turn their attention to politics, science, art and religion; that therefore the production of the immediate material means of life . . . forms the basis on which the State institutions, the legal principles, the art, and even the religious ideas of the people . . . have developed and out of which they must be explained . . . (15:531).

Marx described nineteenth-century industrial society as comprised essentially of two classes: the capitalist bourgeoisie—industrialists, manufacturers and merchants, all engaged in the business of profit; and the proletariat—laboring men who worked for a wage, whose production made the profits for the capitalists. Marx recognized, naturally, that there were still aristocratic and peasant remnants of an earlier social order, but he did not regard them as determinative; they were not in the center of the economic stage.

In Marx's diagnosis, exploitation is the essence of class relations in capitalism. Without the work of the propertyless masses there would be no profit, yet the profit they produced went into capitalist pockets, property, bank accounts, and the accumulation of still more capital. By owning mines, factories and other means of production, the capitalist class had a monopoly on the control of the economy. The proletariat was at the mercy of the capitalists.

Marx and Engels judged the capitalist system to be essentially un-just in theory and completely dehumanizing in practice. They saw that the conditions of life and work for the proletariat were intolerable, and this notwithstanding the fact that mid-nineteenth century Britain was the leading industrial and commercial power of the world. During the 1840's —the time Engels wrote his book on the English working class—the conditions of life of the common member of the working mass may be sketched as follows: without job security and for subsistence wages he works twelve to thirteen hours a day, six days a week; his wife probably does likewise, and his children begin working six and one half hours per day at age nine, increasing to twelve hours per day at age thirteen; his education is extremely primitive, with the result that he cannot write and can barely read; he lives in a densely crowded slum of dilapidated houses lining unpaved streets strewn with stinking rubbish; for six days a week a pall of industrial smoke hangs over his town, and the river that, in Engel's words, enters it "crystal-clear and undefiled . . . leaves it thick, black and stinking with every imaginable kind of refuse" (1:48); he is ill fed, often eating spoiled and adulterated food; he is unable to afford adequate clothing and not infrequently is clad in rags, while many women and children in his town have no shoes; infant mortality and fatal childhood accidents have a high incidence in his family, and little medical care is available; among his fellow workers unemployment and indigence is often widespread, death from starvation and fatal illness resulting from undernourishment is not uncommon, while begging and petty theft to get the barest necessities of life are everyday phenomena.[4] Surveying this picture of wretchedness and degradation, Engels concludes, with eloquent brevity, that the factory hand has been turned into "a soulless factor of production and . . . deprived of his humanity" (1:116). It is no wonder that in 1848 the *Manifesto* summoned the workers to revolution: "Let the ruling classes tremble at a communist revolution. The proletarians have nothing to lose but their chains. They have a world to win. Working men of all countries unite!" (9:168)

What role were the Christian churches playing in such a society? Since we cannot go into the complex historical details, we must take an example of the sort of attitude which impressed Marx as typical. Rather than setting up a straw man, we will select someone of recognized stature, a progressive leader who expressed a Christian social conscience in his lifelong efforts to ameliorate degrading social conditions. Such a man was William Wilberforce, the English statesman, humanitarian and philanthropist.[5] Wilberforce is best remembered for leading the long and successful campaign in Parliament to abolish first the slave trade and then the very institution of slavery itself. He also pressed for more humane criminal laws, and advocated legislation giving the same civil rights to British Catholics as those enjoyed by the Protestant majority. How, then, does this devout, progressive leader view the bearing of religion on the miserable life of the working class.

In 1797 Wilberforce published a book with one of those marvelous, and in this case revealing, eighteenth-century titles: *A Practical View of the Prevailing Religious System of Professed Christians in the Higher and Middle Classes in this Country contrasted with Real Christianity*. In it he argues that Christianity roots out man's "natural selfishness" in order to plant in its place a humble but vigorous benevolence. Christianity therefore teaches the affluent to be liberal, and those in authority to be restrained.

> Thus, softening the glare of wealth, and moderating the insolence of power, she renders the inequalities of the social state less galling to the lower orders, whom also she instructs, in their turn, to be diligent, humble, patient: reminding them that their more lowly path has been allotted to them by the hand of God; that it is their part faithfully to discharge its duties, and contentedly to bear its inconveniences; that the present state of things is very short; that the objects about which worldly men conflict so eagerly are not worth the contest; that the peace of mind which Religion offers to all ranks indiscriminately, affords more true satisfaction than all the expensive pleasures which are beyond the poor man's reach; that in this view, however, the poor have the advantage, and that if their superiors enjoy more abundant comforts, they are also exposed to many temptations from which the inferior classes are happily exempted; that, "having food and raiment, they should be therewith content," for that their situation in life, with all its evils, is better than they have deserved at the hand of God; finally, that all human distinctions will soon be done away, and the true followers of Christ will all, as children of the same Father, be alike admitted to the possession of the same heavenly inheritance. Such are the blessed effects of Christianity on the temporal well-being of political communities.[6]

While Wilberforce wrote at a time of considerable social unrest, industrial conditions were probably worse half a century later in Marx's time. But Wilberforce's sentiments had an enduring appeal, since the book was regularly reprinted during Marx's lifetime, running to over twenty editions throughout the nineteenth century. Needless to say, such religious sentiments were typical of those Marx totally repudiated.

On the international scene Marx saw heads of state employing religion in a similarly oppressive way. As one who had been brought up on the anti-monarchical ideals of the French Revolution—liberty, equality, fraternity—he observed the marriage between throne and altar which resulted in the birth of the Holy Alliance in 1815. Fathered by Czar Alexander I of Russia, assisted by Francis I of Austria and Frederick William III of Prussia, the alliance was later joined by other European nations who pledged themselves to base their relations on "the sublime truths which the holy religion of our Savior teaches" so that "the precepts of justice, Christian charity and peace . . . would have an immediate influence on the Councils of Princes and guide all their steps." European liberals saw it as a mask for less exalted ends, such as the Russian desire to contain British sea power, and Austria's determination to retain its possessions in Italy. So the Holy Alliance became a symbol of the pursuit of imperial interests by the monarchies of the great powers, their buttressing of traditional aristocratic society against radical social change, and the autocratic repression of revolutionary ideals and movements—all sanctioned by "the holy religion of our Savior." The banner of religion flew at the head of a royal crusade of reaction and counter-revolution. The meaning of such pious pretenses is clear; we have every reason to believe that the point was not lost on Marx.

2. PHILOSOPHICAL BACKGROUND TO MARX'S CRITIQUE

One of the anvils on which Marx hammered out his thought was the German philosophical tradition. In particular, his response to the writings of two philosophers, G. W. F. Hegel (1770–1831) and Ludwig Feuerbach (1804–1872), was decisive for his thinking about society and religion.[7] Each of them strongly influenced Marx, and also provoked sharp disagreements from him. We will consider four topics which emerge from this philosophical background and bear upon Marx's critique of religion: materialism, history, alienation, and Feuerbach's philosophy of religion.

Materialism

Marx's materialism was in direct opposition to Hegel's philosophical idealism. "Idealism" here is not a social and moral category suggesting reforming zeal and ethical commitment; it is a technical term expressing the view that *ideas*, mind, intellect, and consciousness are ultimate and are the essence of reality itself. When Hegel said that man is essentially "spirit" (*Geist*), he was not denying man's body and the material world or invoking the popular religious notion of the soul and its other-worldly destiny; he meant that man is essentially a being of conscious mind and ideas, and that these are the decisive elements in society and history.

Marx rejected this idealism in favor of "materialism," which also needs explanation. Marx did not mean, of course, that man is simply a body of matter devoid of freedom, creativity, thought, feeling, and imagination; on the contrary he valued these highly.[8] Nor did he suggest that the acquisition of goods and possessions was the chief purpose of life—which is what "materialism" tends to suggest in a consumer society. He was arguing, rather, that the economic structure of society was the "foundation" or "basis" on which the whole of life is built. The other aspects of life are shaped and conditioned by the foundation on which they stand. Specifically, the organization of the means of production—not spirit, mind, and ideas—is determinative for society. Marx's opposition to any "idealistic" philosophy is apparent in his famous statement:

> The mode of production in material life determines the general character of the social, political and spiritual processes of life. It is not the consciousness of men that determines their existence but, on the contrary, their social existence determines their consciousness (12:11f.).

Marx built his analysis of ideology on this insight that all forms of human consciousness are conditioned by economic organization and relations between social classes. Since religion cannot be understood apart from its role in capitalist ideology, we must examine this concept further. All the ideas of consciousness—including religious ideas—are informed and determined by the socioeconomic conditions out of which they grow. Consciousness is consciousness *in* and *of* the existing order, and reflects that order. The dominant ideas of a society, therefore, are the ideas of its dominant class; they comprise the *ideology* which legitimates and rationalizes the self-interest of the particular dominant class. Political theories are not based on self-evident truths, legal systems are not founded on the axioms of natural law, philosophical positions are not established by pure reason, and religious beliefs are not given by divine revelation; they all fundamentally reflect the economic relations of society. In Marx's terms, consciousness is a "superstructure" built on the foundation of the mode of production. Ideas do not determine society; society determines ideas. So long as ideas and thought merely reflect the economic self-interest of the dominant social class, they remain ideological and constitute a "false consciousness."

In making this sociological critique of ideas as ideology, Marx's argument is similar to Freud's psychological critique of reason as rationalization of unconscious psychic drives and processes. Like Freud, Marx also held that it was possible for men to free themselves from the unconscious determination of their reason and to think rationally and scientifically; he made precisely this claim for his own thought. By making an empirical study of the economic organization of society and its class structure, the social analyst can expose the ideological function of legal, philosophical, economic, moral, and religious idea systems; his analysis reveals their unconscious socioeconomic determinants. Such a scientific analysis enables him to propose a new social system, not designed to further the self-interest of the capitalist elite, but rationally planned for the well-being of all.

History

Marx borrowed from Hegel and also reacted against him in formulating his own view of history. For Hegel, life and reality is not static—it is a historical process. History is the process in which reality is realizing itself. It is a process in which spirit differentiates and develops itself. History, however, is not simply the development of finite human spirits. Immanent in the history of human spirit is the creative power of the Absolute Spirit, or God. Hegel's idealism not only gave primacy to the human mind and its ideas in the historical process, it also produced a view of history which was essentially religious. History was, in the last analysis, the unfolding of the Divine Spirit.

Marx agreed with Hegel that history was a social process. In rejecting Hegel's idealism, however, he not only attacked the view that spirit, both finite and Absolute, was the driving power of history; he also abandoned the religious approach to history which it entailed. History for Marx is made by the work of man, who transforms nature for his own purposes and creates human society for the fulfillment of mankind. His philosophy of history is humanistic, naturalistic, and secular. Religion does not aid man's historical work and destiny, or empower his creativity; it suppresses and impoverishes him.

Hegel held that history did not develop gradually in a straight line of progress; rather, the new in history emerged out of the old by a process of tensions and conflicts. It is a dialectical *process* which proceeds, according to the familiar formulation, by a movement of thesis, antithesis, and synthesis. As a modern example, Hegel might offer the following: against an established system, a movement of protest arises which sets freedom and individual conscience in opposition to traditional authority and power. This thesis is countered by an antithesis: an appeal to law and order and the suppression of dissent. Out of this confrontation comes a resolution, or a synthesis. What it will be, or what forms of thesis and antithesis will follow the synthesis, cannot be predicted. We can know, however, that the historical process as a whole discloses this dialectical pattern. Hegel understood this historical dialectic as a dramatic conflict and development in which Absolute Spirit came to self-realization and self-consciousness. *Concept of fate*

For Marx, Hegel's view that Spirit is the mover of history is a piece of mystification. The mystification, however, conceals a truth, for history *is* a dialectical process in which the new emerges out of oppositions and negations. But these are not the dialectics of the inner life of Spirit; they are the dialectics of material forces, i.e., economic classes: masters and slaves in antiquity, feudal lords and serfs in the Middle Ages, and bourgeoisie and proletariat in modern times. In the struggle of socioeconomic classes we see not the mystified but the real dynamics of history. Hegel's dialectic had been the philosopher's analytical principle for interpreting social history; Marx transformed it into a revolutionary weapon for changing the world.[9]

Alienation

In Marx's view, man was intended to realize his authentic humanity through his work. Man is able to project goals and to actualize them by his labor. He is not static and predetermined once and for all; he is an historical being with the power to create. In his work man can transform nature to serve human well-being, he can build a human society for the good of all, and in doing this he fulfills and realizes his true nature. Man is *homo faber.*

Yet this is hardly what Marx sees happening among his fellows. He sees their work not as self-realization but as alienation. "Alienation," and the related notion of "objectification," was a central philosophical concept in Hegel and Feuerbach which Marx transformed in typical fashion.

There are several components in Marx's description of alienation. Under the capitalist system of production, the worker is alienated from *himself* as a human being. He is an instrument of production, an anonymous unit in the labor pool. He is hired and paid according to the market laws of supply and demand, which apply as much to human beings as to soulless raw materials like coal and iron ore. Similarly, the worker is alienated from the *purpose* of work. He cannot be a free and creative human being since the goal of the system is profit, not human fulfillment. Likewise he is alienated from the *process* of work. Since the capitalist owns the means of production as his private property, he dictates how work shall be done for maximum efficiency and productivity. The worker is depersonalized and becomes, in Marx's words, "the flesh-and-blood appendage to a steel machine" (6:60). Further, the worker is alienated from the *product* of his work; he is a maker of commodities which are ruled by the laws of the market, not a contributor to common human projects which he personally supports.

The cause of alienation, Marx holds, is the capitalist system of private ownership of the means of production. This, in itself, is a fundamental alienation. The elite capitalist class not only has control over human resources, technology, and the economy; it has a monopoly on centuries of human achievement. Roger Garaudy states the point nicely:

When a man works, his activity partakes of all previous humanity; his work is the expression of the species-life of man, of all the creations accumulated by the human race. Now, when the means of production are private property, all this patrimony in which the creative work of all past humanity is embodied . . . is in the hands of certain individuals who thus control all the contributions accumulated by millenia of human labor and genius (6:60).

Under capitalism the worker is alienated from the heritage of mankind.

In being alienated from the purpose, the process, and the product of his work, the worker is alienated from himself and from his fellowmen. He is an object, not a person; competition, not co-operation, characterizes human relations under this system. While Marx saw many forms of alienation pervading and perverting every aspect of human life, the origin of it all is the alienation of labor. This negated man at the point where he should be most truly and creatively himself. Religion was for Marx a symptom and an ally of alienation. Ludwig Feuerbach first gave him an insight into religion as alienation. Marx then radicalized Feuerbach's theory.

Feuerbach's Theory of Religion

Feuerbach's criticism of Hegel's philosophical idealism was the catalyst that enabled Marx to develop his own materialism. Feuerbach's writing concentrated on the interpretation of religion, and this was the point of his most radical inversion of Hegel.[10] According to Hegel, the whole of history is a process in which the Divine Spirit is immanent in the spirit of mankind as the creative, moving power. The truth symbolized in religion, Hegel explained, is that the Absolute Spirit "objectifies" itself and eventually comes to self-consciousness in the human mind. Mankind, we might say, is a means for the self-realization of God.

Feuerbach turns this reasoning upside down. Religion is not the Divine Spirit coming to self-realization in man; rather, in the idea of God, men have expressed human qualities and powers to come to an awareness of themselves. The ideas of God and his attributes, Feuerbach contends, are nothing other than the objectified powers and attributes of *man himself*. God is, so to speak, the projection of universal humanity in a cosmic image. The secret of theology is that it is nothing other than a "mystified" form of anthropology.

> Man—this is the mystery of religion—projects his being into objectivity, and then again makes himself an object to this projected image of himself thus converted into . . . [an independent] subject . . . God is, *per se*, his relinquished self . . . (3:29ff.).

This means that when religious man speaks of the Divine power, knowledge, wisdom, and love, he is speaking of precisely those qualities in himself which he has objectified and projected as a Supreme Being. Man deludes and deprives himself if he imagines that God is anything other than the objectified form of his own humanity.

Yet this is exactly what Feuerbach believed was happening in modern religion. Whereas in earlier stages of religion men were able to reappropriate the objectified image in a magnified form, infused with love and grace, this was no longer possible. What was objectified had now become alienated. Man's own powers, objectified in God, are alienated from his own being. But if religion results in man relinquishing his powers, it impoverishes him; its effect is not man's salvation, but his degradation. Over against this fantastic Supreme Being upon whom he has conferred all his own powers, man is a weak and emasculated creature. Therefore Feuerbach writes:

> Religion is the disuniting of man from himself; he sets God before him as the antithesis of himself. God is not what man is—man is not what God is. God is the infinite, man the finite being; God is perfect, man imperfect; God eternal, man temporal; God almighty, man weak; God holy, man sinful (2:33).

If man is to find his true fulfillment, Feuerbach concludes, he must take back and reintegrate into himself his own powers which have been alienated from himself in religion. God must be "humanized" that man may become man. Atheism is the prerequisite for salvation. In denying God, Feuerbach explains, he is not regressing to the antiquated theistic controversy about the objective existence of God; he is registering his rejection of the religious negation of man. For Feuerbach, then, religion is the expression of man's feeling toward his ideal of his true nature. True religion is a natural, humanistic religion of love.

Marx appropriated Feuerbach's view that religion was a mode of man's alienation from his own true nature. However, Marx radicalized this position. Religious alienation was only a symptom, not an independent and self-explanatory phenomenon.[11] Marx diagnosed the real source of all forms of alienation in the dehumanizing conditions of labor under capitalism. For this reason, Marx had no interest in Feuerbach's naturalistic, true religion; even atheism was *passé*. Since the communist revolution would abolish the social conditions which produced alienation, there would be no foundation for religion of any kind. Unlike Feuerbach, Marx did not criticize religion to reform or transform it, but to abolish it.

"The *criticism of religion* . . . is the premise of all criticism" (14:41), Marx said in a famous statement. But what is the purpose and nature of his criticism? Its purpose is to clear the way for revolutionary thinking and action. Since Marx holds that social existence determines consciousness, it necessarily follows that social existence must be changed before a new consciousness can emerge in a society. In the meantime, there is no point in academic religious debates with believers; criticism of religion is designed to serve those open to revolutionary thinking. For them, the criticism of religion cannot be an end in itself; [12] it is only the beginning, the premise, of all criticism because Marx sees religion as the reactionary, ultimate sanction in an exploitative society. If this premise is contradicted, then the whole theory and practice of capitalism can be undermined. From the criticism of religion the revolutionary moves on to the criticism of politics and the revolutionary struggle.

The nature of Marx's criticism is therefore a diagnosis of a false ideological consciousness. The diagnosis is like the process in psychotherapy by which the patient gains insight into the unconscious factors determining his life, and so is helped to change. Marx's social diagnosis of religion helps to clear the way for revolution and the new communist society. In this society religion will become dysfunctional; like the state apparatus (police, courts, army), religion will "wither away." This being the case, there is no reason for a crusade against religion. True revolutionary action is directed to changing socioeconomic conditions. It does not involve persecution and personal attacks on religious people. That would be a contradictory and self-defeating strategy which only produces enemies and religious martyrs.

One additional observation should be made about Marx's critique. Here we shall concentrate on the characteristically "Marxist" attack on religion in his writings. Like other thinkers in the Enlightenment tradition, Marx naturally used new scientific and historical findings to discredit religious beliefs and the authority of the Bible and the Church.[13] Such criticism he shares in common with many others. Yet while his use of Enlightenment criticism is interesting and while it is a general support for his own position, it is not distinctive of his original contribution to the analysis of the social function of religion. What is distinctive and original is his theory of religion as a social epiphenomenon, a variable of the socioeconomic system.[14]

Since Marx discusses the role of religion in a two-class society, it is appropriate to examine his theory of religion from two angles: its function for the proletariat, and its function for the capitalists.[15] As we shall see, it is Marx's general model of the economic relations between the two classes in capitalist society which links these two aspects together. We begin with the proletariat, for the theory serves as a social diagnosis to liberate this class from its present oppression.

3. OPPRESSIVE COMPENSATION:
RELIGION AS A SOCIAL NARCOTIC

Marx holds, like Feuerbach, that "*man makes religion, religion does not make man*" (14:41). Religion does not originate from a source independent of man, such as Divine revelation in the Christian and Jewish traditions, or even the Absolute Spirit of Hegel's philosophy. Nor is there any aspect of human nature itself which necessitates religious activity, analogous, for example, to the way sexual instincts lead to sexual behavior. In no sense does religion have an independent source; it is an epiphenomenon, a by-product of other processes.

Marx describes the religious consciousness, or idea system, as arising out of actual human conditions. He calls it a "reflection," "reflex," and "superstructure" of the real world. Though not comprising the whole of religious consciousness, the idea of a heavenly realm independent of and superior to the earthly world is seen by him as central to the Christian religious consciousness. This is a duplicate world, but it is the sort of duplicate to be found in a mirror which inverts the object it is reflecting. Thus, Marx explains, the sufferings of earth are reversed in the expectation of heavenly bliss; or, human suffering is said to be ultimately caused by God's punishment of sin, whereas in reality that suffering results from the oppression and exploitation of other men.

Why do men make a religious fantasy world of this sort? Why do they cherish these illusions of the religious consciousness? Marx believes that Feuerbach was on the track of the answer. Feuerbach had argued that in religious objectification modern man becomes alienated from his own powers, that the projected divine and heavenly world comes into existence as man divests himself of his own being. Marx argues, however, that Feuerbach does not give an adequate explanation of man's alienation. He has described the growing process and fruit of the religious tree, but has not laid bare its roots and soil and nourishment. If the projected religious realm reflects human conditions, and if the reflected image involves an alienation, then, Marx contends, we must find in society itself the actual alienation which is reflected in religion.

> The fact that the secular foundation detaches itself from itself and establishes itself in the clouds as an independent realm is really only to be explained by the self-cleavage and self-contradictoriness of this secular basis (14:70).

For Marx alienation can only be fully explained in terms of the social class alienation in a capitalist society. "Feuerbach," Marx writes, "does not see that the 'religious sentiment' is itself a *social product,* and that the abstract individual whom he analyzes belongs in reality to a particular form of society" (14:71).

Capitalist society, as a two-class system of an exploiting and an oppressed class, has social alienation in its very heart. More particularly, since the worker is treated merely as a producing commodity in the labor pool, he is alienated from his own humanity. Even what he produces is alienated from him, since it is not a fulfillment of his own creativity, nor for his personal use, nor is he in any way involved in the decisions governing production; he is only a producer of commodities made for the purpose of capitalist profit.

This is the proper context to understand the celebrated dictum of Marx with which we began. But we must consider the full statement.

> *Religious* distress is at the same time the *expression* of real distress and the *protest* against real distress. Religion is the sigh of the oppressed creature, the heart of a heartless world, just as it is the spirit of a spiritless situation. It is the *opium* of the people (14:42).

The word "people" here, it should be stressed, does not include everybody; it specifically refers to the proletariat. Marx does not use the opium metaphor when speaking of the function of religion for the capitalist class. It is notable that Marx's description of religion in this passage is full of sympathy, and indeed, of pathos. Religion is the "sigh" of the oppressed, the beating "heart" and life of a cold body politic, and a manifestation of "spirit" in a dispirited human condition. For religion is a form of protest, and any sort of protest, however misguided, however sublimated, however self-defeating, is nevertheless a sign of life in opposition to intolerable exploitation. If men create a glorious fantasy-world of religion and set it over against the real world, this amounts to a judgment upon and a rejection of prevailing conditions, a will to negate what negates their humanity, and a spark of hope for better things.

This makes it evident that for Marx religion is not just an arbitrary and meaningless construction, but an expression of real distress. It is rooted in the real needs of men, and has an intelligible function in life. Religion may be an illusory and self-defeating response to human problems, but it is not an accidental and meaningless one. The proletariat takes its religious opium in response to actual pain. Just as the drug addict or the alcoholic is simultaneously seeking relief from his sufferings and making a protest against his social and personal condition, so it is with religion.

Hence Marx does not hold that the narcotic of religion is violently imposed upon the unwilling proletariat by an opportunistic capitalist class. While he certainly believes that the only real and tangible benefit of religion is that which accrues to the capitalists, this does not deny that the proletariat takes the opium of religion willingly as a relief from suffering and a protest against it. While Marx argues that there is a necessary component of deception and illusion in religion, it is above all *self-deception* which he has in mind. While he regards religion as a fraud, it is not a deliberate hoax knowingly perpetrated by scheming priests upon an unwilling and gullible populace. Marx was familiar with this viewpoint, but regarded it as giving an inadequate explanation of even the disguising and deceiving function of religion. Engels put it as follows:

> A religion that brought the Roman world empire into subjection and dominated by far the larger part of civilized humanity for 1800 years cannot be disposed of merely by declaring it to be nonsense gleaned together by frauds (14:195).
>
> Religions are founded by people who feel a need for religion themselves and have a feeling for the religious needs of the masses (14:197).

What, then, is the particular need to which religion appeals in the proletariat, and why does this sublimated protest take the form that it does?

The need is above all for *compensation*, or, to use Marx's own term, "consolation" (14:41). Just as the alcoholic may in his drunken fantasy imagine himself to be everything which he is not in actual life—a hero, a great lover, a business tycoon—so religious imagery provides compensation for the intolerable conditions of the worker's life. He anticipates redress in the heavenly world after death. In that blessed state there will be no pain, misery and suffering; poverty will be replaced by an extravagant abundance of mansions and golden streets; eternal rest will replace ceaseless labor; man will no longer oppress his fellows as inferiors, but, as Wilberforce put it, "all human distinctions will . . . be done away" when all men are "children of the same Father." Under the influence of religious opium the proletarian enters the sleep in which present misery is forgotten, and he dreams of the heavenly world in which he will be vindicated and fulfilled. He thereby gains a fantasy compensation and consolation.

For this dubious benefit, however, the worker pays an inordinately high price. The price he must pay for his religious drug is addiction to the status quo. For it is not possible to have the compensatory images without the other ingredients of the religious consciousness, and the social function of these ingredients is precisely to justify and reinforce the established socioeconomic system which exploits him. We can group the functions of these other ingredients, which make the addiction an oppressive one, under two main heads: the *rationalization* of the existing order, and the *inculcation of servile virtues.*

Religious *rationalization* of the status quo takes the form of various teachings which explain and sanction existing conditions of life, and which minimize the sufferings these conditions bring upon the proletariat. Marx's writings on this aspect of the function of religion focus on two main points: what is rationalized is the suffering of the oppressed, and the order of society as a whole, particularly its institutions of authority.

There are several arguments used by religion to explain and minimize suffering. Christianity, Marx argues, teaches that the sufferings of the present life are as nothing compared with the bliss of heaven; and the former are short, while the latter is everlasting (14:35). In line with this, if the proletarian poor should complain that it is unjust for so much wealth, property, and power to be concentrated in the hands of so few, religion teaches them that spiritual blessings are of far greater and lasting worth, and that the treasure on which they should set their hearts is not of this world (14:35).

Furthermore, Christianity has some ready arguments which explain to the proletariat why the present state of affairs is as it is. Since men are in a condition of sin, their sufferings can easily be rationalized as justly deserved divine punishment. According to Marx, Christianity regards "all vile acts of the oppressors against the oppressed to be . . . the just punishment of original sin and other sins" (14:84). There is also another useful variation of this argument. What reply can be given to the believer who says that since he has renounced his sin and has turned to God in faith, he should no longer be subject to the same sufferings as the unrepentant? The church answers, Marx observes, that such sufferings are a test of the genuineness and perseverance of his faith; they are "trials that the Lord in his infinite wisdom imposes on those redeemed" (14:84). Whether a man is an unbeliever or one of the faithful, such religious teaching removes any reasons he might give for rebelling against sufferings and inequities in his earthly life; they reconcile him to his miserable condition.

Taking society as a whole, Marx contends that religion legitimates the authority of the state and gives an ultimate rationalization for the powers that be. Furthermore, Christianity, as Marx sees it, does not do this conditionally, by supporting some forms of the state in preference to others, but unconditionally. Whether the state is an absolute monarchy, a constitutional monarchy, or a republic, Christianity indiscriminately teaches that it is the duty of men simply to "submit to the authority, for *all authority* is ordained by God" (14:37). As we have seen, Wilberforce employed a variant of this argument when he stated that the "station in life" of the poor was divinely ordained (cf. Engels, 14: 303). Similarly, in our own day it is by no means uncommon for religious sanctions to be invoked to justify the superiority claims of one racial group against another.

One particularly important instrument of state power is the army. Here too, Marx saw that religion was in no way expected to disturb its orderly and efficient operations; on the contrary, religion is supposed to keep up its morale, and to reinforce military discipline by teaching unqualified obedience to authority (14:39).

This function of rationalizing the existing order of society Marx regarded as a constant throughout the history of the church in changing socioeconomic orders:

> The social principles of Christianity justified the slavery of Antiquity, glorified the serfdom of the Middle Ages and equally know . . . how to defend the oppression of the proletariat, although they make a pitiful face over it.
>
> The social principles of Christianity preach the necessity of a ruling and an oppressed class, and all they have for the latter is the pious wish that the former will be charitable (14:83).

Marx sums up the rationalizing aspect of the social function of religion as follows:

> Religion is the general theory of that [alienated] world, its encyclopaedic compendium, its logic in a popular form . . . its moral sanction, its solemn completion, its universal ground for consolation and justification (14:41).

Corresponding to the social order thus rationalized there is an internalization of the attitudes which are required to perpetuate that order. Religion *inculcates servile virtues* which reinforce a man's submission to the class that exploits him. Although the practice of Christians may not always be one of non-resistance to evil, Marx notes that the true teaching of Christianity is "that suffering in patience and the bliss of hope are cardinal virtues" (14:35). Christians are taught to turn the other cheek when struck, not to institute legal proceedings when cheated by others, and to love and pray for enemies, not fight against them.

This is an obvious point which clearly fits into Marx's theory and does not need further elaboration. His polemic, of course, does not stem from an abstract concern for human self-regard. Servile virtues are perfectly fitted to maintain the status quo, while Marx is working for the revolutionary creation of a new order which requires a completely different set of personal qualities. He summarizes the point and the contrast in these words:

> The social principles of Christianity preach cowardice, self-contempt, abasement, submission, dejection, in a word all the qualities of the

canaille [riff-raff]; and the proletariat, not wishing to be treated as *canaille*, needs its courage, its self-feeling, its pride and its sense of independence . . . (14:84).

The religious opium not only imparts a fixed and stable character to the established social order, it also immobilizes those energies which are necessary to change it, replacing them with passive submission. In contrast to Marx's demand for radical social revolution, religion yields only a drugged lassitude.

We have now seen how Marx understands the actual social roots of religion in the proletariat; it is based in real need and distress, and provides both a compensation and a protest in the face of that suffering. But the price paid for this is inordinate, since the religious rationalization of society and the internalization of servile virtues only serve to reinforce the condition of the proletarian, not to free him from it. He is trapped in a vicious circle, and his use of the religious drug requires that he continue to take it. His dose is not like an antibiotic which changes conditions and so renders further use unnecessary; religion is addictive.

Marx's theory of religion is in fact a concise paradigm of his whole analysis of capitalism. The worker gets a subsistence wage out of religion, but a huge "surplus value" accrues to the capitalist as profit from this activity. We must now consider the social function of religion for the capitalist class.

4. RELIGION AS CAPITALIST IDEOLOGY

"The ruling ideas of each age have ever been the ideas of its ruling class" (14:88). This aphorism concisely states Marx's concept of ideology. To understand Marx's view of religion as capitalist ideology, we must briefly supplement our earlier discussion of this concept.

Popular usage frequently uses "ideology" to mean a system of social and political ideas which contains the convictions, assumptions, values and goals of a given movement, party, or government. As we have seen, Marx speaks of ideology in a more specific sense. For him it is the idea system of the dominant class, it reflects the socioeconomic interest of that class, and its function is to reinforce the status and self-interest of that class.

This analysis rejects, of course, the view that members of the dominant class have about their ideas. A judge, for example, may believe that his legal thought is based upon fundamental axioms of justice which transcend the socioeconomic order of his society; he thinks that the legal system is an independent and impartial power which regulates the economic practices of business corporations, guarantees equity for all racial groups, and so forth. But this view, Marx argues, is the exact opposite of the real dynamics of ideas. Legal ideas—and other aspects of consciousness, including religion—are not independent regulators and evaluators of the economic system; rather, they primarily reflect and rationalize precisely that system.

Ideological thinking, in believing that consciousness and ideas determine society, has turned the picture upside down. "In the whole of ideology, men and their relations appear upside down as in a *camera obscura*" (14:74; cf. Engels, 14:263,283). For this reason ideology functions unconsciously, and members of a dominant class are usually quite unaware that their idea system is simply an intellectual reflection of their socioeconomic status. As we examine how the various components of religion serve capitalist ends, it is important to remember that Marx saw ideology as an *unconscious*—though not for that reason less effective—instrument of the self-interest of the dominant class.

When religion is considered in its function for the capitalist class, Marx interprets it precisely as ideology. Indeed, in nineteenth-century Europe Marx saw religion as the summit of the ideological super-structure of law, morality, philosophy, art, and all other aspects of human consciousness. Religion is the integrating factor, the keystone which holds the whole edifice together. It provides the ultimate sanction for the existing social order, and it legitimates the values, goals, and basic principles of the capitalist system. It functions to reinforce the social dominance, privilege, and profits of the capitalist class. Marx's whole purpose in showing the self-defeating way religion appealed to the exploited proletariat is to expose it as a self-serving instrument of the capitalists. Since ideology reflects the basic economic relations between social classes, it is obvious why Marx holds that the dominant ideas of a society are the ideas of its dominant class, and why he argues that the real profit of religion benefits the capitalist class. We will now examine these benefits in detail.

First, the capitalist is handsomely served when religion deflects to a heavenly world the proletarian hopes for a better life and an equitable distribution of wealth and power. Religious eschatology channels the hopes of the dispossessed to a safe place, far removed from the tangible treasures and luxuries of the capitalists.[16] The expectation of heavenly blessings and abundance involves no threat whatsoever to the exploiting class; but the absence of this alternative source of redress and compensation would re-direct such hopes and expectations towards the wealth and position which the capitalists now hold. Insofar as religion gives some compensation to the dispossessed proletariat, it serves as a safety valve for potentially revolutionary frustrations and demands. The eschatology of heavenly bliss defuses earthly frustrations at least enough to protect the exploiters from outbursts of revolutionary hostility. So long as there is a guaranteed eternal income in heaven there is little point to a "revolution of rising expectations" in the transitory life on earth.

Second, religious rationalization of the existing socioeconomic system clearly pays dividends to those who own, control, and profit from that system. If the industrial worker really believes that the class structure of society, with its "superior" and "inferior" classes, is the result of an absolute if inscrutable Divine will, he is not likely to entertain the heretical thought that his miserable condition actually derives from the lust for profit which motivates his earthly master, the capitalist. If he is taught to value spiritual blessings above all others, he will not set his heart on the material goods which the capitalist possesses in abundance. If he regards his suffering as penance for sin or as a test of his faith, why then should he jeopardize his eternal salvation for a changed economic order which, while attractive, would after all be of short duration? That would risk losing his soul for a mess of pottage.

Such attitudes, Marx objects, are as beneficial to the capitalist as they are self-defeating for the proletarian. It is the capitalist who profits from the religious belief that a man's social status derives not from a dominant exploiting class but from the Divine will. It is the capitalist who profits from the religious devaluation of material goods and economic power. It is the capitalist order which is preserved by the religious teaching that the suffering of want and oppression is necessary in the divine plan of salvation. Religion thus conceals from the proletarian the true explanation of his present social condition; the necessity for social revolution to change radically his economic status is completely hidden from him by religious teachings. Further, by substituting spiritual blessings for material goods and physical well-being, religion fosters vain hopes in the proletariat, and these hopes protect the economic power and possessions of the capitalist from attack. In short, religious rationalization is an ideology which inverts and thereby totally misinterprets social reality and desirable human goods to the detriment of the worker and to the direct benefit of the ruling, capitalist class.

The same must be said for the religious rationalization of state authority and the apparatus of social coercion like the army, the police and the courts. Who, more than the members of the ruling and profiting class, stands to lose by the overthrow of the established order? Who but the capitalist stands to gain from the belief that revolution is a sin against the divine "law and order"? Engels underlines this point in his comments on religious activity in England after the European revolutionary uprisings in 1848:

> If the British bourgeois had been convinced before of the necessity of maintaining the common people in a religious mood, how much more must he feel that necessity after all these experiences? Regardless of the

sneers of his Continental compeers, he continued to spend thousands and tens of thousands, year after year, upon the evangelization of the lower orders; not content with his own native religious machinery, he appealed to Brother Jonathan [Uncle Sam], the greatest organizer in existence of religion as a trade, and imported from America revivalism, Moody and Sankey, and the like (14:308).

When the bourgeois capitalist feels the whole order of society threatened by revolutionary movements, he quickly moves to shore up the whole edifice by the ultimate sanction of religion.

Third, it is perfectly evident how the servile virtues function to the great advantage of the capitalist class. Marx drew the contrast between the revolutionary virtues of courage, self-esteem, pride, and independence, and the submissive virtues of self-contempt, abasement, patience, and non-resistance of enemies. Whereas the former pose an obvious threat to privileged classes and those in authority, the servile virtues of religion are perfectly suited to the maintenance of the status quo and deference to its authorities.

Considering the net result of these three major components of religion, it is clear why Marx regarded the paltry and illusory compensation derived from the religious opiate to be purchased at a price which brings enormous social and economic profits to the capitalist class. The capitalist society thereby possesses a guaranteed, socially functioning insurance for its system and can continue to make its profits without fear of overthrow.

One further question needs an answer to understand fully the function of religion as capitalist ideology. Marx pointed to a quite specific and genuine need of the proletariat which religion filled: it was a compensatory protest against a completely degraded and hopeless situation. But the capitalists, after all, were not suffering under hardships and exploitation like the proletariat, and had no cause for protest or need for compensation. That is why Marx did not apply the opium metaphor to the capitalist class. So the question is: does the capitalist have a genuine, personal need for religion? Why is the bourgeoisie religious?

Marx never gave an exhaustive, systematic treatment of religion, for the obvious reason that he considered it an epiphenomenon. His magnum opus, *Das Kapital*, was on economics, not religion. In identifying with the cause of the proletariat, he was interested in religion only to show that it was a significant factor in capitalist exploitation. But he does suggest an answer, and it has two parts.

The first part is historical, and is spelled out more fully by Engels. The capitalists were already religious people as they came into their modern position of economic power, for they had found in religion an ally for their own social revolution. Indeed, Engels argues, since the medieval Catholic Church had "surrounded feudal institutions with the halo of divine consecration," the battle against feudalism by the rising middle class naturally took the form of a religious revolt against the Church of Rome. This, he contends, is the real significance of the Protestant Reformation which, while begun by Luther, produced in Calvinism the most suitable ally in the fight against kings and aristocratic lords [17] (14:299ff.).

Having served as an effective weapon for a class "on the make," religion now underwent a mutation, for the capitalist was quick to learn that the same weapon can be used to protect his gains by holding down the lower class.

> He was not long in discovering the opportunities this same religion offered him for working upon the minds of his natural inferiors, and making them submissive to the behests of the masters it had pleased God to place over them. In short, the English bourgeoisie now had to take a part in keeping down the "lower orders," the great producing mass of the nation, and one of the means employed for that purpose was the influence of religion (14:303).

But this historical observation does not explain the continuing personal need that religion satisfies for the capitalist.

The more operational factor is found in the second part of the answer. The fact is that *ideology itself* meets a deep, personal need for the members of the class who hold the ideology. The religious rationalization of the established order not only holds the proletariat in submission; it simultaneously sanctions the whole way of life of the capitalist class, and supports its mentality. The capitalist has religious sanction for believing in the superiority of his own class; the success of his worldly work can be viewed as a sign of Divine election and blessing; in short, his values, world view, and social position are first expressed in religious ideology and then reflected back to him in a way that confirms his belief in the rightness of the prevailing order. Such belief produces security, self-confidence, solidarity, and trust among members of the dominant class. Further, it serves to blind them to the injustices and sufferings of those who do not belong to the privileged class, and this in turn makes it all the easier to believe in the essential rightness and goodness of the prevailing system. In this sense, then, religious ideology plays a valuable role for the capitalist class; if the proletariat needs *compensation*, the bourgeoisie needs *confirmation*, and this is what religion gives. That this ideological confirmation was bought at the price of considerable hypocrisy—especially with respect to the humble and submissive virtues, more conspicuously urged on the proletariat than practiced by the bourgeoisie—is something Marx never tired of pointing out (14:35,128).

The aim of Marx was not simply to diagnose the evils of capitalist society, but above all to overthrow the system itself. His critique of Christianity exposes the two sides of the reactionary social function of religion. On the one hand he shows how it can support the dominant position of the exploiting capitalist class. On the other hand he demonstrates that religion offers a narcotic compensation to the proletariat, thereby disguising the true source of their suffering and siphoning off their revolutionary energies.

Since his aim was a revolutionary change of the society in which religion had social and psychological viability, Marx saw no point in attacking religious people and institutions directly, as in persecutions and coercive restrictions of religious practice. Rather, the criticism of religion is a preparation for revolution which gives man a true insight into social reality and a new understanding of his own dignity and powers.

> The criticism of religion ends with the teaching that *man is the highest being for man,* hence with the *categoric imperative to overthrow all relations* in which man is a debased, enslaved, abandoned, despicable being (14:50, translation altered).

The criticism of religion will not, of itself, change society; but revolutionary social change will abolish religion. Looking to the past, Marx wrote:

> It was not the downfall of the old religions that brought about the downfall of the old states, but the downfall of the old states which brought about the downfall of the old religions (14:23).

While, throughout history, the downfall of old religions accompanied social upheavals, new forms of religion arose which were adapted to the ensuing social orders.

But now a new "revelation" has appeared in history. Marxist analysis has discovered the secret of social history, uncovering the laws of economic relations and class struggle (14:94). This discovery of social truth makes superfluous and reactionary any future expression of social reality in mystifying and ideological religious terms. The criticism of religion, Marx said, is the premise of all criticism. Once the criticism of religion is complete, the next stage is the criticism of law and politics. Yet even this criticism is not an end in itself; it is necessary in order to understand the nature of class conflict in capitalist society which, once understood, must be "revolutionized in practice by the removal of the contradiction" (14:70). Nowhere is the movement, purpose, and force of Marx's criticism of religion better expressed than in the concluding paragraphs of his classic "opium" passage. It is fitting to conclude this section by quoting them in full.

> The abolition of religion as the *illusory* happiness of the people is required for their *real* happiness. The demand to give up the illusions about its condition is the *demand to give up a condition which needs illusions.* The criticism of religion is therefore *in embryo the criticism of the vale of woe,* the *halo* of which is religion.
>
> Criticism has plucked the imaginary flowers from the chain not so that man will wear the chain without any fantasy or consolation but so that he will shake off the chain and cull the living flower. The criticism of religion disillusions man to make him think and act and shape his reality like a man who has been disillusioned and has come to reason, so that he will revolve round himself and therefore round his true sun. Religion is only the illusory sun which revolves round man as long as he does not revolve round himself.
>
> *The task of history,* therefore, once the *world beyond the truth* has disappeared, is to establish the *truth of this world.* The immediate *task of philosophy,* which is at the service of history, once the *saintly form* of human self-alienation has been unmasked, is to unmask self-alienation in its *unholy forms.* Thus the criticism of heaven turns into the criticism of the earth, the *criticism of religion* into the *criticism of right* [i.e., law] and the *criticism of theology* into the *criticism of politics* (14:42).

5. THE PROVOCATIVE LEGACY

Without a doubt, Marx's analysis is the most serious and damaging critique of the social function of religion ever mounted against Christianity during its long and complex history. In its ancient, medieval, and modern periods Christianity had been the subject of numerous philosophical criticisms, to which it had responded with great intellectual creativity and power. But never had a social thinker trained his critical analysis upon the social function of establishment Christendom with the perceptiveness and incisiveness of Marx. Marx, furthermore, had placed his opponent in a particularly vulnerable position by changing the ground rules of criticism. For it was no longer possible for Christianity, or any other religion, to respond to Marx in the traditional manner of intellectual apologetics and philosophical debate. Counter-questions and criticisms might indeed be raised against Marx, but these would not be sufficient response to his fundamental challenge. For, although Marx himself did not expect any response from a religion he regarded as doomed, the only adequate response to his challenge would be a religion which could demonstrate that its *actual social function* was radically different from what he described and attacked. While it is one thing for religious intellectuals to reformulate their thinking about the social role of religion, it is quite another matter to translate theologies of radical social change into active, practical movements which engage the energies and resources of traditional religious institutions and their popular constituencies. Indeed, precisely whether this should and can be done is a most divisive issue in churches and synagogues, in comparison to which denominational divisions are revealed as relics of a past age. In the 1970's, while the struggle is still quite open-ended, there is no reason to think that Marx would be favorably impressed by the social attitudes and actions of most religious people and institutions.

Nevertheless, we must observe that some decisive developments in Christian thought have taken place which are directly relevant to Marx's theory of religion, and which have evoked much interest among present-day Marxists. Karl Barth's theology of freedom explicitly subverts that ideological form of religion which absolutizes the self-interests, natural prejudices, economic systems, and political pretensions of any social group in order to gain an ultimate, divine sanction and justification.[18] Dietrich Bonhoeffer sets his "religionless Christianity" in diametrical opposition to any religion which, by its obsession with consolation and compensation, holds a man in childish dependence and diverts him from assuming a mature responsibility for his fellowmen.[19] From these two seminal thinkers has come an impressive group of younger theologians working in the area which might be described as the theology of radical politics, and including among them such writers as Paul Lehmann, Richard Shaull, James Cone, Harvey Cox, Jürgen Moltmann, Johannes Metz, and Rubem Alves.[20] Perhaps it is not surprising that such theological questions have become central when it is widely recognized that in most countries of the West, the sociocultural establishment of Christendom has been virtually replaced by a secular society.

In noting this development towards a much more independent, critical, and socially transforming role for Christianity in society, which is expressed in movements and new communities as well as in thought, two further observations are pertinent. The first is that a criticism of Christianity exactly opposite to that of Marx has also been made, namely, that rather than legitimizing the self-serving power structure of an exploiting dominant class, Christianity has been, on occasion, subversive of it. Precisely this charge that Christianity was subversive of the Roman *imperium* was what stimulated Augustine to write his classic, *The City of God*.

The second observation is that the criticism of religion and its reactionary social role is by no means new with either Marx or modern Christian theologians. Indeed, it would be difficult to surpass the pungent, radical, and satirical criticism of religion which is found in the Bible itself. This is particularly the case in the Hebrew prophets, where there are repeated attacks on the way degenerate religion is invariably connected with social injustice and exploitation.[21] The extent to which such writings might have influenced Marx is an interesting question; at least he is reported to have advised his wife and daughters that, rather than going to church, it would be far more religious of them to stay home and read the prophets (11:379).

Now that we have indicated the force of Marx's critique and the radical nature of any effective response to it, we will conclude by posing four questions about problems in Marx's thought.

First, does Marx's concentration upon man in his socioeconomic activities and relations result in a serious neglect of the psychological factors which operate in class behavior and social conflict as well as in interpersonal relations? Do social groups never act against their economic self-interest because of the psychic make-up of the members of the class? Granted that social structures intimately effect personal psychic structures, are the latter reducible to the former? [22] To put the question in its most general form, which does not restrict it to the psychological dimension of man: is Marx a sociological reductionist?

Second, Marx does not deny that once men have been disabused of a false, socially determined class consciousness, their imaginative visions, ideas, and social theories can serve to motivate and precipitate radical social change. If this was indeed the purpose of Marx's own thought and vision, can he exclude the possibility that religious symbols and ideas may play an exactly analogous role? Is it unlikely that the critical, nonconformist, and prophetic attitudes in the scripture of Christianity and Judaism might function analogously to Marx's own social theory? A too-hasty negative answer to this question might well boomerang on Marx, since it has often been observed that there are some intriguing similarities between salient aspects of his own thought and the ideas and symbols of the Western religions: compare the classless society of justice, equality, peace, and abundance with the biblical imagery of the Kingdom of God; or the role of the proletariat in the revolutionary coming of the communist society with the various Jewish and Christian themes of the saving remnant and the messianic liberator; or the social demands of Marx for justice and the lifting of oppression from the exploited with the biblical motif of the Exodus from oppression, the prophetic demand for justice, and the special solicitude for the socially vulnerable.

The third question follows from the first two. Can the socially revolutionary sects of the left-wing in the Protestant Reformation be understood *only* as class phenomena and not also as independently grounded religious movements? Were their religious ideas only by-products of a class ripe for revolution, or were the religious aspirations significant, independent impulses in these radical social movements? [23] Similarly, why is it that at the present time the religious advocates of radical social change in both white and black communities are led by predominantly middle- and upper-middle class people who presumably have most to gain economically by maintaining the status quo? Can Marx's thesis that religion is a social epiphenomenon be validly generalized without qualification?

The final question concerns an issue which has consistently exercised the religious mind. Marx protested vehemently against man's inhumanity to man, giving an acute documentation of the economic and social dynamics of exploitation and ideological self-justification. This oppression must be overthrown in the revolutionary transformation of the prevailing system, thus inaugurating the society of justice, equality, voluntary cooperation, reason, and peace. If, as Marx thought, man's inhumanity is only a variable of the social system, it is indeed logical to suppose that a complete transformation of society will also eradicate exploitation, injustice, prejudice, self-seeking, suspicion, and antagonism. But the question is precisely whether man's inhumanity to man is only a variable of a social system, or whether, more fundamentally, it is found in social systems because it is a variable of man himself? With all good will towards the aspirations of Marx and his followers, without any attempt to excuse Western hypocrisy and self-righteousness, and without any theological determinism or philosophical fatalism, the very history of the Marxist movement itself obliges us to face this question. No social analysis can be adequate which does not candidly face this problem in the creative and provocative legacy of Karl Marx.

NOTES

[1] *Divini Redemptoris,* the 1937 encyclical of Pope Pius XI, bore the English title "On Atheistic Communism," and this undoubtedly contributed to the widespread currency of this phrase.

[2] Fortunately, the "Christian-Marxist dialogue" marks an important step beyond the rigid and self-righteous attitudes of the cold war. See the Secondary Readings in the "Suggested Readings" for this chapter.

[3] "Atheism," Marx once wrote, "has no longer any meaning, for atheism is a negation of God and postulates the existence of man through this negation; but socialism *qua* socialism no longer stands in need of any such a mediation" (cited in 11:304).

[4] For further discussion of social conditions in Britain, see Edwin P. Thompson, *The Making of the English Working Class* (New York: Pantheon Books, 1964) and E. J. Hobsbawn, *Labouring Men: Studies in the History of Labour* (New York: Basic Books, 1964).

[5] William Wilberforce (1759-1833) was the father of Bishop Samuel Wilberforce mentioned in chapter three, above.

6 Wilberforce, *A Practical View* (London: Cadell and Davies, 1797), p. 405f.

7 Sidney Hook, *From Hegel to Marx* (Ann Arbor: University of Michigan Press, 1962), is an outstanding study in intellectual history. The "Introduction" by Richard Kroner to Hegel, *Early Theological Writings* (Philadelphia: University of Pennsylvania Press, 1971), contains extensive discussion of Hegel's philosophy of religion. A selection from Hegel, *The Philosophy of Religion*, and a brief introduction, is found in B. M. G. Reardon, *Religious Thought in the Nineteenth Century* (Cambridge: University Press, 1966). Karl Barth, *From Rousseau to Ritschl* (London: S.C.M. Press, 1959), contains a chapter on Hegel; and Emil Fackenheim, *The Religious Dimension in Hegel's Thought* (Bloomington: Indiana University Press, 1967), is a recent, major study.

8 Marx the humanist must be set over against the caricature of him as a mechanistic materialist. Discussions in recent years, stimulated particularly by the publication of early manuscripts of Marx, have discredited the caricature. The manuscripts, together with personal reminiscences by his family and friends and an introductory discussion of Marx's humanism, may be studied in Erich Fromm, *Marx's Concept of Man* (4).

9 This transformation of the Hegelian dialectic of spirit leads to the "dialectical materialism" of Marxist philosophy.

10 For Feuerbach's philosophy of religion, see the two books in the chapter bibliography and also Feuerbach's *The Essence of Faith According to Luther* (New York: Harper & Row, 1967), with an introduction by Melvin Cherno. Karl Barth, in addition to his introductory essay to Feuerbach, *The Essence of Christianity*, also has a chapter in *From Rousseau to Ritschl*. B. M. G. Reardon, *op. cit.*, also contains a selection from Feuerbach, with introduction.

11 For Marx's criticisms, see his "Theses on Feuerbach" (14:69-72), especially theses IV, VI and VII.

12 In a famous aphorism Marx said: "The philosophers have only *interpreted* the world differently; the point, however, is to *change* it" (14:72, translation altered).

13 See the following themes in Marx and Engels, *On Religion* (14): science is opposed to obscurantist religious authority, dogma, and suppression of unorthodox views (23ff., 38); historical study discloses myth, legend, and manipulation of historical facts in the Bible (119, 194, 223, 327); empirical reason rejects miracles, superstition, and spiritualism (63, 161, 175ff., 326); an irreligious or atheist position is not inconsistent with morality, social well-being, and human dignity (63).

14 In common with other eighteenth- and nineteenth-century thinkers, Marx also speculated about the historical origins of religion; like them, he did so by projecting into the past the conclusions he had reached about contemporary religion. Hence, since religion reflects social life, and since primitive man is believed to live an animal-like existence in herds, human consciousness is a "sheep or stock consciousness." Accordingly, primitive religion is "nature worship"; man's attitude to nature is "a purely animal one and . . . he submits like a beast" (14:75; cf. 147).

15 This exposition will primarily draw upon the writings of Marx himself, supplementing these occasionally by material from Engels. While they both agree on the central theses of the theory of religion, there are aspects of Engels' position which diverge somewhat from Marx. A detailed comparison, however, cannot be made here.

16 During the 1960's, a new understanding of biblical eschatology and its radical political implications came to the fore. Jürgen Moltmann, a leading participant in the Christian-Marxist dialogue, stimulated this thinking with his *Theology of Hope* (New York: Harper & Row, 1967); for further discussion and bibliography, see chapter seven below.

17 It is worth noting here the tacit admission by Engels that, prior to its reactionary use by an established class, religion can serve as an ally, if not an independent cause, in the process of social change.

18 Barth was an architect of the Confessing Church in Germany which rejected precisely such an ideological perversion of Christianity by Hitler and the Nazis. See Barth, *The German Church Conflict* (Richmond, Va.: John Knox Press, 1965) and Arthur C. Cochrane, *The Church's Confession Under Hitler* (Philadelphia: Westminster Press, 1962). For post-war writings urging Christians to seek an alternative to the ideological captivity of the cold war, see Barth, *Against the Stream* (New York: Philosophical Library, 1954), particularly the correspondence with Emil Brunner, "The Church between East and West," and "Political Decisions in the Unity of the Faith"; see also Karl Barth and Johannes Hamel, *How to Serve God in a Marxist Land* (New York: Association Press, 1959). Georges Casalis, *Portrait of Karl Barth* (Garden City, N. Y.: Doubleday, 1963), is a fine, brief introduction to Barth.

19 See chapter nine below on Bonhoeffer's theology of Christian adulthood, autonomy and social responsibility. Both Bonhoeffer and Barth have awakened considerable interest among European Marxists.

20 For a discussion of several themes shared by most of these theologians, and for further bibliography, see chapter seven below.

21 I hate, I despise your feasts,
    and I take no delight in your solemn assemblies.
Even though you offer me your burnt offerings and cereal offerings,
    I will not accept them . . . .
But let justice roll down like waters,
    and righteousness like an ever-flowing stream.
Amos 5:21ff., (R.S.V.); cf. Isaiah 1, Jeremiah 7.

22 In *Civilization and Its Discontents* (New York: W. W. Norton, 1962), p. 60, Freud specifically makes this sort of criticism against Marxist social thought.

23 In this context we may note Engels' interesting views on the revolutionary tradition in Christianity. Primitive Christianity was a revolutionary movement of the masses (13:345,316) whose congregations were rather like local sections of the International Working Men's Association (13:318); unfortunately this incipient socialism was sublimated to another world. Late medieval heretical sects were radicals who "from the 'equality of the children of God' . . . inferred civil equality, and partly even equality of property" (13:101); they represent nothing less than an "anticipation of communism by fantasy" (13:103). Thomas Münzer (1490-1525) is Engels' religious hero, a precursor of the modern proletarian movement, and a revolutionary organizer of peasants and plebians who is not reluctant to threaten princes with both the wrath of God and the armed force of his followers (13:103ff.). Engels, however, can only praise Münzer by virtually isolating him from the Christian tradition and painting him as a great heretic who was on the verge of atheism. It is difficult to avoid the conclusion that here Engels is begging the question of the relation between Münzer's religious ideas and social actions, and reading the facts to fit his theory.

BIBLIOGRAPHY

1. ENGELS, FRIEDRICH, *The Condition of the Working Class in England,* translated and edited by W. O. Henderson and W. H. Chaloner. Oxford: Basil Blackwell, 1958.

2. FEUERBACH, LUDWIG, *The Essence of Christianity,* trans. George Eliot. Foreword by H. Richard Niebuhr. Introductory essay by Karl Barth. New York: Harper, 1957.

3. ———, *Lectures on the Essence of Religion,* trans. Ralph Manheim. New York: Harper & Row, 1967.

4. FROMM, ERICH, *Marx's Concept of Man.* With a translation from Marx's *Economic and Philosophical Manuscripts* by T. B. Bottomore. New York: Frederick Ungar, 1961.

5. GARAUDY, ROGER, *From Anathema to Dialogue: A Marxist Challenge to the Christian Churches,* trans. Luke O'Neill. New York: Herder & Herder, 1966.

6. ———, *Karl Marx: The Evolution of His Thought,* trans. Nan Apotheker. New York: International Publishers, 1967.

7. HOOK, SIDNEY, *Marx and the Marxists: The Ambiguous Legacy.* New York: D. Van Nostrand, 1955.

8. LACHS, JOHN, *Marxist Philosophy: A Bibliographical Guide.* Chapel Hill: University of North Carolina Press, 1967.

9. LASKI, HAROLD J., ed., *Communist Manifesto.* Introduction by Harold J. Laski. London: George Allen & Unwin, 1948.

10. LENIN, V. I., *On Religion.* Moscow: Progress Publishers, 1969.

11. LOBKOWICZ, NICHOLAS, ed., *Marx and the Western World.* Notre Dame: University of Notre Dame Press, 1967.

12. MARX, KARL, *A Contribution to the Critique of Political Economy.* Translated by N. I. Stone from the second German edition, 1897. Chicago: Charles H. Kerr, 1904.

13. ———, *Early Writings,* translated and edited by T. B. Bottomore. London: C. A. Watts, 1963. ["On the Jewish Question," pp. 1-40, is Marx's discussion of two writings by Bruno Bauer: *The Jewish Question,* and "The capacity of the present-day Jews and Christians to become free."]

14. ———, and FRIEDRICH ENGELS, *On Religion.* Introduction by Reinhold Niebuhr. New York: Schocken Books, 1964.

15. MEHRING, FRANZ, *Karl Marx: The Story of His Life,* trans. Edward Fitzgerald. Introduction by Max Schachtmann. Ann Arbor: University of Michigan Press, 1962.

16. WEST, CHARLES C., *Communism and the Theologians.* New York: Macmillan, 1963.

SUGGESTED READINGS

1. *Primary Readings*

Karl Marx and Friedrich Engels, *On Religion* (14). The writings of Marx and Engels on religion are, for the most part, incidental in character. The collection in this volume is therefore arranged chronologically, not systematically. The following selections, sometimes quite brief, indicate the most important passages from which a comprehensive understanding can be gained: pp. 23, 35-37, 41-42, 50-54, 69-89, 94, 97-118, 127-137, 142-143, 145-151, 194-212, 226-227, 237-241, 263-267, 299-309. These may be supplemented by Engels' essay "On the History of Early Christianity," *On Religion*, pp. 316-347. Another supplementary reading is Marx's essay "On the Jewish Question" in Karl Marx, *Early Writings* (13).

2. *Secondary Readings*

The literature of the "Christian-Marxist dialogue" continues the present discussion of Marxism and religion. The following books introduce many of the major participants in the dialogue, the central issues, and further bibliography: Herbert Aptheker, ed., *Marxism and Christianity* (New York: Humanities Press, 1968); Herbert Aptheker, *The Urgency of Marxist-Christian Dialogue* (New York: Harper & Row, 1970); J. B. Metz, ed., *Is God Dead?* (New York: Paulist Press, 1966); Roger Garaudy, *From Anathema to Dialogue* (5); Roger Garaudy and Quentin Lauer, *A Christian-Communist Dialogue* (Garden City, N. Y.: Doubleday, 1968); Giulio Girardi, *Marxism and Christianity* (New York: Macmillan, 1968); Helmut Gollwitzer, *The Christian Faith and the Marxist Criticism of Religion* (New York: Scribner's, 1970); J. M. Lochman, *Church in a Marxist Society; a Czechoslovak view* (New York: Harper & Row, 1970); Thomas W. Ogletree, ed., *Openings for Marxist-Christian Dialogue* (Nashville: Abingdon Press, 1968); Paul Oestreicher, ed., *The Christian Marxist Dialogue: An International Symposium* (New York: Macmillan, 1969); John C. Raines and Thomas Dean, eds., *Marxism and Radical Religion; Essays Toward a Revolutionary Humanism* (Philadelphia: Temple University Press, 1970).

3. *Additional Bibliography*

John Lachs, *Marxist Philosophy: A Bibliographical Guide* (Chapel Hill: University of North Carolina Press, 1967), is a comprehensive, annotated bibliography including a chapter on "Marxism and Religion." More bibliography on the Christian-Marxist dialogue is found in *Study Encounter*, vol. IV, no. 1, 1968 ("Dialogue between Christians and Marxists"), published by the Division of Studies of the World Council of Churches.

Religion Fosters Social Criticism
and Promotes Social Justice

Reinhold Niebuhr (1892–1971) was profoundly concerned about the role of religion in society. Could religion be an agent for social change? Could it expose inequity and promote social justice? Or was religion a reactionary force in society? Was it a barrier to change, an ideological mask for unjust self-interest, a forbidden habitation for people of good conscience? Through the title of his first book Niebuhr asked pointedly, *Does Civilization Need Religion?* His reply was that sensitive spirits scorn those forms of religion that fail "to challenge recognized social inequities" (6:14). Civilization needs no religion that exacerbates or ignores pressing social problems.

Because of this social sensitivity, Niebuhr listened carefully to Karl Marx's scathing indictment of religion. His own experience as a minister in Detroit, Michigan, between the first world war and the great depression led him to conclude that Marx's analysis of the role of religion in society was often correct. Niebuhr observed that Marx's charge concerning the reactionary role of religious institutions was too often "unequivocably true" (11:Autumn, 1935, 14). Both in the past and the present religion often

creates a reverence for authority and encourages a humble obedience toward and a patient acceptance of the exactions of power, thus aggravating the injustices of a social system and retarding their elimination (*ibid.*).

For the most part, religion is counter-revolutionary. It endows repressive governments with auras of sanctity; it justifies suffering in social life as a just punishment for sin; it dampens social unrest by offering other-worldly rewards. It smothers the cry of the ethically sensitive revolutionary, and turns a deaf ear to the groans of the oppressed. It protects the status quo and fosters social inequity by encouraging an unconscious, but hypocritical feeling of righteousness in those who benefit from oppression. In too many cases, religion indeed is an opiate of the people and an ideological companion for established authorities.

Nevertheless, through his acquaintance with the prophetic sources of biblical religion, Niebuhr became convinced that religion could become an agent for social change. In contrast to its reactionary role, religion can become a power that encourages revolution and the amelioration of social ills. From the biblical literature and his own creative experience he developed a realistic, socially responsible "prophetic religion" in sharp distinction from the forms of religion identified by Karl Marx. This "prophetic" or "high" religion has three concrete social functions.

First, prophetic religion stimulates a critical assessment of the real nature of human existence. In radical opposition to the assertions of Karl Marx and Sigmund Freud that religion offers man an illusionary escape from the real problems of human existence, Reinhold Niebuhr argued that religion sponsors an incisive, realistic, insightful depiction of man and the world (6:47-149; 9:xii-xxv; 3:11). It describes man's depravity and dignity and unmasks the sentimental illusions of all idealistic social schemes, including the utopian vision of the self-designated social scientist Karl Marx.

Second, prophetic religion reveals and sustains absolute ethical standards that may become the foundation for prophetic criticism and social unrest. Since these norms can never be completely realized in any social system, they give prophetic religion the power to "criticize and condemn the partial achievements of any historical movement" (11:Autumn, 1935, 18). "Prophetic spirits" arise in many generations and cultural contexts and indict all established social, political or religious positions. They break free from the confines of class and nation and denounce anyone—king, priest, educator, executive—who betrays the rights of men and resists the cries of conscience (ibid.:18-19; 4:51,163-164).

Third, aided by its critical realism, prophetic religion functions in society as a catalyst for social change. Like Marx's acid test for philosophy, Niebuhr believed that religion should help transform the world, not just analyze it (6:165-189; 11:Spring, 1938, 18). Like yeast in dough, the reformist principles of religion can become implanted in political and social structures and then effect transformation and change (11:Winter, 1936, 10; 10:II, chap. IX). Prophetic religion is neither reactionary nor impotent. It is "the most radical force in social life" (11:Spring, 1938, 13).

How and why did Reinhold Niebuhr appropriate the indictment of Marx, yet also vindicate prophetic religion's positive social roles? Niebuhr's American context led him to search for a critically realistic perspective from which he could understand political, social and religious institutions. Marx became an intrinsic part of that quest. Yet at the same time, Niebuhr believed that Marx's critique had excluded prophetic criticism from religion. However obscured or submerged it might become, prophetic judgment constantly appears within religion. Impelled by transcendent ethical perspectives, fiery-eyed prophets arose to denounce old orders and proclaim and portray new ones. Indeed, Niebuhr argued, Marx borrowed from and secularized that heritage. Marx created a new, secular religion which was less viable and realistic than that which Niebuhr found within the biblical literature. Behind the searing social critic was Marx the religious romantic.

1. NIEBUHR'S INTELLECTUAL, HISTORICAL, AND SOCIAL SETTING

Two theological traditions and two sets of historical experiences deeply informed Niebuhr's thought and influenced his response to Marx. Protestant liberalism and the social gospel movement became Niebuhr's theological parents. The young Niebuhr was nurtured by liberalism and the social gospel movement, and the maturing Niebuhr developed his later perspectives over against them. World War I and its aftermath was an eye-opening experience that initiated the collapse of Niebuhr's early optimistic world view. Then his parish activities in industrial Detroit between the war and the great depression left an indelible impression on Niebuhr's mind that made him receptive to the thought of Marx.

With his father as his tutor, Niebuhr was schooled in the religious liberalism of the famous German historian and theologian Adolf von Harnack (1851–1930) (3:3).[1] Harnack characterized the essence of Christianity as an attachment to the paternal love of God made known through the actions and teachings of Jesus. Characteristic of liberal Protestant theology, Harnack's dominant concern was to make faith fully compatible with the modern world. The rigid, dogmatic, literalistic faith of the past had to be fundamentally revised. The Bible was to be read in light of ordinary historical and literary criteria, hopefully without losing its religious value. Traditional beliefs would be updated by new scientific, philosophical, historical and moral truths. Specifically, the criteria for liberal religious beliefs included: 1) conformity to the scientific world of Newtonian physics and Darwinian biology; 2) compatability with modern philosophy represented by David Hume, Immánuel Kant and others; 3) consistency with the reigning assumption that man had evolved from a crude, primitive past and was becoming progressively enlightened and moral; and 4) substitution of traditional beliefs about the sovereignty of God and the depravity of man with convictions concerning God's immanence in the natural world as evident in mankind's innate capacity for goodness and rationality (2:37-34,57-69,88-95).[2] For liberalism, the essence of religion lay in its ethical principles of love and brotherhood, not its disclosure of the tragedy and mystery of human life.

Niebuhr was further exposed to religious liberalism through his teachers at Yale Divinity School, particularly Douglas Clyde Macintosh.[3] From Macintosh and Harnack, Niebuhr inherited a high evaluation of man, an attachment to the principles of tolerance and openness towards other positions, a desire to find meaning in the Bible apart from orthodox literalism and passion for relating religion to modern secular culture (8:40-41,58; Williams in 3:194,203-205). The humanistic concerns of Protestant liberalism were shared by secular liberals like John Dewey, and Niebuhr always remained intensely aware of their similarities and influence (9:xii-xxv).

The term "social gospel" highlighted the shift from the older, individualistic, conversion-oriented evangelism to a new, corporate concern for the social problems of the modern world (2:108-111,115-116).[4] This involved a movement away from questions relating to personal ethics—profanity, drunkenness, sexuality and the like—to a primary concern for social ethics—fair wages, unemployment, child labor, welfare, and urban slums (2:112-113). The term "gospel" was retained because the Protestant supporters of the movement still believed that the life and teachings of Jesus formed the central core of religious faith. Nevertheless, a momentous shift had occurred. For the social gospel movement, religion was to find its primary *raison d'être* in the social sphere. Concern for individual salvation was not denied, but that concern was to be related inextricably to larger questions concerning the humanization and transformation of society.

Significant lines of continuity existed between the liberal theology of Harnack and Macintosh and the ideology that supported the social gospel. The denial of original sin was accompanied by a belief in the malleability of humanity, or, in the words of the famous social gospel leader, Walter Rauschenbusch, "the plastic possibilities of mankind" (2:112). Man comes into the world morally neutral and has the ability to internalize and practice altruism (1:224-225,260-275; 2:109,215; 4:138-140). Society, if led by strong men and women of good will, could move progressively toward an ideal future. The long-expected and proclaimed kingdom of God could—and would—be created on this earth (1:151-154; 2:115). The stubborn sins of the social order could be eradicated by love and brotherhood (4:130-134). American biblical scholars in the social gospel era claimed that these themes lay at the heart of the original proclamation of Jesus.[5]

The tactics of social gospel leaders fit hand-in-glove with their religious ideology and concern for social issues. They first made exceedingly careful, scientifically accurate analyses of social problems and then called for religiously inspired action to solve them. They had great expectations about the social power of religion once it secured the aid of the social sciences. Their enthusiasm led them to undertake impressive studies of social problems in which penetrating criticisms of the social order were offered (e.g., 4:19-25). However, their excessive confidence in human rationality and goodness encouraged them to believe that the solutions to social ills could be attained by the scientific analysis of society coupled with altruistic service. The legacy of this liberalism is still everywhere apparent. Malleable man, if transformed and inspired by religious faith, could break the chains of *laissez-faire* capitalism. The church as "a society of free men acting together in the spirit of intelligent good-will" could change the world (1:292).

During Reinhold Niebuhr's student years at Yale (1913–1914), this form of the social gospel movement was reaching its peak in America. The dean of the Yale Divinity School, Charles Reynolds Brown, along with several younger faculty members, was attempting enthusiastically to use the resources of religion to forge social change (1:149-152,169-170,225-234). After leaving Yale, Niebuhr found a focus for his own ministry in social concerns (8:27). He also sharply criticized a fellow clergyman's preoccupation with the personal ethics of his parishioners rather than with real problems of "essential Christianity" (8:96-97).

The picture of religion drawn by Marx was alien to that of theological liberals and social gospel advocates. For these two American theological traditions, religion was no illusionary, futuristic, other-worldly pie in the sky. Indeed, distinct continuities linked the basic religious concerns of social gospel liberals with Karl Marx. Both were devoted to critical rationality, ethical values, this-worldly concerns, social activism and the goodness and malleability of man. When liberal activists took their students to visit urban slums or to man social-service centers in the midst of cities, little did they realize that they were taking some of their students into the world of Karl Marx.

Niebuhr began his ministry in Detroit shortly after the start of the first world war, and although his parish activities consumed much of his energy, the war and the diplomacy that followed it made vital impressions upon his mind. Throughout his life, Niebuhr's thought was informed by the larger movements of world history.[6] History served as a testing ground upon which he worked out his understanding of man, society and religious institutions. In this he was not unlike the Hebrew prophets.

The war was a sobering experience. Niebuhr said at one time that it "created" his world view. "It made me a child of the age of disillusionment" (15:1161). When the war started, he was a "young man trying to be an optimist without falling into sentimentality." When it ended, he had become a "realist" trying to save himself from "cynicism" (*ibid.*).[7] It influenced his thinking in several ways.

First, it showed Niebuhr how wrong some of his former convictions had been and pushed him into a search for other insights. Like most second generation German-Americans, he had fervently supported America's war effort only to find that the noble rationale behind Allied participation was as false as the propaganda about the inequality of the Axis powers (8:14,18,42; 15:1161). The folly of uncritical patriotism began the process of Niebuhr's disenchantment.

Second, the patriotic involvement of the churches in the war led Niebuhr to begin revising his assessment of the moral value of organized religion. By 1918 he sensed that American chaplains were confusing loyalty towards Jehovah with loyalty towards the great war god, Mars (8:14-15) He later became convinced that American religious institutions had supported the fight with uncritical vengeance. "Good men," he cried, were "often the mouthpieces of Satan and the instruments of hell" (15:1162).

Third, the horrors of the first world war made it impossible for Niebuhr to make any easy connections between Western civilization and the expected kingdom of God (15:1162-1163). "Vanished were all the hopes of automatic progress." Western civilization had heightened, not pacified, man's brutal self (15:1161; 8:45-47). The war was a veritable "revelation of the internal anarchy of Western civilization" (14:542). Patriotism, organized religion and Western culture did not offer eternal verities. Niebuhr's mind had been "sunk into a sea of relativities" (15:1161).

As a result of his disillusionment with state, church, and Western civilization, Niebuhr's optimistic view of man was severely qualified. Religious man, Western man, all men exhibited at best dubious morality. In the war, rulers and diplomats had played a half-childish, half-ignorant ego game, brutally callous toward humanity (8:42-43). Individuals are already morally ambiguous, but political, racial and religious *groups* "are always less ethical than the individuals that compose them" (15:1162). Simple, liberal, moralistic views of man could not account for the tyrannies and historical blunders of the twentieth century (14:542-543).

If the war relativized many of Niebuhr's former beliefs, his experiences in Detroit offered him new certainties. Four of those experiences suggest the emerging shape of his new convictions.[8]

In 1924, Bishop Charles David Williams died, leaving Niebuhr in a state of numb despair (8:72). Williams had been a "fearless protagonist" for the "cause of democracy in industry." His leadership in this cause won him the affection of industrial workers but the opposition of industrialists and many clergy. With the death of Williams, Niebuhr became determined "to strive for the reformation of society rather than one's own perfection" (8:73). To that end, his attention was turned increasingly to questions pertaining to social ethics (8:73ff.). But his own struggles for social change in Detroit seemed "futile." Niebuhr's sense of hopelessness was reenforced by his realization that an influential clergyman like Bishop Williams had not been able to "change the prevailing attitudes of Detroit industry by a hair's breadth" (*ibid.*).

In 1925, Niebuhr made his first visit to an automobile factory. In the foundry the heat was horrible. The men were weary and their labor seemed to be the "drudgery and toil of slavery" (8:78). Niebuhr recalled Markham's poem, "The Man with the Hoe." The face of the laborer is empty.

> Who made him dead to rapture and despair
> A thing that grieves not and that never hopes,
> Stolid and stunned, a brother to the ox? (*Ibid.*)

This experience in the factory impressed two images on his mind: the brutality of modern industry and the irrelevance of contemporary religion. Institutionalized religion seemed only interested in cultivating piety "in the more protected areas of society." It was impervious to the brutalities of modern industrial civilization; its whole ethic seemed "anachronistic" (8:77).

In 1926, the American Federation of Labor held its annual meeting in Detroit, and its leaders announced their intention of organizing the auto industry. Unscrupulously, business leaders branded the A.F. of L. as a communist organization and began to pressure churches to cancel any invitations to labor convention speakers (Niebuhr in 3:5). In response to industrial pressure, the churches lost whatever courage they had and "lined up solidly against labor" and unionization (8:111). Niebuhr concluded that the

> churches in America are on the whole thoroughly committed to the interests and prejudices of the middle classes. I think it is a bit of unwarranted optimism to expect them to make any serious contribution to the reorganization of society (8:112).

If religion were to play a constructive role in industrial society, "a more heroic type of religion" must be developed (8:113). The maturing Niebuhr had identified a central theme of his future life's work.

In a caustic article in 1926, Niebuhr exposed some of the deceptive and brutal policies of Henry Ford. The Ford organization adopted new policies which it claimed were humanitarian: daily pay was raised to five dollars, the work week was reduced to five days, and five thousand young men between sixteen and twenty years of age were employed to keep them out of crime. Niebuhr knew that Ford publicity grossly distorted the intention and purported benefits of these policies. A laborer and his family could not possibly live on five dollars a day in Detroit. The celebrated five-day week was actually adopted in order to limit working time because of plant production cutbacks. Young men were hired, not to keep them out of mischief, but to replace workers over forty-five, thus exploiting the superior stamina of the young (16:98-101). In Niebuhr's view, these policies of the Ford Company manifested "criminal indifference on the part of the strong to the fate of the weak" (8:94). At the heart of capitalism was power, and "an industrial overlord will not share his power with his workers until he is forced to do so by tremendous pressure" (*ibid.*).

These and similar experiences in Detroit comprised the foundations of Niebuhr's new certainties: the moral pretentions of industrialists, the horror of working conditions, the impotence and reactionary role of religious institutions, the irrelevancy of the moral optimism of the social gospel and liberalism, and the centrality of power in modern society. By 1928, Karl Marx had become for Niebuhr a healthy antidote for his earlier idealisms and illusions.

2. MARX AS SECULAR SEER AND MENTOR

By the time that he left Detroit and began his career as a professor of ethics at Union Theological Seminary (1928–1960), Niebuhr had begun to utilize Karl Marx's analysis of ideology and ethics as a critical principle in his own thought. His disillusionment with liberalism and the resistance of churches to progressive social roles also led him to Marx's critique of religion. In 1928 he recommended that every religious leader subscribe to several radical, socialist journals, "preferably the ones extremely inimical to religion" (8:177). These journals exposed some of "the fundamental defects of modern society" as well as many of the illusions of liberalism. An examination of Niebuhr's understanding of ideology and the class origins of ethics, together with his application of these concepts to American middle-class religion, disclose his indebtedness to Marx.

Karl Marx had maintained that economic factors ultimately gave rise to political, philosophical and religious ideologies. Economic conditions give birth to social classes which in turn develop patterns of thought that rationalize and justify the respective social positions of each class. The resulting ideologies are illusionary in that they are a "reflex" (reflection) of the real world of economics and society, not the substantially valid principles that they are assumed to be. Religion reflects the social status of its adherents and functions negatively by preserving oppressive social systems. Religion keeps man from becoming aware of the primary significance of social and economic factors in life and discourages social change by insisting on the supreme importance of other-worldly rewards.

In a pregnant quotation, Reinhold Niebuhr demonstrated substantial agreement with Marx's analysis. Niebuhr argued that it is

> impossible to deal intelligently with the social problem of man if the whole world of culture . . . does not give more generous understanding of the truth which Marxism has discovered, or at least rediscovered: The truth that all human ideals and ideas are conditioned by the physical, geographic, economic and political circumstances in which they rise and that the final religious effort to escape this relativity may frequently become no more than the final rationalization, and justification of the partial and relative value of class, race and nation. In that sense the ultimate dishonesty of a culture is always a religious one [11:(Autumn, 1935), 19].

Ideologies are conditioned by economic and social factors. Religion, by endorsing—indeed divinizing—the respective statuses of each social class (extended also to race and nationality) preserves the social status quo and obscures the degree to which the values of each class reflect social circumstance rather than God-given truth (9:116). Religion and other ideological systems are frequently counter-revolutionary, and they foster illusions about the nature of life.

Niebuhr, however, did not agree with Marx's "economic determinism," that is, with the belief that ideologies were only reflections of economic forces. Niebuhr believed that economic and social circumstances greatly influence, but do not delimit, human ideas and ideals (9:145; 11:Autumn, 1935, 4,18; 8:Spring, 1938, 17). This position was similar to that of Friedrich Engels and of a growing number of American economists and historians after 1913 (9:145).[9] Niebuhr's fundamental divergence from Marx's determinism allowed him to draw heavily upon the latter's thought without accepting his reductionism.

Niebuhr applied Marx's critique of ideology to the subject of morality. In his book *Moral Man and Immoral Society* (1932), Niebuhr coursed through history showing how the respective class conditions of the proletariat and the bourgeoisie within industrial society led them to develop different moral systems. Proletarians idealize the group and its need for solidarity (9:152). They are thus willing to limit personal freedom by subsuming individualism under the cherished hope of an egalitarian society. The proletarian turns to his own group in order to qualify the greed and power of privileged groups. He also sanctions violence to secure social change (9:176-179). His ideals do not spring from some "pure ethical imagination," but from the specific circumstances of proletarian life (9:160). The proletarian's symbol of hope is a classless society which

> gives moral dignity to the dream of the victory of his class. By that vision the proletarian escapes the partial and the relative and bestows the value of universality upon his efforts (9:161).

These are the principle ideals of Marxism and are readily received as the creed of the oppressed masses.

Due to their radically different social situation, dominant social groups develop other ethical values. The bourgeoisie idealize individual liberty and insist on respect for individual life and rights (9:178). They become "the apostles of law and order," abhoring violence and adoring civil peace. They assume that civil disorder and violence are intrinsically evil and that civil peace is inherently virtuous (9:130). Little do members of the ruling class realize that they are in fact idealizing the forces that enable them to maintain power. They claim that their superior ability and education, combined with their thrifty, diligent life-style, are deserving of special economic rewards and social power (9:118,123). In fact, their idealizing of order and peace allow them to retain the power that they have gained and to deplore morally any attempts to change by force the system that they control. If, however, they were truly and intrinsically opposed to violence, why do their cries for civil peace turn into international sword-rattling when their economic interests abroad are threatened (9:139)? "More than one ruling class," cried Niebuhr, "has saved itself by an opportune war" (*ibid.*).

Niebuhr concluded that the conscious and often unconscious "ethical outlook of members of given classes is invariably colored, if not determined, by the unique economic circumstances which each class has as a common possession" (9:116). Any class, therefore, that assumes its values alone are correct is self-deceived (9:117). Privileged groups mouth class-colored, race-informed ideals, not universal ones (9:117-141). These relative, class-originated values are manifest in all primary Western institutions—law, education, politics and religion.

Between 1926 and 1928, Reinhold Niebuhr had become intensely aware of the degree to which American religious institutions reflected "the interests and prejudices of the middle classes" (8:112). When he published his first book in 1927, he utilized the insights of the famous sociologist of religion and student of Marx, Max Weber, in arguing that Protestantism sanctified "the peculiar interests and prejudices of the races and classes" which dominated the industrial, commercial West (6:65-67).[10] Niebuhr observed how religious institutions frequently gave "a pseudo-absolute character" to national, class and racial values (6:61-71). This indictment did not exclude Protestant liberalism, which Niebuhr said "grew out of the intellectual and religious needs of the privileged classes" and was in danger of becoming a "spiritual sublimation of the peculiar interests and prejudices of the commercial class" (6:72).

By 1935, Niebuhr began to make a fundamental distinction between "prophetic religion" and acculturated forms of religiosity (11: Autumn, 1935, 3-6). He regarded prophetic religion as a socially radical, realistic form of religion that transcended its culture origins, including the influence of social class. Niebuhr identified the polar opposite of prophetic religion as "culture religion" or acculturated religion, that is, any religion that knows no God or has no moral system that transcends the culture in which it finds itself (11:Autumn, 1938, 9). Acculturated religion is a "form of tribalism" which makes the nation or the civilization into God. It is "a form of idolatry in which God has become domesticated into a tame icon," sanctifying and preserving the values of a given culture (*ibid.*) Niebuhr's category of acculturated religion was precisely parallel to what Marx had assumed about all religion: it is an ideological reflection of socioeconomic existence.

Niebuhr identified two forms of acculturated religion which were precisely like the two basic types of religion analyzed by Karl Marx. The first is the traditional religion of the masses, identical with most non-Protestant, pre-industrial forms of faith. This religion encourages servile virtues of reverence for authority and a patient endurance of, and humble obedience to, those holding power (11:Autumn, 1935, 14). In believing that evil rulers were sent by God as punishment for sin, in beguiling mankind away from mundane problems through promising other-worldly rewards, and in sanctifying class divisions, this religion defuses revolutionary change and endorses injustice in the social sphere. Russian Orthodoxy before the advent of communism typified this kind of acculturated religion. Its almost complete identification with socially reactionary political forces made it "an easy prey" to the proletarian revolt against the old order (6:69, 9:184 also). Marx's charge that religion was counter-revolutionary was "broadly true" for this form of institutionalized religion (11:Autumn, 1935, 14-18).

A second form of acculturated religion—and the one to which

Niebuhr gave his greatest attention—is the faith of the middle-class and upper middle-class in industrial capitalist society. This faith, best represented by Protestantism, supports bourgeois ethics. It endows individuality, diligence, education, civil order, and peace with cosmic significance. By giving divine sanction to the self-interests and needs of those who control the social order, middle-class religion offers security and solidarity to those who benefit most from the capitalist system.

Niebuhr gave several specific examples of capitalist religiosity. He observed how the churches of Detroit eschewed social change and possible disorder by lining up solidly against the collective labor movement and in support of business and management (8:112).

A vivid new example appeared in 1935. With several other clergymen, Niebuhr was invited to Pineville, Kentucky, after Congress had passed a bill requiring an investigation of coal mines in Kentucky. Niebuhr found himself in the middle of a "class war" with "the poor mining community arrayed against the middle-class community" of mining operators and owners (Niebuhr in 16:110). The self-designated "good people" of the middle class looked down upon the impoverished miners as ignorant, lazy and immoral enough to steal and perpetrate violence. Predictably, the middle-class churches stood "pretty unqualifiedly on the side of the operators" who were rabidly opposed to any unionization of the mines (ibid.). Clergy of the local white churches united with the mining owners and operators of Pineville against the "communist" unionizers. Sensing the social opinions of Niebuhr and other members of the committee, town leaders began to accuse the committee of being theological "modernists," alien to the self-confessed "fundamentalism" of the people in the town. Pineville leaders made it clear that they stood unswervingly upon the "inerrancy of the Scripture as the absolute Word of God" and considered violence-prone communists as deserving of no civil liberties (16:109-111).

In that small Kentucky community Niebuhr observed religion functioning as the bastion of social conservatism, preventing "a thorough analysis of the human problem" and resisting any alteration of the status quo. One operator was quoted as saying

> I am a good Christian and a member of the Christian church, but I would just as soon tie a communist in a sack and throw him in the river as do anything else I know (16:111).

Town leaders considered themselves justifiably moral because they sponsored a charity program for some of the miners and because several weeks before the committee's arrival, a religious revival had brought "salvation" to most of the individuals in the middle-class community

(16:112). Individual conversion experiences, acts of charity, educations superior to the poorer members of society, thrifty life-styles and hard work defined what it meant to be religious in Pineville. Niebuhr concluded that if

> one notes the fact that economic circumstances invariably color religious convictions and moral and social ideals, one may well come to the conclusion that no middle-class church will ever espouse the cause of the dispossessed with full vigor (16:112).

Middle-class religion was acculturated to the social patterns of the dominant class.

Niebuhr's critique of the morality of philanthropy was directly indebted to his conviction that it expressed and preserved the individualistic, class values of middle- and upper middle-class capitalists. Acts of charity by altruistic individuals—as manifest in Pineville—were assumed to represent the essence of civic virtue. In fact, Niebuhr argued, such philanthropy is directly related to injustice and inequality (6:103-108). "Christian love in a society of great inequality means philanthropy," and philanthropy always compounds the display of economic power with expressions of pity (7:183). Charity unwittingly invests an unjust social system with a moral aura. Wealthy, self-serving, self-justifying capitalists are made to appear religious and democratic. There is no deeper pathos, Niebuhr once observed, than the unconscious cruelty of a righteous people, a self-appointed moral aristocracy (7:225-226).

Through Reinhold Niebuhr the spirit of Karl Marx traveled from industrial England and holy Russia to the United States. A gigantic conceptual revolution was initiated. Those influenced by Niebuhr no longer took for granted the inviolable morality of white-steepled chapels and little brown churches in the dale.[11] An American myth about its middle-class religious institutions was exposed. These institutions were not merely perpetuators of moral virtue—supposedly but mythologically "separate" from the dirty realism of politics—but were also the expression of the self-interest of the dominant groups in society.

Niebuhr's passionate desire was to be a *realist*, to expose all "illusions" and "pretensions" (two favorite terms) by critical analysis. The moral "pretensions" of statesmen and business leaders should be unearthed and the "illusions" of former idealists like himself must be exposed. Religious institutions could not be exempt from this criticism. In this context, Marx became a secular seer, a severe realist who felt no need "to save either God's or man's reputation" (6:209). His voice served as an antidote to liberal self-deception and offered an analytical perspective that helped expose the immoral dimensions of modern industrial society. In mind and in spirit Niebuhr found a comrade in Karl Marx.

Nevertheless, Niebuhr's practical work in Detroit, his native intelligence and force of character gave him a critical, discriminating independence from Marx which he never lost (19:117-125, 3:139). On the subjects of ideology, class-shaped ethics, and the reactionary role of religion, Marx was Niebuhr's teacher. However, Niebuhr developed proto-Marxian ideas about industrial society and acculturated religion on the basis of his own experience as illuminated by the biblical literature. His view of man and his understanding of prophetic religion further underline the mature Niebuhr's intellectual independence.

3. THE NATURE OF MAN IN PROPHETIC RELIGION

Given Niebuhr's Marxist critique of religion, why did he remain committed to religion? Given his indictment of American religious institutions, how could he hold a professorial chair in ethics in a major American seminary for 32 years?

In part, the answers to these questions lie in Niebuhr's intellectual independence and his refusal to accept Marx's reductionism. Niebuhr felt the temptation of a "complete capitulation" to Marx's materialistic humanism, particularly when so many of his former liberal beliefs had disintegrated. However, he believed that Marx's determinism did "violence to the real dialectic between nature and spirit . . . which all history reveals (11:Autumn, 1935). In contrast with Marx, Niebuhr discerned in man a creative power enabling him to transcend the constraints of his economic or social conditions. In addition, Niebuhr recognized a pervasive and intractable proclivity toward evil which could not be eradicated simply by changing the social structure. In brief, Niebuhr was both more optimistic and more pessimistic than Marx. He discerned resources of freedom in man concealed by Marx's determinism and limits to human goodness concealed by Marx's optimism.

Niebuhr developed this distinctive view of man from the classical Christian literature, especially the Bible. Basic to his thought were the biblical stories of the creation and the fall of man. Niebuhr recognized that these stories were not "actual history," the literal stories of Adam and Eve as the first man and woman. However, because these stories were "myths" and not historically true, he would not dismiss them as did secular and religious liberals.[12] For myths, while not true to history, were true to human nature; they depicted the irreducibly transcendent and tragic dimensions of human life. Religious liberals who ignored the myth of the fall—because it was historically not true—also missed its profound insights into human nature.

The stories of the creation and the fall appear in the first three chapters of Genesis. In these narratives, God creates a good world and creates man—and subsequently woman—in his image. A serpent then appears who tempts Eve with the promise that she will "be like God" if she eats of the forbidden fruit of the tree of good and evil. After Eve eats the fruit, and induces Adam to eat also, they know themselves to be guilty and are expelled from the garden to a life of labor and suffering.

Niebuhr interpreted the story of creation to mean that man is both body and spirit, with animal and divine qualities. As spirit, he has the power and the freedom to transcend himself. His high degree of consciousness and reason allow him to triumph over other creatures, to remember, analyze and initiate self-directed action. His self-consciousness grants him the power of introspection and moral direction (10:I,12-14). Human dignity lies in these potencies that are actualized in radical freedom. Because he is endowed with the transcendent "image of God" or "spirit," man is a majestic creature (10:I,122; also Wolf in 3:234-235). This biblical story served as a paradigm for Niebuhr's rejection of Marx's determinism. To bind man to economic and social conditions was to dismiss the freedom intrinsic to mankind's creation. According to Niebuhr, Marx's own thought illustrated this freedom. For Marxism grew out of the philosophical reflection and historical investigations of "educated members of the propertied class" and was not a mere reflection of proletarian experience (9:148).

Nevertheless, human dignity comprises also the ground of human depravity. Adam and Eve, representing humankind, refused to accept their limitations as creatures. At the heart of their rebellion was *hubris,* the desire to overcome finitude by playing God. Characteristically, man transmits his "partial and finite self and his partial and finite values into the infinite good. Therein lies his sin" (11:I,122). The driving force of sin is egotism or pride, expressed as dishonesty or pretension (7:71-79,85-87; 18:459). Human life measured by its possibilities is majestic, but measured by its actualities is tragic.

This paradoxical vision of the majesty and tragedy of human life as preserved in the myths of creation and the fall form an essential aspect of Niebuhr's "prophetic religion" (7:74). He believed that the virtue of classical and Reformation thinkers, like Augustine and Martin Luther, lay in their realistic presentations of the pervasiveness of evil in the world (7:74-75). Yet he criticized them for losing the paradoxical balance between man's self-transcendence and his abuse of that power through pride. By denying man's capacity for transcendence and by focusing too strongly on original sin as an "inherited" corruption, classical Christian theologians minimized the dimension of human freedom and encouraged too much pessimism and social passivity (7:74,90). Niebuhr was neither a thoroughgoing pessimist nor a traditionalist.

Reinhold Niebuhr used this biblical view of man as an interpretive perspective for understanding the dynamics of human history. Like Charles Darwin's theory of natural selection, Niebuhr's view of man became the organizing principle for his extensive observations. For example, Niebuhr discerned that when middle-class business and religious leaders called for law and order, they really asked to place their own interests at the center of that order. This self-aggrandizement was characteristic of Adam, whose inordinate pride led him to make his finite, limited powers and values into ultimate ones (7:85). Man's pretentiousness affects the way he reasons, the way he is patriotic, the way he worships. Against Enlightenment rationalists, who regarded reason as the great road by which learned man leaves bigotry and injustice behind, Niebuhr argued that rationality itself was often corrupted by egotism (9:23,40). It can be simply an instrument for shoring up individual or group insecurity. It can be a scepter by which humans legitimate their rights to oppress their fellows (11:Autumn, 1935, 19-20).

Nationalism is even more frequently distorted by egotism. Weak, "average" little people, unable to achieve individual power and glory, turn to patriotism in order to achieve importance vicariously through the achievements of their nation (9:18). Fathers and mothers project their unfilled ego ambitions on their children. Males avoid mutuality with females lest they expose the weakness of their own humanity (9:46-47). The list of examples is almost endless—class, race, age, profession, culture. Man's infinitely varied creativity is used to find ingenious ways to rival God and rebel against the moral claims of conscience. Man's majesty has become the basis for his tragedy, his self-transcendence the grounds for his darkest pretensions.

As a brilliant extension of this innovative anthropology, Niebuhr distinguished between the egotism of individuals and that of groups.[13] His years as a bachelor in Detroit enabled him to observe how love flourished with much greater ease between individuals within families than between groups of people within larger communities (8:49). In interpersonal relationships, humans are able to transcend egoism and demonstrate genuine care and empathy. However, Niebuhr warned that in social groups there is always

less capacity for self-transcendence, less ability to comprehend the needs of others and therefore more unrestrained egoism than the individuals, who compose the group, reveal in their personal relationships (9:xi-xii).

This "collective egoism" compounds the pride and insensitivity already intrinsic to individuals. Pride, and its consequent display of power and dishonesty, is thus inseparably bound up with social institutions. In Niebuhr's hands this observation became the basis for a cogent critique of all uncritical and idealistic schemes that claim to transform the social problems of industrial society by increasing individual knowledge and benevolence (9:xii-xxv).

Through biblical and classical religious literature Reinhold Niebuhr developed an independent perspective that enabled him to jettison much of his liberal past, yet reach new certainties.[14] Niebuhr's criticism of his own liberal heritage constituted the cutting edge of his intellectual growth (6:205; 7:169,175; 14:544). At the same time, the view of man he developed from his own experience and his appropriation of biblical literature provided a solid basis for his social criticism. Freedom and *hubris* were "irreducible" characteristics of human life. Human behavior manifested "perennial" sources of conflict, "inevitable" tragedies, "irreducible" irrationalities, and constant sources of freedom for self-transcendence (11:Autumn, 1936, 4; Niebuhr in 3:435-436).

This perspective convinced Niebuhr that both the Protestant liberals and Karl Marx were wrong in assuming that humankind was infinitely malleable. Liberals believed that man could be educated and morally cajoled out of his ignorant and immoral past (9:xi-xxv; 11: Autumn, 1936, 4-5). Marx believed that evil resided ultimately in the economic order. For Niebuhr, "the most grievous mistake of Marxism" lay in its assumption that economic and social manipulation could produce altruistic citizens who would "give according to their ability and take according to their need" (7:201). Marx's man was too plastic, too easily reshaped. Marx and his followers were therefore blind to the degree to which new forms of pride and greed would pervade even their own socialist societies (11:Spring, 1936, 28; 10:II,253,261).

While Niebuhr accepted much of Marx's critique of religion, he clearly had an independent point of view which enabled him to criticize Marxist thought and practice. The biblical view of man as free but perverted exposed the fallacy of Marx's economic determinism and utopian illusions. Prophetic religion, like Marx, is able to unmask the sentimental illusions and reactionary social roles of traditional and middle-class acculturated religion. Yet beyond Marx, prophetic religion points to the deeper roots of injustice in all human societies (11:Autumn, 1935, 4). It is able to appreciate Marx as a seer, but also considers him a disguised romantic (9:193-199). Prophetic religion is, therefore, not illusory, not an opiate of the people, but a source of insight and realism not limited by any social system. Through its incisive realism it illumines the dynamics of human society, but can it do more? Can it become an instrument for changing society?

4. LOVE, JUSTICE, AND POWER

Human history for Reinhold Niebuhr was enacted in a mountainous terrain which displayed the depths of incorrigible self-interest and the heights of a transcendent love. Even as his analysis of human nature yielded resources for social criticism, so also his articulation of the transcendent love of God contained principles and resources for criticism and change.

Further informed by the biblical heritage, Niebuhr identified the transcendent norm of prophetic religion as love. This ultimate norm is not to be equated with mutual love (eros) which is born of human need and always "seeks to relate life to life from the standpoint of the self and for the sake of the self's own happiness" (10:II,82). The transcendent norm of ethical religion is self-giving love or agape (the Greek word for this love in the New Testament), a love not concerned for reciprocity, heedless about the needs of the self and directed towards the good of the other (7:57, 10:II,71-72). As a Christian, Niebuhr believed that agape was portrayed supremely in the death of Christ on the cross, symbolizing the suffering of one who sought nothing for himself and everything for the neighbor (7:37,120; 10:II,58,71).[15]

Niebuhr considered agape as much more than a human ideal. He called it the "quintessence of the character of God," and, although he did not believe that agape was the exclusive possession of the Christian heritage, he said that it was "clarified" by the New Testament literature and was embodied in the life, teachings and death of Christ (9:58-59; 7:39; 10:II,70-71). Such persons as the Indian saint Ramakrishna conceived of selfless concern for the other as an ultimate ethical ideal for human conduct (9:58). But through the life and death of its founder, Christianity had agape woven into the fabric of its existence. With a kind of heedless charity, St. Francis of Assisi kissed lepers and trusted robbers, and Paul the apostle cried that Christian communities should make no value judgements between Jew and Greek, male and female, slave and free (9:58).

Nevertheless, Niebuhr did not believe that self-giving love was an ideal "attainable in history" (7:117; 10:II, 68). Agape is a divine, transcendent, "ecstatic" form of love which defines the "ultimate heroic possibilities of human existence," not "the common possibilities" of historical behavior (16:28; 9:263).

While Niebuhr regarded self-giving love as an ideal transcending the calculating compromises of ordinary human transactions, he was convinced that it was still a powerful ingredient in shaping man's life in history. Niebuhr did not relegate *agape* to some other-worldly status with no relevance to this-worldly existence. Throughout his life Niebuhr was concerned about the "relevance of an impossible ideal" (7:103-135; 10:II,68-97; Bennett in 3:54-57).

In the first place, part of the genius of *agape* lies in its organic relation with "every moral aspiration and achievement" (7:105). Human moral systems that prohibit stealing and murder or that affirm human rights and equality are "grounded in" *agape* and fulfilled and refined through it (7:105-107). Prohibitions and positive moral systems are based on hopes for greater social unity and mutuality and presuppose concern for the other as well as the self. Self-giving love sensitizes the way parents treat their children, the way school systems educate, and the way societies should treat criminals not as enemies but as genuine human beings (7:109-111). Niebuhr developed the notion of "mutual love" *(eros)* as the norm that most directly and consistently relates *agape* to human experience. Mutual love, expressing the reciprocal needs of neighbor and self, is the highest norm that is realizable by man in natural human communities (10:II,81-82). *Agape* "completes" mutual love by pointing to an always more perfect form of brotherhood (10:II, 82-86).

In the second place, like the biblical view of man, *agape* serves as a norm for social criticism. Precisely because this love can never be fully embodied in human history, it always preserves its integrity as a transcendent ideal. Self-giving love thus exposes the egotistical limits to any form of social justice and keeps men from imparting "unqualified worth to qualified values" (7:105; 10:II,86-95). It is "precisely in a high religion, which sees the whole world of history as relative to the absolute and final goodness of God" that the "dishonesties and deceptions of culture can be best discovered" (11:Autumn, 1935, 19). Thus, *agape* provided Niebuhr with a norm for criticizing any acculturated religion which served the self-interests of its participants rather than the needs of all men. Any secular or religious system that supposes that it realizes altruism within history is self-deceived. No social program, like universal education or the secular society of Marxism, is able to embody self-giving love (10:II,86-87). Because of its transcendence, *agape* exposes and opposes all past and present attempts to endow any society with absolute moral goodness and divine sanction.

Driven by the ideal of self-giving love, prophetic religion possesses the power to challenge social inequities and to create social unrest. Niebuhr identified himself with a long heritage of radical spokesmen. The herdsman Amos of the Old Testament cried out against the merchant aristocracy of his age and their priestly supporters; he was charged by the king of Israel with political conspiracy (Amos 2:6; 7:10-17). Jesus offended the religious establishment of first-century Judaism and the political power of Rome; he was crucified as a messianic pretender. During the Reformation, the Anabaptists took up the "left wing" political heritage of biblical faith; they became political exiles for their cause. Later in England, the Puritans, propelled by the egalitarianism latent within their faith, joined ranks with Oliver Cromwell in a revolution against the monarchy (11:Spring, 1938, 14). In all these instances, Niebuhr saw the transcendent norm of *agape* inspiring prophetic spokesmen to take up the cause of social criticism or political revolution. Indeed, religion of this kind was the opposite of a passive ideology sustained only by hopes for a heavenly reward. Niebuhr viewed Marx himself as a prophet in this tradition, sharing "exactly the same faith," although in secular form (11:Autumn, 1935, 17).

Niebuhr had no illusions concerning the adequacy of love as the sole norm for transforming oppressive social systems (9:34; 16:44). His realistic view of man and his understanding of the moral limits of groups led him to view social problems in terms of corporate self-interest and power conflicts.[16] Therefore, if prophetic religion was to address the significant social issues of the day, it was necessary to develop a moral norm that would be rooted in love and appropriate to the competing self-interests and power conflicts of social groups. For Niebuhr, the notion of justice provided the mediating norm between the ideal of love and the realities of power.

Consistent with the Enlightenment tradition, Niebuhr understood justice in terms of equality. Yet maintaining a more dynamic perspective than Enlightenment thinkers, Niebuhr believed that equality was a transcendent principle behind justice, since genuine equality could never become fully embodied in the varied historical manifestations of justice (11:Spring, 1938, 16; 7:108; 10:II,254). As a "pinnacle of the ideal of justice," equality pushes the historical forms of justice toward higher levels (10:II,254).

Niebuhr once called "equal justice" an "approximation of brotherhood under the conditions of sin" (10:II,254). He meant by that phrase that justice ultimately pushes people—however reluctantly—to treat others as their equals. This is a kind of second-level golden rule—acting for others as you wish them to act for you (16:13,26-27). Equal justice is fulfilled in mutual love, and mutual love finds its ultimate ideal in *agape* (7:108; 10:II,247). Justice, therefore, enjoys a dialectical relationship with love. On the other hand, love serves as a transcendent magnet that draws justice towards higher and higher levels. In this process, the concept of "justice" is transformed in history (10:II,246). The sensitizing power of unselfish benevolence means that today's "justice" may appear unjust tomorrow (10:II,246ff.). On the other hand, justice keeps love honest. It keeps love from degenerating into sentimentalism or from being undermined by subtle forms of self-interest. For example, the meaning of a "love" relationship between a man and woman can easily be informed more by customs and stereotypes than "by a fresh calculation of competing interests" and mutual rights (10:II,248, Bennett in 3:60). Similarly, what appears to be "love" in philanthropy is shown to be something less by the criterion of justice. Justice shows that much philanthropy is predicated upon illegitimate social inequalities (16:26).

Justice, however, is not only in dialectical relation with love but also is in close proximity to the real world. Personal self-interest and group egotism constantly express themselves in the world through many types of conflict. Equal justice is the best norm for evaluating these conflicts. It recognizes realistically that the differing interests of individuals and groups must be respected and calls upon reason to assess and balance conflicting needs and desires (7:196; 16:28; 10:II,252). The Enlightenment legacy of "critical intelligence" is a "veritable prerequisite of justice" in its ability to adjudicate competing interests (7:163-164; also 9:57,59). Justice thus utilizes reason and deals forthrightly with self-interest and egotism.

Moreover, justice includes a consideration and use of power or coercion, and Niebuhr regarded power as an absolute necessity for effecting social change (9:esp. xxiii). Legal systems, governmental structures, the popular will, economic resources and even the force of arms are means of power available in society to adjudicate the competing self-interests of groups (10:II,256-269). Learning from Marx that disproportionate power often lay at the root of social injustice, Niebuhr emphasized that the struggle for justice in society would have to consist in a redistribution of power, particularly by giving greater strength to the less powerful victims of injustice (10:II,258,262-265; 9:163; Bennett in 3:60). In this respect, his thought was a prophetic forecast of many of the social crises of the 1960's and 1970's.

Niebuhr believed that the redistribution of power must be accomplished either through governmental and legal action or violent revolution. These were the embodiments of coercion necessary to change society, and Niebuhr saw no "absolute distinctions between non-violent and violent types of coercion or between coercion used by governments and that which is used by revolutionaries" (9:172,179). In opposition to Marx, Niebuhr did not believe that violent revolution was inevitable, but opposing middle-class presuppositions, he argued that violence was not "intrinsically immoral." For example, violence was not inevitably an expression of hatred or ill-will, nor did it always produce more suffering than forms of non-violent coercion like blockades or boycotts (9:171-179; cf. also p. 230).

While Niebuhr was committed to augment justice within society by legal and political means, he was willing in the 1930's to entertain the possibility of utilizing violence. He argued that the Russian Revolution, rather than representing the first, worldwide revolution, occurred under a set of unique conditions that could not be duplicated in America or Western Europe (9:187). Uncannily, he predicted in 1932 that although communism would probably not sweep the West, it very likely would "gain its victories in the agrarian Orient" (9:191). He expected American society to be reshaped along the lines of political and economic reform evident in England and Germany in the 1920's and early 1930's (9:187-219). Niebuhr himself considered nonviolent forms of political coercion as "clearly preferable" to violent readjustments of power (9:220). Yet in the 1930's he believed that violence, hopefully executed without blind self-righteousness and with the quick "tempo of a surgeon's skill," could justifiably be used to effect social change (9:220; 12:165-189).

His commitment to win justice by altering the balance of power in society led Niebuhr to become involved in politics. On the economic front, he was an active supporter of organized labor throughout his career. At times he would leave his lectures at Union Theological Seminary in order to appear on a picket line for a local New York union. Niebuhr invited and won support from many other church leaders in this cause. As early as 1934 he wrote that Christians need to "stop fooling themselves." If they really want to reconcile men to each other and help create a more just society, they must recognize "the perennial necessity" of this-worldly, political involvement (16:43; Schlesinger, Jr. in 3:135). Niebuhr himself helped initiate several political organizations and politically-oriented journals. One was the liberal political group, Americans for Democratic Action; another was the journal, *Christianity and Crisis*.[17] His life incarnated his own principle: there must be "conscious political contrivance in human history to mitigate conflict and to invent instruments for the enlarging mutualities of social existence" (10:II,265).

Niebuhr's commitment to the liberal wing of the Democratic political party was a relatively late development in his career. It was a commitment that expressed his confidence in the ability of Franklin Delano Roosevelt's New Deal politics to humanize *laissez-faire* capitalism as well as his revulsion towards the fascism of Germany and Italy and the Stalinism of the Soviet Union (cf. 11:Winter, 1938, 44-45; Schlesinger in 3:142-150 and Bennett in 3:72-75).

Prior to 1944, Niebuhr's political position was far more radical. From 1929–1944 he described his position as that of a "Christian Marxist."[18] With Marx, Niebuhr found capitalism brutal and dehumanizing. He understood capitalism to embody self-interest and inequality, while socialism thrived on enlightened self-interest and equality. For Niebuhr in the 1930's, only the "socialization of property" could provide an adequate "prerequisite of basic justice" (14:545; 11:Spring, 1936, 28; 7:184; 9:170). And only a violent or legislative socialist revolution could establish a "tolerable equilibrium of economic power" (14:545). World War I and the great depression had convinced Niebuhr that capitalism suffered "an organic and constitutional sickness," surviving crises in unemployment only by resorting to warfare (12:24-35,77-81; 11:Spring, 1938, 15-17; 14:545; 4:166-185).[19]

After 1944, Niebuhr greatly altered his political beliefs. He became, in fact, a national spokesman and defender of pragmatic, Western democracy.[20] Under Franklin D. Roosevelt's New Deal, labor began to enjoy more of the fruits of democracy (Schlesinger in 3:142-145). At the same time, Niebuhr's realistic view of man led him to become increasingly critical of socialist power systems (cf. Bennett in 3:72-75). He defended democratic capitalism because it allowed for the expression and adjudication of group conflicts under the ideals of equality and love (see esp. 10:II,263-64; 5:xii-xv). One of Niebuhr's famous dictums expressed the close relationship between his realistic view of man and his commitment to democracy: "man's capacity for justice makes democracy possible; but man's inclination to injustice makes democracy necessary" (5:xiii).

Apart from his changing political loyalties, Niebuhr relied upon his systematic love–justice–power ethic to change status quo relationships in a variety of areas. He taught, preached, wrote and acted so that men and women, inspired by *agape* love, would create and support structures of power that would enable labor, the poor, women, blacks, Jews and ethnic minorities to win their just rights in society (see the bibliography in 3:459-478). This entailed the support of specific and "proximate" economic and political policies, as well as leadership in various agencies like the National Council of Churches and the NAACP. Niebuhr could criticize Martin Luther King's "sentimentality," yet he deeply influenced King and strongly supported his quest for social justice.[21]

Throughout his life, Niebuhr was a staunch critic of institutional religion. He hoped that dynamic preaching of prophetic religion would help prepare middle-class Christians for social justice (cf. 16:153). However, he was never convinced that this transformation would occur. In the late 1920's and the early 1930's, the focus of his criticism fell upon the irresponsibility of middle-class, acculturated religion toward industrial conditions and labor. In the mid-1940's, he rightly complained that this same middle-class church had "failed miserably" in its response to racism. Indeed, the church in America, declared Niebuhr in 1944, was "almost consistently Jim Crow in its pattern of segregation (16:37,143).

Nevertheless, Niebuhr recognized certain institutionalized forms of religion that did serve as instruments of social justice. The Puritan churches in England, propelled by the ultimate norm of the sovereignty of God, had become a revolutionary, "left-wing" social force in opposition to the monarchy (11:Spring, 1938, 14). Niebuhr also conjectured that lower-class white American churches might become socially dynamic, but, for the most part, their activism was hindered by ignorance (16:112-113). Later in his life, he believed that black churches were developing genuine social vitality (16:20). However, these institutions tended to be the exceptions, rather than the norm, in Niebuhr's understanding of the social role of institutionalized religion. While he continued to believe in the power of prophetic religion to promote social justice, he was always keenly aware of the gulf between the biblically based, prophetic religion he espoused and the acculturated practice of religion in American churches.

5. CRITIQUE OF MARX

Several of Niebuhr's criticisms of Marx have already been noted. On the basis of his biblical view of man, Niebuhr objected to Marx's socio-economic reductionism which did not take account of man's freedom or his perennial evil proclivities. Moreover, as an historian, Marx did not acknowledge the fact that religion had inspired many revolutionary prophets and movements. Niebuhr therefore concluded that Marx was not correct in his contention that religion was only a superstructure reflecting the socioeconomic substructure of life or that religion functioned solely as a weapon for established oppressors and a psychological crutch for the working masses.

However, Niebuhr's critique of Marx was far more devastating than these cogent criticisms. For Niebuhr exposed the religious basis of Marx's self-proclaimed scientific empiricism. While Marx had a realistic, empirically based appreciation of economic influence and while he rightly recognized the centrality of power and conflict in human life, he had to leap over "the bounds of rationally verifiable possibilities" to establish the essential contentions of his position: the inevitability of revolution, the necessity for the ultimate victory of the proletariat, and the establishment of an egalitarian society free from destructive egotism (9:156,167; 13:462,468). Undiluted Marxism, Niebuhr argued, was actually "a religious interpretation of proletarian destiny."

> To make the degradation of the proletarian the cause of his ultimate exaltation, to find in the very disaster of his social defeat the harbinger

of his final victory, and to see in his loss of all property the future of a civilisation in which no one will have privileges of property, this is to snatch victory out of defeat in the style of great drama and classical religion. . . . Marxism is another kind of slave revolt. It exalts not the virtues but the estate of the lowly. . . . It is not the meek but the weak who are given the promise of inheriting the earth (9:154).

Marx thus created "an apocalyptic vision," a confident prophecy of a utopian future for the disinherited, a secularized version of Christian eschatological hope (9:155-156).

Beyond the incipient religious ideology of Marx himself, Niebuhr discovered in Russian communism the fully developed characteristics of a major religion. Stalinism included the absolute ethic of loyalty to the proletariat; it disseminated a sacred scripture consisting of the writings of Marx and Lenin to be studied and revered by all; the Communist Party functioned as a dogmatic, heresy-hunting organization, expelling and sometimes executing party members holding deviant beliefs; Stalin himself ruled as a priest-king, endowed with mystical powers and demanding dutiful reverence from the masses; the people's confidence depended upon faith in a higher, providential power, in this case the dialectic of history, leading to worldwide victory for the communist cause; and the future of a classless society was envisioned in terms reminiscent of the traditional expectations of paradise (13:466-468; 9:155-162; 11:Autumn, 1935, 15). The post-Stalinist establishment of a sacred shrine containing the body of Lenin and attracting pilgrims from all over Russia and elsewhere further confirmed Niebuhr's analysis of the religious dimensions of Russian communism.

While Niebuhr considered communism a religion, he always recognized that this new religious movement has promoted social change. Communism tapped the hopes and despairs of the laboring masses and directed their energy towards the building of a new, egalitarian society. Like Puritanism or black churches, Marxism fused the self-interests of a social group with an inspired faith (9:161-162). Communism also joined together a critical, realistic analysis of social oppression with an idealistic vision of a new future society. The combination of these two factors—critical realism and transcendent hope—is closely analogous to Niebuhr's own version of prophetic religion. The pessimism of the communist social analysis called for violence and total commitment, while the optimism of its future hope sustained self-denial for the sake of building a new society. Niebuhr regarded the Marxist criticism of the old order and its devotion to social change as its most constructive aspects.

Nevertheless, considered as a whole, Niebuhr found the religion of Marxism to be highly destructive of basic human values. Because Marxism imagined itself to be purely scientific and therefore necessarily true, it encouraged a rigid and ruthless dogmatism. Because Marxist idealism viewed man as infinitely malleable, it was blind to the egotistic and repressive use of power within socialist societies. There simply was no room in the dogmatic expressions of Marxism for ideological or social criticism once revolutionary power had been established. Like older religious and secular liberals, the Marxist placed a naive trust in human rationality and espoused a romantic view of human nature which ignored man's perennial lust for power (9:155,194; 11:Spring, 1938, 17-18).

Finally, Niebuhr objected to Marxism as another form of acculturated religion. Just as middle-class, Western religious institutions tended to absolutize the values of their class, so Marxism made the values of the proletariat infinite (9:161-192). By uncritically absolutizing the self-interests of the working masses, Marxism created new forms of vindictiveness, violence and egotism (9:155,157). While Niebuhr sought to abolish the social injustice intrinsic to middle-class domination of society, he was not willing to absolutize the values of any single social class, including the proletariat. For Niebuhr, any religion based on a particular class, any exaltation of the finite to the infinite, was necessarily destructive both for individuals and for society as a whole.

Through this critique of Marx, Niebuhr exposed yet another set of pretensions and illusions. While claiming to be scientific, Marx was shown to rely deeply on nonempirical hopes. While claiming to be realistic, Marx also propagated utopian dreams. By means of Niebuhr's prophetic realism, Marx was unmasked as a reductionist and romantic, not so much the propounder of a new, social-scientific synthesis as the prophet of a new form of acculturated religion.

6. NIEBUHR'S PROPHETIC LEGACY

At a time when the social policies of traditional religion appeared irrelevant and those of liberalism naive and ineffectual, Niebuhr gave a new impetus to the prophetic legacy of the Bible. He became an American Amos whose discoveries were also rediscoveries of the critical, revolutionary voices of ancient Hebrew prophets. His writings show that religion has been and can be a catalyst for social unrest and change. This potency of religion had been overlooked by Karl Marx.

Yet Niebuhr's delineation of prophetic religion was more than a reaffirmation of the past. While his own convictions concerning the social role of religion were informed by Hebrew prophets and advocates of the social gospel, Niebuhr added to that heritage his own incisive, critical realism. Through his analysis of individual and group behavior, he enabled a generation of religious thinkers and political theorists to become partners in the mitigation of social ills (Schlesinger, Jr., in 3:126-150).[22]

Niebuhr's insistence on the centrality of self-giving love was faithful to his Christian tradition and germane to the problems of social change. Love meant more to Niebuhr than the highest ideal of tradition or liberal Christianity. It became a critical norm for judging all the relative and finite approximations of justice in society. Moreover, the fusion of love with the norm of justice and the tactics of power led to the birth of a new generation of socially active religious leaders in America. These people were committed to remake old institutions or create new ones in order to realize more inclusive forms of justice. As we have seen, among those deeply influenced by Niebuhr was Martin Luther King, who combined the religious traditions of American blacks with the nonviolence of Mahatma Gandhi and Niebuhr's power-oriented realism.

The form of prophetic religion developed by Reinhold Niebuhr proved to be an effective instrument for social criticism. His analysis of mankind's diverse expressions of egotism unmasked intractable self-interest and aggressiveness in all social systems. As a result, many social critics who reject the religious origins and claims in Niebuhr's thought use his analysis as a critical perspective.[23] They have become rightly suspicious of the claims of any group that identifies its self-interest with ultimate ethical principles: capitalist and Marxist societies; middle-class or proletarian economic strata; ethnic, racial, religious or sexual groups. In short, like Marx's anti-religious social philosophy, Niebuhr proved that prophetic religion can clarify the dynamic forces shaping human existence, criticize oppressive social orders and cultivate programs designed to promote a more just society.

Niebuhr's elaboration of the reactionary role of much religion has been confirmed by recent research. Gibson Winter's *Suburban Captivity of the Churches* set forth a careful, sociological analysis, showing how middle-class religion was captive to the ethos of suburbia; sociologists Charles Y. Glock and Rodney Stark have presented evidence indicating that strong religious commitment varies inversely with a high concern for revising society; and studies by Charles Reimer and Jeffrey Hadden have shown respectively how churches have nurtured racism and have resisted active involvement in controversial social issues.[24] Enclaves of Niebuhr-informed social activists in denominational superstructures or in organizations like the National Council of Churches have often discovered painfully that they are shepherds without flocks. Their sophisticated studies and carefully designed social policies have simply failed to attract broad-based, grass-roots support from members of middle-class religious institutions. The analysis of Niebuhr that seemed radical and pessimistic in the 1930's has proven, unhappily, to be true for the 1970's.

Nevertheless, a careful consideration of Niebuhr's thought suggests four problematic points. First, does Niebuhr's pervasive application of his realistic image of man tend to restrict and inhibit social change? Over against the moral optimism of his liberal theological predecessors, Niebuhr insisted on the dominant role of self-interest in all human behavior and on man's tendency to use his power to exploit others. This theological perspective tended to make Niebuhr conservative in his expectations for political and social change. He was extremely cautious about any revolutionary program which was oriented towards a utopian hope for a new society. Given the genuine innovations within history, was he too cautious? Critics of Niebuhr like Richard Shaull have argued that the eschatological hope of the Bible is oriented towards a radical transformation of society in the future, a transformation that cannot be confined to a pragmatic program of relative increments in social justice. Did Niebuhr's disillusionment with social gospel idealism and his pessimism concerning man's evil proclivities prevent him from taking seriously the radical hope proclaimed in the Bible? [25]

Second, does Niebuhr's identification with the post-World War II American social context limit his ability to understand problems of social change in underdeveloped societies? Was Niebuhr after the mid-1940's a social prophet relevant only to America and other economically developed, politically stabilized democracies? Before 1940, in his "socialist phase," Niebuhr spoke of the bankruptcy of *laissez-faire* capitalism and of hope for a new social order more consistent with the norms of love and justice in prophetic religion. But the specters of fascism and Stalinism, the acid of his own realistic view of man and the social changes evident under the New Deal led him to temper his hopes and limit his visions. Pragmatism, prudence and order replaced in part his earlier pleas for radical justice and love (16:152ff.). Today, many social ethicists question the applicability of post-World War II American experience to underdeveloped societies.[26] It may be impossible to develop more humanized social orders in other nations within an American type of political democracy or within the economic style of democratic capitalism. Because Niebuhr chose to direct his thought to the specific issues of the post-World War II context, he may be less relevant than others to a quite different economic and political situation. This problem is highlighted in the following chapter. Should there be a movement from Christian realism to Christian radicalism in the application of prophetic religion to new social and political contexts?

Third, given Niebuhr's enthusiasm for relating his thought to "biblical religion," did he overlook the rich diversity of resources for social change within the biblical literature? Did he take seriously the eschatological visions of a new age predominant in much of the biblical literature? Did he fail to recognize sufficiently the biblical vision of God who identifies himself fully with the poor and the oppressed? James Cone develops both of these biblical themes—the identification of God with the disposessed and the eschatological vision of a new society—in his exposition of a theology for black American Christians.[27]

Fourth, in light of Niebuhr's critique of middle-class religion and his conviction that social change requires the utilization of power, what social agencies are available for prophetic religion's quest for justice? Throughout his life, Niebuhr was suspicious of the social role of most forms of institutionalized religion. He chose to cast his lot with shrewd, informed pressure groups that occupied positions of power in denominational, intradenominational and political organizations—the religious and ethical brain trusts of national church bodies and political parties. The unity and power once achieved by the concerted activity of national church agencies behind Martin Luther King and black churchmen now appear to be fragmented and weakened. If prophetic religious leaders do not trust local religious groups because they tend to be bastions of middle-class values, and if the national churches have been divested of both prestige and economic power, the question as to who will implement the prophetic quest for social justice becomes pressing indeed. Can social change result from the agitation of radical "cell" groups or the legislative activity of "well-placed" political leaders? Will social change be produced by those groups intrinsically self-interested in change—the religious institutions of the dispossessed? The latter suggestion is consistent with Niebuhr's own thought, for it links together self-interest with a religious hope for justice.

It is still an open question whether religious institutions will respond to the criticisms of Marx and the prophetic judgments of Niebuhr. For religious believers, Niebuhr's vision of prophetic faith offers a decisive challenge. Will these believers transform their communities by their self-proclaimed, highest ideals? Or instead, will they, as the prophetic Isaiah said, hide their eyes from the visions of seers and demand that prophets speak "smooth things," and "prophesy illusions?" (Isaiah 30:10)

NOTES

[1] Harnack gave a classic statement of his theology in his published lectures entitled in English, *What Is Christianity?* (New York: Harper & Row, 1957, originally published in 1900). A succinct discussion of Harnack's thought is found in Dean B. Peerman and Martin E. Marty, eds., *A Handbook of Christian Theologians* (New York: World, 1965), pp. 86-111. A sketch of Harnack's theology in relation to the development of liberalism is found in John Dillen-

berger and Claude Welch, *Protestant Christianity* (New York: Scribner's, 1954), pp. 173-231. For a more thorough study of Harnack as an historian and theologian, see G. Wayne Glick, *The Reality of Christianity* (New York: Harper & Row, 1967).

2 For introductions, selected primary sources and bibliography on American liberals, see H. Shelton Smith, Robert T. Handy and Lefferts A. Loetscher, *American Christianity*, II (18:255-308); and William R. Hutchison, *American Protestant Thought: The Liberal Era* (2). A more elaborate discussion is found in Kenneth W. Cauthen, *The Impact of American Religious Liberalism* (New York: Harper & Row, 1962).

3 The best available recent discussion of Macintosh's thought is in Peerman and Marty, *A Handbook of Christian Theologians*, pp. 212-232. For his mature thought, see Macintosh, *Theology as an Empirical Science* (New York, 1919), and *The Reasonableness of Christianity* (New York: Scribner's, 1926).

4 For accounts of the rise and maturation of the early social gospel as well as other phases of social involvement by religious groups in America, see Charles Howard Hopkins, *The Rise of the Social Gospel in American Protestantism, 1865-1915* (New Haven, 1940); Henry F. May, *Protestant Churches and Industrial America* (New York, 1949); and Aaron I. Abell, *Aberican Catholicism and Social Action* (Notre Dame, Ind.: University of Notre Dame Press, 1963). For briefer discussions with selected writings and bibliography, see Smith, Handy, and Loetscher, *American Christianity*, II (18:359-416); and Robert T. Handy, ed., *The Social Gospel in America, 1870-1920* (New York: Oxford University Press, 1966).

5 See, for example, the discussion by Hopkins, *The Rise of the Social Gospel*, pp. 205-214. Niebuhr's later attempts to refute these claims are found in his *An Interpretation of Christian Ethics* (7:43-64), and his essay in D. B. Robertson, ed., *Love and Justice* (16:29-40).

6 At one time Niebuhr served on the Advisory Committee for the Policy Planning Staff of the U. S. State Department. He once remarked that he spent as much time dealing with the field of international politics as with theology. See Ronald H. Stone, *Reinhold Niebuhr: Prophet to Politicians* (Nashville: Abingdon Press, 1972), p. 245. For an impressive collection of Niebuhr's writings on political, social and ethical issues, see Harry R. Davis and Robert C. Good, eds., *Reinhold Niebuhr on Politics* (New York: Scribner's, 1960). For the best analyses of his thought in relation to politics, see Stone, *Reinhold Niebuhr.* See also the articles by Arthur Schlesinger, Jr., and Kenneth Thompson in Charles W. Kegley and Robert W. Bretall, eds., *Reinhold Niebuhr: His Religious, Social, and Political Thought* (3).

7 For indications of disenchantment—sometimes less severe—among other American religious leaders, see Hutchison, *American Protestant Thought* (2:147-196); and Smith, Handy and Loetscher, *American Christianity*, II (18:426-428). In 1935 the journal *Christian Century* contained the autobiographical statements of twenty-four prominent religious leaders on how the War had affected their thinking. For the broader cultural setting and the rejection of the cult of optimism in America, see Merle Curti, *The Growth of American Thought*, 3rd ed. (New York: Harper & Row, 1964), pp. 685-709, and Dixon Wecter, *Age of the Great Depression, 1929-1940* (New York: Macmillan, 1948).

8 These experiences are drawn from Niebuhr's fascinating diary as a minister in Detroit, *Leaves from the Notebook of a Tamed Cynic* (8), and his autobiographical statement in Kegley and Bretall, eds., *Reinhold Niebuhr* (3:3-23).

For detailed accounts of Niebuhr's intellectual journey, see Stone, *Reinhold Niebuhr*, pp. 17-167, and the intellectual biography by June Bingham, *Courage to Change* (New York: Scribner's, 1972). For the social and economic conditions of the American worker and the history of the Ford company, see Irving Bernstein, *The Lean Years: A History of the American Worker, 1920-1933* (Boston: Houghton-Mifflin, 1960); and Allen Nevins, *Ford: Expansion and Challenge, 1915-1933* (New York: Scribner's, 1957).

9 The famous economic interpretation of the American revolution by Charles A. Beard was first printed in 1913. Marxian-informed, economic interpretations of history flourished for several decades after that time. For a discussion and bibliography of this phase of historiography in America, see Oscar Handlin, *et al., Harvard Guide to American History* (Cambridge: Harvard University Press, 1954), pp. 15–22.

10 Although the focus here is on Niebuhr's exchange with Karl Marx, Niebuhr was genuinely influenced by the sociologists of religion, Max Weber and Ernst Troeltsch. Surely part of that influence came through the exchanges between Reinhold and his brother, H. Richard Niebuhr. The latter wrote his famous book, *The Social Sources of Denominationalism* in 1929, in which he outlined the degree to which divisions within Christianity were informed by social and economic factors. In that book H. Richard Niebuhr recognized his great indebtedness to Weber, Marx and Troeltsch, as well as to his brother Reinhold.

11 For a collection of Niebuhr's writings from 1931-1957 in which he evaluated and criticized institutionalized religion in America, see *Essays in Applied Christianity*, ed. D. B. Robertson (New York: Meridian Books, 1959), pp. 69–196. Reinhold Niebuhr was not alone in his criticism of the church as captivated by status quo concerns. See, for example, Smith, Handy and Loetscher, *American Christianity*, II (18:443-447), a selection taken from the essays by H. Richard Niebuhr, Wilhelm Pauck and Francis P. Miller published in *The Church against the World* (Chicago, 1935).

12 The most important statements by Niebuhr concerning the positive meaning of myth are his essays, "The Truth in Myths" in *The Nature of Religious Experience* (New York: Harper and Brothers, 1937), edited by J. S. Bixler, *et al.;* and "As Deceivers, Yet True," given in full in Smith, Handy and Loetscher, *American Christianity*, II (18:455-465). The first essay was written in opposition to the avowed "empirical" theology of Niebuhr's Yale professor, Douglas Clyde Macintosh.

13 Niebuhr's classic analysis of the dynamics of entrenched, group egoism is given in his still impressive *Moral Man and Immoral Society* (9). By relating the theme of human depravity to the dynamics of social existence, Niebuhr laid the ground work for breaking the social gospel movement away from its former alignment with pacifism and for moving the attention of church leaders more squarely into the arena of political theory and action. See the discussion in Smith, Handy and Loetscher, *American Christianity*, II (18:509-512), and the selections from Niebuhr in Davis and Good, eds., *Reinhold Niebuhr on Politics*, pp. 43-151, 193-238.

14 The emergence of post-liberal, neo-orthodox spokesmen like Niebuhr brought a resurgence of biblical study in America. Cf. the discussion and bibliography in Smith, Handy and Loetscher, *American Christianity*, II (18:431 and 503).

15 Although Niebuhr shunned the title of "theologian" (3:240), his two-volume work, *The Nature and Destiny of Man* (10), explores in depth classical themes in Christian thought. Paul Lehmann has argued persuasively that Niebuhr's understanding of Jesus Christ was central to his work in social ethics and the-

ology; Lehmann in Kegley and Bretall, eds., *Reinhold Niebuhr* (3:252-280). Cf. also the impressive study in Part One of Gordon Harland, *The Thought of Reinhold Niebuhr* (New York: Oxford University Press, 1960).

[16] Niebuhr played a central role in renovating—via the analytical depth and social realism of his thought—the earlier American social gospel movement (see note 4 above). See the discussions, readings and bibliography in Smith, Handy and Loetscher, *American Christianity*, II (18:505-562); and particularly the books by Paul A. Carter, *The Decline and Revival of the Social Gospel* (Ithaca, N. Y.: Cornell University Press, 1954); and Donald B. Meyer, *The Protestant Search for Political Realism, 1919-1941* (4).

[17] For more elaborate discussions of Niebuhr's political thought, involvement and influence, see the articles by Arthur Schlesinger, Jr., and Kenneth Thompson in Kegley and Bretall, eds., *Reinhold Niebuhr* (3:125-176); and the books by Ronald H. Stone, *Reinhold Niebuhr: Prophet to Politicians;* and Gordon Harland, *The Thought of Reinhold Niebuhr.*

[18] For the background to Niebuhr's Marxism and the reception of socialism in America, see the following: Stone, *Reinhold Niebuhr*, pp. 54-91; Robert T. Handy, "Christianity and Socialism in America, 1900-1929," *Church History*, 21 (March, 1952), 39-54; Henry F. May, *Protestant Churches and Industrial America;* and Donald B. Meyer, *The Protestant Search for Political Realism.* Further bibliography can be found in Nelson R. Burr, *A Critical Bibliography of Religion in America* (Princeton: Princeton University Press, 1961), pp. 711-714.

[19] Niebuhr's disenchantment with pre-New Deal capitalism became a virtual jeremiad in his *Reflections on the End of an Era* (12).

[20] See particularly Niebuhr's *The Children of Light and the Children of Darkness* (5), *The Irony of American History* (1955), and Niebuhr and Paul E. Sigmund, *The Democratic Experience Past and Prospects* (New York: Frederick A. Praeger, 1969), as well as the discussions by Stone, *Reinhold Niebuhr*, pp. 92-167, 204-210, and Schlesinger in Kegley and Bretall, eds., *Reinhold Niebuhr* (3:125-150). These sources prove that Niebuhr's appreciation of democracy was always a discriminating one.

[21] For the mutual relationships between King and Niebuhr, see Martin Luther King, *Strength to Love* (New York: Harper & Row, 1963), pp. 135-143; and Niebuhr in Davis and Good, eds., *Reinhold Niebuhr on Politics*, pp. 235-238, and Robertson, ed., *Love and Justice* (16:20). The aged Niebuhr's longer reflections on racism in America are found in *Social Action/Social Progress*, XXXV (October, 1968), 53-64.

[22] For the great influence of Niebuhr on George F. Kennan, Hans J. Morgenthau and others, see Stone, *Reinhold Niebuhr*, pp. 9-10, 169-217.

[23] See note 22 above and the comments by John C. Bennett in Kegley and Bretall, eds., *Reinhold Niebuhr* (3:48-49).

[24] See, for example, Charles Y. Glock and Rodney Stark, *Religion and Society in Tension* (Chicago: Rand McNally, 1965), pp. 201-226 (see also their negative assessments of the social roles of institutionalized religion in pp. 170-200); David M. Reimer, *White Protestantism and the Negro* (New York: Oxford University Press, 1965); Jeffrey Hadden, *The Gathering Storm in the Churches* (Garden City, N. Y.: Doubleday, 1969). Very recent studies suggest that the degree of pessimism manifested above may be over-drawn. See the review by Joseph C. Hough, Jr., "The Church Alive and Changing," *The Christian Century*, 89 (January 5, 1972), 8-12.

25 Cf. the analysis by Shaull in "Theology and the Transformation of Society" (17:26-36), which at points draws heavily from the work of Paul Lehmann. Niebuhr's relationship to Jürgen Moltmann, Rubem A. Alves and others is discussed briefly in Stone, *Reinhold Niebuhr*, 235-240.

26 See the discussion of Dom Camara in the next chapter and the analysis by Stone in *Reinhold Niebuhr*, pp. 204-211. Niebuhr's own sensitivity to this problem is evident in his joint study with Paul Sigmund entitled *The Democratic Experience: Past and Prospects* (New York: Frederick A. Praeger, 1969).

27 See the discussion of Cone in the next chapter.

BIBLIOGRAPHY

1. Brown, Charles Reynolds, *The Social Message of the Modern Pulpit*. New York, Scribner's, 1910.

2. Hutchison, William R., ed., *American Protestant Thought: The Liberal Era*. New York: Harper & Row, 1968.

3. Kegley, Charles W., and Robert W. Bretall, eds., *Reinhold Niebuhr, His Religious, Social, and Political Thought*. New York: Macmillan, 1956.

4. Meyer, Donald B., *The Protestant Search for Political Realism, 1919-1941*. Los Angeles: University of California Press, 1960.

5. Niebuhr, Reinhold, *The Children of Light and the Children of Darkness*. New York: Scribner's, 1944; edition with new foreword, 1960.

6. ———, *Does Civilization Need Religion?* New York: Macmillan, 1928.

7. ———, *An Interpretation of Christian Ethics*. New York: Harper and Brothers, 1935.

8. ———, *Leaves From the Notebook of a Tamed Cynic*. New York: Willett, Clark and Colby, 1929.

9. ———, *Moral Man and Immoral Society*. New York: Scribner's, 1960. Originally written in 1932.

10. ———, *The Nature and Destiny of Man*, Vols. I and II. New York: Scribner's, 1943.

11. ———, *Radical Religion*. Numerous Articles from this Journal between 1935-1938.

12. ———, *Reflections on the End of an Era*. New York: Scribner's, 1936.

13. ———, "The Religion of Communism," *Atlantic Monthly*, 147 (April, 1931), 462-470.

14. ———, "Ten Years That Shook My World," *The Christian Century*, 56 (April 26, 1939), 542-546.

15. ———, "What the War Did to My Mind," *The Christian Century*, 45 (September 27, 1928), 1161-1163.

16. Robertson, D. B., ed., *Love and Justice*. Cleveland: World, 1967 [1957].

17. Shaull, Richard, "Theology and the Transformation of Society," *Theology Today*. 25 (April, 1968), 23-36.

18. SMITH, H. SHELTON, ROBERT T. HANDY, and LEFFERTS A. LOETSCHER, *American Christianity*, II. New York: Scribner's, 1963.
19. WEST, CHARLES C., *Communism and the Theologians*. London. SCM Press, 1958.

SUGGESTED READINGS

1. *Primary Readings*

Readings from *Moral Man and Immoral Society:* pp. xi-35. Niebuhr's critique of liberal optimism, moralism, and rationalism in the light of his analysis of human depravity, as heightened and institutionalized in society. pp. 116-141, 144-168, 193-199. Niebuhr's appropriation and critique of Marx: the influence of social and economic factors on ethical systems; Marx as an antidote to liberal naiveté; Niebuhr's emerging critique of Marx.

Readings from D. B. Robertson, ed., *Love and Justice:* pp. 25-46: Niebuhr on love, justice, and power. pp. 89-113: Niebuhr's expose of Ford company policies and his negative assessment of much institutionalized religion. pp. 142-158: Niebuhr on racism and religion.

2. *Secondary Readings*

For brief discussions concerning Niebuhr's social ethics, his political thought and influence, and his theology, see the essays by John C. Bennett, Arthur Schlesinger, Jr., and Paul Lehmann in Charles W. Kegley and Robert W. Bretall, eds., *Reinhold Niebuhr: His Religious, Social and Political Thought* (3:45-77,125-150,251-280).

The two best, lengthy analyses of Niebuhr's thought are: Gordon Harland, *The Thought of Reinhold Niebuhr* (New York: Oxford University Press, 1960); and Ronald H. Stone, *Reinhold Niebuhr: Prophet to Politicians* (Nashville: Abingdon Press, 1972).

3. *Additional Bibliography*

An excellent bibliography of Niebuhr's writings up to 1956 has been done by D. B. Robertson in Kegley and Bretall, eds., *Reinhold Niebuhr* (3:455-478).

Christians in the
Revolution of the Oppressed

At a time when a prophetic social witness and realistic liberal ethic were needed, Reinhold Niebuhr found critical resources for this task in biblical insights and perspectives. At the center of his thought was a strong emphasis upon theological criteria for a transcendent judgment upon society as well as a realistic assessment of the historical limitations of all finite, social achievements. In developing these themes, Niebuhr was led to selectively appropriate Marxist criticisms of society, although he rejected Marx's analysis of religion as distorted and his utopian vision as illusory.

During the 1960's and 70's, a new breed of Protestant and Catholic churchmen felt compelled by the social crises of the era to extend and to intensify earlier theological criticisms of society.[1] Profoundly disturbed by white racism, social inequities, worldwide poverty, and the Vietnam War, the new religious radicals rediscovered a broad range of radical biblical themes beyond the norms of love and justice utilized by Niebuhr.[2] Armed with these fresh biblical insights, the new breed abandoned the much celebrated pragmatic and realistic stance of modern liberalism for a far more revolutionary perspective than that offered by the mature Niebuhr. In employing these themes to challenge traditional interpretations of social reality and to issue a clarion call for thoroughgoing social change, radical churchmen moved closer to Marx than even the young Niebuhr, although they obviously differed from the founder of communism in finding theological justification for their insights in traditional Judeo-Christian affirmations.

As one would expect in any broad social movement, members of the new breed came from diverse backgrounds. They included Roman Catholics, Protestants, and Jews from the developed countries of Europe and North America as well as religious spokesmen for the deprived masses in the Third World nations of Africa, Asia, and Latin America. Despite their diversity, however, they were by and large not only intensely critical of the status quo, but socially active. Most of those in the United States, like the Berrigan brothers and Father James Groppi, joined or led demonstrations for civil rights, open-housing, and peace.[3] In Europe, Protestant and Catholic clergy involved in the Marxist-Christian dialogue participated in student uprisings and supported trade-union demands. Throughout Latin America, some Catholic churchmen joined underground revolutionary movements. Although few followed the example of the Colombian priest-guerrilla, Camilo Torres, who actually took up arms to fight against reactionary government forces, fifty Bolivian priests openly espoused armed revolution, while a group of Maryknoll priests and nuns assisted Guatemalan guerrillas.[4] Given these and other activities, it is scarcely surprising that the major cultural symbol of religious radicalism, by the end of the nineteen sixties, had become the socially active clergyman (16:122).

How have religious radicals justified their commitment to leftist activities? Is it not true that religion is primarily concerned with the eternal salvation of man's soul? Is it not also true, as Marx observed, that traditional religions have generally supported the status quo at the expense of social reform? If these claims are true, how have religious radicals squared their so-called "meddling in politics" with historically sanctioned beliefs? Most have argued that authentic biblical faith demands radical action on behalf of the poor and the oppressed, thereby contesting Marx's claim that religion is necessarily a social opiate. In what sense is this position justified? Is it legitimate to speak of the sociopolitical claims of biblical faith or is this merely a modern distortion of the biblical message designed to sanctify contemporary leftist activities? These are some of the issues with which the present chapter on religious radicalism in general and its articulation by two outstanding spokesmen is designed to answer.

In justifying their commitment to radical social activities, members of the new breed cite a tremendous variety of theological themes. Diversity in theological commitment rather than homogeneity characterizes the movement. Yet, religious radicals are united by several shared concerns and common theological perspectives that are frequently articulated by their leading spokesmen. Among Roman Catholics, prominent spokesmen are Dom Helder Camara, the Berrigans, Peter Riga, and James Groppi, while Protestant radicals include Rubem Alves, James Cone, Vincent Harding, Jürgen Moltmann, Richard Shaull, and Joseph R. Washington, Jr. Taken together, the common perspectives expressed by these and other churchmen signal the emergence of a new type of religiously inspired social thought, the main lines of which constitute "the theology of radical politics." [5]

The first element in this new theology is the intense dissatisfaction with the status quo that permeates the language of religious radicals. This dissatisfaction derives in part from existential commitment to the biblical concept of justice as divine vindication of the poor, the needy, and the helpless. In contrast with Niebuhr's Enlightenment or rationalist definition of justice as "the ideal of equality" transcending social realities, religious radicals speak of God's righteous vindication of the poor and the oppressed against the rich and the powerful. The God of the Old and New Testaments, they maintain, is not to be seen as a spokesman for transcendent ideals, but, rather, as the Holy One working in history on the side of the "have-nots" of the world against their oppressors. This is the message of Amos, Hosea, Isaiah, and Micah; it is also the "good news" embedded in the New Testament story about Christ's identification with, and ongoing work on behalf of, the poor, the hungry, the naked, and the imprisoned. Profoundly impressed by this biblical emphasis upon divine vindication of the dispossessed, religious radicals are outraged by the subhuman existence of peasants in the Third World, the dehumanized lot of blacks in America, and the plight of the unemployed in rich and poor nations alike. Seeing deprivation not simply as a fact of life, but as a consequence of social injustice, they frequently condemn the rich and the powerful who, as Amos says, "oppress the poor," "crush the needy," "turn justice into poison," "deal deceitfully with false balances," "buy the poor for silver and the needy for a pair of sandals." With the zeal of the eighth-century prophets, who condemned the whole of Israel for collective oppression of the poor and the needy, they indict the entire social system, including characteristic attitudes and dominant institutions, for hindering what God is doing to humanize the lot of the dispossessed.

Prophetic dissatisfaction with the status quo is combined with a strong emphasis upon liberation from oppression. Here the Exodus of Israel out of Egyptian slavery and the Christian gospel of liberation from oppression (Luke 4:18-19) are central motifs in the new theology. "The Exodus," writes Harvey Cox, "is the event which sets forth 'what God is doing in history.' He is seen to be liberating people from bondage, releasing them from political, cultural, and economic captivity, providing them with the occasion to forge in the wilderness . . . a new set of values" (17:132). The Christian gospel of liberation, writes the black theologian, James Cone,

> means the irruption of a new age, an age which has to do with God's action in history on behalf of man's salvation. It is an age of liberation, in which "the blind receive their sight, the lame walk, the lepers are cleansed, the deaf hear, the dead are raised up, the poor have the good news preached to them" (Luke 7:22). This is not pious talk, and one does not need a seminary degree to interpret the message. It is a message about the ghetto, and all other injustices done in the name of democracy and religion to further the social, political, and economic interests of the oppressor. In Christ, God enters human affairs and takes sides with the oppressed. Their suffering becomes his; their despair, divine despair. Through Christ the poor man is offered freedom now to rebel against that which makes him other than human (11:36).

What makes this ancient Judeo-Christian emphasis upon liberation so revolutionary is its association with sociopolitical liberation. In place of the old pietistic emphasis upon freedom from worldly concerns for the sake of heavenly salvation, religious radicals speak of God's action in history liberating men from oppressive institutions. In keeping with this understanding of liberation, they urge fellow believers to join the divine action in the good fight for freedom and justice. "Therefore, whoever fights for the poor, fights for God; whoever risks his life for the helpless and unwanted, risks his life for God" (11:47).

Liberation is interpreted by most religious radicals as involving the participation of all social groups, especially the poor and impotent, in the life of the community and nation. Liberation is meaningless, they contend, unless individuals are involved in the decision-making processes by which their lives are determined. The oppressed are deprived of this opportunity insofar as their lives are determined by others, whether the "others" be WASPs in North America, political dictators in Latin America, or unscrupulous businessmen throughout the Third World. With Hannah Arendt, religious radicals see participatory democracy as a major thrust of all revolutionary movements (see:3). Unlike Arendt, however, theologically informed radicals trace this participatory ideal to biblical themes, like the theological notion that man is called to be a co-creator with the Deity in shaping his social destiny. With Pope Paul VI in *Populorum Progressio*, they contend that "man is only truly man in as far as master of his own acts and judge of their worth, he is author of his own advancement" (2:15). This theme underlies the radical religious claim that men only live meaningful lives insofar as they become participants in shaping their own history and the history of their groups. Participation in history, however, is only possible through power. Hence, radicals believe that the new man and the new society can only be created in and through activities that are political in character (2:16). "In this context," comments the Brazilian Protestant, Rubem Alves,

> politics is no longer understood as the activity of the few, the play of power among the elites. It is the vocation of man, because every man is called to participate, in one way or another, in the creation of the future. Politics thus becomes for this consciousness the new gospel, the annunciation of the good news that, if man emerges from passivity and reflexivity, as the subject of history, a new future can be created. It challenges man: "Seek first the kingdom of politics and his power, and all these things shall be yours" (2:16).

In short, human liberation is seen as the result of active involvement on the part of all citizens in the decision-making processes by which men recreate the world.

The goal of liberation through participatory democracy is not freedom for freedom's sake, but liberation for the creation of a more human world. The new breed envisions not only liberation from present restrictions, but a totally transformed social order that stands in dramatic contrast with existing social patterns. Over against Niebuhr's emphasis upon the limited achievements of all finite societies, the religious radical is captivated by a vision of a totally new society characterized by peace, brotherhood, worldwide solidarity, and justice. Enthralled by this vision, he is acutely aware of the gap separating the status quo from the ideal social order. He is thus extremely critical of the liberal argument that man is inherently incapable of building a society in conformity with ideals that transcend what appears to be realistically possible. Against liberal realism, the religious radical contends that youthful dreams are not only desirable, but the stuff of which revolutions are made. This vision tends to be theologically justified by references to the eschatological orientation embedded in Hebrew and Christian scriptures. The God of Israel was not the static Eternal Order of Greek ontology, but a deity who led his people towards a new day, in which they discovered new opportunities for human fulfillment within a transformed society.[6] As Isaiah puts it, "God is doing a new thing" or, to use the language of St. Paul, "the creation waits with eager longing . . . , because the creation itself will be set free from its bondage to decay and obtain the glorious liberty of the children of God" (Romans 8:19-21). The theology of most radicals is, therefore, a theology of hope.[7] In light of future expectations generated by eschatological hopes for a totally transformed world, the task of the responsible believer is to act as a midwife of the future, just as the proletariat were challenged by Marx to be the midwife of the Communist revolution.

This concern for a radically new society represents a return to the future-oriented social thought of pre-Niebuhrian liberalism, without the latter's unrealistic, and hence superficial, optimism. Unlike his nineteenth-century precursors, the new religious radical is very much aware of the power of reactionary forces in society and the problems involved in attempting a new beginning. He vividly refers to inhibiting forces, like apathy and self-interest, as sinful or demonic. Yet, he does not believe that awareness of these difficulties justifies narrow calculations about what can be accomplished through compromise. Against the tendency of the social realist to limit social possibilities to the clearly realizable or politically expedient, he calls for creative new visions plus a willingness to risk innovative initiatives. In the words of Richard Shaull, a Protestant theologian of revolution:

> To build a new society requires a "new beginning." We must develop new ideas and perspectives on life and society by the cultivation of the creative imagination. So often the social thinking of many of us is sterile because we allow ourselves to be boxed in by a logic of our own making. We remain bound by presuppositions that are no longer valid, and are slow at finding alternatives for obsolete institutional patterns. The new revolutionary rightly senses that our historical experience has not exhausted all the possibilities that exist for the ordering of society. He shatters our complacency and challenges us to forge new models and respond to the impact of the future (27:194-195).

This call to envision new social possibilities is congruent, Shaull further maintains, with biblical messianism, namely, the hopeful expectation that new possibilities for human life will appear in history, even after all human possibilities appear to have been played out (27:217).

Commitment to thoroughgoing social change calls for practical initiatives designed to overcome misery and injustice. Religious radicals therefore call all believers to join the dispossessed of the world in their just struggles against the rich and the powerful. In other words, these new thoughts about the radical nature of biblical theology are joined with appeals for practical action. With Marx, religious radicals believe that the task of systematic reflection—in this case, theology—is not only to think about existence, but to change it. "Truth," they contend, "must be practicable" (26:138). Christians, they believe, dare not dream about freedom and justice beyond time, rather, they must bring "the hoped-for future into practical contact with the misery of the present. This is . . . a demand of Jesus himself. He not merely announced the Kingdom of God, but practiced it in his love of sinners and publicans" (26:139).

The church, from this perspective, cannot remain above politics or stand aside on a neutral platform. Against those who maintain that the church should stay out of politics either to celebrate pietistic dreams of eternal salvation or to reconcile people with diverse political opinions, religious radicals stress the church's responsibility to enter into the struggle for power, for example, by giving funds to Saul Alinsky or black power groups. This active political involvement of churches is often justified by the claim that the church of Jesus of Nazareth, who sided with the poor and the powerless, must follow her Lord's example. It is only by taking sides with the poor, the dispossessed, and the humiliated that the church fulfills her mission not only to the poor, but to the powerful as well. For the mission of the church to the powerful, as radicals understand it, is not simply to terminate their oppressive activities, but to liberate them from enslavement to anxieties about preserving wealth, status, influence, and the like. As long as these anxieties enslave a man, he is determined by fears that lead him to sacrifice his own humanity by oppressing others. The goal of the church's involvement in politics is not simply to liberate the poor and the powerless, then, but to end the subtle captivity of the rich as well. As the German theologian, Jürgen Moltmann states, the church "is not out to turn the slaves into masters but to subvert and abolish the whole master-slave relationship so that in the future men will be able to treat one another as men. . . . In this sense, Christianity's taking sides with the 'damned of the earth' is a way to the redemption and reconciliation of the damned and the damners" (26:142-143).

Despite the seriousness of their commitment to radical action, most spokesmen for the new religious left do not neglect the lighter, including the humorous, side of life. Indeed, some are extremely critical of the compulsive moralism of many secular radicals. As one theological critic of "up-tight," secular revolutionaries states:

> I would expect from Christians, who believe in God's presence in the midst of revolution, that they would laugh and sing and dance as the first to be liberated in creation . . . Jesus was no Zealot like Bar Kochba, nor a preacher of repentance like John the Baptist. He was called "a glutton and a wine-bibber." His disciples did not fast: together with Jesus and the outcasts, and in full view of the enemies, they celebrated the heavenly banquet of the righteous. Is this foolish? Do we have time for that in a revolution. . . . I think this is the way that revolutionary movements can be redeemed from the coercion of the law and of good works (26: 146).

Indeed, the freedom to laugh and sing in the midst of sociopolitical activities is viewed by some as an anticipation in the present of the desired future state of affairs.

In developing these various common themes, the new breed of religious radicals have succeeded in bringing to the fore biblical perspectives that have lain dormant for many years. They have thereby reminded others that Western religious history includes not only popes who crowned emperors and ministers who blessed troops, but rebels and revolutionaries who, like the biblical prophets and Jesus of Nazareth, condemned the existing order or, like Thomas Münzer and early Calvinists, actively tried to transform the world in the name of a new vision.[8] Though this part of Judeo-Christian history has been neglected by many orthodox theologians and clergy, it has been appropriated in fresh, and often surprisingly effective, ways by the new Christian left.

Despite their shared concerns, religious radicals differ in style, focus, emphasis, and strategy. The Christian humanism of the Latin American Archbishop, Dom Helder Camara, for example, is quite different from the theology of liberation formulated by the black American Protestant, James Cone. In turning to these two representatives of the new theology of radical politics, we shall, therefore, encounter major differences as well as striking similarities in their justification of revolutionary change.

1. DOM HELDER CAMARA

Dom Helder Camara (b. 1909), the Archbishop of Olinda and Recife in desperately poor Northeast Brazil, is a leading Roman Catholic spokesman for the deprived masses in the Third World. A hero of the Catholic left everywhere, he is representative of the small but growing group of radical Catholics that surfaced following the reformations wrought by Pope John XXIII and the Second Vatican Council (1962–1964).[9] Like most other newly radicalized Catholics, Dom Helder has remained profoundly committed to his faith and church while rebelling, in the name of Christian values, against the inhuman practices of many traditional institutions. Although less extreme than the Colombian priest-turned-guerrilla, Camilo Torres, who became a martyr after being killed during an ambush in 1966, Dom Helder believes that nothing less than a global revolution is demanded by genuine Christian faith. Yet he advocates aggressive nonviolence in the great tradition of Mahatma Gandhi and Martin Luther King, hoping that peaceful change may occur before violence becomes inevitable.[10]

Like Gandhi and King, Dom Helder's vigorous nonviolent pursuits have won him the affection of his miserably deprived constituency as well as the international recognition symbolized by a Nobel peace prize nomination. At the same time, he has kindled the wrath and violence of reactionary forces on the extreme right in his native Brazil. A man of peace with the selfless qualities of a saint, he has been condemned to death by both the Commandos for the Hunt of Communists (an extreme right-wing group with ties to the Brazilian military) and the Squadron of Death (an illegal execution squad of police officers responsible for the assassination of hundreds of "enemies of the public order"). Thus far, he has escaped assassination, though several of his associates have been kidnapped by extermination squads, cruelly tortured, and brutally murdered. Far from intimidating Dom Helder, these acts of violence have instead served to increase his prophetic anger and vigorous work on behalf of the dispossessed.

From Ecclesiastical Politics to Social Action

Dom Helder was not always an innovator of radical change. Having received a conservative theological education in Brazil during the 1920's, he began his professional career, like most Latin American clergy, as a proponent of right-wing politics. In the early 1930's he actively campaigned for the neo-fascist Integralist movement, for which he was rewarded with an appointment, while still in his mid-twenties, as Secretary of Education in his home state of Ceará. Although he shortly thereafter resigned from the Integralist movement, he continued for several decades to provide implicit religious support for the establishment by accepting key government appointments to the Ministry of Education in Rio de Janeiro. Within the church, his major activities during the 1940's and 50's involved high level, intra-ecclesiastical affairs. Indeed, he gradually became one of the leading church bureaucrats in Latin America in his capacity as secretary general of the Brazilian Conference of Bishops, which he helped found, and as the chief organizer of the 1955 International Eucharistic Congress in Rio de Janeiro. It was not until the mid-50's that Dom Helder began to devote himself primarily to solving the pressing problems of the poor by means of radical social activities.

What influences led Dom Helder to abandon the relative security of ecclesiastical politics for the perilous arena of social action? Like other rebellious laymen and priests in Latin America, he appears to have been affected by several major stimuli. The first was the call for social justice sounded by the papal encyclicals of Pope John XXIII, *Pacem in Terris* and *Mater et Magistra*, and subsequently by Vatican II's "Pastoral Constitution on the Church in the Modern World" (*Gaudium et Spes*), and by Pope Paul's radical social encyclical, *Populorum Progressio*.[11] As a clergyman profoundly committed to the social teachings of his church, Dom Helder felt compelled to implement the directives set forth by the Vatican.

A second stimulus was the urgent concern for the vitality of the church in Latin America voiced by leading European Catholics during recent decades to Latin American churchmen.[12] This concern, which has occasionally taken the form of heavy pressure for change, derives in part from the fact that over a third of the church's worldwide baptized membership lives in severe poverty in Latin America. It is feared, for good reason, that this constituency is "particularly susceptible to political seductions of the communist variety" (33:62). In Dom Helder's case, this concern was convincingly communicated by Cardinal Pierre Gerlier (Archbishop of Lyons, France) who urged him, after the International Eucharistic Conference in 1955, to devote his considerable organizing abilities to solving the problems of the *favelas* (slums). "Cardinal Gerlier," Don Helder recalls, "was the one who gave me the push that plunged me into this action. Formerly, I had felt the problem, but had not been involved in the battle" (18:152).

A third stimulus was the rise of the New Left in the Third World.[13] Especially among university students, with whom Dom Helder has always maintained close communication, there began to emerge in the mid-50's a refusal to be boxed into the cold war ideological divisions of East and West. A new identification with other oppressed peoples in the Third World—the world of poverty and deprivation—began to be felt, which gave rise to sharp condemnation of the growing gap between rich and poor nations perpetrated by the unjust interference of major powers in the affairs of marginal peoples.

Fourth, Dom Helder found early sustenance and support among an influential group of concerned Brazilian politicians and churchmen who, like himself, were beginning to appreciate the need for internal, domestic reforms.[14] When the housing projects, educational reforms, and other social initiatives begun by these liberal politicians and clergy were abruptly terminated by the military dictatorship that came to power following the *coup d'état* of April 1, 1964, Dom Helder was further radicalized by the realization that reactionary forces were brutally repressing just programs for human liberation.

While these predominantly external influences were important in leading Dom Helder to join the activist battle for social change, his growing conviction of Christ's special love for the poor and the oppressed was even more decisive. As he stated in his inaugural message to the people of his diocese at the time of his installation as Archbishop of Recife and Olinda in 1964, "It is clear that, loving everyone, I must have special love, like Christ, for the poor" (5:6). To follow Christ meant not only loving the poor, but seeing the suffering Lord's literal identification with the outcasts of the world. "What value can there be in venerating pretty images of Christ, or even recognizing his disfigured face in that of the poor," he asked rhetorically in his message, "if we fail to identify him with the human being who needs to be rescued from his underdeveloped condition? . . . Christ in the North-East is called José, António, Severino . . . Behold the man! This is Christ, the man who needs justice, who has a right to justice, who deserves justice" (5:11-12). Ultimately, we shall all be judged, he further asserted, "by our treatment of Christ, of Christ who hungers and thirsts, who is dirty, injured and oppressed" (5:6). Deeply convinced that imitating Christ involved openly identifying with the dispossessed with whom the Lord is eternally present, Dom Helder took the unusual step, after becoming Archbishop, of abandoning the medieval pomp, ceremony, and luxury of the Episcopal Palace for an inconspicuous apartment among his deprived parishioners. By living close to his people, Dom Helder has made himself ever available to the multitudes who flock to him for advice and assistance.

Dom Helder's identification with Christ's special concern for the poor led the new Archbishop to vividly appreciate the plight of the dispossessed in his native land and, by extension, that of the two-thirds of humanity living in "subhuman conditions." The term "subhuman" continually recurs in Dom Helder's speech. It refers, on one level, to the appalling physical conditions of the poor, that is, the stink and squalor of teeming slums, the miserable housing and scant clothing of peasants, and the malnutrition that kills some thirty-five or forty million people per year in underdeveloped countries. "Subhuman" also refers to the moral destitution of those living in these conditions, to the sense of dejection, impotence, and sadness that is the legacy of deprivation: the misery of parents unable to save their children from crippling diseases and early deaths, the sense of powerlessness of peasants in debt to rich landlords, and the despondency of laboring men unable to care for their families.

These experiences are intolerable in Dom Helder's eyes not only because of the cruel suffering involved, although this is bad enough, but also because misery destroys the image of God in man. Every man is entitled, according to Dom Helder's theology, not only to the bare minimum of food, clothing, and housing, but to the full dignity, freedom and intelligence that are God's special gifts to man. Because these gifts were bestowed upon man with his being created in "the image of God," they are universal, inviolable, and inalienable (7:53). Insofar as the misery of poverty annihilates these divine gifts and the inalienable rights to humane work, political association, and education associated with them, severe poverty represents a fundamental "disorder" in human society. To rectify this disorder by creating opportunities for a richer, freer, and more responsible way of life is, therefore, no less than to enable men to realize their potential as "sons of God" and brothers of Christ, who entered the disorder of human existence so that men might have "life and have it to the full" (5:22).

Committed to realizing human rights by identification with Christ's special love for the poor and by belief in the inherent dignity of man created in God's image, Dom Helder found additional theological support for social action in the ancient concept of man's responsibility as a co-creator with the deity. According to this concept, which was repeatedly stressed during the Second Vatican Council, man made in the image of God is essentially a creator. As such, man's vocation is to continually transform the world in accordance with God's humanizing purposes. In the first place, this means that man is not an "object" to be manipulated by forces beyond his control, but rather a "subject" within history who realizes his innate capacities only insofar as he actively participates in the humanization of the natural and social forces which inhibit full realization of his potential. Concretely, this involves refusing to be dominated by natural forces or by social institutions which enslave men, while risking the apparent benefits of security for the hazards of a socially active life. Secondly, man's vocation as a co-creator implies that the world to which he is related is not a fixed order in which everything is determined. Instead, the world that man has received from the hands of God is an unfinished realm in which men fulfill their responsibility by continually reforming and recreating their environment. This unfinished character of creation is especially apparent in the social realm, where so many imperfections remain to be eradicated. To live as a co-creator, then, is to reject domination by the status quo in favor of a vocation devoted to transforming society in the direction of fuller and richer forms of individual and social existence.

The Goal of Development

In seeking a remedy for subhuman conditions, Dom Helder came to see that they were not accidental, but rather a result of underdevelopment. At first, he believed that poverty in the Third World was simply a failure on the way towards development. As a corollary, it followed that Western forms of industrialization and technological modernization were the appropriate means for solving the development problem. With this in mind, he more or less uncritically advocated economic and technical assistance from North America and Europe, hoping thereby to upgrade the have-not nations of the world to the level enjoyed by the haves. He thus rebuked developed countries for giving less than a fraction of the 1 percent in gross national product recommended by the United Nations to aid underdeveloped lands. Gradually, however, he came to see that economic aid and technical assistance were insufficient, for international economic and political institutions were such that rich nations were getting richer while poor nations were scarcely developing at all. He was distressed, for example, by United Nations statistics showing that the average per capita income in the developed countries was increasing several hundred dollars every five years, while that in underdeveloped nations scarcely advanced beyond $150 per year. He was equally disturbed by statistics on economic relationships between the United States and Latin America indicating that the latter had actually "loaned" the richest nation in the world almost fourteen billion dollars during a recent eleven year period, this "loan" being paid in profits on United States investments, falling prices for raw materials, and similar economic exploitations (5:52-53).

These and other facts forced Dom Helder to realize, with other international observers, that the Third World was not only poor, but that it had been made and kept poor by international economic colonialism. Their poverty was the consequence of an economic system which enabled powerful nations to dominate and exploit the weak. Colonialism had not ended with the rise of autonomous political states; it had continued in the subtle, and not so subtle, relationships by which rich nations planned programs, including the Alliance for Progress, in accordance with their own interests, not in accordance with the needs of developing states. For Dom Helder, these harsh realities indicated that the problems of the Third World could not be resolved without a thoroughgoing overhaul of existing international institutions and relationships. He thus became increasingly critical of the economic imperialism by which rich nations, especially the United States and the Soviet Union, exploit the Third World.

In searching for ways of improving conditions in the Third World, Dom Helder realized that the goals of many development programs needed drastic revision. Too many were based on the uncritical assumption that development is exclusively a matter of economic and technological modernization, whereas genuine development always involves realization of moral and cultural values. In fact, economic and technical innovations are not desirable, unless they upgrade the quality of human life. For example, the introduction of modern mass means of communication (like the transistor radio) may represent a progressive step if employed to educate illiterate peasants. But human progress is scarcely served when the media are used by dictators, as they are currently in Brazil, to suppress criticism and dissent. Here, the introduction of advanced technology represents a retrogressive step in the quality of life among the Brazilian masses. Because realization of human values is essential to genuine, as opposed to specious, development, Dom Helder has increasingly insisted on careful scrutiny of the goals implicit in all development programs.

Realizing that specific development goals could only be evaluated within a broad historical context, Dom Helder felt compelled to articulate the general direction of authentic human progress. Over against the materialist goals of some modernization theorists and reformers, Dom Helder's theologically informed historical scheme views development as involving nothing less than both the restoration of the image of God in man and the gradual divinization of the human race. From this perspective, progress involves not only provision of sustenance for every man, but also recovery of those divine-like human attributes, such as intelligence and choice, that are seriously diminished by the miseries of poverty and oppression. Progress along these lines also entails fulfillment of man's vocation as a co-creator through social programs designed to transform the world in accordance with values of love, justice, and peace. Ultimately, Dom Helder's historical scheme envisions the "divinization" of the race through full realization by every man of his highest potentialities. Such divinization cannot be condemned as idolatrous, Dom Helder contends, precisely because it is the purpose of creation and the goal of Christ's mission for all men to realize the divine plenitude latent within them.

This clarified understanding of development led Dom Helder to realize that neither the dominant institutions of the democratic West nor those of socialist countries were sufficiently humanistic to serve as models for emerging nations. Deeply aware of the plight of the thirty million poor in the United States and the dissatisfaction of the politically powerless living under socialist regimes, Dom Helder saw that deprived nations had to create their own sociopolitical institutions. In his opinion, only new forms of democratic socialism could successfully avoid the errors of East and West. But first there had to be a thoroughgoing rejection of prevalent dehumanizing institutions plus a willingness to experiment with new forms of participatory socialism:

> Without agrarian reform, the almost inhuman misery of the rural workers will persist. Without banking reform, little will be done for the development of the country, and without fiscal reform, the rich will continue to grow richer while the poor will continue to suffer. Without electoral reform, the elections will appear to be free but in fact will be subjected to the power of money. Without administrative reform, bureaucracy will continue to sap the strength of public life (18:ix).

These reforms could not be imposed from above; rather, they had to be instituted with the help of those who suffer exploitation. For the oppressed not only have more knowledge than other groups about the inadequacies of unjust institutions, they have an inalienable right as co-creators to participate in the political processes by which their future, as well as that of the rich, is determined. Whether or not this inclusion of the dispossessed in the political process is acceptable to the powerful, the disenfranchised have an unquestionable right, in Dom Helder's view, to organize to implement their just demands and to determine the future direction of development.

Strategy for Change: Violence versus Non-violence

As an advocate of mass participation in social action, Dom Helder had to confront the unavoidable issue of violence in collective protest. Like other contemporary radicals, he has come to see the question of violent redress by the oppressed in light of the subtle forms of violence perpetrated by unjust societies. In his vocabulary, as in that of the New Left everywhere, violence occurs whenever power is used unjustly. Violence is involved not only in the unfair use of physical force by the police, but also in conspiracies among landlords to fix slum rents and in the exploitation of entire continents by unfair international trade relationships. Because hidden violence of the latter sort is ubiquitous in the Third World, Dom Helder has developed a deep respect for those who feel obliged by conscience to opt for physically violent means of redress and reform. "In my opinion," he stated in 1968, "the memory of Camilo Torres and of Che Guevara merits as much respect as that of Martin Luther King. I accuse the real authors of violence: all those who, whether on the right or left, weaken justice and prevent peace" (5:109).

Yet, Dom Helder goes on to express his own vocation as that of "a pilgrim of peace" armed with nonviolent means. "I do not believe in violence, I do not believe in hatred, I do not believe in armed insurrections" (7:37). There are four main reasons for this commitment to nonviolence, three of them pragmatic, one theological. To take the theological one first, Dom Helder believes that the New Testament, especially the Beatitudes, clearly indicates that Christians should be on the side of nonviolence. Christians are called to believe "more passionately in the force of truth, justice and love than in the force of wars, murder and hatred" (5:110). Second, Dom Helder is convinced that a violent revolution in Latin America today would be quickly crushed by the powerful forces aligned on the side of the status quo. A popular revolution in Brazil, for example, would probably lead the United States to intervene, as it did in the Dominican Republic and Vietnam. "I have no interest," he states, "in causing a war to break out, even a war of liberation, if I am convinced that it would be immediately crushed" (18:75). Third, Dom Helder fears the masses would suffer more than any other group in a war of liberation. Fourth, even a successful revolution would be undesirable in Dom Helder's opinion, because the resulting social chaos would force the reintroduction of totalitarian practices, as in the cases of the French and the Russian revolutions.

For these reasons, and because he feels a successful people's revolution in Latin America will not occur for at least ten or fifteen years, Dom Helder has requested his more radical associates to allow him the remaining time to experiment with nonviolent means. These means are scarcely passive, however, including, as they did until recently repressed, consciousness-raising activities among the masses, especially through basic education, radical social criticism of the establishment, and large-scale pressure groups that "risk everything," along the lines pursued by Gandhi and Martin Luther King, Jr.

The first major goal of Dom Helder's nonviolent strategy is a massive "revolution of ideas," for ideological change is a necessary prerequisite for the peaceful transformation of unjust institutions. Mass ideological commitment is also desirable for protecting new or changed institutions from easily reverting to older, unjust practices. Ultimately, Dom Helder hopes his contribution to the rise of radically new ideas in Brazil will aid the emergence of a global revolutionary consciousness that will permit the reconstruction of unjust international institutions on genuinely ethical foundations.

In underdeveloped countries, this revolution in ideas occurs through *conscientização*, an untranslatable word meaning a "demystification" as well as a "powerful awakening" of consciousness among the deprived masses.[15] The aim of *conscientização* is to raise the masses to the human level by making them conscious not only of living at a subhuman level, but of their inalienable right to a better life, worthy of man. It involves opening the eyes of the deprived masses to their misery, and telling them: "No, the life you live is not just, something must be done" (5:42). In attempting to foster this awareness, Dom Helder helped initiate during the early 60's the now famous Movement for Basic Education (MBE). A clearly revolutionary enterprise, MBE used transistor radios to teach illiterate people to read textbooks designed to open their eyes to their fate, to their human rights, and to the appropriate means for obtaining justice. Peasants learned to read passages like the following from the basic textbook, *To Live Is to Struggle:*

> Pedro's family is hungry. The people work and are hungry. Is it just that Pedro's family should be hungry? Is it just that the people are hungry?
>
> The people of Brazil are exploited. They are exploited not only by Brazilians but by many foreigners. How can we rescue the country from this condition? (18:40)

Given this sort of fare, it is scarcely surprising that MBE was the first target of the military dictatorship that came to power in April, 1964.

Equally important to raising the social consciousness of the masses is consciousness-raising among the inhabitants of developed nations.

Myths about the so-called "free" world and communism scale the eyes of the relatively rich in both East and West, just as acceptance of deprivation blinds the poor. In the United States, for example, the illusion persists that there is a free world to be vigorously defended at all cost against communism, although most peoples within this sphere of American influence are enslaved by hunger, disease, malnutrition, and ignorance, if not by actual dictators. Within the Soviet bloc very different myths about the just struggle of the proletariat prevail, despite Russian intervention in weaker states like Hungary and Czechoslovakia. According to Dom Helder, both myths, by falsifying the nature of reality in East and West, foster the arms race, promote neo-colonial imperialism in the Third World, and hinder international progress towards the elimination of global poverty. The results of these very different myths are virtually identical, therefore, in their negative impact on genuine development in the world and in the perpetration of dehumanizing institutional structures, relationships and actions.

Believing in the enormous power of myths and ideologies in history, Dom Helder fears that these differing illusions, by widening the gap between East and West, will eventually bring about a Third World War, or, barring that catastrophe, an explosion among the neglected masses in the Third World. Defusing these myths is, therefore, one of the most urgent of contemporary tasks. One way of defusing a myth is to expose and denounce the unjust practices carried out in its name. Dogmatic anticommunism, for example, should be exposed for pharisaically ignoring the equally inhuman character of capitalistic investment policies, which also crush human beings by perpetuating the miseries of poverty. A second strategy is to dramatize the way in which these ideologies waste national resources, produce fruitless international tensions, and neglect the real problems of the proletariat in the Third World. A third strategy, one frequently employed by Dom Helder, is to demonstrate that democratic and communist myths express a longing for similar goals: peace, freedom, equality, brotherhood. Why not challenge both parties to get on with implementing these values on a worldwide scale? If we could, in these ways, "destroy the myths directed against the socialist world, and if the socialist world, for their part, could exorcise themselves of the anti-capitalist myths, the effect would certainly lead to an end of the suicidal arms race, to a general prohibition on using the atom for war purposes, and to a real respect for the self-determination of nations" (5:66).

What is to be done following consciousness-raising? In his early lectures and writings, Dom Helder called for dialogue between universities, churches, legal associations, and business groups in underdeveloped and developed countries. His hope was that a pooling of resources by concerned professional groups would lead to new strategies for the reform of unjust social structures. In this context, Dom Helder frequently cited Pope Paul to the effect that "sincere dialogue fosters brotherhood," among institutions as among persons (7:42). Indeed, he dared to look forward to an inclusive, worldwide dialogue not only among professionals in varying parts of the world, but also among former antagonists: capitalists and socialists, businessmen and laborers, technical experts and peasants, Christians and non-Christians, even young and old. In this spirit, he suggested that every individual could contribute to this process by initiating encounters about significant problems in their own backyards, for "the lack of dialogue between individuals leads to lack of dialogue between groups and eventually to a lack of dialogue between peoples and nations" (7:64).

While Dom Helder apparently still believes in dialogue, he has considerably modified his earlier hopes. With blacks in the United States, he has come to appreciate the impossibility of genuine dialogue among unequal partners. He now increasingly stresses the necessity for deprived peoples to gain an equal footing with their oppressors before entering into conversations about desired reforms. Accordingly, he urges students in the Third World to recognize the meaninglessness of dialogue between the very strong and the impotent (7:74). Calling for the consolidation of power before the initiation of joint projects with the powerful, he recommends that deprived peoples begin by dropping their illusions about alliances, which only end up being dominated by the powerful. The first task of the oppressed is to support one another, for only after they gain collective moral strength and power will genuine dialogue with the powerful be possible.

Christian-Marxist Rapprochement

In working for *conscientização* through the Movement for Basic Education and a variety of other channels, Dom Helder came to appreciate the way in which the widespread religious fatalism of the masses, by preventing an accurate appreciation of their situation, destroyed their desire to change it. Seeing God's hand in everything, the fatalistic peasant would passively accept the status quo as ordained by God, thinking he was thereby humbly submitting to the Divine will. He would ascribe to God not only natural phenomena (floods, harvests, droughts), but social injustices as well. Dom Helder quickly perceived that this fate-determining deity was not an authentic expression of Judeo-Christian beliefs, but, as Marx observed, an "expression" of socioeconomic conditions of deprivation.

A man who vegetates in such deplorable conditions without a minimum of education, or independence from his employer, tends to abandon all hope and to identify his religion with a sad fatalism: "These things are ordained by God; some are born poor, some are born rich. We were born poor. It was written in the heavens" (5:74).

Christianity "protests" against this fatalistic deity not by offering illusory hopes as a narcotic compensation, as Marx claimed, but by challenging "religious" fatalism itself.

The fate-determining deity of the subhuman masses is not God, Dom Helder contends, but a fictitious creation of men. Unlike "the ingenuous, spiteful, magic-working God" of the superstitious poor, the Creator Father, far from creating and determining everything himself, set creative evolution in motion by providing boundless opportunities for men to participate in the continuing perfection of the creation (7:23). Instead of requiring servile submission, the Creator Father calls the beings made in his likeness out of object-like existence into the glorious liberty enjoyed by subjects of history. By challenging the poor to abandon a fictitious god for One who calls them to assume their responsibility as co-creators charged with perfecting and finishing the work of creation, Dom Helder believes that the Christian churches have a unique role to play in the advancement of *conscientização* and concomitantly worldwide social change.

Dom Helder has not failed to criticize his own church's complicity in supporting religious fatalism. "It is true," he confesses, "that in the past our preaching, catechism, and liturgy led consciously or unconsciously to conformity and kept the masses in a subhuman condition" (7:49). Insofar as this has generally been the case, Marxists are correct in their critique of religion:

> Marxists regard religion as the great alienated and alienating force. We should have the honesty to acknowledge that in our preoccupation with eternal life, we can easily forget terrestrial life; in our concern for the social order, we do not always notice that it is often synonymous, in the Third World, with injustice and stratified disorder; in our anxiety to avoid profound and violent change, we use and abuse prudence, and almost always we act as the brake rather than the accelerator. And to carry honesty to extremes, we should recognize that it is always a temptation for us, difficult to determine yet interfering with our judgment and our work, that the wealthy and the government contribute to our social works and even to worship itself (5:68).

This complicity has led the Archbishop to plead with his church to renounce her sinful participation in the fatalistic ideology and unjust structures for which she shares partial blame. Counseling ecclesiastical repentance and conversion, he argues that the church's strength lies not in her cultural prestige, but in her willingness to renounce all advantages for the risks entailed in arousing the masses and vigorously acting on their behalf. This can happen, however, only if the church, following the lead of Vatican II, realizes that she cannot stand apart from history, and accepts her divine mission to participate with men in the everyday world, where Christ is carrying the underdeveloped world on his shoulders. The church witnesses to Christ whenever she serves, without dominating, movements to humanize unjust social conditions. In concrete terms, the hierarchy should "openly side with the underdeveloped masses, helping them to become a people . . ." (5:55).

If this Christian justification of consciousness-raising and radical reform sounds like Marx in theological robes, it is probably because Dom Helder has discovered, with other recent students of the founder of communism, that Marxism is essentially humanistic: "its aim is to elevate mankind to the highest degree of self-fulfillment. It would banish whatever dehumanizes or alienates man, the better to release the vast innate possibilities latent in him" (7:69). Dom Helder does not hesitate, therefore, to appropriate Marx's critique of religion, for this criticism, despite its nontheological source, expresses Christian love for one's neighbors as well as a concern for their fulfillment. Indeed, Marxists are said to challenge Christians to distinguish the humanistic essence of their faith—namely, the call to be co-creators with God through participation in Christ's humanizing work in the world—from its passing cultural forms and from the errors of Christians. Critical Marxists help Christians to remain true to their faith by forcing them to ascertain whether their beliefs are merely a reflex or a protest, an opiate or an illuminating guide, an alienating ideology or a genuine challenge, a justification of the status quo or of the Apocalypse (7:71).

For Dom Helder, what is to be rejected in Marxism is not its just criticism and humanistic goals, but its atheism. A deeply pious man, who rises every day at 2 a.m. to read his breviary, pray and write, Dom Helder holds that man cannot fully realize his potential without enriching his life through faith in, and love for, God. Indeed, Dom Helder believes atheism to be an historically conditioned, rather than an essential, aspect of communism. Marx, he argues "would never have presented religion as the opium of the people and the Church as alienated and alienator if he had seen around him a church made flesh, continuing the incarnation of Christ; if he had seen Christians who really and practically loved men as the primary expression of their love for God; if he had seen the days of Vatican II, which sums up what theology can say about terrestrial reality" (5:112). Whatever Marx may or may not have said about religion if Christians had not vindicated his critique, Dom Helder believes contemporary Marxists will appreciate Christianity, when they see the gospel inspiring dedicated churchmen to work, with other radicals, on behalf of the proletariat.

> The great mass of communists will give to religion their attention and sympathy when they see it resolved never to give cover to absurd injustices committed in the name of the right to property and private initiative. The great mass of communists will be pleasantly surprised to discover that the gospel inspires a thirst for justice and a desire to end the absurd situation of two-thirds of humanity sinking deeper every day into underdevelopment and starvation (5:59).

Dom Helder's appropriation of, and response to, Marx has been motivated, in part, by a desire to create a theistic alternative to communism. The only way of combating the mass appeal of communism, he maintains, is to teach a religion which is not "the opium of the people" by drawing out the revolutionary implications of Christianity and courageously tackling the most urgent problems of the day (5:75, 5:35). It is noteworthy, however, that the main themes in this Christian alternative are drawn directly from recent social teachings of the Vatican, not from reading the Bible with Marx in hand. According to Dom Helder, Christians would have a duty to stir up the masses "even if there were no agitation and revolutionary intrigue (and there is), even if communism were not at work (and it is)" (5:42). In response to criticism that this is to play into the hands of communists, he replies that nothing could be more democratic than goading a man's intelligence and encouraging his sense of freedom (7:133). If his own nonviolent, democratic methods do not work, Dom Helder believes democracy will have failed a crucial test, thereby vindicating Marxists. With regard to the argument that his methods will ferment revolt, he responds that "the eyes of the masses are being opened whether we like it or not, with us, without us, against us. It is ingenuous to try to halt a movement which is by now uncontrollable. When a river is in full flow, either you channel it in the right direction or it sweeps away everything" (5:42-43).

Whether Dom Helder has gone far enough in formulating this radical Christian alternative to Marxism has been questioned from several directions. Theologians find his affirmations of faith few in number and lacking the systematic coherence and sophistication expected from major Christian theorists. Few see anything especially innovative in Dom Helder's basic theology, although they generally respect his heroic stand in Brazil as well as his demonstration of the revolutionary implications of recent Vatican social thought.

Social ethicians criticize Dom Helder's acknowledge confidence in the ability of ideas to radically change those in power, arguing that he fails to appreciate the primacy of "interests" over ideas in determining social behavior. Against this criticism, Dom Helder contends that he has scarcely neglected this obstacle to his hopes. "I am scarcely so naive as to think," he states, "that brotherly counsel and pathetic appeals are enough to make the socioeconomic structures crumble like the walls of Jericho." Citing the New Testament story about the obstacles facing the rich man seeking the kingdom of God, he observes, "how very hard it is to be rich and still keep the milk of human kindness. Money has a dangerous way of putting scales on one's eyes, a dangerous way of freezing people's hands, eyes, lips, and hearts" (7:142-143). Yet Dom Helder clearly has more confidence in appeals to those in power than most radicals indebted to Marx and to Reinhold Niebuhr are willing to grant.

Dom Helder's nonviolent alternative to Marx has also been criticized by those who believe that violence is sometimes justified in opposing entrenched injustice. Protestant theologian Richard Shaull, for example, questions Dom Helder's identification of nonviolence with the Christian way (18:x), while Professor James Cone, for reasons explained in the following section, actually defends the use of violence by Christians against unjust societies.

These criticisms of Dom Helder's revolutionary credentials aside, he has clearly succeeded in responding to Marx by appropriating the critique of religious fatalism within a radical theology devoted to the realization of high human values. At the same time, he has exhibited the ideological potentiality of the major preoccupations of the new religious left with divine vindication of the poor, liberation from oppression, participatory democracy, eschatalogical hope, and creative sociopolitical initiatives. For these achievements as well as for his heroic stand against totalitarianism, Dom Helder clearly deserves the title: religious spokesman for the Third World (18:79).

2. JAMES CONE

The Black Theology of James Cone (b. 1938), the young American Professor at Union Theological Seminary, is similar in some respects to Dom Helder's Christian humanism. But there are crucial differences in background, focus, life-style, theology, and strategy between the two men. Whereas Dom Helder was radicalized by the rise of political dictatorship in Brazil, Cone was mobilized by the emergence of Black Power following the failure of Martin Luther King's nonviolent civil rights movement.[17] Like Dom Helder, Cone desires liberation for all oppressed peoples, but he concentrates exclusively on the problems and needs of

North American blacks. Cone's prophetic anger contrasts dramatically with the Archbishop's quiet, saintly intensity. Theologically, Dom Helder is dependent upon recent social teachings of the Vatican, while Cone is primarily indebted to the black church in America and to twentieth-century Protestant theologians, like Karl Barth, Paul Tillich, and Dietrich Bonhoeffer. For reasons related to all these differences, Cone rejects Dom Helder's nonviolent premises and strategy, arguing that blacks may use "any means necessary" in their just fight for human liberation.

Black Power as the Gospel

Cone's anger and righteous indignation derive from personal experiences as a black in racist America. In childhood, Cone experienced the humiliating inner contradiction between professed American beliefs about human equality and the actual practice of racial bigotry. As a schoolboy, he read with pride the lofty ideals of the Declaration of Independence: "We hold these truths to be self-evident, that all men are created equal, that they are endowed by their Creator with certain unalienable Rights, that among these are Life, Liberty and the pursuit of Happiness." But he also read and heard innumerable statements suggesting that blacks are subhuman, deserving of their deprived status. Like other young blacks in the 1960's, Cone was mobilized by the Civil Rights movement and Black Power not only to affirm his "black being" as beautiful, but to fight back with dignity and self-respect.[18]

Understandably, Cone believes that Black Power is the most important movement in contemporary American life. Because Black Power is an emotionally charged expression with a variety of meanings, Cone defines it as the *"complete emancipation of black people from white oppression by whatever means black people deem necessary"* (11:6). The tactics employed in the destruction of white oppression may legitimately include boycotts, marches, looting, even rebellion, as long as these means advance the twin goals of Black Power: complete freedom from the debilitating psychological consequences of negative social stereotypes (e.g., the "good Nigger") and authentic black self-determination in all major areas of life. "Black Power," Cone writes,

> means black freedom, black self-determination, wherein black people no longer view themselves as without human dignity but as men, human beings with the ability to carve out their own destiny. In short, as Stokely Carmichael would say, Black Power means T.C.B., Take Care of Business —black folk taking care of black folks' business, not on the terms of the oppressor, but on those of the oppressed (11:6).

This involves a negation of white dominance as well as vigorous affirmation by blacks of themselves as fully human, in spite of white attempts to treat blacks as objects to be manipulated. "This is Black Power, the power of the black man to say Yes to his own 'black being,' and to make the other accept him or be prepared for a struggle" (11:8).

How should Christians view Black Power? Cone not only believes that Black Power is *consistent* with the gospel, he argues that Black Power *is* the gospel. Several theological arguments are employed in supporting this novel claim. In the first place, the gospel, like Black Power, is essentially a message of liberation. In the man Jesus, God himself became a slave for the sole purpose of striking the chains of enslavement, thereby freeing men from ungodly principalities and powers.[19] Born in a stable manger ("the equivalent of a beer case in a ghetto alley"), Jesus' entire life and work was directed toward the poor and against the rich (12:204). "The conflict with Satan and the powers, the condemnation of the rich, the insistence that the Kingdom is for the poor, and the locating of his ministry among the poor—these and other features of the career of Jesus show that his work was directed to the oppressed for the purpose of their liberation" (12:19-20). Jesus himself defined the nature of his ministry in these terms rather than in the language of "spiritual" liberation employed by white middle-class churches:

> The Spirit of the Lord is upon me,
> because he has anointed me to preach good news to the poor.
> He has sent me to proclaim release to the captives
>   and recovering of sight to the blind,
> to set at liberty those who are oppressed,
> to proclaim the acceptable year of the Lord (Luke 4:18-19, RSV).

Because this message was originally proclaimed, not as an abstract theory for intellectual debate among scholars, but as an existential message to the suffering masses, the gospel of liberation is expressed wherever men rebel against whatever negates their humanity.[20] To say "No" to oppression and "Yes" to liberation is nothing less than to encounter the essence of the Christian message. Therefore, Cone argues that secular movements, like Black Power, genuinely express the gospel insofar as they liberate men from oppressive conditions.

A second argument supporting Black Power as an expression of the gospel involves the affirmation, which Cone shares with Dom Helder, that Christ is currently present among the oppressed, continuing his work of liberation there. He is not shrouded in the historical dust of the first century. "He is our contemporary, proclaiming release to the captives and rebelling against all who silently accept the structures of injustice" (11:38). From this perspective, Christ is not a static being to be approached through abstract philosophy; He is rather actively involved in liberating, historical movements where men are related to him less by intellectual belief than by participation in the divine fight for social justice (11:47). In other words, men encounter Christ in liberating *praxis* of the Marxist sort. In America, Christ is not to be found in the suburbs, but in the ghetto where blacks are struggling in the quagmire of misery and humiliation. "We must therefore be reminded that Christ was not crucified on an altar between two candles, but on a cross between two thieves. He is not in our peaceful, quiet, comfortable suburban 'churches,' but in the ghetto fighting the racism of churchly white people" (11:66). To be involved in Black Power is thus to encounter "the Oppressed One," who is also "the Liberator *par excellence*" (12:213-214).

Third, Cone sees the ultimate aim of Black Power as a genuine contemporary representation of the eschatological hopes of the Christian gospel. Because Black Power anticipates not only full realization by blacks of their humanity, but also redemption of the humanity lost by their oppressors, Black Power expresses God's this-worldly intentions for human fulfillment better than the non-biblical, other-worldly expectations of many nominal Christians.[21] Like genuine biblical hope, Black Power relates eschatology to history, that is to the *"hope of justice, the humanizing of man, the socializing of humanity, peace for all creation"* (11:126). In this historical reading of eschatology, the heavenly rewards promised by pious literature are illusions born of hopelessness about decisive improvements in history. Heavenly rewards imply, Cone writes, "that absurdity has won and that one is left merely with an unrealistic gesture toward the future. Heavenly hope becomes a Platonic grasp for another reality because one cannot live meaningfully amid the suffering of this world" (11:123). Against this other-worldly orientation, Cone asserts that Black Power, like biblical eschatology, looks forward to sociopolitical transformations in time. Eschatology thus comes to mean making the world what it ought to be. It involves looking to the future not for a reward or punishment, but as a means of making men fundamentally dissatisfied with the present. The principal purpose of envisioning the future is to disclose the intolerable injustices of the present. The hope shared by Black Power and biblical theology is thus a *practical ideal*, its main purpose being to revolutionize those suffering from despondency in the present.

The Church and Black Power

If the church exists wherever the gospel is accurately expressed, the community of saints is not to be found in the buildings, institutions, and worship services usually identified with the ecclesia. The church is therefore redefined by Cone through a fresh reading of the three essential functions of the church discussed in the New Testament: preaching (*kerygma*), service (*diakonia*), and fellowship (*koinonia*). Preaching occurs wherever the liberation of man is proclaimed. "The Church, then, is men and women running through the streets announcing that freedom is a reality" (11:66-67). The church not only exists where the word of liberation is sounded, it also exists wherever men actively work for liberation. This is service, *diakonia*. To serve this cause, a group must do more than talk and pass resolutions, it must back up its verbal commitments with active involvement on the side of the oppressed in their just struggle for humanization. For the oppressed are God's people, and, "in America, that people is a black people" (11:69). The church as fellowship, *koinonia*, exists where the internal relationships of a community are based upon justice and mutuality. Thus the church, by definition, exists where racism has been eliminated, which also means that Christ has broken down "the dividing walls of hostility" (Eph. 2:14, 11:70). From this perspective, the Black Power movement appears to qualify as the church in ways that many ecclesiastical institutions do not.

This reinterpretation of the church does not entail a total rejection of the institutional ecclesia. Cone recognizes the necessity of preaching, service, and fellowship in a Christian community explicitly committed to traditional teachings and practices. For people to know the truth of the Christian gospel, it must be preached and lived, as it is in authentic black churches as well as in other churches identified with the oppressed. But Cone denies the ascription of "church" to ecclesiastical institutions that fail to exhibit the three essential marks of the church.

In Cone's view, the white church in America not only fails to manifest the signs of the true church, it actually contradicts them—"if not by word, certainly by 'moral' example" (11:74). Instead of preaching the gospel of liberation to the oppressed, the white church either explicitly condones racism or implicitly supports it by perpetrating segregation within its doors.[22] Service to the poor is undermined by a narrow moralism that is "more concerned about drinking or new buildings or Sunday closing than about children who die of rat bites or men who are killed because they want to be treated like men" (11:71). As a fellowship, the white church leads the segregated institutions of American society by perpetuating all-white congregations. Even politically liberal white clergy are criticized by Cone for passing harmless resolutions instead of pressing for vigorous social action. Imagine, he writes, "men dying of hunger, children maimed from rat bites, women dying of despair—and the Church passes a resolution" (11:79). For these reasons, Cone concludes not only that Christ is working outside the denominational white church, but that the latter is the Antichrist or enemy of Christ. "The real Church of Christ is that grouping which identifies with the suffering of the poor by becoming one with them. . . . The Church includes not only the Black Power community but all men who view their humanity as inextricably related to every man" (11:80-81).

Love, Power, and Justice in Black Power

In claiming that Christ is at work in Black Power, Cone is not contending that every advocate of Black Power is a preacher of the gospel in disguise. Committed as Cone is to Black Power, he appreciates the fact that some black leaders advocate views contrary to the gospel:

> It is not my thesis that all Black Power advocates are Christians or even wish to be so. Nor is it my purpose to twist their language or to make an alien interpretation of it. My concern is, rather, to show that the goal and message of Black Power, as . . . articulated by many of its advocates, is consistent with the gospel of Jesus Christ. Indeed, I have even suggested that if Christ is present among the oppressed, as he promised, he must be working through the activity of Black Power (11:48).

Black Power is only consistent with the gospel insofar as it expresses the "love," "power," and "justice" at the heart of the Christian message. These terms, each of which has a very specific meaning for Cone, thus provide the criteria by which he distinguishes between genuine and inauthentic secular as well as religious expressions of the Christian faith.

Christian love, as Cone understands it, is neither sentimental romanticism nor superficial friendship; rather, love is grounded in God's radical decision to be totally "for man" in Jesus Christ.[23] To accept this love means first of all to affirm one's personal dignity and worth, precisely because God's love bestows value on human existence as such. The universal nature of divine love also means a radical identification with all men. Because the self-realization of every man is God's will for his creatures, universal identification entails commitment to the self-actualization of all peoples. For the black man in particular, the radical nature of divine love means that "God has made him somebody" by imparting intrinsic value to his black existence, despite internalization of negative self-definitions imposed by white society (11:52). "In a world which has taught blacks to hate themselves, the new black man does not transcend blackness, but accepts it, loves it as a gift of the Creator" (11:53). He now "knows that until he accepts himself as a being of God in all of its physical blackness, he can love neither God nor neighbor" (11:53). As for neighborly love, black love for white men is expressed through *confrontation*, acting as "a Thou without any intentions of giving ground by becoming an It" (11:53). This may entail conflict, but radical confrontation bothers Cone less than the denial of self implicit in submission to racial oppression. Moreover, self-affirming confrontation, by destroying what is against love, makes neighborly love possible; for true mutuality only exists among equals who recognize the full dignity and worth of each other.

Christian love is not inconsistent with power, Cone argues, following Tillich, because "love without the power to guarantee justice in human relations is meaningless" (11:53).[24] The inseparability of love and power, in fact, is what prevents the radical love at the heart of the gospel from being falsely understood as a resignation of power. This joining of love with power also precludes the mistaken identification of power with a denial of love (11:54). Cone, therefore, rejects the common association of love with powerlessness, arguing that love involves using power to overcome estrangement within the self and from others. For example, the racially oppressed counter the psychic divisions resulting from negative self-definitions not by passively accepting stereotypes, but by forcefully rejecting them. Estrangement from oppressors is similarly overcome by aggressive actions designed to repudiate the mastery but not the humanity of antagonists. Black Power is an indispensable vehicle for healing black-white estrangement, precisely because it seeks to use power to destroy what is against love while affirming the common value of humanity on both sides. Power conflicts with love only " 'when it prevents the aim of love, namely, the reunion of the separated' " (11:54).

Neither love nor power can be separated from justice, for justice is the goal of both. God's loving decision to be for man in Jesus Christ is no more separable from His righteousness than human love for the neighbor is from social justice. Both divine righteousness and human justice refer specifically to liberation of the oppressed, which is "the essence of divine activity" (12:121). Specifically, this means God is currently working through Christ to vindicate oppressed groups, like American blacks, in their just rebellion against the crumbling structures of social decadence.

If God is at work in Black Power, vindicating blacks against white oppression, the most valuable symbol for pointing to God's activity is the Black Christ.[26] According to Cone, use of the Black Christ symbol does not imply that God is literally black, for man cannot directly describe the transcendent nature of the deity. All theological speech is necessarily of a symbolic nature.[27] Yet the symbol of Christ as black is indispensable for an analysis of where God is at work in a racist society in which men are related to him by political action rather than by belief. What the Black Christ manifests is succinctly summarized in the following manner:

The blackness of Christ . . . reveals that the achievement of full humanity is consistent with his being. Man was not created to be a slave, and the appearance of God in Christ provides man with the possibility of freedom. By becoming a black man, God discloses that blackness is not what the world says it is. Blackness is a manifestation of the being of God in that it reveals that neither divinity nor humanity reside in white definitions but in the liberation of man from captivity. The Black Christ is he who threatens the structure of evil as seen in white society, rebelling against it, thereby becoming the embodiment of what the black community knows that it must become. Because he has become black as we are, we now know what black empowerment is. It is black people determining the way they are going to behave in the world. It is refusing to allow white society to place strictures on black existence as if their guns mean that blacks are suppose to cool it. Black empowerment is the black community in defiance, knowing that he who has become one of them is far more important than threats from white officials. The Black Christ is he who nourishes the rebellious impulses in black people, so that at the appointed time the black community can respond collectively to the white community as a corporate "bad nigger," lashing out at the enemy of man (12:215-216).

Revolution, Violence, and Reconciliation

Whenever a society seriously violates God's loving and just purposes for man, either civil disobedience or revolution become genuine Christian obligations. For the Christian's ultimate allegiance to God transcends loyalty to all laws and customs that contradict the human dignity bestowed upon every man by the Creator. "Through disobedience to the state," Cone writes, the Christian "affirms his allegiance to God as Creator and his willingness to behave as if he believes it" (11:137). In racist America, Cone believes obedience to God requires revolution, since it is not a particular wrong that needs to be rectified —as traditional civil rights groups falsely suppose—but an unjust pattern beyond minor repair. Revolution is necessary to create a totally new system out of a hopelessly corrupt social order.

Since revolutions involve coercion, the question naturally arises: may Christians employ violent means? Against the widespread notion that Christians should decide the question of violence by looking at what Jesus did in the first century, Cone argues that they should consider where Christ is at work in the twentieth century, namely, his activity in the midst of revolutions of the oppressed. Faith in Christ's ongoing work directs believers to the appropriate type of activity, but it does not provide absolute guidelines regarding the use of violence in particular circumstances. Each specific case, Cone argues, must be decided not only in light of Christ's ongoing work, but also in view of the probable consequences. If the Christian "decides to take the 'nonviolent' way, then he is saying that revolutionary violence is more detrimental to man in the long run than systematic violence. But if the system is evil, then revolutionary violence is both justified and necessary" (11:143). Cone himself believes violence is justified against the American system of racism whenever it represents an attempt by an oppressed person to "say Yes to his being as defined by God in a world that would make his being into nonbeing" (11:55). If violence derives from "the black man's courage to say Yes to himself as a creature of God, and if in affirming self he affirms Yes to the neighbor, then violence may be the black man's expression, sometimes the only possible expression, of Christian love to the white oppressor" (11:55).

Anticipating the argument that revolutionary violence is incompatible with the classical Christian virtues of patience, suffering, and hope, Cone reinterprets each in conformity with his fresh reading of the gospel. Inasmuch as the gospel is essentially a message about the liberation of the oppressed, patience is a resolute determination to resist the oppressor. Suffering by the oppressed is not the will of God, except insofar as it is experienced while fighting the injustices of the status quo. Hope in Christ is not an illusory compensation for current miseries, but a protest against whatever conflicts with the divine promises of liberation and fulfillment (11:101–102). Hope is "not patience but impatience, not calmness but protest" (11:102). In short, the really virtuous Christian is not quiet in the face of injustice, but actively engaged in conflict with the world.

As for the ancient Christian concept of reconciliation, Cone observes that threatened oppressors invariably employ the word to justify peace on their own terms in lieu of full justice for their opponents. This use of "reconciliation" conflicts, however, with the meaning of the New Testament passage, "God was in Christ reconciling the world to himself" (II Cor. 5:19). For God to be reconciling "means that the wall of hostility is broken down," making color and other intra-human differences irrelevant to social relationships (11:147). Genuine racial reconciliation, by definition, involves an equality that rejects one-sided white criteria for dialogue and embraces the unique values that blacks bring to the relationship. Because reconciliation of this sort is impossible until blacks are fully accepted and treated as equals, Cone argues that black people cannot consider "the possibilities of reconciliation" in a racist society "until full emancipation has become a reality for *all* black people" (11:146).

In developing these several themes of his Black Theology, James Cone has formulated a more radical theological alternative to Marxism than Dom Helder. By eschewing the latter's confidence in the ability of ideas to persuade the powerful as well as Dom Helder's arguments in support of nonviolence, Cone challenges the status quo with ideological support for the oppressed as vigorous as that issued by Marxists. Yet Marx had virtually no influence on Cone's theology, which was forged out of an encounter with the Bible, contemporary Protestant theology, and the black experience in America. By his creative use of traditional Christian beliefs, Cone has demonstrated that Christianity, far from being only an opiate of the masses, can be enlisted in support of violent revolution. He has also implicitly responded to an important Marxist critique of religion by showing that theology can proceed in accordance with Marx's dictum that reflection be embedded in *praxis,* thought in revolutionary action. His Black Theology both arises from the experience of oppression and reflects upon the movement for black liberation. Yet, Cone maintains a commitment to Christianity that preserves the dialectical relationship between theological criteria and the commanding claims of the black political movement.

3. CRITICAL EVALUATION

There can be little doubt that spokesmen for the new theology of radical politics have discovered extremely effective ways of responding to Marx's critique of religion without abandoning either his basic insights or their own Christian convictions. By and large, religious radicals agree with Marx's analysis of the socially dysfunctional consequences of many prevailing religious beliefs, arguing that ecclesiastical institutions have frequently undercut social criticism and action by offering illusory heavenly compensations as well as by supporting a naive fatalism that views all things, including the sociopolitical status quo, as ultimately in accordance with the good intentions of a benevolent deity. By denouncing these beliefs as perversions of the central message of the Bible and by drawing out the revolutionary implications of biblical theology, radical churchmen have rediscovered Judeo-Christian resources legitimating activities as radical as those advocated by Marxists.

The theological resources employed by religious radicals are sufficiently similar to suggest the emergence of a new theology of radical politics centering on divine vindication of the poor, liberation of the oppressed, participatory democracy, eschatological hope, and creative use of secular and ecclesiastical structures for social change. Nonetheless, religious radicals differ widely in their specific responses to Marx. Dom Helder's Christian humanism, for example, concentrates on countering the alienating effects of religious fatalism by specifying the revolutionary implications of fairly traditional beliefs in the *imago Dei* in man and Christ's identification with the poor. James Cone is less concerned with countering alienating illusions than with a Christian equivalent of Marx's proclamation of liberation to the oppressed. By using traditional theological categories to interpret secular realities, like Black Power, Cone succeeds better than Dom Helder is rooting theology in *praxis*, although this also means that his thought diverges more sharply than the Archbishop's theology from traditional Christianity. Cone's justification of violence also moves him closer to Marx than Dom Helder, who represents the more traditional, but still defensible, Christian commitment to nonviolence. It is diversity of this sort that has enabled religious radicals to effectively respond to very different aspects of Marx's challenge.

Despite the heterogeneity of the new religious left, several criticisms apply generally to their work. First, religious radicals, for reasons related to their commitment to dramatic change, have failed to develop sophisticated theologies comparable to those of seminal theologians like Barth, Bultmann, Bonhoeffer, and Tillich. For some socially active men, like Dom Helder, this failure appears to be due to exceptionally heavy leadership responsibilities. Others, like James Cone, apparently eschew traditional forms of academic sophistication because they feel it is more important to motivate commitment through emotionally charged rhetoric than to engage the intellect alone. In both cases, however, the result is the same, namely, a tendency to simplify excruciatingly difficult moral problems. A case in point is the issue of violence in social protest. Dom Helder simply asserts that violence is incompatible with the gospel, without considering the careful arguments for the legitimate uses of violence advanced by just war theorists, like Augustine, Aquinas, and Calvin. Taking the opposite track, Cone contends that violence is justified, but he nowhere analyses the specific conditions for its legitimate use. Consequently, we look in vain to most radical theologians for arguments that might illumine our specific moral dilemmas beyond general ideological perspectives.

A closely related problem is the failure of many religious radicals to fully consider the likely implications of their views, especially the ancient problem of the relationship between the means employed in social action and the ends sought. For example, if love is to be temporarily confined within an oppressed group before it is expressed towards others, how does one prevent the "poisoning of the spirit" which is willed towards some men and not towards others (21:7)? If self-defense justifies the use of violence by the oppressed as Cone suggests, how does an oppressed person avoid becoming a slave to another man's initiative, answering the opponent on his terms? Is bondage really avoided when men respond to violence with violence? Traditionally, religions have stressed the importance of finding new grounds for responding to danger, grounds that bring something new into being beyond the animal capacity to strike back (21:22). Assuming that violence is eventually employed, although reconciliation is the final goal, what is the nature of the binding process that will eventually result in reconciliation? How can we assure that the powerless, when they get their hands on coercive weapons, will use them with greater integrity than their former oppressors? There are no easy answers to these questions, but they cannot be avoided simply by failing to ask them.

A further criticism derives from the tendency of religious radicals to ignore the obstacles to their hopes represented by the deeper psychological motivations that are as much a part of the human condition as the external social environment. Because radicals implicitly assume that most problems—like man's exploition of man—can be eliminated within the right institutional structures, they concentrate on social change, neglecting the concomitant need for deeper psychological insight and motivational transformation. Considerable psychoanalytic evidence suggests, however, that men will have to learn to deal with their unconscious processes, especially aggressive feelings, before they will be capable of being as gentle and non-exploitative as most radicals hope.

Finally, most religious radicals are extremely vague about the exact goals being sought, despite eloquently expressed hopes for worldwide justice, solidarity, peace, and the like. One reason for this vagueness is the shared conviction among many radicals that human beings must remain continually open to new possibilities in history. This position has much to commend it, yet skeptics have a point when they ask for further specification of the constituent characteristics of the desired future state of affairs. After all, more than a few revolutions have failed precisely because their adherents lacked a clear vision of the new model to be implemented.

These shortcomings of contemporary forms of the new theology of radical politics are serious, but it is important to remember that the movement is scarcely more than a decade old. Many of those involved within it are both acutely aware of these criticisms and committed to rectifying them.

NOTES

[1] The new breed in American Protestantism is described in Harvey Cox, *On Not Leaving It to the Snake* (16:119-135).

[2] In recovering new biblical themes, religious radicals have been influenced by

several scholarly works on the revolutionary impact of biblical theology on Western history. See, for example, H. and H. A. Frankfort, "Interrelationships between Religion and Nature in the Ancient Near East," in William Lessa and Evon Vogt, eds., *Reader in Comparative Religion,* 2nd ed. (New York: Harper & Row, 1965), pp. 488-494; Arend Van Leeuwen, *Christianity in World History,* trans. W. H. Hoskins (New York: Scribner's, 1964); Dietrich Von Oppen, *The Age of the Person* (Philadelphia: Fortress Press, 1969), esp. ch. 1.

[3] For the Berrigans, see Daniel Berrigan, *The Dark Night of Resistance* (Garden City, N. Y.: Doubleday, 1971), *Night Flight to Hanoi* (New York: Macmillan, 1968), *No Bars to Manhood* (Garden City, N. Y.: Doubleday, 1970), *The Trial of the Cantonville Nine* (Boston: Beacon Press, 1970); Philip Berrigan, *American Catholic Exodus,* ed. John O'Connor (Washington: Corpus Books, 1968), *Prison Journals of a Priest Revolutionary,* with an Introduction by Daniel Berrigan (New York: Holt, Rinehart and Winston, 1970); William Casey and Philip Nobile, eds., *The Berrigans* (New York: Avon Books, 1971); Daniel Berrigan and Robert Coles, *Geography of Faith* (Boston: Beacon Press, 1971); Francine du Plessix Gray, *Divine Disobedience: Profiles in Catholic Radicalism* (19:45-228).

[4] For material on Torres, see Germán Guzmán, *Camilo Torres,* trans. John D. Ring (New York: Sheed and Ward, 1969); Camilo Restrepo Torres, *Camilo Torres: His Life and His Message,* eds. John Alvarez Garcia and Christian Restrepo Calle (Springfield, Ill.: Templegate Publishers, 1968); Camilo Restrepo Torres, *Revolutionary Writings* (New York: Herder and Herder, 1969).

[5] For an alternative description of the theology of contemporary religious radicals, see Richard Shaull, "Revolution: Heritage and Contemporary Option," in Carl Oglesby and Richard Shaull, *Containment and Change* (New York: Macmillan, 1967), pp. 179-248.

[6] Arend Van Leeuwen contrasts the dynamic concept of the biblical God with the ontocratic view of the cosmos shared by other ancient civilizations in his *Christianity in World History,* esp. chs. 2, 3, and 4.

[7] Major contributions to the theology of hope during the 1960's were made by Jürgen Moltmann, *Theology of Hope* (25), *Religion, Revolution, and the Future* (26), *Hope and Planning* (24); Rubem A. Alves, *A Theology of Human Hope* (2). For a critical discussion of the theology of hope, see Frederick Herzog, *The Future of Hope: Theology as Eschatology* (22).

[8] For a brief discussion of Müntzer, see Lowell H. Zuck, "Fecund Problems of Eschatological Hope, Election Proof, and Social Revolt in Thomas Müntzer," in Franklin Hamelin Littel, ed., *Reformation Studies* (Richmond, Va.: John Knox Press, 1962), pp. 238-250. Michael Waltzer presents an excellent history of radical Calvinism in *The Revolution of the Saints* (Cambridge, Mass.: Harvard University Press, 1965).

[9] For general accounts of the Second Vatican Council, see Henri Fesquet, *The Drama of Vatican II,* trans. Bernard Murchland (New York: Random House, 1967); Robert Blair Kaiser, *Pope, Council and World: The Story of Vatican II* (New York: Macmillan, 1963); Michael Novak, *The Open Church: Vatican II, Act II* (New York: Macmillan, 1964); Xavier Rynne, pseud., *Letters from Vatican City* (New York: Farrar, Straus, Giroux, 1963), *The Second Session* (New York: Farrar, Straus, Giroux, 1964), *The Third Session* (New York: Farrar, Straus and Giroux, 1965), *The Fourth Session* (New York: Farrar, Straus and Giroux, 1966). For interpretations of the achievements of Vatican II, see Herbert Vorgrimler, ed., *Commentary on the Documents of Vatican II*

(New York: Herder and Herder, 1969), vols. 1-5; Edward Schillebeeckx, *The Real Achievement of Vatican II,* trans. H. J. Vaughan (New York: Herder and Herder, 1967); Peter Riga, *The Church Renewed* (New York: Sheed and Ward, 1966); Leo Westow, *Introducing Contemporary Catholicism* (Philadelphia: The Westminster Press, 1967).

10 For the nonviolent philosophies of Gandhi and King, see Joan Bondurant, *Conquest of Violence: The Gandhian Philosophy of Conflict,* rev. ed. (Berkeley: University of California Press, 1965); Mohandas K. Gandhi, *Non-violent Resistance* (New York: Schocken Books, 1961); Martin Luther King, Jr., *Stride Toward Freedom* (New York: Harper & Row, 1958), *Why We Can't Wait* (New York: Harper & Row, 1963), *Where Do We Go From Here: Chaos or Community?* (New York: Harper & Row, 1967).

11 For an excellent history of papal social encyclicals, see Jean Yves Calvez and Jacques Perrin, *The Church and Social Justice: The Social Teaching of the Popes from Leo XIII to Pius XII* (4). Also see Anne Freemantle, *The Papal Encyclicals in Their Historical Context,* with an Introduction by Gustave Weigel (New York: New American Library, 1956); Anne Freemantle, *The Social Teachings of the Church* (New York: New American Library, 1963). For comments by American Catholic scholars on the significance of the social encyclicals of Pope John XXIII, see Joseph N. Moody and Justus George Lawler, ed., *The Challenge of Mater et Magistra* (New York: Herder & Herder, 1963). "The Pastoral Constitution on the Church in the Modern World" may be found in Walter Abbot, ed., *The Documents of Vatican II* (1); it is critically evaluated in *The Church Today; Commentaries on the Pastoral Constitution on the Church in the Modern World,* trans. John Drury, D. Barrett, and Michael Mazzarese, and edited by Group 2000 (Westminster, Md.: Newman Press, 1967). Barbara Ward discusses the significance of *Populorum Progressio* in her Commentary on *The Encyclical Letter of His Holiness Pope Paul VI: On the Development of Peoples* (New York: Paulist Press, 1967).

12 Useful material on the social situation of the Roman Catholic Church in Latin American can be found in Leslie Dewart, *Christianity and Revolution: The Lesson of Cuba* (New York: Herder & Herder, 1963); Henry A. Landsberger, ed., *The Church and Social Change in Latin America* (Notre Dame, Ind.: University of Notre Dame Press, 1970); Donald Eugene Smith, ed., *Religion, Politics, and Social Change in the Third World* (32); Frederick Turner, *Catholicism and Political Development in Latin America* (Chapel Hill: University of North Carolina Press, 1971); Ivan Vallier, *Catholicism, Social Control, and Modernization in Latin America* (33). For further bibliography, see Frederick Turner, *Catholicism and Political Development in Latin America* (Chapel Hill: University of North Carolina Press, 1971), pp. 225-259.

13 For a characterization of the New Left in the Third World, see Rubem Alves, *A Theology of Human Hope* (2:ch. 1).

14 A brief history of Catholic radicalism in Brazil may be found in Emanuel de Kadt, "JUC and AP: The Rise of Catholic Radicalism in Brazil," in Landsberger, ed., *The Church and Social Change in Latin America,* pp. 191-219.

15 Dom Helder's concept of *conscientização* as well as his educational theories were influenced by Paulo Freire with whom he was associated in the Movement for Basic Education. For the latter's views, see Paulo Freire, *Pedagogy of the Oppressed,* trans. Myra B. Ramos (New York: Herder & Herder, 1970).

16 For background material on the black church in America, see James Cone, *Black Theology and Black Power* (11:ch. IV); E. Franklin Frazier, *The Negro*

Church in America (New York: Schocken Books, 1963); Franklin Loescher, *The Protestant Church and the Negro, a Pattern of Segregation* (New York: Association Press, 1948); Benjamin E. Mays and J. W. Nicholson, *The Negro's Church* (New York: Institute of Social Research, 1933); Howard Thurman, *The Negro Spiritual Speaks of Life and Death* (New York: Harper & Row, 1947); Joseph Washington, *Black Religion* (Boston: Beacon Press, 1964).

17 Useful background information on the history of black protest in the 1960's can be found in August Meier and Elliott Rudwick, eds., *Black Protest in the Sixties* (Chicago: Quadrangle Books, 1970); Richard P. Young, ed., *Roots of Rebellion: The Evolution of Black Politics and Protest since World War II* (New York: Harper & Row, 1970).

18 The principal books on Black Power are: Floyd B. Barbour, ed., *The Black Power Revolt* (Boston: Porter Sargent, 1968); Joseph R. Barndt, *Why Black Power?* (New York: Friendship Press, 1968); Stokely Carmichael and Charles Hamilton, *Black Power: The Politics of Liberation in America* (New York: Random House, 1967); Stokely Carmichael, *Stokely Speaks: Black Power Back to Pan-Africanism* (New York: Random House, 1971); Malcolm Little, *The Autobiography of Malcolm X* (New York: Grove Press, 1965); Malcolm Little, *Malcolm X Speaks* (London: Secker and Warburg, 1966); Bobby Seale, *Seize the Time: The Story of the Black Panther Party and Huey Newton* (New York: Random House, 1970); Nathan Wright, Jr., *Black Power and Urban Unrest* (New York: Hawthorn Books, 1967).

19 Following the great Swiss theologian Karl Barth, Cone argues that Christology is the point of theological departure (11:34). Yet he also accepts Tillich's emphasis upon the importance of contemporary culture for theology, arguing that it is also "a source and norm of theology." Cone has recently attempted to combine these two hermeneutical principles, in his "The Sources and Norm of Black Theology," *A Black Theology of Liberation* (12:ch. 2, 50-81).

20 Cone is indebted to Moltmann's discussion of the "political hermeneutics of the gospel for this joining of the freedom of faith with political liberation. See Jürgen Moltmann, "Toward a Political Hermeneutics of the Gospel," *Union Seminary Quarterly Review*, vol. 23, no. 4 (Summer, 1968), 313-314.

21 Moltmann's theology of hope is an important source of Cone's eschatology. See Jürgen Moltmann, *Theology of Hope* (25), *Religion, Revolution and the Future* (26).

22 Cone agrees with George Kelsey's contention that racism is an alien faith. See George Kelsey, *Racism and the Christian Understanding of Man* (New York: Scribner's, 1965).

23 Cone considers Anders Nygren, *Agape and Eros* (Philadelphia: Westminster Press, 1953) to be the classical treatment of the Christian idea of love.

24 For Tillich's discussion of the inseparability of these values, see Paul Tillich, *Love, Power, and Justice* (New York: Oxford University Press, 1960).

25 Cone contends that "white theology is not Christian theology." For his explanation of this position, see *A Black Theology of Liberation* (12:28, n. 4).

26 For a somewhat different interpretation of the Black Christ, see Albert B. Cleage, Jr., *The Black Messiah* (8).

27 Cone is indebted to Paul Tillich for his understanding of symbolism in religious discourse. See Tillich, *Dynamics of Faith* (New York: Harper, 1957).

BIBLIOGRAPHY

1. ABBOTT, WALTER, ed., *The Documents of Vatican II*. New York: America Press, 1966.
2. ALVES, RUBEM A., *A Theology of Human Hope*. New York: Corpus Books, 1969.
3. ARENDT, HANNAH, *On Revolution*. New York: Viking Press, 1963.
4. CALVEZ, JEAN YVES, and JACQUES PERRIN, *The Church and Social Justice: The Social Teaching of the Popes from Leo XIII to Pius XII*, trans. J. R. Kirwan. Chicago: Henry Regnery, 1961.
5. CAMARA, DOM HELDER, *The Church and Colonialism*, trans. William Mc-Sweeney. Denville, N. J.: Dimension Books, 1969.
6. ————, *Race Against Time*, trans. Della Couling. Denville, N. J.: Dimension Books, 1971.
7. ————, *Revolution Through Peace*, trans. Amparo McLean, ed. Ruth Nanda Anshen. World Perspectives Series, Vol. 45. New York: Harper & Row, 1971.
8. CLEAGE, ALBERT B., JR., *The Black Messiah*. New York: Sheed and Ward, 1968.
9. COLAIANNI, JAMES, *The Catholic Left: The Crisis of Radicalism Within the Church*. Philadelphia: Chilton, 1968.
10. CONE, JAMES, "Black Theology and Black Liberation," *Christian Century* (September, 1970), 1084-1088.
11. ————, *Black Theology and Black Power*. New York: Seabury Press, 1969.
12. ————, *A Black Theology of Liberation*. Philadelphia: J. B. Lippincott, 1970.
13. CONE, JAMES, and GAYRAUD S. WILMORE, "Black Theology and African Theology: Considerations for Dialogue, Critique and Integration" (unpublished paper).
14. COX, HARVEY, ed., *The Church Amid Revolution*. New York: Associated Press, 1967.
15. ————, *The Feast of Fools*. Cambridge, Mass.: Harvard University Press, 1969.
16. ————, *On Not Leaving It to the Snake*. New York: Macmillan, 1967.
17. ————, *The Secular City*. New York: Macmillan, 1965.
18. DE BROUCKER, JOSÉ, *Dom Helder Camara: The Violence of A Peacemaker*, trans. Herma Briffault. Maryknoll, N. Y., Orbis Books, 1970.
19. GRAY, FRANCINE DU PLESSIX, *Divine Disobedience: Profiles in Catholic Radicalism*. New York: Alfred A. Knopf, 1970.
20. HALL, BARBARA, and RICHARD SHAULL, "From Somewhere along the Road," *Theology Today*, Vol. 29 (April, 1972), 86-101.

21. HARDING, VINCENT, "The Religion of Black Power," in *The Religious Situation: 1968,* ed. by Donald R. Cutler. Boston: Beacon Press, 1968.

22. HERZOG, FREDERICK, *The Future of Hope: Theology as Eschatology.* New York: Herder & Herder, 1970.

23. MARTY, MARTIN, and DEAN PEERMAN, eds., *New Theology No. 6: On Revolution and Non-Revolution, Violence and Non-Violence, Peace and Power.* New York: Macmillan, 1969.

24. MOLTMANN, JÜRGEN, *Hope and Planning.* New York: Harper & Row, 1971.

25. ———, *Theology of Hope.* New York: Harper & Row, 1967.

26. ———, *Religion, Revolution and the Future.* New York: Scribner's, 1969.

27. OGLESBY, CARL, and RICHARD SHAULL, *Containment and Change.* New York: Macmillan, 1967.

28. RAINES, JOHN C., and THOMAS DEAN, eds., *Marxism and Radical Religion.* Philadelphia: Temple University Press, 1970.

29. RIGA, PETER, *The Church and Revolution.* Milwaukee: Bruce Publishing Company, 1967.

30. ROBERTS, J. DEOTIS, *Liberation and Reconciliation: A Black Theology.* Philadelphia: Westminster Press, 1971.

31. SHAULL, RICHARD, "Theology and the Transformation of Society," *Theology Today.* 25 (April, 1968), 23-36.

32. SMITH, DONALD EUGENE, ed., *Religion, Politics, and Social Change in the Third World.* New York: Free Press, 1971.

33. VALLIER, IVAN, *Catholicism, Social Control, and Modernization in Latin America,* Modernization of Traditional Societies Series (Englewood Cliffs, N. J.: Prentice-Hall, 1970).

SUGGESTED READINGS

1. *Primary Readings*

James Cone captures the challenge of radical theology in his *Black Theology and Black Power* (11), chs. 1, 2, 3, 5, and 6. Dom Helder Camara's basic position is explained in his *Revolution Through Peace* (7), chs. 1, 3, 4, 6, and 7.

2. *Secondary Readings*

For a helpful general discussion of revolutionary consciousness and a sympathetic theological appraisal of it, see Richard Shaull, *Containment and Change* (27), 170-248. For an historical survey of the religious and secular roots of revolutionary movements since the Reformation, and a critical evaluation of major theological perspectives on modern society, see Rosemary Radford Ruether, *The Radical Kingdom: The Western Experience of Messianic Hope* (New York: Harper and Row, 1970).

For a readable account of the diverse personalities and the varying interests of selected Roman Catholic radicals (e.g., David Kirk of Emmaus House, the Berrigan brothers, and Ivan Illich), see Francine du Plessix Gray, *Divine Disobedience: Profiles in Catholic Radicalism* (19). Daniel Berrigan explains the influences leading to his commitment to political radicalism in his *No Bars to Manhood* (New York: Doubleday, 1970).

For a sympathetic portrait of Dom Helder Camara, including a description of his political activities, see José de Broucker, *Dom Helder Camara: The Violence of a Peacemaker* (18). The efforts of Dom Helder and other Christian revolutionaries in Latin America are briefly criticized by Ivan Vallier in his sociological study of the roles that religions play in impeding or facilitating modernization, *Catholicism, Social Control, and Modernization in Latin America*, chs. 1 and 4.

For a critique of dominant secular and theological interpretations of black-white relations as well as a constructive black theology, see Joseph R. Washington, Jr., *The Politics of God* (Boston: Beacon Press, 1967). For a careful analysis and critique of black power as a religion, see Vincent Harding, "The Religion of Black Power" (21). For a critical assessment of Cone, Washington, and Harding from a more traditional confessional position, see J. Deotis Roberts, *Liberation and Reconciliation: A Black Theology* (Philadelphia: Westminster Press, 1971).

3. *Additional Bibliography*

On the Roman Catholic Church and social change in Latin America, see Frederick Turner, *Catholicism and Political Development in Latin America* (Chapel Hill: University of North Carolina Press, 1971), pp. 225-259. On American blacks, see Elizabeth W. Miller, *The Negro in America: A Bibliography* (Cambridge, Mass.: Harvard University Press, 1966). On black protest, see Richard P. Young, ed., *Roots of Rebellion: The Evolution of Black Politics and Protest Since World War II* (New York: Harper and Row, 1970). On black protest and religion, see Arnold Schuchter, *Reparations* (Philadelphia: Lippincott, 1970), pp. 265-74.

IV

PSYCHOANALYSIS AND RELIGION

8

The Psychoanalytic Diagnosis: Infantile Illusion

Sigmund Freud (1856–1939)—the founder of psychoanalysis and father of modern psychology—is one of the truly remarkable figures in the history of science. In the course of almost fifty years of dedicated research, he constructed—from empirical insights, therapeutic encounters, and speculative hypotheses—a comprehensive and highly original theory of the human psyche and its development in relation to the organic and social environment. Like Darwin, with whom one is tempted to compare his revolutionary discoveries, Freud formulated a seminal conception of man's origins.[1] Unlike the author of *The Origin of Species*, however, Freud focused not upon man's ancestral descent as an organic creature, but, rather, upon the unconscious and infantile origins of his conscious thoughts and deeds. By demonstrating the relation of conscious beliefs and acts to unconscious processes and by further tracing these processes to early stages of development, Freud succeeded in radically altering modern man's self-understanding. Thanks to Freud even the man on the street is now aware that slips of the tongue, dreams, and myths conceal sentiments of an unconscious, and frequently infantile, nature.

Freud's challenge to religion was three-pronged. In the first place, he sketched a portrait of man that was clearly incompatible with the classical religious doctrine that man's aesthetic, moral, and religious attributes transcend the realm of nature and scientific explanation. Freud was not, to be sure, the first to challenge this traditional doctrine of man.

Darwin, for instance, had previously attempted to explain, in *The Expression of Emotions in Man and Animals,* how man gradually attained his most exquisitely human characteristics. By the time Freud began the study of biology and psychology in the waning decades of the nineteenth century, however, scientists were beginning to question Darwin's explanation. A serious lacuna thus appeared at the heart of the theory of evolution. How, it was asked, are we to explain those qualities of human spirit that elevate man above other animals? The general failure of biologists to respond adequately to this central question left the scientific door ajar for several enterprising theologians who—desirous of preserving the traditional doctrine of man's unique status in nature—proceeded to formulate an interesting compromise with the Darwinian theory. The Deity, these theologians contended, created man's body, but not his soul, by means of the complicated evolutionary process described by Darwin.[2] As a corollary, it was argued that Divine intervention in the evolutionary process was necessary in order to endow man with his distinctive spiritual attributes and to establish man's unique and special relationship with his Creator.

Freud approached the problem of explaining man's spiritual attributes from a new and quite different direction. The human psyche, he contended, is like an iceberg. The so-called higher regions of the human spirit are simply the superficial surface that happens to be accessible to consciousness. Below this surface lurks a dangerous, unknown mass of primal instincts, amoral passions, and repressed memories—in short, a great underworld of dynamic, hidden forces which exert imperious control over the conscious life and behavior of man.[3] With this fresh perspective as his starting point, Freud spent more than forty years mining the unconscious for the hidden origins of rational, aesthetic, moral, and religious beliefs and practices. In doing so, he closed the still remaining gap in the Darwinian theory of evolution and thus rendered superfluous the theological notion that the Deity, by a special act of creation, endowed man with his spiritual characteristics. It is primarily for this reason that Freud's biographer, Ernest Jones, confers upon him the title: "the Darwin of the Mind" (19:304).

In addition to challenging the classical religious doctrine of man's unique status in nature, Freud also challenged the validity of numerous religious beliefs by unmasking their "real," but unconscious, origins. Belief in God's providential care, for example, was traced by Freud to man's desire to be protected, as he once was as a child, against the dangerous, uncontrollable, and unknown forces that threaten his existence.[4] When the average adult discovers that his existence is threatened by disease, death, and so forth, he feels overwhelmed by his own weakness and helplessness. This state of helplessness reminds him, as it were, of a similar state of weakness when as a child he felt protected by a father to whom he attributed superior wisdom and strength. These memories evoke a similar longing for protection against the hazards of adult existence. This powerful longing or wish engenders, in turn, the illusory notion that he is protected by a fatherly deity whose love and protection can be won by obeying his commandments. In short, according to Freud, belief in Divine Providence has its origins in anxiety, helplessness, infantile desires, and unconsciously generated fantasies.

If it had not been Freud, the father of modern psychology, who posed these and other arguments regarding the emotional and, hence, irrational origins of religious beliefs these several propositions probably would not have produced much excitement, for some of them were neither new nor powerful in themselves. The role of fear, ignorance, and imagination in the genesis of religion had been previously suggested by David Hume. But in the context of psychoanalytic theory, as an application of this extremely persuasive theory to religious beliefs, the ancient arguments of gifted, but unscientific scholars, such as Hume, acquired a new aura of scientific plausibility. Thus, where it had been possible to discount the insights of Hume as those of a speculative philosopher, it became difficult to disavow the magnitude of the evidence Freud amassed in support of somewhat similar conclusions.

Finally, Freud challenged the widespread assumption that religious beliefs and practices yield positive psychological benefits.[5] By uncovering the immature and irrational attitudes perpetrated by religious institutions, Freud showed how religion impoverishes a believer's ability to effectively cope with the threatening forces impinging upon him from the natural world without, and from the unconscious impulses within, himself. Instead of dealing with these forces in a mature and rational manner, Freud demonstrated that the religious person frequently turns to a divine father-figure whose protective love is sought through prayers, penances, confessions, and so forth. For example, when a religious student becomes anxious about an exam and utters a prayer for divine help, it may be that he is retreating from the realistic task of studying into an emotionally charged, infantile world of fantasy. Freud discovered that the impoverishment of a person's critical ability in one area such as this impedes the use of reason in other areas as well. In addition to demonstrating the immature and irrational attitudes perpetrated by religion, Freud also showed the damaging psychological effects of the strict moral codes sanctioned by religious institutions. Freud found in treating disturbed patients that rigidly righteous believers, who feel that any expression of anger or hostility is sinful, invariably live constricted, guilt-ridden, unhappy, and unfulfilled lives.

In explicating these and other damaging psychological consequences of religion, Freud raised several issues with which religious laymen and theologians have been forced to grapple throughout the middle decades of the twentieth century. Is religious faith incompatible with psychological maturity? Are religious institutions responsible for perpetrating undesirable patterns of human existence? In short, are the psychological effects of religion necessarily dysfunctional? When we turn to Dietrich Bonhoeffer and Erik Erikson, we will see the importance of these questions.

In this three-pronged assault on the classical religious doctrine of man, the validity of religious beliefs, and the psychological consequences of faith, Freud reminds one of Marx, who, it will be recalled, also uncovered deep irrationalities in human behavior and questioned the functional consequences of religion. There are, however, several crucial differences between Marx and Freud. Whereas Marx interprets religion as a by-product of social, especially economic, conditions, Freud sees religion as primarily a product of intra-psychic processes dating back to infantile dependency needs. In consequence of this disagreement about derivations, Freud disagrees with Marx regarding the false religious consciousness from which man must be freed if he is to achieve maturity and fulfillment. Whereas for Marx false religious consciousness stems from ignorance concerning the oppressive social functions of religious ideologies, for Freud religious illusions derive from failure to appreciate the unconscious, infantile origins of religious ideas and their damaging psychological results. This unique Freudian diagnosis leads to an equally unusual prescription. Rather than looking with Marx into the future for a liberating social movement, Freud chose to examine the unconscious past of religious believers with the ultimate aim of emancipating them from their abnormal infantile fixations. Thus, while Marx saw our religious present as pregnant with a non-religious future, with the proletariat as the midwife of history, Freud viewed present-day religiosity as pregnant with the past, with the psychoanalyst as the abortionist of history.

Having sketched Freud's challenge to religion and having indicated, in a very general way, several of his principal arguments, we now turn to a closer analysis of his personal orientation towards, and contributions to, the study of religious phenomena. We will consider separately Freud's personal attitude towards religion and the contributions he made towards understanding its psychological roots.

1. FREUD'S PERSONAL ORIENTATION TOWARDS RELIGION [6]

There was no obvious psychological reason why Freud should have been so disturbed by religion. The future critic was not himself raised in a religious household; no superstitious beliefs or tiresome family pieties stifled his development. His freethinking parents, emancipated from their own rabbinic heritage, raised their children in a secular atmosphere devoid of Jewish dietary observances and other customary rituals. The sole exception to this general neglect of traditional religious customs in the Freud household was the festival meal of Seder over which Freud's father, Jakob, presided on the eve of Passover. The young Freud thus never passed through the religious phases so frequent in the development of most children. Indeed, he never seems to have taken religious beliefs very seriously at all—a fact which may account for his lifelong curiosity about the religious beliefs of other people.

Given this secular background, one would not expect Freud to be particularly sympathetic towards religious issues; but neither would one expect particularly strong hostility. Yet, his animus is clear to anyone acquainted with his writings. To what can we attribute this animosity?

Several biographers have made a great deal of the influence of Freud's Roman Catholic "Nanny" in the genesis of his negative attitude towards religion. This elderly Nanny, whom Freud refers to as "that prehistoric old woman," apparently instructed her young charge in the primitive religious beliefs current among the lower classes in Austria in the middle decades of the nineteenth century (18:6). This instruction included biblical stories, ideas about Heaven and Hell, and threats of severe punishment for moral transgressions. She also took the young Sigmund to her church services, although the precocious young child was uniquely unimpressed. Upon returning from church, he would imitate what he had seen and heard, much to the amusement of his parents. There is little evidence to suggest, however, that this Nanny's theological beliefs had any lasting influence on the young Freud beyond possibly setting the stage for his later contempt for the superstitious beliefs of naive believers. His contact with her ceased when he was two and a half years old.

Much more important than his Nanny in the genesis of Freud's hostility towards religion was the fact that he was raised as a Jew in the predominantly Roman Catholic and intensely anti-Semitic city of Vienna, where he lived for almost eighty years until the city was overrun by the Nazis in the late 1930's.[7] As a boy, he quickly came in contact with naive beliefs about Jews being the killers of Christ. At school, he was subjected to the most primitive anti-Semitic prejudices. At home, he learned from his parents something about the persecution of his people. One can readily understand the basis of Freud's later polemics against the irrationality and immorality of many religious believers from the following account of a memorable childhood experience:

> I may have been ten or twelve years old, when my father began to take me with him on his walks and reveal to me in his talk his views upon things in the world we live in. Thus it was, on one occasion, that he told

me a story to show me how much better things were now than they had been in his days. "When I was a young man," he said, "I went for a walk one Saturday in the streets of your birthplace; I was well dressed, and had a new fur cap on my head. A Christian came up to me and with a single blow knocked off my cap into the mud and shouted: 'Jew! Get off the pavement!' " (5:107)

It is scarcely surprising that the son who heard this, and other stories, and who personally experienced less brutal, but no less real, forms of discrimination as an adult, turned his polemical weapons against the superstitious and patently immoral beliefs partly responsible for engendering such persecution.

Equally important in the formation of Freud's negative attitude towards religion was his devotion to science as the sole road to truth.[8] To Freud, science represented—as it still does to many people—not only the sole legitimate method of obtaining valid knowledge, but also the supreme expression of rationality and the prime remedy for human ills. Science thus appeared to offer the only legitimate means of realizing what Freud describes as his early "overpowering need to understand something of the riddles of the world in which we live and perhaps even to contribute something of their solution" (18:28). Yet, curiously, this devotion to science did not entail any great interest in the physical and biological sciences. To these disciplines Freud felt little or no strong attraction. His own concerns were, rather, with the great psychological and cultural issues—especially with the great problem of how man evolved psychologically. In explaining his choice of profession and directions, Freud observes that he felt no "particular predilection for the career of a physician," that he was "moved, rather, but a sort of curiosity, which was, however, directed more towards human concerns than towards natural objects" (18:28).

Curiosity of this sort invariably leads beyond strictly empirical findings, and Freud was no exception to this general principle. His irrepressible desire to contribute to our understanding of the riddles of human existence impelled him to speculate far beyond the normal reaches of science and to draw moral conclusions from his speculative ventures. "In psychoanalysis," Philip Rieff shrewdly observes, "Freud found a way of being the philosopher he desired to be, and of applying his philosophy to himself, humanity, the cosmos—to everything, visible and invisible, which as a scientist and physician he observed" (20:1). Yet, Freud never ceased to insist that his views—in contrast with the unverifiable speculations of metaphysicians—were based on proven empirical evidence and subject to continual revision in the course of scientific progress. Accordingly, Freud disparaged the unverified and unverifiable beliefs of religious people by contrasting them with his own empirically based scientific theories.

To summarize the main elements in Freud's basic attitude towards religion is to unravel his own most cherished beliefs and values: his lifelong atheism, his sensitivity to moral injustice, and his commitment to the truths revealed by science. These beliefs and values were endangered, Freud felt, by the superstitious, immoral, and nonverifiable elements in popular religion. It was for this reason that Freud reserved his greatest contempt for the childish irrationality of popular religion and ignored the trust, kindness, and reasonableness that has characterized religion at its best.

It would be a grave mistake to suppose, however, that Freud's critique of religion was conditioned solely by his personal animus. Although the religious phenomena he chose to study and the vehemence with which he attacks religion derive from his personal predilections, most of his views are based upon his psychoanalytic discoveries. To understand Freud's interpretation of religion, then, we must first carefully explore those psychoanalytic insights that pertain to his investigations in this area. Having done so, we shall be in a position to follow Freud's application of these insights to a variety of religious beliefs and practices.

2. FREUD'S PSYCHOANALYTIC THEORY

Unravelling the psychological views of a theorist as complex as Freud is always difficult. His writings contain not only a complex network of interrelated hypotheses regarding psychic processes and personality development, but also a rich vocabulary of esoteric concepts, such as repression, regression, projection, and so on. In addition, Freud's assertions are written in an aggressive, often shrewd, style that compels the reader to look at his own base desires. His prevailing tone is a cunning "you've misunderstood yourself from the ground up," accompanied by an even more disturbing willingness to begin our education anew. Yet Freud knows how to be fruitfully disturbing—rather in the way Socrates knew how to lead his fellow Athenians into a deeper self-understanding. If we begin, as we do here, with Freud's earliest discoveries, it is primarily because his mature psychoanalytic theory reaches out from these early insights.

It was a highly intelligent, imaginative, and very disturbed young woman, known in history as Anna O, who first utilized the technique for exploring the human mind which Freud later developed into psychoanalysis.[9] The patient in question, who had become ill while caring for her sick father, manifested serious symptoms such as speech defects, phobias, paralysis of an arm, and an inability to converse in her mother tongue. At Anna's own request, her Viennese physician, Josef Breuer, hypnotized her. During the resulting hypnotic trances, Anna insisted on talking in detail about the manifold real and hallucinatory experiences she had accumulated since her physician's last visit. Although neither Anna nor Breuer had any preconceptions as to the possible consequences of such a unique doctor-patient relationship, it developed that their conversations had the beneficial effect of at least temporarily relieving Anna's symptoms. The young woman herself called the new treatment a "talking cure" or "chimney sweeping."

Surprised by the improvements observed after these hypnotic trances, Breuer conceived the idea, which he communicated to his young friend and colleague Sigmund Freud, that his patient's symptoms were caused by certain emotional, but unconscious, experiences which were released or discharged during hypnosis. A prototypic example of such unconscious motivation was Anna O's repugnance, during a particularly hot summer, to the act of drinking from a glass of water. For no apparent reason, the girl suddenly found herself unable to drink from a glass of water despite a tormenting thirst. She would take the glass in her hand, but, as soon as it touched her lips, she would put it down again in utter disgust. After six weeks of this (during which she quenched her thirst by eating succulent fruits), Anna recalled under hypnosis an incident regarding her English governess whom she disliked. This governess had once allowed her dog, that the girl abhorred, to drink from a glass of water. Out of politeness Anna had said nothing about her anger; subsequently, she had forgotten the incident. But once the memory was recalled under hypnosis, she gave vent to her long suppressed annoyance, asked for a drink, and swallowed a large quantity of water without the slightest difficulty. Afterwards, the symptom completely disappeared.

Deeply impressed by this form of therapy, Freud collaborated with Breuer, adopted his hypnotic technique, and amplified his initial discoveries.[10] The results were published in their 1895 book, *Studies On Hysteria*. Foreshadowing things to come, Breuer and Freud concluded: first, that an emotionally significant event, if sufficiently painful to everyday consciousness, may be so thoroughly excluded from the conscious mind as not to be accessible to normal recollection. Anna, for instance, was incapable of remembering the incident regarding her governess's dog. Second, Freud and Breuer concluded that hysterical symptoms, such as those Anna experienced, are connected with an emotionally traumatic occurrence in the past (psychic traumatism). Symptoms such as Anna's inability to drink, are the "remnants" or "memory symbols" of earlier traumatic experiences. Finally, they showed that if the traumatic event could be vividly re-experienced under hypnosis, it would no longer exert an unconscious influence and the symptom would disappear. This curative method they called the *cathartic method*.[11]

From these insights, it was a relatively short step to Freud's fundamental concept of the self in conflict. The self, Freud realized early in his career, is not a static entity, but a battlefield of intrapsychic conflicts between hidden impulses on the one hand, and conscious pursuits on the other. Unconscious drives, images, fantasies, and emotions are forever pressing toward often irrational goals. Yet, these drives are seldom experienced in their pristine state. For the conscious surface of the mind reacts against the disruptive forces emanating from the unconscious "cauldron of seething excitement" by driving them below the threshold of consciousness and impeding their discharge. The drives and memories that are driven out of consciousness in this manner, however, do not lose their dynamic force. From their home in the unconscious workshop of the psyche they continue to demand some form of expression, sometimes manifesting themselves in devious forms such as peculiar symptoms, nightmares, slips of the tongue, and the like. Thus, Anna O's anger at her governess for allowing her dog to drink from a glass, although deeply buried in her unconscious, found expression in her own inability to drink.

Freud and Breuer finally parted company, partly because of the former's dissatisfaction with hypnosis, but primarily because of Breuer's refusal to dig ever-deeper into the seamy unconscious motivations of his patients. At the time of the break, Freud had discovered that a great many unconscious feelings, which at first seemed accessible only under hypnosis, would be remembered by the patient if his physician listened sympathetically. This discovery led to the development of the now famous *free association* technique of therapeutic treatment.[12] As developed by Freud, free association became the keystone of psychoanalytic therapy and the principal method, which it remains today, of discovering unconscious motivations.[13] The fundamental assumption of this technique is that there are two distinct ways in which ideas are associated in the human mind: (1) the logical association of ideas characteristic of ordinary rational thought, and (2) the emotional association of ideas typical of dreams, poetry, plays, and so forth (17:30-33). The latter type of association occurs both in states of reverie, such as daydreams and sleep, as well as in waking life—as when a boy likes a girl because she reminds him of his mother. This second type of association provided the basis of Freud's free association method. By asking his patients to ignore ordinary logical thought processes and by encouraging them to give free reign to whatever emotionally related thoughts came into their minds, Freud found that his patients were capable of bringing forgotten memories to mind without the aid of hypnosis. One thought led to another until they finally touched deeply buried materials.

Freud also discovered, however, that his patients erected internal *resistance* to the communication of certain ideas. Patients would suddenly discover all sorts of reasons for not reporting certain associations, saying they were illogical, unimportant, or immoral. The materials which resisted recollection in this way were found to be painful to remember because they were either guilt-evoking or anxiety-producing. The resistance, however, was not deliberate; it was more like a defensive maneuver to avoid psychic discomfort. The presence of resistance convinced Freud that a psychic obstacle or censor existed which prevented the forgotten material from being recalled. The process by which unacceptable desires or painful memories were forced into the unconscious by this censor was called *repression*. Although Freud initially thought that repression was exerted by the conscious ego, he later came to recognize repression as largely an unconscious process arising from the superego. Nevertheless, the central importance of this process was realized at the outset; in Freud's own words, "the doctrine of repression is the foundation stone on which the whole structure of psychoanalysis rests" (2:61).

Early in his investigations, Freud observed that the unconscious desires and conflicts which were causal factors in pathological problems were invariably related to deeply repressed sexual instincts and desires.[14] This observation led to one of his most significant psychoanalytic discoveries: the importance of sex in the make-up of the human psyche. It should be observed, however, that the term "sexuality" as used by Freud refers to a much broader group of phenomena than its usual referent in ordinary speech—the genital desires of the normal adult for the pleasures of sexual intercourse.[15] Sexuality includes such specifically genital desires, but it also comprises other pleasant bodily sensations such as those produced by stimulation of the various erogenous zones—the mouth and related structures, the anus, and so forth. Sexuality also refers to the complex emotions to which the term love is commonly applied—friendship, admiration, self-love, parental love, and love of abstractions. Freud thus widened the conception of sexuality by, on the one hand, extending it to a variety of pleasurable bodily sensations, and, on the other hand, associating it with affection and tenderness. In the ordinary adult, however, genital sexuality was recognized by Freud as an extremely potent unconscious force.

Numerous examples could be cited where unconscious sexual motives are the effective determinants of behavior. The unattractive co-ed who maligns the stupidity of the school football hero cannot consciously admit her real motive: "I am sexually attracted to him, and hate him for ignoring me." Similarly, the mother-in-law who vigorously criticizes her daughter's husband cannot consciously admit her real desire: "I love him, and would like to take my daughter's place." In both these illustrations, a repressed and, hence, unconscious erotic wish is the effective motivation of behavior. The student is unaware of her erotic desires; the mother-in-law of her so-called "unnatural" love. Nevertheless, these repressed impulses eventually force the individuals to indirectly discharge their emotions by disguising their true feelings. The frustration of being ignored by the beloved hero is expressed by disparaging his scholastic abilities; the unnatural love of a son-in-law by condemning him as unlovable.

Freud extended his novel method of interpretation to the interpretation of dreams after observing that his patients often mentioned dreams while associating freely. Applying the technique of free association to the dreams of his patients as well as to his own dreams, Freud accumulated a fascinating amount of data which he published in 1900.[16] He found that dreams were substitute expressions for sexual desires and memories which had become unconscious through repression. The dream regularly represented a hidden desire in a disguised form, that is, it expressed in dramatic form an unconscious wish of the dreamer represented as fulfilled. For example, a German statesman, during wartime, dreams that he is riding along an Alpine path which narrows until a rocky cliff makes it impassable (5:378-381). He dismounts, strikes a rock with his whip, and calls on God. The whip immediately grows to an endless length and the rocky obstacle drops away giving a view over the landscape in Bohemia where Prussian troops are waving victory banners. According to Freud's interpretation of this dream, the major elements in it are unconsciously associated with the biblical story in which Moses strikes water from a rock in violation of God's command. The whip, like Moses's rod, is a phallic symbol; seizing it in masturbation is a forbidden and rebellious act. God is called upon as though to deny as ostentatiously as possible any such wish. Unlike Moses who was punished for violation of God's commandment, the statesman's desire is fulfilled. "A dream such as this of victory and conquest," Freud notes in conclusion, "is often a cover for a wish to succeed in *erotic* conquest" (5:381). An extremely important consequence of this method of interpreting the unconscious elements in dreams was that it suggested to Freud the possibility of explaining religious symbols and myths in an analogous fashion.

Application of the method of free association to the sexual desires and conflicts of his patients led Freud to the discovery of memories which went further and further back into childhood. Exploration of these early memories brought to the fore one of the most fundamental of all Freud's discoveries, namely, *infantile sexuality.*[17] The unconscious sexual wishes of disturbed, as well as normal, adults were found to be linked with the sexual impulses of the first five years of life. In other words, infantile sexual desires which were not gratified or altered in the course of maturation into suitable forms of adult genital behavior were shown to persist in the adult unconscious from whence they motivate many aspects of adult behavior. The erotic desires adults sought as children to gratify through masturbation, play, and fantasy find expression in their symptoms, superstitions, dreams, literary works, and religious myths.

For example, a patient suffered severely from an impulse to yell obscenities during church services (3:302). Analysis disclosed that once, in childhood, when his father was ill, the patient was told to be extremely quiet. It was on this occasion that the compulsion to disrupt a "holy" silence first appeared. The compulsion had its origins in his infantile incestuous desire to possess his mother sexually, a desire that could only be fulfilled by the removal of his father. By breaking the imposed silence, he thought he might bring about his father's death and fulfillment of his incestuous wish to replace him. Subsequently, God unconsciously represented his father, and the impulse to yell in church indicated his wish to kill his father in order to possess his mother sexually.

Freud discovered three major stages in the normal development of infantile sexuality.[18] The first, stretching from birth to the end of the fifth year, is a period of active interest in the pleasures associated with the different erogenous zones, i.e., the mouth, the anus, and the genitals. This first period is followed by the latency period which lasts for a period of five or six years. During this phase, erotic desires are repressed and earlier sexual memories dismissed from consciousness (infantile amnesia). Finally, with the advent of puberty, erotic desires erupt again and the period of adult genital behavior begins to develop as the adolescent matures.

According to Freud, the first period is decisive for personality formation. It is in this period, extending from birth to the sixth year, that many character traits and unconscious problems develop, even though they may not manifest themselves until later. Freud distinguished three stages in this first period. The first, the oral stage, is characterized by the fact that the mouth and related structures provide the principal source of pleasurable stimuli. During the second, the anal stage, the anus supplants the mouth as the chief source of pleasure. The expulsion of the feces, by removing the discomfort resulting from the accumulation of digested foods in the lower intestinal tract, produces a feeling of relief. During the phallic stage, the sexual feelings associated with masturbation come into focus. The degree to which an adult is able to work, love, and enjoy life depends to a large degree on the relative balance between satisfaction, frustration, and repression of these infantile desires.

Further exploration of the infantile past of his patients led Freud to conclude that dependency needs are among "the oldest, strongest and most urgent wishes of mankind" (13:47). Since the human infant, unlike other species, goes through a long period of dependence upon his parents for sustenance, love, and protection, profound feelings of *dependency* arise during his extended infancy which persist into adulthood. These feelings of dependency are first experienced in relation to the mother, who initially satisfies the infant's oral needs and provides protection against external dangers and bodily discomforts. Somewhat later, the father replaces the mother as the child's chief protector, a status which he retains in the child's estimation until early adulthood. Curiously, however, the child's attitude to its father is colored by a peculiar ambivalence. The father seems to constitute a danger for the child, perhaps because of his superior strength and his role as a disciplinarian. These feelings of ambivalence in the attitude to the father are so deeply etched on the unconscious that a sense of dependency upon, and fear of, authority figures persists throughout life, despite the fact that the child, as he matures, becomes increasingly independent. These early ambivalent feelings are apt to come to the fore whenever the adult feels anxious, weak, or helpless. That is, the average adult longs for protection in anxiety-provoking situations, but fears any authority figure who attempts to serve as his protective agent.

Summarizing our interpretation thus far, Freud, having begun with Breuer's theory of unconscious motives, went on to discover the free association method. Application of this method eventually disclosed the phenomena of resistance to, and repression of, hidden impulses and desires. Further investigation showed that these unconscious impulses were often of a sexual nature, and that they dated back to unsolved sexual conflicts in infancy. This final discovery of the decisive importance of the remote past in the formation of the unconscious led Freud to suggest that dependency needs are among the strongest wishes of mankind.

As he built upon these early discoveries, Freud speculated about the structural regions of the psyche, and formulated a highly plausible theory of how their interaction affects human behavior.[19] In one of his last major works, he suggested that the human psyche is made up of three major systems, the id, the ego, and the superego.

The *id* is the most primitive, deepest, and most inaccessible part of the psychic apparatus. It is the great reservoir of instinctual drives, and the unconscious storehouse of the repressed erotic impulses and memories of childhood that continue to seek conscious expression. The id continually endeavors to abolish the intrapsychic tensions resulting from its various impulses. It does so by forming images of objects that will gratify these demands. For example, the id of a hungry person may attempt to eliminate its nutritional deficit by forming a mental image of a steak or a chocolate bar. Wish-fulfilling, hallucinatory images of this sort are the only reality the id knows, since it has no access to, or knowledge of, objective reality. The id is thus constitutionally incapable of satisfying its own desires. A hungry person cannot eat his mental image of steak. Consequently, a second psychological system develops which is primarily responsible for transactions with the external world.

The *ego* is that part of the infant's original id that has been molded and modified by direct contact with the objective world. It comes into existence because the needs of the organism require realistic transactions with the external environment. In order to survive, the hungry child eventually has to learn how to seek, find, and eat appropriate foods. This means that he has to learn to control unconscious id demands until appropriate means can be employed to gratify these internal strivings. In performing these realistic functions, the ego utilizes perceptions of reality, conscious memories, abstract reasoning, and so forth. In short, the ego is the conscious system of the personality; its basic function is to mediate between reality and id demands, controlling the latter until they can be gratified in some way consonant with the limitations imposed by the environment.

The *superego* is the moral arm or conscience of the personality. According to Freud, the moral prohibitions and ideals of the superego are not innate; they are internal representations of the moral norms and ideals of society as interpreted to the child by parents and other authority figures. The internalization or "introjection" of parental moral standards occurs in response to the punishments which are inflicted on the young child for disobedience and the rewards which are meted out for good behavior. As the child seeks to avoid punishments and obtain rewards, the superego emerges as a third component of the personality representing moral prohibitions and values. The introjected mandates of the superego include, but are not limited to, consciously recognized standards; most superego mandates are, in fact, unconscious. The basic functions of this third psychic structure include: 1) prohibition of id impulses, particularly those of a sexual and aggressive nature, 2) insistence that the ego strive towards moral perfection, 3) critical self-observation and self-punishment, and 4) self-praise as a reward for virtuous thoughts and deeds. In performing these functions, the superego attempts to dominate both the id and the ego by making them conform to its ideal morality.

The *Oedipal complex* is of profound importance for superego development and, as we shall see, for the formation of religious beliefs. Briefly, the Oedipal conflict erupts when the child of five or six becomes sexually attached to the parent of the opposite sex, the boy to his mother and the girl to her father. As this attachment intensifies, the parent of the same sex is increasingly viewed as a rival and jealous, even murderous, impulses are aroused. The boy wants to remove his father in order to possess his mother, the girl wants to displace her mother and to be possessed by her father. These sexual and aggressive desires arouse severe conflicts within the child on two counts. First, the child fears brutal punishment for these unacceptable impulses. Secondly, the child's hostile feelings conflict with feelings of love and admiration for his rival, and, frequently, with feelings of dependency. In addition, the young boy fears castration by his angry father while the young girl fears genital injury from intercourse with him.

These and other fears induce internalization within the superego of parental prohibitions against incest and aggression. By making the prohibitions and threats of his parents his own, the young child defends himself against sexual fantasies and imagined threats of punishment. Henceforth, the superego says in effect: "Thou shalt not commit incest or contemplate aggression against parents." Simultaneously with this first acceptance of parental prohibitions, the child succeeds, with the help of the newly formed superego, in driving his earlier incestuous desires and murderous wishes into his unconscious. Subsequently, for reasons that are not clearly understood, the normal child begins at this stage to develop a straightforward identification with the parent of the same sex. One reason for this is that the boy's identification with his father as well as the girl's identification with her mother afford vicarious satisfaction of now unconscious desires towards the parent of the opposite sex. Several important consequences follow from these identifications. In the first place, the superego begins to introject not only parental prohibitions, but ideal patterns of parental behavior. The young boy, for instance, begins at this stage to idealize the manifold character traits represented by his father, while the young girl takes her mother as her ideal. In consequence, the child's superego is subdivided into two parts: 1) the "conscience," which represents parental prohibitions, and 2) the "ego-ideal," which represents the parental ideals the child seeks to emulate. The conscience punishes the person by making him feel guilty, the ego ideal sets forth the idealized qualities the person should emulate. Second, identification with parental ideals sets the stage for future identification with the moral values represented by other authority figures. Examples of such authority figures are teachers, political figures, and religious instructors. Subsequent identifications of this sort mold the individual's ego ideal in the direction of conformity with the moral values of the various social groups, including religious groups, to which he belongs. Numerous adult ideals are a result of these later identifications.

The psyche, then, has three main systems: the id, the ego, and the superego. Behavior is a result of the complex interaction of the various processes associated with these diverse psychic structures. From the id arise demands for gratifications of instinctual and other unconscious impulses. From the superego issue uncompromising demands that frequently conflict with id drives, especially those of an erotic and aggressive nature. The ego seeks modes of behavior which satisfy id impulses and superego demands within the opportunities and limitations imposed by the external world. The ego is thus pictured as a reactive agent serving three masters: the id, the superego, and reality.

When the ego feels unable to cope with the stimuli arising from its three masters, it become flooded with *anxiety*.[20] According to Freud, ego anxiety is one of the most painful experiences of the conscious mind. In his later works, Freud distinguishes three types of ego anxiety: realistic anxiety, neurotic anxiety, and moral anxiety. The first, realistic anxiety, results from fear of dangers in the external world such as disease, death, earthquakes, floods, and so forth. Neurotic anxiety has an internal origin; it arises from the id, that is, from fear that unconscious impulses will get out of control and force one to perform acts for which one will be severely punished. For example, a patient experienced acute anxiety whenever his teachers gave out especially difficult assignments. Analysis showed that his anxiety resulted from a fear of unconscious hostility towards authority figures, overt expression of which would be punished. Moral anxiety is fear of guilt. A person with an overly developed superego fears moral condemnation for thoughts as well as deeds prohibited by his firmly entrenched moral code.

In endeavoring to avoid these several forms of anxiety the ego resorts to a variety of *defense mechanisms,* one of which has previously been noted. Repression is perhaps the most common of these mechanism; it occurs when a person attempts to reassure himself that a danger no longer exists by forcing the disturbing idea out of his mind. Other defense mechanisms include regression—retreating to earlier stages of development—and projection—attributing the source of anxiety to the external world rather to one's own id or superego. Both regression and projection, as we shall see, are important defense mechanisms in the formation of religious beliefs and practices.

3. THEORY OF RELIGION

The foundations of psychoanalysis were laid when Freud discovered the unconscious origins of conscious thoughts and deeds. The theoretical insights built upon this basic discovery proved applicable not only to the explanation of pathological symptoms, dreams, and personality traits, but to the study of artistic, political, and religious phenomena.[21] The utilization of psychoanalytic insights in these latter areas of study has come to be known, by common usage, as *applied psychoanalysis.*

Central to Freud's own application of psychoanalysis were his studies of religion.[22] Early in the development of his most distinctive theories, Freud realized that many religious phenomena could be elucidated by his dramatic discoveries. In 1901, Freud gave an early indication of what such an application of his psychoanalytic insights to religion might entail:

> I believe that a large part of the mythological view of the world, which extends a long way into the most modern religions, *is nothing but psychology projected into the external world.* The obscure recognition . . . of psychical factors and relations in the unconscious is mirrored—it is difficult to express it in other terms . . . —in the construction of a *supernatural reality,* which is destined to be changed back once more by science into the *psychology of the unconscious.* One could venture to explain in this way the myths of paradise and the fall of man, of God, of good and evil, of immortality, and so on, and to transform *metaphysics* into *metapsychology* (6:258-259).

In this early passage Freud not only gives voice to his basic approach to the study of religion, he also gives expression to several of his fundamental presuppositions regarding the nature and origin of religion. In the first place, religious beliefs are associated with a mythological world view. In contrast with Freud's own scientific philosophy, this world view entails belief in a supernatural reality of some sort, mythological stories, moral prescriptions and prohibitions, immortality, and so forth. Secondly, the "otherness" of this supernatural realm and the validity of the diverse myths associated with it are assumed to be a fictional creation of the unconscious basement workshop of the psyche. As a corollary, it follows that psychoanalysis—the science of the unconscious—is in a peculiarly unique position to explain the genesis of religion.

Several years later, in his study of Leonardo da Vinci (1910), Freud made a significant contribution to these early assumptions by specifying the unconscious conflicts responsible for the genesis of religious beliefs. In this study, Freud observed that religions arise out of, and are a means of dealing with, unconscious conflicts generated by man's relations with his father. "The psychoanalysis of individual human beings," Freud stated shortly thereafter, "teaches us with quite special insistence that the god of each of them is found in the likeness of his father, that his personal relation to God depends on his relation to his father in the flesh and oscillates with that relation, and at bottom God is nothing other than an exalted father" (cf., 9:190). Religious symbols and rituals represent a return, in adult life, of the infantile feelings of love and fear, awe and guilt, obedience and rebellion resulting from man's infantile relations with his father.

The infantile attitudes that lie at the basis of the religious need are further explicated in Freud's now-classic essay, *The Future of an Illusion*. The thesis of this small, but extremely influential volume is that religion has its origins in "the oldest, strongest and most urgent wishes of mankind" (13:47), namely, man's desire to be protected, as he once was as a child, from the dangers that threaten his existence. This powerful desire is triggered by anxiety in face of the realistic, instinctual, and moral demands that threaten to overwhelm the adult ego. When man discovers, as an adult, that his existence is continually threatened by natural forces that impinge upon his existence from without (such as death and disease) as well as by the instinctual and moral forces that batter his ego from within, he develops a profound sense of his own helplessness and weakness. In the resulting state of ego anxiety, he regresses to an earlier stage of development when, as a small child, he felt protected by a father whom he both loved and feared as an all-powerful, but essentially benevolent, being. These memories, by evoking a longing for similar protection in adulthood, engender projection of a Divine father-figure in the likeness of the earthly father. Like the infant who reacts to his helplessness by picturing his father as an omnipotent being whose love and protection can be obtained by obeying his commandments, the anxious adult projects the image of a heavenly being who possesses the attributes his father once seemed to possess—omniscience, omnipotence, the power to love, protect, and punish.

Why should an adult maintain this infantile attitude towards his father by projecting paternal characteristics on a deity? There are several reasons. In the first place, he realizes, as he grows older, that his earthly father does not in fact possess the attributes he once attributed to him. As a result, he loses the protection he once imagined his seemingly omnipotent father possessed. Secondly, he discovers as he grows older that he is destined to remain a child forever, in the sense that he continues to unconsciously yearn for protection against unknown and mighty powers. Driven by this unquenched id longing, the religious adult invests the universe with the traits of his father. Thus, "a store of ideas is created, born from man's need to make his helplessness tolerable and built up from the material of memories of the helplessness of his own childhood and the childhood of the human race" (13:25).

By regressing in this manner to an earlier stage of development and projecting a divine being on the model of his father, man humanizes the dangerous forces that impinge upon his existence. The powers of nature are personified, in the sense that natural catastrophes—earthquakes, floods, diseases, and death—are envisioned as ultimately the manifestation of an infinitely wise and omnipotent Being or Beings. Moral demands are similarly personified. They are the will of God who compensates for the moral sufferings, privations, and injustices of this life by ultimately rewarding the good and punishing the evil. The erotic and aggressive impulses of man's nature are attributed to the devil or to human sinfulness, but they can be atoned for by acts of contrition, confession, penance, and other rituals. It is an enormous relief to the human psyche, Freud states, when dangerous forces within and without the self are explained and handled in this manner. For "if everywhere in nature there are Beings [or a Being] around us of a kind that we know in our own society, then we can breathe freely, can feel at home in the uncanny and can deal by psychical means with our senseless anxiety" (13:22).

A projection like this not only provides immediate psychic relief, it also points the way to a further mastery of the situation. For if the natural and moral forces that impinge upon human existence are ultimately directed by God or the gods, we can try to influence the relevant deity through sacrificial offerings, prayers, and other ritualistic acts. According to Freud, all such acts follow an infantile model. The believer "has learnt from the persons in his earliest environment [particularly from his father] that the way to influence them is to establish a relation with them; and so, later on, with the same end in view, he treats everything else that he comes across in the same way as he treated those persons" (13:31). These acts of propitiation and entreaty are not performed, however, without a touch of hostility towards the deity that makes them necessary. When, therefore, the god fails to grant a favor or permits a catastrophe, feelings of hostility come to the fore just as they once did in childhood when the father failed to satisfy the infant's desires. The deified image of the father thus inherits the hostility as well as the affection the adult, as a child, directed towards his real father.

In the process of personifying the forces at work in the world, *homo religiosus* develops what Freud calls an "illusion." Since the term "illusion" has a very specific meaning in Freudian thought, it is important to be clear about its precise definition. By an illusion is meant a set of beliefs motivated primarily by powerful wishes or desires (13:48). An illusion in this special Freudian sense is not necessarily false, for the beliefs so generated may be true despite the fact that wish-fulfillment was a prominent factor in their genesis. For example, a soldier prays that he will survive the war. His belief in an omnipotent deity capable of providing such protection is an illusion in the Freudian sense, insofar as it is born of his profound longing for self-preservation. The presence of this desire in the formation of religious beliefs does not itself disprove the existence of God; a benevolent deity may exist, although human beliefs about him are caused solely by unconscious id longings. When Freud says that religious beliefs are illusions, then, he is not saying that they are erroneous, but rather that wish-fulfillment is a prominent factor in their motivation (13:49). Freud, nevertheless, felt that his demonstration of the "real," but unconscious, origins of religious illusions constituted a serious challenge to their validity.

Thus far, Freud's explanation of religion seems simple enough. "When the growing individual finds that he is destined to remain a child forever, that he can never do without protection against strange superior powers, he lends those powers the features belonging to the figure of his father; he creates for himself the gods whom he dreads, whom he seeks to propitiate, and whom he nevertheless entrusts with his own protection" (13:35). There are, however, several important modifications of this seemingly straightforward interpretation which complicate Freud's explanation of religion.

The most important of these complications is Freud's contention that the religious myths that grow up around the supernatural father reflect the conflicts associated with the Oedipal complex. Religious myths not only express infantile dependency needs, then, they also reflect, often in disguised forms, the Oedipal child's hostility towards and subsequent reconciliation with his father.[23] All religions, according to Freud, express the love and hate, awe and fear, obedience and rebellion generated in man's Oedipal relation to his father.

An example of a religious myth which expresses unconscious Oedipal sentiments is the central Christian drama, repeated in the Eucharist, of Christ's crucifixion and resurrection.[24] Viewed from the perspective of psychoanalysis, the Christian story of a son of God sacrificing himself for the guilt of other sons gives oblique expression to the Oedipal son's desire to do away with his father in an effort to possess his mother. In the crucifixion, Christ atones for the Oedipal desire to murder the father by sacrificing his own life. Christ's death, by expiating the original sin of the Oedipal complex, reconciles other sons with the father against whom they once wished to rebel. Simultaneously with this reconciliation with the father, the myth expresses the ambivalence which is always displayed in Oedipal situations; the very act which is said to atone for sinful desires fulfills the original wish to take the place of the father. For, through the resurrection, a human son is placed at God's side and made a co-deity with the father. In other words, the Oedipal wish to displace the father is symbolically expressed in the Christian myth insofar as a son becomes God. By identifying with Christ in the communion, Christians give expression to their unconscious Oedipal conflicts by, on the one hand, recognizing their guilt and longing for reconciliation with the father, and, on the other hand, vicariously experiencing fulfillment of their primitive desires to take the place of the father.[25]

This theme of identification with Christ in the Eucharist brings us to another complication in Freud's interpretation of religion. To the

Christian, Christ is not only a glorified redeemer, he is also a moral teacher (10:33-35,86). Through identification with his moral precepts, the believer introjects Christ's ideals and commandments into his superego. This process also has an infantile prototype. Just as the young boy, at the conclusion of the Oedipal crisis, introjects his father's superego by identifying with him, similarly, the Christian adult alters his superego in line with Christ's moral teachings. Subsequently, his ego ideal says in effect: "you ought to be like this, like Christ, and love all other men as Christ loves them." His conscience represents the prohibition: "you may not do what Christ has prohibited." As a result, the ego assumes the same sort of passive and obedient attitude towards Christ's teachings that the ego always assumes towards the superego. There is a feeling of triumph when something in the ego coincides with the perfection represented by Christ, and guilt when the ego falls short of this lofty goal.

Christianity, of course, is by no means unique in calling forth superego identification with the standards taught by moral spokesmen for the deity. According to Freud, Moses and the prophets, Buddha and Confucius represent the moral teachers of their respective religions. The psychological consequences of internalizing these various moral standards, in Freud's view, are always the same. By establishing exalted standards by which both the id and the ego are judged, the believer's superego succeeds in severely repressing id impulses and in summoning the ego to strive for an exceptionally high standard of perfection. The intense sense of inferiority, humility, and guilt that accompanies religious commitment is an expression of the resulting tension between the superego on the one hand, and the id and ego on the other.

Freud provides a convenient illustration of these complex processes in his discussion of the central commandment of Christianity in *Civilization and Its Discontents*. According to Freud, Christ's command to "love thy neighbour as thyself" so enormously inflates the ethical ideal of love that it cannot be fulfilled. For man is not essentially a gentle being, but an erotic and aggressive creature (14:90). His love is always mixed with baser motives, and its scope is always limited. His neighbour is often seen, not as a potential brother, but as someone who tempts him to satisfy his aggression on him, "to exploit his capacity for work without compensation, to use him sexually without his consent, to seize his possessions, to humiliate him, to cause him pain, to torture and to kill him" (14:58). When, therefore, man is summoned to universal love, he is really being asked to gain "unlimited mastery over his id" as well as over his ego (14:90). This, however, is impossible. The self-judgment which declares that one has fallen short of this sublime goal produces the religious sense of humility and guilt which lies at the basis of the permanent state of unhappiness from which many Christians suffer.

Because religious ideals and commandments invariably engender instinctual repression and guilt feelings, Freud refers to religion as an *obsessional neurosis.* The reason for applying to religion a term originally coined to describe a form of mental illness is that religious prohibitions, by blocking id impulses, produce intrapsychic conflicts identical with those found in those neurotic patients who suffer from excessive repression of sexual and aggressive instincts. The painful attacks of anxiety suffered by these patients derive from the overwhelming influx of forbidden stimuli arising from blocked id desires. Because these desires, if consciously expressed, would result in intense guilt feelings, the neurotic feels psychically compelled to ward off severe punishment from the superego by engaging in stereotyped ritualistic acts of handwashing, confession, self-mutilation, and so forth. A prototype of a neurotic symptom is the psychic compulsion to bathe frequently in an effort to wash away sinful desires and thus avoid punishment. The similarity of compulsive acts of this sort with religious rituals such as baptisms, confessions, and stereotyped prayers was not missed by Freud (9:39-40). In *Totem and Taboo,* he demonstrated the similarity of many primitive religious practices to the compulsive rituals observed in his neurotic patients.

From what has been said thus far regarding Freud's interpretation of religion, it is obvious that religion represents a counterproductive means of dealing with anxiety. For the anxious adult, who deals with the overwhelming internal and external forces that threaten his ego by projecting a deity in the image of his father, invariably creates a Being whose love and protection cannot be won without obeying his inflated moral commandments. Whatever temporary psychic relief is gained by the illusion of Divine Providence and the forgiveness of Oedipal sin is thus purchased at an enormous psychic cost. The price is excessive repression of id impulses which, in turn, engender neurotic anxiety and bizarre symptoms. A vicious cycle of anxiety, regression, projection, moral repression, and anxiety is thus set in motion.

Up to this point our analysis of Freud's interpretation of religion has focused exclusively on his psychological explanation. Religious beliefs and practices, however, have a social history. Realizing this, Freud devoted several important works to the historical origins and cultural evolution of totemism, Judaism, and Christianity. Although a detailed analysis of Freud's studies in this area would take us beyond our present interests, several pertinent conclusions are noteworthy.

In *Totem and Taboo,* Freud sought to ascertain the historical origins of the religious customs in primitive societies.[26] These customs include the worship of sacred animals called "totems," taboos against killing the totem, and special ritualistic occasions when the totem is both killed and eaten. A partial clue to a genetic explanation of these strange practices was suggested to Freud by his study of a five-year-old boy by the name of little Hans whose ambivalent awe and fear of horses was shown to be a symbolic expression of his admiration for, and fear of, his father (7:149-295; 9:167-168). If Hans displaced his feelings towards his father onto an animal, Freud postulated, the totem animals of primitive peoples might also unconsciously represent the father. This conclusion seemed strengthened by examination of the two principal prohibitions associated with totemism: (1) the taboo against murder of the totem animal, and (2) the taboo against incest. These taboos seemed to coincide with the prohibitions against murder and incest normally introjected at the conclusion of the Oedipal stage. In attempting to link the genesis of totemic customs with Oedipal phenomena, Freud postulated that totemism had its historical origins in a primordial Oedipal complex when the sons of the chieftain of the primal horde banded together, killed their father, and ate his body.[27] Later, when guilt feelings for this act came to the fore, the brothers attempted to undo their deed by setting up the totem as a surrogate father and by declaring that killing the father substitute was not allowed. The result was totemic worship, a sort of symbolic compromise with the father in which the latter grants everything that the child's fantasy could expect from him—protection, care, and forebearance—in return for which a pledge is given to honor his life by not repeating the act of murder against the father surrogate. At the same time, however, the brothers instituted an occasional ceremony when they could express their hostile wishes by reenacting the crime of patricide by killing the totem.

In the conclusion of *Totem and Taboo* and again in *Moses and Monotheism,* Freud developed his now famous hypothesis about the inheritance of unconscious *racial guilt* for this primal murder. According to this now discredited hypothesis, all later religions are attempts to palliate inherited guilt for the murder of the primal father (9:187). Years later, in *Moses and Monotheism,* Freud supplemented this theory of inherited guilt by adding the notion of *the return of repressed racial memories.* The origins of Hebraic monotheism, Freud argues, represents a return of repressed memories of the one great primal father. "When Moses gave to his people the conception of an Only God it was not an altogether new idea, for it meant the reanimation of primeval experience in the human family that had long ago faded from the conscious memory of mankind" (15:166-67). In the same volume, Freud extended this thesis regarding the return of repressed racial memories to the origins of Christianity. According to this interpretation, St. Paul's doctrine that Christ atones for original sin represents a return in Paul's mind of the repressed psychological truth that "it is because we killed God the Father that we are so unhappy" (15:174). In Freud's view, St. Paul correctly realized that only the sacrificial death of a son could expiate this guilt, since the primal sin had been murder of the father. One becomes a Christian, according to this interpretation, because the inherited primal guilt, reexpressed in one's own Oedipal fantasies, is reenacted and resolved in images appropriate to the unconscious processes involved.

Fortunately, the validity of Freud's major contributions to the study of religion is not affected by these dubious metapsychological hypotheses regarding the primal murder, inherited guilt, and the return of repressed racial memories. As Freud himself suggests in *Civilization and Its Discontents*, whether or not the father is actually killed is not really the decisive point, inasmuch as one is bound to experience guilt in either case given the universal experience of the conflicts associated with the Oedipus complex (14:79). Had Freud applied this insight to his cultural studies of religion, he might well have dispensed with the primal horde, inherited guilt, and the racial unconscious, and simply observed that the unconscious memories and Oedipal conflicts mirrored in totemism, Judaism, and Christianity stem from common experiences in infancy.

Two principal criticisms of religion emerge from Freud's various psychoanalytic explorations of the psychological origins and consequences of religious beliefs and rites. The first is his contention that religious beliefs are illusory insofar as they are a product of infantile longings and wish-fulfillment. This argument consists largely in connecting religion with the helplessness and weakness that adults experience in relation to the dangerous, unknown, and seemingly uncontrollable forces that threaten human existence. Adults cope with the overwhelming anxiety generated by these forces as if still children, by projecting a father deity or deities. Because religion corresponds to the childhood of the human psyche, it is contrasted by Freud with the heroism of true maturity. The moral Freud draws from this is that maturity entails a fundamental break with the religious illusions that detain man at "the parental house where he was so warm and comfortable" (13:81). If infantalism is to be surmounted and maturity achieved, Freud argues, adults must first "admit to themselves the full extent of their helplessness and their insignificance in the machinery of the universe; they can no longer be the centre of creation, no longer the object of tender care on the part of a beneficent Providence" (13:81).

Freud's second major psychoanalytic argument against religion is that its moral standards have been abnormally repressive. The thrust of this criticism is not that mankind can do without moral standards. In the total absence of moral restraints, Freud observes, one could choose any woman who took one's fancy as a sexual object, one could kill one's rival without hesitation, and one could seize another man's goods without asking his leave (13:19). Under these conditions, not only would society be impossible, but life would be cruel and brutish. The problem with religious moral standards, in Freud's estimation, is not that they inhibit sexual and aggressive drives, but that they go too far. Religious codes are excessively repressive. If we wish to live less repressed and constricted lives, we must begin by abandoning the restrictive moral codes sanctioned by religious institutions.

Freud thus challenges *homo religiosus* on two fronts. In the first place, he asks him to abandon the infantile dependency needs and illusions at the basis of the religious need, to leave his father's house, and to face up to his aloneness and insignificance in the universe. Second, Freud challenges the religious individual to emancipate himself from the overly repressive and restrictive moral standards sanctioned by religion. If and only if *homo religiosus* grows up and abandons his infantile dependence upon, and fear of, divine moral authority can he hope to become psychologically healthy.

4. A CRITICAL EVALUATION

No critical assessment of Freud's contribution to our understanding of religion would be adequate if it did not begin with an acknowledgment of his immense perspicacity as a student of both man and religion. As a student of human nature, Freud was undoubtedly correct in recognizing the existence of unconscious impulses. As an interpreter of religion, Freud was certainly correct in emphasizing the role of anxiety, weakness, and helplessness in the genesis of religious commitment. He was also right in observing that early childhood impressions, especially the universal human need for security and protection, has had an immense influence upon religion. Freud was further right in holding that religious ideologies and institutions have frequently perpetrated excessively repressive moral codes.

In explicating these several aspects of religion, Freud has contributed not only to our scientific understanding, but also to religion itself. For "image-breaking" of this sort is, in the final analysis,

> no less part and parcel of human life and history than image-making; it is also no less part and parcel of man's religion, and no less essential to it. . . . The painful recognition of the clay feet of the old idols is indispensable to human growth; it is also indispensable to the emergence of more appropriate figures for human awe, devotion, and service (21:27).

Precisely because Freud was a relentless critic of religion, he inadvertently contributed, as we shall see in the next two chapters, to the emergence of "more appropriate figures for human awe, devotion, and service."

Nonetheless, three major objections may be raised regarding the validity of several central Freudian assumptions. The first concerns his image of man. The picture of the human person that emerges from Freud's work is that of a being largely determined by intrapsychic forces beyond his control. Several questions are raised by this portrait. Is this an accurate characterization of the real men and women we know and are? Is it reasonable to suppose that our conscious thought and deeds are determined by sexual and aggressive impulses, unconscious memories of infantile conflicts, and so forth? Are our seemingly spontaneous moments of intellectual creativity spurious? Is our ordinary sense of moral responsibility illusory? In short, are human beings devoid of an irreducible personal center, a seat of genuine spiritual creativity, decision, energy, and action? Given the widespread human experience of such an irreducible center, Freud's conception of man, while not entirely false, is apparently incomplete.

A second major objection concerns Freud's definition of religion. According to Freud, all religious beliefs deify the attributes of the earthly father. The question arises, therefore, whether this uncritical assumption does justice either to the non-paternal religious beliefs found in many cultures or to the sophisticated doctrines of theologians like Augustine and Aquinas. For the latter, Freud has nothing but contempt. Their elaborate intellectual superstructures, he contends, are nothing but attempts to rationalize essentially infantile convictions. Is such a position sufficient, however, to explain the complicated beliefs of Bultmann, Teilhard, Reinhold Niebuhr, Bonhoeffer, and Tillich? Interpreted in their own terms, these theologians scarcely appear to reflect the primitive fantasies described by Freud.

A third and final objection concerns Freud's assumption that religious ideologies and institutions invariably foster excessively repressive forms of moral behavior. By focusing exclusively on the excessively strict moral codes perpetrated by some religions, Freud lends credence to his assertion that all religions engender intense guilt feelings. This analysis completely ignores, however, the trust, the kindness, the love, and the forgiveness which are also the fruits of religion.

Taken together, these several objections suggest that Freud finally fails to conclusively demonstrate either the infantile or the repressive nature of every religion. His observations seem to apply to those religious ideologies and institutions that fit his description, but this description scarcely covers all forms of religion. Freud's conclusion that the abandonment of religion is necessary in order to achieve healthy psychological maturity, therefore, cannot be accepted. There are religions that are compatible with and contribute to precisely that form of psychological maturity Freud had in mind.

NOTES

1 Freud compared himself with Darwin as well as with Copernicus. See, for example, "A Difficulty in the Path of Psychoanalysis," *The Complete Psychological Works of Sigmund Freud, Standard Edition* (London: Hogarth Press, 1953-1964), vol. XVII, pp. 140-141; and "The Resistances to Psychoanalysis," *Collected Papers of Sigmund Freud* (London: Hogarth Press, 1949-1950), vol. V, p. 173.

2 For a brief discussion of this theological response to Darwin's theory of evolution, see Ernest Jones, *The Life and Work of Sigmund Freud* (New York: Basic Books, 1957), vol. III, pp. 303-304.

3 For a summary of pre-Freudian literature on the unconscious, see Henri Ellenberger, *The Discovery of the Unconscious: The History and Evolution of Dynamic Psychiatry* (New York: Basic Books, 1970), chs. 1-6; Henri Ellenberger, "The Unconscious before Freud," *Bulletin of the Menninger Clinic*, XXI (1953), 3-15; and L. L. Whyte, *The Unconscious before Freud* (New York: Basic Books, 1960).

4 Freud's analysis of the infantile origins of religion is most succinctly explicated in *The Future of an Illusion* (13:23-27, 31-32, 34-35, 47-48, 70-71).

5 Freud treats the dysfunctional consequences of religion in *The Future of an Illusion* (13:60-61, 67-68, 70-72, 77-79, 81-82); and *Civilization and Its Discontents* (14).

6 The best biography of Freud is the three-volume work by Ernest Jones, *The Life and Work of Sigmund Freud*. For Freud's attitude toward religion, see *ibid.*, vol. I, pp. 5-6, 19-20, 22-23, and vol. III, pp. 349-374; Philip Rieff, *Freud: The Mind of the Moralist* (20:281-287); and Gregory Zilboorg, *Psychoanalysis and Religion* (New York: Farrar, Straus and Cudahy, 1962), pp. 195-243.

7 Material on Freud's Jewish identification and the social conditions of Jews in Vienna can be found in David Bakan, *Sigmund Freud and the Jewish Mystical Tradition* (Princeton, N. J.: D. Van Nostrand, 1958), esp. chs. 4-8; Sigmund Freud, "Address to the Society of B'nai B'rith" [1926] *Standard Edition*, XX, p. 273; Henri Ellenberger, *The Discovery of the Unconscious*, pp. 418-444, 463-464; and Philip Rieff, *Freud*, 281-287.

8 In adopting this strictly scientific approach to truth, Freud followed his teachers, Brücke and Meynert, who advocated an exclusively scientific or positivist approach to the study of man. For background material on the scientific environment in which Freud worked, see Peter Amacher, *Freud's Neurological Education and Its Influence on Psychoanalytic Theory, Psychological Issues*, vol. 4, no. 4 (New York: International Universities Press, 1965); Siegfried Bernfeld, "Freud's Earliest Theories and the School of Helmholtz," *Psychoanalytic Quarterly*, vol. 13 (1944), 341-362; Henri Ellenberger, *The Discovery of the Unconscious*, pp. 418-550; Henri Ellenberger, "Fechner and Freud," *Bulletin of the Menninger Clinic*, vol. 20 (1956), 201-214; Ernest Jones, *The*

Life and Work, vol. I, chs. IV, X, XI; and Ernst Kris, *The Origins of Psycho-analysis* (New York: Basic Books, 1954), pp. 1-47. Freud was trained in neurology and began by assuming, with Brücke and Meynert, that psychic processes are quantitatively determined. For a sophisticated discussion of the development of Freud's thought away from materialism, see Paul Ricoeur, *Freud and Philosophy*, trans. Denis Savage (New Haven: Yale University Press, 1970), Book II.

9 The story of Anna O. is discussed by Josef Breuer in the book he published with Freud, *Studies on Hysteria* [1895]; in *Standard Edition*, vol. II, pp. 21-47; and by Freud in his *Five Lectures on Psychoanalysis* [1910], *Standard Edition*, vol. XI, pp. 10-20.

10 Freud was favorably impressed by Breuer's work partly because he was familiar with the use of hypnotic techniques and the interpretations of traumatic paralyses advanced by several leading French psychologists, especially Jean-Martin Charcot, Hippolyte Bernheim, and Pierre Janet. Freud studied Charcot's use of hypnosis in the treatment of hysteria in Paris from October, 1885, until February, 1886. He visited Bernheim in Nancy, France, in July, 1887. For Freud's own account of his indebtedness to, and criticism of Breuer, see his *Five Lectures on Psychoanalysis* [1910], *Standard Edition*, vol. XI, pp. 9-20; "On the History of the Psychoanalytic Movement" [1914], *Standard Edition*, vol. XIV, pp. 1-15; and *An Autobiographical Study* [1925], *Standard Edition*, vol. XX, ch. 2.

11 Today, there is some doubt whether Anna O. was in fact cured. For secondary discussions of her treatment, see Ernest Jones, *The Life and Work*, vol. I, pp. 223-225; and Henri Ellenberger, *The Discovery of the Unconscious*, pp. 481-484.

12 For a discussion of the historical roots of free association, see L. Béllak, "Free Association: Conceptual and Clinical Aspects," *International Journal of Psychoanalysis*, 41 (1961), 9-20; and Sigmund Freud, "A Note on the Prehistory of the Technique of Analysis," *Standard Edition*, vol. XVIII, pp. 263-265.

13 For information on the classical psychoanalytic technique, see Edward Glover, *The Technique of Psychoanalysis* (New York: International Universities Press, 1955); S. Lorand, *The Technique of Psychoanalytic Therapy* (New York: International Universities Press, 1946); and Karl Menninger, *Theory of Psychoanalytic Technique* (New York: Basic Books, 1958). For the development of psychoanalytic technique since Freud, see R. Ekstein, "A Historical Survey on the Teaching of Psychoanalytic Technique," *Journal of the American Psychoanalytic Association*, VIII (1960), 500-516; and K. Eissler, "The Effects of the Structure of the Ego on Psychoanalytic Technique," *Journal of the American Psychoanalytic Association*, I (1953), 104-143.

14 For early articles by Freud on the role of unconscious sexual impulses in psychic life, see his "Heredity and the Aetiology of the Neuroses" [1896], *Standard Edition*, vol. III, pp. 143-156; "Further Remarks on the Neuropsychoses of Defense [1896], *Standard Edition*, vol. III, pp. 162-185; and "The Aetiology of Hysteria" [1896], *Standard Edition*, vol. III, pp. 191-221.

15 For this widening of the concept of sexuality in Freud's thought, see his *Group Psychology and the Analysis of the Ego* [1921] (New York: Bantam Books, 1960), pp. 29-31; *Beyond the Pleasure Principle* [1920] (New York: Liveright, 1950), pp. 68-73, 83-84n55; and "An Outline of Psychoanalysis" [1938], *Standard Edition*, vol. 23, pp. 152-154.

16 Freud's self-analysis during the period of severe neurotic suffering that he experienced between 1894 and 1899 was an extremely important source of the ideas contained in his now classic work, *The Interpretation of Dreams*, a book

which has been aptly described as a disguised autobiography. In interpreting his own dreams as well as those of his patients, Freud was influenced by a large body of nineteenth-century literature on dreams. As Ellenberger points out, Freud was apparently familiar with the work of Karl Scherner, "who maintained that dreams can be interpreted scientifically according to rules inherent in their nature, and that certain dream symbols have general value. Among others were sexual symbols, which were much the same as those later described by Freud. The mechanism of displacement and condensation had been described under other names by many authors. The term 'dream work' (*Traumarbeit*) was used by Robert. Much of Freud's theory was found in Maury, Strümpell, Volkelt, and particularly Delage. Delage propounded a concept of dynamic energy, implying that the representations loaded with psychic energy repress or inhibit each other, or can fuse together, that there are in dreams chains of associations that can sometimes be partially reconstructed, and that old memories can be called forth from dreams through association with recent images.

Freud's originality resides in four innovations. The first is his model of the dream with its distinction of manifest and latent content and its specific pattern of being lived simultaneously in the present and the remote past. The second is Freud's contention that the manifest content is a distortion of the latent content, resulting from repression by the censor . . . Freud's third innovation was the application of the free association as a method for the analysis of dreams, and the fourth was the introduction of systematic dream interpretation as a tool of psychotherapy." Ellenberger, *The Discovery of the Unconscious*, p. 493.

For recent developments in the interpretation of dreams, see R. Fliess, *The Dream: A Post-Freudian Reader* (New York: International Universities Press, 1953); and E. Gutheil, *A Handbook of Dream Analysis* (New York: Liveright, 1951).

[17] In addition to the practice of free association, Freud was indebted to a number of nineteenth-century psychologists for ideas that were fused in his explanation of the infantile sexual sources of neurosis. Janet had argued that the treatment of hysterical patients involved retracing a chain of unconscious ideas. Herbart's associationist psychology had explained how chains of association could converge on nodal points. Benedekt had emphasized the importance of fantasy, frequently of a sexual sort, in the normal as well as the neurotic. Finally, several psychologists were in the process of turning to childhood sexuality. In 1894, for example, "Dallemagne had contended that many sexual deviations in adolescence resulted from childhood sexual experiences, which had been revived in puberty." Ellenberger, *The Discovery of the Unconscious*, p. 489.

[18] For an early treatment by Freud of these stages of development, see his *Three Essays on Sexual Theory, Standard Edition* [1905], vol. VII, pp. 173-206.

[19] Freud distinguished this structural or topographical aspect of his theory from the dynamic and economic points of view. The typographical referred to distinctions among psychic systems whereas the dynamic meant the conflict of psychic forces. The economic referred to the regulation of psychic forces through the pleasure-unpleasure principle. Freud's topographical analysis evolved from a distinction between the unconscious, the preconscious, and the conscious (designated respectively as Ucs, Pcs, Cs) in his "Papers on Metapsychology," *Collected Papers*, vol. IV, pp. 13-170) to the distinction between id, ego, and superego presented in *The Ego and the Id* [1923] (New York: Norton, 1962). For a careful critique of Freud's theory of human nature, see Daniel Yankelovich and William Barrett, *Ego and Instinct: The Psychoanalytic View of Human Nature—Revised* (New York: Random House, 1970).

[20] Anxiety is a major theme in Freud's work. In his early writings, anxiety is regarded as transformed libido in contrast with his mature interpretation of ego

anxiety. For his mature views, see *The Ego and the Id* (New York: Norton, 1962), pp. 56-59; and *Inhibitions, Symptoms, and Anxiety* [1926], *Standard Edition*, vol. XX, pp. 87-174. For a review of Freud's theory of anxiety, see Rollo May, *The Meaning of Anxiety* (New York: Ronald Press, 1950), pp. 122-127. For a discussion of Freud's theory of anxiety and existentialist interpretations, see Rollo May, ed., *Existence, A New Dimension in Psychiatry and Psychology* (New York: Basic Books, 1958), chs. 1-2.

21 Freud has had a major impact on psychological interpretations of art. His own works in this field include: "Creative Writers and Daydreaming" [1908], *Standard Edition*, vol. IX, pp. 143-153; "Leonardo da Vinci and a Memory" [1910], *Standard Edition*, vol. XI, pp. 63-137; and the selections in *On Creativity and the Unconscious*, ed. Benjamin Nelson (New York: Harper & Row, 1958). For other works in this field, see Ernst Kris, *Psychoanalytic Explorations in Art* (New York: International Universities Press, 1952); Otto Rank, *Art and the Artist* (New York: Tudor, 1932); Hanns Sachs, *The Creative Unconscious* (Cambridge, England: Sci-Art Publishers, 1942); H. Slochower, "Psychoanalysis and Literature," in D. Brower and L. Abt, eds., *Progress in Clinical Psychology* (New York: Grune and Stratton, 1960).

Freud applied psychoanalysis to social and political issues in a variety of works. For his central thesis that civilization presupposes renunciation of sexual and aggressive impulses, see *The Future of an Illusion*, chs. 1-2, and *Civilization and Its Discontents*. For secondary interpretations of Freud's sociopolitical theory, see Thomas Johnson, *Freud and Political Thought* (New York: Citadel Press, 1965) and Paul Roazen, *Freud: Political and Social Thought* (New York: Alfred A. Knopf, 1968). For post-Freudian social and political theories partly inspired by psychoanalysis, see Norman O. Brown, *Life Against Death: The Psychoanalytic Meaning of History* (Middletown, Conn.: Wesleyan University Press, 1959); Erich Fromm, *Man for Himself* (New York: Rinehart, 1947); Erich Fromm, *The Sane Society* (New York: Rinehart, 1955); Herbert Marcuse, *Eros and Civilization: A Philosophical Inquiry into Freud* (Boston: Beacon Press, 1955); Herbert Marcuse, *Five Lectures* (Boston: Beacon Press, 1970); and Roger Money-Kyrle, *Psychoanalysis and Politics* (London: G. Duckworth, 1951).

22 Freud's principal works on religion are: "Obsessive Actions and Religious Practices" [1907], *Standard Edition*, vol. IX, pp. 115-127; *Totem and Taboo* [1912-1913] (New York: Random House, 1946); *Group Psychology and the Analysis of the Ego* [1921] (New York: Bantam Books, 1960), esp. chs. 5-12; *The Future of an Illusion* [1927] (New York: Doubleday, 1944); *Civilization and Its Discontents* [1930] (New York: Norton, 1963); and *Moses and Monotheism* [1939] (New York: Random House), 1939).

23 For a sophisticated discussion of the universality of the Oedipal complex and its influence on religion, see Anne Parsons, "Is the Oedipal Complex Universal," in her *Belief, Magic, and Anomie: Essays on Psychosocial Anthropology* (New York: Free Press, 1969).

24 The following account of Oedipal themes in the Christian myth modifies Freud's own account, which is complicated by assumptions yet to be discussed (the primal horde, the racial unconscious, and inherited guilt). Cf. 9:198-199, 15:111-114.

25 For an excellent cross-cultural comparison of Oedipal features in Christianity with those in Chinese Confucianism, see Robert Bellah, *Beyond Belief* (New York: Harper & Row, 1970), ch. 5, pp. 76-99.

26 Freud's introduction of psychoanalysis into ethnology in *Totem and Taboo* stimulated a great deal of psychologically informed anthropological studies.

Leading anthropologists who have been influenced by Freud include George Devereux, A. Kardiner, Margaret Mead, Warner Muensterberger, Géza Róheim, and John M. Whiting. For a brief review of Freud's impact upon anthropological studies of religion, see Clifford Geertz, "Religion: Anthropological Study," *International Encyclopedia of the Social Sciences* (New York: Macmillan and Free Press, 1968), vol. 13, pp. 398-406.

27 This idea of primitive mankind living in hordes under the tyrannical leadership of a dominant male was originally suggested by Charles Darwin, whose description was enlarged upon by J. J. Atkinson.

BIBLIOGRAPHY

1. BRENNER, CHARLES, *An Elementary Textbook of Psychoanalysis.* Garden City, N. Y.: Doubleday, Anchor Books, 1955).

2. CAPRETTA, PATRICK J., *A History of Psychology.* New York: Dell, Delta Books, 1947).

3. FENICHEL, OTTO, *The Psychoanalytic Theory of Neurosis.* New York: Norton, 1945).

4. FREUD, SIGMUND, with JOSEF BREUER, *Studies on Hysteria,* trans. A. A. Brill. New York: Nervous and Mental Disease Monographs, No. 61. First published in German, 1895.

5. FREUD, SIGMUND, *The Interpretation of Dreams,* trans. and edited by James Strachey. New York: Science Editions, 1961. First published in German, 1900.

6. ———, *The Psychopathology of Everyday Life,* trans. Alan Tyson. New York: Norton, 1965. First published in German, 1901.

7. ———, "Analysis of a Phobia in a Five-Year-Old Boy," in *Collected Papers,* Vol. III. London: Hogarth Press, 1933, pp. 149-295. First published in German, 1909.

8. ———, *Leonardo Da Vinci: A Study in Psychosexuality.* New York: Random House, 1947. First published in German, 1910.

9. ———, *Totem and Taboo,* trans. A. A. Brill. New York: Random House, Vintage Books, 1946. First published in German, 1913.

10. ———, *Group Psychology and the Analysis of the Ego,* trans. James Strachey. New York: Bantam Books, 1960. First published in German, 1921.

11. ———, *The Ego and the Id,* trans. James Strachey. New York: Norton, 1962. First published in German, 1923.

12. ———, *The Problem of Anxiety,* trans. Henry A. Bunker. New York: Psychoanalytic Quarterly Press and Norton, 1963. First published in German, 1926.

13. ———, *The Future of an Illusion.* Garden City, N. Y.: Doubleday, Anchor Books, 1944. First published in German, 1927.

14. ———, *Civilization and Its Discontents, trans.* James Strachey. New York: Norton, 1963). First published in German, 1930.

15. ———, *Moses and Monotheism*, trans. Katherine Jones. New York: Random House, Vintage Books, 1939. First published in German, 1939.

16. FROMM, ERICH, *Psychoanalysis and Religion*. New Haven: Yale University Press, 1950.

17. HENDRICK, IVES, *Facts and Theories of Psychoanalysis*, 3rd ed. New York: Dell, Laurel Books, 1966.

18. JONES, ERNEST, *The Life and Work of Sigmund Freud*, vol. I. New York: Basic Books, 1957.

19. ———, *The Life and Work of Sigmund Freud*, vol. II. New York: Basic Books, 1957.

20. RIEFF, PHILIP, *Freud: The Mind of the Moralist*. Garden City, N. Y.: Doubleday, Anchor Books, 1961.

21. WHITE, VICTOR, *God and the Unconscious*. London: Collins Clear-Type Press, Fontana Books, 1952.

SUGGESTED READINGS

1. *Primary Readings*

Freud's projective theory and critique of religion is most succinctly set forth in his *The Future of an Illusion* (13:1-92).

For additional material on the repressive nature of religion, see Freud's *Civilization and Its Discontents* (14). For the historical origins of religion, see Freud, *Totem and Taboo* (9), ch. 4, 130-207, and *Group Psychology and the Analysis of the Ego* (10), ch. 10, 69-76. For a highly suggestive analysis of the psychic bonds uniting a religious community, see *Group Psychology and the Analysis of the Ego* (10), chs. 4-12.

2. *Secondary Readings*

For a concise, basic introduction to Freudian theory, see Calvin Hall, *A Primer of Freudian Psychology* (New York: The New American Library, 1954). For an analysis of Freudian theory from the standpoint of existential psychology, see Rollo May, ed., *Existence: A New Dimension in Psychiatry and Psychology* (New York: Basic Books, 1958). For an excellent philosophical criticism of Freud's basic assumptions about the nature of man, see Daniel Yankelovich and William Barrett, *Ego and Instinct: The Psychoanalytic View of Human Nature—Revised* (New York: Random House, 1970).

For two psychological responses to Freud's theory of religion from the point of view of religious maturity, see Gordon Allport, *The Individual and His Religion* (New York: Macmillan, 1950), and Erich Fromm, *Psychoanalysis and Religion* (New Haven: Yale University Press, 1950). For a careful Roman Catholic response to Freud, see Roland Dalbiez, *Psychoanalytical Method and the Doctrine of Freud*, trans. T. F. Lindsay (London: Longmans, Green, 1941). For an important Protestant response to Freud from the standpoint of theological existentialism, see Paul Tillich, *Dynamics of*

Faith (New York: Harper and Row, 1958), chs. 1-3; *The Courage To Be* (New Haven: Yale University Press, 1966), chs. 2 and 6; *Theology of Culture* (New York: Oxford University Press, 1964), ch. 8; *Systematic Theology,* II (Chicago: University of Chicago Press, 1957), pp. 51-55. For a general discussion of Protestant responses to Freud, including those of Reinhold Niebuhr and Paul Tillich, see Peter Homans, *Theology After Freud* (Indianapolis: Bobbs-Merrill, 1970).

3. *Additional Bibliography*

The most comprehensive bibliography of Freud's work is in *The Index of Psychoanalytic Writings,* ed. Alexander Grinstein (New York: International Universities Press, 1957). A selected chronological list of Freud's major writings appears in Reuben Fine, *Freud: A Critical Re-Evaluation of His Theories* (New York: David McKay, 1962). For an annotated bibliography on Freud's theory of religion and critical responses to it, see Peter Homans, *Theology After Freud* (Indianapolis: Bobbs-Merrill, 1970), pp. 233-245.

9

Religionless Christianity: Maturity, Transcendence, and Freedom

Freud's new understanding of personality did not remain confined within the limits of psychoanalytic treatment. After World War II, a host of dramatists, novelists, educators, and social critics popularized psychoanalytic motifs in a variety of cultural forms that exposed a significant portion of American society to Freud's basic insights. Changing sexual mores were, in part, an expression of the cultural impact of this Freudian legacy. New suspicions and doubts concerning the credibility of religious beliefs were another by-product. Even the most conservative and psychologically unsophisticated believers could not completely ignore the Freudian shadow cast on their faith: Is belief in an omnipotent deity illusory? Is the conflict between religious belief and psychological maturity unresolvable? Has religion no future, or one confined exclusively to marginal groups?

Among contemporary theologians who have wrestled with the psychological gulf between modern man and traditional religion, few have been as radical or as influential as Dietrich Bonhoeffer (1906–1945). Bonhoeffer did not confront Freud's analysis of religion directly; he was apparently unfamiliar with Freud's personality theory as well as his critique of religion.[1] However, Bonhoeffer discovered, through his own experience and reflection, the same psychological problems with religion previously noted by Freud. Like Freud, Bonhoeffer concluded that belief in an omnipotent deity was more expressive of psychological needs than

284

genuine transcendence. Bonhoeffer also found religious dependency to be in conflict with psychological maturity. With Freud, Bonhoeffer regarded immature religiosity as a dysfunctional illusion destined to disappear in the near future.

While agreeing with Freud on these points, Bonhoeffer moved beyond Freud in two important respects. First, Bonhoeffer clearly differentiated between a mature faith which nourishes human autonomy and an immature religiosity symptomatic of regression to infantile dependency. His personal aversion to religious personalities, who used their beliefs to justify weak and selfish behavior, led him to reexamine the biblical and theological bases of Christianity. He concluded that the Bible presents God as an ally of genuine strength and maturity, although beliefs about God have been distorted, throughout the ages, by psychic needs and desires. Consonant with his biblical findings, Bonhoeffer began formulating a "non-religious interpretation of Christianity," that is, a version of biblical faith explicitly excluding theological imagery engendered by immature, psychological dynamics. Second, while Freud understood man in terms of individual psychological processes, Bonhoeffer regarded man as a social being inseparably bound to others. This social view of human life gave an ethical focus to all his writings, including his psychological reflections.[2] As a result, the psychological maturity of which Bonhoeffer speaks includes man's "freedom for others." A responsible life with others, informed by freedom and love, is not for Bonhoeffer an unrealistic command of an alien superego, but a realistic possibility leading to human fulfillment.[3] This version of maturity is informed by Bonhoeffer's Christian faith and includes socioethical dimensions ignored by Freud.

The last few years of Bonhoeffer's life dramatically depict this life of commitment to others. At the age of thirty-three, Bonhoeffer arrived in New York from Berlin as a promising young scholar-theologian. Friends had arranged a position for him in this country since his opposition to Nazi policies had already threatened his career in Germany.[4] With the outbreak of war between England and Germany imminent in 1939, Bonhoeffer abruptly decided to terminate his anticipated residence in America. Returning home, he resumed work with fellow Christians in the Confessing Church, a group which protested the religious-moral claims of the Nazis.[5] By the summer of 1940, however, Bonhoeffer had moved beyond the protest of the Confessing Church and committed himself to the Resistance Movement.[6] Its center was based in the German military intelligence agency, the famed *Abwehr* of World War II spy thrillers. Its plot was to assassinate Hitler, establish a new government by a *coup d'état*, and negotiate a surrender with the Allies. Bonhoeffer's role in this political conspiracy was primarily that of a secret diplomat. During the war, he made several trips to Switzerland and Sweden, purportedly to seek intelligence for *Abwehr*, but actually to meet with leaders of the ecumenical movement who, in turn, sought to win the support of British and American governments for the German underground.[7] As a double agent for *Abwehr* and the Resistance Movement, Bonhoeffer lived through these years in a complex and many-layered web of deception. For example, one mission involved plans for the escape of certain Jewish families to Switzerland, an escape financed by *Abwehr* funds deposited by Bonhoeffer in a Swiss bank. Arrested in 1943, he was first held for questioning on minor charges until the Gestapo learned, after the attempted assassination of Hitler on July 20, 1944, of his membership in the conspiracy. Moved from one prison to another to avoid the invading Russian army, Bonhoeffer was executed by hanging on April 9, 1945, less than a month before the surrender of Nazi Germany.

As a pastor, theologian, double agent, and martyr, Bonhoeffer was neither interested in nor trained for deep psychological self-exploration. He preferred the posture of a psychological agnostic, a man who was relatively comfortable with himself without knowing his unconscious motivations (4:162). His aristocratic, Prussian background led him to scorn the psychoanalytic exploration of the secret parts of human life, like sexuality. Nevertheless, in spite of these vocational commitments and personal inclinations, Bonhoeffer was led, during his captivity in prison, to develop a careful critique of the psychological infrastructure characteristic of traditional Christianity. While the loose style of *Letters and Papers from Prison* may sometimes conceal the thrust of Bonhoeffer's argument, a careful reading of this text suggests that Bonhoeffer's most significant contribution to contemporary theology appears precisely at the point of his new psychological model of Christian maturity.

1. RELIGION AND MATURITY: PSYCHOLOGICAL AND HISTORICAL PERSPECTIVES

Bonhoeffer's critique of religion appears in a series of letters written to a friend during a five-month period of his prison life, from April through August, 1944.[8] He describes his own reflections on the themes of religion and maturity as being

> in the early stages; and, as usual, I am being led on more by an instinctive feeling for questions that will arise later than by any conclusions that I have already reached about them (4:325).

Executed by the Nazis a year after beginning this process of exploration, Bonhoeffer never had an opportunity to sort out the complex web of ideas proposed in his correspondence. The informal style of his letters allowed him to fuse three distinct themes of his critique of religion: 1) a psychological typology of religious and mature personalities; 2) a developmental interpretation of Western history leading to the ascendancy of post-religious man; and 3) a theological-biblical critique of religion. This section describes the first two themes, while the next section presents the third.

While Bonhoeffer was not a psychologist by professional training or personal inclination, he suggests in his prison letters a sketch of two distinct personality types. The first type he calls religious, the second, mature or adult. In Bonhoeffer's view, religious man is basically an immature, dependent personality, disturbed by emotional conflicts within and anxious about the world without, liable to intellectual dishonesty and moral irresponsibility. Mature man, in contrast, is fundamentally an autonomous personality, relatively free of inner conflict and confident in his dealings with the world, a person of intellectual integrity and moral reliability. From this brief sketch, it should be clear that the terms "religion" and "religious" have a very special meaning for Bonhoeffer. Instead of referring to all forms of belief, devotional practice, and ecclesiastical institutions, these terms describe a particular personality type.

Bonhoeffer's observations concerning religious and mature personalities grew out of his experiences in Germany during World War II. As a member of the German Resistance Movement from 1940 until his arrest in 1943, Bonhoeffer came in contact with a group of men who held no particular religious beliefs, but whose conduct demonstrated unusual strengths of courage and compassion in situations of extreme stress. He acknowledged that "a Christian instinct often draws me more to the religionless people than to the religious," not for the sake of converting them, but simply "in brotherhood" (4:281). Later, during his years in prison, he also observed how often religion seemed to support personal weakness and selfishness (4:204f.). During bombing raids, many prisoners, filled with religious piety, cried out the name of God and fell on their knees in prayer, while ignoring the real distress of others around them (4:199). In sorting out his personal affinity for the religionless men he had known in the Resistance as well as his distaste for the immature religiosity of some of his fellow prisoners, Bonhoeffer found it necessary to distinguish his own faith from that religion "of weakness that Christianity does not hold with, but which people insist on claiming as Christian" (4:205).[9]

Bonhoeffer describes the religious personality in terms reminiscent of Sigmund Freud. Just as Freud describes religious believers as infantile and regressive, Bonhoeffer views them as immature and dependent. While chronologically adult, the religious personality uses his beliefs to evade the normal processes of growing up. Such people have not yet "come of age," to use Bonhoeffer's characteristic phrase. Since their psychological development is retarded, they remain fixed in the status and attitude of childhood dependency. As a result, they find their lives unhappy. They tend to be preoccupied by a sense of despair, anguish, and morbid introspection. Like children, they have not yet found a satisfactory way of coping with their needs. Hence, they find themselves always disturbed by "problems, needs, and conflicts" within themselves (4:341).

The religious personality experiences his world primarily as a source of anxious concern. Intellectually, the world is enigmatic and confusing, a world in which the name of God constantly needs to be invoked to fill gaps in human knowledge. Existentially, religious people experience the world as a hostile and threatening environment. Anxious about the unknown future, they expect that their own meager share of happiness will always be threatened.

In terms of morality, Bonhoeffer finds the religious personality to be selfish and amoral. After reading Dostoevski's *The House of the Dead,* Bonhoeffer writes

> May not this amorality, the product of religiosity, be an essential trait of these people? (4:358)

One reason Bonhoeffer links religiosity with moral irresponsibility is because religious people are still bound by the chains of infantile narcissism. They are the "people who regard themselves as the most important thing in the world, and who therefore like to busy themselves with themselves" (4:326f.). They are the same people who remain concerned about the individualistic question of personal salvation, "redemption from cares, distress, fears, and longings, from sin and death" (4:336). They still expect to find some kind of religious salvation from their inner needs and conflicts, and this wish only preserves and extends their infantile self-concern. A second reason for linking religion and amorality grows out of the weak character of religious personalities.

> Is not people's weakness (stupidity, lack of independence, forgetfulness, cowardice, vanity, corruptibility, temptability, etc.) a greater danger than evil? (4:392)

In either case, because of infantile self-love or weakness of character, Bonhoeffer views the religious personality as incapable of effectively caring for others.

The mature personality differs from his religious counterpart in every respect. He is an autonomous person who enjoys a "wholeness of independent existence" (4:310). He accepts full responsibility for his own life and actions, and does not need to assign a portion of that responsibility to a vague but powerful deity. In contrast with the discontent of religious believers, mature man is relatively "content" with his life at work, with his family, and with his leisure time; he does not experience his "modest share of happiness as a trial, a trouble, or a calamity" (4:327). In contrast with the anxiety of religious personalities, mature man has "grown self-confident in what seems to us to be an uncanny way" (4:326). Partly, this self-confidence reflects his proven competence in changing his environment, especially by scientific knowledge and technical means. This self-confidence is further enhanced by an ability to cope with personal and emotional crises. Mature man also has vulnerabilities; he must come to terms with "death, suffering, and guilt" (4:311). However, these threats do not drive him to abandon his autonomy for the sake of religiosity.

At the core of the religious personality is a particular kind of relationship to God. Bonhoeffer describes this "religious relation" to God in terms of its psychological dynamics and theological imagery. Psychologically, the religious relation with God is rooted in the dynamics of anxious self-concern and projection. Finding themselves no longer able to cope with the conflicts raging within and the threats of the world without, men turn to God for help. In his poem, "Christians and Pagans," Bonhoeffer describes the psychological origins of the religious relation to God:

> Men go to God when they are sore bestead,
> Pray to him for succour, for his peace, for bread,
> For mercy for them sick, sinning, or dead;
> All men do so, Christian and unbelieving (4:348f.).

Hunger, illness, guilt, death and war: these are the human experiences out of which the religious relationship with God is formed.[10] In response to such situations of need, men project an all-powerful deity whom Bonhoeffer calls the *deus ex machina*, a phrase which literally means the mechanical God. The phrase is derived from the god figure manipulated by levers and wires so as to float across the ancient Greek stage. The *deus ex machina* was employed to solve a dilemma of the play which the human actors were not able to resolve. By referring to this device of Greek drama, Bonhoeffer suggests that men individually and collectively construct a deity who is just as mechanical and unreal as the one artificially introduced to resolve crises on the Greek stage.

Not surprisingly, the most prominent theological attribute associated with the *deus ex machina* is power. The impotence characteristic of immature and dependent personalities has its corollary in the symbol of omnipotence for their deity. Indeed, the God of religion must be, above all else, a God of absolute and unqualified power, for only such a deity can meet the needs of the religious personality for deliverance from the terrors of the world and the conflicts within himself. For Bonhoeffer, the God of power is identical with the *deus ex machina*, the artificial construct engendered by the crises of immature, dependent personalities.

Bonhoeffer's psychological insights might have remained confined within the private sphere of his personal experience, if these observations had not become linked with a larger vision of Western historical development. For Bonhoeffer does not regard religious and mature personalities as two groups of individuals isolated from the larger course of history; rather, he views the emergence of psychological maturity as the most recent development in a continuous pattern of history.[11]

Bonhoeffer finds the movement toward autonomy evolving through four stages to be the dominant trend of Western history. First, he identifies a series of pre-modern social theorists who, beginning as early as the thirteenth century, set forth a new vision of man freed from the authority of religious claims and institutions. Second, this vision of a humanity independent of a divine tutor acquired intellectual expression in the Enlightenment. For the Enlightenment clearly articulated the autonomy of the intellect; reason was sufficient in itself and did not require a higher religious authority to support its truth claims. Third, in the nineteenth and twentieth centuries, human autonomy was embodied in a new technology designed to control the forces of nature and new forms of social organization which were, in fact as well as theory, independent of any ecclesiastical jurisdiction. In addition, new secular institutions arose which, by providing a more secure natural and social environment, reenforced human autonomy. Fourth, the last stage in the process of "the world coming of age" is the interiorizing of autonomy in the mature personality type. Even after the intellectual articulation of autonomy and its social realization, most men remained sufficiently bound by inner problems and conflicts to sustain religiosity. Only with the appearance of psychic maturity as the dominant personality type of the twentieth century has the movement toward autonomy reached its completion.

Bonhoeffer's version of Western history differs considerably from the older Enlightenment accounts, e.g., as represented by David Hume or Rudolf Bultmann. First, Bonhoeffer regards "the movement . . . towards the autonomy of man" as a process which began in the thirteenth century rather than in the eighteenth century (4:325). He includes a variety of late medieval and Renaissance thinkers, as well as familiar Enlightenment philosophers, as spokesmen for the new vision of man.

Second, Bonhoeffer locates the emergence of autonomy as a major theme in the sphere of social philosophy. His list of prophets who announced man's new status of independence and self-determination include religious and ethical thinkers, political theorists, and philosophers of society and international law.

> In theology one sees it [the movement toward autonomy] first in Lord Herbert of Cherbury, who maintains that reason is sufficient for religious knowledge.[12] In ethics it appears in Montaigne and Bodin with their substitution of rules of life for the commandments. In politics Machiavelli detaches politics from morality in general and founds the doctrine of "reasons of State." Later, and very differently from Machiavelli, but tending like him towards the autonomy of human society, comes Grotius, setting up his natural law as international law, which is valid *etsi deus non daretur* ("even if there were no God") (4:359).

By way of contrast, Rudolf Bultmann, who adopted the Enlightenment version of Western history, identified the eighteenth century as the turning point in human history and regarded the fields of natural science and scientific philosophy as the decisive loci for the appearance of the autonomy of reason. Bonhoeffer's quite different reading of history suggests two characteristics of his thought. First, social theorists rather than natural scientists initiate the theme of autonomy; second, autonomy is not exclusively attached to rationality, as in the Enlightenment, but is a quality of personality which emerges with those secular institutions that support it.[13]

In spite of his disagreement with the Enlightenment interpretation of Western history and his stress on the autonomy of the total personality, Bonhoeffer recognizes the attainment of intellectual independence in the eighteenth century as a decisive step in the world coming of age. For Bonhoeffer, autonomy is not given man by nature, revelation, or even the articulation of a new vision of humanity. It is an arduous achievement which requires the exercise of an independent intellect. Eberhard Bethge has called attention to the close similarity between Bonhoeffer's idea of the "world come of age" and Immanuel Kant's explanation of the meaning of Enlightenment. Bethge quotes Kant as follows:

> Enlightenment is the departure of man from his self-inflicted immaturity. Immaturity is the inability to use one's own reason without the guidance of someone else (12:77).

For Bonhoeffer, as well as Kant, men initially attain autonomy by the exercise of reason "without the guidance of someone else." As they gain knowledge of the world "and the laws which govern its . . . existence," they also gain confidence concerning the sufficiency of reason (4:326).

Does he D.V.N. Revelation + inspiration?

we do use God to fill the gaps, however, will our eventually preclude any need for God - not hypothesis.

They are able to seek knowledge and truth on their own, without recourse to the divine tutor-guardian whose inspiration and authority was formerly sought in man's quest for truth (4:326). Furthermore, as reason expands into ever new territories of inquiry, solving questions and problems which had remained unresolved for generations, the need for the "God-hypothesis" to fill the empty holes of human knowledge decreases (4:326).[14] As a result, Bonhoeffer sees a steady expansion of rational autonomy and an equally consistent retrenchment of God in modern intellectual history.

Because Bonhoeffer recognizes man's status as a social being, his analysis of the transition from the age of religion to the age of maturity includes a description of changing social organizations. Bonhoeffer suggests some of these social developments in the outline of a book he began to write in prison, but never completed. This outline describes the development of "technical organization" as the principal means by which modern man has become "independent of nature" (4:380). "Our immediate environment is not nature, as formerly, but organization" (4:380). While technical organization frees man from his former dependency on nature, new social organizations safeguard human life "against 'accidents' and 'blows of fate'" (4:380). Bonhoeffer cites insurance policies of various kinds as one social instrument designed to mitigate—if not eliminate—the insecurities of human life (4:380). As a result of these developments, modern man enjoys a larger sense of corporate security than his ancestors. Autonomy and maturity are continuously supported and reenforced by man's self-confident standing before nature and fate. This is not to say that modern man may not feel dependent upon, and helpless before, impersonal social systems, especially oppressive societies, but the latter are not able to undermine his achieved autonomy and maturity.

Modern man is not only less vulnerable to the terrors of life than were his religious ancestors but he has new resources available to assist him in coping with perennial vulnerabilities. Suffering, death and guilt, "the so-called ultimate questions" in Bonhoeffer's terminology, have not disappeared from human experience with the emergence of the modern age. The limits of human strength and autonomy continue to be threatened by these perennial crises. However, in modern society, Christianity no longer offers the only answer to such "ultimate questions." "It may be that Christian answers are just as unconvincing—or convincing—as others" (4:311f.). Alternative resources are available for healing the wounds in man's sense of well-being: "It is now possible to find, even for these questions, human answers that take no account whatever of God" (4:311). Therefore, modern man need not be driven to religion as the only solution for remaining vulnerabilities. He may avail himself

God Point

instead of therapeutic resources which support, rather than negate, his personal autonomy.

Like other prophets of history, Bonhoeffer identifies his present historical context as the transition from one epoch of history to another. Since the time of the thirteenth century, "the world come of age" has been developing, while the religious stage of humanity has been withering away. This world historical process has, in the mid-twentieth century, "reached an undoubted completion" (4:326). Intellectual autonomy has long been a *fait accompli*. "In questions of science, art, and ethics this has become an understood thing at which one now hardly dares to tilt" (4:326). Similarly, the independence of social, political and economic institutions from religious authority has long been acknowledged as a basic principle of Western society. The last sanctuary for religion had been man's "inner life"; the mixture of hopes and fears, conflicts and crises which besiege, and sometimes overpower, a person. However as contemporary men developed a sense of inner autonomy, this last bastion of religion also fell. In light of this final development in the world historical movement towards autonomy, Bonhoeffer declares that we are now "moving towards a completely religionless time" (4:279). Indeed, this future is already so imminent as to be present. "I think that that is already more or less the case" that man has become "radically religionless" (4:280).

Bonhoeffer thus uses the categories of maturity and religion to identify two distinct epochs in human history: the age of maturity designates the historical successor of the age of religion. Some readers may question Bonhoeffer's historical generalization by pointing to the number of immature, dependent people who still need religion to cope with inner conflicts, anxiety, suffering or death. Bonhoeffer clearly does not intend to say that all men have "come of age" and he gives a vivid description of the religious personalities whom he encountered in prison. However, Bonhoeffer does contend that the cultural, political, intellectual and moral leaders of the twentieth century are increasingly autonomous personalities. While dependent religious personalities continue to survive, especially in religious subcultures, they have receded into the background of our public life. For our age, it is not religious man but autonomous man who provides the paradigm for the normal, healthy human being.

2. RELIGION, MATURITY, AND FAITH: A THEOLOGICAL ANALYSIS

Bonhoeffer's repudiation of religion as psychologically regressive and historically obsolete does not lead him to reject his faith as a Christian.

At the same time that he is writing about "the end of the age of religion," he is also living a disciplined spiritual life shaped by the traditional resources of the Christian community. He reads daily those biblical texts and commentaries fixed by the liturgical calender of the church; his letters are filled with biblical references that illumine his personal experience in prison and the theological issues of concern to him; when permitted, he leads worship services and preaches sermons for a congregation of fellow prisoners; and he extends pastoral care to other prisoners, and friends in the outside world, as the need arises. In brief, the whole of his life is permeated by the actions, beliefs, and attitudes characteristic of a Christian man.

Obviously Bonhoeffer finds no contradiction between his life of faith and his radical critique of religion; faith, for him, is clearly not a form of religion but a source of human maturity and strength. To clarify this seeming paradox, it is necessary to explicate three theological convictions which inform Bonhoeffer's understanding of the relation between faith, maturity, and religion. First, Bonhoeffer believes that the Christian faith must be clearly separated from religion because the former alliance of the two compromised and distorted the unique character of faith in Christ.[15] Second, on the basis of the distinction between faith and religion, Bonhoeffer develops a critique of the religious theologies dominant in the modern period. Third, Bonhoeffer presents a "non-religious interpretation of Christianity" in which faith is allied with maturity in opposition to religion.

While Bonhoeffer argues for a clear distinction between faith and religion, he recognizes that the two have been thoroughly mixed in the past.

> Our whole nineteen-hundred-year-old Christian preaching and theology rests on the "religious a priori" of mankind (4:280).

Indeed, the fusion of primitive religious attitudes with Christian commitment has been so complete that the disappearance of religion "means that the foundation is taken away from the whole of what has up to now been our Christianity" (4:280).

While acknowledging that "Christianity has always been a form of religion," Bonhoeffer does not regard the past religious form of Christianity as determinative for its future (4:280). The reason for this curious claim is that Christianity was not religious in its essence; its religiosity was only an expression of the historical epoch in which it was born and developed. During the Christian period of history, the religious posture of dependency and weakness was appropriate to the real situation in which men found themselves. Most men felt relatively helpless before the threatening forces of their world. And, they lacked the resources necessary for developing the intellectual and personal strengths of mature autonomy. Christianity, like other world religions, responded to this situation by incorporating within itself the psychological dynamics of need and projection, along with the theological imagery of an omnipotent *deus ex machina*. In Bonhoeffer's terms, religion became the "garment" of Christianity or its "form of expression" (4:280). However, this religious form of expression is no longer appropriate today. Since religion is only "an historically conditioned and transient form of human self-expression" and not identical with the substance of faith, Bonhoeffer proposes to "dereligionize" Christianity (4:280).[16]

Bonhoeffer bases his proposal for a "nonreligious interpretation of Christianity" on three biblical-theological arguments. First, he cites the New Testament rejection of law as a precedent for his rejection of religiosity. In the early Christian Church, many Jewish-Christians argued that it was necessary for all Christians, Gentiles as well as Jews, to accept the religious law of Judaism as a first step in the new life of faith. Paul successfully argued against this position, especially in his letter to the Galatians, by contending that Christians were freed from the claims of Jewish religious law. In a similar manner, Bonhoeffer argues that the cultivation of religious dependency is not a necessary precondition for faith (4:329). "Freedom from circumcision [as demanded by the Jewish law] is also freedom from religion" (4:281). To demand that men become religious first as a condition for faith is

> Unchristian, because it confuses Christ with one particular stage in man's religiousness, i.e., with a human law (4:327).

Second, Bonhoeffer argues that, in the Bible, man is consistently regarded as a whole person; religion, in contrast, is concerned only with a partial aspect of human existence. For example, religion is concerned with man's soul or spirit but not his body; in the Bible, however, man is presented as a unity of body and spirit. Hence, the biblical promise of ultimate vindication is not the immortality of the soul but the resurrection of the embodied person. Similarly, religion may separate man's inner feelings from his external behavior or isolate his individuality from his corporate existence whereas the Bible never cuts man into segmented parts. The Bible has a wholistic view of man while religion is dualistic, dividing man into body and soul, internal and external, individual and corporate.

Third, Bonhoeffer contends that the Bible presents God as an ally of human strength. Unlike the *deus ex machina* of religion, the biblical God does not require his people to become weak, dependent or guilty as a precondition for doing his will. The Old Testament specifically identifies God with a series of blessings which he bestows upon his people. These blessings include health, long life, prosperity, progeny, land, and nationhood. These blessings are not given by a deity who is an enemy of human strength. The New Testament presents Jesus in a similar light. Far from disparaging health and strength, Jesus is a healer who restores the minds and bodies of those afflicted with diseases and debilitating weaknesses (4:341f.). Nor does Jesus require every man to become guilty before becoming a disciple (4:341). To document this contention, Bonhoeffer presents a list of New Testament personalities who never confessed their sin or guilt, but were presented as models of faith: the shepherds and wise men, the children whom Jesus blessed, the centurion and the "rich young man" whom Jesus loved, the eunuch and Cornelius, Nathaniel, Joseph of Arimathea, and the women at the tomb (4:362).

The biblical God does not require a religious sense of weakness, dependency, or guilt; he, rather, blesses men with new strength, frees them from the bondage of sin, and calls them to an active life of love. "Never did he [Jesus] question a man's health, vigor, or happiness . . . or regard these as evil fruits, else why should he heal the sick and restore strength to the weak" (4:341)? While the *deus ex machina* is a corollary of man's sense of inadequacy and helplessness, the biblical God enables men to realize their maximum strength: "Christ not only makes people good; he makes them strong too" (4:392).

In light of these considerations, Bonhoeffer concludes that biblical faith is qualitatively different from religious attitudes and beliefs. Religion functions oppressively as a kind of law, a transient form of human self-expression appropriate for one age of history but dysfunctional and destructive in another. Faith in Christ frees men from all religious laws which attempt to fix the human spirit in a particular mold. Because religion is rooted in only a part of human life, such as unresolved dependency-needs and inner conflicts, it finds expression in isolated segments of human behavior: worship attendance on the Sabbath, private morality, and rituals designed to guarantee the salvation of the soul beyond death. Faith grasps men in the center of their lives, finding expression in their secular activities as well as specifically religious concerns. Finally, belief in the religious *deus ex machina* tends to support and encourage infantile attitudes of dependency, anxiety and guilt, while the biblical God enhances the strength and responsibility of those who believe in him. For all these reasons, Bonhoeffer rejects the former alliance of Christianity with religiosity. Not only are religious attitudes and beliefs obsolete in a world come of age, they also conceal and distort the distinctive quality of biblical faith. For this reason, the end of the age of religion may mark the beginning of a new age of faith.

In contrast with this elimination of religion from faith, Bonhoeffer finds that the predominant forms of modern Christian theology have identified religion and faith. As a result, each new step toward autonomy in modern Western history has been viewed by Christian theologians as a loss of faith. Because they erroneously confused faith with religion, and because autonomy was clearly undermining religious attitudes, they concluded that the direction of history was in conflict with faith. Bonhoeffer vigorously criticizes this modern religious brand of theology. He depicts the decline of this theology in three stages: attack, surrender, and exploitation.

In the early period of modern history, the Christian church and its theological spokesmen attacked each new assertion of autonomy as an enemy of Christian faith. This response is evident in the Catholic attack on Copernican astronomy and the Protestant polemic against Darwinian biology (4:341). However, this theological belligerence was not confined to particular cases, but extended to the movement toward autonomy as a whole. "Roman Catholic and Protestant historians agree that it is in this development [toward autonomy] that the great defection from God, from Christ is to be seen" (4:326). One result of this theological polemic was the emergence of an anti-Christian orientation among spokesmen for intellectual and personal autonomy. Because they were seen by the church as playing the role of the anti-Christ, they identified with this position (4:326). A second result of this attack on autonomy was the growing alienation of the church from the mainstream of modern culture. In Bonhoeffer's view, only a "few intellectually dishonest people" continued to surrender their autonomy to the authoritarian claims of religion (4:280). Secular culture became increasingly godless, while the church became confined to a social ghetto of unhappy misfits.

The ecclesiastical strategy of attack failed to stop the movement toward autonomy. In some instances, the church was able to delay, but never to prevent, man's growth toward self-determination. As a result, each new historical advance toward autonomy meant a new retreat for religious theology. The strategy of surrender gradually replaced the more aggressive posture of attack. In intellectual matters, Kantian theology set the pattern of surrender by excluding God from the sphere of rational knowledge (4:341). Henceforth the name of God was invoked only to answer unresolved problems of human thought. What men did not know or could not explain at any given moment of time was accounted for by the "God-hypothesis," a convenient device for temporarily filling gaps in knowledge (4:360). In the everyday world, God was also pushed to the periphery. Political, economic, and cultural matters were handled without reference to God and his rule. As a result, Bonhoeffer finds that religious theology has "surrendered on all secular problems," consenting to the gradual exclusion of God from the thought and activity of modern men (4:326).

Having lost the battle for religion in the public spheres of culture and society, religious theology focused upon the ambiguities and vulnerabilities of the individual's inner life. This last-ditch stand of religious theology was itself a testimony to the accuracy of Bonhoeffer's historical diagnosis. In his corporate life, man found his autonomy sufficient to dispel his religious needs. Only in the hidden depths of his inner life were there still unresolved problems and conflicts for religion to exploit. As a result, religious theology in this third phase of development became highly individualistic both in theory and practice. For in the last days of the age of religion, only the individual and his interior life appeared to provide a safe place for God (4:374).

At a theoretical level, Bonhoeffer found this final strategy of religious theology expressed in the concept of "the boundary situation." First developed by the philosopher, Karl Jaspers, the notion of the boundary situation was appropriated by a wide variety of Christian theologians contemporary with Bonhoeffer. These theologians described the point of contact between man and God in terms of "the boundary situation." According to this view, man does not meet God in the exercise of rational autonomy, but at the vulnerable fringes of existence which disclose his interior complexity. In his confrontation with the enigmas of the cosmos, man encounters the limitations of his knowledge; in the vicissitudes of historical experience, he discovers the limits of his autonomous will as he finds his destiny shaped by powers greater than his own; in the ambiguities of his emotional life, he finds himself besieged by conflicting drives and prohibitions which elude the limits of his control; finally, and most decisively, in the anticipation of death, he comes upon the ultimate boundary of his autonomy. Each of these situations disclose the finitude of human nature and so provide occasions for man's encounter with God. For, according to this theory, man meets God precisely at these exposed edges of his life, these boundary situations.[17]

Bonhoeffer repudiates this apologetic theology which attempts to convince autonomous man of his need for religion. He rejects it as unbiblical, because the God of the Bible does not claim to meet man at the tattered fringes, but at the center of his life. Nor does the biblical God retreat from the public sphere of history to the isolated and partial sphere of interiority. Rather, the biblical God invites men to use their strength as responsible agents in shaping the corporate history in which they participate. A biblical prophet like Amos, for example, addresses the landowners and rulers of Israel precisely in terms of their corporate responsibility, charging them with exploitation of the poor and the destruction of innocent women and children in war. Bonhoeffer also rejects a theology of the boundary situation because its premise is fast becoming obsolete. It is no longer true that the so-called ultimate threats to human autonomy—death, guilt and suffering—will necessarily drive men to religion. As men utilize their reason to illumine the mysteries of their inner life and discover new resources for self-transformation, religious conversion becomes an increasingly unattractive and unnecessary solution to the universal dilemmas of human life.

Bonhoeffer's critique of the theoretical effort to justify man's need for religion is mild in comparison with his scathing indictment of the ministry. In Bonhoeffer's judgment, the Christian minister too often tries to justify religion by "spying out" the weakness and meanness of his people (4:345). He thinks he must convince people of their need for religion by first undermining their sense of self-confidence. For a frightened and anxious man is in need of religion. Or, if this attack does not work, the minister may seek to convince his relatively happy and healthy congregation that they should really be quite miserable with their lot in life (4:341). For a desperate man is also in need of religion. If this strategy is still not effective, the minister may always count on some latent guilt feelings, ready to be aroused by the clergyman "sniffing-around-after-people's-sins in order to catch them out" (4:345). Again, a guilty man is also in need of religion. If none of these efforts drive a man to religion, then, as Bonhoeffer sarcastically observes,

> it is a case of having to do with a hardened sinner of a particularly ugly type, or with a man of "bourgeois complacency," and the one is as far from salvation as the other (4:341).

For the sake of common human decency and the Lord Jesus, Bonhoeffer pleads with all who are entrusted with the care of souls, ecclesiastical as well as secular counselors, to cease and desist from this exploitation of human vulnerability.

Bonhoeffer rejects all three of these strategies of religious theology —attack, surrender, and exploitation of individual weakness—because they are alien to biblical faith and counterproductive in a world come of age. He considers

> the attack by Christian apologists on the adulthood of the world [to be] pointless, because it seems to me like an attempt to put a grown-up man back into adolescence, i.e., to make him dependent on things on which he is, in fact, no longer dependent, and thrusting him into problems that are, in fact, no longer problems to him (4:327).

He deplores the strategy of surrender, which displaced God from the public world of history to confinement within the private life of the individual, because it is unbiblical and expressive of an inferior, vulgar mentality (4:345). Finally, he condemns the theoretical and practical effort to exploit individual vulnerabilities for religious purposes as

> ignoble, because it amounts to an attempt to exploit man's weaknesses for purposes that are alien to him and to which he has not freely consented (4:327).

All three of these theological strategies share a common premise: all assume that faith and maturity are necessarily in conflict with each other. Bonhoeffer was free to repudiate this apologetic theology precisely because he had discovered, through his experience in the Resistance Movement and his reflection on biblical themes, the basic difference between the infantile dynamics of religion and the maturity nourished by Christian faith.[18] By clearly distinguishing faith from religion, he was able to propose a quite different pattern of theological polemics, namely, one which attacked religiosity while embracing maturity as an offspring of, and fit partner for, the Christian faith.

Bonhoeffer therefore begins his "non-religious interpretation of Christianity" by establishing the positive connection between biblical faith and the world come of age. Contrary to religionists, the movement toward autonomy is not the work of the anti-Christ nor is it an accident of modern Western history. Rather, Bonhoeffer discerns the hand of the biblical God in the world's coming of age. This God, who blessed Abraham and David with strength to do his will in history, is also active in our age. It is this biblical God who "would have us know that we must live as men who manage our lives" without recourse to any *deus ex machina* (4:360). It is also this biblical God, "before whom we stand continually, . . . who lets us live in the world without the working hypothesis of God" (4:360). The movement of world history toward autonomy is therefore theologically, as well as psychologically and historically, significant. For

> the development towards the world's coming of age, . . . which has done away with a false conception of God, opens up a way of seeing the God of the Bible (4:361).

The psychohistorical changes of the modern world have increasingly compelled men to question religiosity and to deny the deity born of human deficiencies. In the process of abandoning the projected and illusory god of religion, men have also been freed to discover anew the God of the Bible. For this reason, the end of the age of religion is not a time for mourning, but for celebrating the advent of a new era of faith.

This is the distinctive insight which runs throughout Bonhoeffer's letters from prison: religiosity is an enemy of autonomy, but faith in the biblical God is an ally of human strength and maturity. In terms of man's intellectual life, this means that faith is not to be identified with unresolved problems and gaps in human knowledge. Rather,

> we are to find God in what we know, not in what we do not know; God wants us to realize his presence, not in unsolved problems, but in those that are solved (4:311).

With respect to society, Bonhoeffer enjoins the Christian to exercise his faith in the midst of secular culture and politics. The Christian need not confine his life of faith to the narrow limits of religious institutions, their rites and obligations; he is free to live a secular life because "he has been liberated from false religious . . . inhibitions" (4:361). Indeed, the Christian "must live a secular life" for it is only in the area of man's corporate history that he participates in the drama of God's dealings with men (4:361). "God should not be smuggled into some last secret place"—the secret guilts and anxieties of the inner life, the individualistic hope of an other-worldly salvation (4:346). Rather, Christians should enact their faith in the open, in the public arena of actions which constitute our social reality.

With regard to man's personal existence, the Christian may expect to meet God, not in immature dependency needs, but at "his strongest point" of maturity (4:346).

> Here again, God is no stop-gap; he must be recognized at the centre of life, not when we are at the end of our resources; it is his will to be recognized in life, and not only when death comes; in health and vigor, and not only in suffering; in our activities, and not only in sin (4:312).

To paraphrase Bonhoeffer in psychoanalytic terms, the deity of religion is rooted in man's unconscious life: his infantile wish for happiness and security, his childish sense of dependency and helplessness, his inner conflicts, anxiety, and guilt. The God of whom Bonhoeffer speaks is active in and through the ego and its strengths (4:282). He is at the centre of life, not its unconscious peripheries; he is known in and with the ego's apprehension of real experience, not a neurotic construct of pseudoreality; his presence is acknowledged in the midst of physical health, emotional vitality, and a sense of self-integrity, not in sickness, depression, and a state of personal disintegration. Finally, God is acknowledged through the decisions and actions which shape the world we share with others; his presence is not confined to those moments of remorse for sin and guilt.

In all these ways, Bonhoeffer emphasizes the affinity between faith and maturity. However, he does not simply identify the two. The world come of age is not the same as the kingdom of God; the maturity of ego strength is not identical with the Christian life. Bonhoeffer also speaks of the "godlessness" of the world come of age (4:362). He derides that secular hedonism which is "a shallow . . . banal . . . comfortable . . . lascivious . . . this-worldliness" (4:369). Bonhoeffer's proposal for secular Christian life is as different from mere secularism as it is from religiosity. Our attention in this section, however, has focused on distinguishing faith from religion and linking faith with maturity. The following section describes the particular characteristics Bonhoeffer associates with Christian life in a world come of age.

3. "RELIGIONLESS CHRISTIANITY": TRANSCENDENCE AND FREEDOM

Bonhoeffer's critique of religiosity grew out of the mature faith that informed his own life and thought. He did not intend simply to shock pious readers by exposing, as a fraud, the deity born of human weakness. His exposé of religion and its exclusion from the domain of faith was only the first step in clearing the way for a recovery of genuine transcendence. The goal of Bonhoeffer's theology is, therefore, not the critique of religion but a restatement of Christian faith as a viable option for a post-religious world: what he calls "a nonreligious interpretation of Christianity" or more simply, "religionless Christianity" (4:282). His constructive theological alternative to religion treats two distinct, but related, questions: 1) How may one speak of God, of transcendence, in a nonreligious way? 2) What are the distinctive chararacteristics of a Christian life-style in a secular age?

Bonhoeffer clearly specifies criteria for religious ways of speaking about God. First, religion employs symbols of power in referring to the deity: omnipotence is the distinguishing characteristic of God in religion (4:381). Second, religious speech about God is infused by the psychological dynamics of need and projection: men do not speak religiously about God out of strength and maturity but out of weakness and desperation. God appears, like the *deus ex machina,* as an all-powerful father figure, who rescues his children from their afflictions and who compensates for their inadequacies. Third, religion uses metaphysical concepts in speaking about God (4:280). God is described as a distinct and transcendent Being—"the highest, most powerful, best Being imaginable"—whose relationship to the world is explicated philosophically (4:381). While there is a wide gap between the naiveté of the religious believer who calls on God in time of need and the sophistication of metaphysical speculation, Bonhoeffer, like Freud, groups both under the single rubric of "religion."

Bonhoeffer's nonreligious interpretation of God involves two basic changes from this prevalent religious pattern. First, Bonhoeffer insists that men do not know genuine transcendence in relation to an omnipotent deity or an abstract, metaphysical Being; rather, men encounter genuine transcendence in the concrete figure of Jesus. By making Jesus the point of disclosure for transcendence, Bonhoeffer eliminates all the characteristics of religious speech. Jesus, quite clearly, is not a symbol of power; on the contrary, Bonhoeffer repeatedly insists, Jesus discloses the weakness and suffering of God.

> Here is the decisive difference between Christianity and all religions. Man's religiosity makes him look in his distress to the power of God in the world: God is the *deus ex machina*. The Bible directs man to God's powerlessness and suffering; only the suffering God can help (4:361).

Nor does Jesus qualify psychologically as the father figure who rescues men from, and compensates for, human inadequacies; Jesus is more like an older brother who paves the way for his younger siblings. To follow Jesus is not to take comfort in an all-powerful deity, but to stand fast with those in need, even through suffering and death. Finally, Jesus is not a fit subject for metaphysical speculation; his being appears through narrative accounts of his relationships with others, not from a list of metaphysical attributes. By substituting the concrete figure of Jesus for an abstract deity or Being, Bonhoeffer eliminates the theological imagery, psychological dynamics, and metaphysical categories of religious speech about God.

Second, Bonhoeffer changes the grammatical function of transcendence from a noun object of belief to a verbal act in the lives of men: transcendence means the power of ultimate transformation. Christian faith, therefore, is not a belief in transcendence, but a participation in the "transformation of all human life . . . given in the fact that 'Jesus is there only for others'" (4:381). Bonhoeffer's notion of transformation is not so vague as to include any radical change in human life. The specific meaning of transformation is directly related to the figure of Jesus. Jesus is the man who is above all else free for others.[19] "His 'being there for others' is the experience of transcendence" (4:381). Transformation, therefore, means "a new life in 'existence for others,' through participation in the being of Jesus" (4:381).

Bonhoeffer's discussion of transcendence constitutes a major break in the prevalent pattern of Christian theology, as he was the first to acknowledge. The story of Jesus has replaced man's psychological need for God as the point of departure for the life of faith. Men do not become Christian by first thinking about their "needs, problems, sins, and fears" (4:361). Rather, to "learn what God promises and what he fulfills, we must persevere in quiet meditation on the life, sayings, deeds, sufferings and death of Jesus" (4:391). Furthermore, Bonhoeffer breaks with attempts to express the transcendent meaning of Jesus by means of mythological titles, dogmatic theological formulas, or metaphysical attributes.[20] Rather, he explicates the role of Jesus as the bearer of transcendence by means of this-worldly socioethical categories.[21] Jesus is the transcendent one because he is "the man for others" (4:381). His transcendence is manifest in the transformation of all those who find "a new existence for others through participation in the being of Jesus" (4:381). In Bonhoeffer's formulation, transcendence is divested of its other-worldly status as a discreet reality infinitely distant from human life. Transcendence occurs within the fabric of man's historical life with others. "The transcendental is not infinite and unattainable tasks, but the neighbor who is within reach in any given situation" (4:381).

Bonhoeffer's prison writings present only a brief sketch of the non-religious interpretation of transcendence which he began to develop for a future book. He had not formulated his thought on this subject in a detailed and systematic manner before his death. As a result, many interpreters of Bonhoeffer have speculated concerning the theological implications of his radical revision of transcendence. Their conclusions vary considerably; some believe Bonhoeffer was moving toward a Christocentric dogmatic theology while others find support for a churchless Christianity in his thought.[22] However, there is an alternative to guessing about the possible future development of Bonhoeffer's incipient ideas. The transcendence of which Bonhoeffer speaks may be illumined by following the indirect route of describing segments of his life in prison as concrete expressions of that transcendence which is transformation.

This approach reflects the new model of transcendence which Bonhoeffer himself proposed. As long as God was understood as a discreet being located in heaven, it was possible to understand his transcendence by means of direct conceptual analysis. The categories of philosophical metaphysics and dogmatic theology have long been employed for just this purpose. However, if God is understood as an agent of transformation, active in the lives of men here and now, then one may gain insight into his transforming function only by following the indirect route of examining the lives of those who bear witness to him. Throughout his prison writings, Bonhoeffer repeatedly interprets his personal life and public deeds in relation to his participation in the being of Jesus. He also recognizes the insufficiency of ideas and the importance of human deeds in the life of faith. Following this suggestion, Bonhoeffer's life may be examined as a mode of transcendence as transformation.

Even a cursory reading of Bonhoeffer's prison writings disclose a salient characteristic of the author: the extraordinary freedom of the prisoner. For Bonhoeffer, freedom is the distinctive characteristic of Christian life. To participate in the being of Jesus is to be free; transcendence shows itself in human life as liberation. This freedom, to be sure, has a specific orientation; it is not freedom from any particular set of restrictions but it is a freedom for others.[23] For Bonhoeffer, freedom functions as the middle term between transcendence and acts of love; freedom is rooted in God and provides the necessary human condition for effectively caring for others. In delineating this kind of Christian freedom which is at the center of Bonhoeffer's life, we will describe a pattern of expanding concentric circles, beginning with personal-psychological modes of freedom moving through its interpersonal-social forms of expression to its political-ethical dimensions.

In its psychological modes, freedom entails the capacity to enjoy a personal sense of wholeness which includes conflicting inner drives, a rich diversity of external experience, and contradictory aspects of the self. Bonhoeffer contrasts his own sense of "wholeness of independent existence" with the behavior of fellow prisoners driven by overwhelming inner needs.

> I notice repeatedly here how few people there are who can harbour conflicting emotions at the same time. When bombers come, they are all fear; when there is something to eat, they are all greed; when they are disappointed, they are all despair; when they are successful, they can think of nothing else. They miss the fullness of life and the wholeness of an independent existence (4:310).

Bonhoeffer's concern for a whole self that transcends its partial drives and needs does not lead him to advocate a stoical renunciation of passion or emotion. He values the inclusion of the Song of Songs within the Bible precisely because it portrays the "ardent, passionate, sensual love" that he regards as an intrinsic part of human life (4:303). He deplores that kind of religious piety which scorns genuine sensuality as something alien to the will of God. "For a man in his wife's arms to be hankering after the other world is, in mild terms, a piece of bad taste, and not God's will" (4:168). At the same time, however, he warns a friend, recently forced to leave his bride for military duty, of the dangers of intense love (4:303). Intense passion and separation from a loved one can overpower a man, leading him to self-pity, anxious concern for his beloved, and a compulsive quest for a substitute (4:303). While desire is a good to be enjoyed, it can be destructive, if it dominates the entire self.

Bonhoeffer understands this freedom to include conflicting emotions within a personal sense of wholeness to be rooted in God. As long as the whole self has a transcendent center, all its parts can be fully expressed without dominating or determining the entire personality. Bonhoeffer uses polyphonic music as an analogy for the freedom of the whole self and the vitality of its parts. The *cantus firmus* (basic theme) of polyphonic music is like the love of God in the life of man. As long as this is clear, all the other affections may be played out to their limits (4:303). Man's love toward God does not negate his earthly affections, but provides a "firm support" for the varied loves of the heart (4:303).

The diversity of experience of which Bonhoeffer speaks includes not only inner feelings, but also the richness of the world outside the self. How does the self retain a sense of identity without excluding those experiences which are genuinely new and different? Bonhoeffer once described his open-ended, inclusive life style as "an uninterrupted enrichment of experience" rooted in faith (4:272).

> Christianity puts us into many different dimensions of life at the same time; we make room in ourselves, to some extent, for God and the whole world. . . . We have to get people out of their one-track minds; that is a kind of preparation for faith, or something that makes faith possible, although really it is only faith itself that can make possible a multidimensional life (4:310f.).

The mixture of interests which flows together in Bonhoeffer's letters—music, friends, glimpses of nature, theological ideas, and political maneuvers—provide a vivid illustration of what he means by a multidimensional life.

Bonhoeffer's distinctive sense of wholeness includes contradictory aspects of himself. This is expressed in his short poem, "Who am I?" In this poem, Bonhoeffer portrays the contradiction between the way others view him and the way he felt about himself. He first describes the attributes imputed to him by fellow prisoners and guards: a calm, cheerful, firm man, who steps from his cell's confinement like a squire from a country house; a man who speaks to his warders in a friendly, clear, and free way, as if he were in command; a smiling, proud, equable man, like one accustomed to win (4:347f.). In sharp contrast with this external appearance, he expresses his subjective experience as

> restive and longing and sick, like a bird in a cage,
> struggling for breath, as though hands were compressing my throat,

yearning for colors, for flowers, for the voices of birds,
thirsting for words of kindness, for neighborliness,
tossing in expectation of great events,
powerlessly trembling for friends at an infinite distance,
weary and empty at praying, at thinking, at making,
faint and ready to say farewell to it all (4:348).

Although he contrasts the confidence and strength observed by others
with his inner feelings of weariness and frustration, Bonhoeffer does not
deny either aspect of himself. He does not indicate a compulsion to act
out inner feelings before others or to internalize what others attribute
to him. He accepts the discrepancy between feeling and behavior as
belonging to the mystery of selfhood. Hence, in place of simplified self-
definitions of identity, Bonhoeffer ends his poem with a confession of
faith:

Who am I? They mock me, these lonely questions of mine.
Whoever I am, thou knowest, O God, I am thine (4:248).

Freedom not only means a sense of wholeness, in relation to conflicting drives, diverse experience, and contradictory aspects of the self,
freedom also includes a sense of self-continuity, especially in the midst
of an alien and destructive environment. One of the striking features of
Bonhoeffer's letters is their tone and mood. They do not sound as if
they were written by a man in prison awaiting execution. He writes
with joy about the simple pleasures to be found in nature—in a bird's
nest, an anthill, and flowers—and in music heard on the radio or, more
frequently, committed to memory. He also writes about the work he
is doing, the books he is reading and the writing projects in which he
is engaged. He speaks constantly of friends and family, sometimes in
response to their occasional visits, but, more often, in recollection of
shared holidays, birthdays, trips, and conversations. In brief, his letters
convey the impression of a man surrounded by the joys of freedom rather
than a prisoner scheduled to die.

This distinctive sense of self-continuity reflects the close personal
relationships which Bonhoeffer enjoyed with his family and friends. He
had a keen sense of the discipline necessary to keep in touch with the
past which he shared with them.

This dialogue with the past, the attempt to hold on to it and recover it,
and, above all, the fear of losing it, is the almost daily accompaniment of
my life here (4:319).

In contrast, some of his fellow prisoners seemed to lack a "moral
memory"; they enjoyed no sense of continuity in relations of love, marriage, friendship and loyalty (4:203).

Nothing sticks fast, nothing holds firm; everything is here today and gone tomorrow. But the good things of life—truth, justice, and beauty—all great accomplishments need time, constancy, and "memory" or they degenerate. The man who feels neither responsibility towards the past nor desire to shape the future is one who "forgets," and I do not know how one can really get at such a person and bring him to his senses (4:203).

Those who forgot past personal relationships were wholly determined by their immediate environment. Bonhoeffer, in contrast, was able to transcend prison life, not only because of a felt continuity with friends and family, but also because of his trust in God. As he reviewed his past, including his years in prison, he found no part of it meaningless or wasted (4:289).

Someone said that the last years had been completely wasted. . . . I am very glad that I have not yet had that feeling, even for a moment. Nor have I ever regretted my decision in the summer of 1939 [to leave America and return to Germany], for I am firmly convinced—however strange it may seem—that my life has followed a straight and unbroken course. . . . If I were to end my life here in these conditions, that would have a meaning that I think I could understand; on the other hand, everything might be a thorough preparation for a new start and a new task when peace comes (4:272).

Bonhoeffer's sense of self-continuity is embedded in a larger purpose that transcends the limits of his particular life history. He does not look back upon the past with regrets or anticipate the future with dread, for "as I see it, I am here for some purpose and I only hope I may fulfill it" (4:289).

While Bonhoeffer's sense of self-continuity allowed him to transcend the debilitating effects of prison life, he had a firm grasp of the reality of his situation. He neither denies the harsh reality of prison life nor wishes for a magical escape from the fate that awaits him. On the contrary, he understands maturity as involving a clear acceptance of one's situation, regardless of how bad it might be.

Is it not characteristic of a man, in contrast to the immature person, that his centre of gravity is always where he actually is, and that the longing for fulfillment of his wishes cannot prevent him from being his whole self, wherever he happens to be? . . . There is a wholeness about the fully grown man which enables him to face an existing situation squarely (4:233).

This contrast between "the immature person" and "the fully grown man" parallels Bonhoeffer's correlation between the freedom of faith and human maturity.

Bonhoeffer's discussion of freedom is not confined to personal-psychological modes of maturity. Indeed, freedom is not defined primarily negatively—as freedom from psychic problems or social pressures—but positively, as freedom for others. In interpersonal relationships, this means both the freedom to commit oneself to others as well as the freedom to be oneself within the context of these relationships. Bonhoeffer's letters reveal the depth of his involvement with other persons: friends and relations in the world outside, and fellow prisoners who were close to him. Bonhoeffer contrasted this concern for personal relationships with the impersonal, detached posture of the scientific bureaucrat.

> In the long run, human relationships are the most important thing in life; the modern "efficient" man can do nothing to change this, nor can the demi-gods and lunatics who know nothing about human relationships (4:386).

While Bonhoeffer's personal commitments to others were strong, they were also free from guilt and sentimentality. He was not driven by a sense of obligation to be nice to all men. He was free to be angry, to speak frankly with those he loved, and, at times, to speak harshly to those who would become dependent on his kindness and burden him with their self-pity. His love for others was, above all else, a free love, a love that did not require him to violate his own integrity, a love rooted neither in the duty of conscience nor the dependent needs of childhood.

Bonhoeffer's commitment to other persons, and his sense of interdependence with them, qualifies his theme of autonomy. Bonhoeffer obviously did not regard the human self as autonomous in the sense of being absolutely independent. On the contrary, he saw the self as inseparably bound to others. He made no pretense of being self-sufficient himself. He repeatedly acknowledged the many ways in which he was dependent upon his family and friends: for their gifts of food, books, and small luxuries to sustain him in prison, for their visits, and for their continuing concern and love (4:150). From this experience, he realized that "wholeness of independent existence" was not acquired by a person in isolation, "but only together with others" (4:200). The lonely individualist or the self-made man was an abstract entity for Bonhoeffer, bearing little resemblance to the reality of his experience.

To accept one's interdependence with others is also to accept responsibility for them. Thus, "wholeness of independent existence" is not an end in itself but a condition of life which enables men to be free for others. Without this sense of wholeness, people tend to

> cling to their own desires, and so have no interest in others; they no longer listen and are incapable of loving their neighbor (4:233f.).

Similarly, a person needs a sense of personal continuity and autonomy to sustain him in moments of anxious concern and crisis; otherwise he becomes so overwhelmed by the pressures of the moment as to be incapable of caring about what is happening to others (4:372). Indeed, all the personal-psychological modes of freedom are not simply goals for an isolated individual, but necessary resources for man's distinctive "freedom for others."

Just as freedom may not be construed as an individual attribute, so "freedom for others" may not be confined within the sphere of interpersonal relations.[24] Bonhoeffer was imprisoned and executed because he enacted his "freedom for others" in the political arena. The exercise of this political freedom was decisive in shaping his thought, especially his ethics. During the time he was an agent of the Resistance Movement and a political prisoner of the German state, Bonhoeffer formulated a distinctive ethical position which directly reflected his political experience.

As a member of a political conspiracy committed to the assassination of Hitler and the overthrow of the Nazi government, Bonhoeffer was clearly violating both the laws of the state and the "laws of conscience," most obviously the prohibition against murder. It is not surprising, therefore, that he formulates his ethics during this period as a "contest between conscience and concrete responsibility" (3:247). Natural conscience, which is seemingly altruistic, was interpreted by Bonhoeffer as a deceptive device for the preservation of entrenched self-interest. This conscience was not a resource leading men to serve the concrete needs of their neighbors, but a means for undermining genuine responsibility for others (3:242).

Fear of transgressing the moral laws of conscience led many of Bonhoeffer's fellow citizens to give passive support to the Nazi regime. Such people had to be content "with a salved instead of a clear conscience" (4:4). Unwilling to accept the guilt involved in political disobedience, they became unwilling supporters of the evils perpetrated by the state. Others, who gave active support to Nazi policies, justified their deeds by claiming that they were only doing their duty by following orders. As Bonhoeffer notes, "The man of duty will in the end have to do his duty by the devil too" (4:5). Neither the laws of the state, the moral laws of conscience, nor the claims of duty and obedience were sufficient resources to guard against the dehumanizing consequences of Nazi rule. On the contrary, these sources of traditional morality were utilized by the Nazis as allies in their cause.[25]

Bonhoeffer therefore articulated his ethic of "free responsibility" in explicit opposition to the prevalent morality of natural conscience. He described his ethic in terms of freedom because, for the free man, nothing can become the governing law of his action, a law to which he can withdraw, to which he can appeal as an authority, and by which he can be exculpated and acquitted. For in that case he would indeed no longer be truly free (3:248-249).

No principles of morality, no system of moral teachings, and no religious authority is available as a self-justifying basis for ethical decisions. This ethic is also described in terms of responsibility, for man is called upon to exercise freedom from conscience in response to the concrete needs of others.

> The conscience which has been set free is not timid like the conscience which is still bound by law, but it stands wide open for our neighbor and his concrete distress (3:244).

To be sure, the responsibility of the free man is not exercised in the crystal clear light of good and evil, right and wrong. Only a moralistic conscience, concerned more with its own sense of security than responsibility for the lives of others, believes that ethical decisions are made in terms of moral absolutes. For Bonhoeffer, free responsibility necessarily involves one in ambiguous ethical decisions. One does not choose between right and wrong, but between right and right, or one wrong and another. Responsible freedom "is performed wholly within the domain of relativity, wholly in the twilight which the historical situation spreads over good and evil" (3:249). As a result, the exercise of free responsibility may entail guilt. "The conscience which has been set free from the law will not be afraid to enter into the guilt of another man for the other's sake" (3:244). Indeed, Bonhoeffer sees the process of moral maturation in terms of personal growth from a morality oriented toward personal innocence and determined by laws of conscience to an ethic of free responsibility capable of assuming guilt and directed toward action on behalf of the neighbor (3:247).

The critique of natural conscience and defense of free responsibility, which grew out of Bonhoeffer's experience in the Resistance Movement, was reinforced by his prison experiences. During his first year and a half in prison, the German authorities were not fully informed of the scope and plot of the Resistance Movement (2:703ff.,714ff.). While suspicious of the activities of Bonhoeffer and others arrested with him, they only had evidence to support minor charges, such as the possible misuse of government funds and Bonhoeffer's alleged illegal exemption from military service. As a result, Bonhoeffer and other imprisoned conspirators engaged in a systematic deception to protect the continuing work of the Resistance as well as the lives of those involved.

In this situation, Bonhoeffer wrote his essay "On Telling the Truth" in explicit response to Immanuel Kant's ethic of duty. According to Kant, if a murderer broke into a house and asked if the owner's friend, whom he was pursuing, was in the house, the owner would be obliged to answer that he was. To do otherwise would violate the general norm of truth-telling; no specific detail about the situation, such as the fact that one man is a known murderer and the other a friend, could legitimately qualify the demand for truth. Bonhoeffer rejects the Kantian claim that an abstract moral principle—like truth-telling—is an ultimate and sufficient norm for human conduct.

> Telling the truth is not simply a matter of moral character; it is also a matter of correct appreciation of real situations and of serious reflection upon them (3:364).

One cannot exclude reality considerations from moral decision-making, even if its inclusion muddies the purity of moral principles.

> The ethical cannot be detached from reality, and consequently continual progress in learning to appreciate reality is a necessary ingredient in ethical action (3:365).

Moral principles, for Bonhoeffer, are situational in their origin and function. We learn the demand for truthful speech in the context of the family. We soon learn that contexts other than the family require a different kind of truth from us. For example, if a teacher asks a child in front of his class whether his father comes home drunk, the child may answer with "a lie . . . that contains more truth . . . than if he had betrayed his father's weakness in front of the class" (3:368). Preferable to lying in response to questions of this sort is to furnish answers which avoid formal lies while concealing the real truth (3:368). This, in fact, is precisely what Bonhoeffer did in response to daily interrogations. He became highly skilled in providing factually true information for his inquisitors while simultaneously slanting this information so as to conceal the actual truth of the conspiracy plot. Like Kant's householder confronting a known murderer and an embarrassed child facing his class, Bonhoeffer confronted a situation which called for skills in not lying while concealing the truth.

Bonhoeffer understood freedom from the claims of conscience and for the concrete reality of others to be an expression of his participation in transcendence. "Natural conscience," he wrote, "is overcome by the conscience which is set free in Jesus Christ" (3:244). Because "Jesus became a breaker of the law," Bonhoeffer felt he could also violate the law (3:244). Because Jesus entered fully into the shared guilt of humanity, Bonhoeffer accepted the guilt of political conspiracy and deception

(3:244). For Bonhoeffer, the natural conscience of man, with its timidity, concern for personal innocence, and fear of risk, does not naturally or easily disappear. The liberation of man from the tyranny of conscience is not a process which a man can effect by himself or for himself; rather, for Bonhoeffer, it is a process which happens in and for the man who finds his life rooted in the reality of God in Christ. Bonhoeffer has no more confidence in the free and independent conscience of secular man than he has in the moralistic conscience of his fellow German citizens. Both are equally untrustworthy.

> Who stands fast? Only the man whose final standard is not his reason, his principles, his conscience, his freedom, or his virtue, but who is ready to sacrifice all this when he is called to obedient and responsible action in faith and in exclusive allegiance to God—the responsible man who tries to make his whole life an answer to the question and call of God (4:5).

Freedom, for Bonhoeffer, has its corollary in commitment, commitment not to laws but to Christ (3:252). Otherwise, freedom becomes nothing but arbitrary self-will (3:252).

The transcendence to which Bonhoeffer pointed is not an alien deity lodged in the distant heavens and awaiting the arrival of disembodied souls. Rather, Bonhoeffer's transcendence is inseparably bound up with human life, incarnate in the Person of Jesus and known through the transformation of all those who find their lives shaped by his story. This transformation, in turn, is not a vague spiritual experience—some kind of mystical ego trip—but a fleshing out of radical freedom expressed in the personal, interpersonal, and political dimensions of human life.

4. RESISTANCE WITH COMPASSION

During Bonhoeffer's confinement in the Tegel prison, a fellow prisoner asked him how he as a Christian pastor could participate in the active resistance against Hitler. Bonhoeffer answered with a story. If he, as a pastor, saw a drunken driver racing at high speed down a street crowded with people, he did not consider it his only or chief duty to bury the victims or comfort their relatives; it was more important to wrench the wheel out of the hands of the madman driving (14:82).

This vignette expresses in a simple way the distinctive character of Bonhoeffer's thought. Christians of most persuasion would find Bonhoeffer's compassionate concern for others to be congenial with their faith. Throughout the ages, Christians have accepted responsibility for aiding those oppressed by the inequities of history. Few Christians, however, would feel comfortable with Bonhoeffer's suggestion that compassion also entailed a responsibility to alter the course of history, "to wrench the wheel out of the hands of the madman driving." In contrast, political revolutionaries would find Bonhoeffer's active resistance of evil more familiar. Mao, Che and their fellow revolutionaries have long accepted their responsibility for stopping the "madman drivers" of history, for stripping oppressive governments of power, · and for establishing better conditions of life for their people. However, political revolutionaries would find Bonhoeffer's concern for compassion alien to their own ventures. In revolutions, the end justifies the means, and as Frantz Fanon has argued, people may enact on others their most violent instincts as a cathartic ritual. For compassion is as alien to revolution as resistance is to traditional Christianity.

Bonhoeffer's distinctive form of faith provided a new basis for Christian social concern. Unlike traditional Christianity, which passively accepted the status quo while busily meeting individual religious needs, Bonhoeffer's version of "religionless" Christianity invites men to commit themselves to the liberation of the oppressed in their society. Christian faith, for Bonhoeffer, includes both a particular view of social reality, which identifies arenas of oppression and human misery with the presence of the biblical God, and a commitment to act with the oppressed to change their fate. At the same time, Bonhoeffer's vision of Christian social action differed considerably from the more optimistic programs of liberal theology and the Social Gospel movement of the 1920's. Bonhoeffer did not envision a new society freed from injustice and inequity emerging as a result of Christian social action; his commitment to resist evil by intervening in political processes was far more limited than this older Utopian goal. Even in relation to the limited goal of resistance, Bonhoeffer was aware of the dubious chance of success. He learned of the failure of the Resistance Movement while he was himself in prison, and this failure dramatized the vast discrepancy in power between established governments and individuals organized in groups for political purposes. Bonhoeffer, therefore, invites others to stand with the oppressed and suffering, not on the basis of pragmatic calculations of success, but on the basis of faith alone. For Bonhoeffer, "participation in the sufferings of God in the secular life" is at the heart of Christian faith (4:361). As an action of faith, the commitment to "share in God's sufferings at the hands of a godless world" is self-authenticating, and not measured by norms of victory or defeat (4:361).

For many American Christians who protested against government policy in Vietnam and racism at home, Dietrich Bonhoeffer offered a decisive model of resistance and compassion. Father Daniel Berrigan, the Jesuit priest arrested at Catonsville, Maryland for destroying draft files, suggested something of his identification with Protestant Bonhoeffer in a review of the latter's biography.[26] Berrigan began writing his poem-review on April 9, 1970, the twenty-fifth anniversary of Bonhoeffer's death and the first day in which Berrigan himself became a "fugitive from injustice," hiding in the homes of friends and hunted by the FBI (1:17).

> I think I know the direction of Bonhoeffer's life—even from afar! Sitting on the floor of a bedroom in a country area, curtains drawn, totally dependent on the risk-taking of a few friends, reading and meditating, realizing in one's deepest being how few will understand, speaking the truth even when the ears of men seem turned to stone. I think I understand (1:20).

Like Bonhoeffer, Berrigan had first to learn the ineffectiveness of "churchy stuff . . . corporate decisions . . . waiting on the awakening of others . . . the hope for gradualism, for church or state reform" (1:17-18). Like Bonhoeffer, he was suspicious of the authenticity of his church, "no more than a state function (a White House Sunday morning), the state flag its emblem also, the cross bent at its four extremities, a swastika" (1:18). Finally, like Bonhoeffer, Berrigan had also come to learn that

> Political man is a synonym for believing man. . . .
> Perhaps the matter should be put more simply: political man is the natural term of man, his adulthood (1:20).

Believing man is political and adult man: this conjunction comes naturally to Berrigan and also to Bonhoeffer. It is a conjunction which explains how Bonhoeffer could meet both the psychological agenda of Sigmund Freud and the political concerns of Dan Berrigan. For psychology and politics were simply two different sides of Christianity, as Bonhoeffer knew it. On the one hand, he rejected both the regressive psychological dynamics of religion and its corresponding privatized, apolitical form of expression. Those who refused to accept responsibility for the future shape of history were, in Bonhoeffer's eyes, something less than mature men: like religious personalities preoccupied with questions of individual salvation, their normal development had stopped sometime before reaching its natural goal. "Religious" Christianity was, therefore, rejected by Bonhoeffer, because of both its politics and psychology. On the other hand, Bonhoeffer's faith in Christ led him to join the Resistance Movement and to suffer the consequences of this decision. Entering the arena of political action, however, did not mean the loss of his personal faith. On the contrary, his writings clearly disclose the importance of this faith as a resource of strength in coping with the incredible difficulties that befall a double agent and political prisoner. Like religion, faith has its psychological dimensions as well as its political form of expression. While faith in Christ may not appear as a compensation for individual inadequacies, it most assuredly is a source of strength for those whose commitment to others have exposed them to situations of extreme stress.

Robert Coles, who works in the psychoanalytical tradition of Sigmund Freud and Erik Erikson, has explored the role of faith as a resource of strength for persons in situations of unusual stress. Coles has published a study of children in the South and North who lived through school integration crises. He also conducted a series of interviews with college students whose short-term summer work with rural communities in the South led them to make long-term commitments as "community-organizers." A series of interviews with one of these young men during the years 1962 through 1970 discloses the emergence of a pattern of faith similar to Bonhoeffer's. Like other young blacks from the South, this man rejected the religion of his childhood during his college days. His old religion gave God's blessing to social and economic oppression, as if black people were "lucky to suffer, to be poor, and have no rights, because they'll get into Heaven later on" (5:4). Like Bonhoeffer, he had chosen to accept a position laden with incredible dangers and difficulties. He lives his daily life in the midst of "fear and danger and threats" (5:4). He becomes disappointed and angry with fellow blacks who fail him and themselves. Each year of his work discloses new complexities and problems which elude any quick, easy solution. And, to add to all this, he has given up his private ambition for a college degree and future career. At times, he doubts his decision:

> Maybe the best thing to do is to go along and live as comfortably as you can—with just enough political involvement to soothe your conscience, but not enough activity to get you into real trouble and cause you to jeopardize yourself, take real risks—I mean risks that shake up your whole way of living (5:4).

In the midst of his fear, anger, disappointment and self-doubt, the young man discovers two sources of strength. The first is "the community, the sense of shared suffering and sometimes joy"; "they're all my people, my family, and I'm one of them" (5:10). The second is the faith he learns from the people of his community.

> But they "keep the faith," they'll say to you. And I guess they've taught me to do so—pray as they do and try to match in my mind their ability to talk with God and "gain some of His strength," as they'll put it (5:10).

He gives all he can and receives a great deal from people who give much, though they are poor. And he prays. He prays for himself, for his people, for the whole world, and especially "for the little children I've seen get born since I've been living in this county" (5:10). Like Bonhoeffer, his faith and prayer is not directed toward a distant and all-powerful deity, but to the suffering God of the Bible present with his people.

> I pray to God that He sees His brothers here, His sons and daughters here. . . . They're suffering like He did, like His son did. They are the poor and the meek, but they're fed up underneath, I'll tell you (5:4).

The voices of Dan Berrigan and an anonymous southern black highlight the particularity and universality of Bonhoeffer's theology. The faith of which Bonhoeffer speaks is clearly rooted in a matrix of commitment and compassion. Those who remain detached from the suffering of others may intellectually understand Bonhoeffer's critique of religion, but miss the existential relevance of his positive statement of faith. However, Berrigan and the young community-organizer also disclose the universality of Bonhoeffer's vision. "Religionless" Christianity is obviously not confined to the aristocratic, German, Protestant, scholarly traditions represented by Bonhoeffer; clearly he is speaking of a faith which transcends the limits of class, nation, denomination and education. A medieval figure like St. Francis or a modern American like Martin Luther King also represent a faith active in resisting human oppression and degradation. While Bonhoeffer made many new observations concerning the psychological dynamics of religion and Christianity, the faith which shaped his life and death were not new but rooted in a larger tradition to which he also bore witness.

NOTES

[1] Dietrich Bonhoeffer's father, Karl Bonhoeffer, was the first professor of psychiatry at the University of Berlin. Because of his father's profession, some authors have speculated that Dietrich became familiar with Freud's psychoanalytic writings through his father; see, for example, Thomas C. Oden, "Theology and Therapy: a New Look at Bonhoeffer," *Dialogue*, V (Spring, 1966), 98-111. However, Eberhard Bethge has pointed out that Karl Bonhoeffer, because of his empirical orientation and neurological training, was suspicious of the validity of Freud's work (2:11-12). In Dietrich's own writings, there are no references to Freud's works nor were Freud's books in Dietrich's personal library. While he offers some superficial criticism or psychotherapeutic concerns for sexuality, it seems clear that Dietrich was not versed in Freud's general theory or his writings on religion.

[2] As early as his doctoral dissertation, Bonhoeffer stressed "the social intention of all the basic Christian concepts"; see Dietrich Bonhoeffer, *The Communion of Saints: a Dogmatic Inquiry into the Sociology of the Church* (New York:

Harper & Row, 1963), p. 13. In this difficult book, Bonhoeffer explicates both the interpersonal and corporate dimensions of the self; see, especially, pp. 30-37; 52; 82-85. A more readable introduction to Bonhoeffer's social view of the self may be found in his *Creation and Fall. Temptation* (New York: Macmillan, 1965); see esp. pp. 35-40 and 57-63.

3 Freud's criticism of Christian love as an unrealistic and repressive demand of the superego appears in *Civilization and Its Discontents* (New York: W. W. Norton, 1962), p. 56ff.

4 For a description of the circumstances that led to Bonhoeffer's proposed residence in America and his sudden return to Germany, see Bethge's biography (2:552-565).

5 For a study of the Confessing Church movement in Germany, see Arthur C. Cochrane, *The Church's Confession under Hitler* (Philadelphia: Westminster Press, 1962).

6 Several excellent historical studies of the German Resistance Movement have been written: Harold C. Deutsch, *The Conspiracy against Hitler in the Twilight War* (Minneapolis: University of Minnesota Press, 1968); Constantine Fitz Gibbon, *20 July* (New York: Berkley, 1956); Fabian von Schlabrendorff, *The Secret War against Hitler* (New York: Pitman, 1965) and *They Almost Killed Hitler* (New York: Macmillan, 1947). For a critical view of the ethics and strategy of the Resistance Movement focusing on Bonhoeffer's role and writings, see Larry L. Rasmussen, *Dietrich Bonhoeffer: Reality and Resistance* (Nashville: Abingdon Press, 1972).

7 Bonhoeffer's most effective link with the Allies was George Bell, Bishop of Chichester. After Bonhoeffer met with Bell in Sweden in June, 1942, Bell communicated with Anthony Eden, foreign secretary of England, and J. S. Winant, the American ambassador to England. For a variety of diplomatic and internal political reasons, both the British and the American governments were unwilling to meet with representatives of the Resistance Movement, or even publicly to acknowledge the existence of such a movement. Bishop Bell gives a brief account of these negotiations in "The Church and the Resistance Movement" (14:196-212). Correspondence in English between Bonhoeffer, Bell, and Anthony Eden has been published in *Gesammelte Schriften*, ed. E. Bethge (Munich: Chr. Kaiser, 1965), vol. I, pp. 372-417.

8 In his earlier writings, Bonhoeffer had articulated several themes in his criticism of religion which were most fully expressed in the *Letters and Papers from Prison*. He rejected religion as a purely spiritual, inner, pious feeling which offered "emotional uplift" and was based in human needs and desires; see, for example, *The Cost of Discipleship* (New York: Macmillan, 1963), pp. 63 and 98; *Life Together* (New York: Harper & Row, 1954), pp. 26f., 37; and *The Way To Freedom* (New York: Harper & Row, 1966), pp. 70 and 230f. In other writings Bonhoeffer was critical of religion as wishfulness which expected God to satisfy men's personal needs and bolster their social institutions, a theme central in the prison letters: see *Gesammelte Schriften* IV, pp. 65f. and 142, and *No Rusty Swords* (New York: Harper & Row, 1965), pp. 66 and 244f. Another theme developed further in the *Letters* is the provincial, limited character of religion, in contrast to genuine faith which informs the whole life: see, for example, *The Way to Freedom*, p. 232, note 1. Again, his attack on the otherworldliness of religion is found in a 1932 address, "Thy Kingdom Come!"; otherworldliness is rooted in human weakness whereas Christ "makes man strong" (7:28-29). The early writings, however, do not develop the comprehensive historical, psychological and theological critique of religion found in the *Letters and Papers from Prison;* prior to the letters Bonhoeffer had not

articulated the insight of "man's coming of age" which is decisive for his later critique. Therefore, this chapter focuses on the analysis of religion developed in the *Letters and Papers from Prison.* I am indebted to my colleague, Professor Clifford Green, for these references to Bonhoeffer's early writings on religion and also for sharing insights and other information from his Bonhoeffer research. Green's dissertation on Bonhoeffer is being prepared for publication. Meanwhile, one of his articles is directly relevant to this chapter: see "Bonhoeffer's Concept of Religion," *Union Seminary Quarterly Review,* 19:1 (November, 1963), 11-21.

[9] Friedrich Nietzsche consistently identified Christianity as a religion of weakness; see, for example, *Beyond Good and Evil* (New York: Random House, 1966), pp. 57-76, or *The Genealogy of Morals* (Garden City, N. Y.: Doubleday, 1956), pp. 166-188. Bonhoeffer read Nietzsche throughout the course of his life, a reading habit reflected in his own criticism of religion.

[10] David Hume identified similar natural conditions as constitutive for the origins of religion; see Chapter 1, pp. 18-19.

[11] A German scholar, Ernst Feil, has demonstrated that Bonhoeffer's version of the development of Western history reflects his reading, while in prison, of the writings of Wilhelm Dilthey.

[12] *De Veritate* by Lord Herbert of Cherbury was published in 1624. This book became the most influential source for the development of English natural theology in the seventeenth and eighteenth centuries. See Chapter 1, pp. 26-27, notes 9 and 10.

[13] From Bultmann's Neo-Kantian perspective, autonomy is an attribute of reason rooted in the history of scientific thought. From Bonhoeffer's social perspective, autonomy is an attribute of personality rooted in changing patterns of psychosocial history. Bultmann, therefore, related the Christian faith to the autonomy of modern man by stripping away the pre-scientific world view of the New Testament or demythologizing. Bonhoeffer's view of autonomy, however, required him to go beyond Bultmann by criticizing the psychological dynamics of man's religious relation to God. Hence, Bonhoeffer is critical of Bultmann because "he did not go far enough" (4:285).

[14] For the origins of the phrase "God-hypothesis," see the discussion of Newton and Laplace, Chapter 1, note 12.

[15] The theological grounds for the separation of "religion" and "faith" was first articulated by Karl Barth in his 1918 *Epistle to the Romans* (London: Oxford University Press, 1933), esp. ch. 7, and, in a revised form, in his *Church Dogmatics,* I:2 (Edinburgh, T. & T. Clark, 1956), pp. 297-324.

[16] Bonhoeffer does not use the term "dereligionize"; as a parallel to Bultmann's "demythologize," it is a convenient term to suggest his intention.

[17] Bonhoeffer would have to include Bultmann in his criticism of "religious theologies." Bultmann affirmed the Kantian separation of rational knowledge and religious faith and insisted that men met God precisely in encounter situations which disclosed their limits.

[18] For a brief comment on the way in which Bonhoeffer's Resistance partners, including his brothers, provided the occasion for his reflections on "religionless Christianity," see Eberhard Bethge, "Turning Points in Bonhoeffer's Life and Thought" (13:88-89; 96-97).

[19] For Bonhoeffer, the freedom of God was shown in the freedom of Jesus for other men. This was not a new theme of *Letters and Papers.* . . . Previously,

Bonhoeffer had criticized Barth's early writings because of a formalistic interpretation of the freedom of God. Against Barth, Bonhoeffer insisted that Jesus disclosed God's freedom as a freedom for man: *Act and Being* (New York: Harper & Row, 1962), p. 90f. This is a theological root for Bonhoeffer's understanding of Jesus and the Christian life in the prison letters.

20 While Bonhoeffer's theological criticism of religion takes up many themes first stated by Karl Barth, Bonhoeffer is also critical of Barth because he still presents the Christian faith in terms of classical dogmas like the Virgin birth and the Trinity (4:286).

21 From the beginning of his theological writings, Bonhoeffer always interpreted transcendence in socioethical terms. The social formulation of transcendence in terms of Jesus' "being free for others," so characteristic of the prison writings, is a strong echo of Bonhoeffer's early writings; see, for example, *The Communion of Saints*, pp. 33 and 127-130; or, *Christ the Center* (New York: Harper & Row, 1966), pp. 28, 30f., 48, and 51.

22 John Godsey interprets Bonhoeffer as developing a Christocentric theology: *The Theology of Dietrich Bonhoeffer* (London: SCM Press, 1960). John Phillips sees the later Bonhoeffer as a proponent for a churchless Christianity: *Christ for Us in the Theology of Dietrich Bonhoeffer* (New York: Harper & Row, 1967).

23 As early as 1932, Bonhoeffer insisted that human freedom be understood in strictly social terms as man's freedom for others: *Creation and Fall*, esp. pp. 37f. and 48.

24 From the time of his early writings, Bonhoeffer has insisted that both the individual and the Christian community have a responsibility for ethical action on behalf of corporate bodies like the state; see for example, the abstruse discussion in *The Communion of Saints*, pp. 82-85, and the more popular statement in *Preface to Bonhoeffer* (ed. Godsey), p. 33.

25 Bonhoeffer's brief essay, "After Ten Years," provides a convenient introduction to several ethical approaches which he judged to be bankrupt in light of his experience with Nazism (4:1-17).

26 Berrigan also has a chapter discussing Bonhoeffer in his book, *No Bars to Manhood* (New York: Doubleday, 1970), part two, ch. 3.

BIBLIOGRAPHY

1. BERRIGAN, DANIEL, "The Passion of Dietrich Bonhoeffer," *Saturday Review.* (May 30, 1970), 17-22.

2. BETHGE, EBERHARD, *Dietrich Bonhoeffer.* London: Collins, 1970.

3. BONHOEFFER, DIETRICH, *Ethics.* New York: Macmillan, 1965.

4. ———, *Letters and Papers from Prison.* Enlarged Edition. New York: Macmillan, 1972.

5. COLES, ROBERT, "What Is Right Has to be Done." Adapted from "Psychological Sanctity and Social Protest," a William James Lecture on Religious Experience. *Harvard Today.* (March, 1971), 3-10.

6. DUMAS, ANDRÉ, *Dietrich Bonhoeffer: Theologian of Reality.* New York: Macmillan, 1971.

7. GODSEY, JOHN, ed., *Preface to Bonhoeffer.* Philadelphia: Fortress Press, 1965.

8. MARTY, MARTIN E., ed., *The Place of Bonhoeffer.* New York: Association Press, 1962.

9. MOLTMANN, JÜRGEN, and JÜRGEN WEISSBACH, *Two Studies in the Theology of Bonhoeffer.* New York: Scribner's, 1967.

10. RASMUSSEN, LARRY L., *Dietrich Bonhoeffer: Reality and Resistance.* Nashville: Abingdon Press, 1972.

11. REIST, BENJAMIN, *The Promise of Bonhoeffer.* Philadelphia: Lippincott, 1969.

12. SMITH, R. GREGOR, ed., *World Come of Age.* Philadelphia: Fortress Press, 1967.

13. VORKINK, PETER, ed., *Bonhoeffer in a World Come of Age.* Philadelphia: Fortress Press, 1968.

14. ZIMMERMAN, WOLF-DIETER, and R. GREGOR SMITH, eds., *I Knew Dietrich Bonhoeffer.* New York: Harper & Row, 1966.

SUGGESTED READINGS

1. *Primary Readings*

The basic sources for Bonhoeffer's criticism of religion and his "nonreligious interpretation of Christianity" are: *Letters and Papers from Prison* (4:esp. 3-17; 278-410); and *Ethics* (3:esp. 196-206, 354-373).

2. *Secondary Readings*

Eberhard Bethge, who edited *Letters and Papers from Prison* and *Ethics,* has also written several helpful introductions to Bonhoeffer's life and thought. Two brief essays by Bethge discuss the changing shape of Bonhoeffer's theology in relation to events in his life: "The Challenge of Dietrich Bonhoeffer's Life and Theology," in *World Come of Age* (12:22-88); and "Turning Points in Bonhoeffer's Life and Thought," *Bonhoeffer in a World Come of Age* (13:73-102). Bethge's biography, *Dietrich Bonhoeffer* (2), includes sections summarizing and interpreting Bonhoeffer's theological writings as well as giving an interesting and thorough account of his life.

3. *Additional Bibliography*

English translations of Bonhoeffer's writings as well as books and articles about Bonhoeffer in English appear in *Bonhoeffer in a World Come of Age* (13:133-140).

ERIK H. ERIKSON 10

Psychosocial Resources for Faith

If Bonhoeffer provides a theological response to Freud's critique of religion, Erik H. Erikson (b. 1902) presents an alternative psychoanalytic reading of religious phenomena. Like Bonhoeffer, Erikson responds to Freud by focusing upon mature forms of religion as contrasted with the immature phenomena analyzed by the founder of psychoanalysis, but he does so from the perspective of a trained analyst rather than from the standpoint of Christian theology. While many of Erikson's conclusions regarding the adulthood of religious leaders, like Luther and Gandhi, are strikingly similar to those associated with Bonhoeffer's mature Christian man, Erikson does not confine religious maturity to Christian forms of existence.

Erikson's seminal contributions to psychology and to the scientific study of religion contain responses to each of Freud's three-pronged challenge to 1) the classical religious doctrine of man, 2) the validity of religious beliefs, and 3) the psychological benefits of faith. With respect to the classical portrait of man, Erikson views Freud's alternative portrait as truncated. While he accepts the validity of Freud's basic thesis regarding the influence of unconscious factors upon the so-called higher mental and spiritual processes, Erikson argues that the real men and women we know and are have capacities ignored by Freud. In addition to unconscious memories and drives, ego anxieties, and superego constraints, Erikson emphasizes man's capacity for creativity, inventiveness, ingenuity, and resourcefulness.[1] Because man is endowed with these and other ego capacities, man (and this *does* include woman) is not only pushed from behind by unknown causal processes in the basement workshop of the psyche, he is also able to creatively transcend these forces by positing new forms of existence and behavior. In contrast with Freud, who always looked in the past for the driving, unconscious forces determining behavior, Erikson endeavors to uncover those strengths that enable individuals to transcend these powerful influences. How, he asks, does a child from an emotionally impoverished home and a destructive slum environment somehow overcome these seemingly overwhelming handicaps? What creative strengths in man enable a psychic cripple to become a great leader of men, even a world-famous hero? These are some of the questions that derive from Erikson's altered perspective on human nature.

In addition to modifying Freud's concept of human nature, Erikson also responds to Freud's assertion that religion is an illusion caused by unconscious desires, like the wish for a father substitute. He does so by pointing to the complex causal factors involved in the formation of religious beliefs.[2] In addition to ego anxieties, infantile memories of parental protection, and desires to be similarly protected in adulthood, religious beliefs are influenced by a variety of other causal variables: cultural beliefs and values, institutional patterns (especially culturally diverse family relationships), interpersonal dialogue, cognitive judgments, existential dilemmas, and creative innovations. Socially shared religious beliefs cannot be reduced to, or explained by, purely intrapsychic processes, Erikson maintains, because these beliefs are in large part the achievement of generations of men interacting in social groups. Even the highly idiosyncratic beliefs of a religious innovator cannot be accounted for exclusively in terms of infantile memories and unconscious processes, for these beliefs are invariably altered forms of traditional social concepts. Erikson, therefore, refuses to restrict himself to strictly psychological explanations of religion, arguing that numerous other factors must also be taken into account.

Erikson also objects, in responding to Freud's treatment of religion as an illusion, to the assumption that the meaning of religious beliefs can be re-interpreted exclusively in terms of unconscious motivations. For the meaning of religious symbols—like "God," the "Torah," and the "Cross"—are simply too complex to denote a single, even unconscious, referent. What is at stake in this argument with Freudian reductionism is the crucial difference between a sign and a symbol. When Freud interprets religious symbols, he tends—although not exclusively—to view them as signs, that is, they are interpreted as pointing, like a roadsign, to a single phenomenon, e.g., an unconscious memory. A snake or a tower in a myth, for instance, are representations of the penis, while a dark well represents the vagina. In contrast with this mode of interpretation, Erikson views symbols, like God and the flag, as having more than one referent or meaning.[3] The word "God" conjures up a rich range of associations, including cosmic love, the power of justice in the world, the image of a great monarch on a heavenly throne, Christ on the cross, universal forgiveness, the Last Judgment, and so on. Because religious symbols invariably express multiple meanings, they cannot be reduced to a single set of meanings, such as those suggested by the father of the Oedipal complex. Consequently, Erikson rejects all forms of reductionism, despite his belief that psychoanalysis can shed considerable light on some of the unconscious meanings associated with religious beliefs. In other words, Erikson admits that psychology can uncover previously unconscious meanings expressed by religious beliefs, but it cannot, as reductionists suppose, translate the entire meaning of religious beliefs in terms of unconscious psychic phenomena. For the religious words and images by which men deal with the manifold experiences of human life transcend unconscious meanings.

Third, and finally, Erikson responds to Freud's claim that religion is psychologically dysfunctional—i.e., infantile and repressive—by pointing to religious beliefs that support mature ego strengths, like intimacy, generativity, and integrity, as well as adult virtues, such as mutual love, care, and wisdom.[4] Immature and repressive forms of religiosity exist, but religion at its best reenforces highly desirable, mature, ego strengths. Indeed, Erikson goes so far as to suggest that every mature adult needs some sort of religion, whether it be a traditional one or a form of secular humanism, to render ideological support for mature love, intimacy, and personal integrity. Religious ideologies not only suppress drives and guide their sublimation, then, they also support the primary function of every mature ego, which is to transform instinctual energies into ethically desirable patterns of thought and action—in short, into a mature identity with a core of integrity which derives in part from belief in a meaningful religious or secular ideology.

1. PERSONAL AND PROFESSIONAL BACKGROUND

Why did an analyst who was associated with Freud in the 1920's and 30's, when the latter was writing *The Future of an Illusion* and other critical essays on religion, eventually revise the master's understanding of human nature as well as his interpretation of religion. In citing personal experiences as well as professional contacts in seeking to answer this question, it will be assumed, following Eriksonian lines, that there is a close link between the work and the inner experience of every man who deals with the great problems of the human psyche and religion. As we shall see, Erikson's most distinctive contributions to psychoanalysis—especially ego psychology, adolescent identity, and adult maturity— were directly related to personal experiences.[5]

Erik Erikson was born near Frankfurt, Germany, on June 15, 1902, of Danish parents. His mother had left Copenhagen, after being abandoned by his father, to be with artist friends in Germany. When Erik was three, his mother, who was then an artist, married a Jewish pediatrician, Dr. Theodor Homburger, who gave the young Erik his last name. Throughout his childhood, Erik's parents kept secret from him the fact that his stepfather was not his real father. This strategy of deception was apparently well intended, but it profoundly strained Erik's sense of identity and belonging in an otherwise comfortable, middle-class environment. Writing of this period in his life, Erikson recalls:

> My stepfather was the only professional man (and a highly respected one) in an intensely Jewish, small bourgeoisie family, while I (coming from a racially mixed Scandinavian background) was blond and blue-eyed, and grew flagrantly tall. Before long, then, I acquired the nickname "goy" in my stepfather's temple; while to my school mates, I was a "Jew" (20:743).

Because the young Erik realized, as children generally do in such circumstances, that he was not his stepfather's son, he carried into adolescence and beyond the negative identity of a bastard, namely, one who never feels that he quite belongs anywhere (20:744). Erikson himself has recently suggested that this may be one reason why he became such a maverick in psychoanalysis—he never really felt that he belonged entirely within psychoanalysis either.

During adolescence, Erik attended the type of elite German high school called the *Gymnasium*, where he received a thorough training in the humanities and classical languages, which appears to have contributed to the broad humanistic perspective that was later to characterize his work. Upon graduation from the *Gymnasium*, Erik's stepfather expected him to become a physician like himself. But Erik was too deeply involved in an adolescent crisis of the sort that he was later to discover in other adolescents to accept this easy step into the future. Rejecting the bourgeois values of his family, he dropped out of higher education, left home, and wandered around Europe for five or six years. Later, Erikson was to refer to this period of time during which an adolescent tries to work out an appropriate identity as a "moratorium," a span of time after childhood and before adulthood when young people try out new ideologies and roles, including negative ones, in a determined endeavor to discover who they really are, and what they can truly commit themselves to. While wandering in the Black Forest, the Alps, and Northern Italy as "a sort of transitional beatnik" (1:180), Erikson became "an artist," which he once described as a "euphemism for a young man with some talent but nowhere to go" (21:12). This sense of being on the move with nowhere to go was also to affect his psychological work. "Maybe, because of this," Erikson writes, "I recognized in maladjusted children and youths the need to move and to be moved and not just feel driven and to reflect on it" (1:180).

The fact that Erikson began his career as a wandering artist—with some talent for sketching and for executing huge woodcuts that were exhibited in Munich's Glaspalast—was to significantly affect both the style of his thought as well as his mode of written communication. In studying an individual, for example, Erikson invariably approaches his subject with a keen interest in the subtle "configurational affinity" uniting the rich details of personal experience, style, and expression, and constituting the uniqueness of the human personality. Instead of approaching the psychological study of man armed with abstractly defined concepts and complex theoretical arguments, Erikson tends to be descriptive first and theoretical in the context of elaborating upon impressions. Erikson's writing style also reflects his artistic sensitivities. He writes as an artist sketches, by brushing in the main outline in the process of filling his pages with incredibly rich background detail. Readers with a similar orientation tend to be captivated by this style, while those seeking crystal clear concepts and theories are often frustrated by the difficulty involved in translating his often intuitive insights into abstract propositions. For these reasons, secondary interpretations of his writings invariably fail to do justice to the descriptive depth of his highly artistic mode of communication.

In 1927, at twenty-four, Erikson accepted an invitation from a childhood friend, Peter Blos, to teach art in a small, progressive school for children of Americans associated with Freud in Vienna.[6] Through his work at the school, Erikson came in contact with psychoanalysis at a particularly fertile period in the history of the young movement. Although some of Freud's disciples were beginning to transform the master's innovative ideas into "beliefs" to be rigidly followed, there continued to be considerable ferment within the new discipline. Freud's brilliant daughter, Anna, was endeavoring to shift psychoanalytic interest in the childhood of adults, as recalled in analysis, to an investigation of children themselves.[7] Freud's later writings on the ego were encouraging his students to turn their attention away from an exclusive emphasis upon the unconscious and toward the characteristics of the ego. Indeed, one of the future architects of modern ego psychology, Heinz Hartmann, was associated with the Vienna Psychoanalytic Institute during Erikson's stay. Freud was also becoming increasingly preoccupied, by the late 20's, with the application of psychoanalysis "to literature and art, to psychobiography, and to the general issues that face all civilized men: the alternatives of war and peace, the nature of education, the sources of religious faith" (1:24). During Erikson's stay, Freud wrote *The Future of an Illusion*, *Civilization and Its Discontents*, "Dostoevsky and Parricide," and a postscript to "The Moses of Michelangelo."

In time, Erikson went into analysis with Anna Freud. The appeal of psychoanalysis to the young Erikson went beyond, although it included, intellectual interest in stimulating, new ideas and a personal concern with gaining insight into some of his own problems. Freud, as well as the psychoanalytic community, Erikson confesses, met needs deeply rooted in his unconscious:

> Here was a mythical figure and a great doctor who had rebelled against the medical profession. Here also was a circle which admitted me to the kind of training that came as close to the role of a children's doctor as one could possibly come without going to medical school. What, in me, responded to this situation was, I think, an ambivalent identification with my stepfather, the pediatrician, mixed with a search for my own mythical father. And if I ask myself in what spirit I accepted my truly astounding adoption by the Freudian circle, I can only surmise (not without embarrassment) that it was a kind of favored stepson identity that made me take for granted that I should be accepted where I did not quite belong. By the same token, however, I had to cultivate not-belonging and keep contact with the artist in me: my psychoanalytic identity therefore was not quite settled until much later . . . (20:744).

After his training analysis had ended, Erikson met and married Joan Serson, an Episcopal minister's daughter of mixed Canadian and American background, who was studying and teaching modern dance in Vienna. As Hitler gained power in Germany, the Eriksons decided to emigrate, with their two infant sons, to the United States. In 1933, they settled in Boston, where Erikson became a practicing analyst, primarily of children, with teaching appointments first at Harvard and later at Yale and the University of California at Berkeley. At these institutions, Erikson became friendly with a number of leading anthropologists, sociologists, and psychologists—like Margaret Mead, John Dollard, Alfred Kroeber, and Kurt Lewin—who were deeply committed to interdisciplinary studies.[8] These contacts convinced Erikson that societies mold psychological conflicts in different ways. Consequently, he began to study the ways in which culturally diverse child-rearing practices affect personality development.[9] This was first done during a field trip study of the Sioux Indians in South Dakota, and, later, on a second field trip, with

Alfred Kroeber, to the Yurok Indians in Northern California.[10] Comparing different ways of holding, feeding, and training children, Erikson noted that the young Sioux was encouraged to be independent before social obligations were imposed upon him, in marked contrast with the early regulation of children in middle-class America during the 1940's. At the same time, Erikson noted that the independent personality traits that had once equipped the Sioux for the nomadic life of following the buffalo over the vast plains made it extraordinarily difficult for them to live within the confines of reservation life. This lack of continuity between personality style and reservation life, although a major source of emotional problems among the Sioux, could not be explained by traditional psychoanalytic categories, precisely because it had to do with the ability of the Sioux to relate to a relatively new social environment and only incidentally with unconscious erotic and aggressive drives. Henceforth, Erikson's writings would focus on sociological as well as psychological influences on personality formation.

The impressions of psychosocial conflict that Erikson gained on the reservations, and in his ongoing clinical practice, were reinforced during the second world war, while he was working with emotionally disturbed young men at the Mt. Zion Veterans' Rehabilitation Clinic in San Francisco. The problems encountered in clinical treatment of veterans led Erikson to formulate the term "identity crisis," for which he is now justly famous. Veterans who had returned home often sought out hospital clinics complaining of vague aches and pains, unsettled "nerves," loss of sleep, appetite and interest in life. As they attempted to reconcile their activities and attitudes as soldiers with those required by civilian life, these veterans no longer felt quite "right" about who they were and what they were doing. Because these former soldiers "were impaired in that central control over themselves for which, in the psychoanalytic scheme, only the 'inner agency' of the ego could be held responsible," Erikson began to speak of a loss of "ego identity" (17:17). Afterwards, he recognized similar symptoms in severely disturbed young people whose sense of confusion was due, not to conflicts engendered by an external war, but, rather, by a war within themselves regarding their identity.[12] Many of these conflicts centered on the lack of continuity between childhood experiences and socially approved adult vocational choices. In all these cases, the term "identity confusion" appeared to be aptly descriptive and diagnostically useful.

2. ERIKSON'S EGO-SOCIAL THEORY

Erikson's revision of Freudian theory is based upon an acceptance of the basic tenets of psychoanalysis, rather than a rejection of them.

Unlike Jung and Adler who, when they broke with Freud, rejected his theories and substituted their own, Erikson builds upon the master's work while revising it.[13]

The first of these revisions takes off from Freud's later work on the adaptive functions of the ego as well as from Anna Freud's classic study of *The Ego and the Mechanisms of Defense* (1936) and Heinz Hartmann's *Ego Psychology and the Problem of Adaptation* (1939). Building upon this work and his own clinical observations, Erikson came to regard the ego not only as a defensive and adjusting mechanism, but as a source of relatively autonomous creativity, ingenuity, and resourcefuless in coping with inner and outer realities.[14] These ego strengths enable individuals not only to steer around hazards, they make it possible for men to learn social skills and to use them in mature work, love, play, and friendship. These strengths also enable individuals to use even neurotic conflicts and symptoms to heal themselves while engaging in creative social activities. Thus, whereas Freud concentrated on the etiology of pathological development, Erikson focuses on those strengths and opportunities that enable individuals "to triumph over the psychological hazards of living" (21:17).

A second revision, deriving from his anthropological fieldwork, has to do with the role of society in the development of the individual. At every step in human maturation, Erikson contends, societies influence behavioral patterns through customary child-rearing practices, social roles, institutional patterns, and shared beliefs and values. Individuals develop not only in relationship to the child-mother-father triangle described by Freud, but in relationship to a family conditioned by a specific social setting and a wider historical-cultural heritage. As individuals mature beyond infancy, their lives are decisively influenced by ever more encompassing social institutions than the family, e.g., schools, churches, voluntary associations, political parties, governments, and international organizations.

Taken together, these fundamental revisions of Freudian theory constitute the distinctive ego-social model of personality formation that Erikson helped introduce into psychoanalytic thought and practice. The significance of this altered perspective on psychological development was first explicated in Erikson's now internationally famous *Childhood and Society* (1950). The result of over a decade of careful reflection on the psychic and social forces making for the ego strengths and weaknesses encountered in therapy, this first book by Erikson sets forth the following fundamental propositions regarding personality development.[15] 1) The psychosexual stages of development described by Freud (the oral, anal, phallic, latent, and genital) must be supplemented by psychosocial stages of ego development during which the individual establishes new basic orientations toward himself and his social world. 2) There are eight of these developmental stages, each of which has a positive component involving an increased sense of inner unity, continuity and vitality, as well as a negative component representing the opposite of these ego strengths. The five stages of childhood and adolescence are: basic trust versus mistrust, autonomy versus shame and doubt, initiative versus guilt, industry versus inferiority, identity versus identity confusion. The three phases of adulthood include: intimacy versus isolation, generativity versus stagnation, ego integrity versus despair. 3) These psychosocial stages of ego development follow the epigenetic principle that "anything that grows has a ground plan, and that out of this ground plan the parts arise, each having its time of special ascendency, until all the parts have arisen to form a functioning whole" (17:92). In other words, the human personality develops in steps, each of which deals with a specific psychosocial problem that is salient during the stage in question. Each stage is related to all others, so that "they all depend on the proper development in the proper sequence of each item" (17:93). 4) Despite the ascendency of particular issues at each stage, like trust versus mistrust in infancy, each issue "exists in some form before 'its' decisive and critical time normally arrives" (17:93-95). For example, an infant may show something like "autonomy" from the beginning, but it is not until later that he experiences the decisive alternative between being autonomous versus being dependent (17:95). 5) Each successive step involves a potential crisis; by "crisis" is meant a crucial period of heightened potential and increased vulnerability, not a catastrophe (17:96). 6) Regression is a natural phenomenon that occurs throughout life, particularly as individuals attempt to weather new crises. When temporary, regression often enables an individual to rework unresolved, earlier conflicts. Spontaneous regression, therefore, may be "in the service of the ego," to use the phrase Erikson borrows from Ernst Kris, rather than a necessarily dysfunctional phenomenon.[16] 7) Relatively successful resolution of successive stage conflicts promote an upward movement on the scale of maturity, culminating in the mature phases of adulthood. The natural thrust of the human psyche is thus toward maturity rather than the regression to infancy suggested by the Freudian model.

The complex psychosocial theory of ego development that Erikson builds upon these fundamental propositions is of considerable interest, not only for its revisionist portrait of psychological man but also for the light it casts on the role of religion in human life. Each of the eight stages of development affects and is affected by religious beliefs or ideological substitutes. The capacity for faith, for example, is deeply influenced by the ego capacities acquired in the course of maturation, this being especially true with regard to the formation of trust in infancy and identity during adolescence. Adult religiosity is affected not only by the strength of these acquired ego capacities, but also by the degree to which religion is supported or not supported by prevailing social institutions. The capacity of adults to foster a nascent religiosity in their children depends to a large extent upon the nature of the social institutions in which they participate. Erikson's general theory of religion, as well as his application of this theory in his well known studies of Luther and Gandhi, presuppose the following detailed description of the eight stages of life.

The first stage in Erikson's scheme of development, *trust versus mistrust,* corresponds to Freud's oral stage. Like the latter, it usually lasts throughout the first year. In contrast with Freud's emphasis upon erogenous stimulation of the infant at his mother's breast, Erikson stresses the qualitative nature of the relationship between mother and child. The child who is fondled, cuddled, played with and talked to develops a sense of basic trust, which involves a pervasive attitude toward the world, including others, and oneself. By "trust" is meant "an essential trustfulness of others as well as a fundamental sense of one's own trustworthiness" (17:96). Concretely, basic trust is expressed when the infant is willing to let his mother out of sight without excessive anxiety or rage. If, however, care is inadequate, inconsistent, or hostilely performed, the infant will express fear and suspiciousness—basic mistrust—toward his outer environment, others, and himself. Whether a child is to become a trusting, basically optimistic person, with confidence in his capacity to cope with new situations, or a demanding, insecure person, preoccupied with his own needs, depends, to a large extent, upon the qualitative sense of everything being "all right" that his mother communicates in the handling, care, and training of her child.

The issue of basic trust versus basic mistrust is a matter of relative degree. No one experiences either pure trust or absolute distrust. Like later conflicts, the fundamental issue of trusting versus mistrusting persists throughout life, but its relatively successful resolution during the first year provides the growing individual with a reservoir of ego strength that is crucial for handling later crises. Indeed, some degree of basic trust is a necessary prerequisite for all further development, as cases of severe child neglect clearly verify.[17] Even under the most favorable circumstances, however, loss of the infant's earlier unity with the maternal matrix that occurs at the end of this period leaves every individual with "a dim but universal nostalgia for a lost paradise" (17:101).

To engender basic trust in their children, Erikson maintains, parents must be able to communicate a profound conviction that there is meaning in what they, as parents, are doing (8:249). This requires that parents firmly believe in the goodness of their own strivings and in "the kindness of the powers of the universe" (8:251). Traditionally, such parental trust has found institutional confirmation in religion, which is described by

Erikson as the oldest and the most lasting institution "to serve the ritual restoration of a sense of trust in the form of faith while offering a tangible formula for a sense of evil against which it promises to arm and defend man" (17:106). Although Erikson notes that many adults today derive a vital faith from secular ideologies and pursuits rather than from traditional religious institutions, he also observes that many parents "are proud to be without religion whose children cannot afford their being without it" (8:251). For children require from their parents a profound sense of the trustworthiness of the world and of themselves.

Erikson views the basic trust that arises out of the encounter of mother and infant not only as the foundational ego strength, but also as the basis of mature religious faith. There is something in the nature of even mature faith which suggests to Erikson that it is the most childlike of all ego qualities, and the most dependent for its verification on images of the charity of fate, the affirmation of a hallowed presence, or the unconditional acceptance of a smiling Madonna. The childlike nature of faith is suggested by the fact that all religious practices induce periodic surrender, as in the case of petitionary prayer, to all-powerful, benevolent Beings that dispense earthly fortune as well as spiritual well-being. These images and practices have their ontogenic beginnings in childlike trust in maternal figures, but Erikson disavows any intention to explain adult faith as childish or regressive, although infantilization is not foreign to many religions. In his opinion, religious beliefs sometimes induce childish behavior, but mature faith is a reaffirmation of trust at a higher level of development. Religious forms of regression may occasionally result in infantilization, but they also frequently lead to a rejuvenation of that trust which is the foundational strength of every healthy ego.

Stage two, *autonomy versus shame and doubt,* spans the second and third years of life, a period which Freudians call the anal stage to designate the pleasurableness and willfulness attached to the eliminative organs. While Erikson's description of this stage includes anality, it focuses primarily on the new motor and mental skills acquired by the child during this period. The problem of autonomy versus shame and doubt has to do with the child's need to do things at his own pace and in his own time as contrasted with adult regulations, limitations, and discipline. If the child is granted sufficient freedom within a stable environment, he will develop a sense of autonomy involving self-control, independence, self-expression, and self-esteem. If, on the other hand, elders fail to support the child in his attempt to "stand on his own feet," and to protect him from having foolishly exposed himself to ridicule, he may develop a lasting sense of shame or a permanent loss of self-esteem, combined with hateful self-insistence or compulsive self-restraint. Closely associated with shame is doubt—doubt about oneself and about the perspicacity of adults. Because doubt results from excessively harsh and irrational forms of discipline, it finds expression in fears concerning hidden persecutors and anxieties about one's dirtiness and messiness.

The ability of parents to combine flexibility with self-restraint in their training of children at this stage depends to a large degree upon their own sense of dignity and personal independence. Just as the "infant's sense of trust is a reflection of parental faith; similarly, the sense of autonomy is a reflection of the parents' dignity as autonomous beings. For no matter what we do in detail, the child will primarily feel what it is we live by as loving, cooperative, and firm beings, and what makes us hateful, anxious, and divided in ourselves" (17:113). Social institutions support parental autonomy to the extent that they provide opportunities for authentic self-expression within the limitations of marriage, work, and citizenship. While these opportunities are not necessarily connected with religious institutions, Erikson notes that religions may re-enforce or undermine the parental strengths required for the adequate training of children during this second stage. Religions, like late medieval Catholicism, which place primary emphasis upon sin and shame before God, undermine these adult strengths, while those built upon a simple faith in God's goodness revitalize the trust that precedes all shame and doubt (10:256).

The third stage, *initiative versus guilt,* corresponds to the phallic stage in classical psychoanalysis, when the child, age four to five, begins to move around more freely, to respond to and initiate things, and to expand his fantasy activities. The degree to which the child will leave this stage with his sense of initiative outbalancing his sense of guilt depends largely upon whether his parents permit freedom for self-initiated activities and refrain from deriding his play activities and fantasy life. When parents overly criticize or denigrate these activities, the child tends to develop a punitive conscience that engenders guilt for most self-initiating pursuits. In severe cases, the child will develop a primitive, cruel, and uncompromising conscience that will constrict him to the point of overall inhibition. In later life, internalized prohibitions about initiative may find expression either in severe self-restriction or in overcompensated forms of rageful vindictiveness against others.

As in the other stages, Erikson relates the capacity of adults to successfully encourage the ego strength of initiative not only to their own acquired strengths, but also to their current institutional relationships. Adults generally encourage initiative when society enables them to realize their own innate and developed capacities in the economic ethos. As in the case of autonomy, however, Erikson also notes that adult expressions of initiative or guilt may also be affected by the religious ethos in which they participate. Some religions inhibit initiative by foisting upon believers a life-long sense of guilt, while others nourish the aspirations and imaginations of men by calling for the transformation of individual and social existence.

The fourth stage, *industry versus inferiority*, occurs between the ages of 6 and 11, when children in developed countries attend elementary schools. In classical psychoanalysis, this stage is referred to as the latency phase, because sexual desires are quiescent. As Erikson observes, however, this stage is, from an ego-social perspective, an extremely active period during which children learn how things are made, how they work, and what can be done with them. This budding sense of industry is expressed by an interest in watching and imitating people representing various readily understood occupations, e.g., firemen, policemen, nurses. Industry is also expressed in cooperating with other children in various games involving active physical skills, like sewing and building, and social role-playing.

When children are encouraged and rewarded for these efforts to know and to make things, their sense of industry is enhanced. The result is a lasting sense of competence in making things work and doing things well. When children are denied opportunities to learn and continually made to feel inadequate, they frequently develop a chronic sense of inferiority or unworthiness.

Adults encourage industry to the extent that they are able to meaningfully communicate the prevailing technological ethos of their culture through educational institutions. The meaningfulness of work is threatened when the child learns that it is not productive work that determines his worthiness in this area, but the color of his skin, the background of his parents, or the fashion of his clothes. Meaningful work is similarly undermined when the child is forced to submit to what Erikson, following Marx, calls "craft-idiocy," by becoming a thoughtless slave of technology and of those who are in a position to exploit it (8:261; 17:127). The reigning ideology of an epoch, whether it is a traditionally religious one or a secular surrogate, has a great deal to do with the meaning, value, and worthiness associated with work in a given society.

With the advent of puberty, between ages 11 and 14, childhood comes to an end and youth enters the fifth stage: *identity versus identity confusion*. Faced with a physiological revolution within them and with adult tasks ahead of them, developing youths are now deeply concerned with what they feel they are as compared with how others view them and what others expect from them. With the advent of increased intellectual abilities and a wider social horizon, adolescents are equally concerned with connecting the abilities, roles, ideas, and ideals cultivated earlier with the occupational and ideological prototypes of the day. In attempting to deal with these varied identity problems, "each youth must forge for himself some central perspective and direction, some working unity, out of the effective remnants of his childhood and the hopes of his anticipated adulthood; he must detect some meaningful resemblance between what he has come to see in himself and what his sharpened awareness tells him others judge and expect him to be" (10:14). The key words in this definition of the identity crisis are "forge some central perspective and direction," as it is Erikson's claim that every adolescent must find a meaningful perspective on himself and his world capable of bringing all the varied and conflicting experiences of life into a working whole.

There are two aspects of this central perspective which is psychosocial identity: a personal, subjective side, and a social, ideological or world-view, side.[18] The personal aspect of identity involves integrating and synthesizing what one has learned about one's body, special ego aptitudes, and social abilities in varied childhood roles: as male or female, son or daughter, friend, student, worker, athlete, and so forth. Personal identity also involves matching the inner sense of sameness and continuity gained in childhood with the perspectives of others. Successful achievement of a subjective sense of personal identity occurs when one intensely feels, and trustingly acts—despite risks—out of an inner conviction, that "this is the real me!" The social aspects of identity formation derive from the necessity of gaining a working perspective on the varied, conflicting, and often vague, wider social world that replaces the circumscribed world of childhood at the advent of adolescence. In this new world, individuals must find appropriate social roles and ideological loyalties for which it is meaningful to prove themselves trustworthy. Full psychosocial identity depends on a reciprocity of subjective (ego) synthesis in the individual and ideological integration with an ongoing community.

Before an appropriate identity is formulated, adolescents in developed countries generally go through a period of "identity confusion." The sources of this confusion are diverse, since adolescents have to refight many of the battles of earlier stages in the process of forging an abiding sense of self and a world view capable of guarding a final psychosocial identity. Sources of identity confusion include fears about trusting the adult world, shame vis-à-vis negative aspects of the self, doubts about sexual or ethnic identity, guilt over failures and compromises, problems in finding appropriate life vocations, and difficulties in establishing a coherent ideological perspective. A vigorous rebellion against parental values often marks the onset of identity confusion, since adolescents frequently must say "No" to what others say about them in order to figure out who they are and who they will be. Rebellion is frequently followed by a radical sense of discontinuity between the past, the present, and the future. As the cowboy song quoted by Erikson puts this sense of discontinuity: "I ain't what I ought to be, I ain't what I'm going to be, but I ain't what I was" (21:56). Uncertainties and anxieties of this sort are sometimes accompanied by a loss of appetite and a decline in erotic activities, a slowdown in vitality and an increase in drowsiness, a feeling of depersonalization and a sense of not really being present with others. In Arthur Miller's *Death of a Salesman*, Biff expresses the resulting cumulative sense of being out of touch with reality to his mother: "I just can't take hold, Mom, I can't take hold of some kind of a life" (17:131). To keep themselves together, adolescents "overidentify, to the point of apparent complete loss of identity, with the heroes of cliques and crowds" (8:262). This phenomenon is referred to by Erikson as "totalism," meaning the tendency of youth, when confronted with a loss of personal wholeness, to restructure themselves and their world by recourse to an alien ideology (17:81). The readiness for such commitment helps Erikson to explain the appeal of simple, sometimes cruel, ideologies to adolescents who, feeling at sea within themselves and within the adult world, latch on to an ideological identity opposed to the one prevailing in their society. For young people suffering from severe identity confusion often prefer a "negative identity" to no identity at all.[19]

When societies offer young people a period of time or *moratorium* with sufficient permissiveness to work through these difficulties, adolescents demonstrate a vital capacity or ego strength to integrate that which they have come to be during the long years of childhood with that which others see in and expect of them, that which they have come to believe with that which others find plausible to believe. In so doing, adolescents often reform life styles and rejuvenate traditional ideologies in the process of healing themselves. For adolescents can only adjust to the adult world by adjusting it to themselves. "Adolescence is thus a vital regenerator in the process of social evolution; for youth selectively offers its loyalties and energies to the conservation of that which feels true to them and to the correction or destruction of that which has lost its regenerative significance" (13:126).

Youth's quest for a basic philosophy of life has religious aspects, insofar as it involves trust as faith in a world view capable of confirming the truthworthiness of the wider environment transcending the give-and-take of ordinary experience. Because faith as a freely pledged loyalty to a wider system of meaning first becomes a psychological problem and possibility in adolescence, Erikson implies that genuine faith cannot begin until this stage of development. Indeed, one might characterize adolescence itself as a fundamentally religious crisis since the central problems at stake revolve around the age-old issues of faith and meaning. In any case, Erikson observes that religious institutions have traditionally provided adolescents with ultimate perspectives on which to fasten their growing need for something in which to truly believe, which also means values in whose service it is worthwhile to prove oneself trustworthy. In our day, of course, youth frequently look to secular ideologies as alternatives to traditional religions in their search for a larger perspective in which to believe, but Erikson sees this search for meaning as fully religious, despite its secular form. Once a satisfactory religious or quasi-religious ideology is found, Erikson argues, trust toward existence as such is generally rejuvenated in such a way as to promote the mature ego strengths of adulthood.

Three adult crises follow the crisis of identity; they concern problems of *intimacy, generativity,* and *integrity.* "Intimacy" is the ability of young adults, during the period between late adolescence and middle age, to love others—in sexual unions, marriage, close friendships, and joint experiences of inspiration—without fear of losing themselves in the process. Avoidance of genuine intimacy due to a fear of ego loss leads to a deep sense of "isolation" and consequent self-absorption (8:264). This danger may be countered by religions that invite the realization of man's propensity for mutual love.

"Generativity" is the gradually acquired ability of middle-aged men and women to be deeply concerned about others beyond their immediate social environment, especially future generations and the world in which those generations will live. Where this caring for others fails to develop, "stagnation" in the form of self-concern drains vital energies and estranges individuals from the wider community of mankind. One of several reasons for this excessive self-love is found in the lack of "some faith, some 'belief in the species,'" which would make future generations appear to be "a welcome trust of the community" (8:267).

"Integrity" arises from the individual's accrued ability, toward the end of life, to accept his "one and only life cycle" and "the people who have become significant to it as something that had to be and that, by necessity, permitted no substitutions" (17:139). Failure to develop ego integrity is signified by "*distrust* and by *despair:* fate is not accepted as the frame of life, death not as its finite boundary" (17:140). Religious traditions provide sustenance for ego integrity insofar as they find meaning in life, even in the face of death. "In such a final consolidation," Erikson writes, paraphrasing St. Paul, "death loses its sting" (8:268).

3. ERIKSON'S THEORY OF RELIGION

Erikson's psychosocial theory clearly accords religion an important role in human development. This generally sympathetic view derives in part from the decisive importance attributed to trust in human maturation. According to Erikson, basic trust is not only the earliest ego strength upon which every growing individual builds, it is the foundational strength of every mature ego. In its mature form, trust takes the form of faith, without which man cannot successfully handle the hazards of existence. Faith from this Eriksonian perspective is not cognitive belief in intellectual propositions, but a profound inner conviction of the trustworthiness of oneself within a trustworthy universe. As such, mature faith is childlike in its sometimes naive affirmation and practice of surrender to a Providence or Power, but it is not infantile. For faith occurs beyond the alienations and accompanying anxieties that distinguish adult from infantile existence. Mature faith might be described as trust "in spite of" alienation, since it often includes recognition of "the alienations—from the self and from others—which are the human lot" (13:153). Mature faith also involves trust in the face of anxieties unknown to the infant, especially existential anxiety. The latter is that dread that is occasioned not by intra-psychic, neurotic conflicts, but rather by universally shared threats to the meaning of human existence. In describing the sort of metaphysical anxiety that must be surmounted by mature faith, Erikson borrows a story from Crane Brinton about a small boy who, upon being told about events before he was born, suddenly burst into tears. As Erikson explains this reaction, the boy was suddenly overwhelmed by the sort of "ego-chill" or "shudder" which comes from awareness of our potential nonexistence—the chilly fact that at some time in history we did not and will not exist. Because this threat of nonbeing undermines the meaningfulness of contemporary existence, Erikson follows Tillich in suggesting that faith is a necessary bulwark against the absurdity of the human condition.[20]

For adults to possess a sense of trust as faith, Erikson argues, societal confirmation in the form of a convincing ideology or world view is necessary. From this societal perspective, Erikson defines religion as 1) an ideological system which 2) establishes pervasive motivations in men by 3) formulating a coherent world view convincing enough 4) to counteract alienations and to support individual and collective identity.[21]

Taking the ideological part of this definition first, Erikson does not wish either to denigrate religion by referring to it as an ideology or to imply that religion is primarily intellectual in character. An ideological system, as Erikson understands it, provides the basic, often unconscious, means by which we interpret reality. An ideology is absolutely indispensable, therefore, since, without it, we would live in a bewildering world of chaotic impressions without any sense of coherence or patterned unity. No ideology, even a scientifically informed one, is a completely accurate representation of reality, since all basic orientations are formulated from "a given stage of partial knowledge" (17:226). Yet Erikson postulates that man needs to translate "into significant words, images, and codes the exceeding darkness which surrounds man's existence, and the light which pervades it beyond all desert or comprehension" (10:21-22). Such a translation is not exclusively intellectual; it rather elaborates on "what feels profoundly true even though it is not demonstrable" (10:21).

As for the motivations established by religious ideologies, Erikson places primary stress upon the way in which religions reaffirm childlike— as contrasted with childish—trust as faith. Of all ideological systems, Erikson writes, "only religion restores the earliest sense of appeal to a Provider, a Providence. In the Judeo-Christian tradition, no prayer indicates this more clearly than 'The Lord make His Face to shine upon you and be gracious unto you. The Lord lift up His countenance upon you and give you peace'; and no prayerful attitude better than the uplifted face, hopeful of being recognized. . . . We can see the search for the same smile of peace in the work of Eastern painters and sculptors, although their Buddhas seem closer to being the overall parent *and* the child, all in one" (10:118-19).

In addition to motivating primary faith, religions attempt to overcome, as they give vivid expression to, man's sense of shame, doubt, and guilt. All the experiences that make men feel distrustful, ashamed, doubtful, and guilty are woven into religious imagery, Erikson maintains, because negative experiences must be recognized and integrated with positive ones in an overall perspective on life. Sometimes religions further intensify negative experiences with images of the devil or a vengeful deity; but Erikson sees an attempt to work through these negative feelings in the image of God as a guiding Voice or Word. Belief in an omnipotent Power's ultimate benevolence gives rise to the conviction that even the evil in human life has somehow been mysteriously planned for the best. Such beliefs enable men to live vital lives, despite guilty consciences.

Religious ideologies are distinguished from political and economic ideologies by their concern with the nature of reality as a whole. In formulating an all-embracing world view tying past, present, and future into a convincing ideology, religion meets man's need to fit his everyday activities into the larger context of existence. In discussing the human need for a life-context, Erikson cites this passage by Crane Brinton: "all normal people are metaphysicians; all have some desire to locate themselves in a 'system,' a 'universe,' a 'process' transcending at least the immediate give-and-take between the individual and his environment; for all normal people the conscious lack or frustration of some such understanding will result in a kind of metaphysical anxiety" (10:110). This metaphysical need accounts, Erikson states, "for the acceptance by youth of mythologies and ideologies predicting the course of the universe or the historical trend; for even intelligent and practical youth can be glad to have the larger framework settled so that it can devote itself to the details which it can manage, once it knows (or is convincingly told) what they stand for and where it stands" (17:247). Today, secular ideologies—like Marxism and right-wing Americanism—fulfill this religious function by presenting historical perspectives on the past, present, and future of "chosen people" like the proletariat of Marxism and the youth of middle America. As religions do, this-worldly ideologies counteract alienation with affirmative dogma and positive ritual that support individual and collective identity. Secular ideologies of this sort are therefore fully religious, in Erikson's use of the term, albeit in a non-theistic, this-worldly form.

Erikson's interpretation of religion emphasizes positive characteristics neglected by Freud, yet he is as sensitive as the founder of psychoanalysis to the dysfunctional consequences of religion for both individuals and societies. Religion, Erikson writes, has undoubtedly exploited man's "child-like needs, not only by offering eternal guarantees for an omniscient power's benevolence (if properly appeased) but also by magic words and significant gestures, soothing sounds and soporific smells—an infant's world" (13:153). Religions have also excessively intensified acquired feelings of shame, doubt, and guilt with terrifying images of a vengeful father-God and eternal punishment. On the societal level, religions have fostered intolerance and hatred towards outsiders. Nonetheless, Erikson also maintains that religions at their historical best have frequently promoted desirable ego strengths, like trust, faith, hope, love, fidelity, mutuality, and integrity. Even childlike religious regressions have often served the recuperative powers of the ego by enabling individuals to work through earlier crises and to integrate even negative experiences into a meaningful set of images.[22] Socially, religious ideologies have stressed brotherly love and other virtues frequently neglected by contemporary secular substitutes. As a result of this subtle approach to the various functions of religion. Erikson eschews sweeping assessments of all religions for a careful study of the positive and negative characteristics of particular manifestations of religiosity.

4. ERIKSON'S STUDY OF LUTHER

Erikson's detailed exploration of the varied roles of religion in human life is best exemplified in his studies of major religious figures, like Luther and Gandhi. Characteristic of these studies is Erikson's lack of dogmatism and his sympathetic sensitivity to the complexity of the human personality, especially when it is dealing with religious matters. In each case, Erikson attempts to show how extremely gifted, but disturbed, young men reformulated the traditional beliefs in which they were raised in such a way as to resolve their own psychosocial problems as well as those of their generation. Throughout, Erikson is primarily interested in the vital ego capacities that enable individuals, especially during adolescence and early adulthood, to revitalize themselves as they reformulate and rejuvenate traditional perspectives on the human condition. Although these reformations on the part of great men like Luther and Gandhi served to promote the mature ego strengths of intimacy, generativity, and integrity, Erikson is neither blind to the remaining personal problems of religious innovators nor unaware of the sometimes dysfunctional, as well as extremely functional, consequences of these innovations in the social arena. Indeed, it is one of Erikson's major themes that the tremendous good accomplished by the ideological innovations of religious leaders is frequently combined with potentially deleterious social components. Because these distinctive themes in Erikson's approach to religion are especially clear in his study of Luther, it is most fruitful for our purposes to carefully examine this seminal study of a religious leader.

The story that Erikson tells in *Young Man Luther*, is that of a deeply disturbed young man who, at the end of the Middle Ages, discovered, through intense introspection, a new vision capable of revitalizing the waning religious world view of his era.[23] Just as Freud struggled with the father-complex through a long "moratorium" before freeing himself in the process of making a major creative breakthrough in the history of psychology, similarly, Erikson contends, Martin Luther fought the psychic consequences of late medieval piety until he had won a creative resolution that helped solve for others what he could not initially solve for himself.[24] Both men, despite dissimilarities in personality, had "one characteristic in common: a grim willingness to do the dirty work of their respective ages: for each kept human conscience in focus in an era of material and scientific expansion" (10:9). Luther referred to his earlier years as working "in the mud," and complained that he had worked all alone for ten years; while Freud, also a lone worker for a decade, compared his labor to the plight of a miner in deep shafts wishing for "a good ascent" (10:9). Neither genius knew at the outset what he would discover. The young Luther scarcely expected to become a great Reformer; Freud certainly did not expect to discover a new psychology. Both men, like other highly creative individuals, came across their respective discoveries almost accidentally, and yet, these discoveries were intimately related to their most personal conflicts, to their superior perceptiveness, and to their stubbornness in courting sickness, even insanity, in order to test themselves and their ideas. In both cases, the eventual breakthrough of creativity was accompanied by neurotic suffering, yet Luther emancipated himself and his followers from medieval dogma while Freud freed many from unconscious conflicts. Luther no less than Freud, therefore, represents to Erikson a young man of genius whose powers of resourcefulness, insight, and recovery demonstrate the vital strengths to be found in other young egos.

Erikson is less interested in the infantile and unconscious origins of Luther's beliefs than in his use of the religious tradition in which he was raised to resolve neurotic conflicts, to get himself together, and to break through to mature creativity. Indeed, Erikson begins his study by explicitly opposing psychoanalytic "fatalism, according to which man is nothing but a multiplication of his parents' faults and an accumulation of his own earlier selves" (10:19). With equally sharp words, Erikson opposes the contention of some analysts that the young Luther was neurotically abnormal, stating: "I do not know about the kind of balance of mind, body, and soul that these men assume is normal; but if it does exist, I would expect it least of all in such a sensitive, passionate, and ambitious individual as young Luther" (10:34). To this one might add that normality is scarcely what Erikson expects to find in any great man, as it is his claim that geniuses are born in the midst of an intense struggle frequently involving an infantile "account to be settled," combined with "an unusual energy of body, a rare concentration of mind, and a total devotion of soul, which carries them through trials and errors and near catastrophes," until they arrive at the unique conclusions that are the basis of their greatness (13:203). What interests Erikson about Luther is not his normality, therefore, but the abnormality that enables a disturbed young man to become a world-famous religious leader who continues to be read almost half a millennium after his death.

Following his customary practice in portraying historical figures, Erikson begins his analysis of the young Luther by elaborating upon a particular crisis which divides the subject's previous life from the direction of his future activities. In Luther's case, Erikson focuses upon the "fit in the choir" that the future reformer supposedly experienced during his early or middle twenties, when, falling to the ground in the choir of a monastery, he raved like one possessed, and roared "*Ich bin's nit!*" or "*Non sum!*"—"It isn't me!" or "I am *not!*" (10:23). Explaining this choice of the fit as a major event in the young Luther's life, Erikson observes that it occurred several years after Martin had entered upon the monastic life, in defiance of his father, but before the advent of the intense inner conflicts that were eventually to result in his leadership of the Protestant Reformation. "The fit in the choir, then, belongs to a period when his career, as planned by his father, was dead; when his monastic condition, after a 'godly' beginning, had become problematic to him; and when his future was as yet in an embryonic darkness" (10:24). In other words, the fit reveals the onset of a severe identity crisis which began when the young monk felt compelled to protest what he was not—what his father said he was, namely, deceived, and what his conscience in bad moments confirmed that he was—in order to break through to what he was and would be.

Having briefly focused upon the onset of Luther's identity crisis, Erikson proceeds, as an artist might, to fill in the background leading to this episode and to the decisive events that followed. The point of this background material is not to explain everything that Luther did, but to describe events, conflicts, and trends that give coherence to his life (1:210).

Drawing upon the known facts about Martin's childhood, Erikson notes that he was born in 1483, the first son of Hans Luther, an ex-miner of peasant stock who had found his way into the newly emergent managerial class. Largely as a result of his own humble background, Hans was, like other self-made men in his day and ours, hard-working, thrifty, and intensely ambitious. Anxious to overcome his peasant identity and to encourage even higher ambitions in his children, Hans denigrated his background, fostering in his children the image of the peasant as a "negative identity fragment" (i.e., the identity a family wishes to live down and to suppress in its children, even though it may sentimentalize precisely this past). As Erikson observes in this context, Martin Luther later demonstrated the persistence of this negative identity image both in his sentimental sermons about peasant life as well as in his intense, seemingly irrational, hostility towards the peasant uprising for which he was partly responsible.

Hans and his wife were intensely superstitious, as were most common folk in the middle ages. They firmly believed and taught their children that human life was threatened by the devil, who was continually tricking people, and by legions of demons, sorcerers, and witches, who were deemed responsible for sudden moods of melancholy, sexual fantasies, aggressive thoughts, and the like. Offsetting these sinister forces were angelic mediators and saints who assisted the faithful in distress. These beliefs, Erikson notes in passing, were undoubtedly unconscious projections, but they also provided an understandable, pre-scientific means of making sense out of, and mastering, unknown inner and outer realities.

> In a world full of dangers they may even have served as a source of security, for they make the unfamiliar familiar, and permit the individual to say to his fears and conflicts, "I see you! I recognize you!" He can even tell others what he saw and recognized while remaining reasonably

free. . . . What else do we do today when we share our complexes, our coronaries, and our communists? (10:60-61)

The important point here, however, is the fact that Martin, having absorbed these superstitions from his parents, fell back upon them at the most crucial junctures in his career—"when thunderstorms and 'fits' and 'revelations' had to accompany the decisions he made," despite his sophisticated education in Aristotelian philosophy (1:218).

Martin's parents were also severe disciplinarians, who did not spare the rod in punishing their children. As Martin himself confessed: "My father once whipped me so that . . . I fled him and I became sadly resentful toward him, until he gradually got me accustomed . . . to him again" (10:64). As Erikson interprets these and other passages, Martin's problems focused around his relationship with the authoritarian father who was the usual source of these punishments. This is not to imply that Martin's mother was an insignificant figure in his development; for she clearly provided him with that minimum degree of basic trust without which children cannot survive. Indeed, nobody could later sing, speak, love, and care with the feminine as well as masculine sensitivities of the mature Luther, Erikson maintains, unless he had once enjoyed a profoundly rewarding relationship with his mother. Yet Erikson hypothesizes that Hans' dominance of the household resulted in the young Martin being prematurely driven out of the security of the first stage into the insecurities of later childhood experiences.

If Hans Luther was authoritarian, he was also deeply attached to the eldest son whom he wanted, like upwardly-mobile middle class fathers in our own time, to satisfy his own ambitions. To this end, Martin was well-educated in preparation for a career in law. Like other sons of overly ambitious, authoritarian fathers, Martin began to realize, however, that his father's authority was not always based upon justice. Quite the contrary, Hans' anger for deeds done and accomplishments unrealized was often ruthlessly impulsive and almost alcoholic in its intensity. Here, Erikson suggests

> is the origin of Martin's doubt that the father, when he punishes you, is really guided by love and justice rather than by arbitrariness and malice. This early doubt later was projected on the Father in heaven with such violence that Martin's monastic teachers could not help noticing it. "God does not hate you, you hate him," one of them said; and it was clear that Martin, searching so desperately for his own justification, was also seeking a formula of eternal justice which would justify God as a judge" (10:58).

At the same time, however, Erikson cautions against uncritically assuming that this is the whole story: that "a brutal father beat a sickly or unstable son into such a state of anxiety and rebellion that God and even Christ became for him revengers only" (10:70). For Luther's struggles were not only with his father, but with the prevailing medieval concept of God as a distant judge. In other words, Martin's crisis was not exclusively centered on the moral authority of a father on earth, it also had to do with the predominant cultural belief in the judgment of the Father in heaven.

Martin's conflict with his father came to a head in the spring of 1505 when, after completing his M.A. and starting law school in realization of his father's ambitions, Hans began to make plans for his son's early and prosperous marriage. Deeply dissatisfied with law as a career and driven to the point of open panic by the idea of a life-long marital commitment, Martin was enmeshed in a crisis of having to choose between submission and disobedience to his father when he was caught in a severe thunderstorm on July 2. A bolt of lightning struck the ground near him, perhaps throwing him to the ground, and causing him to be seized by severe terror. Fearing sudden death, Martin called out to his father's saint, "Help me, St. Anne . . . I want to become a monk" (10:92). As Erikson interprets this sudden commitment to the monastic life, Martin was in part rebelling against his father's legal and marital plans, but in this bizarre form because he could not consciously admit his deep psychic ambivalence about obeying and disobeying his father. The fact that Martin called upon his father's saint at the moment he decided to disobey him by going into the monastery is evidence of this conflict-ridden ambivalence.

Martin's years as a monk are referred to by Erikson as the "moratorium" during which the future reformer marked time before deciding what he could really believe about God and himself with complete honesty and integrity. For at least the first year, the monastic life apparently suited the young Luther's needs quite well. Celibacy and daily rituals freed him from burdens he was not ready to assume, while learning the detailed rules and observances of the monastery diverted his attention from personal preoccupations and excessive self-scrutiny. Gradually, however, Martin's problem about obeying and disobeying Hans was shifted to the higher plane of obeying and disobeying God. Many of Martin's problems with Hans then emerged as problems with God. God and even Christ were seen as distant authoritarian judges as Hans had been. And, as Martin had questioned whether Hans' judgments were based on love and justice, so, too, he now questioned whether God is not an irrational judge. Again, as Martin felt guilty for disobeying his father, now he experienced intense guilt as a wretched sinner before God. In Erikson's view, these theological problems were partly a result of projection, but they also involved an existential struggle on Martin's part of personal justification of his existence as such beyond the neurotic guilt generated by the authoritarian prohibitions of an overweening superego. To use the Tillichian terminology with which Erikson is familiar, Martin was struggling for existential courage in spite of the threat of ultimate moral condemnation of his entire being.

A major event heralding the onset of Martin's intense psychic and spiritual struggle occurred on the day of his first Mass. There are various versions of the events of that day, but they all refer to Martin's anxiety attack during the Mass and to Hans' angry disapproval of his son's monastic career during the banquet following. The anxiety attack, as Erikson interprets it, resulted from the double bind in which Martin found himself as he stood at the altar with the Eucharist in front of him and his father behind him. At that moment, when he was about to address both the Father and the father, he felt torn by doubts about his relationship and obedience to both. Later, Hans intensified his son's doubts about his worthiness as a monk by suggesting, during an angry confrontation, that the thunderstorm experience may have been "a devil's spook" (10:145). Faced with doubts about not only the justification of his calling as a monk, but of his existence before both the Father and the father, Martin subsequently made the issue of being justified before God both the center of severe neurotic obsession as well as a basic theological problem.

Initially, this search for justification in the eyes of God took the usual monastic form of confession. Martin, however, went far beyond the usual expectations, even for a monk, by compulsively attempting to confess every intention, no matter how small, as well as every deed. But the more thoroughly Martin examined himself, the more intensely unworthy he felt of precisely the justification that he sought. Martin thus unwittingly confirmed his father's suspicions and his own deepest fears, that he was not only unsuited for "monkishness," but unworthy of eternal salvation. This led him to hate God and to blaspheme against him, but these hostile feelings and acts only drove him further away from the wholehearted love of God that he sought. Eventually, Martin became totally pessimistic about ever being able to gain God's grace even through the most scrupulous discipline. At this point Martin reached what Erikson calls the "rock-bottom" attitude, meaning the insistent and precocious integrity with which adolescents wrestle with their problems in "an attempt to find that immutable bedrock on which the struggle for a new existence can safely begin and be assured of a future" (10:103). Precisely because Martin searched the rock bottom of his sinfulness with an honesty shorn of self-deceit, Erikson suggests, he eventually experienced a creative breakthrough to solutions that had escaped equally tormented, but less brutally honest, members of his era. Martin's introspective suffering was not only neurotic in character, it provided the occasion for his becoming an historical religious hero.

Luther was still struggling with these issues, when, at the age of 25, he was transferred to Wittenberg, where he met the man who was to become his confidant and mentor, Dr. Staupitz, the vicar-general of the province. In Erikson's opinion, Staupitz performed the important role of elder counter-player in relationship with whom adolescents often express their fears and test out newly formed ideas. A kind man, Staupitz was the first benevolent paternal figure Martin had met in a long time. In contrast with Hans and other superiors, Staupitz trustingly accepted Martin as he was without condemnation, yet without giving in to every whim and claim. In response to Martin's central problem of being terrified by God and Christ, Staupitz apparently counselled that "one is not truly penitent because one anticipates God's love, but because one already possesses it" (10:167). This seemingly simple advice, Erikson notes, involved "a totally reversed time perspective which Luther later thought to be strikingly confirmed in the scriptures" (10:167). Staupitz was also responsible for Martin's being made a lecturer at the University where he struggled anew to find a theological position that he could really believe or, as Erikson puts it, "feel to be true" and "really mean it."

In preparing his lectures on the Psalms, Martin was forced by the scriptures themselves to confront once again the theological problem of God's justice and his own justification. As the mature Luther himself confessed in reference to this period:

> When I first read and sang in the Psalms . . . *in iustitia tua libera me* [and deliver me in thy righteousness], I was horror-stricken and felt deep hostility toward these words, God's righteousness, God's judgment, God's work. For I knew only that *iustitia dei* meant a harsh judgment. Well, was he supposed to save me by judging me harshly? If so, I was lost forever (10:202).

Gradually, during what was probably a series of minor crises leading up to a major resolution, Martin began to appreciate God's justice as forgiveness. In any case, his struggles culminated in the famous revelation in the tower when, as Martin was reviewing Romans 1:17, "the last sentence suddenly assumed a clarity which pervaded his whole being and 'opened the door of paradise' to him: 'For therein is the righteousness of God revealed from faith to faith: as it is written, *The just shall live by faith*'" (10:201). The overwhelming significance of these words lay in the new perspective on the nature of God and man that they gave, namely, that God's justice is expressed in the grace and mercy of Christ by which He justifies men through faith. What is needed on the part of man is not meritorious behavior, but trusting faith in the grace freely given in Christ. In reaching this now famous doctrine of justification by faith, Erikson argues, Luther emancipated himself from the debilitating psychic consequences of guilt before God and laid the foundation for a "religiosity for the adult man."

In the process of explaining how Martin's revelation portrays a vigorous recovery of ego-initiative, Erikson focuses on three themes: "the affirmation of voice and word as the instruments of faith; the new recognition of God's 'face' in the passion of Christ; and the redefinition of a just life" (10:207). In Erikson's view, Luther's confidence in the reconciling Word of God embedded in the matrix of scripture represents a mature recovery of the trusting attitude of every healthy infant. Yet it is more than infantile trust, for it occurs at a higher level of psychic complexity after the inner divisions created by the formation of conscience, will, and reason. On the one hand, such trust involves a deep passivity, which Luther found in the state of prayer, wherein one allows the rich phenomena of the inner life to speak, even to the point of being nearly overwhelmed. This is the feminine side of trust which Erikson suggests "mannish men" ignore at the peril of being alienated from their own psychic depths. On the other hand, trust in the form of faith involves actively choosing to affirm the trustworthiness of existence with the whole of one's being. Faith and conviction of this sort, Erikson maintains, are not only necessary for a strong sense of identity, they are also "indispensable tools for strengthening identity in others" (10:209).

Erikson also finds a recovery of ego-initiative in Luther's recognition of God's face in the crucifixion of Christ. In finding God there, Erikson maintains, Luther abandoned both the prevailing concept of Christ as a substitute victim who died "in the place of" others, as well as the representation of Christ as an ideal (superego) model to be imitated or abjectly venerated. In place of these ancient views, Luther substituted the concept of Christ within, "who is dying *in* everyone even as he died *for* everyone" (10:211). From this personalized perspective, Christ is "the core of the Christian's identity," for "Christ is today here, in me" (10:212). What this means is that the Christian daily acknowledges his utter abandonment in sin before God as well as his total acceptance through the unmerited grace of Christ. Stating psychologically what has just been expressed in theological terms, Erikson argues that Luther's negative conscience and active self-observation resulted in a daily sense of guilt, while his newly discovered identification with Christ's passion provided him with a non-neurotic sense of being continually reborn, renovated, and regenerated. In this way, Luther discovered, as did Freud, a healthy means of ego-mastery over a negative conscience which entailed honest acceptance of guilt, while it fostered a daily sense of recovered ego-strength. "Under these conditions," Erikson writes, "apparent submission becomes mastery, apparent passivity the release of new energy for active pursuits" (10:217-128).

Luther's redefinition of the just life is also said to have promoted a recovery of ego-initiative. When Luther spoke against works from the perspective of justification by faith, he argued that no one is just because he does good works; the works are just only if the man is just. Commenting upon the psychological truth contained within this theological formulation, Erikson observes that

> People with "well-functioning egos" do good work if they can manage to "mean" the work (for whatever reason or for whoever's sake) which they must do. This is not always easily arranged, by any means, and we should not be too glib with the term "strong ego." Many individuals should not do the work which they are doing, if they are doing it well at too great inner expense. Good work it may be in terms of efficiency; but it is also bad works. The point is, not how efficiently the work is done, but how good it is for the worker in terms of his lifetime within his ideological world (10:220).

In stressing the theological importance of the spirit with which work is performed by Christians, Luther not only found a new meaning in daily activities for others, he also discovered a vocation in preaching the Word which tapped his own tremendously creative ego capacities.

On October 31, 1517, at the age of thirty-three, Luther nailed his ninety-five theses on the door of the Castle Church in Wittenberg. The event itself was less dramatic than novelists and movie-makers suppose, as this was a rather typical way for scholars to make their opinions known in Luther's day, yet the drama accorded this event rings true in one important sense: it signaled the emergence of a troubled youth who, having fought his own inner battles, was now prepared to stubbornly challenge pope and emperor in the name of his own hard-won insights. When he later stood before the Diet of Worms and spoke the words of conscience that may have included the phrase "I cannot . . . I will not . . . recant! Here I stand," he did so as one whose newly forged religious identity, although still subject to doubts, supported a determination to stand on his own feet, even in the face of ostracism and death. This is not to imply, Erikson cautions, that Luther was henceforth free of conflicts and infantile behavior. Far from this being the case, the mature Luther continued to be tormented by intra-psychic conflicts while his public behavior combined generosity and kindness with vengeful and spiteful behavior. But there can be little doubt that Luther found in a rejuvenated religious tradition a mature identity which, while not devoid of problems, supported strengths ignored by Freud's analysis of infantile religious personalities.

Indeed, Erikson argues that Luther's religious identity not only promoted ego-initiatives, it also provided the foundation for his resolution of later adult crises. As he reorganized his life around his fresh insights, Luther found heterosexual intimacy with his wife Katherine, a former nun, and interpersonal intimacy with a wide variety of male friends to whom he wrote freely about his emotional life, including sexual experiences, "with a frankness clearly denoting a need to share intimacies with them" (10:259). As preacher and writer, he also demonstrated an ability to relate to the intimate lives of others beyond his immediate circle of friends.

As for generativity, Luther became both a loving father and an impressive leader of a wide following. Yet Erikson also notes that the creative productivity and care for others associated with generativity was severely threatened in Luther's middle years by the peasants' revolt occasioned by his own rebellious writings. The peasants followed the revolutionary style of the young Martin, while the middle-aged Luther warned against insurrections against the princely offices established by God. When the peasants continued to disobey, Hans' son responded in fright and anger as his father might, arguing that the only answer a rebel understands is "a fist that brings blood from the nose" (10:236). After 130,000 peasants were massacred during the battles of May, 1525, Luther suffered a protracted state of anxiety and depression, bordering on manic-depression. As Erikson sees it, this was due in part to profound dissatisfaction with what he had generated, or helped to generate, in the peasants' revolt and its aftermath. Luther recovered sufficiently, however, to proceed with building an impressive theological edifice. A generous father, host, and pastor, he devoted himself to the intimacies involved in marriage, friendship, pastoring, and teaching, bestowing on others the feminine warmth he must have received from his mother (10:250).

As for the last stage of integrity, Erikson argues that Luther, like other religious heroes, faced the problem of how to give meaning to life in spite of death from the outset of his identity struggles. Because he experienced a breakthrough to the last problem so early in life, Luther's identity resolution also solved, albeit not finally, the existential problem of integrity. Later, this sense of integrity became problematic again during his "crisis of generativity," when he felt that a large part of what he had generated was undesirable. As previously noted, however, Luther partially recovered from despair before he died at the age of sixty-three.

In setting forth this analysis of Luther, Erikson not only provides an illuminating account of the Protestant reformer's life, he also revises the Freudian theory of religion in several fundamental respects. While recognizing Freud's basic insight regarding the unconscious motivations expressed in religious beliefs, Erikson overcomes the tendency of psychological reductionism evident in most psychoanalytic studies of religion. Unconscious memories and conflicts are undoubtedly expressed in religious symbols, but so are a variety of social and historical experiences as well as existential dilemmas and past theological insights. In fact, religious symbols not only reflect a variety of human experiences, they provide an occasion for constructive innovations that in turn affect the outcome of psychic conflicts by actively redirecting unconscious motivations. At their best, religions revitalize ego capacities and promote mature resolutions of adult stages of development. Erikson therefore concludes that a vital religious faith no less than psychoanalysis may provide the means by which health and maturity are achieved.

5. HOMO RELIGIOSUS

In his various psychosocial studies of religion, but especially in his recent study of Gandhi, Erikson formulates a normative concept of the genuinely religious man, *homo religiosus*. This concept, which is used to describe actual religious figures, also expresses Erikson's own ethical convictions. In his view, a *homo religiosus* is a major cultural figure—like a Luther, a Kierkegaard, or a Gandhi—who squarely confronts problems dealing with the nature of ultimate reality and the meaning of human existence. As such, he is a specialist in the most pressing existential problems confronting mankind, but evaded by most men. The reasons for this widespread evasion are diverse, but most have to do with anxieties involved in tackling excruciatingly difficult metaphysical questions, which drive most men to utter despair or even psychosis (10:262). The *homo religiosus* also experiences these anxieties, which frequently drive him to the borderline of insanity, yet he proves resilient in the midst of confronting the rock-bottom question of trust in existence as such and uniquely gifted in eventually discovering fresh perspectives on the meaning of human life. The enthusiastic response of less precocious men to these fresh religious insights rests, Erikson states, "on the need of all men to find a few who plausibly take upon themselves—and seem to give meaning to—what others must deny at all times but cannot really forget for a moment" (19:397).

Because adolescence is the developmental stage during which questions regarding the meaning of existence are most pressing, this stage tends to be decisive for the formation of the *homo religiosus*. Unlike his contemporaries, the *homo religiosus* finds traditional religious formulations problematic. Rather than conform to them, "he acts as if mankind were starting all over with his own beginning as an individual, conscious of his singularity as well as his humanity" (10:262). To begin again, he often starves himself, "socially, erotically, and, last but not least, nutritionally, in order to let the grosser weeds die out," and make way for the growth of his "inner garden" (10:44). In other words, he confronts both his inner self as well as the traditional beliefs of his culture with a searching honesty that persists until he discovers that which he can really feel to be true. In searching for what "feels effectively true" about himself and his world, the *homo religiosus* deals with a level of reality which, because it cannot be empirically demonstrated, is distinguished by Erikson from the factual reality with which the sciences deal (19:396). Unlike the scientist, the vocation of *homo religiosus* is to give expression to empirically nonverifiable dimensions of reality by the use of significant words and images which convincingly illumine the mystery surrounding man's existence in the world. Because this vocation is always exercised within a particular social context, the symbolic resources available to the *homo religiosus* vary according to his culture, although it is his special task to decisively rejuvenate these resources by reformulating his cultural heritage. Gandhi, for example, drew upon the traditional resources of Hinduism in forging a fresh politico-religious ideology, just as Luther depended upon the symbols of Christianity for his reformation.[26]

In *Gandi's Truth*, Erikson goes beyond the foregoing description of *homo religiosus* and sets forth his own views, in dialogue with Gandhi, regarding the type of nonviolent, "all-human identity" for which he feels genuine *homines religiosi* in our day are, and ought to be, working. In doing so, Erikson forges Gandhian and psychoanalytic insights into a fresh perspective intended to suggest a universal identity whereby modern men might transcend the all-pervasive violence that threatens the continuation of the human species.

In Erikson's opinion, Gandhi, like all great *homines religiosi*, realized that truth is revealed in action, that genuine religion ethically renews and regenerates men in the present. At the center of Gandhi's religious actualism was his belief that "man should act in such a way that he actualizes both in himself and in the other such forces as are ready for a heightened mutuality" (19:413). Thus, *"truly worthwhile acts enhance a mutuality between the doer and the other—a mutuality which strengthens the doer even as it strengthens the other"* (13:233). This ideal, which Erikson identifies with the Golden Rule in Christianity and similar maxims in other religions, represents the goal which he believes all contemporary *homines religiosi* should convincingly articulate and actively apply in their varying social contexts.[27] For the ethical substance of religion can only become actual in specific cultural settings where it is reinforced by different and yet analogous traditions, and where religious innovators vividly express in meaningful contemporary terms the highest human ideals.

A central concept at the heart of Gandhi's nonviolent and mutuality-centered protest against British rule in India was the traditional Hindu concept of *ahimsa.*[28] Literally translated, *ahimsa* is the refusal to do violence to another living creature. In actuality, as Erikson points out, *ahimsa* came to mean more than this in Gandhi's reformulation. It also expressed his commitment not to do violence to the essence of another person, even his enemies, for such violence only evokes counter-violence, which may end in an uneasy truce, but not in a higher form of inter-personal communion. Respect for his opponents as equals and for their capacity to acknowledge the truth was a working premise of Gandhi's political tactics. In addition, Gandhi's concept of *ahimsa* included a willingness to suffer, not for masochistic purposes, but as a means of revealing the truth latent within his opponents, as well as within con-flict situations. This voluntary acceptance of self-suffering included a willingness to be changed by the other in the process of trying to change him. Because of the religious roots and cultural pervasiveness of *ahimsa* in India, Gandhi was able to adopt this ideal not only for himself, but as the ideological basis of a new popular movement. Prior to planned confrontations, all participants entered upon a spiritual discipline during which they internalized voluntary acceptance of self-suffering, even unto death, as the means to a heightened mutuality. To Erikson, this use of *ahimsa* represents a creative ritualization which enables men to avoid destructive violence while maximizing the creative resources and latent unity among participants.

Erikson was attracted to *ahimsa* not only as a specific cultural ex-pression of the ethical ideal of caring mutuality stressed by religious traditions at their best, but also because of the inner affinity between this method of resolving sociopolitical conflicts and the implicit ethic employed by psychoanalysts in interpersonal therapy. Like *ahimsa,* psy-choanalysis is a method for nonviolently overcoming destructive forces within the self, for example: overbearing conscience and instinctual rage. Like Gandhi, the analyst presupposes a relation of equality with the patient, recognizing in himself similar psychic conflicts as well as the patient's capacity for accepting the truth about himself. The analyst, like the adherent of *ahimsa,* seeks to avoid violating the personal essence of the patient by refraining from manipulative practices and overbearing interpretations. Respect for the potential strength of the patient is as basic for the analyst as it was for Gandhi. Because analysts seek to enable people to deal with themselves and others in a nonviolent way, Erikson believes that the ethic of psychoanalytic practice and *ahimsa* are mutually compatible, even necessary complements of one another.

The importance of this mutuality is indicated by Erikson's criticism, from a psychoanalytic perspective, of the ruthless way in which Gandhi imposed severe moral asceticism (e.g., abstinence from sexual intercourse) on himself and his followers. Gandhi's appreciation of the desirability of nonviolent political activities was combined with a severe moralism involving intra-psychic violence. Far from avoiding hostility, Erikson argues, asceticism of this sort merely drives our worst proclivities underground, where they endeavor to find expression in subtle and not so subtle forms of self-hatred and sadism towards others. To avoid these psychic consequences, Erikson believes modern man must eschew strict moralism in favor of conscious acknowledgment of sexual and aggressive impulses within the self. For strict moralism invariably fosters violent reactions among those upon whom it is imposed, while conscious insight enables men to be more gentle with themselves and with others. For these reasons, Erikson believes Gandhi's nonviolent sociopolitical tactics need to be complemented by Freudian insights regarding nonviolent acceptance of oneself and others, just as psychoanalysis needs to be complemented by nonviolent sociopolitical tactics in the social arena.

Erikson's criteria for a genuine *homo religiosus* today include not only psychic and social nonviolence, but a universal appreciation of the oneness of mankind. Disturbed by the prevalence of what he calls "pseudo-species," namely, the assumption that a segment of humanity possesses the values and attributes of the whole, Erikson criticizes former ideologies, including religions, for promoting narrow parochialism at the expense of a worldwide human identity. Mankind, however, is one species, regardless of these attempts to subvert recognition of this fact. Today, acknowledgment of this species-wide identity on the part of every *homo religiosus* is indispensable, if mankind is to survive the very real threat of nuclear annihilation. Therefore, a principal function of the contemporary *homo religiosus* is to disarm the pseudo-species mentality of warring groups by an inspired search for an inclusive human identity supported by a new world vision.

6. ERIKSON AS A HOMO RELIGIOSUS

Erikson interprets religion from a revised psychoanalytic and humanistic perspective rather than from the theological tradition of a particular religious community. Perhaps for this reason, his work provides the most comprehensive reformulation of the central issues raised by Freud's critique of religion. As previously indicated, Erikson responds persuasively to each of the three major challenges posed by the founder of psychoanalysis. Moreover, he is as sensitive to the inner experiences and constructive consequences of religious life as are most contemporary theologians. His discussion of faith as a mature form of trust, like Bonhoeffer's treatment of Christian adulthood, is a creative antidote to Freud's interpretation of infantile religiosity. With contemporary critics of psychoanalytic reductionism, Erikson recognizes the non-neurotic, existential issues at the heart of the mature religious quest. He also regards religious symbols as creative resources for the resolution of psychosocial problems, including the transformation of psychic drives in the direction of more realistic, ethical motivations. Indeed, religion, or a surrogate, is necessary, in Erikson's opinion, to support the adult virtues of loving mutuality, caring generativity, and full integrity. His sympathetic treatment of this broad range of religious concerns combined with his own suggestions regarding a universal, nonviolent human identity, indicates that Erikson himself is a *homo religiosus,* albeit one whose convictions are based on psychoanalysis and humanism rather than a specific historical religion.

In exploring the psychic depths of human nature, including the underlying motivations of religious figures, and in reformulating the established conclusions of his own psychoanalytic profession, Erikson not only performs functions analogous to those of a *homo religiosus,* he also sets forth a new variant of this model. In contrast with Bonhoeffer, who formulated one of the most creative theological responses to Freud in the process of becoming a *homo religiosus,* Erikson delves much deeper into the underlying psychic motivations expressed, and worked through, by religious personalities. Bonhoeffer, it will be recalled, broke through to a new form of mature self-actualization (including personal and political dimensions) from within the Christian tradition. He thus became an influential model for other contemporary Christians, like the Berrigan brothers. While a variety of personal relationships and social experiences influenced this reformulation, Bonhoeffer integrated these experiences around his central concept of Jesus as "the man for others." Yet Bonhoeffer remained psychologically naive, despite this successful identity resolution. Indeed, he valued that naiveté as intrinsic to his personal and theological identity. Erikson, by way of contrast, is a psychologically sophisticated *homo religiosus,* who explores his own inner depths and those of others with psychoanalytic categories. Yet Erikson recognizes that religious men, like Bonhoeffer, successfully resolve psychosocial conflicts with religious symbols and without explicit recourse to psychoanalytic perspectives.

Erikson also goes beyond Bonhoeffer in formulating a new model of maturity. For Bonhoeffer, adulthood involves resolute personal autonomy free of dependency on others as well as the exercise of rational processes in technical and social organizations. In contrast, Erikson's model of maturity joins personal autonomy with caring mutuality. It also calls not only for the exercise of rational processes, but for acceptance of those infantile, sexual, and aggressive components of personality never fully integrated by the rational ego. He even suggests that the mature man is free to regress without jeopardizing his developmental achievements; indeed, temporary regression, being in the service of the ego, is an essential aspect of maturity. In other words, Erikson's ideal of maturity is more inclusive, incorporating, as it does, deeper psychic processes and childlike responses. Bonhoeffer, to be sure, exhibited many of these characteristics in his personal life, but his explication of adulthood did not encourage the appropriation of these more primitive processes.

While these several achievements of Erikson are clearly seminal, one might legitimately question whether basic trust is really the central religious sentiment. If so, how is this trust related to the perception of radical evil in the world and in man that is central to some religious formulations, like apocalypticism? How does one maintain a balance of mature faith over radical distrust in a social milieu characterized by seemingly endless exploitation and oppression? Within the biblical tradition, faith in the goodness of creation was modified by apocalyptic sensitivity to the thoroughgoing evil of the present order. In light of this theme and contemporary expressions of it in the theology of radical politics, Erikson's emphasis upon trust seems optimistically one-sided. There can be no doubt, however, that Erikson has succeeded in bringing forth central aspects of religious experience for careful and illuminating analysis.

NOTES

1 In emphasizing these traits, Erikson is partly indebted to several major figures in the development of ego psychology, especially to Anna Freud, *The Ego and the Mechanisms of Defense* [1936] (New York: International Universities Press, 1946); Heinz Hartmann, *Ego Psychology and the Problem of Adaptation* [1939] (New York: International Universities Press, 1958); and David Rapaport, "Some Metapsychological Considerations Concerning Activity and Passivity," unpublished paper, 1953, "The Theory of Ego Autonomy: A Generalization," *Bulletin of the Menninger Clinic*, XX (1958), 13-35. Erikson himself, however, was one of the most influential pioneers of ego psychology.

2 Erikson's opposition to reductionism is central to his exploration of cultural, historical, and theological factors in his psychosocial study of *Young Man Luther* (New York: W. W. Norton, 1958). At the outset of this study, Erikson explicitly rejects narrowly psychoanalytic causal theories in favor of an inter-

disciplinary approach that recognizes the numerous factors influencing Luther's religious beliefs. See *ibid.*, chs. 1-2, *passim.*

3 Throughout his study of *Young Man Luther*, Erikson insists that the Protestant reformer's concept of God was far more complex than the projection theory would suggest, although projection was partly responsible for Luther's theological beliefs. See, for example, *Young Man Luther*, pp. 70-71.

4 For illustrations of the positive consequences of religion, see Erikson's *Childhood and Society* (New York: W. W. Norton, 1963), pp. 250-251; *Young Man Luther*, pp. 264-266; *Identity: Youth and Crisis* (New York: W. W. Norton, 1968), p. 106; *Insight and Responsibility* (New York: W. W. Norton, 1964), pp. 116-117, 152-153.

5 For biographical material, see Erik Erikson, "Autobiographic Notes on the Identity Crisis," *Daedalus* (Summer, 1970), 730-759; Robert Coles, *Erik H. Erikson, The Growth of His Work* (Boston: Little, Brown, 1970), esp. chs. 2, 3, 4, 5, 7, and 9.

6 The school was established by Dorothy Burlingham, a wealthy American, whose maiden name was Tiffany, and Anna Freud. Peter Blos, like Erikson, later became a well-known American child analyst and author. His major work is *On Adolescence: A Psychoanalytic Interpretation* (New York: Free Press, 1962).

7 Anna Freud and Melanie Klein were the first child analysts. For their writings on child analysis and education, see Anna Freud, *The Psychoanalytical Treatment of Children* (London: Imago Publishing Co., 1946); "Observations on Child Development," *The Psychoanalytic Study of the Child* (New York: International Universities Press, 1951), vol. 6, pp. 18-30; *Psychoanalysis for Teachers and Parents*, trans. Barbara Low (New York: Emerson Books, 1954); and Melanie Klein, *The Psychoanalysis of Children* (London: Hogarth Press, 1932).

8 Margaret Mead, who set sail for Samoa in 1925, was the first anthropologist to commence fieldwork with the avowed intention of studying socialization. In this work, Mead increasingly drew upon psychoanalytic resources. See, for example, *Sex and Temperament in Three Primitive Societies* [1935] (New York: Mentor Books, 1950). John Dollard (1900-   ), a prominent American sociologist with psychoanalytic training in Europe, was an early advocate of studies of personality combining psychoanalytic and cultural approaches. See his *Criteria for the Life History* [1935] (New York: P. Smith, 1949), esp. ch. 1. Alfred Kroeber (1876-1960) was one of the leading American anthropologists of his generation. Like other anthropologists during the 1920's, Kroeber was initially extremely hostile to Freud's attempt, in *Totem and Taboo*, to introduce psychoanalytic theory into ethnology. This negative response to Freud's work is especially apparent in his 1920 review, *"Totem and Taboo:* An Ethnologic Psychoanalysis," *American Anthropologist*, New Series, Vol. 22 (1920), 48-55. Nevertheless, Kroeber underwent a brief analysis himself and subsequently practiced psychoanalysis in San Francisco. Subsequently, he argued in favor of joining psychology and anthropology, although he warned against simplistic approaches to this extremely complex field. See Alfred Kroeber, *The Nature of Culture* (Chicago, University of Chicago Press, 1952). Kurt Lewin (1890-1947) is best known for his interdisciplinary "field theory" approach to psychological and social reality. In a variety of experimental studies on cognitive learning, psychological motivation, group leadership, adolescence, and social restraints, he continually crossed the traditional boundaries dividing the human sciences. For a brief review of his work, see Ronald Lippitt, "Lewin, Kurt," *International Encyclopedia of the Social Sciences* (New York: Macmillan and Free Press, 1968), vol. 9, pp. 266-276.

9 Erikson was in the vanguard of child socialization theory when, in the 1930's, he studied the child-rearing practices of the Sioux. Partly as a result of his work, anthropologists subsequently began to devote considerable attention to the ways in which culturally diverse child-rearing practices affect personality development. For a comprehensive bibliography of anthropological reports on child care and child-rearing, see Margaret Mead, "Research on Primitive Children," in L. Carmichael, *Manual of Child Psychology* (New York: John Wiley, 1946).

10 Géza Róheim and Erikson were the first psychoanalysts to engage in anthropological fieldwork. Róheim set out on a field trip to central Australia in 1928, Erikson studied the Sioux in 1938. Both of them studied child-rearing practices and interpreted customs, rituals, and values, but their impact upon anthropologists was very different. "Róheim was so arbitrary and dogmatic in his interpretations that he antagonized many anthropologists and gave the study of socialization a bad name among the more conservative members of the profession. Erikson's interpretations were, by contrast, sensitive, illuminating, and nondogmatic—a fact which did much to counteract the influence of Róheim." J. M. Whiting, "Socialization, Anthropological Aspects," *International Encyclopedia of the Social Sciences*, vol. 14, pp. 545-546. For Erikson's fieldwork findings, see *Childhood and Society*, Part II, pp. 111-186.

11 For a case history of a soldier with these symptoms of disturbed ego identity, see *Childhood and Society*, pp. 38-47.

12 For a discussion of adolescent identity, see *Childhood and Society*, pp. 261-263; *Identity: Youth and Crisis*, pp. 15-44, 128-135. In turning to the problems of adolescents, Erikson was influenced by Anna Freud and August Auchhorn. See, Anna Freud, *The Ego and the Mechanisms of Defense*, chs. 11 and 12; Anna Freud, "Adolescence," in *The Psychoanalytic Study of the Child* (New York: International Universities Press, 1958), Vol. 13, pp. 255-268; August Auchhorn, *Wayward Youth*, with a Foreword by Sigmund Freud (New York: Viking Press, 1935). This influence aside, Erikson's own work greatly stimulated new psychological research on adolescence. Today, most psychological literature on adolescence is heavily indebted to Erikson's work, especially his concept of identity. For a general survey of literature on adolescence, see Dorothy Eichorn, "Adolescence," *International Encyclopedia of the Social Sciences*, vol. I, pp 85-96.

13 For Erikson's view of Freud, see *Insight and Responsibility*, ch. 1, pp. 19-41.

14 Anna Freud focused upon the defensive functions of the ego, while Heinz Hartmann initially stressed the ego's adaptation to its environment. In contrast, Erikson emphasized the resourcefulness and creativity of the ego. Subsequently, this concept of ego creativity has been widely accepted.

15 For Erikson's theory of psychosocial development, see *Childhood and Society*, ch. 7, pp. 247-274; *Identity: Youth and Crisis*, ch. 3, pp. 91-142. For a critique of this psychosocial theory, see Robert W. White, "Competence and the Psychosexual Stages of Development," *Nebraska Symposium on Motivation*, VIII (1960).

16 Ernst Kris (1900-1957) became a psychoanalyst after receiving a Ph.D. in the history of art from the University of Vienna (1922). He developed his now famous notion of "regression in the service of the ego" to describe the inspirational phase of the creative act. See "On Inspiration," *International Journal of Psychoanalysis*, XX (1939), 377-389.

17 For material on child neglect and its consequences for basic trust, see John Bowlby, *Child Care and the Growth of Love*, 2nd ed. (Harmondsworth, En-

gland: Penguin Books, 1965), esp. ch. 1, pp. 13-74; Lawrence Casler, "Maternal Deprivation: A Critical Review of the Literature," *Society for Research in Child Development*, Monograph 26, no. 2; Erikson, *Childhood and Society*, ch. 5, pp. 195-208.

[18] For a clear discussion of these personal and social aspects of identity, see Erikson, "Identity, Psychosocial," *International Encyclopedia of the Social Sciences*, vol. 7, pp. 61-65.

[19] Erikson employs his concepts of "totalism" and "negative identity" to explain aspects of juvenile delinquency. See, for example, *Identity: Youth and Crisis*, pp. 253-256. Also see Peter Blos, "Delinquency," *Adolescents: Psychoanalytic Approach to Problems and Therapy*, ed. Sandor Lorand and Henry Schneer (New York: Harper & Row, 1961).

[20] Erikson's concept of metaphysical anxiety appears to have been influenced by Tillich's discussion of the existential threat of non-being in the latter's *The Courage To Be* (New Haven: Yale University Press, 1952). For a general discussion of existential anxiety in contemporary theology, philosophy, and psychology, see Rollo May *et al.*, eds., *Existence, a New Dimension in Psychiatry and Psychology* (New York: Basic Books, 1958), chs. 1-2.

[21] This composite definition of religion as viewed by Erikson was suggested to the writer by Clifford Geertz's formulation, which is remarkably similar to Erikson's view of religion. According to Geertz, "a religion is a system of symbols which acts to establish powerful, pervasive and long-lasting moods and motivations in men by formulating conceptions of a general order of existence and clothing these conceptions with such an aura of factuality that the moods and motivations seem uniquely realistic." Clifford Geertz, "Religion as a Cultural System," in Michael Banton, ed., *Anthropological Approaches to the Study of Religion* (London: Tavistock Press, 1966), p. 4.

[22] For a discussion of the recuperative value of temporary regression, see Erikson, *Young Man Luther*, p. 265.

[23] For a good general biography of Luther, see Roland H. Bainton, *Here I Stand* (New York: Abingdon-Cokesbury Press, 1930).

[24] The crisis in Freud's life that Erikson has in mind occurred during his friendship with Fliess. See Erikson, "The First Psychoanalyst," *Insight and Responsibility*, pp. 19-46; Sigmund Freud, *The Origins of Psychoanalysis: Letters to Wilhelm Fliess, Drafts and Notes: 1887-1902*, eds. Marie Bonaparte, Anna Freud and Ernst Kris (New York: Basic Books, 1954).

[25] The well-known sociologist of religion, Robert Bellah, sees this symbolic redirecting of unconscious motivations as a central function of religious beliefs. See, for example, Robert Bellah, *Beyond Belief* (New York: Harper & Row, 1970), pp. 3-17, 76-97.

[26] For Erikson's psychosocial analysis of Gandhi's life, see his *Gandhi's Truth: On the Origins of Militant Nonviolence* (New York: W. W. Norton, 1969), pp. 97-226; pp. 229-392. For a good secondary exposition of Erikson's study of Gandhi, see Robert Coles, *Erik H. Erikson*, ch. XI, pp. 293-399.

[27] Mutuality is the central value in the ethical theory that Erikson joins with his psychosocial theory. As a corollary, it follows that exploitation, especially the exploitation of children, is "the most deadly of all possible sins" (*Young Man Luther*, p. 70). For Erikson's reinterpretation of the Golden Rule as mutuality, see "The Golden Rule in the Light of New Insight," *Insight and Responsibility*, ch. VI, pp. 217-243.

[28] For Gandhi's ethics of nonviolence, see Mohandas K. Gandhi, *Non-violent Resistance* (New York: Schocken Books, 1961); Joan Bondurant, *Conquest of Violence: The Gandhian Philosophy of Conflict*, rev. ed. (Berkeley: University of California Press, 1965); Erikson, *Gandhi's Truth*, pp. 373-377, 410-423, 436-440.

BIBLIOGRAPHY

1. COLES, ROBERT, *Erik H. Erikson: The Growth of His Work*. Boston: Little, Brown, 1970.

2. ERIKSON, ERIK H., "Observations on Sioux Education," *Journal of Psychology*. 7 (1939), 101-156.

3. ———, "Hitler's Imagery and German Youth," *Psychiatry*. 5 (1942), 475-493.

4. ———, *Observations on the Yurok: Childhood and World Image*. Monograph, University of California Publications in American Archaeology and Ethnology. 35 (1943), 257-301.

5. ———, "Plans for the Veteran with Symptoms of Instability," in *Community Planning for Peacetime Living*, ed. Louis Wirth. Stanford, Calif.: Stanford University Press, 1945.

6. ———, "Childhood and Tradition in Two American Indian Tribes," in *The Psychoanalytic Study of the Child*, vol. I, pp. 319-350. New York: International Universities Press, 1945.

7. ———, "Ego Development and Historical Change," in *The Psychoanalytic Study of the Child*, vol. II, pp. 359-396. New York: International Universities Press, 1946.

8. ———, *Childhood and Society*. New York: W. W. Norton, 1950. Second, enlarged edition, 1963.

9. ———, "Freud's 'The Origins of Psychoanalysis,'" *International Journal of Psychoanalysis*. 36 (1955), 1-15.

10. ———, *Young Man Luther: A Study in Psychoanalysis and History*. New York: W. W. Norton, 1958.

11. ———, "Identity and the Life Cycle: Selected Papers," in *Psychological Issues*, vol. I. New York: International Universities Press, 1959.

12. ———, ed., *Youth: Change and Challenge*. New York: Basic Books, 1963.

13. ———, *Insight and Responsibility*. New York: W. W. Norton, 1964.

14. ———, "Gandhi's Autobiography: The Leader as a Child." *The American Scholar* (Autumn, 1966).

15. ———, "The Human Life Cycle," in *International Encyclopedia of the Social Sciences*. New York: Macmillan, 1968.

16. ———, "Psychosocial Identity," in *International Encyclopedia of the Social Sciences*. New York: Macmillan, 1968.

17. ———, *Identity: Youth and Crisis*. New York: W. W. Norton, 1968.

18. ———, "The Development of Ritualization," in *The Religious Situation*, ed. Donald Cutler. Boston: Beacon Press, 1968.

19. ———, *Gandhi's Truth*. New York: W. W. Norton, 1969.

20. ———, "Autobiographic Notes on the Identity Crisis": *Daedalus*. (Summer, 1970), 730-759.

21. MAIER, HENRY W., *Three Theories of Child Development*. New York: Harper & Row, 1965.

SUGGESTED READINGS

1. *Primary Readings*

Erikson's most important psychosocial analysis of religion may be found in his *Young Man Luther* (10), pp. 49-97, 98-125, 125-169, 201-222, 251-267. For another example of Erikson's interpretation of a religious figure, see his discussion of Gandhi's childhood and maturation in *Gandhi's Truth* (19), pp. 97-226, 229-392. For Erikson's discussion of *homo religiosus*, see *Young Man Luther* (10), pp. 34-35, 37, 39, 40, 261-262; *Insight and Responsibility* (13), pp. 202-205, 208; *Gandhi's Truth* (19), pp. 194-195, 395-409.

2. *Secondary Readings*

For an intellectual biography of Erikson, see Robert Coles, *Erik H. Erikson* (1). For a brief overview of Erikson's psychological theory, see Henry W. Maier, *Three Theories of Child Development* (21), ch. 2, pp. 12-74. For a critique of Erikson's eight stages of development, see Robert W. White, "Competence and the Psychosexual Stages of Development," *Nebraska Symposium on Motivation*, VIII (1960). For a careful philosophical discussion of the significance of Erikson's contribution to a general theory of human nature, see Daniel Yankelovich and William Barrett, *Ego and Instinct: The Psychoanalytic View of Human Nature—Revised* (New York: Random House, 1970), esp. chs. 8 and 9. For Erikson's contribution to the understanding of faith, see Leland Elhard, "Living Faith: Some Contributions of the Concept of Ego-identity to the Understanding of Faith," *The Dialogue Between Theology and Psychology*, ed. Peter Homans (Chicago: University of Chicago Pres, 1968), pp. 135-161.

3. *Additional Bibliography*

For a complete bibliography to 1970 of Erikson's writings, see Robert Coles, *Erik H. Erikson* (1), pp. 421-425.

V

HISTORY AND RELIGION

11

Modern Historical Thought and the Challenge to Individual Religions

People who vacation or live near an ocean or a lake now and then have occasion to witness the sun shining across the water, either at dusk or dawn. When the sun is right at the horizon its rays seem to concentrate in a single pathway across the water, moving directly to the point where the observer stands. As you watch, for a time, the intense solar light appears to shine across the water on *you* alone. Everywhere else, it seems, all over the water and along the shore, the gray pall of the twilight is hovering.

Obviously, a person positioned a mile down the shoreline perceives the sun in exactly the same way. How foolish it would be, then, for either one of the observers to deny that the sun was shining directly on the other. How foolish it would be for one of the observers to maintain that he alone, not the other, sees the pathway of light.

What is obvious about the sun shining across the waters has not always been considered obvious in the sphere of religion. Sometimes, when a religious tradition is young, or when it is isolated for a long time, the question about what the other man sees does not even arise. But usually, sooner or later it does: Do not other men also have a direct revelation of God? Has God chosen to disclose himself only at the point where *we* are standing?

For a number of religious traditions this kind of question causes little, if any, anxiety. The Hindu for example, assumes that God as a matter of course reveals himself in differing ways to all peoples. The Hindu has a place in his schema for the Lord of Judaism, and his Torah, for the Christ of the Church, and his message of Love, for the Prophet of Islam, and his holy Truth, and so on. The vision of the Hindu is *inclusivistic*.[1] As he understands religion, the rays of the sun shine across the waters to everyone. But there are other religions, especially the three aforementioned faiths, which have held that the truth about the rays of the sun shining across the water is not at all the truth about their own particular religious standpoints. Judaism, Christianity, and Islam, in their classical forms and in various ways, have been self-consciously *exclusivistic*. They have generally affirmed that the light of Divine truth and reality has shined directly on them alone, and that other religions live either in the twilight or altogether in the darkness.

This, then, is the general shape of a religious question which has become particularly pressing in the West: Do other faiths have any validity? If so, in what sense? Does my own faith have absolute validity? This kind of question first emerged in the West during the late nineteenth century, when knowledge of "non-Western religions" began to grow, both through comprehensive scientific study and greater opportunities for firsthand contact. By the second half of the twentieth century, the question came alive for most religiously oriented people who have been touched by the contemporary intellectual and cultural milieu. In universities today, courses in "world religions" are immensely popular. Also, the mass media, such as the famous *Life* magazine series on world religions, are having an extensive impact. Opportunities for travel, also, have made possible a new kind of direct contact with diverse religions. The citizen of today's world, for all intents and purposes, lives in a "global village." Hence the question of the validity of other religions is virtually inescapable.

It was the greatness of Ernst Troeltsch (1865-1923) to recognize the import of the question of the validity of other religions, and to deal with the question with a breadth of knowledge and a depth of sensitivity which set him apart from others who have dealt with the same set of problems. Like many scholars in German universities at the turn of the century, Troeltsch's interests and knowledge were comprehensive. His writings deal with religion, society, history, culture, ethics, and a variety of related topics. He even found time for an active political life and was once mentioned publicly as a possible candidate for the Presidency of the Weimar Republic.

But Troeltsch's most fundamental concern throughout his distinguished career was historical thinking and the impact of that mode of thought on the modern consciousness. He identified the birth of a *new kind of historical consciousness* in the modern period, a consciousness which he referred to as "historicism." [2] According to this mode of thought, all historical phenomena must be approached empathetically and objectively. They must be interpreted in their own terms before any value judgments are applied to them; no religion or no set of values should be denied its own significance, indeed, its own irreducible significance. Troeltsch was convinced that this kind of historical thinking was bound to have radical ramifications within the spheres of religion and values. Troeltsch's lifework was an effort to insure that those ramifications would be creative, not destructive. He believed, on the one hand, that modern man cannot avoid a thoroughgoing historical consciousness. "Historicism" is an unavoidable element in the cultural atmosphere of modernity. More particularly, Troeltsch was convinced that the historicist approach to human life raised legitimate questions about the traditional exclusivist claims of Christianity, and also about the claims Western men were wont to make for the ultimate validity of their values generally. Troeltsch was deeply troubled, on the other hand, by the rise of a thoroughgoing "cultural relativism," occasioned by the historicist approach. In a word, if historically "everything is relative," does that not mean that "anything goes"? Does not cultural relativism, which seems to arrive fast on the heels of historical thinking, result in total anarchy in the area of values?

The issue of cultural relativism, however, was not merely an intellectual one for Troeltsch. It was profoundly personal and practical. This is one of the reasons why Troeltsch is such a significant figure. He sought to take the claims of traditional religion with utmost seriousness. His own personal history was a history of struggle, for a viable faith, as well as for an uncompromising intellectual honesty. Although a critic of religious exclusivism, Troeltsch was nevertheless a deeply religious man.

Already as a student Troeltsch began to feel the force of the relativizing tendencies of the modern intellectual milieu. He developed, as he says, "a deep and vivid realization of the clash between historical reflection and the determination of standards of truth and value." He felt the profound anguish of the committed believer who is completely open to truth, from whatever source, who then comes upon certain truths that seem to radically undermine his own faith. Troeltsch recounts how thoroughly he was influenced, at a very early age, by historical and humanistic studies. At the same time, however, he was consistently and passionately concerned, as he explains, to reach "a vital and effective religious position, which could alone furnish my life with a centre of reference for all practical questions, and could alone give meaning and purpose to reflection upon the things of this world" (24:5).

It was the latter interest that led Troeltsch to study philosophy and theology, with an engulfing personal concern. But these studies, he found, only plunged him further into the clash between intellectual truth and religious conviction. "I soon discovered," he writes, ". . . that the historical studies which had so largely formed me, and the theology and philosophy in which I was now immersed, stood in sharp opposition, indeed even in conflict with one another" (24:6). Troeltsch found himself confronted, on the one hand, with "the perpetual flux of the historian's data, and the distrustful attitude of the historical critic towards conventional traditions," and on the other hand with the reality of the "impulse in men towards a definite practical standpoint—the eagerness of the trusting soul to receive divine revelation and to obey divine commands." "It was largely out of this conflict," Troeltsch states, "which was no hypothetical one, but a fact of my own practical experience, that my entire theoretical standpoint took its rise" (24:6). Troeltsch's own soul became an arena for the conflict between the relativizing tendencies of the modern intellectual milieu and the demands of the religious consciousness for certainty.

1. WESTERN APPROACHES TO "NON-CHRISTIAN RELIGIONS"

To understand Troeltsch's approach to the truth-claims of individual religions, it is important to have a concrete picture of his own cultural inheritance. Most of Troeltsch's historical study, and most of his personal concern likewise, focused on the history of Western Christendom. Accordingly, whenever he dealt with the question of the truth-claims of individual religions, it was Western Christianity that was foremost in his mind. This was the framework and the focus of his scholarly and personal explorations and reflections.

Within Western Christendom three major approaches to non-Christian religions may be identified: Christian traditionalism, rationalism, and historicism. Each one of these, in differing ways, markedly influenced the shape and the substance of Troeltsch's thought.

On the whole, the representatives of *Christian traditionalism* have been only dimly aware of other religions. On occasion even this general awareness has tended to be missing. Accordingly, the traditionalist usually has shown little evidence of concrete knowledge of the actual beliefs and practices of non-Christian religions. Rarely if ever has the traditionalist broken through to any kind of empathetic appreciation for non-Christian religions. His approach has been dominated by an unquestioned sense of superiority.

The roots of traditionalist approach are to be found in the New Testament itself. The first generation of Christians, like Jesus himself, expected a speedy end to the whole cosmos. They had a strong "eschato-logical consciousness." Related to this sense of the impending end of the world was a strong "election consciousness," inherited from the traditions of Judaism. This is expressed most vividly perhaps in the Book of Revelation, which depicts a community of elect ones surviving the final catastrophic judgment that is about to be loosed on the world. This kind of eschatological and election consciousness frequently fused with feelings of hostility toward other more powerful religions, such as Judaism and the various official Roman religions. These dominant religions had apparently been persecuting the new Christian sect, in varying degrees, from the very beginning. This made mutual understanding exceedingly difficult.

A century later several early Church fathers did discuss non-Christian religions, but—ironically—this mainly took the form of analysis and criticism of *Homeric* religion, not of the living non-Christian religions in their immediate proximity. This kind of non-awareness of non-Christian religions became even more pronounced with the coming of the Constantinian era, when Christianity became the official state religion. And, it reached the point of virtual ignorance during the Middle Ages. True, there was always an awareness of the so-called heathen and the Jews, but this was hardly a sympathetic appreciation of non-Christian religions or even an awareness of their particularities. Dante, for example, consigned Muhammed to the twenty-eighth sphere of his Inferno, as the arch protagonist of damnable schism. The political counterpart of this theology was the Crusade and the forced conversion of the Jews, which hardly represented any sympathetic knowledge of, or any positive appreciation for, non-Christian religions.

This lack of knowledge, and lack of appreciation, of other faiths persisted generally in Christendom through the Reformation and the Counter-Reformation periods. Contact with non-Western peoples in the decades of world exploration, in the fifteenth and sixteenth centuries, did not appreciably change the situation. The impulse to conversion, accompanied by a lack of real understanding of the culture and religion of those to be converted, was the dominating religious factor. Even as late as 1860 at the first ecumenically representative Christian missionary conference in Liverpool, hardly a word was said about the non-Christian religions, with which the missionaries were to be dealing every day. Ignorance of non-Christian religions, and an unquestioned sense of superiority, continued to be the characteristic marks of the Christian consciousness.

Official Christianity did not really begin to take cognizance of non-Christian religions until toward the end of the nineteenth century. What seemed to be a dramatic departure from the traditionalist stance of the

Church occurred in 1893. This was the momentous Parliament of World Religions, which met in conjunction with the Columbian Exposition in Chicago.[4] The famous historian of religion, Max Mueller, hailed this vast gathering of representatives from all the world's religions as a world-historical event. He was convinced that it signaled the dawning of a new era of mutual understanding. This 1893 Parliament is, indeed, worth careful consideration.

The Parliament was a grandiose affair. Ten religions were represented by leaders from all over the world. It lasted for seventeen days. Over 150,000 people attended its sessions. Its organizer and director, a certain John Henry Barrows, said in retrospect that "the Parliament gave mankind the first opportunity of studying religion, not in its fragments, but in its entirety, as represented in one historic assemblage." Barrows also spoke enthusiastically about the openness of the meeting. He contrasted it with the closed-mindedness of much of traditional Western Christianity. The Parliament, he observed, "was certainly a protest against the exclusiveness of feeling, the ignorant pride, the ecclesiastical aloofness, and the dogmatic haughtiness, which often prevail" (2:304,309). These are glowing words.

Upon closer examination, however, the basic premise and the final conclusion of the Parliament appear to be consistent with missionary Christianity of the nineteenth century, namely, the unquestioned superiority of Christianity to all religions.[5] The only difference was that, in this instance, some effort was made to understand non-Christian religions. As Barrows himself describes the Parliament, it was "a great Christian demonstration with a non-Christian section which added color and picturesque effect." "Only Christianity," he writes, "proclaimed itself the missionary and absolute religion with the world for its field." More specifically, Barrows describes the results of the Parliament this way:

> it was generally felt and said by Christian ministers, journalists, and teachers, that the Christianity of Christ displayed its glorious supremacy, its peerless character from first to last, and some went so far as to affirm that the non-Christian religions would never be willing to appear again in a great world congress, and show their little tapers by the side of Christianity's solar orb.

"When at the closing meeting," Barrows observes, "one speaker ventured to suggest that no religion should henceforth seek to make converts of the others, that strange remark received applause from only one person" (2:312,313).

So, notwithstanding the opportunity for firsthand conversation with representatives of nine non-Christian religions, the Christian participants did not appreciably move away from their traditionalist perspective. They did not, by and large, seek to approach other faiths empathetically. One can even wonder how much they truly sought to understand the language and the concrete convictions of other faiths. The Parliament resulted, in any case, in the reaffirmation of the set of convictions that most of the Christian participants had brought with them when they arrived, namely, that Christianity without any question is the supremely valid or even exclusively valid religion in the world. Even more, the Parliament had the further effect of assuring its Christian participants that they could afford to be *less* concerned about non-Christian religions in the future!

Those are the contours of the approach of Christian traditionalism to other religions, at least until the turn of the twentieth century. Given the monolithic force of this approach within official Christianity for some 2000 years, it is easy to understand how Troeltsch's work—merely by raising the *question* of the absoluteness of Christianity—might be perceived as a radical undermining of the classical faith of the Church.

In contrast to the traditionalist approach, sustained within the life of the Church, the *rationalist approach* to non-Christian religions flourished mainly outside the walls of official Christianity. It was predicated on the premise that there is a rational core or universal structure behind the accidental "historical shell" of all religions. It presupposed that such phenomena as rites, doctrines, and organizational hierarchies are secondary to the processes of human reason. Sometimes the rationalist approach was antithetical to the "historical shell" of religion, seeking to strip it away in order to allow for a "more rational" existence for the believer. Other times the rationalist approach was more irenic, more positively disposed to concrete religious phenomena; yet it sought nevertheless to lay bare the underlying "rational religion" or universal rational essence of religion.

The rationalist approach did not emerge fully in the West until the dawning of the Enlightenment. Intimations had appeared in earlier times, particularly in the fifteenth-century Renaissance.[6] But in the eighteenth century, for the first time in a thoroughgoing way, pure reason was employed as a tool to analyze religion. David Hume's *Natural History of Religion* is one example of the rationalist approach to religion typical of this era. Hume was concerned with other religions, like primitive polytheism, not for their own sake, but only as a means to attack Scottish Calvinism and British Deism, the two types of religious belief predominating in Hume's own milieu.[7]

Other Enlightenment writers took a more positive interest in non-Christian religions. Following the rationalistic method, a number of thinkers sought specifically to identify the "essence of religion," that is, the essential rational kernel behind the accidental historical shell. Thus Gotthold Lessing and Immanuel Kant distinguished between the abiding truths of pure reason and the transient forms of historical religion. And, both affirmed that the rational truth of religion is its impulse to the good life, whereas such forms as rites and dogmas, institutions and holy places, were accidental. So in his 1779 play, *Nathan the Wise*, Lessing spins the tale of a solid gold ring, which has two exact replicas. He identifies these rings with the good moral life. According to the story, somehow the original ring is confused with the replicas, and neither the Jew nor the Muslim nor the Christian, who are wearing the rings, knows who has the original. What really matters, Lessing suggests, is the fact that each one is wearing the ring, living the good life, not whose is the original. With this judgment Kant generally concurs, and that concurrence is worked out in heavy philosophical prose in his 1793 essay, *Religion within the Limits of Reason Alone*. Lessing and Kant gave attention to non-Christian religions, but not primarily to understand those religions themselves. Lessing and Kant were chiefly interested in using non-Christian religions in order to make a case for the rational morality which constituted the "essential core" of all religions.

Perhaps the most sensitive and fruitful use of the rationalistic method as applied to non-Christian religions was made by the great English anthropologist, Sir James George Frazer, in his monumental study, *The Golden Bough*. He saw his chief task to be the collection of data about primitive religions. This he did on a massive scale, and for the most part with conspicuous objectivity. Yet, inevitably he had to choose some principle to organize his data: and this Frazer found in the idea that the key to religion is its origin in magic. For Frazer, the movement of thought in human history has on the whole been from magic through religion to science. This principle of interpretation presupposes that the inmost meaning of religious practices lies in their tendency to give way, under the right circumstances, to "more rational" forms of life. And Frazer occasionally drew on this schema, and data from primitive religions along with it, to mount a polemic against Christianity. Nevertheless the focus of his research consistently fell on the acquisition of new knowledge concerning many diverse religious practices. This brought the study of non-Christian religions to a new plateau. Although many religions, particularly the major world religions, still remained to be studied in detail, the effect of Frazer's work was to make it impossible for any educated Westerner to legitimately dismiss other religious traditions out of ignorance.

The work of writers such as Hume, Lessing, Kant, and Frazer undoubtedly did much to set the stage for, and to support the flourishing of the *historicist approach* to non-Christian religions. In particular, the studies of Frazer and an increasing number of scholars who had similar interests, provided the proponents of the historicist approach with a vast body of significant data. But none of the aforementioned moved explicitly into the arena of the historicist approach. Each of them, variously, remained within the confines of the rationalistic method. The historicist approach to religion, which so concerned and captivated Ernst Troeltsch, and which is so fraught with questions for exclusivist Western religions, began to grow in a different, somewhat anti-rationalistic context. It was destined, surely, to employ reason, to be highly methodical, and to strive for objectivity, but it took shape inspired by a certain pre-rational impulse.

The historicist approach, in contrast to the rationalism of Hume, Lessing, Kant, and Frazer, did *not* presuppose the distinction between a rational core of human experience and an accidental, historical shell. Whereas the rationalist approach generally was shaped by a search for universally valid structures of meaning, the historicist approach was driven by a passion for the concrete and the particular. The historicist approach rejected the assumption, so clearly stated by Hume, that religion is something secondary in human experience. On the contrary, the historicist approach presupposed that religion is as essential to human experience as reason. The historicist thus accepts the overall testimony of the religious believer concerning his own experience. The actual religious believer, at least in moments of intense religious experience, would never say that his faith is something secondary. Hence if study of religious phenomena is to be empathetic, if it is to deal with religions on their own terms, if it is to be objective in this sense, it must take seriously their concrete "historical shell" as believers themselves do. This is what the proponents of the historicist approach generally sought to do.

In the late eighteenth century a wide variety of thinkers, especially in Germany, felt repelled by what they considered to be the sterility of the Age of Reason. This feeling was buttressed by the Enlightenment's inglorious collapse in the terror perpetrated by the "enlightened" leaders of the French Revolution. Many thinkers therefore turned away from the allegedly enlightened present, so celebrated by men like Hume, to the past; and not only to the more immediate past, particularly the Middle Ages, but also to the distant past, the age of primitive man and his mythology. By immersing themselves in what they considered to be the mysteries of the past, as well as by communing in a mystically perceived world of nature around them, they sought to find wellsprings for a new and more vital kind of life. These thinkers are frequently identified by the term "romantics," although this nomenclature sometimes can be confusing.

Interestingly, many of these scholars began their careers as students of language. This, we can see, was the necessary first step toward a fully historical approach to the religions of the world. In order to understand foreign religions, the original languages had to be mastered. And this kind of study was pursued with great intensity, roughly from the first decades of the nineteenth century. In those decades Oriental and Asiatic societies were established throughout Europe and in England, as were chairs for the study of Sanskrit. It was the German philosopher Schopenhauer who said, in the middle of the nineteenth century, that the study of Sanskrit could do for the modern era what the study of classical languages did for the Renaissance of the fifteenth century.

Perhaps the most significant early figure in this context was the German philologist and philosopher, Johann Gottfried Herder. Herder produced studies of ancient Hebrew poetry and other newly discovered types of poetry from the ancient Orient. But it is not these particular studies which are memorable today as much as the method which underlay them. This was the romantic method of *Einfühlung,* empathy. The romantic thinker felt capable of transcending his own cultural context and intuiting the meaning of cultures removed from his own, much as he felt himself capable of transcending his own standpoint and entering into an empathetic relation to nature. So Herder describes the proper historical method: "First sympathize with the nation, go into the era, into the geography, into the entire history, feel yourself into it (*einfühlen*)" (11:23). The observer looks first of all at the phenomena themselves in order to apprehend and understand them in their own terms. He does not first establish, by reason alone, a conception or a model by which to identify and to evaluate the phenomena. This is the most evident difference between the typical Enlightenment and the typical Romantic approaches to religious phenomena.

There is a further difference, more subtle, but no less important. The rationalistic method of the Enlightenment is predicated on a philosophy of history dominated by the concept of progress. For the Enlightenment thinker, the present age, and the reign of reason in particular, are an immense advance over all preceding ages, especially over the time of primitive man, the time of "superstition." Not so for the romantic thinker. For him, no one age is any better than any other. As Herder wrote:

> Every nation, like every age of life, has in itself the central point of its well-being. The youth is no happier than the innocently contented child, nor is the graybeard unhappier than the vigorously striving man (11:23).

Every historical era, however primitive, has its own characteristic value and uniqueness. The empathetic observer intuits, as carefully as he can, what that value and uniqueness is.

The romantic impulse came to its most prominent historicist flowering in the work of the great German historian, Leopold von Ranke. Two German expressions are often associated with von Ranke's historical method, and both are worth citing, for they rather precisely describe the intent of his scholarly work. First, von Ranke wanted to write history *wie es eigentlich gewesen* ("as it actually happened"). Here is the romantic impulse to attend to the phenomena first, before applying the evaluative and analytical constructions of reason. Secondly, von Ranke affirmed that *jede Epoch ist unmittelbar zu Gott* ("every epoch is immediately present to God"). Here is the romantic impulse to find uniqueness and value in every historical era.

Von Ranke was quite conscious of the method he was adopting. As he explains in a fragment in the 1830's:

> There are really only two ways of acquiring knowledge about human affairs: through the perception of the particular, or through abstraction. The former is the method of history; the latter is the method of philosophy (20:58).

At the same time, von Ranke was convinced that the historian should not rest content with a collection of unrelated facts, but that he should seek to discern their intrinsic relations. Nevertheless, von Ranke emphasized, this search for a meaningful pattern should never take the historian beyond or behind the phenomena to something allegedly more original. The meaningful interrelation of the phenomena is to be found, if it is to be found at all, *in* the phenomena themselves.

Von Ranke, like Herder, gave his empathetic historicist approach a certain theological underpinning. Both thinkers were concerned not only to affirm that every epoch is immediately related to God, but—like the German poets Goethe and Novalis, and behind them the tradition of German mysticism—they were expressing their mystical sense for the immediacy, the omnipotence, and the fecund creativity of the Divine. Von Ranke saw history as "God's march through the world." But for von Ranke, as for Herder, God in himself remained unknown. God, said von Ranke, is as "a sacred hieroglyph, conceived and preserved in his most external" (20:318). This also suggests that there is no going behind the accidental "historical shell" to some more original rational or psychological or economic or theological level. The meaning of the phenomena is in the phenomena themselves. The German historicist tradition thus reflects the famous mystical saying of Martin Luther, that the whole creation is the *mask of God*. Luther's statement gives testimony to both the omnipresent creativity of God and to God's hiddenness in himself.

Although von Ranke himself did much to advance the science of history, it remained for others to apply his method to the study of religion in a thoroughgoing way. The most prominent name in this connection is that of the German-born English philologist, Max Mueller. Today Mueller is generally acknowledged as the founder of the study of "the history of religions" (German: *die Religionsgeschichte*).[8] The tenor of Mueller's work is well indicated by a comment he made in 1867:

> There is to my mind no subject more absorbing than the tracing of human thought; not theoretically, or in accordance with Hegelian laws of thought . . . , but historically, and like an Indian trapper, spying for every footprint, every layer, every broken blade that might tell and testify of the former presence of man in his early wanderings and searching after light and truth (10:ix).

This careful, empathetic work of research Mueller pursued with steady devotion. His task as he saw it was to highlight the concrete phenomena of religious history, to attempt to see them from the inside, to see them as much as possible as actual believers saw them, and then—and then only—to raise the question of meaningful patterns of historical events. As Mueller wrote, "Religion escapes our firm grasp till we trace it to its real habitat, the heart of one true believer" (10:ix).

Herder, von Ranke, and Mueller, clearly, were not Christian traditionalists. They eschewed the hostility toward non-Christian religions characteristic of much of Christian history. Unlike Christian traditionalists, they were unwilling to accept indifference towards, and ignorance of, non-Christian religions. At the same time, Herder, von Ranke, and Mueller believed that the rationalistic approach spawned by the Enlightenment had significant limitations. While the rationalistic method had uncovered important factual findings, it did not permit them to interpret the world with what they considered to be full scientific objectivity. In particular, it did not allow interpretation of the religions of the world "from the inside," from the perspective of the concrete events of history itself, that is, empathetically. In this respect, it did not allow a full account of events from the past "as it really was." In addition, the rationalistic approach occasionally resulted in serious historical distortions, as when early forms of human religion were more or less discounted as "magic" or "superstition," and not studied with attention to their religious particularity. So Herder, von Ranke, Mueller, and others began to forge a new method, which—with a view to their commitments to objectivity as well as their commitments to historical empathy—may be called the method of historical reason. This approach to historical data came to be the central commitment in the historicist attitude toward non-Christian religions.

Christian traditionalism, rationalism, and historicism are the matrix from which the thought of Ernst Troeltsch emerges. Troeltsch was well aware of the exclusivist claims that traditional Christianity was wont to make, frequently with little or no understanding of non-Christian religions. While he was highly critical of that exclusivist mentality, he nevertheless sought to identify positive elements in traditionalism. Troeltsch did not want to reject his particular religious tradition. That would be destructive, he felt, and would lead to aimless relativism. Troeltsch also valued the rationalist approach to religion, championed by thinkers such as Lessing, Kant, and Frazer, as a fruitful method for identifying and analyzing ethical and social aspects of religious traditions. However, Troeltsch's major concern was undoubtedly most closely related to the work of Herder, von Ranke, and Mueller. From the beginning to the end of his scholarly career, Troeltsch was captivated and challenged by the method of historical reason. He was also influenced by the religious perspective of German historicism, which mediated to him some of the religious intuitions of German mysticism and Luther. Troeltsch's writings, scientific as they always are, at times give expression to a deep mystical passion, to a sense that the whole historical process is the "mask of God": an expression of an infinitely creative Divine Ground of Being, yet inscrutable in its ultimate depths.

2. REASSESSING EXCLUSIVIST RELIGIOUS CLAIMS

At the turn of the twentieth century, seven years after the memorable but essentially traditionalist World Parliament of Religions, and four years before the publication of John Mott's famous book, *The Evangelization of the World in this Generation,* Troeltsch produced his searching study, *The Absoluteness of Christianity and the History of Religions* (23). Looking back over his entire career, he described this book as the "nucleus" of all his writings. In this work, and in a variety of related studies, Troeltsch set forward a thoroughgoing reassessment of all exclusivist religious claims. That is the scope of his concern, although as the title indicates, Troeltsch focuses his attention on the particular exclusivist claims of Christianity.

Troeltsch began the discussion of the question of religious exclusivism by underlining the significance of the modern historical consciousness. This consciousness, he emphasizes, is something "new in principle" in history. It takes for granted that all cultures and all periods have their own intrinsic validity. In particular, the modern historical consciousness prohibits any "dogmatic approach" to history, any approach which assumes that one particular tradition is absolutely valid. Accordingly, the modern science of history ("historiography") attempts to judge all phenomena empathetically and justly, uniting them in a coherent picture of the overall development of mankind. Specifically, Troeltsch sees the historical study of religion proceeding "from the general to the special, from an investigation of religion as a unique contact with God occurring everywhere, to an investigation of special, concrete areas of religion" (28.II:314f.). Troeltsch is well aware that his understanding of historiography has its own presuppositions. For him, indeed, it is not a question of whether one has presuppositions or not, but whether one's presuppositions are good or bad, better or worse. Dogmatic Christian presuppositions are to be rejected, Troeltsch argues, because broader, less-committed and therefore more objective presuppositions are available, namely, those of modern historical science. Even these, Troeltsch stresses, must continually be subjected to scrutiny and revised where necessary. In this sense, Troeltsch concludes that modern historiography makes a traditional approach to Christian history untenable.

Troeltsch then identifies two characteristic ways in which Christians have claimed absoluteness for their religion. The first, the more tradition-directed, he calls the "miracle-apologetic." Proponents of this view argued that Christianity is absolute because it is, or has been, attended by miracles. Troeltsch rejects this as an unacceptable isolation of Christianity from the history of religions. Many religions claim to be accompanied by miracles. Troeltsch also rejects what he considers to be a reinterpreted form of the old miracle-apologetic in the writings of nineteenth-century Protestant theologians. These thinkers argue that Christianity brings with it a miracle in the heart of every believer. The miracle is internalized. Troeltsch rejects this approach, since it places the essence of Christianity in some other-worldly supra-historical dimension, distinct from the concrete history of mankind. Moreover, he suggests, other religions have their claims for intense inner experiences, too. How are we really to judge between all these "inner miracles"?

The second major argument for the absolute validity of Christianity is what Troeltsch calls the "evolutionary-apologetic." This type of thinker sees some validity in all religions; nevertheless Christianity appears as the highest religion, at the apex of a universal, rationally structured process of religious evolution. The proponent of the evolutionary-apologetic claims that the essence of religion is an immanent law *in* all religious phenomena and that it *produces* all religious phenomena. Christianity is seen as the final realization of that universal essence of religion. In Troeltsch's view, history cannot be grasped by such a rationalistic principle, it does not have a universal rational structure (it is not "panlogistic").[9] The evolutionary-apologetic does violence to the particularity of history. It does not see the manifoldness of psychic causation, nor its mystery. Indeed, says Troeltsch, the founders of this theory were only able to give it plausibility because so little was known about the history of religions in their day. Actually, Troeltsch observes, "the modern study of history gives us no indication whatever of any graded progression such as this theory might lead us to expect" (23:69).

Troeltsch then underlines the fundamental reason for his challenge to the miracle-apologetic and the evolutionary-apologetic. Here he indicates how seriously he takes the historicist approach to religion. He elevates the notion of historical *individuality* to a dominating position in his thought. History, for Troeltsch, is the realm of individual agents, individual events, and individual cultures, each one of which has its own intrinsic structure of validity. As Troeltsch said in his last lecture, history is an "immeasurable, incomparable profusion of always-new, unique, and hence individual tendencies, welling up from undiscovered depths, and coming to light in each case in unsuspected places and under different circumstances" (24:14). Accordingly, Troeltsch can state categorically: History is no place for "absolute religions" or "absolute personalities." Such terms are self-contradictory (23:78). Christianity, for this reason, can be viewed only as "a purely historical phenomenon subject to all the limitations to which any individual phenomenon is exposed, just like the other great religions" (23:85). If someone wishes to use the word "relative" with regard to Christianity, Troeltsch notes, there can be no objection: "for the historical and the relative are identical" (23:85).

Closely related to this notion of history is Troeltsch's understanding of God. For Troeltsch, God is the infinitely creative Absolute, which is the source and the goal of the cosmos, and more particularly of human history. God is not reason but immediately creative *will:* "God is Act, living, creative Act" (29:162–163). The Divine will, says Troeltsch, is the "ground of ground, law of laws; its 'why' knows no reason" (29:151). This "voluntaristic" approach to God recalls von Ranke's statement that God is the eternal hieroglyph, that God's eternal ways are never known in themselves, but only externally in history. So Troeltsch says repeatedly that the Absolute is never fully known in history; that only beyond history will the Absolute be comprehensively known. Moreover, the manifestations of God are infinitely varied within history, as history moves towards its Final End. The religious experience of mankind is thus unified, insofar as it is all grounded in the manifestations of God, but it takes a wide variety of forms in response to the particularity of each Divine manifestation, as God works to bring history to its Final Goal. Troeltsch describes this universal religious process in vivid terms:

The unity of all religious manifestations is grounded in a common, differentiating, forward-pressing tendency of movement of the human spirit and completes itself though the mysteriously working movement of the Divine in the unconscious depths of the unified human spirit. Uncapable of reaching its goal in the short span of an individual life, it completes its own movement through the work of innumerable people who work together and who are grasped and led by the Divine activity . . . (28. II:340).

In Troeltsch's perspective, this is emphatically not a unilinear process. It is not a logical, universal succession of stages, but a simultaneous manifestation and creative working of the Divine in a profuse variety of individualizations.

The universal law of history consists precisely in this, that the Divine Reason, or the Divine Life, within history, constantly manifests itself in always new and always peculiar individualizations—and hence that its tendency is not towards unity or universality at all, but rather towards the fulfilment of the highest potentialities of each separate department of life (24:14).

This again is reminiscent of von Ranke, and indeed Troeltsch refers to the former's dictum with appreciation, that every epoch is immediately related to God. No epoch, or no culture, Troeltsch affirms, is merely a step on the way to something better. Every epoch and every culture has its own individuality, its own self-sufficient meaning, and therefore its own value. On the basis of this kind of historicist understanding of God as well as history, Troeltsch affirms that no religion can ever legitimately claim to be *the* final religion. History, while constituted by the infinitely variegated expressions of the Absolute, is never able to contain the Absolute. Historicity and absoluteness are simply incompatible.

In *The Absoluteness of Christianity*, Troeltsch qualifies the "relative" status he assigns to Christianity by arguing for its role as the "highest" religion in the world today. Of the major religions in the world, Troeltsch argues, Christianity is the strongest and most intensive revelation of passionate religiousness. More than this, Christianity successfully relates reverence for God to the worldly life and to the problems of guilt-stricken souls. Also, its "higher world" is an infinitely valuable, all-conditioning personal life. These points lead Troeltsch to conclude that Christianity, though relative, is the highest religion history has thus far produced. In his judgment, Christianity has the clearest understanding of the interrelation and distinction of God, the world, the soul, and an other-worldly life. Of course, Troeltsch grants, the certainty of Christianity's normative character is a *confession*. It is not based on scientific proof. It is an affirmation made on the basis of careful study of history, and also a personal decision. But even so, the normative character of Christianity among religions in the world today can be historically validated.

At the same time, Troeltsch is well aware of the implications of his historicist principles. Hence he states that Christianity, like all historical facts, need not remain forever. Its status as the highest religion in the world is therefore tentative. A higher revelation, Troeltsch feels, may yet discover deeper postulates. Conceivably Christianity may even disappear, although this seems unlikely, he says. The Absolute is not fully present in Christianity any more than it is fully present in any other phenomenon in history. The Absolute lies on the "other side" of history.

This was the shape of Troeltsch's reassessment of the exclusivist religious claims of Christianity in 1901, a stance which he continued to take in 1912, when the second edition of *The Absoluteness of Christianity* appeared. But in the interim, and in the decade following the second edition, Troeltsch immersed himself in further historical research. In the course of this study, he became more and more convinced of the determinativeness of historical individuality. As a result he began to doubt whether a member of one culture can truly understand another culture. On the one hand, Troeltsch came to believe that Christianity is totally a Western phenomenon in its present form. On the other hand, through careful study of non-Christian religions, he became convinced of the genuineness of their claims for validity for themselves. It is as if Troeltsch concluded that no man can be culturally bilingual in the profoundest sense. We may learn to speak the language of other cultures—this is what Troeltsch thinks sensitive historical study can do—but we cannot fully and truly participate in them unless we join them, a decision which then requires us to leave our own culture behind.

Interestingly, Troeltsch came to see historical individuality as being determinative not only for religion, but also for science and logic. "Even the validity of science and logic," he writes, "seem to exhibit, under different skies and upon different soil, strong individual differences present even in their deepest and innermost rudiments." This ever more deepening sense for historical individuality led Troeltsch to reformulate his earlier view of the finality of Christianity. In 1901 he had argued that Christianity is the highest religion in the world, compared to all others. In 1923 he dropped the comparative element entirely and argued that Christianity is the final religion for us (Christians), because *we know no other*. As he said, "It is final and unconditional for us, because we have nothing else . . ." (24:26). *Other religions, moreover, may have the same kind of finality for their adherents.* Only God knows when one religion is more valid than another. No human being can jump out of his historical skin and make legitimate, demonstrable value judgments between individual religions.

The schema Troeltsch offers for coming to terms with the exclusivist claims of Christianity, and by implication with any religious claims for exclusive validity, might be described in summary as—"Religion, between Rationalism and Historicism." Troeltsch sought to distill rudimentary elements from the three major streams of his cultural inheritance—Christian traditionalism, rationalism, and historicism. From the very beginning of his life, he took religious commitment with utmost seriousness. His life was a search for religious certainty. This intense, existential search reflects what might be called the "absolute tone" of religious exclusivism. At the same time, Troeltsch rejected the idea of a religious retreat from modern culture. He sought to construct "a genuinely scientific theology." He sought to employ, and do justice to, both the rationalist and the historicist approaches to human experience, particularly religion. "The Enlightenment," Troeltsch writes, "fixed its gaze on the universal and the valid." Accordingly, in the spirit of thinkers like Lessing and Kant, Troeltsch continually sought to identify expressions of value, religious and ethical, amidst the flux of history. Yet Troeltsch could not fully accept the results of Lessing's and Kant's moral rationalism. History itself, Troeltsch felt, discredits any generalized, universalized rationalism. As Troeltsch states, "the discoveries made by the modern study of history have presented us with a world full of depth, richness and vitality" (23:106). Above all, the modern historical consciousness has bequeathed the idea of history as the arena of individuality. To take this seriously, is to seek valid norms and an understanding of the logic of history not in some abstract or panlogistic rational interpretation, but in the relativities of history itself, where no universally valid set of norms or universal logical schema of historical development can ever be identified:

> History is a unique sphere of knowledge because it is the sphere of the individual and the nonrecurrent. But within the individual and the nonrecurrent, there is something universally valid—or something connected with the universally valid—which makes itself known at the same time. The problem is to hold these two elements together in the right relation (23:106).

Troeltsch was, indeed, concerned to find this "right relation." Having subjected exclusivist religious claims to a thoroughgoing critique, Troeltsch also attempted to reaffirm and reestablish the viability and vitality of the religious life.

3. REESTABLISHING THE VALIDITY OF INDIVIDUAL RELIGIONS

Troeltsch was no debunker of religion, like Hume, nor was he an irenic critic and universalizing moral rationalist like Kant. Troeltsch had an unshakable allegiance to the concrete religious tradition of his fore-fathers. He wanted to show that that kind of exclusivist tradition could attain a viable and vital expression in the present, once it had internal-ized the modern historicist critique of religious exclusivism. How did Troeltsch seek to build up a new historicist form of religious piety?

Troeltsch naturally focuses his concern to reestablish the validity of individual religious claims on his own particular tradition. Troeltsch would say, indeed, that as a Christian it would be presumptuous of him to try to reestablish, let us say, the validity of Judaism. But at the same time, Troeltsch's mode of procedure at this point surely could be adopted, in a parallel way, by exponents of other exclusivist traditions.

Like an experienced mountain climber who has just led a novice up a perilous trail, and who then sits down with the novice to reflect about the climb, Troeltsch raises the question near the end of *The Ab-soluteness of Christianity* whether his treatment of the problem "can satisfy ordinary religious people whose modes of perception and reflec-tion are those of the modern world, and above all whether it can serve our clergymen and theologians" (23:118). He answers in the affirmative. The ordinary religious man does not really require an absolute religion, Troeltsch maintains. Indeed, does not a person who requires an absolute religion reflect the demands of "the natural, human presumptuousness that would vault over the boundaries and conditionality of life and transpose itself at once to the perfect goal where there is a cessation of toil, conflict, and difficulty?" "Is not the principal need of the religious man," Troeltsch asks, "rather, the real and innermost certainty of having encountered God and heard his voice? . . . of committing to God the question of how He will proceed from this point on?" (23:119). The religious man, Troeltsch continues, does not need to believe that he pos-sesses the truth exclusively or that he possesses it in a complete and final form.

What, then, does Troeltsch's position offer the ordinary believer? Everything he needs, says Troeltsch. The ordinary believer can be cer-tain that in the prophetic and Christian word he actually has found God *and* that consequently, "no matter what God may do with men, this faith will never deceive him" (23:121). More than that, the ordinary man of faith may be certain that the position of Jesus Christ in his life will remain central, as it was in the past. In the present, the man of faith

> is summoned to rely on Jesus, who is the source and illustration of this entire world of life, and without whose central position in our faith no religious community that perpetuates him is conceivable. The commitment of any imaginable future to Jesus is, for him, a matter that is given with and follows from faith, not a dogmatic theory that one must espouse in order to be a Christian at all (23:122).

Although Troeltsch calls for an abandonment of "the attitude which regards Jesus as the center of the universe, or even the center of human history" (31:239), he reveals a deep piety focusing on Jesus as the historical source and continuing historical fountain of life for Christianity. For Troeltsch, Jesus Christ is the Alpha and the Omega of the Christian religion.

Troeltsch even points to Jesus as the preeminent example of the vitality of the kind of faith he, Troeltsch, is highlighting. Jesus—here was no harsh fanatic, here was no zealot or dogmatist! "Wherever Jesus went," Troeltsch writes, "he referred in a completely unprejudiced way to the revelation of God present in those he met with, and he drew them into the challenge and promise that he, as the definitive word of the Father, proclaimed as the highest truth, the truth decisive for man's eternal destiny." And what was the content of Jesus' preaching? "Only the future would bring complete deliverance, perfect knowledge, and permanent victory." Jesus, Troeltsch insists, "relegated the absolute religion to the world to come" (23:123). Interestingly, recent biblical scholarship and some contemporary theologians have placed more and more emphasis on the theme to which Troeltsch is pointing here, the importance of the future Kingdom of God in the teaching of Jesus.[10]

The ordinary believer can thus be certain that his experience of God is real and that it will never be denied, that Jesus Christ is and will continue to be the historical font of his faith, and indeed that the teaching and life of Jesus himself provides a warrant for a historicist position. With these basic points established, Troeltsch turns to two other questions: the status of the Christian missionary enterprise and the validity of ethical norms.

Regarding missions, Troeltsch states that in the modern world "there can be no talk of a universal mass of sinful people everywhere, lost and damned, beyond the pale of Christianity" (28.II:789). Such a monolithic, exclusivist approach is simply impossible for the historically conscious man of today. At the same time, men of faith, who have found a vital religious position in Christianity, cannot help but want to share their religious life with others. Along with this impulse to share, Troeltsch continues, believers with authentic religious convictions will naturally seek to deepen their faith, to grow in every possible creative way. Indeed, Troeltsch emphasizes, today Christianity desperately needs to grow out of its self-enclosed European milieu. "Precisely the crisis of the Christian faith at home," he writes, "must drive us out into foreign lands" (28.II:792). In this world context, in a few instances, the impulse to seek conversion may still be appropriate. But in the case of the major religions of the world, the proper missionary approach should be not to aim at conversion, but to seek mutual understanding. "It is their duty to increase in depth and purity by means of their own interior impulses," Troeltsch says of these major faiths, "a task which the contact with Christianity may prove helpful, to them as to us, in such processes of development from within." On the basis of increased mutual understanding, unforeseeable developments may occur, on the side of all participants in the encounter. All may find new kinds of vitality, each in its own way. "If each strives to fulfil its own highest potentialities, and allows itself to be influenced by the similar striving of the rest, they may approach and find contact with each other" (23:29,33). Although Troeltsch does not anticipate that an increase of mutual understanding among the higher religions of the world will entail any essentially new religious formations in the foreseeable future, he nevertheless hopes that this new kind of "missionary work" will lead to more vital religious impulses and convictions, which will bring mankind closer to the realization of its final, eschatological unity in God, beyond history. That is Troeltsch's reinterpretation of traditional Christian missionary theology. By the second half of the twentieth century, it is an approach that has found more and more acceptance.

With regard to the method of identifying valid ethical norms in a context of relativized historical consciousness, Troeltsch's solution parallels his treatment of religious validity. In both cases he emphasizes that the Absolute *is* to be found in the relative events of history, yet *never fully* manifested in history. Hence there can be no absolute vantage point, whether it be the Bible or the Papacy, for establishing valid ethical norms. Normative values for the present, Troeltsch maintains, can be attained first of all through historical study of the values of our own past. In Troeltsch's mature view, our own past means our *Western* past. This is the largest possible cultural context, the largest "individual totality," which our historical situation permits us to work with. Beyond this, we cannot truly know and experience the religious intuitions and the values of other peoples. This vast cultural European-American totality is the primary source of valid ethical norms for our present life. Yet, as Troeltsch was well aware, history moves on. The Absolute, which has been manifesting itself in history, continues to manifest itself in the present. Hence reference to our *past* alone is not enough. Valid ethical norms emerge, Troeltsch states, only when careful study of our past is made to come alive, through present personal experience. Immersed in the present situation, the sensitive student of history takes the risk, by personal decision, of selecting and reinterpreting norms from the past as valid for his own time. In this way he creates a new synthesis. In this sense, as a present participant in history, he "overcomes history with history." Within the relativities of history, tutored by his past, he affirms what is valid *for him*. Of course, Troeltsch is not suggesting that the establishment of valid norms is a matter of individual whim. It presupposes a sensitive, critical interpretation of both the past and the present. Even so, the affirmation of valid norms presupposes the personal conviction of the student of history. Ethical norms cannot be demonstrably identified as final any more than religions can. Norms have their validity, in the past and in the present, only in a specific historical milieu. In a sense, Troeltsch was an early protagonist of the "situational" approach to ethics, which has become so dominant in contemporary Christianity.[11]

Yet one may legitimately ask, how can Troeltsch so confidently assert that his position is consistent with a vital and captivating Christian faith; that Jesus himself proclaimed a relativized type of faith; that the traditional Christian missionary impulse can be legitimately reshaped; that there is a valid situational way of reinterpreting the absolutist ethical norms of the past; and that therefore Troeltsch's own position manifestly stands *within* the flow of the Christian tradition? The entire Christian tradition, it seems, has made exclusivist claims and grounded both its beliefs and its morality in those exclusivist claims. In what way, if any, can Troeltsch legitimately maintain that he is still within the pale of the Christian tradition?

In response to this question, Troeltsch draws on two central concepts of his thought: *naive religion* and *critical reason*. In affirming these notions, Troeltsch is also defending the *independence of religion*. By invoking the latter idea, he seeks to disassociate himself from those who would claim that the validity of religion lies in some internal rational kernel (Lessing, Kant) or that religion as such has little or no validity at all (Hume, Marx, Freud).

Religion, for Troeltsch, is qualitatively independent of all other aspects of man's historical life, although it may be thoroughly influenced by them. Religion is not a primitive form of thought. Nor is it to be explained fundamentally by reference to sociological or psychological forces. Nor can it be reduced to morality or aesthetics. That is what religion is *not*. But to say what it *is*, in Troeltsch's perspective, is no easy undertaking. There is no readily identifiable "essence of religion" in the flux of human history.

Troeltsch approaches religion as an essentially a-rational experience. "Religion in itself," he states, "is without ideas and without scientific method" (27:405). Religion is a "fundamental life experience" (*Erlebnis*) (28.II:348). "Feeling" (*Gefühl*) is a word which Troeltsch also uses frequently in this regard, but he stresses that that term is not to be construed merely in a psychological way. Religious feeling, he stresses, is far from a simple reality: it entails dedication, reverence, fear, renunciation, and awe, together with wonder, joy, trust, love, and ecstasy, all of which are mixed together in a thousandfold way. This notion of religion as fundamentally a-rational, clearly, is closely related to Troeltsch's view of God as supra-rational, creative will. Religion is communion with this Deity, the Absolute, which is never fully manifest in history, which is manifest only in an infinite variety of forms. Religion is an experience of the incomprehensible Ground of history (*Urgrund*), which Ground can be totally known only beyond history. Religion is an experience of a God who is "ever pressing the finite mind toward further light and fuller consciousness," not by any universally evident logic, but by a plethora of individual manifestations.

Within history, Troeltsch explains, most religious experience is reproductive or derivative. It depends on earlier, more powerful experiences of the Divine, as well as on immediate experience. Religion in its purest form, however, is always *naive*. This is a technical term in his vocabulary. It is used neutrally, he claims, not as a value judgment. It is used to refer to unpremeditated and unreflective intercourse with the Divine. This is generally possible only for a few, the "heroes"—such as Jesus of Nazareth —who become vessels that pour forth new religious power. These heroes usually belong, moreover, to the lower strata of society, for here is where the necessary lack of rational sophistication for a pure religious experience is to be found. In the moment of revelation, which for Troeltsch, emphatically, is not the communication of supernatural truths by God, but immediate communion with the living Divine presence, the religious hero mediates vital new forms of religious expression. These concrete forms of expression, Troeltsch stresses, are always present; the hero's communion with the Divine presence is invariably garbed in mythological or cultic forms as soon as he gives expression to it. A further and decisive characteristic of naive religion, in Troeltsch's view, is that it always comes to the fore in the form of absolute claims. "Absoluteness," Troeltsch says, "is a universal characteristic of the naive way of thinking" (23:132). Claims for absoluteness as a matter of course flow from the initial naive moments of profound religious ecstasy. Troeltsch asserts that, given the power of originating religious experiences, these claims are surely understandable and in that sense justifiable.

Yet naive religion, in Troeltsch's view is an unstable historical compound. Its justifiable initial claims for absoluteness will give way to a kind of second generation authoritarianism; they will lapse into various forms of parochialism; or they will be subjected to the restraining and universalizing influence of *critical reason*. The last option, as far as Troeltsch is concerned, is clearly the only fruitful one. Although reason like religion, according to Troeltsch, is grounded ultimately in the Absolute, it is qualitatively different from religion. Reason properly is concerned with the relative, with the world of historical experience as such, whereas religion seeks and experiences the Absolute. The exact relations of reason and religion, Troeltsch maintains, are unclear and will always remain so. Nevertheless, religion, especially in its naive form, very much needs reason, in order to avoid the extremes that enthusiastic naive experience can produce. Naive religion, Troeltsch says, is mostly one-sided, cultureless, spiritually narrow, unharmonious, and confusing. Critical reason need not purge those elements in naive religion which have the mark of genius. But, generally, naive religions need

> the corrective of scientific education and rearing, quietness and harmony, material knowledge of the world, and a genuine, carefully considered tolerance, together with a broadening of horizons to the surrounding world and a harmonization of its contents (33:10).

On the other hand, critical reason is never meant to replace or create religion, for it can do neither. It must continually make way for the naive. Indeed, if reason does not make a place for religion it has by that fact extended itself beyond its own limits.

On the basis of the distinction between naive religion and critical reason, Troeltsch explains how his relativizing historicist position is not inimical to Christian traditionalism but in agreement with it. He distinguishes between two kinds of absolute claims. The first is the justifiable naive claim for absoluteness. Later on, however, when Christianity became established, the naive claim was no longer necessary, and a more scientific way of thinking should have been allowed to come to the fore. But at that time, Troeltsch notes, there was a total lack of historical understanding. Hence an *artificial* claim for absoluteness arose. This took a variety of forms, all of them essentially defensive and apologetic, many of them tending toward dogmatism. In the modern period, the artificial claim for absoluteness took on the form of evolutionary thought. But in all and through all, these later claims for absoluteness *were* artificial, notwithstanding the fact that they originally arose for an understandable

reason, and persisted understandably in the absence of a critical, historical sense. But in the modern era, that critical historical sense *has* arisen.
And, as a matter of course, it has become a base for the criticism of
absolute claims. At the same time, Troeltsch believes, the emergence of
historical criticism has freed Christianity from the task of preserving
absolute claims, which are no longer necessary or appropriate.

In Troeltsch's view, then, not only does the ordinary intelligent believer have everything he needs for his faith—the certainty of God,
dependence on Jesus as the source and life of his religion, a new interpretation of missions, and a new method for establishing valid ethical
norms—but that believer also can understand why his stance, which is
not founded on claims for absolute validity, is fundamentally in conso-
nance with the whole tradition, howevermuch his position may seem to
diverge from the tradition on the surface. The modern believer knows,
according to Troeltsch, that Christianity's original claim for exclusive
validity was legitimate at first; and that the secondary, artificial claims
for absoluteness only arose because the faith was not yet established in
the world and because, thereafter, its adherents lacked a critical, historical sense. Of course, the modern believer need not trouble himself
with establishing Christianity; it is well established. Nor does the modern
believer lack a critical, historical sense. Hence he is in a position both to
accept a relativizing historicist position and at the same time to understand the reasons which make it possible for him to adopt this stance.

But Troeltsch's defense of his own position does not stop here. He is
concerned to show not only that the ordinary believer has everything he
needs for a viable, vital faith, but also that the historicist position is the
only possible position, at least within Protestantism. Protestants, Troeltsch
says at various points, surely do not wish their tradition to disintegrate
into skepticism or veer into religious authoritarianism (Troeltsch has in
mind the Roman Catholic Church of his own day). Those seem to
Troeltsch to be the two major alternatives to his own position. Why? Because *the modern historical consciousness is so pervasive*. The man who
is at all conditioned by modern culture is by that fact conditioned
thoroughly by historical thinking. He takes it for granted that every culture, past and present, has its own meaning and its own internal validity.
He is aware of the relativity of his own cultural milieu. That awareness
is given with his very sociocultural existence in the modern world. This
modern historical consciousness, Troeltsch contends, is "something new
in principle" in human history. "The modern idea of history is no longer
merely one aspect of a way of looking at things or a partial satisfaction of
the impetus to knowledge." People, to various degrees, have always had
a certain interest in the past. No, the modern historical consciousness is a
new stage in history, because it is so comprehensive, so much the pre-

supposition of everything modern man thinks and does and feels. It is, Troeltsch writes, "the foundation of all thinking concerning values and norms. It is the medium for the self-reflection of the species upon its nature, origins, and hopes. . . . The modern idea of history is a dynamic principle for attaining a comprehensive view of everything human" (23:45-47). Troeltsch holds, as we have seen, that any intelligent modern religious man cannot escape historical thinking, unless he wishes to deny his own identity as a modern man. Hence any modern man cannot help but approach religion with the relativizing historicist sense that "every epoch is immediately related to God." Given this new historically pervasive mind-set, Troeltsch argues, Protestantism cannot remain uncommitted. If it continues to assert the (artificial) claim for exclusive validity of traditional Christianity, it will become literally incredible. The only result, then, would be to drive its intelligent members into a position of unlimited relativism and skepticism, or to push them toward an arbitrary "absolute" religious authority.

In this way Troeltsch not only argues that his position supplies the ordinary intelligent believer with everything he needs. He not only seeks to reestablish the validity of traditional Christian claims in a new historicist form. But he also maintains that for the intelligent Protestant, *there is no other way.* The latter point could perhaps be extended to our own day. In the wake of the Second Vatican Council, the Roman Catholic Church, too, has been increasingly feeling the pressures of the modern historical consciousness. A new, somewhat relativized understanding of the Church's teaching authority seems to be appearing. Even the absolute authority of the Pope is being reinterpreted. The Catholic Church is also producing more and more searching historical studies, and seeking out more and more contacts with "non-Christian religions." Perhaps Troeltsch's statement could be taken today to refer to Roman Catholicism as well as to Protestantism: there is no other course than assuming the kind of historicist position Troeltsch is advocating, if the Christian tradition is not to give way to skepticism or to an arbitrary new authoritarianism, from one end of the ecumenical spectrum to the other.

4. THE CONCRETE CHALLENGE OF TROELTSCH'S THOUGHT

In a time when Christian traditionalism was being revived and extended with a worldwide missionary fervor, Ernst Troeltsch prophetically questioned the validity of any religious exclusivism. In his own time, however, few religious people felt the force of his question. Seven decades later, the situation has radically changed. Scientific study of the religions of the world, past and present, and ever more frequent opportunities for firsthand interreligious confrontation and dialogue around the planet, have made it practically impossible to ignore the problem posed by Troeltsch. Insofar as Troeltsch's thought presses the question of the validity of any religious exclusivism on the contemporary believer, it remains compellingly relevant.

Yet the concrete challenge which Troeltsch's thought poses to twentieth-century religious man, particularly in the West, is not Troeltsch's criticism of religious exclusivism as such. Any number of critics from Voltaire to the present have seriously questioned religious exclusivism. That general kind of critique certainly has to be considered. But the concrete challenge of Troeltsch's thought is something else, perhaps something even more radical, as far as the traditions of religious exclusivism are concerned. It hinges on the fact that Troeltsch writes from *within* an exclusivist religious tradition. He is not on the outside looking in, with critical eyes. His criticism is immanent criticism; it arises within the flow of the tradition. He is speaking from the standpoint of a *believer,* whose criticism cannot therefore be piously dismissed because he "lacks true understanding" (faith). From the perspective of an insider, he is affirming that the tradition of religious exclusivism is *not* valid, that the believer must *reject* his exclusivist stance in favor of a faith tempered by historical thinking. Troeltsch is also claiming that apart from his kind of position, the inevitable result will be the disintegration and the dissipation of the tradition, either in the direction of more and more skepticism, or in the direction of an irrational surrender to some arbitrary authority.

Still, the question can be raised whether Troeltsch's mediating position, between exclusivism and skepticism, between absolutism and relativism, actually is one of those compromises that gains us not the best of both worlds, but a mediocre combination—or even the worst—of both worlds. The thought of the twentieth-century theologian, Karl Barth, offers a vivid contrast at this point.[12] Barth's theology represents perhaps the most thoroughgoing expression of Christian exclusivism in the modern period. For Barth, when all has been said, there is no validity in any non-Christian religion. It was this highly exclusivistic Barthian theology, significantly, that inspired and informed the thought and action of the so-called Confessing Church in Nazi Germany. This group stood apart from, and over against, the mores and the institutions of the Nazis. By denying any validity to the nationalistic nature religion fostered by the Nazis, the Confessing Church was able to oppose a monstrous fascist dictatorship, vigorously and consistently. Other Christians in Germany, who were less exclusivistic in their own faith, found it more difficult to stand apart from the Nazi religious claims. To have asked the Confessing Church to grant that other religions also had validity, then, would have been to have asked it to give up the foundation of its protest against

National Socialism. This is why the theology of Karl Barth is so note-worthy in this context. In this one instance, at least, religious exclusivism bore some memorable, impressive fruits.

The stance of the Confessing Church and the theology of Barth hearkens back to the figure of Martin Luther. Both the Confessing Church and Barth looked to Luther as a theological mentor and paradigm of protest. In the name of "the Word of God," Luther battled Pope and Emperor. For Luther, the Word of God provided a *transcendent religious criterion* which enabled him to judge both the Church and society of his time. On this basis, he initiated a rebellion against the whole of the medieval "cultural synthesis." Like Barth, Luther's example raises again the question of the religious necessity for a transcendent criterion able to evaluate the cultural synthesis of any time.

In the spirit of Luther, Karl Barth rejected the kind of position Troeltsch espoused as "culture-Protestantism." [13] In his famous *Epistle to the Romans,* written about the same time when Troeltsch was producing his lecture "The Place of Christianity among the Religions of the World," Barth claimed that culture-Protestantism had sold out to the world, that it was overly optimistic in its acceptance of the "best values of its time" as normative, that it was sinking deep into a stagnant pool of bourgeois religiosity, and that it was out of touch with a culture-transcending commitment to what the Bible calls "righteousness." [14] In retrospect, indeed, when one thinks of the *Western* record in our century —Dachau and Buchenwald, Dresden, Hiroshima, Nagasaki, and Viet-nam—and if one has any sympathy for Christianity, one can only deeply shudder to hear Troeltsch saying that Western culture and Christianity are inextricably bound up with each other. One can sympathize with Barth's call for some more comprehensive frame of reference than European-American culture. This raises the question for Troeltsch, do men not require some kind of transcendent religious criterion? Can a religious and ethical position developed solely in terms of one's own culture ever be sufficient? If, moreover, some kind of unified global culture does develop, can that culture itself be an adequate basis for religious and social commitments? As in the case of individual cultures of the past, will not some transcendent religious criterion still be needed to judge the life of religious communities and the forces of society? A global culture gone mad, with totalitarianism and war, is as conceivable as a German nation gone mad in the 1930's, a nation which embodied "the best" of the classical humanistic traditions of the West. Who can imagine a situation when some kind of transcendent religious criterion is not required?

Such a criterion may or may not be "the Word of God." To begin with, that is a peculiarly Western symbol. It will by no means be self-evidently relevant around the planet. Within Western culture, moreover, one of the effects of our modern historical consciousness has been the increasingly widespread realization that the Bible is in history, that we are in history, and that therefore for us to read the Bible as a transcendent religious norm is difficult, perhaps impossible. It has become just as problematic to accept the Bible as some kind of "paper Pope," as it has been for many to accept the Pope as some kind of "living Bible."

Mindful of the problems involved in approaching the biblical writings as a transcendent religious criterion, then, certain biblical motifs can still legitimately be cited, as a way of further clarifying Troeltsch's concrete challenge to religious exclusivism. Troeltsch opens his thought to this kind of reference to biblical sources, since he claims that his position is a valid expression of the Protestant tradition. In his view, his relativizing historicist position offers the ordinary believer everything he needs, above all a certainty of God and a sense that the source of his faith continues to be Jesus. With the biblical writings in view, one may ask: *which* God, and *which* Jesus?

In a biblical perspective, Troeltsch's voluntaristic suprarational conception of God appears suggestive, but one-sided. Undoubtedly the notion of God as creative will is important for biblical thinking. Troeltsch's picture of God as creative, living Act is reminiscent of much biblical imagery. Yet at the same time the God depicted in the Bible, from the first page to the last, is the God who speaks his *Word,* his *Logos.* Moreover, this God discloses himself through his Word to his chosen people, *and* discloses his historical purposes to them. He discloses, as it were, a certain Divine logic in history. The God depicted in the Bible, then, seems to have a certain kind of rationality, a *ratio,* which, while it is higher than man's rationality, *is* affirmed and confessed as having been disclosed to those who trust in Him. In the New Testament, the man Jesus is viewed in this context, as the incarnation of the Divine Word, the embodiment of a universal meaning. Jesus is also depicted, surely, as pointing to the Future of God for the final realization of the Divine Will; but the New Testament takes it for granted that that final realization will be the consummation of the very "logic" of history revealed in the history of Israel and preeminently in the man Jesus.

Troeltsch's voluntaristic suprarationalistic conception of God may be an overreaction to Hegelian rationalism which excessively universalized the Logos, over against the more particularistic biblical perspective. The lack of any expressible notion of a universal Divine rationality may be the missing keystone in Troeltsch's thought which makes it impossible for him to build the archway of a transcendent religious criterion over Western-Christian culture.

One may also question Troeltsch's distinction between naive religion and religion which has been "harmonized" by reason. Pure religion, according to Troeltsch, is sheer, undifferentiated a-rational experience of the Divine. At the same time, paradoxically, Troeltsch frequently states that the Judeo-Christian tradition is characterized by its personalism, by its understanding that both God and man are personal and that they commune with each other personally. As Martin Buber has shown, personal encounter involves *speaking;* and speaking, in turn, involves a certain kind of rationality. Speaking, surely, is not a-rational. Is it a coincidence, then, that in the biblical writings a primary mode of Divine-human communication is the Word/word? In biblical thinking a Divine-human encounter frequently has a *content,* a message; it is not simply an overwhelming, captivating, ecstatic kind of experience. On what does Troeltsch base his notion that the experience of the Divine is a-rational, that it is "naive" in that sense? Furthermore, is the idea of the a-rational character of religious experience true to the historical data of biblical religion? Was primitive Christianity "without ideas"? Or is it not historically more accurate to say that primitive Christianity was characterized by a plethora of ideas (law, love, obedience, resurrection, etc.)? Does this not suggest a variety of profound personal encounters, each with some kind of verbal/rational content? From within the Protestant tradition, and from the perspective of historical biblical studies, one may question the legitimacy of Troeltsch's definition of naive religion as essentially a-rational.

In light of the apparent verbal-rational content given in the personal encounter of primitive Christian experience, moreover, were the second generation claims for absoluteness only *artificial?* Could they not be legitimately interpreted as a *translation* of original claims into a new language, rather than an *imposition* of an artificial language on to an original vital experience? Is Troeltsch's distinction between naive and artificial claims for absoluteness all that convincing? Is there not much more continuity in Christianity's tradition of exclusivistic claims than he wants to allow? Is it not conceivable, indeed, that second-generation Christians would have *still* continued to make exclusivistic claims—as some contemporary Christians have—even if they did have some kind of critical, historical sense? What reason can Troeltsch supply to sustain his judgment that those second-generation claims for absoluteness were artificial, other than his own *a priori* distinction between naive and artificial claims?

Troeltsch's concept of naive religion thus seems to be open to a number of queries, as is his closely related concept of God as supra-rational will. Both these concepts, naive religion and God as will, are closely tied to Troeltsch's historicist framework. Historicism presupposes that "every epoch is immediately related to God" and that there is no universal logic of history, behind the "bewildering diversity" of historical phenomena. Because of this framework, Troeltsch would understandably gravitate toward a notion of religion as essentially a-rational experience and an idea of God as supra-rational will. In light of the question concerning a transcendent religion criterion and Troeltsch's failure to establish such a criterion, together with his evidently one-sided view of God and religion, a more comprehensive question arises: *Has Troeltsch absolutized the modern historical consciousness?* Has he taken what is essentially a relative phenomenon of history and baptized it with absolute validity? Has he taken modern historical thinking as a finally valid dogma of faith?

With this comprehensive question in mind, related questions of a similar scope also arise. If Troeltsch has absolutized historical thinking, has he thereby been overly hasty in ruling out the possibility of a final, universal revelation in history? On what basis is Ernst Troeltsch really able to say—to speak for God as it were—that God will never in principle reveal himself finally in history?

On the other hand, the experience of religious diversity is undoubtedly a permanent feature of our global village. Is that experience to be taken seriously, or is it to be repressed? Howevermuch Troeltsch's own resolution of the problem of religious exclusivism may justly be criticized, the concrete challenge he embodied in his life and work remains. What contemporary believer can seriously and wholeheartedly maintain that his own is the only valid religious tradition? Who today would really want to maintain that the sun of eternity is shining across the waters of history on him and him only?

NOTES

1 For a sympathetic treatment of Hinduism and other major world religions, see Huston Smith, *The Religions of Man* (17).

2 Troeltsch's unfinished magnum opus dealing with historicism has not yet been translated into English: *Der Historismus und seine Probleme* (28:vol. III).

3 Troeltsch's most famous historical study, a classic in its own right, is his two-volume work, *The Social Teachings of the Christian Churches* (32).

4 Materials dealing with this interesting event were collected by its organizer, John Henry Barrows, *The World's Parliament of Religions* (3).

5 The Christian missionary movement grew geometrically in the nineteenth century, along with the imperialistic expansion of the West. In 1814 there were only a few hundred Protestant missionaries in foreign countries. A century later

there were some 22,000. This was the century that came to be called "the Christian Century" (there is still a liberal Protestant journal by that name).

6 The fifteenth-century Cardinal, Nicolas of Cusa, was perhaps the first to attempt a first-hand study of a non-Christian religion, Islam. In the same century the Platonist philosopher, Marsilio Ficino, postulated and searched for a "primordial revelation," prior to the Christian revelation and the source of all religions, including Christianity. But efforts by men like Nicolas of Cusa and Ficino were against the stream of their times and had no substantive impact.

7 Hume's position is paralleled by the much more biting polemic of Voltaire. In his 1769 "Essay on the Manners and Character of the Nations," Voltaire says to the reader, with some irony: "You are looking for useful truths and have found, you say, scarcely anything but useless errors. Let us try to enlighten ourselves together; let us try to disinter some precious monuments from the ruins of the centuries" (11:4). Then Voltaire proceeds to compare a variety of religious traditions, his chief purpose being the debunking of established Christianity. He holds up the religions of the East chiefly to denounce the dominant religion of the West. Seen against the East, he writes, the West stands out as a "heap of crimes, follies, and misfortunes . . ." (11:15).

8 The familiar term "comparative religion" may most instructively be understood to apply to the rationalistic method of scholars like Frazer. The term "history of religions" can best be applied to the empathetic historicist approach of thinkers like Herder, von Ranke, and Mueller.

9 At various places in his writings, including *The Absoluteness of Christianity*, Troeltsch takes special pains to distinguish his own position from that of the immensely influential nineteenth-century German philosopher of history, Georg Wilhelm Friedrich Hegel. Hegel sought to take the "accidental" historical dimension of the religions of the world with full seriousness. For Hegel, the Absolute—which he identifies as ultimate Reason—works *through* the concrete forms of various religions, in all their diversity. At the same time, however, Hegel postulates a universal logic (interpretation) of history, which is for him the ground or inmost core of everything that happens: history is the process of the Absolute coming to self-consciousness through the extended and infinitely complex events of history. The philosopher, according to Hegel's perspective, *can* grasp that universal logic and articulate it. Troeltsch rejects the latter notion; for him, the Absolute is inscrutable Will, not Reason, hence no universal logic of history can be identified; only intra-cultural meanings are ascertainable.

10 See, for example, Jürgen Moltmann, *The Theology of Hope: The Ground and the Implications of a Christian Eschatology*, trans. James W. Leitch (New York: Harper & Row, 1967).

11 Importantly, however, the "situation" for Troeltsch is not merely interpersonal or ecclesiastical; it is cultural and historical.

12 A brief introduction to Karl Barth's thought is conveniently available in *A Handbook of Christian Theologians*, eds. Dean G. Peerman and Martin E. Marty (New York: Meridian Books, 1965), pp. 396-409.

13 Troeltsch would not have been happy with this charge, especially since he himself mounted an attack on "culture Protestantism."

14 Karl Barth, *The Epistle to the Romans*, trans. E. C. Hoskyns (New York: Oxford University Press, 1933).

BIBLIOGRAPHY

1. BAECK, LEO, "Revelation and World Religions," *The Essence of Judaism.* London: Macmillan, 1936.
2. BARROWS, JOHN HENRY, *Christianity, the World Religion.* Chicago: A. C. M. Clurg, 1897.
3. ———, ed., *The World's Parliament of Religions.* Chicago: Parliament, 1893.
4. "Decree on the Church's Missionary Activity" and "Decree on the Relationship of the Church to Non-Christian Religions," in *The Documents of Vatican II,* ed. Walter M. Abbott. New York: Herder & Herder, 1966.
5. ELIADE, MIRCEA, and JOSEPH KATAGAWA, eds., *The History of Religions: Essays in Methodology.* Chicago: University of Chicago Press, 1967.
6. ———, *The Sacred and the Profane: The Nature of Religion,* trans. Willard R. Trask. New York: Harcourt, Brace, 1959.
7. KIRKPATRICK, DOW, ed., *The Finality of Christ.* Nashville: Abingdon Press, 1966.
8. KRAEMER, HENDRIK, *The Christian Message in a Non-Christian World.* London: James Clarke, 1938.
9. LEEUW, G. VAN DER, *Religion in Essence and Manifestation.* New York: Harper & Row, 1963.
10. MUELLER, F. MAX, *Chips From a German Workshop,* vol. I. London, 1868.
11. NEFF, EMERY, *The Poetry of History: The Contribution of Literature and Literary Scholarship to the Writings of History Since Voltaire.* New York: Columbia University Press, 1947.
12. NEWBIGIN, LESSLIE, *The Finality of Christ.* Richmond, Va.: John Knox Press, 1969.
13. NIEBUHR, H. RICHARD, *The Meaning of Revelation.* New York: Macmillan, 1941.
14. OGLETREE, THOMAS W., *Christian Faith and History: A Critical Comparison of Ernst Troeltsch and Karl Barth.* Nashville: Abingdon Press, 1965.
15. RAHNER, KARL, and HERBERT VORGRIMMER, "Absolutist Claim of Christianity," "Non-Christian Religions," in *Theological Dictionary,* ed. Cornelius Ernst. New York: Herder & Herder, 1965.
16. ———, "Christianity and Non-Christian Religions," *Theological Investigations,* V. Baltimore: Helicon Press, 1967.
17. SMITH, HUSTON, *The Religions of Man.* New York: Harper, 1958.
18. SMITH, WILFRED CANTWELL, *The Meaning and End of Religion: A New Approach to the Religious Traditions of Mankind.* New York: Macmillan, 1963.

19. Steinberg, Milton, "Israel and the Nations," *Basic Judaism*. New York: Harcourt, Brace, 1947.

20. Stern, Fritz, ed., *The Varieties of History*. New York: Meridian Books, 1956.

21. Tillich, Paul, See the bibliography following the next chapter.

22. Toynbee, Arnold, *Christianity among the Religions of the World*. New York: Scribner's, 1957.

23. Troeltsch, Ernst, *The Absoluteness of Christianity and the History of Religions*, trans. David Reid. Richmond, Va.: John Knox Press, 1971.

24. ———, *Christian Thought: Its History and Application*, ed. Baron F. von Huegel. New York: Meridian Books, 1957.

25. ———, "Contingency," "Historiography," in *Hastings Encyclopedia of Religion and Ethics*.

26. ———, "The Dogmatics of the 'Religionsgeschichtliche Schule'," *American Journal of Theology*. 17 (1913), 1-21.

27. ———, "Empiricism and Platonism in the Philosophy of Religion," *Harvard Theological Review*. 5 (1912), 401-422.

28. - ———, *Gesammelte Schriften*, vols. I-IV. Tuebingen: J. C. B. Mohr, 1912-1925.

29. ———, *Glaubenslehre*. Munich: Duncker and Humbolt, 1925.

30. ———, *Protestantism and Progress: A Historical Study of the Relation of Protestantism to the Modern World*, trans. W. Montgomery. Boston: Beacon Press, 1958.

31. ———, "On the Possibility of a Free Christianity," in *Fifth International Congress of Free Christianity and Religious Progress (Berlin): Proceedings and Papers*, ed. Charles W. Wendte. London: 1911, pp. 233-249.

32. ———, *The Social Teachings of the Christian Churches*, trans. Olive Wyon. New York: Harper, 1960.

33. ———, "Das Wesen der Religion und der Religionswissenschaft," in *Die Kultur der Gegenwart*. Berlin: 1907.

SUGGESTED READINGS

1. *Primary Readings*

The Absoluteness of Christianity (23). The major source, only recently translated into English.

"The Place of Christianity Among the World Religions," in *Christian Thought: Its History and Applications* (24). Troeltsch's last lecture, lucidly written, a good introduction to his thought. He here alters the position he took in the preceding work.

2. *Secondary Readings*

Adams, James Luther, "Introduction," *The Absoluteness of Christianity* (23).

————, "Ernst Troeltsch as an Analyst of Religion," *Journal for the Scientific Study of Religion*, I, 1 (October, 1961), 98-108. Adams is the foremost American interpreter of Troeltsch.

KRAEMER, HENDRIK, *The Christian Message in a Non-Christian World* (8). A lengthy study, drawing on the exclusivistic perspective of Karl Barth. The standard statement of this position.

NIEBUHR, H. RICHARD, *The Meaning of Revelation* (13). Seeks to do justice both to the historicism of Troeltsch and the exclusivism of Barth. Highly readable, a minor theological classic.

RAHNER, KARL, "Christianity and Non-Christian Religions," in *Theological Investigations* (16). A forceful statement of a traditional perspective by a leading contemporary Catholic theologian.

STEINBERG, MILTON, "Israel and the Nations," *Basic Judaism* (19). A short survey of various attitudes toward the finality of Judaism within the Jewish tradition.

TILLICH, PAUL, See the Suggested Readings following the next chapter.

3. *Additional Bibliography*

REIST, BENJAMIN A., *Toward a Theology of Involvement: The Thought of Ernst Troeltsch* (Philadelphia: Westminster Press, 1966), pp. 257-262. Complete citation of Troeltsch's works, including his several encyclopedia articles. Some secondary studies also cited.

12

The Relative and the Ultimate
in the Encounter of Religions

How can a religion avoid making intolerant, naive, and bigoted claims of superiority for itself? If a religion is intrinsically involved in a particular culture, can it still have sufficient independence to bring transcendent ethical claims to bear on that culture? If a religion recognizes its historical and cultural relativity, can it still have the confidence and power to give creative meaning to human life? Is there a danger that religious-cultural relativism will lead to an "aimless relativism," an extreme individualism with no shared meaning for communities and peoples? To what extent do all religions deal with the same basic issues of human existence? To what extent are their answers distinct, and to what extent are they similar? How are the various religions related to the Ultimate, to God, to the Absolute?

Many of these questions were treated by Troeltsch. Some of them are more recent variations of his concerns. All of them found a place in the wide-ranging thought of Paul Tillich (1886–1965).[1]

Tillich, one of the leading religious minds of the twentieth century, spent the first half of his life in Germany, his native land. As a young professor at the University of Berlin in the 1920's, he was a junior colleague of Troeltsch. Tillich acknowledged that Troeltsch had deeply influenced him, and dedicated one of his early major books to the memory of Troeltsch after his death in 1923. Nevertheless, Tillich felt dissatisfied with Troeltsch's form of historicism and relativism.

The year 1933 brought Hitler and National Socialism to power, and Tillich was forced to leave his professorship in Germany. He came to the United States, where he taught at Columbia and at Union Theological Seminary (where Reinhold Niebuhr was his colleague), at Harvard as a University Professor, and at the University of Chicago. Throughout his long and distinguished career, Tillich described his work as a "theology of culture"; he continually probed the interaction of religion with philosophy, politics, history, art, psychoanalysis and other aspects of human culture.[2]

In his earlier years Tillich was immersed in questions of religion and Western culture. To be sure, he approached those questions with characteristic openness. He felt that the isolation and conflict between Catholics and Protestants was sterile, and often said that he tried to combine in his own thinking the "Catholic substance" of Christianity with the "Protestant principle" of prophetic protest. Also, he was much concerned about relations between Christians and Jews; he wrote on the subject, and his uncompromising opposition to Nazism led him to lose his position at the University of Frankfurt. Again, all forms of ecclesiastical exclusivism and institutional imperialism were foreign to him; he repeatedly criticized this authoritarian attitude of "heteronomy," to use his own word. It was not until the last years of his life, however, that he became actively involved in inter-religious dialogue and detailed study of non-Western religions. In 1960 he travelled to Japan for lectures and meetings with Buddhist and Shinto leaders. This visit influenced his lectures on "Christianity and the Encounter of the World Religions" which he gave the following year. In the last two years of his life he conducted a joint seminar with Mircea Eliade, the history-of-religions scholar at Chicago; in fact, his last lecture, given ten days before he died in October, 1965, was on the subject of the history of religions. So, although he knew Troeltsch in Berlin at the beginning of his career, it was not until many years later that he became directly involved in discussions with leaders of non-Western religions. He died, as he had always lived, exploring a new frontier, standing on a new "boundary" and asking new questions.[3]

Eliade wrote that "we will never know what would have been the result of Paul Tillich's encounter with primitive and oriental religions" (12:35). We do know, however, how Tillich responded to Troeltsch, and how this response affected his own approach to the encounter of the world religions. Tillich once said that the work of Ernst Troeltsch was the negative premise of all future constructiveness, clearly a two-sided remark. He wanted to face up to the issue of historical particularity and cultural relativism, but he wanted to give a better answer than the one he found in Troeltsch.

Several of Troeltsch's fundamental convictions were shared by Tillich. He held, with Troeltsch, that the idea of the "absoluteness of Christianity" was a "questionable concept," to put it mildly (16:233). He agreed with Troeltsch and Max Weber that religion was an *independent* factor in human life, not just a by-product of social or psychic processes, as Marx and Freud held. Indeed, Tillich stressed perhaps more forcefully than Troeltsch that religion was a fundamental factor in everyone's life, basic to personal and cultural life alike. Like Troeltsch, Tillich accepted the findings of the "history of religions school" at the turn of the century, namely that the central symbols of the biblical religions had been influenced by the other religions which surrounded Judaism and Christianity during their rise and growth.

On the critical side, Tillich thought that Troeltsch overemphasized the *individuality* of history and the *relativity* of cultures, while neglecting the *universal* dynamics of life found—in individualized forms of course,—in people of all cultures and historical ages. By so stressing the particularity and distinctness of human experience, Troeltsch underestimated the significance of certain fundamental concerns which all people in all times share in varying ways; historical-cultural relativism ignores the great and recurrent themes of history in all periods. Extending this criticism, Tillich opposed the ultimate relativism of Troeltsch's historicism. It is easy, Tillich argued, to criticize relativism in the idea of truth, and to point out that every radical relativism had self-defying consequences. He therefore concluded that "here indeed is a point in which Troeltsch is not sufficiently protected. This is so because he does not dare to rise to the level . . . of a metaphysics and theology of history" (11:113). Against Troeltsch's relativism, Tillich proposed a metaphysical, or better, a symbolic view of history. This "finds in representative, symbol-creating events a meaning of all history which is free from the difficulties of relativism and leads to ethical consequences which are rooted in an ultimate meaning of life" (11:113).

In these quotations from an early review (1924) of a major book by Troeltsch, Tillich shows his own characteristic emphasis. Tillich's is a religious, symbolic and typological approach to history and culture. Without in the least denying historical particularity and cultural relativity, he tries to discern the universal *in* the particular, the ultimate *in* the relative, the eternal *in* the historical. This disagreement discloses the basic perspective of each man's thought. Troeltsch stresses the *individual, distinct* and *particular* character of all historical experience; Tillich stresses the *universal*, common and shared elements which pervade the concerns of humanity in their infinite variety of expression. Almost forty years later, during his discussions in Japan, this same basic approach appears.

To understand Tillich's approach to the encounter of religions, some basic questions must be answered. These concern his definition of religion, his criticism of prevalent misunderstandings and distortions of words like "faith" and "God," his view of the relation of religion to culture and to specific religious organizations, and his understanding of religious symbols.

1. TILLICH'S THEORY OF RELIGION: ULTIMATE CONCERN

What is religion? [4] Tillich's answer begins by saying what religion is not. First, Tillich repudiates the theistic definition of religion. The traditional, theistic view is that God is the supreme, all-powerful being, and that belief in the existence of such a God is the essence of religion. However Tillich counters, one should not "define religion as man's relation to divine beings" (18:4) whose existence is asserted by believers and denied by critics.

> A God about whose existence or non-existence you can argue is a thing beside others within the universe of existing things. . . . Theologians who make of God a highest being who has given some people information about Himself, provoke inescapably the resistance of those who are told they must subject themselves to the authority of this information (18:5).

Here Tillich argues that religion is not belief in a highest being. God is not a thing, a being, or even a supreme being, alongside or above everything else that exists; if God is regarded this way, he remains one among many finite beings.

Tillich expands this critique of traditional theism by showing that it vacillates between viewing God as both *object* and *subject*. But if God is regarded as an object, then he has no existential, religious meaning for man. Yet if he is regarded as the supreme, all-powerful, and all-knowing subject, then all human freedom and subjectivity is endangered. Such a God is an "invincible tyrant."

> This is the God Nietzsche said had to be killed because nobody can tolerate being made into a mere object of absolute knowledge and absolute control. This is the deepest root of atheism. It is an atheism which is justified as the reaction against theological theism and its disturbing implications (8:185).

This critique of theistic religion leaves open for the moment how Tillich will constructively speak of God to avoid these problems. [5]

Second, Tillich rejects the view that religion is only "a special function of the human spirit" (18:6). Religion is not confined to some aspect of life, like morality or feeling. Nor is it, to state the point in popular terms, restricted to the "soul," or to what some religious believers mean by "the spiritual life." In the same vein Tillich argues that religion is not limited to the activities of religious institutions. Without denying the need for organized churches and synagogues, and their functions of worship, teaching and fellowship, Tillich holds that religion is distorted if confined to special religious institutions and excluded from the whole range of human life—politics, art, education, philosophy, science, and so on. The sacred and the secular cannot be divorced from each other.

How, then, is religion properly described? Religion is *ultimate concern*. Here we meet the first of Tillich's efforts to mint a new language, and so overcome the misleading and often meaningless associations of much traditional religious terminology. By the word "concern" Tillich stresses that religion is existential; it involves the *whole* person and includes much more than belief. Religion is "the dimension of depth" that undergirds and informs every aspect of life. The metaphor "depth" links up with the word "ultimate." Religion as the dimension of depth "points to that which is ultimate, infinite, unconditional in man's spiritual life" (18:7). In our daily lives we have many concerns: food, home, friendship, work, leisure, health, security, freedom—the list could be greatly extended. While these concerns are important, they are nevertheless preliminary; though religion informs the way one handles these concerns, none of them would be the proper aim of an *ultimate*, religious concern. All these concerns of daily life are part of a larger, more serious, concern: *life itself*, our true being. So Tillich writes:

> Religion is the state of being grasped by an ultimate concern, a concern which qualifies all other concerns as preliminary and which itself contains *the answer to the question of the meaning of our life*. Therefore this concern is unconditionally serious and shows a willingness to sacrifice any finite concern which is in conflict with it. The predominant religious name for the content of such a concern is God—a god or gods (7:4f., italics added).

This definition can, of course, include nontheistic religions such as Zen Buddhism; ultimate concern about "the meaning of our life" is evident even though it is not focused upon a deity.

From this definition it follows that ultimate concern is expressed in all the preliminary, daily concerns, in all the activities which make up human culture.[6] Hence "religion as ultimate concern is the meaning-giving substance of culture, and culture is the totality of forms in which the basic concern of religion expresses itself" (18:42).

In light of this definition, the question naturally arises: what is the status of special religious institutions? If the ultimate concern of religion is to be expressed in all aspects of life, what need is there for special religious communities and practices? The answer is that they are *necessary*, though *relative*. Tillich's ideal would be a "theonomous" culture, that is, a culture which is transparent to the "ground of being." But culture is not theonomous; the light of the holy does not shine transparently into all our experience. On the contrary, there is a strong tendency for the religious and secular aspects of life to be separated and estranged from each other; culture often lacks the depth-dimension of religion, and religion is often divorced from real cultural relevance. The *necessity* for special religious communities and activities derives from the fact that culture is not theonomous. Religious communities have an emergency function, so to speak, a particular vocation to recall culture to its roots in the ground of being. But in fulfilling this vocation, they must remember that their function is not to swallow up the freedom of culture in a spiritual imperialism. Special religious communities and activities are therefore *relative*, because their vocation is to point beyond themselves to the ground of being, which is greater than religion, and is the only proper focus of ultimate concern.

Tillich's definition of religion also obliged him to deal with the issue of "quasi-religions." If religion is "ultimate concern," and if it is expressed in culture, do not some secular movements function very much like a religion? Think about communism. In spite of all its polemics against religion, many observers have suggested that in a strange, secular way, it has "religious" characteristics. The similarity is real, even if unintended. Communism expects an unconditional allegiance from its party members. It promises a new life and a new world in the "classless society"; indeed, this symbol has a striking similarity to the eschatological symbol of the Kingdom of God in the Bible—though now translated into secular-political form. Communism offers a way of overcoming the estrangement, or alienation, of capitalist society, and this offer is like the religious offer of salvation. These and other characteristics justify for Tillich the description of communism as a "quasi-religion." Like communism, a radicalized socialism, fascism was a radicalized nationalism, and also a quasi-religion. Here, concern for the nation was elevated to the status of "ultimate concern." The totalitarian character of German fascism consisted precisely in the absolute and unconditional status given to the nation, and to the unqualified claim of obedience and sacrifice laid upon the citizen. The warrant for speaking of communism and fascism as quasi-religions consists in their elevating social ideology or nation to the status of ultimacy, and in their making unconditional claims upon people in the name of these concerns. However, his distinction between finite and ultimate concern provides Tillich with a critical criterion for judging quasi-religions.

Nothing finite, however important it may be in itself, is entitled to claim ultimacy; demonic consequences always follow the consecration of finite concerns to the status of ultimacy, for a finite concern is always made ultimate at the expense of other legitimate, finite concerns. The ultimacy of German nationalism, the Aryan race, and the dream of "the thousand-year Reich" were purchased at the enormous cost of Jewish blood and worldwide war.

In discussing the two extreme quasi-religions of German fascism and Stalinist communism, Tillich highlights the destructive consequences which follow when a finite concern is made ultimate. Similar examples, if not always quite so drastic, can be found in scientism and anti-communism. However, a quasi-religion may occasionally have a more benign form, and this is what Tillich sees in liberal humanism and democracy; even so, he warns against the danger of radicalizing—that is, making more ultimate—the concerns and claims of liberal humanism, for this would be a self-defeating contradiction. Such quasi-religion is benign to the degree that its claim is not absolutized. Tillich's position here is basically the same as his previously stated attitude to religion proper: it must never make itself the ultimate concern, but should direct ultimate concern beyond itself to the ultimate, to the ground of being, to God. Religion is a medium, not the Ultimate itself. As Tillich once put it, speaking about Christianity: the greatness of Christianity is that it can see how small it is.

Central to Tillich's theory of religion is his understanding of religious *symbols*.[7] A symbol is not a sign, even though both point beyond themselves. A sign conveys information—the highway sign showing the direction to the city, the red light indicating that cars must stop, the mathematical sign indicating the multiplication process. The sign is usually conventional; there is no necessary reason why a blue light, rather than a red one, might not have been chosen to show that cars should stop. A symbol, however, *participates* in the reality it points to. The civil rights song, "We shall overcome," is symbolic in this sense. Born out of a struggle for freedom and justice, and often sung in the face of tremendous opposition, this symbol has a necessary relation to the reality it expresses. This reality, furthermore, is not merely factual and empirical; it is an existential reality, the expression of profound feeling about the meaning of life which gives people courage to persevere in the face of great odds.

The symbol thus discloses aspects of reality which transcend the scientific and technical level: Picasso's "Guernica," which Tillich regarded as a major religious painting, discloses something about the Spanish Civil War which no amount of statistics can convey. At the same time, the symbol opens up dimensions of our lives, "hidden depths of our own being" (10:43), which correspond to the reality thus disclosed. Here one might think of dreams, which present reality symbolically rather than literally, yet really do disclose aspects of reality and dimensions of our being not accessible in other ways. A related characteristic of symbols, especially those which function socially as do political and religious symbols, is that they cannot function without involving the deep and unconscious dimensions of our being. Accordingly, symbols cannot be invented intentionally; they are born in situations where their meaning is relevant, live as long as they have existential power, and they die when they no longer evoke response.

Ultimate concern is always expressed symbolically. The reason for this is that only finite reality can be expressed non-symbolically. But

> the true ultimate transcends the realm of finite reality infinitely. Therefore, no finite reality can express it directly and properly. . . . Whatever we say about that which concerns us ultimately, whether or not we call it God, has a symbolic meaning. It points beyond itself while participating in that to which it points. In no other way can faith express itself adequately. The language of faith is the language of symbols (10:44f.).

All religious expression, then, is symbolic. Traditionally one might think of an object, like a cross, as a religious symbol. But Tillich reminds us of other types of religious symbols. The *story* of Adam, for example, created by God and then falling into sin, is a symbolic story. *Myth* is a story of divine-human interaction in which a number of symbols are joined together to make a narrative: an example is the Christian myth of the Messiah who was born of a virgin, performed miracles during his life, was crucified and resurrected, ascended into heaven, and who will come again as the judge and savior of the world. Religious *concepts,* above all the concept of God and his attributes of power, love and justice, are symbolic; so too is a creed, like the Apostle's Creed. Symbol, then, is the native language of religion. Clearly, Tillich does not regard symbol and myth as perjorative terms; on the contrary, symbols are rich in power and meaning, transcending in potency all empirical, literal and technical forms of communication. Indeed, to literalize a symbol is to betray the greatest misunderstanding of its nature, and to deprive it of its existential potency.[8] Symbol for Tillich is not a primitive form of expression which has been superseded by modern, scientific thinking; it is a perennial form of human consciousness which conveys profound insights into the nature of reality and the depths of human being.

Religious symbols give content to ultimate concern. They are the media by which man is able to participate in the "ground of being." They open up the ground of being and depth of life, so that the ultimate—life itself, true being—can be related concretely to all aspects of human experience.

2. EXISTENTIAL CONCERNS AND RELIGIOUS SYMBOLS

Ultimate concern is existential concern about the meaning and fulfillment of our lives.[9] As existential, this concern underlies and informs every
human concern and activity. There is no question which is more necessary, elemental and inescapable than the question of *my being*. Hamlet's
"to be, or not to be?" is a profoundly religious question. And, if one
answers "to be," this is immediately followed by another equally serious
question: "how shall I be?" that is, what is the real meaning of life, and
how shall I find my true being? This existential question is not only
ultimate in its importance for man. It is ultimate above all because it
points beyond finite man and asks: is man's quest for life and true being
supported by a "ground of being," an ultimate and unconditional reality
in whose power, meaning and love man participates? The term "ultimate
concern" thereby unites man's most urgent existential questions with the
concern about "being-itself" as the answer to these questions; in traditional terms, it refers both to faith and to God.

Tillich's use of the concepts "being," "ground of being," and "being-
itself" needs explanation. To begin with, "being" is best approached not as
an abstract noun, but as an active participle of the verb "to be": "be-ing."
Generally speaking, be-ing refers to the *life process*. To live, to exist, is
a way of be-ing. I am, she is, you are, they are—we be! As we live we find
ourselves in a great ocean of being. Together with all the millions of
people in the world, with all the animal and plant life, and with all the
processes which abound in nature, we share in life, we "live and move
and have our being." With all our rich varieties of culture, geography,
history, nation, race and religion—Hindu, Jew, Buddhist, Moslem, Christian, Confucianist, Taoist, animist, polytheist, monotheist—we share together in a great ocean of being.

To be sure, this enormous, rich ocean of being is comprised of finite
be-ings, and even in its totality it is still finite. Yet being and living
gives rise to questions and concerns about the meaning of our be-ing.
These are the religious questions. The religious question is *not* whether,
in addition to all the finite being we experience, there is another infinite
Being, *a* Supreme Being. The religious question is *not* whether, in addition to everything that exists, God also exists. The religious question is:
what is the true nature of be-ing, what is the "essence" of being, what
does it mean truly to be? Again, the religious question is *not* whether a
Supreme Being exists. It is, rather: what is the true and essential nature
of what actually exists and manifestly *is*? What is the essential character of that be-ing we call life? In other words, can we symbolize the

"ground of being," or "being-itself," which gives meaning to our life and satisfies our ultimate concern? Is there, so to speak, an infinite spring of life which continually feeds into the great ocean of finite being? [10]

To answer this question Tillich identifies three basic dimensions of life which are involved in our ultimate concern about being: *finitude*, anxiety, and the courage to be; *existence*, estrangement, and healing; and *life*, ambiguity, and integration. In each case, the first term specifies the dimension of human life under consideration, the second term refers to the problem, and the third to its resolution. Tillich's usage will become clear in the course of the exposition which shows how these three dimensions of life involve ultimate concern, and how religious symbols correlated to these existential questions disclose something about ultimate reality, being-itself. [11]

Finitude, Anxiety, and the Courage To Be [12]

To be a finite human being is, *per se*, to experience anxiety. "Anxiety is finitude, experienced as one's own finitude. This is the natural anxiety of man as man, and in some way of all living beings. It is the anxiety of nonbeing, the awareness of one's finitude as finitude" (8:35f.). Anxiety, then, is intrinsic to being finite. But anxiety is distinct from fear, for fear normally focuses on a specific source of danger—a burning house, serious illness, rejection by a significant person, and so on. One can come to terms with fears by taking precautions against potential dangers, struggling against a particular threat, or working to overcome a serious setback. But anxiety, while it is often expressed in particular fears, is different. Anxiety does not derive from any specific object; its source is nameless and faceless, it is rooted in the awareness of what existentialist philosophers like Heidegger and Sartre call "nothingness." The anxiety about nonbeing has several different expressions, particularly death, guilt and meaninglessness.

Death, obviously, represents a threat to our being, and death is the lot of every finite mortal. In the awareness of death, it is not just fear of being killed in an accident or war, or fear of the pain in a fatal illness, which produces anxiety; the anxiety derives from the realization that, faced with eventual death, there is nothing we can do to preserve our being—we are not immortal, like gods, but are mortal by nature. Here, then, "awareness of one's finitude" clearly involves "the anxiety of nonbeing." While awareness of death is the most obvious manifestation of the anxiety of finitude, there are others. Closely related is the experience of fate—the sense that one's life is contingent upon powerful forces which, despite heroic efforts to change them, often render one powerless and helpless in the face of an intractable situation. Nowadays, deep frustration about efforts for political and institutional change illustrates this type of anxiety.

Guilt is another major form in which the threat of nonbeing is experienced. Guilt is not simply remorse for a particular act which is contrary to a moral code of society and the internal norms of conscience. Guilt is more profound and pervasive, striking at the whole self; it is the awareness that one's moral self-affirmation is undermined, that one is rejected and condemned as a person, that one is threatened by nonbeing in the feeling of worthlessness. Even short of extreme forms of guilt, like that experienced by the young Luther in the monastery, this anxiety is present in the awareness of the ambiguity of good and evil which is found in all moral life. Guilt, as a profound sense of self-rejection, is the anxiety of nonbeing in the form of despair about losing one's destiny.

Meaninglessness is the third major form of anxiety about nonbeing which Tillich finds intrinsic to all finite existence. Indeed if, in a large historical perspective, the concern with fate and death was typical of the early centuries of Christianity, and if concern with guilt and condemnation was typical of medieval Christendom, then meaninglessness and emptiness is the most characteristic experience of the anxiety of nonbeing in the modern age (8:57ff.). "Man's being includes his relation to meanings. He is human only by understanding and shaping reality, both his world and himself, according to meanings and values" (8:50). But what happens when social and political values, long assumed valid, are flouted by a government? What happens when law is used to oppress rather than to promote justice? What happens when traditional family and personal roles are found unsuitable in a different stage of society, and no new meanings are readily available? What happens when the culture of a minority group is suppressed? What happens when traditional religious symbols no longer engage the real experience of life? In all these cases one becomes aware of emptiness and meaninglessness as a threat to one's being, and one senses another form of the anxiety of nonbeing threatening life. In an achievement-oriented society, for example, guilt and condemnation may be experienced if one fails to attain the expected level of performance—as every student knows!

> Guilt is produced by manifest shortcomings in adjustments to and achievements within the creative activities of society. It is the social group in which one participates productively that judges, forgives, and restores, after the adjustments have been made and the achievements have become visible (8:111).

The anxiety of fate in a competitive society is felt, Tillich believes, especially in the threat of exclusion from the process of economic production. The anxiety of doubt and meaninglessness is known to anyone who has experienced the impact of the question: what is the *purpose* of the whole enterprise of technical civilisation and capitalist economics? On the more personal side of experience, the anxiety of meaninglessness— and the necessity to create one's own meaning in the face of despair—has repeatedly been expressed by modern existentialist philosophers, and also by artists and writers. Sartre's *No Exit,* T. S. Eliot's "The Waste Land," *The Stranger* of Camus, Kafka's *The Trial,* and Auden's *Age of Anxiety* all express the anxiety of meaninglessness which Tillich regards as the most critical concern of the twentieth century.

These examples show that "nonbeing" is not simply "nothing." Perhaps it can be concisely restated as "negation," the threat to life, the negative pole to being. This negativity, which finite man experiences in the several forms of underlying anxiety, can lead to despair. Usually, however, man does not simply despair and give up, but struggles to affirm his being: hope struggles with despair, meaning with meaninglessness, life with death, being with nonbeing.

This struggle implies a question which is of ultimate concern: is it possible to have a "courage to be," a courage which can take the threat of nonbeing into itself and lead to self-affirmation in spite of ever-present anxiety? Indeed, is there a "ground of being" which en-courages and sustains human self-affirmation in spite of the negating threat of nonbeing?

This is not a speculative question, but one which emerges in the existential struggle of people wrestling with their lives. In fact, Tillich answers, we repeatedly find courageous self-affirmation in spite of negation, and this is a clue both to human being and also to "being-itself," the "ground of being" in which human be-ing participates. Human courage, the *power* to affirm one's being in the face of negation and anxiety, is rooted in being-itself. In other words, *power of being* is an essential characteristic of reality itself; power belongs to the essence of being. The infinite spring of life which feeds into the great ocean of finite being is the power of being which continually overcomes nonbeing. Traditionally stated, the divine power is the ground and source of all human courage and affirmation of life in the face of nonbeing. Speaking metaphorically or symbolically, as one always must when talking about being-itself, Tillich writes:

> being "embraces" itself and nonbeing. Being has nonbeing "within" itself as that which is eternally present and eternally overcome in the process of the divine life. The ground of everything that is is not a dead identity without movement and becoming; it is living creativity. Creatively it affirms itself, eternally conquering its own nonbeing. As such it is the pattern of the self-affirmation of every finite being and the source of the courage to be (8:34).

The traditional Christian symbol which expresses this power of being which sustains finite being and gives courage for overcoming nonbeing is God the Creator and Preserver of the world. Faith, seen in relation to the problem of finitude, is not " 'belief in something unbelieveable' "; "faith is the state of being grasped by the power of being-itself. The courage to be is an expression of faith. . . ." Faith is the experience of the power of self-affirmation as rooted in the power of being-itself which is found in every act of courage (8:172).

The courage to be, then, is the resolution to the anxiety of finitude. Precisely because this courage to affirm oneself in spite of anxiety is rooted in the ground of being, it is manifest in all human experience, whether its religious character is acknowledged or not.

> Every courage to be has an open or hidden religious root. For religion is the state of being grasped by the power of being-itself. . . . Everything that is participates in being-itself, and everybody has some awareness of this participation, especially in the moments in which he experiences the threat of nonbeing (8:156).

The experience of courage is not limited to those who profess an explicit religious faith; the religious root may be "passionately denied" or "deeply hidden," but it is never totally absent. Whenever someone affirms life in spite of the negation of nonbeing, there being-itself is present and effective to some degree. This means that no matter how secular one's attitude, or no matter what religion one follows, he can never be totally divorced from being-itself—for simply to be, is to participate to some degree in being-itself; how, Tillich asks, could one have any being at all if one did not participate in being-itself? While this assertion still leaves unanswered questions about the criteria for evaluating various forms of courageous self-affirmation, it nevertheless highlights the *universal* scope of Tillich's theory of religion. The vehicle for this universal approach is his religious *ontology*, or theory of being. Because all people participate in being, they experience its common dynamics.

Existence, Estrangement, and Healing [13]

Man's life agenda requires him to bring his true nature into existence, as well as to affirm himself courageously as a finite being. The process of self-actualization brings with it the problem of estrangement. In estrangement man is at odds with his true being, and so he seeks for healing.

The category of "existence" introduces another dimension of life. Of course, one who experiences the anxiety of finitude is an existing being, and his courage to be is an affirmation of his being. But if finitude simply poses the question of be-ing in the face of nonbeing, existence poses another question: *how* shall I be, how shall I actualize my *true* self? In addition to constantly affirming his being, man seeks fulfillment. Tillich calls this the process of actualizing one's essence, or true nature; it involves fulfilling one's human potential.

Man has many potentialities: to be a free and independent individual, to love, to participate meaningfully with others in communities of work, art and science, to create justice in political and economic orders, and so on. Human potentialities for good, however, are not really real until they have been actualized; potential must become actual, man's true nature (or "essence") must come into actual existence.

But when man proceeds to actualize his potential, what comes into existence always includes estrangement. While self-actualizing is as necessary through man's whole life span as resisting the anxiety of finitude, a good example of actualization and estrangement can be seen when a growing child or adolescent seeks to establish independence in relation to parents. He must gain his autonomy as the basis for further development, psychic health, and adult responsibility. Yet often the process of actualizing independence and gaining personal freedom also brings estrangement. The young person may accuse the parents of domination, neglect, hypocrisy, distorted values, and the like; these charges may include both truth and distortion. Or the young person may expect from the parents an exalted moral perfection and a quite unrealistic capacity for love and understanding. The parents, for their part, may be quite unwilling to have their values challenged, or to come to terms with their own anxieties. From both sides, then, and taking account of the freedom and limits with which all parties act, estrangement results. A good potential, in this case freedom and autonomy, has been actualized, but not without estrangement. The innocent unity, metaphorically speaking, which once characterized relations between others and oneself, has now become estranged existence. Tillich is never closer to existentialism than when he argues that there is a "gap" between man's true nature and his actual life, between his "essence" and his "existence." This gap, or split, is what he describes as "estrangement."

Many examples of estrangement in individual and corporate actualization come quickly to mind. Social and political revolutions, necessary for freedom and justice, almost invariably involve an excess of violence, gross oversimplification of complex human experience, and severe compromise of the precious quality of compassion. That the anti-Fascists in the Second World War could claim impressive moral legitimacy for their cause did not prevent, but rather contributed to, their excessive self-righteousness and to wanton destruction of the most dubious sort. The therapeutic process of psychoanalysis often includes a stage of deep hostility before acceptance and healing is possible.

Surprising though it may seem at first, Tillich finds that the symbolic biblical myth of Adam opens up the problem of estrangement. Adam, of course, is not regarded literally as the first human being whose fall into sin sealed the fate of all humanity. Adam is Everyman, symbolic of us all. "The fall" symbolizes the estrangement, and loss of innocent goodness, which distorts all human existence. The fall is not a primeval event, but "a symbol for the human situation universally" (17.II:29). Furthermore, the estrangement from one's own true being which it entails does not refer to one particular stage or event in a person's life history. While man's true being and essential goodness is a constant reality in all his attempts at self-actualization, estrangement is an ever present factor distorting his essential being in his actual existence.

Tillich sees three main types of estrangement: *hubris*, concupiscence, and unbelief. *Hubris*, a Greek term usually translated as "pride," is expanded by Tillich to include all human attempts to overleap the limits of finitude, to make oneself the center of reality, to elevate oneself into the divine sphere. Because *hubris* is a denial of man's finitude, Tillich regards it as the typical form of man's estrangement from himself. *Hubris* appears in many guises. For example, unbridled personal ambition which tramples upon others, or a social group identifying its morality with absolute goodness, are both forms of *hubris*. *Hubris* is also evident when a nation gives its political or economic system ultimate status and universal validity. Any individual or corporate self-absolutization is *hubris* because this makes a finite concern ultimate.

While *hubris* denotes self-estrangement, *concupiscence* refers to man's estrangement from his world; it is the other side of *hubris*. The Latin term "concupiscence" is normally used to mean inordinate sexual desire. Tillich expands its meaning to include every expression of an unlimited desire to absorb reality into oneself. For example, when a system of philosophy—or theology!—pretends to finality or completeness of knowledge, this is concupiscence. So too is a nation's imperialistic urge to dominate neighboring peoples, or even to rule the whole world.

These two postures exemplify and perpetuate man's estrangement from himself and from everyone and everything which make up his world. Such alienation from one's true self and one's right relation to the world is rooted in man's estrangement from the ground of being. Tillich calls this type of estrangement *unbelief*. "Unbelief" means man's alienation from being-itself, not "disbelief" in the church's authoritative doctrines; distrust ("un-faith") and distorted love ("un-love") are constitutive of man's alienation from his ground of being. These three inter-related forms of estrangement are involved in all man's achievements of actualizing his potential. "In his existential self-realization he turns towards himself and his world and loses his essential unity with the ground of his being and his world" (17.II:47).

Estrangement is the universal predicament of human existence. Adam symbolizes the profound insight about human being, namely that the process of self-actualization always leads to an existence which is estranged. This is *not* to assert that man is evil by definition, and corrupt in all his ways; nor does it mean that he is forced by some predetermining structure of being to be estranged—though the inescapable and tragic element in estrangement must be acknowledged together with freedom and responsibility. The symbol of fallen Adam means that in the midst of everything that is great and good and noble in human existence, we also find the contradiction of estrangement.

As with the experience of anxiety, so estrangement gives rise to a crucial question: can estrangement be overcome, can the contradiction in human existence be healed? In other words, is there *New Being,* beyond the split of essence and existence? Like the question about the courage to be, this problem is of ultimate concern. The answer likewise reveals something decisive about the nature of being-itself.

To share in New Being is to begin the process of healing. Both man's inordinate exaltation of himself and his cultural creations (*hubris*), and his attempt to draw the whole of reality into himself (concupiscence) need to be healed. But this is possible only when the deepest estrangement is overcome, that is, when man is re-united with the ground of being, with being-itself. Just as the courage to be ultimately rests upon the *power* of being-itself flowing into finite life and resisting nonbeing, so overcoming existential estrangement depends ultimately upon New Being manifesting itself in a healing presence.

For Tillich, the quest for New Being is as universal as the experience of estrangement. It is found in all cultures, in all historical ages, in all religions, and also in secular movements such as Marxism or psychoanalysis.

> The quest for the New Being is universal because the human predicament and its ambiguous conquest are universal. It appears in all religions. Even in the few cases in which a completely autonomous culture has developed—as in Greece, Rome, and the modern period of the Western world—utopian expectation of a new reality is present. The religious substance is effective under the secular form. The character of the quest for the New Being changes from religion to religion and from culture to culture (17.II:86f.).

Because he regards the quest for New Being as universal, Tillich meets a fundamental problem: is New Being sought in an *historical* or *non-historical* form? Western religions—Judaism, Christianity, Islam—expect to find New Being *within* history, while Eastern religions—Hinduism, Buddhism, Taoism—seek New Being by *transcending* history as a whole. In Eastern religions, Tillich finds:

> the misery of mankind in history is not to be changed, but individuals may transcend the whole sphere of existence—things, men and gods. *The New Being in this interpretation is the negation of all beings and the affirmation of the Ground of Being alone.* One could say that the price paid for the New Being is the negation of everything that has being. *This is the root of the difference in the East and the West in the feeling for life* (17.II:87, italics added).

Western religions, however, affirm the essential goodness of finite reality despite estrangement, and believe in the possibility of historical transformation, so that New Being is actualized primarily through historical groups to which individuals belong (17.II:86ff.). In Judaism, God makes his covenant with Israel, and salvation is faithfulness to the covenant as God leads his people through history; in Christianity, the Messiah appears in history, and salvation is found in the community of the church which anticipates the Kingdom of God as the goal of history. Tillich tries to overcome the difference between these two types of religion by arguing that the historical expectation can embrace the non-historical, whereas the reverse is not possible. One can imagine Troeltsch smiling as Tillich wrestles with this difficult issue.

The Christian answer to the question of estrangement and the expectation of New Being is given in the symbol "Jesus as the Christ." Specifically, Tillich describes the central Christian symbol as "the New Testament picture of Jesus as the Christ," a picture focused on the cross and resurrection. "Cross" does not simply refer to an instrument of execution in the Roman empire; nor does "resurrection" mean the resuscitation of a corpse as a miracle believed by pre-scientific minds, as literalistic defenders and critics would have it. Cross and resurrection are symbolic in that they refer to being-itself and not to a past event or miracle. The symbol of the cross points to the complete participation of Jesus in the conditions of human existence: he is subject to contingency, anxiety, insecurity, loneliness, weariness, error, self-doubt and the final desolation of death (17.II:125ff.). Yet the biblical picture does not portray Jesus as estranged. The symbol of the resurrection expresses his victory over estrangement, even while subject to the conditions of existence: in his life and death he is portrayed as completely united with God, serenely and majestically resisting the attacks of estrangement on this unity.

The Christ symbolizes New Being. Here in an actual human life man's true nature is fulfilled without any form of estrangement. This also means that in the Christ, being-itself discloses its healing and saving dimension. Human life is rooted in an ultimate reality which not only has the power to resist nonbeing, but which is also present to heal the estrangement of existence. The symbol of the New Being points to this source of healing, and unites man existentially with the ground of his being which can begin to heal estrangement.

Tillich's discussion of the Christ discloses the centrality of the Christian symbols of cross and resurrection to his thought. He is not embarrassed or apologetic about his particularistic Christian focus. However, he attributes *universal* significance to the particular symbol of the Christ. *"The manifestation of saving power in one place implies that saving power is operating in all places"* (17.II:96, italics added). The symbol of the Christ discloses that being-itself, in which all men participate, operates to heal estrangement. If this is true for the ground of being in which all finite beings share, then one must affirm that the healing presence of the divine is everywhere at work. The particular has universal significance. The healing symbolized in the New Being, then, is not confined to professed Christian believers. The symbol points to the possibility and reality of healing present everywhere. Tillich sees this overcoming of estrangement in all religions. It also occurs in secular modes such as psychological therapy, artistic developments, and political movements.

> In some degree all men participate in the healing power of the New Being. Otherwise, they would have no being. The self-destructive consequences of estrangement would have destroyed them (17.II:167).

While Tillich finds that the healing of estrangement in history is only partial, he insists that it is real. The biblical symbol of the Christ calls attention to the healing presence of being-itself.

Life, Ambiguity, and Integration [14]

In human life there are a host of ambiguities: various elements of life compete and conflict with each other. Both man's essential nature and estrangement are present in all the activities of human life, resulting in ambiguities, particularly in the moral, cultural and religious dimensions of life.

Tillich sees the human spirit to be preeminently constituted in the *moral* act. A person becomes a "centered" self especially through his ethical encounters with others; man's moral life, when grounded in love, establishes both individual self-integration and his participation in community with others. But in fact, ambiguity pervades moral life. The popular question of how to love those you don't like shows this ambiguity. So too does the relationship of personal integrity and reconciliation with others: do I keep my own integrity at the risk of alienating those I must resist, or do I sacrifice my own position—even for enemies—at the risk of losing my own integrity? The moral imperative of universal love is itself caught up in the ambiguities of life, and offers no self-evident solutions to them.

Culture also exhibits the ambiguities of life. Human expressions of meaning, for example, are ambiguous when they not only communicate truth but also conceal psychological rationalizations or social ideologies (17.III:71). Freud and Marx both stress the deceptive aspects of much apparent meaning, and thus document ambiguity. Technology has not only a great capacity to enhance life, but also to vulgarize and destroy it. In personal relationships, the mutual projection of images and roles —deliberately or unconsciously—mixes genuine communication with distortion and concealment. In the social search for justice, there is an ambiguity between the claim of a given group to maintain its cohesion against disintegration, and the rightful claim of dissenters, nonconformists or newcomers to belong to the group.

Religion also is subject to the ambiguities of life. In religion man's freedom transcends mere finitude and strives toward the infinite. But this self-transcendence is ambiguous. "One can say that religion always moves between the danger points of profanization and demonization, and that in every genuine act of the religious life both are present, openly or covertly" (17.III:98). Religion becomes profane when it pretends to capture the infinite within finite forms such as dogma, rites and organization. Religion becomes demonic when it identifies itself with the ultimate. Religious persecutions, inquisitions and crusades illustrate how religion can become demonic, elevating itself to ultimate status instead of showing that it is symbolic of genuine transcendence.

Ambiguity, like anxiety and estrangement, is inescapable. It gives rise to the quest for wholeness and integration. The symbol of the "Divine Spirit" that overcomes ambiguity in the unity of love points to the dimension of the ground of being which answers this quest. Being-itself has, along with power and meaning, the quality of love which is the ultimate source of wholeness.

By the symbol "Divine Spirit," or "Spiritual Presence," Tillich refers to an aspect of being-itself, not to *a* divine Spirit as a "separated being" (17.III:107). The Divine Spirit is being-itself present in the human spirit in the mode of love which integrates life. "Love" for Tillich is more than an emotion. Ultimately it is that quality and activity of divine being which "reunites," or integrates. So, by being united with the transcendent ground of being (in which there is no conflict or ambiguity), man can experience moments of unambigous life even though in history this is partial rather than perfect. Like the power of being resisting nonbeing and the New Being overcoming estrangement, the Divine Spirit is operative among all men.

Tillich believes that Divine Spirit is universally present in all religions; however, it is present in no religion without ambiguity. The quest for

> the Spiritual Presence . . . is effective in all religions and the answer received underlies all religions, giving them their greatness and dignity. But both quest and answer become matters of ambiguity if expressed in terms of a concrete religion. It is an age-old experience of all religions that the quest for something transcending them is answered in the shaking and transforming experiences of revelation and salvation; but that under the conditions of existence even the absolutely great—the divine self-manifestation—becomes not only great but also small, not only divine but also demonic (17.III:110).

This combination of universality and ambiguity leads Tillich to suggest the unusual notion of a "religion beyond religion." It also prompts him to engage in dialogue with people of religions other than his own, a dialogue presupposing that the divine is both present and distorted in all religions. Because of this, the idea of "religion beyond religion" informs his whole discussion of the encounter of the religions.

3. THE ULTIMATE IN THE ENCOUNTER OF WORLD RELIGIONS

Like Troeltsch, Tillich acknowledges the particularity of all human experience and the relativity of all cultures and religions throughout changing historical eras. At the same time, against Troeltsch, he affirms that all men participate in the *one* ground of being, and that being-itself is not beyond history but manifest *within* the structures and dynamics of all human life. Therefore all human life fundamentally involves certain common issues of ultimate concern. The religions of the world deal with these common, basic issues. Several consequences follow from this point of departure.

First, Tillich *relativizes relativism*. In one of his last articles, he defended his position against a critic who, like Troeltsch, had argued for a thoroughgoing relativism. The critic contended that the pluralism and relativity of world religions required Tillich to give up any talk of a "final" revelation in Christianity. Tillich replied that the critic was caught in a logical contradiction: by "affirming the relativity of one's own and every other religion one makes a statement which is not supposed to be relative" (9:177). In other words, relativism claims "universal validity" and ironically becomes itself a hidden absolutism. Tillich concludes that simple relativism offers no better solution to the diversity of religions than simple absolutism did in a previous era. Beyond both of these, Tillich proposes a dialectical approach to the relative and the ultimate in religions.

Drawing on his conversations with Japanese Buddhists, Tillich concluded that the dialogue between religions was more fruitful when participants acknowledged the particularity of their own faiths, including "implicit absolutism." Each dialogical partner should try to see how the distinctive emphases of his own religion pointed beyond itself to that which *is* ultimate and absolute, being-itself.

> I believe, through my conversations with Buddhists in Japan, that this way of dealing with the problem of religious absolutism and relativism makes an inter-religious dialogue more creative than an unanalysed and dogmatically affirmed relativism; and I was assured by my partners in the dialogue that they also felt that way (9:178).

Tillich, then, did not deny the relativity of all religions, but he did reject the contradiction of absolute relativism. He restated the question of relativism and absolutism to become: what is the relation between the relative and the Ultimate in religions, and how does this affect the way religions relate to each other? How do the explicit or implicit universal claims of all religions relate to one another? What *sort* of *universality* do the particular religions offer?

Second, Tillich rejects what he calls the "orthodox-exclusive" attitude shown when Christianity, or any other religion, claims sole truth for itself. "Revelatory experiences are universally human. Religions are based on something that is given to a man wherever he lives. He is given a revelation which always implies saving powers. . . . There are revealing and saving powers in all religions" (12:81). Specifically, the presence of being-itself which gives the courage to be, heals estrangement, and integrates ambiguities, is found in all religions in some form.

However, each religion is genuinely distinct in the way it manifests being-itself; ultimate concern does not have the same form in every religion. The Buddhist goal of Nirvana is quite different from the Jewish hope for the messianic age, or the Christian symbol of the Kingdom of God. Likewise, individual personality, and history, are viewed quite differently in Eastern and Western religions. Therefore, it is altogether too simplistic to say that all religions are aiming at the same goal. They give different weight to the common concerns of human life, and they offer different solutions to fundamental human problems. For example, the relation of the individual with his world is resolved in Hinduism by identifying the individual with the absolute: *atman* ("individual" soul) is identical with *Brahman* (cosmic "soul"). Christianity and Judaism, on the other hand, both seek to preserve the individuality of man while uniting him to a new community overcoming estranged individuality. The one approach locates the problem in individuality itself, and proposes to resolve it by transcending individuality in ultimate identity; the other locates the problem in the egocentric distortion of individuality, and proposes a new form of selfhood ("faith," or "following Torah") as the right relation with God and others. So, though each religion is distinct from any other, Tillich nevertheless believes that no essential aspect of the divine is ever completely lacking in any genuine religion. Each religion is distinctive in its concrete form, and every religion is a manifestation of being-itself.

Tillich's dialectical approach, recognizing both the distinctive and relative character of each religion as well as its relation to the Ultimate, or being-itself, provides a distinctive resolution to the questions posed at the beginning of this chapter. By emphasizing the *one* ground of being, the universality of certain basic, human concerns, and the universality of revelation, Tillich prevents any religion from claiming for itself absolute validity and sole possession of truth. This is a powerful antidote to religious bigotry and intolerance. By insisting that the religions point beyond themselves to the ground of being which they symbolize in their traditions, beliefs and rites, he holds all religions and cultures accountable to a transcendent norm; not superiority and self-righteousness, but humility is the proper attitude of man in relation to the Ultimate. At the same time he does not ask any religion to compromise its particular claims. Like Troeltsch, he recognizes the distinctiveness and individuality of each religion and culture. Accordingly, he does not support the naive opinion that all religions are virtually the same, nor advocate a synthesis of religions to produce a new religion embodying the insights of them all. While protecting this particularity, however, Tillich is anxious to avoid a simple relativism and pluralism: these offer no solution, for they weaken the seriousness of *ultimate* concern; they bracket questions of truth and goodness; and they sidestep the quest for universal meaning, an urgent quest for a humanity aware as never before of its common destiny and interdependence.

How can these major themes be held together, and what do they mean concretely for relations between members of the several religions?

Tillich answers with a proposal for *dialogue;* but since this overworked word often refers only to aimless talk, he quickly spells out the specific purpose and method of this encounter. It is a process of mutual questioning, understanding and criticism in which representatives of the various religions seek to discern the strengths and weaknesses of their symbols as expressions of ultimate reality, being-itself. The primary purpose of this dialogue is to penetrate to the depths of their own respective visions of the divine so that they become more transparent to the infinite and unconditional reality which transcends and is present in them.

For this dialogue to be fruitful, Tillich proposes several ground-rules.

> It first presupposes that both partners acknowledge the value of the other's religious conviction (as based ultimately on a revelatory experience), so that they consider the dialogue worthwhile. Second, it presupposes that each of them is able to represent his own religious basis with conviction, so that the dialogue is a serious confrontation. Third, it presupposes a common ground which makes both dialogue and conflicts possible, and, fourth, the openness of both sides to criticisms directed against their own religious basis (7:62).

These presuppositions reflect Tillich's basic theory of religion. There is one ground of being in which all men participate and which all religions symbolize in varying ways; this gives the "common ground" which makes dialogue possible. It also leads each partner to respect the religious conviction of the other "as based ultimately on a revelatory experience." At the same time, being-itself is revealed in the particular experiences of historical cultures; therefore, their expressions of the Ultimate will be partial and distorted. Accordingly, the partners should present their insights with seriousness and conviction, not compromising their religious particularity, and should be open to criticism of their own religious traditions. The ground rules, in short, concern the interplay of the *Ultimate* and the *relative,* the *universal* and the *particular.*

Tillich proposes that dialogue proceed by using an explicit method based upon a typology of religions. Briefly, a typology is a model which, from the wealth of empirical data, abstracts typical elements considered essential for understanding that data. Tillich organizes his typology by means of the different elements intrinsic to the nature of the Holy—the sacramental, the mystical and the prophetic.[15] "There are elements in the experience of the Holy which are always there, if the Holy is experienced. These elements, if they are predominant in one religion, create a particular religious type" (12:86). He calls his typology "dynamic" rather than static because each of these three elements is present in all religions although one of them tends to be predominant in any particular religion. Because the three elements are present in each religion, and since each religion highlights a different element of the Holy, it is necessary for the religions to enter into a dynamic relationship with each other.

The *sacramental* element is the manifestation of the Holy in a special way and in a finite form. The Eucharist and the Bible in Christianity, the Torah in Judaism, and the Koran in Islam exemplify the "sacramental" elements of the Holy; in these special forms the divine is expressed and the finite is open to the infinite ground of being. However, because such sacraments can be treated as holy in themselves, critical elements also belong to the nature of the Holy. One is the *mystical*. The mystic seeks to transcend every finite embodiment of the Holy in order to rise above its concrete expressions so as to experience immediate unity with the Ultimate. The mystical element is critical of the demonic distortion of the sacramental: the identification of the Ultimate with its finite embodiment. The third element is the *ethical* or *prophetic*. This criticizes any view of the Holy which minimizes the claim of justice; holiness without justice is not holy, but demonic, as mystical union with God which neglects justice also is demonic. These three elements are found to some degree in all religions. In a given religious tradition one of the three elements may be more prominent than the others in a particular historical age. And, if one element tends to predominate throughout a religion's history, it thereby locates that religion within the typology. So, Tillich writes, "the predominance of the mystical element in all India-born religions is obvious, as well as the predominance of the social-ethical element in those born of Israel" (7:59).

Tillich uses this typology as a framework or point of reference for inter-religious dialogue. In his essay "A Christian-Buddhist Conversation," Tillich described his own experience of dialogue in Japan (7:53ff.). The Kingdom of God and Nirvana, Tillich suggests, are the respective Christian and Buddhist symbols which express the aim to which each religion points. Both involve a critical evaluation of the actual conditions of human life: the Kingdom of God is counterposed to the kingdoms of the world, and Nirvana is set over against the illusion (*maya*) of an independent self and the seeming reality of the world. This shared critical perspective, however, also includes serious differences; the Kingdom of God symbol is predominantly personal and ethical, while the Nirvana symbol is predominantly transpersonal and mystical. These symbols inform quite different experiences of life and the world. Christianity sees man and the world as essentially good, and estrangement as a distortion of essential goodness. Buddhism tends to locate the human problem in finitude itself, and to look for salvation from "finitude, separation, blindness [and] suffering" in a "blessed oneness of everything, beyond finitude and error" (7:64f.).

Realizing these basic differences, the dialogue partners may wonder if their perspectives are incompatible and mutually exclusive. The Christian then discovers that his tradition, taken as a whole, has a significant mystical element; Christianity has not only used personal symbols for God, like Father and Lord, but also transpersonal symbols, like the *esse ipsum* (being itself) of medieval theology. Further, the Christian tradition speaks not only of divine revelation but also of the incomprehensibility of God. By recognizing the mystical element in his own tradition, the Christian gains some appreciation for the Buddhist notion of the Ultimate as "Absolute Nothingness." The Buddhist also recalls that his tradition does not lack the personal element with its ethical implications; Mahayana Buddhism speaks of the manifestation of the Buddha-Spirit in personal forms, thus making possible a non-mystical relation to the divine. In this exchange, members of the two religions see significant similarities and important differences between them; they examine their own traditions and sometimes discover elements which have been neglected or overlooked. They also ask themselves and each other about the adequacy of their own symbols for expressing the Ultimate which is present in yet transcends them both. Not synthesis, but scrutiny and self-evaluation is the nature of this dialogue.

The symbols of the Kingdom of God and Nirvana also have important implications for *ethics*. The Kingdom of God includes the individual person who *participates* in it, whereas Nirvana involves an *identity* of everything thereby negating individuality. In the relation of man and nature, the Buddhist principle of identity emphasizes the unity of man with his natural environment. It thus serves as a criticism of those forms of Christianity which radically sunder man from nature or sanction an irresponsible exploitation of nature. The Buddhist identity-principle calls technical, Western man back to his lost intimacy with nature, and to a nature-mysticism exemplified by Francis of Assisi; this could be the basis of a new human respect for nature in the West.

On the other hand Christian symbolism poses critical questions for Buddhist ethics in the personal and political spheres. The Christian principle of participation involves the understanding of love as *agape:* based on the divine love for man, of the holy for the sinner, this is a love which extends to the unloved, the rejected, and the enemy. Such love accepts the unacceptable, and seeks to provide resources for transforming the one who is estranged. Buddhist *compassion*, Tillich feels, follows from the principle of identity. It can be a very active way of love, and much more helpful than a moralistic distortion of the *agape* commandment. Compassion is an empathetic identification with the suffering of another. However, it does not yield the insight that the suffering of the other involves some distortion of life. Therefore it lacks the motivation to *transform* life, whether by direct influence on the other, or by transforming the social and psychological conditions which affect the other person's suffering. For all its appeal, there is something almost fatalistic, Tillich suggests, in the Buddhist notion of compassion; it leads to an undue acceptance of the given, what simply *is*, whereas a greater appreciation of human freedom would lead to an ethic with a greater will to transformation.

The differing attitudes to *history* are related to this exchange on ethics. Under the Christian symbol of the Kingdom of God, history is seen as the locus of individual destiny and corporately as "a movement in which the new is created and which runs ahead to the absolutely new, symbolized as 'the new heaven and the new earth' " (7:72). This can have transforming effects in society, some liberal and some quite revolutionary. But

> there is no analogy to this in Buddhism. Not transformation of reality but salvation from reality is the basic attitude. This need not lead to radical asceticism as in India; it can lead to an affirmation of the activities of daily life—as, for instance, in Zen Buddhism—but under the principle of *ultimate detachment*. In any case, no belief in the new in history, no impulse for transforming society, can be derived from the principle of Nirvana (7:72f., italics added).

This does not mean that Buddhism lacks concern for the victims of society; however, this concern does not seek to transform society or create new social orders.

The Buddhist, from his standpoint, may ask the Christian an important question about *detachment*. Detachment is by no means unknown to Christianity; for centuries it has been institutionalized most conspicuously in monastic communities. But the Buddhist may question whether some forms of Christianity have become so activist in their concern for social transformation that they have lost perspective and critical distance, thereby jeopardizing their religious substance. A religion can sell its birthright for a mess of political pottage. More distance, or detachment, need not be in conflict with the impulse to historical transformation; it may protect the religion from becoming secularized, and so lose its distinctive contribution to society. Tillich himself did not suggest the relevance of the Buddhist attitude of detachment for Christianity, but it is consistent with the spirit of his dialogue.

These discussions exhibit the basic purpose of the dialogue as

Tillich conceives it: to let religions encounter each other in their particularities, let mutual questioning stimulate self-criticism, and self-criticism lead each religion to explore its own depths. This is thoroughly consistent with other emphases in Tillich's position as a whole. It accords with his idea that special religious institutions and activities have a *"relative necessity"* only, their vocation being to symbolize the ground of being which transcends everything finite, including religion and religious symbols. It is also consistent with his repeated warning that the greatest temptation of religion is to make itself absolute, thereby becoming demonic rather than manifesting the Holy.

How, in this light, may the history of religions be characterized? It is, writes Tillich, "the fight of God within religion against religion" (12:88). In this colorful and telling phrase Tillich points to a dimension of dialogue now made explicit. The dialogue is not simply a dialogue between religions. Above all, it is the dialogue of men of all religions with the transcendent and living reality which is the ground of their being. The Ultimate is living, not dead; being-itself is the living depth of life. To be open and receptive to this reality is proper ultimate concern.

It may be, Tillich continues, that there is a *telos*, an inner aim of the whole history of religions. This could be described as "The Religion of the Concrete Spirit" (12:87ff.), which would express the unity of the sacramental, mystical and ethical elements. "We cannot identify this Religion of the Concrete Spirit with any actual religion, not even Christianity as a religion" (12:88). But neither should it be regarded only as a future possibility, since "it appears in a fragmentary way in many moments of the history of religions" (12:88). For Tillich, one of these unsurpassed, historical moments is Paul's New Testament doctrine of the Spirit. For the Christian, the victory of the cross symbolizes victory in the "fight for the Religion of the Concrete Spirit, a fight of God against religion within religion" (12:88). The victory of the cross symbolizes "the negation of any demonic claim," including demonic claims of religion; this gives grounds for hope that authentic and self-transcending religion, uniting the three elements, will continue to appear. Speaking out of his own tradition, Tillich points to the dialectic of the *particular* and the *universal.*

> The criterion for us as Christians is the event of the cross. That which has happened there in a symbolic way . . . also happens fragmentarily in other places, in other moments, has happened and will happen even though they are not historically or empirically connected with the cross (12:89).

"Not conversion, but dialogue" (7:95). This is for Tillich the appropriate relation between the religions of the world. The conclusion

to his lectures on Christianity and the world religions provides a concise and lucid summary of his position.

> Does our analysis demand either a mixture of religions, or the victory of
> one religion, or the end of the religious age altogether? We answer: None
> of these alternatives! A mixture of religions destroys in each of them the
> concreteness which gives it its dynamic power. The victory of *one* religion
> would impose a particular religious answer on all other particular an-
> swers. The end of the religious age . . . is an impossible concept. The
> religious principle cannot come to an end. For the question of the ultimate
> meaning of life cannot be silenced as long as men are men. Religion can-
> not come to an end, and a particular religion will be lasting to the degree
> in which it negates itself as a religion. . . .
>
> The way to achieve this is not to relinquish one's religious tradition for
> the sake of a universal concept which would be nothing but a concept.
> The way is to penetrate into the depth of one's own religion, in devotion,
> thought and action. *In the depth of every living religion there is a point
> at which the religion itself loses its importance, and that to which it points
> breaks through its particularity, elevating it to spiritual freedom and with
> it to a vision of the spiritual presence in other expressions of the ultimate
> meaning of man's existence* (7:96f., italics added).

4. AN OPEN QUESTION?

Tillich's work has been hailed as one of the outstanding contributions to religious thought in the twentieth century. His translation of
worn, traditional concepts into fresh language has made, as he hoped
it would, an impact beyond the narrow confines of conventional theology. A conspicuous example is his interpretation of religion as the
ultimate concern which underlies and is expressed in all cultural forms;
so is his analysis of the nature and function of religious symbols.
Sociologists like Robert Bellah, psychoanalysts like Karen Horney, and
leaders in several other disciplines have drawn extensively on Tillich's
work.[16]

In the specific issues of the encounter of world religions, and the
impact of historical relativism on religious beliefs, Tillich has made
several significant contributions. He has undercut the grounds of religious bigotry, intolerance, and persecution; for those who take Tillich
seriously, naive exclusivism, parochial particularity, and insensitive superiority are no longer acceptable. Imperialistic notions of missions and
conversion are also excluded. At the same time, he has cogently criticized
the equally naive approach which would simply dispense with the distinctiveness and integrity of particular religious traditions. The Ultimate
is revealed *in* the particular, the absolute *in* the relative. This further
provides a basis for the confidence a religious community needs if it is

to bring creative meaning to human life. This also makes possible a transcendent ethical critique of a culture, and not only of culture, but also of the religion itself.

In his religious analyses of finitude, estrangement, and ambiguity, Tillich has developed a flexible set of categories which allows him to make a strong case for the universality of basic human concerns in all cultures and religions. Because he also acknowledges the rich variety in which these concerns appear in different cultures and through historical changes, he has increased the persuasiveness of his case. In arguing for these universal elements of ultimate concern, however, Tillich takes seriously the individuality and relativity of religious questions and their answers. Similarly, he argues that all religions manifest the Holy, but that these manifestations are conditioned by the relativities of history and culture.

Tillich's proposal for dialogue between the religions also commands a good deal of respect. Its clear philosophical basis makes it not only practical but also amenable to criticism and modification. Its ground rules are viable, and its dynamic typological method makes a creative encounter possible. It does not violate the integrity of particular religious traditions. Above all, it requires the religions to be constantly accountable to the essential nature of authentic religion, by subjecting themselves to self-criticism and pointing to the Ultimate which transcends even religion itself.

Especially important is Tillich's critical analysis of the problems inherent in radical relativism. In a sense, Tillich takes the crisis of relativism more seriously than Troeltsch himself. For Troeltsch was convinced by his historical studies that he could identify an enduring and comprehensive *matrix of meaning* within each culture and religion. This unifying center was apparent in the shared values, commitments, priorities and sense of purpose shaping and guiding a given society. Today, many people question this assumption. Within most modern societies, there are profound conflicts about the society's matrix of meaning and historical purpose. As a result many people have turned away from any unified cultural meaning toward an individualistic and subjective set of meanings and values; this is a relativism far more radical than Troeltsch espoused. Contemporaneous with this cultural fragmentation, and in conflict with it, is the emergence of a profound longing for a new vision of humanity as a whole which is able to meet the common crises of our age. The survival of spaceship earth in the face of nuclear holocaust and environmental rape is a concern which transcends the self-interests of individual societies. The need for trans-cultural bonds of meaning, coupled with the turn towards individualistic values, gravely intensifies the crisis of relativism. Contemporary relativism, compared with that of Troeltsch, is often so radical and individualistic that the birth of new and universal meaning is aborted at the moment of conception.

Tillich was acutely sensitive to both aspects of the contemporary crisis of relativism. He argued persuasively that individuals found enduring patterns of meaning for themselves only by relating to meaningful symbols shared with others. By definition, the religious symbol is always social; there is no purely individualistic religious symbol. Tillich was always careful, however, to protect the individual from the arbitrary and authoritarian imposition of any symbol system; by definition, the religious symbol is freely appropriated by the individual. In relation to the transcultural aspect of the question, Tillich always insisted that the essential content of every valid religious symbol was itself universal. He also recognized that religious symbols are born in the existential context of urgent human questions. If our present religious symbols are parochial rather than universal, and if man's existential needs seek symbols which foster the unity of humanity, Tillich would be the first to expect that new symbols appropriate to a new age of humanity would be born.

In spite of these impressive contributions, there is a fundamental problem which remains in Tillich's effort to relate the claims of the particular and the universal, the relative and the ultimate. Troeltsch's basic question returns in this form: to what extent does Tillich's own position reflect the *particularity* of his Western Christian perspective? The issue involves more than the centrality of the Christ as the New Being. It is rooted in the very structure of his thought itself. Tillich's whole dialectic of the particular and the universal, and his proposal for dialogue between world religions, is based on his ontology, his theory of being. Built in to this ontology, for which he claims universal validity, are certain convictions: that *individuality* is one of the basic elements of all being, and that *history* is an inescapable reality of life which cannot be denied. These convictions inform the critical questions which Tillich as a Christian posed in his encounter with Buddhists. *Individuality* lies behind Tillich's preference for the principle of *participation*, rather than the principle of *identity*, in the exchange on ethics. Individuality also underlies the different valuations of the *ethical* and the *mystical* in Christianity and Buddhism. *History* is so important for Tillich precisely because this is the temporal arena in which being is actualized as the new and the individual.

Elements like individuality and history, then, are intrinsic to Tillich's theory of being. But what happens when another religion cannot accept this account of the essential nature of being? What happens, for example, when Buddhism cannot accord personal individuality and history the same status that Tillich gives them? This surely exposes the inescapable particularity of Tillich's Western theory of being, whatever its universal implications may be. Of course, dialogue is not inhibited by such particularity. Nevertheless Tillich was perhaps less troubled by this problem than he might have been. We are left, finally, with an open question: can particularity, which Troeltsch stressed so vigorously, really be transcended?

Did Tillich, finally, feel the force of this question? In the last lecture he ever gave, he discussed his own position in relation to several modern attempts to take the history of religions seriously. Immanuel Kant epitomizes the Enlightenment claim to evaluate the validity of all religions according to the criterion of modern rationality. Hegel, building on the romanticist view of history as progressive development, held that all religions culminated in his philosophical version of Christianity. Arnold Toynbee proposed a synthesis of the world religions. More recently, Teilhard de Chardin taught "the development of a universal, divine-centered consciousness which is basically Christian." Reflecting on these diverse conclusions about the religions of the world, Tillich expressed both confidence and humility about his own position. Believing that the Ultimate is present in all finite human reality and that true religion always points beyond itself to the infinite ground of being which relativizes all human perspectives, Tillich said that he was dissatisfied with previous attempts to answer the question of the diverse claims of world religions. However, he concluded, "I am also dissatisfied with my own [attempt], but I will give it in order to induce you to try yourself because that is what one should do if he takes the history of religions seriously" (12:86).

NOTES

1 For introductions to Tillich's position in relation to modern Christian thought, see Alexander J. McKelway, *The Systematic Theology of Paul Tillich* (6:ch. I); David H. Hopper, *Tillich: A Theological Portrait* (2:chs.1-III); and Tillich's own *Perspectives on 19th- and 20th-Century Protestant Theology* (16).

2 In Tillich's earlier years in Germany, he was very active in the movement of Religious Socialism—not to be confused with Hitler's National Socialism. Tillich's volume, *The Interpretation of History* (New York: Scribner's, 1936), sets forth philosophical and theological aspects of his thinking on history and politics as developed in connection with Religious Socialism. A related collection of essays is his important book *The Protestant Era* (Chicago: University of Chicago Press, 1957).

3 "The concept of the boundary," Tillich wrote, "might be the fitting symbol for the whole of my personal and intellectual development"; cf. his *On the Boundary: An Autobiographical Sketch* (New York: Scribner's, 1966).

4 James Luther Adams has edited a collection of early articles by Tillich under the title *What Is Religion?* (New York: Harper & Row, 1969), with a helpful

introduction. In these articles the reader will find many ideas typical of the later Tillich.

5 Further criticism of theism, and an explanation of Tillich's concept of "the God beyond God," is found in *The Courage to Be* (8:182ff.).

6 In this interpretation of the way authentic religion infuses and informs all human culture, Tillich shares Troeltsch's understanding of the "synthesis" between religion and culture.

7 Discussions of religious symbols occur throughout Tillich's writings; to supplement the present discussion, see *Theology of Culture* (18:ch. V).

8 Tillich regarded literalism as one of the grievous errors of fundamentalism. His popular impact in America derives to a considerable degree from the appeal of his alternative to fundamentalism. Two volumes of sermons helped to gain a wide audience for his thinking: *The Shaking of the Foundations* (New York: Scribner's, 1948) and *The New Being* (New York: Scribner's, 1955); these remain helpful for readers who have some difficulty with his more abstract, systematic writings.

9 For a concise and illuminating discussion of Tillich's relation to existentialist currents in Heidegger, Bultmann, Marx and Nietzsche, see James Luther Adams' "Introduction" to Paul Tillich, *Political Expectation* (New York: Harper & Row, 1971); and Tillich's own discussions of existentialism in *Theology of Culture* (18), *The Courage to Be* (8), and *Systematic Theology* (17). See also Tillich's discussion of his "method of correlation" in which Christian symbols engage "existential questions" in *Systematic Theology* (17: vol. I, p. 59ff.; and vol. II, p. 13ff.).

10 These questions point to the fundamental importance of Tillich's "ontology," or theory of being. The "existentialist" dimension of his thought functions *within* his religious theory of being; his ontology, therefore, gives Tillich a distinct position in the broad current of modern existentialism. Further study of Tillich's ontology may begin with Part II ("Being and God") of the *Systematic Theology* (17:vol. I, p. 163ff.). A sophisticated, philosophical discussion of Tillich's ontology and its roots in his early dissertations on Schelling is found in David H. Hopper, *Tillich: A Theological Portrait* (2:chs. IV and V).

11 Tillich's *Love, Power and Justice: Ontological Analyses and Ethical Applications* (New York: Oxford University Press, 1954) provides access to his ontology from the perspective of ethics. His *Biblical Religion and the Search for Ultimate Reality* (Chicago: University of Chicago Press, 1955) discusses ontology in terms of the abstract language of philosophical theology and the concrete, personal imagery of biblical language.

12 This aspect of Tillich's thought is discussed in *The Courage to Be* and in the *Systematic Theology*, vol. I, Part II.

13 The second volume of the *Systematic Theology* is a comprehensive discussion of this subject.

14 This is the subject of Part IV of Tillich's system, in volume III of *Systematic Theology*.

15 A related typological discussion of the history of religions is given by Tillich in *Systematic Theology*, vol. I, pp. 218-235.

16 See Bellah's *Beyond Belief: Essays on Religion in a Post-Traditional World* (New York: Harper & Row, 1970). Karen Horney's distinction between "neu-

rotic" and "existential" anxiety draws upon Tillich's analysis of anxiety, as seen, for example, in *The Courage to Be*.

BIBLIOGRAPHY

1. ADAMS, JAMES LUTHER, *Paul Tillich's Philosophy of Culture, Science and Religion*. New York: Schocken Books, 1970.

2. HOPPER, DAVID H., *Tillich: A Theological Portrait*. Philadelphia: Lippincott, 1968.

3. KEGLEY, CHARLES W., and ROBERT W. BRETALL, eds., *The Theology of Paul Tillich*. New York: Macmillan, 1952.

4. KELSEY, DAVID H., *The Fabric of Paul Tillich's Theology*. New Haven: Yale University Press, 1967.

5. LEIBRECHT, WALTER, ed., *Religion and Culture: Essays in Honor of Paul Tillich*. New York: Harper & Row, 1959.

6. McKELWAY, ALEXANDER J., *The Systematic Theology of Paul Tillich*. New York: Dell, 1966.

7. TILLICH, PAUL, *Christianity and the Encounter of the World Religions*. New York: Columbia University Press, 1963. Paperback edition 1964.

8. ———, *The Courage to Be*. New Haven: Yale University Press, 1966.

9. ———, "Discussion: Christianity and Other Faiths," *Union Seminary Quarterly Review*. 20, 2, (1965), 177–178.

10. ———, *Dynamics of Faith*. New York: Harper & Row (Torchbook), 1958.

11. ———, "E. Troeltsch: Historismus und seine Probleme," *Journal for the Scientific Study of Religion*. 1, 1, (1961), 109-114. First published in German in 1924.

12. ———, "The Significance of the History of Religions for the Systematic Theologian," *The Future of Religions*, ed. Jerald C. Brauer. New York: Harper & Row, 1966.

13. ———, "Is There a Judeo-Christian Tradition?" *Judaism*. 1, 2, (April, 1952), 106-109.

14. ———, "Jewish Influences on Contemporary Christian Theology," *Cross Currents*. II, 3, (1952), 35-42.

15. ———, "Missions and World History," *The Theology of the Christian Mission*, ed. Gerald H. Anderson. New York: McGraw-Hill, 1961.

16. ———, *Perspectives on 19th- and 20th-Century Protestant Theology*, ed. Carl E. Braaten. New York: Harper & Row, 1967.

17. ———, *Systematic Theology*. Chicago: University of Chicago Press. Volume I, 1951; volume II, 1957; volume III, 1963.

18. ———, *Theology of Culture*, ed. Robert Kimball. New York: Oxford University Press (Galaxy Book), 1964.

19. ———, *What Is Religion?* Edited and with an Introduction by James Luther Adams. New York: Harper & Row, 1969.

SUGGESTED READINGS

1. *Primary Readings*

Paul Tillich, *Theology of Culture* (18), introduces his view of religion and its relation to culture in chapters I and IV; other essays in this book show his approach at work in concrete analyses. His *Christianity and the Encounter of the World Religions* (7) and his essay on "The Significance of the History of Religions for the Systematic Theologian" (in 12) focus on the issues of this chapter.

2. *Secondary Readings*

James Luther Adams' volume on Tillich (1), while written in 1945 and focusing on Tillich's earlier writings, is still the best treatment of Tillich by his foremost interpreter; an erudite book, it has much that is accessible to the student first encountering Tillich. L. Gordon Tait's *The Promise of Tillich* (Philadelphia: Lippincott, 1971) is an easier, brief introduction to Tillich's thought, following the structure of the *Systematic Theology*. Alexander J. McKelway's *The Systematic Theology of Paul Tillich* (6) is a critical, summary exposition of the *Systematic Theology* which Tillich described as "an excellent introduction" to his theology. The books by David Kelsey (4) and David Hopper (2) are analyses of Tillich's thought as a whole, the latter presented in a more historical examination. D. Mackenzie Brown, *Ultimate Concern: Tillich in Dialogue* (New York: Harper & Row, 1965), is based on the transcript of a seminar in 1963 at the University of California, Santa Barbara; this text presents many of Tillich's basic ideas in response to actual questions by students and faculty, and it includes considerable discussion on Judaism, Islam, Hinduism, Buddhism, and "quasi-religions." *The Theology of Paul Tillich* (3), edited by Charles W. Kegley and Robert W. Bretall is a still-useful collection of essays on major aspects of Tillich's thought.

Paul Tillich in Catholic Thought (Garden City, N. Y.: Doubleday, rev. ed. 1969), edited by Thomas O'Meara and Donald Weisser, is a series of scholarly studies of Tillich by Catholic theologians. George H. Tavard, *Paul Tillich and the Christian Message* (New York: Scribner's, 1962), is a scholarly and critical Catholic study of Tillich's Christology. A study by a Jewish scholar, based on the first two volumes of the *Systematic Theology*, is Bernard Martin's *The Existentialist Theology of Paul Tillich* (New York: Bookman Associates, 1963). No full-length study of Tillich's position on the encounter of religions has yet been published. A biography of Tillich will soon be published; meanwhile, Tillich's own "autobiographical sketch," *On The Boundary* (New York: Scribner's, 1966), is a brief yet illuminating account of the interaction of his life and thought.

3. Additional Bibliography

Adams (1) contains a bibliography of works by and about Tillich from 1910-1945; Kegley and Bretall (3) updates writings by Tillich to March, 1952, and Leibrecht (5) contains the fullest bibliography of Tillich's writings through 1958. Selections of Tillich's major writings, and of recent works about him, are found in the bibliographies of D. Mackenzie Brown, *Ultimate Concern: Tillich in Dialogue* (New York: Harper & Row, 1965) and L. Gordon Tait, *The Promise of Tillich* (Philadelphia: Lippincott, 1971).

The Birthing of Post-Modern Religion

Toward the middle of the eighteenth century, Alexander Pope expressed the temper of rational, progressive modernity in his famous epitaph for Sir Isaac Newton:

> Nature and Nature's Laws lay hid in Night:
> God said, Let Newton be! and all was Light.

In 1837, the English historian Thomas Macaulay affirmed the same paean of praise for science, in memorable prose:

> It has lengthened life; it has mitigated pain; it has extinguished diseases; it has increased the fertility of the soil; it has given new securities to the mariner; it has furnished new arms to the warrior; it has spanned great rivers and estuaries with bridges of form unknown to our fathers; it has guided the thunderbolt innocuously from the heaven to earth; it has lighted up the night with the splendour of the day. . . . These are but a part of its fruits, and of its first fruits; for it is a philosophy which never rests, which has never attained, which is never perfect. Its law is progress (33:7f.).

As late as 1933, the sponsors of the Chicago World's Fair chose a motto which surely would have pleased both Pope and Macaulay: "Science Explores, Technology Executes, Man Conforms." In 1933, many in the Western hemisphere still took that motto to be the unquestionable formula for establishing the rule of Reason and Progress for all peoples around the globe.

But the modern era was coming to an end. This fact was deeply inscribed in the faces of those few who survived the German death camps—Dachau, Buchenwald, Auschwitz, and other citadels of technologized barbarism. The same fact was also mundanely disclosed in a 1945 report detailing reactions of the pilot who had just dropped the first Atomic Bomb, which fried thousands alive and maimed countless others:

> He adjusted his polaroids to the mild intensity and looked down at Hiroshima. A large white cloud was spreading rapidly over the whole area, obscuring everything and rising very rapidly. . . . "Jesus Christ," said Lt. Jeppson, "if people knew what we were doing we could have sold tickets for $100,000."

Science had explored. Technology had executed. Man had conformed. Instantaneously efficient, scientifically detached mass murder was the final product. It was no wonder that the septuagenerian Albert Einstein, whose work had paved the way for the Atomic Bomb, wrote to a friend, not long before Einstein himself died: if he had his life to start all over again, he would not choose a profession "that has to do with the search for knowledge." According to the friend, Einstein's aversion to science developed after the events of Hiroshima and Nagasaki. "He left the world without regret," his friend commented. The quiet despair of the aging scientific genius was perhaps the whimper that signaled the last days of modernity. In his lifetime Reason and Progress had been dethroned and decapitated.

Different observers see the causes and the pivotal points at different places, but a consensus seems to be developing in the second half of the twentieth century regarding the era which has been called "modern": it is on the wane, dramatically. Reason and Progress are still treasured values for some, but they are no longer the dominant themes of Western culture. Something new, for better or for worse, is emerging. The new age has been called by many names: "sociotechnic society" (Herbert Richardson), "post-culture" (George Steiner), "post-civilization" (Kenneth Boulding), and "neo-paganism" (Tom Driver). But whatever its name, and whatever its portent, signs of its presence are being identified everywhere.

This moment of historical transition affords as a unique vantage point for assessing the shape of modern religion and for tentatively identifying some new kinds of religious sensibilities. By looking back over the course of the epoch that is now coming to an end, we can gain not only a clearer understanding of where we have been, but also some sense for where we might be going.[1]

1. THE DEMISE OF MODERNITY

The thought and spirituality of the seventeenth-century French philosopher René Descartes provides an appropriate point of departure for a retrospective view of modernity. Early in his life, Descartes became dissatisfied with the speculative philosophy he had inherited. To free himself from bondage to past traditions, he employed his famous method of systematic doubt. In this process, he found that he could indeed doubt everything, except himself. For, in thinking about his own existence, he obtained assurance that *he* did exist. Hence his oft-quoted motto: "I think, therefore I am" (*cogito ergo sum*). While he could not be certain of the existence of God or the objective world, he could be certain of his own existence as a rational self. Descartes thus epitomizes the intellectual and spiritual premise basic to modern culture: what is real is the rational, personal self-consciousness, the ego; not God and nature. God and nature are secondary realities. Hence, the individual thinking ego became the spiritual center of the modern West. And Reason became one of the self-consciously celebrated Western values.

Descartes was also typical of modernity in his view of nature. He depicted nature in strictly mechanical terms, as *res extensa* (extended thing), as something qualitatively different from *res cogitans* (rational self). For Descartes, as for Isaac Newton a generation later, the whole natural cosmos was a vast, impersonal Machine, in itself lifeless, wholly determined by physical laws, without any qualities which pre-modern man had perceived in it: color, smell, taste, and beauty. These were "secondary qualities," rooted in the perceiving activity of the ego. In itself, nature was sheer extension (mass), a field of blind physical forces, a vast mechanism of dead, moving particles. Consistent with this view of nature, Descartes also envisioned the human body in mechanical terms; it was simply the machine for the individual self-conscious rational ego.

Like many moderns, furthermore, Descartes understood the relationship of ego and mechanical world to be that of master to slave. In Cartesian perspective, the ego is intended to dominate and manipulate the world of nature, either by the increase of scientific knowledge or by the technological use of that knowledge. Indeed the very meaning of knowledge *is* power over nature, as Descartes states forthrightly:

> I perceived it to be possible to arrive at knowledge highly useful in life, and instead of the speculative philosophy taught in the schools, to dis-

cover a practical [method] by means of which, knowing the force and action of fire, water, air, the stars, the heavens, and all the other bodies that surround us, as distinctly as we know the various crafts of our artisans, we might also apply them in the same way to all the uses to which they are adapted, and thus render ourselves the lords and possessors of nature (36:4).

How else would a rational, self-conscious personal ego relate to a blind, lifeless impersonal machine than by dominating it? As this domination was articulated and justified in the modern era, the idea of Progress more and more came to the fore, alongside of Reason, as one of the central, self-consciously celebrated Western values. "Progress" generally implied the domination of nature for the sake of human betterment.

Accordingly, the Cartesian emphasis on mechanism and domination came into phase, as a matter of course, with the expanding forces of modern industrialism. As Lewis Mumford has pointed out, "The power that was science [i.e. mechanistic Cartesian-Newtonian science] and the power that was money were, in the final analysis, the same kind of power; the power of abstraction, measurement, quantification" (29:31). Adam Smith himself, the intellectual patriarch of modern capitalism, conceived of the socioeconomic order in terms which would surely have been congenial for Descartes. "Human society," Smith wrote, "when we contemplate it in a certain abstract and philosophical light, appears like a great, an immense machine whose regular and harmonious movements produce a thousand agreeable effects" (36:37). Such was the vision of the self-conscious, rational modern ego: society itself, along with nature, was mechanized. Society, too, could therefore be legitimately dominated and controlled for the sake of Progress.

The Deity of modern theism was also given a definite place in the Cartesian schema. More than a few who came under the spell of Descartes' thought took faith in God very seriously. They viewed God as the Highest Being, a Person, a spiritual Self, not unlike the human ego. God was thought of as existing independently, apart from the whole created order. Like a cosmic clockmaker, God had initiated the world mechanism. He also intervened here and there to repair things in the mechanism which had gone awry; even Newton allowed for Divine corrections of mechanistic deviations. For some believers, God even intervened to work "miracles" when He chose to aid his children *in extremis*, particularly in response to fervent prayer. Most of all, however, God was the final guarantor of the integrity of the human ego, "the infinite value of the individual soul." By relating themselves consciously to God, men and women could find spiritual strength for their struggle to dominate nature. In this way the modern theistic God functioned as the ultimate ground for the values of modernity, especially Reason and Progress.

As the Cosmic Ego who initiates the Cosmic Machine, moreover, who intervenes occasionally to repair it, and who validates the spiritual struggles of man for a life of Reason and Progress, God in the Cartesian schema is also an eternal individual, always the same, never changing. He sets the Cosmic Machine in motion and guides it toward a predetermined end. Likewise, as the moral Lawgiver, God inspires men to faith in Himself, in order to bring them also to his predetermined moral end for them. Furthermore, God is above both time and space; the whole creation is spread before him as an open book. He can read every jot and tittle of its pages, past, present, and future. He has perfect knowledge and perfect power; he is omniscient and omnipotent. He is an infinite, all-powerful Ego, who omnisciently watches over his cosmic domain from his exalted heavenly throne.

That, then, is a retrospective overview of some of the major features of modernity. It is not a complete picture, by any means; a number of important tendencies were deliberately not mentioned, among them the Romantic protest against the Cartesian schema and industrial society. But the themes of the rational ego, nature the Machine, domination and control over nature, and God as the cosmic Ego carried the day in the modern West, howevermuch they may have been challenged. So, overall, there was cultural coherence and harmony: Science, philosophy, social and economic theory and practice, religion and morality—all coalesced into one grand all-comprehending cultural system. Inspired by the publicly articulated values of Reason and Progress, and the passionate inner conviction that "God is on our side," the modern West created an amazingly integrated, self-justifying, and self-propelling culture on the basis of the Cartesian schema. Some even found it easy to reaffirm the conviction of the Enlightenment philosopher Leibniz that theirs was "the best of all possible worlds."

There were visible cracks in the facade of this vast cultural system. Visible, that is, to those who had eyes to see. Right from the start the vast numbers of workers in the factories, not a few of them children, and the many poor people in colonies around the world, never really were given occasion to make their influence felt in shaping modern culture. The American and the French Revolutions, which in a sense were the most dramatic precipitating external events of modern culture, never really had the effect of spreading the rule of Reason and Progress to all peoples. In America in particular, thousands and thousands of black people lived as slaves, *de jure* or *de facto*, throughout most of the modern era. What did Reason and Progress mean to them? Moreover, even within the milieu of the "enlightened" middle classes, who so championed the dominant philosophy and spirituality of the era, severe stresses began to become apparent by the middle of the nineteenth century, above all the experience of a certain profound boredom (*ennui*) (33:1–25). These stresses were articulated in varying ways by prophetic critics such as Friedrich Nietzsche, Søren Kierkegaard, and Henrik Ibsen.

But it was neither the discontent of the proletariat and enslaved masses, nor the direct attacks of the great prophets of cultural crisis that began to undercut the foundations of modernity, howevermuch those forces may have disrupted the external forms of modern culture. Not even a virulent attack, such as the one mounted by Nietzsche, denouncing the dominant Appolonian values of the West and proclaiming the death of God, had a substantive influence. The modern era began to give way, at the deepest levels, in virtue of a much more subtle kind of causality, followed by the prodigious cultural fragmentation of the "Thirty Years' War" of the twentieth century, 1915–1945. That subtle causality was the devastating intellectual attack on the religious and valuational substratum of modernity, the Cartesian world view. The collapse of Cartesian philosophy and spirituality signaled the demise of modernity.

The keystone of the Cartesian world view was the self-conscious rational ego. It was the genius of Freud to identify the ego merely as a visible psychic superstructure of the profoundly irrational or a-rational psychic depths of the unconscious. The influence of Darwin's celebrated "animalization of man" was already widely felt by the time of Freud's discovery and interpretation of the unconscious. It became more and more apparent that the identification of man solely as the self-conscious rational ego was woefully inadequate. The vast submarine regions of unconscious drives and instinctual forces more and more came to be seen as constitutive elements of the self, along with, or sometimes to the exclusion of, the self-conscious rational ego.

The notion that man is primarily the self-conscious rational ego was also called into question by thinkers such as Bultmann, Erikson, and Tillich, from a number of perspectives. Bultmann depicted the human self chiefly as historical, not rational. The self is most authentically the self, for Bultmann, not when it is thinking, but when it is deciding concretely in freedom to love the neighbor. Bultmann surely did not deny that rationality is an important aspect of human existence, but he affirmed that the isolated self of Cartesian rationality was an effete, totally inadequate expression of human possibilities. Erikson, similarly, pointed to the social matrix of the self as constitutive of its identity. For Erikson, an isolated self-conscious ego is a distorted, neurotic human being. The self is constituted from its earliest days in community, by the basic trust developed within the family, by the ability to relate sensitively to society as a whole. Tillich's perspective was even more comprehensive than Bultmann's and Erikson's. For Tillich, authentic selfhood arises not only in human history, whether in relation to the concrete neighbor or in relationship to the structures of family and society, authentic selfhood also has a decisive embodied and cosmic dimension. For Tillich, the polarity of self and world is fundamental; without a world, there is no self, and vice versa. Indeed, for Tillich, in vivid contrast to Descartes, the very being of the self *can* be doubted; it stands under the threat of nonbeing as all finite reality does. Any child, says Tillich, can raise the question why there is something and not nothing. To overcome the threat of nonbeing, the self and its world must be seen as rooted in "being-itself," the "ground of being." The deepest relationship to the Ultimate, for Tillich, is the indispensable ground of both self and world. In his schema, moreover, Tillich makes a place for the reality and power of the unconscious. This is reflected in Tillich's view of God, as "the Abyss of Being," which transcends the Divine Logos, and also contains within itself the reality of nonbeing. For Tillich, so to speak, being-itself has its unconscious depths.

Under the force of criticism such as this, the idea of a self-conscious rational isolated ego increasingly was shown to be inadequate. Similarly, the other side of the Cartesian world, nature the Machine, also came under attack. Hume was among the first to repudiate the mechanical model of nature. For a number of reasons, Hume argued that it was much more adequate to think of nature as an organism, rather than a machine. The mechanical idea of nature was also rejected, passionately, by Teilhard. Nature, for him, is much more a process than a machine. All things in nature, moreover, are not merely "things," lifeless objects, functioning according to blind physical laws. All things in nature have a "within," and they are being drawn forward by the spiritual power of Love emanating from the final Omega point of the universe toward a final, ultimate spiritualization. Nature participates in salvation; it is not a meaningless adjunct or merely a stage for rational existence. For Teilhard, indeed, the world when it is rightly perceived is sacramental. Tillich held similar ideas, particularly in his anti-Cartesian essay, "Nature and Sacrament." Bonhoeffer also developed a consistently positive appreciation for nature. In his theological emphasis on the incarnation, Bonhoeffer affirms that God enfleshes Himself in the whole world, reestablishing the reality and the integrity of the entire concrete order of human existence. It was no accident that Bonhoeffer also personally celebrated human sensuality and the beauties of nature.

Along with the attack on the notions of the rational ego and nature the Machine, a number of intellectuals repudiated the motifs of domination and control, which were so important for the Cartesian schema. Within an existential, interpersonal context, Erikson argued vigorously that trust, not control, is the foundation for growth into maturity. Growth presupposes the ability to give up control, according to Erikson, to risk love and intimacy with others. Conversely, the fixation on control is a sign of immaturity. Bultmann argued, similarly, that the self which is shaped by domination and control is an inauthentic self, imprisoned by a fixation on worldly security. Within the social and economic context, both Marx and Niebuhr mounted a thoroughgoing polemic against the motifs of domination and control. Marx stressed again and again the social and economic results of the ideology of control and domination, namely, the oppression of the proletariat. The basic evil in society, indeed, is the domination exercised by one group over others. This turns members of the proletariat class into mere things, cogs in the industrial machine. This, in turn, results in the alienation of the worker from himself, from his work, and from the whole human species. Neibuhr argued that the fixation on control and domination is a symptom of the inordinate lust for power. He specifically objected to the idea of Progress as it had been developed in bourgeois society. Progress, Niebuhr pointed out, can very well be another name for the domination of the poor by the rich. That ideology of Progress and the resultant domination of the poor must be radically rejected in the name of social justice. Cone and Camara pick up these themes and carry them further. Camara in particular proposes a total restructuring of society, in which a manipulative technology is transformed and becomes the servant of the oppressed peoples in the Third World.

Modern theism has been subjected to a similarly scorching attack. No element of the Cartesian world view was spared. The first waves of criticism came from skeptics like Hume, who questioned the rationality of theism on logical grounds. Freud, with his doctrine of projection, and Marx, with his idea of religion as an opiate, extended and deepened this critique of theism. But the most sustained attack on theism emerged from within the religious tradition itself. Bultmann, for example, argued that the theistic deity of the Cartesian schema is a distortion of the God of biblical experience. Such a deity is an objectification about whose existence, or non-existence, men can hold dispassionate discussions. No, says Bultmann, the God affirmed by biblical experience calls men to decision; the proper response to Him is not argument, but obedience. Addressed by the Word of God, one's very existence is called into question; accordingly, a detached "objective" response is impossible. Bonhoeffer likewise took issue with what he referred to as "the God of the gaps," the theistic deity who allegedly intervenes at times when human knowledge or human power has come to its limits. No, says Bonhoeffer, God is to be found in the center of life, not at its peripheries. God is suffering in the midst of his world; he is no cosmic watchmaker sitting there idly "paring his fingernails" (James Joyce), except when he occasionally works miracles. The notion of the Wholly Other God of theism was also radically challenged by Teilhard. While not denying Transcendence, Teilhard was profoundly concerned with the immanence of God: the working of the cosmic Christ on the "within" of all things, influencing them, drawing them forward to their final fulfillment. Tillich assumed a similar stance, reflected most dramatically by his assertion that God does not exist. By this Tillich means that God is not *a* being among other beings, even the Highest Being. On the contrary, God is the "ground of being," "being-itself." For Tillich, God is not even *a* person; God is *more than* personal; and the personal, like the natural, according to Tillich, is grounded in God as its ultimate source and fountain of being. The God of modern theism was further challenged by the questions raised by Troeltsch. On the basis of painstaking historical research, Troeltsch concluded that Christianity is inextricably implanted in Western culture. Not only did this view allow a certain validity to non-Western religions, it implied that the Wholly Other personal God of the Cartesian world view was a time-bound conceptualization, dependent on the peculiar cultural system of the West and perhaps meaningful nowhere else.

With the self-conscious rational ego thus relativized, with the mechanistic Cartesian view of nature undermined, with the controlling, dominating approach to persons and things repudiated, and, finally, with the whole theistic approach to God undercut, the Cartesian substratum of modern culture began to fragment and disintegrate. So the proclamation of the "Death of God" by a number of self-styled radical theologians in the second decade following World War II is hardly surprising. By that time theism was all that was left of the modern cultural system. As the Divine apex of the whole system, its demise was worthy of a public obituary. "The significance of modern atheism," Herbert Richardson has written "is not in its denial of conceptions of God that are appropriate to other cultural epochs, but in its denial of the God who is appropriate to our own cultural epoch: that is, the God who undergirds democracy and capitalism, the God who makes empirical science possible" (21:10).

With the Cartesian substratum of modern culture decimated, what was left for the future? Religiously speaking, there *was* a legacy. Bultmann, Teilhard, Niebuhr, Cone, Camera, Bonhoeffer, Erikson, and Tillich bequeathed the possibility of new religious beginnings for the postmodern era. While these thinkers consciously and unconsciously related their writings to the shape and substance of modern culture, they also sided with the severest critics of modern culture and its theistic foundation. In this way, they transcended their own cultural matrix—the decline and fall of modernity—and pointed towards a new religious modality and a new sense for the Transcendent. For them, God or the "ground of being" is always acknowledged *within the given historical and natural milieu of human experience.* Their legacy, then, was their emphasis on the matrix of concrete experience as the locus of ultimate meaning. Ultimate meaning is to be found in, with, and under the whole field of human existence, not in some Wholly Other heavenly realm. The Transcendent *can* be experienced in varying ways, they maintain, but always within the parameters of immediacy.

2. THE EMERGING POST-MODERN RELIGIOUS QUEST

The American poet, Theodore Roethke, caught the temper of the post-modern religious situation in a trenchantly lonely poem about an individual's journey in an automobile:

> I dream of journeys repeatedly:
> Of flying like a bat deep into a narrowing tunnel,
> Of driving alone, without luggage, out a long peninsula,
> The road lined with snow-laden second growth,
> A fine dry snow ticking the windshield,
> Alternate snow and sleet, no oncoming traffic,
> And no lights behind, in the blurred side-mirror,
> The road changing from glazed-tarface to a rubble of stone,
> Ending at last in a hopeless sandrut,
> Where the car stalls,
> Churning in a snowdrift
> Until the headlights darken (23:25).

Post-modern religious experience begins with the moment of total aloneness, with the wheels of technological society spinning in a hopeless sandrut, then the moment of stalling in total darkness. So another American poet, Archibald MacLeish, describes a circus scene, that compulsively diversionary busy-ness which seeks to avoid bitter reality, and how that scene is unmasked by the moment of final nothingness. The poem is entitled, "The End of the World":

> Quite unexpectedly, as Vasserot
> The armless ambidextrian was lighting
> A match between his great and second toe,
> And Ralph the lion was engaged in biting
> The neck of Madame Sossman while the drum
> Pointed, and Teenie was about to cough
> In waltz-time swinging Jocko by the thumb—
> Quite unexpectedly the top blew off:
>
> And there, there overhead, there there hung over
> Those thousands of white faces, those dazed eyes,
> There in the starless dark the poise, the hover,
> There with vast wings across the cancelled skies,
> There in the sudden blackness the black pall
> Of nothing, nothing, nothing—nothing at all (15:93).

To begin with, institutional religion is on the decline, almost everywhere. In the United States, which is perhaps the most religiously oriented of the industrialized Western nations, studies have shown that during the decade from 1957 to 1967 the number of Americans who saw religion losing its influence jumped from 14 to 57 per cent. Among theologians a "secular theology" has arisen, which may at times be superficial and histrionic, but which nevertheless reflects a deep theological malaise. One study, published in 1969, depicts the "current revolution in Christianity" in these terms, in its table of contents:

> *The Dimensions of the Revolution:* Theology Without God, Christology Without Jesus, the Bible Without Authority, Church Without Clergy, Salvation Without Immortality, Mortality Without Immortality, Conclusion: No Area Will Escape.
>
> *The Causes of the Revolution:* An Obsolete Theology, A Questionable Ethics, An Antiquated Liturgy, Dubious Institutional Practices, Conclusion: A Crisis for Christianity (34:9).

MacLeish succinctly describes the situation in which organized religion seems to find itself today at the end of his play *JB:* the candles on the altars are out.

Institutional education finds itself in a similar situation. The literary critic, George Steiner, has pointed vividly to the disturbing face of "liberal education" when that hallowed countenance is viewed in the mirror of twentieth-century barbarism:

> We now realize that extremes of collective hysteria and savagery can coexist with a parallel conservation and, indeed, further development of the institutions, bureaucracies, and professional codes of high culture. In other words, the libraries, museums, theatres, universities, research centers, in and through which the transmission of the humanities and of the sciences mainly takes place, can prosper next to the concentration camps. . . . obvious qualities of literate response, of aesthetic feeling, can [even] coexist with barbaric, politically sadistic behavior in the same individual. Men such as Hans Frank who administered the "final solution" in Eastern Europe were avid connoisseurs and, in some instances, performers of Bach and Mozart. We know of personnel in the bureaucracy of the torturers and of the ovens who cultivated a knowledge of Goethe, a love of Rilke (33:77).

In the post-modern era the educational institution, which had been considered to be the very bedrock foundation of Reason in Western culture, has been widely discredited.

More generally in society, the questionable use of technology has begun to create a society of one-dimensional men (Herbert Marcuse). Technology has been allowed to dominate corporate and individual behavior more and more. Behavioral psychologist B. F. Skinner's 1972 magnum opus, *Beyond Freedom and Dignity,* expresses one aspect of the way social and political trends of the second half of the twentieth century may be moving. In general, as new technologies have been developed in the post-modern era, they have been appropriated by the "military-industrial complex" for destructive purposes; or, such positive benefits as new technologies have produced have been channeled to an elite, affluent few. It could indeed be the case that *1984* and *Brave New World* are just around the corner.

One of the most harmful effects of "runaway technology" in the post-modern era has been the accelerating ecological crisis: increasing exhaustion of a finite store of resources, continued exponential population growth, and massive pollution. The whole planet is in an environmental crisis of Gargantuan proportions. The life-support system of the human species is now threatened. At the same time, most industrial nations continue to exacerbate the situation by policies designed to promote increased economic growth, while so-called underdeveloped nations seek to emulate the industrialized nations' successes, with the attendant exhaustion of resources and increase in pollution. All the while, population and world-wide poverty continue to grow. Together with the threat of thermonuclear war, the ecological crisis is slowly poisoning the spirit of many people with a profound despair.

Like the global crisis, the individual is also subject to extreme stress. Identity-forming communities such as the family seem unable to cope with the pressures of the present, and have been giving way to new forms which are as yet unproved. The sociologist Philip Slater has argued that the dominant quest in American society has become the "pursuit of loneliness." As Slater explains,

> We seek a private house, a private means of transportation, a private garden, a private laundry, self-service stores, and do-it-yourself skills of every kind. An enormous technology seems to have set itself the task of making it unnecessary for one human being ever to ask anything of another in the course of going about his daily business. Even within the family Americans are unique in their feeling that each member should have a separate room, and even a separate telephone, television, and car, when economically possible. We seek more and more privacy, and feel more and more alienated and lonely when we get it (32:7).

The controlling ego, so celebrated by Descartes, has been more and more isolated in the second half of the twentieth century. The corollary of this is that the controlling ego has more and more *lost control* of religious and educational institutions, of science and technology, of government and the environment. The "controlling" individual ego is, indeed, in the situation depicted by Roethke's poem, alone in the darkness in a stalled automobile. Nothing seems subject to control anymore; surrounded by exquisite technological grandeur, the individual finds himself powerless.

Even intimate personal relationships somehow seem increasingly difficult to cultivate. In a world of isolated selves, where is the "Thou" in whose presence loneliness can be transcended? So the citizen of the postmodern era is frequently and profoundly alone, with "nothing, nothing —nothing at all." His world has been shredded into a thousand randomly scattered pieces. His own identity is under constant attack, for there are fewer and fewer fixed interpersonal, as well as social and religious, points in relation to which he may find some confirmation of his identity. Even the much discussed psychological fixation on the mother and the father is apparently becoming a thing of the past, since in the compulsively busy, highly mobile post-modern era many children never have had the sustained experience of their parents which allows them to become "fixated," to invest themselves passionately in parental relationships.

The psychoanalyst Rollo May describes the impact of this overall situation on the psyche this way:

> With most patients several decades ago (and with naive patients now), we could assume, when they said they had nothing to believe in anymore, that they were suffering from some unconscious conflict about symbols having to do, say, with "God and the authority of the father," or "mother and protectiveness," and so on. Our problem then was easier: we had only to help them work through the conflict about their symbols in order that they might choose their own; the dynamic was there. My point is that now, however, patients on a much broader scale seem to be reflecting the general disintegration of cultural symbols, a disintegration that percolates down more and more broadly into the members of society.

May goes on to observe that patients today tend to have nothing "they can believe wholeheartedly enough to make commitment of themselves possible." "We often observe in our patients," he explains bluntly, "that they cannot discover any accepted symbol in their culture these days sufficiently accepted even to fight against" (19:97). In this vein, Roethke tells at one point how he seeks to make contact with another human being, but then he immediately turns back to himself:

> I sing the wind around
> And hear myself return
> To nothingness alone (24:42).

Paradoxically, however, this prototypical post-modern experience of nothingness has in some instances become the rich soil for the growth of a new kind of religious quest.

When, to speak with MacLeish, the vast wings of the canceled skies

Theistic God is a product of man's mind — not a product of revelation

show us nothing, nothing, nothing at all, when the individual is radically isolated, when he or she is alone with the Void, then a number of religious alternatives present themselves.

One response is *repression*. The experience of nothingness can give way to religious business-as-usual, cooking the meals, changing the diapers, drinking the martinis, as if everything were as it always has been; seeking, by an act of will, to make the shattered form of religion whole again: preaching the sermon, saying the prayers, keeping the High Holy Days, offering the sacrifice of the Mass, sustaining inherited institutional structures. As if modern theism were not defunct! As if, indeed, the radical experience of the total absence of God were not for real! In America the strategy of repressing the experience of nothingness is perhaps most highly developed in the context of so-called "civil religion," that public piety which informs national politics. Billy Graham at the side of more than one President has been the symbol of unbroken public piety. "God is with us," Graham tells the nation directly and indirectly, again and again, "I spoke with Him this morning." For a relatively sizeable group of people, theism of the Graham vintage is still somehow viable.

Another religious response to the experience of nothingness is *regression*. This entails the return to some pre-modern form of religious experience. Much of the popular fascination with primitive religion and primitive mythology seems to have a regressive character. Similarly, the return to simple Bible-carrying faith in Jesus, the so-called Jesus Movement, which emerged around 1970, also seems to be dominated by regressive tendencies.[2] Likewise for some of the protagonists of drugs and the ecology movement: the popular "return to nature," whether it be by a hallucinatory "trip" or a literary journey to live in the wilderness, seems to be in large measure regressive.[3] In a parallel way, others have occupied themselves almost totally with social activism, rarely allowing themselves time for reflection and meditation, even in times of defeat. They have been "too busy" for the experience of nothingness.

Repression and regression are familiar human responses in times of crisis, and their popularity should not be surprising. Yet they are potentially disastrous if allowed to continue for too long, for they prohibit realistic responses to post-modern reality. And, in a time when even the survival of the human species is in question, unrealistic patterns of behavior entail a risk too high to be sustained.

An alternative response to the experience of nothingness is *ingression*. An individual who experiences radical emptiness need not deny it or flee from it. Rather, he or she may stay within the framework of technological society and the concomitant experience of cultural distintegration in order to enter into that experience, explore it, and wait faithfully for signs of a new beginning.

Add the concept of Transcendence

Thomas Merton, the Trappist monk, student of Zen Buddhism, novelist and poet, wrote an essay in 1966 entitled "Apologies to an Unbeliever," a revealing expression of post-modern religious man. Merton takes issue with all those who speak confidently concerning the message of God for our time, or the acts of God in history. Likewise he distances himself from "the latest routines" designed to celebrate God's presence. Merton confesses that he lives in a world in which God is *silent,* even *absent.* Then this Catholic monk explains his own vocation, how in his solitude he seeks to experience the awesome depths of reality. Merton's milieu is precisely the post-modern territory of nothingness:

> My own peculiar task in my Church and in my world has been that of the solitary explorer who, instead of jumping on all the latest bandwagons at once, is bound to search the existential depths of faith in its silences, in its ambiguities, and in those certainties which lie deeper than the bottom of anxiety.
>
> In these depths there are no easy answers, no pat solutions to anything. Here one lives a kind of submarine life in which faith sometimes mysteriously takes on the aspect of doubt when, in fact, one has to doubt and reject conventional and superstitious surrogates that have taken the place of faith. On this level, the division between Believer and Unbeliever ceases to be so crystal clear. It is not that some are all right and others are all wrong; all are bound to seek in honest perplexity. Everybody is an Unbeliever more or less! (17:4)

The existential corollary of this, in the post-modern era, is that everyone in a certain sense *can* be a believer! Under the pervasive spiritual pressure of nothingness, the religious quest has been radically democratized. It is no longer the special responsibility of those within the pale of institutional religion. Indeed, there are those who would argue that institutional religion in the West is inextricably bound up with the modern era that is disappearing. In any case, it seems clear that the midwives of post-modern religion are not typically Jewish and Christian clergy or other identifiable "denominational leaders," but a variety of new "*gurus,*" who speak a cacophony of religious languages which are anything but traditional.

The music of John Cage provides another point of access to the post-modern religious experience. Cage's music is passionately fixed on the *sound* of music, as distinct from the *idea* of the composer which is mediated through the sound. So Cage rejects virtually all the canons of Western composing. He creates "scores" which do not specify anything about tempo or pitches or dynamics. At the same time Cage seeks to highlight the sounds of everyday experience, allowing them to be heard, liberating them from the pre-perceptive mind-sets of the modern listener. For Cage, all sounds in our environment are intrinsically worth hearing: the automobile horn, the fingernail scraping on the blackboard, the sneeze, the rustle of papers in the wind. In one work, for example, entitled *4′ 33″*, Cage has the pianist simply remain seated for four minutes and thirty-three seconds before a closed piano. Cage seeks to provide the framework for a transfigured perception of the given sounds of human experience. In the midst of nothingness, he seems to be saying, if that nothingness is passionately attended to, there is the possibility of ecstasy: by embracing the meaningless fragment of experience, there is the possibility of a new existential vitality.

Among the growing number of self-styled prophets, experimental poets and scholars, and traveling religious teachers from the Far East, the literary critic and philosopher, Norman O. Brown, is both a representative and an original thinker of some stature. Brown is at home with a number of cultural phenomena: Freudian psychology, Zen Buddhism, Christian theology, primitive mythology, and art and literature from various periods and societies. His pluralistic approach typifies one of the most striking features of emergent post-modern religion. "Faith of our Fathers, Living Still," to instance the traditional Christian perspective, is exploded by Brown, and imploded, too. For Brown seeks a new religious synthesis, which penetrates to the depths of the Christian tradition and draws sustenance from the universal field of human experience.

Like the musicology of John Cage, Brown develops a thoroughgoing critique of the received cultural tradition. The central theme for Brown, as his 1966 book *Love's Body* suggests, is bodily vitality. Instead of the transcending, dominating self-conscious ego of Descartes, Brown highlights the immanent, permeating, unconscious id of Freud. Instead of nature the Machine, as it was for Descartes, Brown depicts an eroticized nature, nature as the greater body of humanity, in which the individual moves and lives and has his being. Instead of an ethics of domination and control by the isolated ego, for the sake of Progress, Brown offers a discipline of participation and cooperation for the sake of a unified mystical life in ultimate reality. Instead of a God who is Wholly Other, a cosmic Ego, Brown proffers a Deity which is as near, as immediate, as the experience of sensual ecstasy.

So Brown writes, in words that are a modern cultural heresy but perhaps becoming a post-modern cultural dogma, "Doing nothing, if rightly understood, is the supreme action" (4:34). By this Brown means that the self-conscious ego must let go, that it must drift down into the vast sea of the unconscious, which is the mystical unity of all people and the whole earth:

> The unconscious is . . . that immortal Sea which brought us hither; intimations of it are given in moments of "oceanic feeling"; one sea of

energy or instinct; embracing all mankind, without distinction of race, language, or culture; and embracing all the generations of Adam, past, present, and future, in one phylogenetic heritage; one mystical or symbolic body (4:35).

With this intense focus on the a-rational, mystical unconscious as the vital substance and the integrating unity of all things, Brown fittingly ends *Love's Body* with some paragraphs on "Nothing." These meditations are the climax of a long aphoristic argument. Brown does not seek to depict or name the Deity, but in the tradition of Zen, to show *the way* to the experience of that which is Ineffable and Unnamable, hence "Nothing." "The world is annihilated," Brown concludes, "the destruction of illusion." Then he raises his eyes to new mystical heights: "The day breaks, and the shadows flee away" (4:261).

Brown's vision exemplifies the emerging shape of post-modern religion in several revealing ways. Above all, Brown highlights *the child* as the primal image for his thinking, rather than the ego-dominated adult. Hence, he calls for "polymorphous perversity." He champions a lifestyle that is holistic, integrated, and sensuous, a lifestyle which resembles the polymorphous sensuality of an infant, with its engulfing unconscious instincts. A wide variety of writers, poets, culture-heroes, and some clergy have been exploring and seeking to embrace a constellation of child-themes, as Brown has done in his own way. Hence, more and more attention has been given to themes like play, fantasy, festivity, sensuality, dreaming, story-telling, ecstasy, wrath, immediacy, narcissism, and anarchism. This concentration on the image of the child is not a return to the sentimental romantic imagery of "the child of nature." It is not a quest for the life of Robinson Crusoe, who escapes to an island paradise far from the woes of civilization. Rather it is a quest to "get in touch with" vitality, spontaneity, and profundity *within* the given technocratic structures, *under* the pressure of the post-modern experience of nothingness, and *with* the given fragments of the tangible world.

The emergence of the child as the primal post-modern religious image has signified a turning away from the cognitive claims of religion towards an immediate involvement with the Ineffable. The widespread "opening to the East" within the matrix of emergent post-modern religion is no accident. Merton was deeply taken by the disciplines of Zen Buddhism. Brown, too, has been thoroughly influenced by the thought and experiential patterns of Eastern religions. These religions are oriented towards *the way*, towards an experience rather than towards *the truth* or right belief. Similarly, they envision a multifaceted cosmic schema with many levels of consciousness, rather than a well-defined, empirical world, known, controlled, and dominated by a rational self-consciousness.

The ascendency of the primal image of the child also signifies the development of a new religious appreciation for the human body and for nature in general. At this point, the ecstatic body imagery of Norman Brown is complemented by a constellation of writers, artists, and "drop-outs" from society who have sought to go beyond the modern isolation of the self-conscious ego and its manipulative approach to the body and nature. Brown speaks for many when he writes, "Dionysius calls us outdoors. . . . The first tabernacle in Jerusalem, the second tabernacle the universal Church; the third tabernacle the open sky" (4:229). In post-modern religion nature the Machine has been dismantled, and its component elements recycled and returned to the earth, "the whole earth."

Within the parameters of this image of the post-modern child of nature, the experience of Divinity is emerging in a fresh way. The human body and the whole earth have now become *sacramental*—"hierophanies everywhere . . . ," says Brown, "in the bread and wine of every meal" (4:230). And this is no "pathetic fallacy," no mere projection of human qualities on an alien mechanical world of nature. No, the experience of nothingness has shattered nature the Machine, as well as man the self-conscious dominating ego. Post-modern religion rests on the intuition "that both the human and the nonhuman modes of existence are animated and empowered by some primal reality, which may be denominated simply as Being itself" (31:85).

The rise of the primal image of the child has also elicited a new appreciation for the childhood religious expressions of the race: *myth*. In the milieu of post-modern religion, myth is no longer viewed as sheer falsehood, primitive science, or nascent philosophy; nor is it simply taken to be the projection of the psyche or the social order. In general, the initiates of post-modern religion approach myth as stories or symbols which evoke elementary feelings for the Ineffable, the Nameless, for Being-Itself, for the Wholeness of ultimate reality. Sociologist Robert Bellah has described symbols like God, Being, Nothingness, and Life as openings to the depth dimension that unites self and cosmos:

> These great summary symbols that refer to the totality of being, to the transcendent dimension of reality, and the differentiated terminologies which have grown up around them, cannot be dismissed as "subjective" just because they are not in a simple sense "objective" in their reference. They are neither objective nor subjective, neither cosmological nor psychological. Rather, they are relational symbols that are intended to overcome precisely such dichotomies of conceptualization and bring together the coherence of the whole of experience (2:202).

Bellah's statement is a reflective scholarly justification for an experience shared by many in the post-modern era. The doors to the storehouse of the earth's mythologies have been thrown open by a constantly increasing body of historical and comparative studies of religion, so that many have been enabled to appropriate religious symbols and mythologies from a variety of periods and cultures. This process of re-mythologizing consciousness has proceeded with growing enthusiasm, encouraged by studies like Mircea Eliade's *The Sacred and the Profane* and Joseph Campbell's *The Hero With a Thousand Faces*.

But the return to myth does not imply a relapse to pre-modern, uncritical modes of thought. On the contrary, the proponents of post-modern religion are quite critical of mythological thinking, just as Bultmann was. They seek to go beyond mere criticism and translation into the genre of philosophy to a new appreciation for myth itself. So Robert Bellah explains, "Only when the symbol has been torn from its experiential context and taken literally as belief 'about' something must we assert its fictional nature. As part of the experience itself it is perfectly and supremely real" (2:204). The post-modern interest in myth, therefore, is by definition *post-critical:* myth is taken to be an authentic and irreplaceable expression of profoundly real experiences, but at the same time myth is never taken literally, either as an objective description of ultimate reality, or as a map of the Ineffable and the Nameless. Myth is that which has the power to evoke and to express powerful experiences of the inexpressible Whole.

Consistent with this approach to myth is the refusal to express religion in a rational set of beliefs. The well-defined Wholly Other God of modern theism, who reveals his purposes in his Word, and who acts discretely in history, has given way in the post-modern era to a much more immanent, much less defined dimension of human experience. The most appropriate post-modern theological term, therefore, is not "God," but "the Sacred." As Sam Keen explains in his 1969 essay, "A Manifesto for a Dionysian Theology":

> "God" language functions to focus celebration and adoration on those sacred dimensions of reality which are known in the ecstatic experiences of love, creativity, hope, joy and thanksgiving. . . . What is ultimately the case about the whole of reality is beyond human powers of perception. At best man can only yield to those experiences in which he senses the presence of a power which urges human life toward a richer harmony (22:47).

This logically modest approach to "God," is like that of a child, as Nathan Scott has pointed out:

> The child is so enchanted with the diversity and multiformity of the world, and his appetite for novelty is so great, that he is not intent on finding principles wherewith to codify and categorize the things and

events which come his way. He is content to be nothing more than a connoisseur of the sheer profusion and variousnss of reality: instead of attempting to classify things and locate them in some system of order, he simply collects them and holds them in juxtaposition, without much regard for questions of logical propriety. He handles the contents of his experience by way of juxtaposition because he feels that "the world is a wedding" in which everything splays off onto everything else (31:96).

The post-modern experience of "God," begotten in the midst of radical cultural disintegration, qualified on every side by the power of nothingness, is a variegated childlike collage of immediate ecstatic encounters with the Sacred, in, with, and under the whole field of human existence.

So a new kind of religious experience is emerging, focusing on *immediacy*. In this respect the proponents of a new religious sensibility have learned a profoundly fruitful lesson from some of the leading religious thinkers of the modern era, and they have built on that lesson with the rich resources of their own imagination. But have the *gurus* of the post-modern era learned *enough* from the religious thinkers of the modern era?

Does post-modern religion sufficiently respond to the realities of *science and technology?* The astronaut or the genetic engineer or the expert on automated warfare may well be the paradigm figures in the post-modern era. How is post-modern religion to exert a humanizing influence on their thoroughly technologized lifestyles and philosophies of life? Is there still something to be learned from thinkers such as Bultmann and Teilhard who wrestled with the issues of science and technology for many years?

Does post-modern religion sufficiently respond to the need for *social justice* throughout the world? "The next generation," Norman Brown proclaims, "needs to be told that the real fight is not the political fight, but to put an end to politics. From politics to metapolitics" (26:458). Is the so-called "politics of experience" which Brown and others champion actually effective in the struggle to alleviate poverty, to transform oppressive social structures, and to establish a sane ecological existence? Perhaps post-modern religion can still afford to be shaped, more than it apparently has been shaped, by the perspectives of theologians like Niebuhr, Cone, and Camara.

Does post-modern religion sufficiently respond to the need for an authentic experience of *Transcendence?* Is post-modern religion eventually destined to be swallowed up by its own passion for immediacy? What is to prevent post-modern religion from becoming a narcissistic fixation on the given order, psychically and socially? Where within the post-modern religious experience is there a genuine opening to real Transcendence, which stands over against self and society in judgment and grace? Perhaps theologians like Bonhoeffer and Tillich, who knew well the fragile nature of religious discourse, but who nevertheless sought to talk about God and Christ and Spirit, still have something to say to the proponents of post-modern religion. Perhaps the time will come when the Nameless will find a new name.[4]

NOTES

[1] The philosopher Hegel once referred to the classical goddess of wisdom enigmatically: the owl of Minerva takes to flight only when the dusk has come. This means a historical period can be adequately interpreted only when it is coming to an end. The deliberations of this chapter, then, which deal with contemporary and future trends, are self-evidently risky. At best they can only be exploratory.

[2] The Jesus Movement, like other phenomena touched on in this section, is a highly complex, many-faceted development. It reflects a widespread thirst for immediacy in contemporary culture, for fulfilling experiences, rather than dry, unsatisfying relationships within the frequently shallow and sterile, even demonic, practices of our established society and established churches. The Jesus Movement may contain within it seeds for an as yet undreamed of renewal of Christianity. It shows signs of a striking kind of sincerity and integrity. It is reminiscent of the simplicity of St. Francis and, indeed, of Jesus himself. At the same time, however, the Jesus Movement seems to share with the "counterculture" generally a number of shortcomings, and then some. It tends to be naively apolitical ("I have dropped out of Ecology-action," one student remarked, "now that I know that Jesus will save the world"). Compare the philosophy of Raymond Mungo's *Total Loss Farm* (New York: E. P. Dutton, 1970) at this point. The Jesus Movement tends, as well, to be naïvely literalistic in its biblical interpretation, negating the struggles of over a century of painstaking scholarly research and the whole modern discussion of mythology and demythologizing. Likewise, the Jesus Movement tends to bypass the insights of depth psychology and sociology in establishing group priorities and patterns of behavior (e.g. overlooking the problems of authoritarianism and manipulative behavior in the guise of religious fervor). Overall, a number of aspects of the Jesus Movement are reminiscent of previous American "awakenings," in New England in the 1740's and 1750's, and on the frontier in the 1800's and 1810's. See further, Lowell Streiker, *The Jesus Trip* (Nashville: Abingdon, 1971).

[3] See H. Paul Santmire, *Brother Earth: Nature, God, and Ecology in a Time of Crisis* (29:chs. I, II).

[4] It may be, although it is far too early to tell, that the foregoing questions about science and technology, social justice, and Transcendence *can* be answered satisfactorily by those who seek to take post-modern religion seriously, *if* one of the most recent cultural developments in the second half of the twentieth century continues to grow and prosper: the movement for women's liberation.

There can be little doubt that modern culture, especially in its specifically religious manifestations, was thoroughly masculine, in the stereotypical sense. That self-conscious dominating ego, ruling over people and things, as if all the world were a cosmic machine; and that Cosmic Ego projected on to the heavens by the modern ego—all of this bears the telltale marks of an excessive influence of the masculine principle (Yang). The rise of post-modern religion, in contrast, represents a break with masculine domination and a movement toward a much more sympathetic appreciation of the feminine principle (Yin). This Yin-character of post-modern religion has been explicitly identified by a number of protagonists of the new religious consciousness, most explicitly perhaps by Allan W. Watts in his book, *Nature, Man and Woman* (35).

Now, concurrent with this feminizing of religion in the post-modern era, one of the major historical tendencies of modern culture, political revolution, is still running its course, indeed with an accelerating tempo. Undoubtedly the latter tendency is the most important "culture-lag" of the second half of the twentieth century. This is how Rosemary Ruether describes the situation: "The power of consciousness, transcendent to nature, by which the male of the ruling class raised himself above the sway of material necessity and subjected the woman, the lower classes and the conquered nations to its rule, together with the mastery of the earth; this revolution is now reaching into the hearts of all peoples, inspiring them to undo this social subjugation by following a similar revolutionary path. All the subjugated and dominated sectors of humanity, upon which the master class rose up to its present achievements, now rise in turn to demand equal share in its power, benefits, and self-development" (28:182).

It so happens that this modern revolutionary tradition carries within it, particularly through the influence of Marx, the drives

1. to take charge of science and technology for the sake of humanization,
2. to elevate the need for social justice to the apex of all values, and
3. the tendency—expressed in various ways, most recently in the writings of the Marxist philosopher Ernst Bloch—to posit an ontological Transcendence in terms of the Final Future (the withering away of the state, etc.).

Now, it is the working hypothesis of Ruether and other feminist theologians that, historically speaking, the domination of *women*, from the first moments of the rise of a human consciousness which was transcendent to nature, has provided "the fundamental psychic and social model for all forms of domination and subjugation" (28:182). If this hypothesis is true, and there seems to be no *a priori* reason to deny it, then the emergence of the feminist movement in the second half of the twentieth century would in fact be potentially not only the revolt of the largest group of oppressed people, it would represent the *final stage* of that revolutionary tradition.

It seems reasonable to state, then, that the movement for women's liberation may be able to unite both the deepest trends of post-modern religion *and* the final realization of the tradition of political revolution, in a way that would take into account the three criticisms of post-modern religion touched on above. Could it not be the case, then, that the present emergent stage of post-modern religion will give way to the stage of maturity, when the initiates and the *gurus* of post-modern religion truly know how to name the Sacred—She?

BIBLIOGRAPHY

1. ALTIZER, THOMAS J. J., and WILLIAM HAMILTON, *Radical Theology and the Death of God.* New York: Bobbs-Merrill, 1966.

2. BELLAH, ROBERT N., *Beyond Belief: Essays on Religion in a Post-Traditional World*. New York: Harper & Row, 1970.

3. BOULDING, KENNETH E., *The Meaning of the Twentieth Century*. New York: Harper, 1964.

4. BROWN, NORMAN O., *Love's Body*. New York: Vintage Books, 1966.

5. CAMPBELL, JOSEPH, *The Hero with a Thousand Faces*. Princeton: Princeton University Press, 1949.

6. DALY, MARY, *The Church and the Second Sex*. New York: Harper & Row, 1968.

7. EISELEY, LOREN, *The Immense Journey*. New York: Vintage Books, 1946.

8. ELIADE, MIRCEA, *The Sacred and the Profane: The Nature of Religion*. New York: Harper, 1957.

9. FALK, RICHARD A., *This Endangered Planet*. New York: Random House, 1971.

10. FERKISS, VICTOR C., *Technological Man: The Myth and the Reality*. New York: George Braziller, 1969.

11. GILKEY, LANGDON, *Religion and the Scientific Future*. New York: Harper & Row, 1970.

12. HOMANS, PETER, *Theology after Freud: An Interpretive Inquiry*. New York: Bobbs-Merrill, 1970.

13. KUHN, THOMAS S., *The Structure of Scientific Revolutions*, 2nd ed. Chicago: University of Chicago Press, 1962.

14. LUKACS, JOHN, *The Passing of the Modern Age*. New York: Harper & Row, 1970.

15. MacLEISH, ARCHIBALD, *Poems, 1924-1933*. Boston: Houghton Mifflin, 1933.

16. MARCUSE, HERBERT, *One-Dimensional Man: Studies in the Ideology of Advanced Industrial Society*. Boston: Beacon Press, 1964.

17. MERTON, THOMAS, "Apologies to an Unbeliever," *Harper's*. (November, 1966).

18. NIEBUHR, RICHARD R., *Experiential Religion*. New York: Harper & Row, 1972.

19. NOVAK, MICHAEL, *The Experience of Nothingness*. New York: Harper & Row, 1970.

20. OGDEN, SCHUBERT M., *The Reality of God and Other Essays*. New York: Harper & Row, 1963.

21. RICHARDSON, HERBERT W., *Toward an American Theology*. New York: Harper & Row, 1967.

22. RICHARDSON, HERBERT W., and DONALD R. CUTLER, eds., *Transcendence*. Boston: Beacon Press, 1969.

23. ROETHKE, THEODORE, *The Far Field*. New York: Doubleday, 1958.

24. ———, *Collected Poems of Theodore Roethke*. Garden City, N. Y.: Doubleday, 1966.

25. ROSZAK, THEODORE, *The Making of a Counterculture: Reflections on the*

Technocratic Society and Its Youthful Opposition. New York: Anchor Books, 1968.

26. ———, *Sources; An Anthology of Contemporary Materials.* New York: Harper & Row, 1972.

27. RUBENSTEIN, RICHARD L., *After Auschwitz: Radical Theology and Contemporary Judaism.* New York: Bobbs-Merrill, 1966.

28. RUETHER, ROSEMARY R., "Male Chauvinist Theology and the Anger of Women," *Cross Currents.* 21, 2 (Spring, 1971).

29. SANTMIRE, H. PAUL, *Brother Earth: Nature, God, and Ecology in a Time of Crisis.* New York: Thomas Nelson, 1970.

30. ———, "Catastrophe and Ecstasy," in *Ecological Renewal* by Paul E. Lutz and H. Paul Santmire. Philadelphia: Fortress Press, 1972.

31. SCOTT, NATHAN A., JR., *The Wild Prayer of Longing: Poetry and the Sacred.* New Haven: Yale University Press, 1971.

32. SLATER, PHILIP E., *The Pursuit of Loneliness: American Culture at the Breaking Point* (Boston: Beacon Press, 1970.

33. STEINER, GEORGE, *In Bluebeard's Castle: Some Notes towards the Redefinition of Culture.* New Haven: Yale University Press, 1971.

34. TODRANK, GUSTAVE H., *The Secular Search for a New Christ.* Philadelphia: Westminster Press, 1969.

35. WATTS, ALAN W., *Nature, Man and Woman.* New York: Pantheon Books, 1958.

36. WHEELIS, ALLEN, *The End of the Modern Age.* New York: Basic Books, 1971.

SUGGESTED READINGS

1. *Primary Readings*

BROWN, NORMAN O., *Love's Body* (4). A post-Freudian *Walden.*

MERTON, THOMAS, "Apologies to An Unbeliever" (17). Identifies a deep religious quest, in short compass.

RICHARDSON, HERBERT W., and DONALD R. CUTLER, eds., *Transcendence* (22). A collection of suggestive, readable essays on a common theme of contemporary religious urgency.

ROSZAK, THEODORE, ed., *Sources* (26). A collection of pieces by many diverse representatives of the counterculture.

RUETHER, ROSEMARY R., "Male Chauvinist Theology and the Anger of Women" (28). An incisive introduction to some of the new theological horizons of feminist thought.

2. *Secondary Readings*

BELLAH, ROBERT N., *Beyond Belief* (2). Cogent essays by a sociologist pointing to new religious possibilities.

FALK, RICHARD A., *This Endangered Planet* (9). A balanced analysis of, and response to, the ecological crisis.

FERKISS, VICTOR C., *Technological Man* (10). A perceptive and sensitive discussion of modern technology and its influence.

ROSZAK, THEODORE, *The Making of a Counterculture* (25). A friendly analysis of the counterculture.

SLATER, PHILIP E., *The Pursuit of Loneliness* (32). A brief, lucid analysis of American society.

Abbott, Lyman, 104, 107, 112n
Adler, Alfred, 329
Alinsky, Saul, 215
Allport, Gordon, 133
Alves, Rubem, 67, 168, 207n, 211, 213
(St.) Anne, 345
Aquinas, Thomas, 116, 121, 144, 240, 276
Arendt, Hannah, 212
Aristotle, 121, 344
(St.) Augustine, 121, 168, 189, 240, 276

Barrows, John Henry, 370
Barth, Karl, 36n, 71n, 120, 137n, 168, 172n, 231, 240, 244n, 319n, 320n, 391, 392, 396
Bayle, Pierre, 16, 35n
Bellah, Robert, 5, 359n, 427, 452
Benz, Ernst, 124
Bergson, Henri, 124
Berrigan, Daniel, 210, 211, 242n, 314-15, 317, 320n, 355
Bethge, Eberhard, 291
Bloch, Ernst, 456n
Blos, Peter, 326, 357n
Bonhoeffer, Dietrich, 1, 2, 4, 5, 7, 8, 36n, 37n, 168, 172n, 231, 240, 254, 276, 284-321, 322, 355, 356, 441, 442, 443, 455
Breuer, Josef, 257-59, 263, 278n
Brinton, Crane, 338, 339
Brown, Norman O., 450, 451, 452, 454
Brunner, Emil, 137n, 172
Bryan, William Jennings, 77, 78, 79, 80, 114
Buber, Martin, 394
Bultmann, Rudolf, 1, 2, 4, 5, 7, 8, 14, 33, 39-73, 107, 108, 115, 116, 117, 118, 137n, 138n, 276, 290, 291, 319n, 431n, 440, 442, 443, 454

Cage, John, 449-50
Calvin, John, 111n, 240
Camara, Dom Helder, 2, 8, 207n, 209-47, 442, 443, 454
Campbell, Joseph, 453
Camus, Albert, 119, 441
Clarke, Samuel, 26, 36n
Cohen, Hermann, 69n
Coleridge, Samuel Taylor, 105, 111n
Coles, Robert, 316
Commoner, Barry, 108
Cone, James, 2, 8, 168, 203, 209-47, 442, 443, 454
Copernicus, 80, 89, 128, 135, 277n, 297
Cowper, William, 110n
Cox, Harvey, 67, 168, 211
Cuvier, Georges, 81, 87, 94, 95

Darwin, Charles, 1, 2, 14, 29, 77-113, 114, 116, 117, 118, 123, 126, 127, 128, 129, 146, 190, 251, 252, 277n, 281n, 440

da Vinci, Leonardo, 267
Descartes, René, 144, 437, 438, 446, 450
Dewart, Leslie, 66
Dobzhansky, Theodosius, 108, 112n
Dollard, John, 327, 357n
Drummond, Henry, 107, 108, 111n

Eichorn, J. G., 43, 44, 69n
Einstein, Albert, 48, 128, 436
Eliade, Mircea, 401, 453
Engels, Friedrich, 144, 145, 146, 147, 158, 159, 162, 163, 164, 171n, 172n, 183
Erikson, Erik, 2, 8, 254, 316, 322-61, 440, 441, 443

Fanon, Frantz, 314
Feuerbach, Ludwig, 36n, 144, 149, 152, 153, 154, 156, 171
Fisk, John, 104, 107, 112n
Fontenelle, Bernard, 16, 35n
(St.) Francis of Assisi, 192, 317, 424
Frazer, James G., 32, 37n, 372, 373, 377, 396
Freud, Anna, 326, 327, 329, 357n, 358n
Freud, Sigmund, 1, 2, 4, 5, 6, 8, 14, 32, 36n, 52, 150, 172n, 176, 251-83, 284, 285, 287, 303, 315, 316, 317n, 318n, 322-24, 326, 327, 328, 329, 330, 331, 340, 341, 342, 354, 355, 386, 402, 418, 440, 442, 450

Gandhi, Mahatma, 201, 216, 224, 322, 330, 340, 341, 351-53, 354, 359n, 360n
Garaudy, Roger, 152
Geertz, Clifford, 359n
Glock, Charles Y., 201, 206n
Goethe, Johann W. von, 375, 445
Graham, Billy, 448
Gray, Asa, 93, 105, 110n
Groppi, James, 210, 211
Guevara, Che, 223, 314

Hadden, Jeffrey, 201
Hamann, Johann Georg, 33, 37n
Harding, Vincent, 211
von Harnack, Adolf, 65, 177, 178, 203n
Hartmann, Heinz, 326, 329
Hegel, George W. F., 121, 124, 144, 145, 149, 151, 152, 153, 156, 171, 376, 393, 396, 420, 430, 455
Heidegger, Martin, 42, 68n, 409, 431n
Heine, Heinrich, 145
Herder, Johann Gottfried, 374, 375, 376, 377, 396
Herrmann, Wilhelm, 65, 69n, 70n
Heyne, C. G., 43, 69n
Hitler, Adolf, 172, 285, 286, 313, 327, 401, 430n
Homburger, Theodor, 325
Horney, Karen, 427, 431n

Hume, David, 1, 4, 8, 13-38, 39, 42, 43, 45, 46, 47, 65, 82, 106, 111n, 116, 117, 118, 178, 253, 290, 319n, 371, 372, 373, 383, 386, 396, 441, 442
Huxley, T. H., 79, 93, 94, 95, 96-97, 98, 101, 102, 104, 106, 108, 110n, 111n

Irenaeus, 124

Jaspers, Karl, 298
Jemmy Button, 101
Joachim of Fiore, 124, 125
Jones, Ernest, 252
Jung, Carl, 329

Kant, Immanuel, 29, 33, 43, 46, 47, 48, 49, 69n, 111n, 138n, 178, 291, 297, 312, 319n, 371, 372, 373, 377, 382, 383, 386, 420, 430
Keen, Sam, 67, 453
Kierkegaard, Sören, 14, 33, 37n, 42, 108, 117, 138n, 351, 440
King, Martin Luther, 197, 201, 203, 206n, 216, 223, 224, 230, 317
Kingsley, Charles, 94, 107, 110n
Klein, Melanie, 357n
Kris, Ernst, 330, 358n
Kroeber, Alfred Louis, 108, 112n, 327, 328, 357n

Laplace, Pierre Simon, 36n
Lehman, Paul, 168, 205n, 206n, 207n
Leibniz, Gottfried Wilhelm, 121, 122, 123, 439
Lenin, 199
Lessing, Gotthold, 371, 372, 373, 377, 382, 386
Lewin, Kurt, 327, 357n
Linnaeus, Carolus, 81, 84, 95
Locke, John, 26, 27, 36n, 110n
Lovejoy, Arthur O., 121, 122, 123, 124
Luther, Hans, 343, 344, 345, 346, 347
Luther, Martin, 111n, 165, 189, 322, 330, 340-51, 352, 357, 359n, 375, 377, 392, 410
Lyell, Charles, 87, 90, 95, 97, 98, 102, 103, 105, 108, 110n

Macaulay, Thomas, 435
MacLeish, Archibald, 444, 445, 447
Malthus, Thomas R., 88
Mao Tse Tung, 314
Marcuse, Herbert, 445
Marx, Karl, 1, 2, 4, 5, 6, 8, 14, 15, 104, 128, 139n, 143-74, 175, 176, 177, 179, 182-88, 189, 191, 194, 195, 196, 198-200, 201, 203, 205n, 209, 213, 214, 226, 227, 228, 229, 230, 239, 254, 386, 402, 418, 431n, 442, 456n
Mead, Margaret, 327, 357n
Merton, Thomas, 449, 451
Metz, Johannes B., 168
Moltmann, Jürgen, 67, 168, 172, 207n, 211, 215, 396n

Moody, Dwight L., 164
Mott, John, 377
Mueller, F. Max, 32, 37n, 370, 376, 377, 396
Münzer, Thomas, 172n, 216

Natorp, Paul, 69n
Newton, Sir Isaac, 26, 27, 35n, 36n, 37n, 39, 89, 435, 437, 438
Niebuhr, H. Richard, 205
Niebuhr, Reinhold, 2, 8, 175-208, 209, 211, 213, 214, 230, 276, 401, 442, 443, 454
Nietzsche, Friedrich, 23, 36n, 319n, 403, 431n, 440

Ogden, Schubert, 68
Origen, 121, 124
Owen, Richard, 79, 94

Paley, William, 82-85, 86, 88, 91, 92, 93, 99, 104, 107, 108
Plato, 34, 121
Plotinus, 121, 122, 124
Pope, Alexander, 435
Pope John XXIII, 216, 217
Pope Paul VI, 212, 217, 226, 243n
Pope Pius XI, 170n

Ramakrishna, 192
Rauschenbusch, Walter, 178
Reuther, Rosemary, 456n
Rieff, Philip, 256
Roethke, Theodore, 444, 446, 447
Róheim, Géza, 358n
Roosevelt, Franklin Delano, 196-97
Rubenstein, Richard, 66
Russell, Bertrand, 135, 137

Sartre, Jean-Paul, 119, 409, 411
Schelling, Friedrich W. J., 121, 124, 431
Schleiermacher, Friedrich, 65, 105, 111n
Schopenhauer, Arthur, 374
Scopes, John T., 77, 109n
Sedgwick, Adam, 78, 79, 80, 84, 93, 104
Shaull, Richard, 168, 202, 206n, 211, 214, 230
Simpson, George Gaylord, 135
Skinner, B. F., 445
Slater, Philip, 446
Smith, Adam, 34, 37n, 438
Smith, Norman Kemp, 21, 36n, 37n
Spencer, Herbert, 97
Spengler, Oswald, 120
Stalin, Joseph V., 196, 199, 202, 406
Stark, Rodney, 201, 206n
Staupitz, Dr., 347
Strauss, D. F., 43, 44, 69n

Teilhard de Chardin, Pierre, 1, 2, 4, 8, 107, 108, 114-40, 276, 430, 441, 443, 454
Tillich, Paul, 2, 5, 7, 8, 107, 231, 236, 240, 276, 338, 346, 359n, 400-34, 440, 441, 443, 455
Tillotson, John, 26, 27, 36n
Tindal, Matthew, 35n, 36n

Toland, John, 27, 35n, 36n
Torres, Camilo, 210, 216, 223
Toynbee, Arnold, 430
Troeltsch, Ernst, 2, 14, 205n, 365-99, 400, 401, 402, 416, 419, 421, 428, 430, 431, 443
Tylor, E. B., 32, 37n

von Ranke, Leopold, 375, 376, 377, 379, 380, 396

Wallace, Alfred Russel, 95, 99, 102, 103, 104, 108, 111n
Washington, Joseph R., Jr., 211
Weber, Max, 185, 205, 402
Wilberforce, Samuel, 79, 80, 81, 84, 93, 94, 104, 114, 170
Wilberforce, William, 147, 148, 158, 159, 170
Winter, Gibson, 201

Yagi, Seiicho, 68

SUBJECT INDEX

Absolute, the, 380, 385, 387ff., 396n, 400.
    See also Ultimate, the; God
Absoluteness of religion, 371, 378, 391, 402, 406, 420. See also Relativism
    critical, 386, 388
    naive, 386, 387ff.
Abwehr, 285, 286
Action:
    and evolution, 128, 133
    political/social, 144, 220, 223, 314
    and truth, 352
Act of God, 48, 59, 71n, 115, 212, 379, 393, 449
Adulthood. See Maturity
Agape, 192, 193, 194ff., 197, 244n, 424.
    See also Love
Agnosticism, 4, 13, 29-32, 104, 106, 286
Ahimsa, 353. See also Non-violence
Alienation. See also Capitalism, exploitation and; Estrangement
    and being, 414, 415
    and religion, 144, 149, 153, 154, 160, 227, 228, 338
    social, 144, 157
    and work, 152ff., 156ff., 442
Ambiguity, Tillich's concept of, 417-19, 428
Americans for Democratic Action, 196
Analogy, principle of, 27, 28
Analysis, Age of, 13, 119, 121
Anglicanism, 26, 32ff., 104, 111n
Anna O., 257, 258ff., 378n
Anthropology. See also Humanity; Man
    discipline of, 32, 108, 280n, 281n, 327ff., 329, 357n, 358n
    science of man, 68nff., 97, 99, 153, 190
Antichrist, 234, 297, 300
Anxiety:
    Age of, 118, 119, 121
    ego, 266, 279n, 322, 338
    existential, 49-58, 409-12, 416, 431n
    metaphysical, 339, 359n
    and regression, 2, 6, 260, 266, 268, 272
    as source of religion, 5, 14, 18, 19, 20, 21, 22, 32, 34, 49ff., 253, 269, 272, 275, 296

Apocalyptic, 199, 228, 356
Atheism, 2, 4, 13, 30, 106, 143, 144, 154, 170n, 171n, 172n, 228, 257, 403, 443
Authenticity. See Autonomy; Ego; Freedom; Maturity
Authority:
    religious, 6, 171n, 391
    religious rationalization for social, 158ff., 175, 176
Autobiography (Darwin), 85
Autonomy, 2, 6, 172n, 285, 287, 288, 290, 291, 292, 298, 299, 300, 301, 309, 319n, 330, 356, 413. See also Ego; Maturity
    vs. shame and doubt, 330, 332-33

Being, 5, 412ff., 429, 431n, 452. See also Existence; Meaning
    Divine Ground of, 377, 443
    Great Chain of, 121, 122, 123, 125, 127
    ground of, 5, 405, 406, 407, 408ff., 411, 412, 415, 416, 419, 421, 430, 441, 443
    New, 415-17, 419
    power of, 411
Belief. See also Faith; Religion
    age of, 13
    Bultmann and, 41ff., 57
    crisis of, 3-5, 8
    in God, 59
    and science, 15
    unbelief, 414-15
Beyond Belief (Bellah), 5, 431n, 452
Bible. See also Eschatology; Evolution; Hope; Man; Miracles; New Testament; Old Testament
    authority of, 1, 7, 82, 155
    and eschatology, 123, 124, 125, 172n, 202, 203, 405
    ethics of, 106, 385
    and evolution, 77, 78, 80, 85
    God of, 55, 242n, 285, 296, 298, 300ff., 303, 314, 317, 393, 442
    in history, 393

Bible (*cont.*)
  literal truth of, 3, 4, 40ff., 42, 58, 65,
    79, 80, 81, 82, 83, 84, 85, 106,
    107, 109n, 112n, 178
  and mythology, 2, 44, 45, 49, 57, 58,
    68, 69n, 115, 171n, 188-89
  prophetic legacy of, 200
  and rationalism, 110n
  and revelation, 44, 45, 83, 120
Biblical criticism, 45, 107, 109n, 177-78
Biblical religion, 2, 32, 53-56, 57, 58,
    125, 138n, 168, 176ff., 188, 191ff.,
    194, 202, 212, 241n, 242n, 294,
    300
Black Power, 230, 231-37, 243n, 244n
Boundary situation, 298, 401, 430n
Bourgeoisie, 42, 67, 146, 152, 163, 164,
    165, 183, 184, 186, 201, 203, 299,
    392. *See also* Capitalism; Middle
    class
Brave New World (Huxley), 446
Brazil, 2, 86, 213, 216, 217, 218, 221,
    223, 224, 229, 230, 243n. *See also*
    Latin America; Third World
Buddhism, 8, 34, 47, 66, 71n, 271, 339,
    401, 404, 408, 416, 420ff., 423-25,
    429, 449, 450, 451

Calvinism, 14ff., 19, 20, 22, 23, 24, 25,
    31, 32, 34, 145, 165, 216, 242n.
    See also Protestantism
Capitalism. *See also* Bourgeoisie; Prole-
    tariat
  alienation and, 144, 152, 154, 156ff.
  exploitation and, 144, 146ff., 155, 157,
    164
  religion and, 150, 155, 158, 161-67,
    179, 186ff., 443
  in society, 146, 161, 182, 186ff., 196ff.,
    201, 202, 206n, 225, 226, 411
Catastrophism, 87, 110n
Cathartic Method, 258
Catholic. *See* Roman Catholicism
Cephalization, 116, 129, 132, 133, 136
Child, as post-modern religious image,
    451ff., 453
Childhood and Society (Erikson), 329
Christ. *See* Jesus Christ
Christendom, 3, 167ff., 168, 410
Christianity, 2, 4, 5, 8, 9, 14, 19, 20, 22,
    23, 41, 45, 49, 58, 61, 83, 106,
    132, 145, 148, 149, 156, 160, 167,
    168, 179, 186, 202, 216, 223, 226,
    229, 232, 237, 272, 294, 295, 300,
    317n, 339, 368, 369ff., 372ff., 392,
    402, 406, 410, 416, 423, 426. *See*
    also Religion
  early, 34, 105, 124, 172n, 394
  religionless, 168, 285, 293, 294, 295,
    296, 300, 302-13, 314, 317
Christian/Marxist dialogue, 159ff., 166ff.,
    170n, 172, 174, 196, 210, 226-30
Church, the, 3, 15, 60, 71n, 116, 124, 132,
    134, 155, 159, 197, 294, 297, 366,
    404ff., 416, 499. *See also* Angli-
    canism; Calvinism; Christianity;

Church, the (*cont.*)
  Confessing Church; Lutheranism;
    Protestantism; Puritanism; Re-
    ligion, institutional; Roman Ca-
    tholicism
  black, 198-99, 201, 203, 231, 233-35,
    243n
  early, 60, 295
  -less Christianity, 304
  and society, 147, 168, 180, 182, 203,
    205n, 214-15, 227, 228, 233-35
  universal, 452
Civilization and Its Discontents (Freud,
    S.), 271, 274, 327
Communism, 143, 145ff., 154ff., 172n,
    185, 196, 199, 200, 209-10, 225,
    228, 229, 405-6. *See also* Com-
    munist; Revolution; Socialism
Communist. *See also* Communism; Marx-
    ism; Socialism
  government, 143
  League, 145, 146
  society, 143, 146, 155, 186, 200, 218
Compassion, 192, 424-25. *See also*
    Ahimsa; Love
  and resistance, 313-17
Complexity and consciousness, law of,
    126-27, 128, 130, 132, 134
Confessing Church, 172n, 285, 318n, 391,
    392
Conscience:
  human, 341
  as inner voice of God, 4
  moral claims of, 190, 310, 311, 312-
    13, 333
  and society, 147, 151, 316
Conscientização, 224, 226, 227, 243n
Consciousness. *See also* Complexity and
    consciousness, law of
  gradations of, 122ff.
  historical. *See* Historicism
  human self-, 189, 440, 441ff., 443, 450
  -raising, 225, 228
  religious, 115, 116, 117, 118, 127, 128,
    156, 162, 171n, 254, 430
  social, 150, 155, 169
Courage, existential, 3, 346, 409-12
Creation, 78ff., 84, 86-93, 95, 106, 107,
    111n., 356. *See also* Evolution;
    God, as Creator; Old Testament
    writings, Genesis
  divine, 3, 115
  of man, 3, 96, 102, 189, 215
  of world, 3, 101
Creationism, 81, 89-90, 93
Cultural meaning, 51
Culture, 101, 415, 418, 436, 439. *See also*
    Anthropology; Modern culture;
    Primitive religion; Relativism, cul-
    tural.
  change in, 50
  primitive, 50, 101
  religion, 185
  and religion, 402, 405, 428, 431n

Darwinism, 8, 116, 117, 126, 134ff., 178,
    252, 297. *See also* Evolution

Darwinism (cont.)
on the nature of man, 93-104
Das Kapital (Marx), 104, 164
Death. See also Finitude; Life after death
and anxiety, 50, 409
existential interpretation of, 70n
and mature man, 289, 292, 337, 350
and rebirth, 61
and religion, 18, 252
self and Nothingness in, 51-52, 409-11, 416
Defense mechanism, 266
Dehumanization, 3, 4, 119, 147, 154, 170, 196, 211, 222, 228, 310. See also Alienation; Humanity, brutalized; Humanization
Deism, 36n, 83, 84, 104, 371
Demystification. See Conscientização
Demythologizing, 2, 8, 42-49, 56, 57, 58, 66, 71n, 319n. See also Mythology
Dependency, 287, 290, 355. See also Regression
infantile, 2, 6, 254, 262-63, 270, 275, 285
and religion, 293, 294, 295, 296, 301
Design, principle of, 80, 84, 90, 86-93, 95, 96, 102, 105, 106, 107, 111n. See also Nature
Determinism, 188, 189, 191. See also Economics; Fatalism
Deus ex machina, 289, 290, 295, 296, 300, 302, 303. See also God, -hypothesis
Developmental hypothesis, 16ff., 35n
Devil. See Satan
Dialectical. See also Materialism
materialism, 152, 171n, 188
process, 151
Dialogues Concerning Natural Religion (Hume), 16, 25, 26, 27, 28, 29, 32, 33
Does Civilization Need Religion? (Niebuhr), 175
"Dostoevsky and Parricide" (Freud, S.), 327
Dream, 407
interpretation of, 261, 262, 266, 278n

Ecological concerns, 108ff., 136, 446, 448. See also Environmental crisis
Economics, 34, 42, 146, 150, 152, 155, 162, 163, 164, 168, 170, 183, 184, 187, 188, 189, 191, 205n, 221, 254, 279n, 316, 410ff., 414, 442. See also Capitalism; Marxism
economic determinism, 183, 191
socioeconomic system, 150, 155, 158, 160, 161, 169, 185, 198, 226, 230
Ecstasy, 133, 192, 387, 450, 451
Ego. See also Anxiety; Autonomy
autonomy, 2
initiative, 348-51
psychoanalytic concept of, 260, 263, 264, 265, 266, 268, 271, 272, 279n, 322, 326, 328, 330, 358n
psychology, 325, 326ff., 329, 356n
-social theory, 328-37, 358n, 359n

Ego (cont.)
strengths, 7, 301, 302, 323, 324, 329, 330, 331, 332, 335, 336, 338, 340, 341, 342, 348, 349, 351, 358n
as thinking self, 58, 437, 438, 440, 441, 446ff., 450, 452, 455n
Egotism, 190, 191, 195, 198, 200, 201, 205n
Emanation, process of, 122, 124
Empiricism, 1, 14-15ff., 47-48, 97, 107, 108, 133, 134, 150, 198, 205n, 256, 352. See also Science
Emptyness, 51. See also Nothingness
Encounter:
and self-understanding, 52, 58, 59
word of God as mode of, 60, 61, 67
Enlightenment, 1, 3, 16, 36n, 39, 41, 84, 111n, 112n, 120, 123, 132, 145, 155, 190, 194, 211, 290, 291, 371, 374, 382, 430, 439
and demythologizing, 42-49, 69n
Environmental crisis, 428, 446. See also Ecological concerns
Eschatology, 47, 60, 67, 71n, 97, 100, 123, 124, 125, 133, 162, 172n, 199, 202, 203, 213, 230, 233, 239, 244, 369, 405. See also Apocalyptic; Bible; Hope
Estrangement, 5, 412-17, 428. See also Alienation
Ethical imagination, 184
Ethical norms, 176, 178
Ethics, 177, 423, 429, 431n. See also Man, moral nature of; Morality
bourgeois, 186
class origins of, 182, 185
evolutionary, 97
personal, 178, 424ff.
and society, 177, 181, 188, 202, 205n, 320n
socioethical categories, 304
Eucharist, 132, 270, 423. See also Ritual and worship
Evidences of Christianity (Paley), 83, 85
Evil, 24, 30, 47, 131, 136, 160, 184, 188, 189, 191, 198, 202, 267, 269, 288, 296, 311, 314, 356, 442. See also Suffering
Evolution, 80, 81, 89, 95, 97, 103, 104, 107, 114, 115, 146, 178, 252, 277n. See also Darwinism; Science
involution of, 130
one main axis of, 126ff., 135
and religion, 1, 2, 77, 86-93, 94, 106, 115-37, 378ff.
Evolutionary-apologetic claims for Christianity, 378-79
Exclusivism, religious, 67, 68, 366, 367, 377-82, 383, 384, 390, 391, 393, 394, 395, 420, 427
Existence, 155, 192, 409, 412-17. See also Existential; Existentialism
authentic, 58-65, 67, 68, 176
Existential:
concerns and symbols, 138n, 408-9ff., 432n. See also Courage; Existentialism

Existential (cont.)
  self-understanding, 49-58, 66, 118,
    280n
Existentialism, 33, 43, 68n, 117, 119,
    121, 138n, 413, 404, 408ff., 431n
Exploitation. See Capitalism

Fable. See Mythology
Faith, 2ff., 5, 7, 23, 111n, 116, 159, 216,
    228, 229, 235, 237, 244, 284,
    314ff., 389, 391, 407, 408. See
    also Belief; Jesus Christ
  vs. belief, 5
  biblical-existential, 42, 55, 57, 58-65,
    68, 71n, 117, 178, 285, 296
  justification by, 348, 349
  and maturity, 293-302, 306ff., 308,
    319n, 338, 340, 355, 356, 412, 414
  vs. myth, 45ff., 57, 58
  prophetic, 203
  psychosocial resources for, 322-61
  and reason, 27, 35, 67, 137
  vs. religion, 294, 300, 302
  and science, 14, 29, 40-41, 65-68, 108,
    118
Fantasy, 4, 20, 34, 53, 279n, 343, 451.
    See also Imagination; Mythology;
    Superstition
Fatalism, 226, 227, 230, 342. See also
    Providence
Father figure, 6, 86, 253, 267, 268, 269,
    270, 273ff., 276, 323, 324, 342,
    343, 344, 345, 346, 347, 350. See
    also God, as Father; Projection
Fear, as motivation for religion, 18, 22,
    35n, 49ff., 99, 253, 267, 270
Feudalism, 152, 160, 165
Finitude, 189, 409-12, 414, 418, 428. See
    also Death
Free association technique, 259, 261,
    278n, 279n
Freedom:
  authentic, 3, 7
  existential, 66ff.
  of God, 320, 319n
  intellectual, 14ff., 34
  for others, 61, 64, 285, 305-7, 309,
    310-11, 312, 319n, 320n, 440
  and society, 24, 42, 136, 146, 151, 188,
    190, 198, 212, 213, 214, 215, 229,
    234
  theology of, 168
  and transcendence, 6, 7, 189, 302-13,
    418
Fundamentalism, 78, 431n. See also
    Bible, literal truth of; Literalism

Generativity vs. stagnation, 330, 337,
    341, 350, 355
-Genesis (Teilhard):
  biblical. See also Old Testament writ-
    ings; Creation
  bio, 128, 129, 131, 133
  Christo, 128, 131ff., 133
  cosmo, 116, 128, 129, 131, 133, 134

-Genesis (Teilhard) (cont.)
  homo, 128, 129, 131, 133, 134
  noo, 129
  ortho, 126, 127, 128, 135
German Resistance Movement, 285, 287,
    300, 310, 311, 314, 315, 318n,
    319n
Germany, 107, 109n, 144, 145, 172n,
    196, 285ff., 287, 308, 310, 311,
    318n, 325, 327, 373, 391, 392,
    400, 401
God. See also Absolute; Act of God;
    Bible; Deus ex machina; Jesus
    Christ; Monotheism; Nature; New
    Testament; Old Testament; Reve-
    lation; Transcendence; Ultimate,
    the
  as ally of maturity, 285, 289, 295, 298,
    301, 313
  benevolent qualities of, 1, 30, 64, 105,
    117, 211, 237, 269, 333
  beyond God, 431n
  as Creator, 1, 2, 14, 15, 16, 17, 25, 27,
    28, 29, 30, 55, 81, 85, 86, 91, 92,
    102, 105, 117, 123, 189, 220, 227,
    235, 237, 252, 412
  death of, 7, 36n, 403, 440, 443
  existence of, 27, 28, 36n, 78, 79, 82ff.,
    104, 105, 106, 107, 111n, 132,
    143, 144, 154, 269, 403, 437
  and faith, 59, 71n, 118, 159, 383, 389,
    408
  and fatalism, 226
  as Father, 2, 4, 6, 124, 148, 158, 177,
    227, 253, 262, 267, 268, 270, 272,
    273, 276, 302, 340, 344, 345, 346,
    424, 447. See also Father figure;
    Projection
  and Great Chain of Being, 121, 123,
    132
  as Ground of Being, 443
  and history, 115, 124, 151, 212, 298,
    300, 375, 379, 380, 394, 395
  -hypothesis, 28, 36nff., 91, 261, 287,
    288, 289, 292, 297, 300, 301, 302,
    319n, 442
  image of, 79, 153, 189, 219, 220, 222,
    239, 339
  as Judge, 25, 55, 81, 156, 345, 347,
    407
  -lessness, 298, 302ff.
  and man, 52, 62, 92, 117, 153, 154,
    178, 190, 202ff., 236, 238, 292,
    375, 441
  and mythology, 39, 46, 47, 48
  omnipotence of, 290, 302
  reality of, 3, 116, 165, 269
  and reason, 43, 48ff.
  sovereignty of, 198
  as Supreme Being, 4, 154, 408
  theistic view of, 5, 6-7, 403, 438. See
    also Theism
  as Wholly Other, 59, 442-44, 453ff.
Golden rule, 194, 352
Gospels. See New Testament
Grace, 154, 346, 347, 348, 455
Ground of Being. See Being

Guilt, 6, 20, 24, 63, 260, 265, 267, 270, 271, 273, 274, 289, 292, 295, 296, 299, 301, 309, 311, 312-13, 345, 346, 348, 410. *See also* Initiative vs. guilt

Healing, 412-17
Heaven, 4, 46, 47, 57, 85, 145, 167, 255, 304, 344, 435, 439, 444
    new, 60, 137, 255, 425
    social function of, 2, 6, 143, 148, 156, 158, 159, 162ff., 194, 233, 316
Hebrew. *See* Judaism; Old Testament
Hell, 4, 47, 85, 255
Hinduism, 105, 352, 353, 365-66, 395, 408, 416, 421, 433
Historical individuality, 379, 381, 402, 429
Historicism (Historical consciousness), 366-67, 368, 372-77, 380, 381, 382, 383, 384, 385, 388, 389, 390, 394, 395, 395n, 400, 402
Historiography, 15ff., 46, 378
History, 41, 111n, 124, 149, 314. *See also* Evolution; God, and history; Relativism, historical
    and eschatology, 47, 60ff., 124
    Ground of, 387
    man and, 42, 50, 55, 60ff., 67, 180, 212, 416, 429, 425
    of mankind, 16, 44, 81, 115, 136, 146, 180, 190, 192, 193
    Marx on, 149, 151ff., 153, 166, 167
    and myth, 45, 49, 69n, 188
    natural vs. supernatural, 14ff.
    personal life, 3, 5, 62, 308, 414
    and religion, 297, 365-99, 426
History of religions, 14, 37n, 378, 396n, 401, 402, 426, 430, 431n
Holy, the, 422, 423, 426, 428
Homo religiosus, 24, 269, 275, 351-56
Hope, 3, 56, 64, 119, 184, 199, 200, 213, 233, 238, 239, 340, 453. *See also* Eschatology
Hubris. See Sin, and *hubris*
Humanism, 97, 126, 128, 151, 154, 166, 171n, 178, 188, 216, 228, 230, 239, 354, 355, 406
Humanity, 130, 429. *See also* Humanism; Man
    authentic, 42
    brutalized, 78, 93, 96, 104, 109, 180, 196
    and work, 153
Humanization, 3, 102, 154, 220, 233, 454. *See also* Dehumanization; Humanity
Hypnosis, 258, 259, 278n

Id, 263-64, 265, 266, 268, 269, 271, 272, 279n, 450
Idealism, 69n, 200
    vs. materialism, 149, 150, 151, 153, 161, 200
Identity, 325, 350, 447. *See also* Autonomy; Ego; Maturity

Identity (*cont.*)
    all-human, 352, 354
    Buddhist principle of, 424ff.
    crisis, 335, 337, 343
    ego, 328
    vs. identity confusion, 328, 330, 334-37, 358n, 359n
    and religion, 348, 350, 352, 425
Ideology, 146, 150, 155, 179, 182, 183, 188, 194, 225, 227, 324, 338-41, 405, 442
    capitalist, 161-67, 168, 172
    and identity, 335, 336, 337
Idolatry, 19, 36n, 48, 185
Ignorance, as condition for birth of religion, 4, 17-18, 19, 20, 22, 34, 43, 253, 254
Illusion. *See* Religion as illusion
Imagination, 101. *See also* Projection
    and religion, 18-19, 22, 34, 43-44, 61, 253
Individualism, 66-67, 68, 71n, 184. *See also* Historical individuality
Industry. *See also* Modern Culture; Technology
    vs. inferiority, 330, 334
    in society, 146ff., 181, 182, 183, 186, 188, 220, 439, 442, 445, 446
Initiative vs. guilt, 330, 333-34, 339, 340
Injustice, 3, 170, 195, 220, 230, 238, 257. *See also* Justice
Insecurity. *See also* Security
    as basic condition, 55, 56, 57, 58, 416
    use of religion to allay, 4, 5, 18, 32, 56
Integrity vs. despair, 330, 337, 340, 341, 345, 350, 355, 418
Intimacy vs. isolation, 330, 337, 341, 350, 355, 359n, 442
Intolerance, 2, 25, 427
Islam, 3, 369, 372, 396n, 408, 416, 423, 433

Jesus Christ, 34, 106, 205n, 299, 366, 384, 387. *See also* Antichrist; -Genesis, Christo; God
    the Black, 236-37, 244n
    Body of, 116, 132ff.
    Chain of Being and, 125, 131
    Cosmic, 132ff., 136, 443
    divinity of, 57
    faith and, 22, 61, 237, 294, 296, 316, 347, 383, 384, 386, 393
    historical life and death of, 41, 57, 60ff., 65, 116, 177, 178, 194
    humanity of, 62
    incarnation of, 79, 212, 228, 232, 441
    life in, 313, 387, 389
    the man for others, 7, 303, 304, 319n, 320n
    as moral teacher, 71n, 271
    as the New Being, 416-17
    as Omega Point, 134, 384
    and the oppressed, 211, 212, 214, 215ff., 218ff., 228, 234, 235, 238, 240
    religion of, 149, 179, 389

Jesus Christ (*cont.*)
  saving work of, 3, 4, 62, 115, 133, 148, 192, 222, 236ff., 238, 270ff., 312, 324, 348, 416, 417
  second coming of, 47, 60
  transcendence and, 303ff.
Jesus Movement, 448, 455n
Jews, 3, 8, 41, 65, 66, 144, 145, 192, 210, 255ff., 277n, 286, 325, 369, 372, 401, 408, 449
Judaism, 19, 49, 106, 156, 169, 194, 212, 216, 239, 272, 295, 339, 369, 383, 394, 402, 416, 421, 423, 433
  customs of, 83, 255, 295
  God of, 19, 366
  messianism in, 169, 214, 420
  scriptures of, 55, 145, 213, 374, 421
Justice, 2, 3, 7, 67, 134, 169, 175, 192-98, 201, 202, 203, 209, 211, 212, 213, 214, 219, 222, 224, 234, 235-37, 238, 241, 324, 344, 345, 347, 410, 418, 423, 442, 454. *See also* Injustice

Kerygma, 234. *See also* New Testament
faith, and authentic existence, 58-65, 66, 67, 68, 71n
Kingdom of God, 60, 128, 133, 169, 179, 180, 214, 230, 232, 302, 318n, 384, 405, 416, 420, 423, 424, 425
Knowledge:
  Divine, 83
  of God, 185
  Kant on, 46-47, 48, 49, 69n, 70n
  limits of, 106

Latin America, 210, 216, 217, 218, 221, 223, 224, 243n. *See also* Brazil; Third World
Legend. *See* Mythology
Letters and Papers from Prison (Bonhoeffer), 286, 301, 304ff.
Liberalism, Protestant, 177, 178, 179, 182, 185, 188, 189, 191, 200, 201, 202, 203n, 204n, 205n, 209, 213, 214
Liberation:
  Christian gospel of, 212, 216, 232, 234, 305
  from oppression, 211, 213, 218, 231, 240, 243n
  psychological, 62-63, 313
  of women, 190, 455n
Life:
  after death, 2, 3, 4, 6
  new, 61
Literalism, 107, 109n, 177, 178, 407, 416, 431. *See also* Bible, literal truth of; Fundamentalism
Logos. *See* Word of God
Love. *See also* Agape
  and Chain of Being, 125
  Christ's, 218, 271, 296, 366
  Divine, 132, 424ff.
  of divine father figure, 253, 268, 270, 272, 344, 345, 347
  of God, 306
  and maturity, 285, 324, 340, 442

Love (*cont.*)
  and others, 53, 55, 64, 190, 228, 240, 307, 309, 337
  parental, 263, 413
  religion as motivating, 34, 56, 99, 154, 178, 276, 387, 394, 453
  and sexuality, 260, 261, 271
  and social justice, 54, 179, 187, 192-98, 201, .202, 209, 222, 235-37, 238, 267
  as transcendent norm, 3, 192-94, 408, 419
Lutheranism, 4, 41, 66

Magic. *See* Superstition
Man. *See also* Anthropology; Evolution; Humanity; Maturity; Transcendence; World come of age
  as animal, 78, 84, 104, 115, 440
  biblical view of, 55ff., 64ff., 188ff., 193, 198, 295
  as co-creator, 220
  cosmic ascent of, 116, 128, 133
  as created, 78, 79, 115, 252
  and the created order, 80, 222, 238
  creativity of, 188ff., 220, 222
  dignity of, 178, 179, 188, 219
  divinization of, 222
  Freud on, 276, 279n, 322, 323
  and God, 154, 222
  moral nature of, 34ff., 78ff., 99ff., 114, 115, 133, 138n, 178, 189, 251, 264, 276, 288, 410, 418
  nature and origin of, 1, 93-104, 107, 166, 251
  post-religious, 287, 293, 302
  as social being, 100, 183, 212, 285, 292
Marxism, 130, 188, 193, 198, 199, 201, 206n, 209, 227, 228, 229, 233, 239, 340, 415, 456. *See also* Communism; Marx; Socialism
Mater et Magistra (Pope John XXIII), 217, 243n
Materialism, 222, 278n. *See also* Dialectical, materialism
  and Marx, 149-51, 152ff., 153, 171n, 188
Maturity. *See also* Autonomy; Man, postreligious; World come of age
  psychological, 2, 4, 6, 254, 274, 276-77, 284ff., 290, 315, 324, 329, 330, 338, 342, 355-56, 441
  religious, 285, 286-302, 308, 311, 315, 322, 324, 348
Meaning, 51, 212, 336, 337, 338, 350, 351, 373, 404, 427, 428. *See also* Being; Existence; Nothingness -lessness, 410-11, 450
Middle class, 185, 186, 187, 191, 195, 200, 201, 232, 328, 340, 439. *See also* Bourgeoisie; Capitalism
Miracles, 3, 4, 7, 17, 18, 21, 45, 48, 49, 57, 62, 83, 378
  and scientific world view, 1, 2, 15, 77, 105, 106, 171n
Missionary movement, 4, 369, 384-85, 390, 395n, 427

Modern culture, 3, 42, 54, 55, 57, 61, 64, 116, 117, 156, 182, 220, 221, 244n, 289, 292, 294, 390, 435, 436, 437-44
and religion, 8, 9, 20, 186, 444-55, 456n
Mono-causal theory, 34. *See also* Reductionism
Monotheism, 19, 21-22, 35n, 273
Moralism, 104, 215, 234, 354
Morality. *See also* Ethics; Man, moral nature of
basis of, 3, 31
and ethical decision, 311-12
and individual, 34-35, 178, 264, 268ff., 290
and nature, 57, 77, 114, 115
norms of, 51, 61, 63, 108, 193, 266, 311, 410
and others, 55, 97, 100, 104, 133, 182, 184, 187, 414, 418
and religion, 4, 24, 31, 33, 134, 162, 171n, 180, 253, 274, 275, 276, 288, 386
slave, 36n
Moral Man and Immoral Society (Niebuhr), 183, 205n
Moses and Monotheism (Freud, S.), 273
Movement for Basic Education (MBE), 224, 226, 243n
Mutuality. *See* Intimacy
Mysticism, 132, 375, 423ff., 429, 450
Mystification, 151ff., 163, 166
Mythological:
form of belief, 5, 8
world view, 2, 24, 43ff., 46, 267, 453. *See also* World view
Mythology, 42-49, 56, 57, 58, 65, 66, 68, 69, 69n, 171, 188-89, 205n, 225, 261, 262, 267, 340, 407, 452-53. *See also* Demythologizing; Paganism; Polytheism; Primitive Religion; Superstition; Symbols

National Socialism, 172, 392, 401, 405ff., 430n. *See also* Nazism
Natural History of Religion (Hume), 371
Naturalization. *See also* Secularization
Natural selection, 86-93, 95, 98, 99, 102, 103, 110n, 126, 129, 190
Nature, 117ff.
argument for God from design of, 27, 78, 82ff., 84, 85, 91, 106, 107, 111n. *See also* Design, principle of
God and, 68, 80, 86, 116, 226, 436
laws of, 44, 89, 118, 435
and man, 98, 109, 116, 292
mechanistic view of, 17, 27, 29, 35n, 82, 431, 437, 439, 441, 442, 443, 450, 452, 456n
organic view of, 28, 29ff., 35n
primitive man's ignorance of, 35n, 42-43
and the supernatural, 39, 40, 49, 50, 59
Nazism, 2, 68, 172n, 255, 285, 286, 310, 320n, 391, 401

Neo-Kantian philosophy, 33, 43, 46, 48, 69n, 70n
New Deal, 196-97, 202, 206n
New Left, 218, 223, 243n
New Testament, 83, 106, 132, 136, 192, 223, 230, 295, 368ff., 393, 426
agape, 192ff.
and eschatology, 71n, 124, 125, 131
and faith, 42, 58, 60
God of, 211, 296, 393
Hellenistic sources and the, 57, 71n, 83, 107, 124, 192, 213, 369
and kerygma, 61, 62, 66, 211, 234
and mythology, 44, 47ff., 57, 58
studies, 41, 42, 70n, 71n
New Testament writings:
Colossians, 131, 136
Ephesians, 131, 136
Galatians, 295
John, 55, 71n,
Mark, 71n
Matthew, 71n
Paul, 55, 71n, 137, 192, 213, 273, 274, 295, 337, 426
Romans, 342, 347
Non-violence, 196, 223-26, 229, 230, 231, 240, 243n, 352, 354, 355, 360n. *See also Ahimsa*
Noosphere, 116, 130
Nothingness, 51, 121, 137, 409, 424, 444, 448, 449, 450, 451, 452. *See also* Emptyness; Meaninglessness

Objectifying, 46, 48, 70n, 71n, 117, 118, 152, 156
Oedipal complex, 264, 270-71, 272, 273, 274, 280n, 324
Old Testament:
Abraham, 300
Adam and Eve, 188, 189, 190, 407, 414-15
David, 300
and eschatology, 124
God of, 211, 213, 296, 300
miracles of, 21, 43-44
Moses, 261, 271, 273
prophets, 106, 168, 180, 200, 211, 216
stories of, 42, 105
Old Testament writings:
Amos, 172n, 193, 194, 200, 211, 299
Exodus, 65, 169, 211
Genesis, 40, 107, 115, 189. *See also* Creation
Hosea, 211
Isaiah, 172n, 203, 211, 213
Jeremiah, 172n
Joshua, 40
Micah, 211
Psalms, 347
Omega Point, 124, 126, 130, 131, 132, 134, 135, 384, 441
One, and the Many, 121-23, 126
Order, principle of, 28, 29, 30, 37n, 57, 59, 80, 89, 213. *See also* Design; Nature
Origin of religion, 14, 15-19, 32, 35n, 65, 253

Origin of religion (*cont.*)
  evolutionism, 16
  historical, 15, 171n
  psychological, 15, 254, 267-75, 277n

Pacem in Terris (Pope John XXIII), 217
Paganism, 23, 36n, 289, 436. *See also*
  Mythology; Primitive religion; Su-
  perstition
Philanthrophy, 96, 147, 187, 195
Planetization, 129, 131
Polytheism, 16-17, 19-20, 21, 22, 23, 31,
  35n
Populorum Progressio (Pope Paul VI),
  212, 217, 243n
Power, social and political, 160, 182, 185,
  192-98, 200, 201, 203, 235-37,
  338, 442
Primitive religion, 8, 14, 16ff., 22, 23,
  24, 36n, 49, 56, 171n, 272, 372,
  401, 488. *See also* Mythology;
  Polytheism; Religion; Superstition
  Greek sources for, 16, 36n, 43
Progress, 16, 120, 123, 124, 135, 151,
  221, 222, 225, 374, 430, 436, 438,
  439, 442, 450
Projection, 5, 257, 266, 269, 442. *See also*
  Father figure; God, as Father;
  Imagination; Objectifying
  and God, 4, 6, 153, 154, 274, 289, 300,
  302, 345, 357n
  as mythological thinking, 44-46, 267
  religion as, 14, 19, 22, 36n, 144, 156,
  267, 272
Proletariat, 6, 144, 146, 147, 152, 155,
  157, 158, 159, 160, 161, 162, 163,
  164, 165, 166, 183, 184, 185, 198,
  200, 201, 225, 228, 340, 440, 442
Prophets. *See* Religion, prophetic; Old
  Testament, prophets
Protestantism, 3, 7, 23, 66, 115, 148, 178,
  185, 186, 209, 210, 211, 241n,
  297, 317, 350, 378, 389, 390, 392,
  393, 396n, 401
Protestant Reformation, 165, 169, 189,
  194, 342, 369
Providence, 78, 79, 84, 252, 253, 272,
  274, 338, 339
Psychoanalysis, 155, 257, 267, 270, 317n,
  322, 325, 326, 340, 354, 355, 414,
  427
  applied, 266, 267, 280n, 316, 327
  of children, 326, 357n, 358n
  practice of, 278n, 284, 353
  theory of, 253, 256, 257-66, 324, 328,
  333
Puritanism, 20, 34, 178, 194, 198

Radicals, religious, 209-47
Rationalism, 84, 108, 110n, 190, 368,
  371-72, 373, 376, 377, 382, 393,
  394, 430
Rationalization of social order, 6, 144,
  150, 158ff., 160, 162ff., 163, 165,
  168, 183. *See also* Ideology, capitalist

Realism, Niebuhr's concept of, 187, 192,
  199, 200, 201, 202, 206n, 209, 214
Reason, 35n, 53, 70n, 101, 195, 291, 292,
  319n, 348, 371, 373, 374, 396n,
  436, 437, 438, 439, 445
  Age of, 373
  categories of, 47, 48
  Divine, 380
  historical, 376, 377
  limits of, 28, 43
  and religion, 4, 15, 17, 27, 35, 66, 120,
  137, 290, 372, 386, 388, 393
Reconciliation, 237-39, 241
Reductionism, 7, 402
  psychological, 7, 8, 323, 324, 351, 355,
  356n, 386
  sociological, 8, 169, 183, 188, 198, 200,
  386
Reformation. *See* Protestant Reformation
Regression, 2, 6, 257, 266, 272, 287, 293,
  330, 332, 356, 358n, 359n, 448.
  See also Dependency
Relativism:
  cultural, 367, 400, 401, 402, 405
  historical, 2, 8, 390, 391, 400, 401, 402
  relativization of, 418, 419-20, 428-29
Religion. *See also* Alienation; Biblical religion; Maturity; Origin of religion; Projection; Reason; Science;
  Society; Symbols; Traditionalism;
  Ultimate concern; World religion
  acculturated, 185, 186, 187, 188, 193,
  197, 198, 200. *See also* Culture,
  religion
  black. *See* Church, black
  Bonhoeffer on, 287, 303, 315, 317,
  318nff
  as compensation, 6, 143, 144, 158, 161,
  162, 164, 165, 166, 167, 271, 216
  Darwin and Huxley on, 104-6
  Erikson on, 331, 337-40, 359n
  essence of, 371, 372, 403
  and faith, 319n
  feminizing of, 455n
  Feuerbach's philosophy of, 149, 153-55,
  171n
  function of, 2, 6, 143, 155, 158, 159,
  161, 162, 166, 167, 198, 200,
  206n, 239, 254, 340
  as illusion, 2, 4, 158, 167, 179, 251-83,
  284, 300, 323
  institutional, 2, 5, 166, 168, 180, 181,
  182, 185, 187, 197-98, 200, 203,
  205n, 206n, 253, 254, 275, 332,
  336, 404, 405, 426, 445
  Marx on, 144, 155, 160, 161, 164, 166,
  168, 175, 179, 191, 209, 227, 239
  naive, 386, 387
  and non-rationality, 16ff., 27, 257
  as obsessional neurosis, 272
  as opiate, 2, 143, 144, 156-61, 164, 167,
  176, 192, 210, 227, 228, 229, 442
  post-modern, 444-55
  prophetic, 176, 177, 185, 188, 189,
  191, 192, 193, 194, 198, 199, 200,
  201, 202, 203
  pseudo, 55ff.

Religion (*cont.*)
  quasi, 46, 199-200, 405ff., 433
  scientific study of, 13, 14, 32, 33, 41,
    378, 390
  Tillich on, 403ff., 418ff., 422, 426ff.,
    428
  Troeltsch on, 386-87
  true, 29-35
Repression, 14, 257, 260, 263, 266, 272,
    273, 276, 318n, 448
Revelation, 166, 419. *See also* Bible
  Christian, 5, 14, 35n, 67ff., 134, 396n,
    420
  and God, 2, 3, 4, 13, 27, 60, 78, 80,
    82, 83, 365, 384
  and reason, 120
  religion of, 36n
Revolution. *See also* Society, change in
  and religion, 2, 155, 162, 166, 172n,
    176, 183, 185, 198, 209, 210, 212,
    214, 216, 237-39
  social, 143, 144, 147, 152, 160, 161,
    164, 170, 194, 195, 200, 202, 223,
    314
Revolutions:
  American, 205n, 439
  Communist, 143, 147, 154, 169, 213
  French, 145, 148, 155, 223, 373, 439
  Russian, 196, 223
Ritual and worship, 31, 67, 272, 340, 353.
    See also Eucharist; Sacramental,
    the
Roman Catholicism, 3, 4, 7, 20, 23, 132,
    136, 148, 165, 209, 210, 216, 217,
    243n, 255, 297, 333, 389, 390,
    392, 393, 401, 449. *See also*
    Vatican II
Romanticism, 83, 105, 108, 373-75, 439
Russia, 143, 148, 149, 196, 199, 225

Sacramental, the, 423ff., 441, 452
Salvation, 5, 69, 115, 154, 163, 169, 178,
    186, 210, 212, 214, 288, 299, 416,
    419, 441. *See also* Jesus Christ,
    saving work of
Satan, 39, 41, 85, 180, 232
Science. *See also* Industry; Technology;
    World view, Cartesian
  and myth, 44-45, 46, 57, 277n
  Newtonian, 25, 36n, 89, 117, 178, 435,
    438
  and religion, 1, 2, 8, 13, 15, 18, 24, 28,
    33, 39, 40-41, 43, 46, 53, 55, 64,
    65-68, 78, 79, 80, 81, 84, 85, 106,
    107, 114-15, 117, 118, 119, 134,
    155, 171n, 256, 291, 372, 381,
    387, 446, 454, 455n
  and self, 54, 55, 310
  of Teilhard, 128, 134, 135
Secularization, 78, 79, 80, 85, 98, 101,
    151, 154, 405, 412, 415
Security, 5, 6, 54, 55, 56, 57, 61, 62, 63,
    64, 165. *See also* Insecurity
Self, the, 7, 23, 42, 49-58, 62, 63, 70n,
    158, 259, 305, 306, 307ff., 318n,
    413, 441, 442. *See also* Autonomy;
    Ego; Maturity

Servility, 144, 160ff., 164, 168. *See also*
    Virtue, servile
Sexism. *See* Liberation, of women
Sexuality, 17, 52, 156, 260, 261, 262, 263,
    264, 278n, 279n, 286
Sin, 3, 20, 179
  conditions of, 194
  and faith, 296, 333
  and *hubris*, 55, 71n, 189, 190, 191, 414
  original, 178, 190, 270, 274
  punishment for, 4, 39, 156, 159, 176,
    185
Skepticism, 1, 13, 28, 33, 391
Social gospel movement, 177, 178, 179,
    182, 200, 202, 204n, 205n, 206n,
    314
Socialism, 143, 145, 170n, 197, 206n, 222,
    225, 430n
Society. *See also* Industry; Technology
  change in, 6, 149, 168, 171n, 174, 176,
    179, 181, 184, 186, 192, 202, 209,
    214, 216-17, 218, 239, 314, 442.
    See also Revolution
  degrading conditions of, 147, 148
  and instincts, 100
  institutions of, 51, 191, 290
  mechanized, 438
  religion and, 6, 8, 14, 42, 144, 155,
    160, 168, 172n, 175, 178, 182, 183,
    184, 200, 438
  and state, 148, 149
  transcendence and conditions of, 6,
    188, 189
Spirit:
  body and, 137, 295
  the Concrete, 426
  the Divine, 124, 232, 418ff.
  Hegelian, 149, 151, 152, 153, 156
  human, 380
  prophetic, 176
Status quo, 118, 144, 158, 159, 160, 164,
    170, 176, 186, 197, 205n, 210,
    211, 213, 223, 226, 239, 314
Sublimation, 144, 157, 172, 185
Suffering, 4, 59, 67, 105, 144, 156ff., 195,
    219, 234ff., 238, 425
  and maturity, 289, 292
  neurotic, 342, 346ff.
  religious rationalization of, 156, 159,
    160, 161, 163, 165, 176, 189
  self-, 353
Superego, 263, 264, 265, 266, 271, 279n,
    285, 318, 322, 348
Superstition, 4, 18, 23, 27, 30, 31, 41, 45,
    69n, 171n, 254, 257, 343, 372,
    374, 376. *See also* Mythology;
    Paganism; Primitive religion
Symbols, 153, 169, 210, 236, 447, 452.
    See also Mythology
  religious, 244n, 261, 267, 323, 324,
    351, 352, 355, 406-7, 408-19, 422,
    423, 424, 426, 427, 429, 431n, 452,
    453

Technology, 3, 42, 50, 53, 55, 64, 130,
    220, 221, 290, 334, 435, 436, 444,

Technology (*cont.*)
445, 446, 451, 454, 455n. *See also* Industry; Society
Teleology, 108, 426
The Absoluteness of Christianity and the History of Religions (Troeltsch), 377, 380, 381, 383
The Communist Manifesto (Marx and Engels), 145, 146, 147
The Descent of Man (Darwin), 98, 102
The Future of an Illusion (Freud, S.), 268, 324, 327
The Golden Bough (Frazer), 327, 372
The Natural History of Religion (Hume), 14, 15, 16, 26, 43, 371
The Origin of Species (Darwin), 78, 79, 85, 89, 90, 91, 93, 95, 251
The Phenomenon of Man (Teilhard), 134
"The Place of Christianity Among the Religions of the World" (Troeltsch), 392
Theism, 26, 28, 30, 105, 106, 110n, 144, 154, 403, 408ff., 431n, 438, 442, 443, 448. *See also* Deism; God
rational. *See* Theology, natural
Theology, 115, 133, 205n, 210
Black, 238, 239
of Crisis, 120
of culture, 400
of Hope, 213, 242n, 244n
natural, 25-29, 31, 32, 35n, 36n, 79, 80, 82, 83, 85, 109n, 110n, 319n
"orang-outang," 81
secular, 445
Third World, 210, 211, 218, 221, 223, 225, 226, 227, 230, 243n, 442. *See also* Brazil; Latin America
Totem and Taboo (Freud, S.), 272, 273
Totemism, 272, 273ff.
Traditionalism, Christian, 368-71, 376, 377, 390
Transcendence, 3, 8, 9, 49, 70n, 407, 419, 426, 428, 430, 454
and *agape*, 193, 194
authentic vs. spurious, 3, 5-7, 285
criterion of, 392, 393
and freedom, 302-13, 320n
and God, 47, 48, 52, 59, 192, 302-5, 442-44, 453-455n
and history, 416
man's capacity for, 52, 80, 189, 190-91, 251, 374, 421
mythological claims of, 56-57
Transformation:
of mankind, 126
political, 67
religious, 3, 22, 303, 304, 313
self, 68, 241, 299, 425
social, 170, 194, 202, 213, 224, 425
Trust, 165
and God, 308
vs. mistrust, 330, 331-32ff., 344, 348, 358n

Trust (*cont.*)
religion as fostering, 34, 56, 336, 337, 338, 339, 340, 348, 351, 355, 356, 387

Ultimate, the, 5, 500, 419-27, 430, 441. *See also* Absolute, the; God
Ultimate concern, religion as, 403-7, 408, 418, 421
Unconscious, 150, 155, 162, 251, 252, 253, 258, 259, 260, 261, 262, 263, 267, 274, 275, 276, 277n, 278n, 322, 323, 324, 326, 327, 328, 338, 342, 350ff., 359n, 407, 440, 450
Uniformitarianism, 87, 91

Vatican II, 216, 217, 220, 228, 242n, 243n, 390. *See also* Roman Catholicism
Violence, 184, 186, 196, 199, 200, 223-26, 230, 231, 237-39, 240, 354, 360n. *See also* Ahimsa; Nonviolence; Revolution
Virtue, 24. *See also* Servility
servile, 158, 160, 161, 164, 185

War, 18, 119, 180, 184, 223. *See also* Revolution
Spanish Civil, 406
Thirty Years', 440
Vietnam, 51, 136, 209, 223, 314
World, I, 51, 177, 197
World, II, 180, 202, 284, 285, 287, 328, 413, 443
Word of God, 3, 4, 34, 59-60, 61, 62, 67, 78, 79, 115, 186, 339, 348, 384, 392, 393, 394, 441, 442
Work:
cosmic, of Christ, 133
ethic of, 42, 54
justification by, 55
man, and history, 151, 152ff.
and mythology, 57
and self-understanding, 52, 54, 56, 58, 70n, 152ff., 334, 349
World come of age, 288, 290, 291, 293, 299, 300, 302, 319n
World religion, 2, 32, 34, 366, 368-77, 385, 419-27, 430
World view:
biblical, 41, 84. *See also* Biblical religion
Cartesian, 437, 438, 439, 440, 441, 442, 443. *See also* Science
culturally conditioned, 49
pre-scientific, 44, 49
primitive, 68. *See also* Mythological world view
scientific, 40ff. *See also* Science

Young Man Luther (Erikson), 341-51